LABOUR AND UNEMPLOYMENT
1900-1914

Labour and Unemployment
1900-1914

KENNETH D. BROWN

Rowman and Littlefield

ISBN 0-87471-039-1

Rowman and Littlefield
81 Adams Drive
Totowa, N J 07512

*Set in eleven point Baskerville
and printed in Great Britain*

To my parents

Contents

List of illustrations

Introduction

VIEWED FROM THE somewhat unreliable standpoint of the 1930s the Edwardian age in Britain assumed for many a quality akin to that of the Garden of Eden: a sort of golden age, untarnished by the horrors of modern warfare, nationalism, financial crises, or mass unemployment. The simple passage of time and a considerable amount of research have both combined, however, to show the other side of this picture, revealing and stressing the insecurities, the tensions, and the social inequalities of Edwardian society. The period saw governments, both Liberal and Conservative, striving to cope with newly revealed social problems—bad housing, old age, undernourishment, and unemployment. The outcome of their strivings was the foundation, albeit somewhat shaky, of the modern welfare state.

It was also in the Edwardian years that the organised working classes emerged as a genuine, independent political force, and this book seeks to examine the attitudes and actions of the British labour movement in just one of the fields with which government was becoming increasingly concerned—unemployment. How far was the movement able to influence government? Was the new Labour Party as feeble as its left-wing critics have often asserted? Did the working-class groups have any realistic proposals of their own and, if so, how did they try to realise them? How did the organised working classes react to new legislation designed for their benefit? These are some of the questions that this book sets out to answer.

CHAPTER 1

The days of the Social Democrats, 1900-1904

BY THE LAST decade of the nineteenth century many Englishmen had come to accept the need for substantial state intervention in order to tackle the problems of poverty. Hitherto,
the poor had been dealt with under the none-too-tender Poor
Law Amendment Act of 1834 or by the numerous private
charitable bodies. The former operated on the principle that
state relief should be made as unpleasant as possible in order
to deter all but the most desperate from applying, and it was
consequently very unpopular. By the late 1860s policy had
been relaxed somewhat towards those who manifestly could
not help themselves, but this was accompanied by a much
more stringent attitude towards those in receipt of out relief,
which in practice usually meant the unemployed. The main
agency of private philanthropy, the Charity Organisation
Society (COS), was also much disliked, largely because of its
underlying philosophy that poverty was the result of some personal defect. 'In charitable work,' wrote Helen Bosanquet, one
of the society's workers, 'we devote ourselves to those who are
weak, who have in some way failed.'[1] Help was given to those
who were deemed deserving, but only after the most rigorous
investigation of the individual's circumstances—which was
again greatly resented—and with the intention of ensuring
that the recipient remained self-reliant.

What really swung public opinion behind the demand for
state action was the revelation that neither the poor law nor
private charity was doing more than scratching the surface of
the problem. Jack London, the American socialist writer who

lived for some months in London's East End in order to see
for himself what conditions were really like, claimed in 1903
that neither relief system had achieved anything 'beyond relieving an infinitesimal fraction of the misery'.[2] The failure of
the existing machinery was made abundantly obvious when
social surveys carried out in London by Charles Booth and in
York by Seebohm Rowntree suggested that over one third
of Britain's urban population was living at or below subsistence level. Such a situation caused even greater concern when
large numbers of recruits for the army had to be rejected as
unfit for service at the time of the Boer War, a lesson with
added import for those who had been watching with some
alarm the growing economic and military strength of Germany
so clearly foreshadowed in the Franco-Prussian War of 1870-1.[3]

Fear for Britain's world position was not the only force working to convince Englishmen that state action was necessary to
deal with the conditions exposed by Booth and Rowntree.
There was a great upsurge of humanitarian sentiment, well
illustrated in the attempts of William Booth to apply the social
content of the Christian gospel through his Salvation Army
movement. Some of this sentiment, however, was less genuinely
altruistic, springing from the fear that working-class poverty
might breed revolution. This is suggested very strongly by the
fact that in 1886 the Lord Mayor's Mansion House Fund,
established to relieve the unemployed, shot up from £19,000
to £72,000 in the two days immediately following demonstrations in the heart of London's clubland. The rioters, most of
them unemployed workers from the East End, were led by
members of the Social Democratic Federation (SDF) who had
been drilling them for some time under the direction of H. H.
Champion, a former soldier. It was not without significance
that shortly after these outbreaks of unrest the President of the
Local Government Board, Joseph Chamberlain, issued a circular making provision for the establishment of unemployment
relief works by local councils, the first attempt to separate the

unemployed from other poor law cases.

One other factor which also contributed to the shift of public opinion was the growing political significance of the working classes. After the Reform Acts of 1867 and 1884 most working men enjoyed the right to vote and by the Local Government Act, also of 1884, the local government franchise was extended and the property qualification for poor law guardians was abolished. All this meant that the voice of the working classes was heard and considered increasingly in the counsels of government. It was, furthermore, a voice which was becoming more articulate and more highly organised. The Trades Union Congress (TUC) had been established in 1867, the SDF in 1883, followed ten years later by a second socialist body, the Independent Labour Party (ILP), and in 1900 by the Labour Representation Committee (LRC).

In 1909 a rising young economist, W. H. Beveridge, wrote that unemployment was fundamental to the whole question of poverty. 'Workmen today,' he said, 'are men living on a quicksand, which at any moment may engulf individuals, which at uncertain intervals sinks for months or years below the sea surface altogether.'[4] Given this, and the fact that socialism came to the fore in England at a time when unemployment was exceptionally heavy, it was not surprising that socialists in particular devoted a great deal of attention to the subject. Indeed, E. R. Pease, an early Fabian representative on the LRC, later suggested that 'excessive attention' had been lavished on the unemployed by English socialists.[5] But unemployment was no respecter of persons and all sections of the organised working-class movement joined, with varying degrees of enthusiasm, in the discussions about social policy which characterised late Victorian England.

They generally agreed that the introduction of labour-saving machinery and its corollary, cheap labour, were among the leading causes of unemployment. Thus the early programme of the ILP included the abolition of child labour, and TUC conferences passed similar resolutions in 1895, 1896, and 1897, although they were usually opposed by textile workers who benefited from cheap child labour. Others felt that the answer to this aspect of unemployment lay simply in a reduction of the hours of work, often associating with this plans for the reduction of systematic overtime, as in the resolution moved by Henry Broadhurst at the TUC conference in 1886. The demand for a statutory eight-hour day was made initially by the SDF in the early 1880s, and after the publication in 1886 of Tom Mann's pamphlet, *What a compulsory eight hour day means to the workers*, it was taken up by London building trade workers and then spread to the whole labour movement. Throughout the late eighties and early nineties the eight-hour cry was raised, but there were frequent clashes at labour conferences between its advocates and those who believed that it would result in smaller wages and a gradual loss of work to foreigners. Although Keir Hardie, founder of the ILP, took the matter up in Parliament in 1894 and a Bill was introduced the following year, nothing had been achieved by the turn of the century. This was due partly to labour's weak parliamentary position and partly to the set-back the campaign received when the Amalgamated Society of Engineers was defeated after a long and costly strike for the eight-hour day in 1897. In any case, trade unionists were divided over both aims and means. Some wanted a general eight-hour day while others preferred a reduction for certain categories of workers as an initial step. They were also split over whether the change was to be secured by legislative action or by collective industrial effort, a division made manifest when the TUC organised a plebiscite on this point in 1888.[6]

Another group of suggestions which found considerable support as possible remedies for unemployment related to the land. Rural immigration into towns undoubtedly was increasing competition for unskilled jobs, depressing wages, and accelerating the descent in the social and economic scale of the older and less able urban workers. To keep agricultural labourers in the countryside, it was argued, adequate facilities should be provided, notably decent housing and security of tenure. For this purpose TUC conferences frequently called for a reform of the country's land laws, for example in 1887, 1889, and 1895. One Social Democrat claimed that the land should be nationalised and the various councils given the power to organise the urban unemployed into the agricultural proletariat of the future.[7] Some envisaged this being done in special labour colonies where the unemployed could be trained for future careers as smallholders. The leading labour advocate of such colonies was George Lansbury, although Keir Hardie and Will Crooks also supported the idea. The latter told his biographer:

> I maintain that even the town wastrel takes more kindly to the land than to anything else. Of course, I know that before he can be made any use of he must be trained, but then it is well known that I favour farm colonies for training him.[8]

A rural note was also evident in the schemes of national works which, it was felt, the government should prepare and set in operation when unemployment grew unusually high. Afforestation was one of the most popular, but harbour construction, coast and land reclamation also found a place in Ben Tillett's resolution at the 1895 meeting of the TUC. The previous year, Hardie, in raising the question in the House of Commons, had suggested that in times of severe distress the government should anticipate works scheduled for some future date, such as the construction of new warships or roads. The TUC was sufficiently interested in the idea of government finance for remunerative local works of a similar nature to organise a members' ballot about it in 1894.

If many Englishmen, workers and otherwise, could give tacit assent to most of these possible reliefs for unemployment,

B

there were few in 1900 who agreed with Hardie, Henry Hyndman, Robert Blatchford, and other socialist leaders, that they were all mere palliatives and that the only solution was the abolition of capitalism in favour of socialism. To socialists, cheap labour, technological redundancy, and trade fluctuations were not basic causes of unemployment at all, but were rather symptoms of capitalist organisation. The programme presented by the ILP to the International Socialist Congress in July 1896 commenced with the assertion that unemployment was the inescapable outcome of capitalism and would only disappear when capitalism itself was overthrown. Only production for use, as opposed to profit, argued socialists, would lead to the eradication of unemployment, hence the frequent demands made for the nationalisation of monopolies and basic economic resources such as mines, railways, and canals.

The logical conclusion of this line of argument was that as the state was responsible for maintaining the economic system which produced unemployment, it should also be responsible for supporting the unemployed. At the ILP's 1895 conference the Huddersfield Branch moved a resolution claiming that one of the citizen's inalienable rights should be the 'right to work' and to enjoy the fruits of his own labours. A similar resolution from the Cardiff Branch stated that as a first step towards amelioration Parliament should recognise its duty to find work for all who needed it. In really bad times Exchequer grants should be made to all local authorities unable to provide work for their unemployed.[9] Earlier in the same year H. Russell Smart, mover of the Huddersfield resolution at conference, had written an article in Hardie's paper, the *Labour Leader*, which, while based on an assumption unacceptable to most socialists, asserted that all men possessed a natural right to work, an idea which appeared in the conference resolutions and which formed the basis of much of the labour movement's unemployment agitation before 1914. Smart argued that socialist theories on unemployment were founded on the fallacy that it was an inevitable product of capitalism. Personally, he believed that capitalism would not die until unemployment had been vanquished, a complete reversal of orthodox socialist doctrine. What was needed, he contended, was a minimum wage and shorter hours to reduce the volume of unemployment. For those still out of work and who had lived for at least six months in one locality the local authority should be legally bound to find work. These proposals he embodied in the form of a 'right to work' Bill.[10]

These then were the main lines along which organised labour felt that unemployment should be tackled, although there were naturally differences of emphasis and not all agreed with the assumptions of the socialists. But in the changing climate of opinion at the end of the nineteenth century the working-class movements readily favoured ideas based on the new premise that in some measure unemployment could be regulated by government control of the amount of work available, and by the re-training of those whose skills had been overtaken by technology. For those still out of work the labour movement wanted a relief system which would provide useful work for wages and be free of the stigma of pauperism and the condescension of the charity workers.

But in bringing the claims of the unemployed before the public the labour movement was hampered to some extent by the fact that the problem was one which fluctuated in intensity and the degree of public interest which could be raised depended very largely on the state of the labour market. Concern was high in the middle 1880s and the early nineties, but by 1897 the economy was entering a period of boom and the ILP national executive reported to the party conference that there had been a 'cessation of public interest in the unemployed problem'.[11] The report went on to exhort party members to be prepared for the inevitable turn of the tide, but the outbreak of the Boer War in 1899 reduced unemployment still further and it soon faded from the public mind in the excitement of war and its accompanying prosperity. It was not until 1902 when the war ended that the tide to which the ILP report had referred began to show signs of turning as the running down of war industry and the return of volunteers and reservists started to dislocate the labour market. Hundreds of demobilised soldiers returned to find their jobs filled and their prospects of finding another greatly restricted by the onset of depression. Early in March 1902 the Association for the Employment of Reserve and Discharged Soldiers contacted the Prime Minister, Lord Salisbury, drawing his attention to this difficulty, but while he promised to give it 'careful attention' he refused the association's request that he receive a deputation.[12] The first working-class organisation to take up the soldiers' cause was the SDF, whose leaders doubtless welcomed the opportunity to embrace a more popular cause after the execration they had suffered for their opposition to the war. In June the SDF paper, *Justice*, predicted that the troops would find 'their places filled and no work staring them in the face', and by October the federation was organising mass demonstrations of unemployed soldiers in Hyde Park.[13] Other SDF agitators were active elsewhere, for example in Bermondsey where meetings were arranged to protest against the council's decision to invite tenders for local authority work rather than give it to the unemployed.

In November the Commander-in-Chief, Field-Marshal Lord Roberts, and John Brodrick, Secretary of State for War, both signed a special public appeal asking employers to remember the soldiers when taking on new labour, but this was as far as anyone in official circles was prepared to go. Arthur Balfour, who had taken over the premiership in July, refused on several occasions to receive deputations from the SDF and the London Trades Council, and when Hardie tried in December to secure a parliamentary discussion on the situation the Prime Minister urbanely dismissed him, suggesting that he was exaggerating its gravity. Two days later the Speaker of the House of Commons refused to allow Hardie to introduce a motion calling on the government to make a grant of £100,000 to the local authorities for the purpose of relieving their unemployed. Shortly before the end of the year the President of the Local Government Board, Walter Long, also refused to meet a deputation from the London Trades Council which wished to place before him evidence of severe unemployment in the capital. Nor was the Liberal opposition any more concerned than the government. On Christmas Eve Sir Henry Campbell-Bannerman told a Scottish audience that the most pressing social problems facing the country were housing and temperance.[14]

In a sense his argument was correct, because the latest Board of Trade unemployment figures showed only 4.4 per cent of trade unionists out of work, and such agitation as had taken place had been of a very spasmodic and local nature. (See Table 1, page 190. All subsequent unemployment percentages are taken from this table.) But the situation was certainly bad in some areas, particularly in parts of London. It was this fact, the general indifference of most politicians, and the inability of Hardie and other Labour MPs such as John Burns to force the government's hand in Parliament, which prompted the Metropolitan District Council of the ILP to convene a meeting of representative public and labour figures on 15 December 1902 in order to consider what could be done for the unemployed and also to investigate the possibilities of establishing some permanent organisation to co-ordinate activity on their behalf. Those present at this conference included Hardie, who took the chair, James Ramsay MacDonald, secretary of the LRC, and several notable radicals such as Percy Alden, Edward Pickersgill, George Bernard Shaw, and R. Cunninghame Graham. The outcome was the creation of a provisional committee of thirty, somewhat unwieldy but necessary to accommodate the various interests present. Among the members of this committee was Alden, who was made secretary,

Hardie, S. G. Hobson of the Fabian Society and his colleague
E. R. Pease, who was also on the executive of the LRC. Thus
the establishment of the new committee did in fact link several
important sources of labour and radical power which were well
able to make their influence felt in different sectors of the
community. Hardie could act as spokesman in Parliament;
Alden was not only a Fabian but also a member of the Mansion House Committee; Pease and MacDonald could utilise
the strength of the LRC; and Hobson could bring in the
sophisticated propaganda machinery of the Fabian Society.[15]

Alden's election as secretary was no surprise, for although
the meeting had been summoned under ILP auspices, his, in
fact, had been the initiative behind it and in an article in the
Labour Leader he proceeded to outline the aims and structure
of the new National Unemployed Committee. Under the
heading of permanent objectives he listed the establishment
of a government department of ministerial status to deal exclusively with unemployment and to be responsible for such
things as the notification of impending distress, the publication of information as to the availability of work, and the
organisation of unemployed labour on road, forest, and farm
colony works. Temporary expedients for which the committee
was to agitate included the opening of local unemployment
offices, shelters to accommodate the homeless poor, and the immediate implementation of works already scheduled by local
authorities. The new central committee was to sit in London
to give information to the press, and it was hoped to set up
similar committees in all the great provincial cities.[16]

Early in 1903 Alden sent out invitations to local authorities,
trade unions, and other interested bodies, inviting them each
to appoint two delegates to a two-day national conference
called to discuss ways and means of realising this programme.
The delegates, 587 of them, duly assembled on 27 February at
the Guildhall and sat politely through long and often contradictory opening speeches delivered by three most unlikely

colleagues—Sir John Gorst, member for Cambridge University and one time Financial Secretary to the Treasury in a Conservative administration, Lady Frances Warwick, one of the SDF's more spectacular converts, and Sir Albert Rollitt, who had been MP for Islington South since 1886. Nor did things improve once the delegates got down to the business in hand. Three resolutions, claiming respectively that unemployment was the joint responsibility of national and local government, that the government should be pressed to take action, and that pressure should also be put on the local authorities, were all moved and debated in a manner described by the *Daily Mail* as 'vague and incoherent'.[17] The fourth resolution, however, moved by George Barnes, secretary of the Amalgamated Society of Engineers, was more practical, suggesting that 'a permanent National Organisation be formed in order to give effect to the decisions of the Conference, and that the Provisional Committee be re-appointed with power to add to its number'.[18]

The SDF regarded this whole enterprise with a very jaundiced eye. Possibly this was because the proceedings had been too mild, disappointing the hope that the conference would result in the unemployed being organised to make a thorough nuisance of themselves.[19] Certainly *Justice* complained that the resolutions had been either irrelevant or too theoretical. Hardie was accused of suppressing the London Trades Council delegates, most of whom were SDF members, for fear of offending the class susceptibilities of such an august gathering.[20] But the federation's apparent hostility to the formation of the National Unemployed Committee may simply have been due to the fact that it had not been consulted about its establishment. Indeed, early in 1903 the Social Democrats had organised their own committee to arrange agitation in London, chiefly in the form of street processions. These processions were not only designed to show the unemployed that the SDF had their best interests at heart, but also to overcome the apathy of the unemployed which had severely restricted the effectiveness of earlier agitation. In November 1902, for example, Harry Quelch, editor of *Justice*, had complained that it was 'idle to expect much help from the unemployed themselves', and it was now hoped to overcome this by organising street collections, the proceeds of which were to be shared out among the marchers.[21] Two brothers named Martin were put in charge

The unemployed in London. *Daily Graphic*, 17 Jan 1903

and they moved around the East End instructing local leaders in an effort to systematise the agitation. The results were impressive. Men from Poplar, Hackney, Tottenham, Shoreditch, Battersea, Lambeth, Edmonton, Mile End, and Southwark soon began to appear almost daily in the West End, sometimes as many as a thousand marching through the city together, and it was claimed that in January alone 20,000 unemployed men had passed through the hands of the SDF organisers.[22] The campaign culminated on the eve of Parliament's re-assembly in February when unemployed workers were marched in from almost every East End district to attend a protest demonstration in Trafalgar Square. *Justice* reported that 3,500 were present and several well-known labour personalities took part, including W. C. Steadman of the London County Council, James Macdonald the Social Democrat editor of the *London Trades and Labour Gazette*, and Harry Quelch.[23]

It would be unwise, of course, to take any of these figures at their face value, especially as both the *Labour Leader* and *The Times* put the attendance in Trafalgar Square at not more than 2,000.[24] But there can be little doubt that the campaign was successful in mobilising London's unemployed and in causing a great deal of inconvenience to the authorities and the general public. Throughout its duration letters appeared constantly in the press, a few couched in terms sympathetic to the unemployed, but the vast majority overwhelmingly hostile to the demonstrations. The main burden of the complaints was that the marchers blocked the streets and caused traffic hold-ups; that the police were far too tolerant; that the marchers were being encouraged to rely for help on public charity rather than on their own efforts, and that in consequence the processions were attracting large numbers of frauds and wastrels. Thus one critical letter claimed that the superintendent of the Clapham and Wandsworth casual wards had recently spotted in a march 'several hundreds' who frequently appeared before him as vagrants.[25] The managing director of the Central

Cyclone Company asserted that many of his employees regularly took time off to join the marches because they were so lucrative.[26] It was hardly surprising, therefore, that one paper could claim that the marches contained 'a small proportion of the deserving, a considerable proportion of hardened and habitual loafers and a good many more on the verge'.[27]

The campaign also disturbed other sections of the working-class movement. At least one trade union proudly boasted that none of its members were taking part because they were all too busy looking for work.[28] The Operative Bricklayers Society, badly hit by unemployment, rejected an SDF appeal for financial help, preferring to organise its own relief for its unemployed members. John Burns admitted that the marches had succeeded in waking London up to the existence of the unemployment problem, but he became so alarmed by the campaign's magnitude that he eventually asked the government to curtail it. Hardie also seems to have been concerned by the identification in the public mind of the unemployed with the militant and annoying tactics of the SDF, particularly as he was due to chair the conference of the National Unemployed Committee at the end of February. He totally disapproved, he said, of the 'way in which these agitations on behalf of the unemployed are taken advantage of to boom some particular organisation'.[29]

The government, too, was alarmed by the danger to public order posed by the unrestricted passage of unemployed East-Enders through the city's richer areas. No doubt memories of 1886 and 1887 were uppermost in the mind of Home Secretary Henry Akers-Douglas, who was giving the matter some serious thought, as he admitted in a letter to Lord Knollys, the King's secretary.

Please assure the King that these Processions have been engaging the most anxious attention of the Commissioner of Police and myself, and that we are using to the utmost the powers which we possess.

The two points in which these Processions are most objectionable are the collecting of money, and the obstruction of traffic.

On the first point our hands are tied by a decision of the High Court in 1886 of which the gist is that if a person, not as a regular mode of living, but for some object not in itself unlawful, goes from house to house and solicits subscriptions that is not within the prohibitions of begging in the Vagrancy Act... Of course if a man with a collecting box resorts to intimidation or otherwise brings himself into conflict with the law the Police can, and will stop him...

On the other point, processions are not in themselves illegal... and until the progress of a procession causes an unreasonable obstruction of traffic the Police have no right to interfere... It has been asserted that the Police are protecting the Processionists, but that is not so. The Police are there to protect the Public by regulating to the best of their ability the whole traffic of the streets... Though I would gladly stop the unpleasantness and inconvenience if I could, there is, I am advised, nothing more that I can do without exceeding my powers, and otherwise incurring great danger of exciting grave disorder.[30]

He went on, however, in a more optimistic vein, saying that the public was at last beginning to realise the futility of giving money to the marchers and that in consequence the incentive to take part in the processions was weakening. But his concern was evidently shared by some members of the government back bench, for shortly after Parliament re-assembled the member for Hanover Square in the West End, Colonel Legge, asked if the government was aware of the inconvenience caused by the processions and whether it was proposed to curtail them by

increasing police powers. Akers-Douglas replied that the police
had done their best to cope, but he agreed that Legge's suggestion was worthy of consideration.[31]

In fact, it was only three months before he presented a
memorandum to the cabinet on the subject. He reported that
police precautions had so far been successful but 'I am assured
by the Commissioner of Police that the margin of safety was
slight, and that the strain on the police, at the best, unduly
heavy'. In London, the memorandum continued, one man in
four had been occupied in marshalling the processions between 1 January and 18 February, and as the situation could
easily get out of hand in another winter Akers-Douglas recommended that the Metropolitan Streets Act of 1867 should be
amended in order to prevent the marchers from collecting
money so freely. If this freedom were limited, he argued, the
marches would probably peter out, and he concluded his
memorandum by stressing that the matter was 'one of great
importance' which should be tackled 'without delay'.[32] Within
three weeks of this cabinet discussion a Bill was introduced,
and it reached committee stage without any debate. Here it
ran into trouble with some Liberals who thought that it would
not be effective, but when Akers-Douglas stressed that he
considered it quite adequate for his purpose they withdrew
their opposition. The Bill then passed rapidly through both
houses and received royal assent on 11 August.

This, of course, was too late to be of use in curbing the
campaign which had provoked the measure's introduction, but,
as it happened, this did not matter, for the Social Democrat
agitation had already foundered on the twin rocks of finance
and doctrine. The unemployed organisers had depended for
their personal income on the results of appeals made in *Justice*
and although it was claimed that the response had generally
been good, the report presented at the annual conference in
April 1903 showed that the federation's financial position was
critical. Considerable inroads had been made into the Central

Election Fund in order to finance all aspects of the work, including the unemployment campaign.[33] Doctrinally the federation was split over the value of pursuing short-term palliative objectives, such as the amelioration of unemployment, a dispute which culminated in the expulsion of the 'impossibilists' at the stormy Easter conference. Although Hyndman and the old guard thus triumphed over those who believed that a palliative policy was a waste of time, their position might well have been strengthened had it been possible to point to any significant increase in membership as a result of the unemployment agitation. But as *The Times* said:

> The federation will, in the long run, gain nothing in popular esteem ... the class which will walk in the processions is traditionally ungrateful, and it seems to be generally understood that it will throw the S.D.F. overboard as soon as it may be convenient.[34]

At the end of the month in which Akers-Douglas finally secured the passage of his Bill unemployment stood at 5.0 per cent, ominously high for midsummer. By October the figure had crept up to 5.6 per cent, and early in November *Justice* appealed to all party members to spare no effort in renewing a vigorous agitation for the unemployed.[35] But the Home Secretary, alerted by his experiences of the previous winter, lost no time in utilising the legislation which he had so recently carried through Parliament, and on 7 November the Commissioner of Metropolitan Police issued regulations under the Metropolitan Streets Amendment Act to enable the police to keep a more stringent check on the activities of the marchers. No collection was to be taken in the streets except as specified in a permit, which could only be obtained from the commissioner. Applications for these permits had to be made at New Scotland Yard ten days in advance of the collection stating its date, purpose, place, and the numbers involved. They were valid only on the specified days and had to be produced on demand. No more than two collectors were to be positioned in any one spot. Tables, and boxes on poles (to reach upper-floor windows) were not to be used unless expressly permitted, and no collector was to annoy passers-by. Breach of any of these regulations was punishable under section twelve of the Metropolitan Streets Act of 1867. Quelch reacted angrily, claiming that 'the seamy side of our civilisation is to be turned in by police brutality, and Mr Akers-Douglas will declare with pride that "order reigns in London"—as in Warsaw'.[36] Certainly the regulations were sufficiently wide, and in some cases vague, to destroy the ease of financial collection which had been the SDF's chief carrot to the unemployed. Although they applied only to areas within six miles of London's centre, thus allowing the collectors still to flourish in the East End and the provincial cities, the decline of Social Democrat agitation in the capital in the winter of 1903 undoubtedly owed much to the cramping effects of this legislation.

To some extent, too, the ground was cut from under their feet by the swift response of many of the London boroughs to the worsening situation, and by the rapid growth of public concern. The London County Council had met on 28 October to discuss what could be done, and charitable appeals were soon appearing in the columns of the daily press with almost monotonous regularity. As November passed into December the monthly journals, particularly the *Toynbee Record*, began to carry numerous articles on the severity of the distress in the East End. On 3 December there came the most striking evidence so far that the city was at last taking the problem seriously. On that date the Mansion House Committee, whose functions had been in abeyance since 1895, was recalled.

This committee, established in 1886 to administer the fund set up by London's Lord Mayor for the unemployed, now resolved to organise a system of relief for a selected number of men on the lines of a plan which had recently appeared in the press. The scheme had been formulated by a number of prominent relief workers and required the selected men, all of whom were to have established homes as a pre-condition of selection, to take work in the country, their wages going to their families. This, it was argued, would avoid homes being broken up and would ensure that no shirkers applied. It had the further advantage that although it required substantial financial backing the work could readily be undertaken on existing farm colonies at Osea Island, Hadleigh, and Lingfield. But it was opposed by Percy Alden, who disliked the proposal to separate the man from his family, and he claimed that the plan's purpose could equally well be achieved by giving each local council twenty shillings per unemployed man in order to finance local relief works. His stand evidently had some effect, for when the sub-committee appointed to consider the plan reported just before Christmas, it was deemed necessary to stress that the borough councils had in fact been approached already but that only one, Poplar, had agreed to establish works of the sort advocated by Alden.[37]

It seems likely that in making his protest Alden was acting as spokesman for the National Unemployed Committee, which had re-convened on 10 October. Although its activities since the Guildhall conference had not been well publicised—one correspondent of the *Labour Leader* inquiring in September if it was still in existence—the committee had been quite busy during the summer.[38] At the October meeting a letter had been read from the Prime Minister refusing to receive a deputation and suggesting that the committee contact the Board of Trade with the resolutions which it had originally forwarded to him. It was thereupon decided to put pressure on the London County Council to call an early meeting of the borough authorities and to ask the President of the Board of Trade, the Free Church Conference, and the Prime Minister to see deputations, the latter on the subject of appointing a labour minister. This last objective was also to be pursued in Parliament by Hardie, and when the legislature re-assembled in 1904 he moved an amendment to the King's Speech regretting that no mention had been made of the need to create such a post with special responsibility for the unemployed.

During his speech Hardie openly admitted his brief for the National Unemployed Committee, confessing that labour men generally were deeply divided about the usefulness of any labour minister. Hardie's admission must have added to the worries of those ILP members who were afraid that their party was drifting rapidly into the Liberal orbit, a path indicated by the co-operation with radicals in the National Unemployed Committee and then by the generous Liberal support given to Hardie's unemployment amendments on the King's Speeches in both 1903 and 1904. Such fears account for the wide support given to one rank-and-file member, H. Wishart, when he suggested in June 1903 that the ILP should launch a national campaign for the unemployed behind the slogan of 'work for all'. Liberals, he contended, could not possibly support such an aim, cutting as it did at the very roots of the capitalism to which they all subscribed.[39] No national campaign was undertaken, however, and ILP agitation on behalf of the unemployed in the last months of 1903 was, like that of the SDF, virtually non-existent, apart from that organised through local initiative. The party's national leaders were concentrating their energies throughout the autumn on attacking Joseph Chamberlain's proposals for tariff reform and imperial preference, organising a series of meetings for this purpose in most of Britain's major cities. But this again attracted adverse comment from the party's unemployment lobby. Fred Wood, an officer in the Huddersfield Branch, appealed for the ILP to forget everything, especially the fiscal controversy, and to lead a national campaign to press the needs of the unemployed.[40] This plea was repeated in January by another member who wanted to know why the national leadership was wasting so much time over Chamberlain's programme.[41]

The answer was partly that, as a constituent section of a

labour alliance hoping to win seats in the next general election, the ILP could neither determine the issues on which an election was to be fought nor ignore a subject which so dominated public interest. But there was also the fact, as Hardie stressed in his speech in the House of Commons in February, that Chamberlain's supporters were making much of the tariff reform proposals as a solution to unemployment. In this they were undoubtedly aided by an unemployment index registering 6.3 per cent in December 1903. Thus Maltman Barry, once a member of the First International but now a Conservative supporter, argued that 'while the present amount of unemployment in this country is very great ... the increased trade which would come to us as a result of Mr Chamberlain's policy would absorb the whole of it'.[42] Leo Maxse, editor of the monthly, the *National Review*, predicted to Sidney Buxton, the Liberal MP for Poplar, that he would find tariff reform exciting 'great enthusiasm among our working classes'.[43] Chamberlain himself admitted more than once that if he failed to win over the working classes he was lost, and it seems clear that some of the ILP leaders appreciated the danger of their mentally associating full employment with a policy of tariff reform, hence their concentration on condemning Chamberlain's programme. Nor were the fears entirely unjustified. In September 1903 the following letter, written by the Chairman of the ILP's Willesden Branch, appeared in *The Times*:

> I crave a corner in your columns to enter my individual protest against the indecent manner in which the organised workers of this country are being cajoled and blustered into passing resolutions condemnatory to any fiscal change ... the so called leaders ... have been peregrinating through the country ... asking the working classes to condemn a proposal on which we have had as yet no definite pronouncement.[44]

Late in 1903 the TUC joined the battle, issuing a statement

C

which condemned as blacklegs all workers who supported Chamberlain. This apparently had little effect in deterring those who were already committed, for in the following April the Tariff Reform League summoned a meeting of trade unionists which resolved itself into the Organised Labour Branch, eventually assuming the name of the Trade Union Tariff Reform Association. Membership, it was decided, was to be confined to *bona fide* trade unionists and a twofold objective was adopted—the strengthening of trade unionism by employing protective tariffs to guard workers against unfair foreign competition, and the consolidation of the British Empire by the use of preferential tariffs. Both, it was argued, would ensure increased employment for British workers. The tariff reform press naturally played up the importance of this meeting, prominently displaying a statement issued at its conclusion in an effort to prove that working-class opinion was behind Chamberlain. The conference had been attended, this communiqué claimed, by representative leaders of 'a great many organisations in the chief industrial towns'.[45] But no attendance figures were given, which prompted a suspicious letter from a member of the Cobden Club. 'Can it be true,' the writer asked, 'as some busybody of a reporter alleges, that only about twenty five gentlemen took part?'[46] It was.

CHAPTER 2

The Unemployed Workmen's Bill, 1904-1905

IN SPITE OF the small attendance at its inaugural meeting, the
Trade Union Tariff Reform Association was launched into
what promised to be a very favourable economic atmosphere,
as the early months of 1904 were marked by an abnormally
high level of unemployment, averaging some 5.7 per cent. Just
what this cold statistic meant in human terms is well illustrated in the following pathetic note left by one George Tagg
who, unable to find work even after long months of searching,
killed himself.

> 'My dear children,
>   I cannot stand this much longer. If I can't get work to
> pay my way and keep you I must do something, for I am
> nearly off my head. If the worst comes, take care of little
> Debbie. Don't put her in the union if you can help it.
> You may manage to keep her between you. God help you
> to do so. You may get on better without me. Goodbye to
> you all. May we meet in Heaven.'[1]

The situation showed no sign of improving as the summer
months drew on and MPs must have been surprised to find
themselves listening to an unemployment debate in July. It
was initiated by Will Crooks, elected on the LRC platform in
1903 as member for Woolwich. He wanted to know what instructions had been given to the various state departments
responsible for coping with unemployment. Balfour replied
that the whole matter was constantly under the government's
surveillance, an evasion which earned him the sharp rebuke of

the *Labour Leader*. It would, said the paper, be a great comfort to 'the hundreds of thousands of men at present unemployed ...all anxiety will now be removed, for they have the assurance that neither the demands of brewers, mine owners, nor landlords ever drive the claims of the unemployed from his mind'.[2] Certainly the Prime Minister's statement did little to calm labour fears. One socialist claimed that the situation in the coming winter would not bear thinking about unless there was an immediate improvement in the labour market.[3]

Nor were working men alone in expressing fears about the position. All through the summer months the unemployed percentage never fell below 5.7, and by September several London poor law unions were making arrangements to increase their casual ward accommodation. On 26 September a special conference of south London guardians was held at Lambeth and the delegates discussed at length whether the government should be asked to take some preventive measures. In provincial cities, too, a similar concern was apparent, and local authorities all over Britain were discussing what could be done to cope with what threatened to be a winter of severe unemployment. In Bradford £5,000 was set aside for the provision of relief works, while in Manchester the Lord Mayor asked the guardians to subsidise the council in setting up similar works, although he admitted that no solution was possible until the government itself stepped in.

In view of these indications that heavy unemployment was widely anticipated, it was not surprising that the delegates at the annual TUC conference in September exhibited a lively concern about the worsening situation. Although there were still those who argued that unemployment could be offset by pursuading everyone to join a trade union, such old-fashioned ideas scarcely accorded with the more radical sentiments of the majority of delegates. Two resolutions were passed, one calling for pressure to be put on MPs and public bodies in order to secure for local councils the power to acquire land and set up works for the unemployed, the other requesting that the parliamentary committee approach the government on the matter of creating a labour minister. The most comprehensive steps of all, however, were taken by the SDF. It was no longer possible to organise street collections in the centre of London, and in any case the federation still could not afford to undertake any sustained campaign of this sort. It intended to nurse its resources until after Christmas and then hold major demonstrations to coincide with the opening of Parliament. But in the meantime the executive decided to sponsor agitation to secure a special meeting of Parliament to deal with the unemployment situation. Local branches were urged to summon public meetings and submit resolutions to the effect that 'the question should be taken up at once and dealt with on a national basis ... the government to summon at once a special Autumn Session of Parliament for the purpose of promoting legislation on behalf of the unemployed'.[4] SDF members on local councils were asked to bring this resolution up for discussion, and circulars were sent to the metropolitan guardians soliciting their support. To provide statistical backing for their case, individual branches were invited to carry out a street-by-street census of the unemployed in the main industrial centres.

Five days after the SDF announced this campaign, the government at last showed signs of responding to the growing pressures and widely expressed fears. On 6 October Walter Long announced that he had received so many representations about the state of the labour market that he had decided to call a conference of all London guardians for 14 October. He claimed that he personally was not worried, but admitted the existence of 'considerable apprehension'.[5] The Social Democrat executive immediately interpreted this as an attempt to draw attention away from the demand for an autumn sitting, and in order to prevent this happening drafted a letter which was forwarded not only to Long himself but also to all the London boards of guardians. It contained a list of proposals for tackling unemployment which included the establishment of labour colonies, an eight-hour day, and the undertaking of harbour and forestry work. It further pointed out that the problem was a national one and as such required treatment and financing on a national scale. All the recipients were asked to press for a special session in order to facilitate the passage of the necessary legislation. This was supported by *Justice* which stressed the point by carrying a large headline, something it

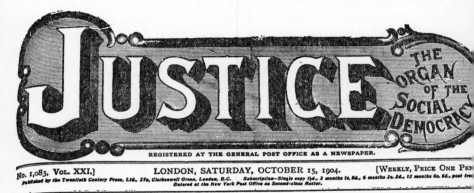

REGISTERED AT THE GENERAL POST OFFICE AS A NEWSPAPER.

No. 1,083, Vol. XXI.]   LONDON, SATURDAY, OCTOBER 15, 1904.   [Weekly, Price One Pen
Published by the Twentieth Century Press, Ltd., 37a, Clerkenwell Green, London, E.C.   Subscription—Single copy 1½d., 3 months 1s. 8d., 6 months 3s. 3d., 12 months 6s. 6d., post free
Entered at the New York Post Office as Second-class Matter.

**WE DEMAND AN AUTUMN SESSION OF PARLIAMEN
TO DEAL WITH THE UNEMPLOYED !**

Justice, 15 Oct 1904

did not normally have. But the guardians of London did not respond very favourably. Only those in Hackney, Shoreditch, Camberwell, Poplar, and Wandsworth passed the Social Democrat resolution, while the Lambeth Board agreed to forward it to its delegates at Long's conference. When George Lansbury tried to secure its passage at the conference itself he was heavily defeated, probably because most of those attending were satisfied by Long's promise of action.[6]

It was noticeable that in opening the conference proceedings Long went to some trouble to assure his audience that he did not share the view, current in some circles, that the country was facing an imminent and grave economic crisis. He simply wanted, he continued, to lay the foundations of a scheme for dealing with unemployment in a more systematic way than ever before. Dealing first with suggestions already put to him, he rejected outright the idea that the government should provide a large sum of money to finance national works, and when Lansbury moved the SDF resolution he successfully opposed it on the grounds that a special meeting of Parliament would not achieve anything. For immediate consideration he proposed that farm colony districts be set up for London and that in each district a local committee should be formed, representing guardians, councils, churches, and charity groups, to sort out those who should be given work in the farm colonies from those to be dealt with under the existing poor law provisions. Over these committees was to be a central body, similar to the Mansion House Committee and elected by the local bodies. The Local Government Board, said Long, would assist the work of all these committees by sanctioning such administrative expenses as were necessary and paying them out of the common poor fund. Borough councils could also make contributions to the central fund from their rates if they wished, and if these were considered to be *ultra vires* they could be similarly sanctioned, under the provisions of an Act of 1867.

On the whole these proposals were well received by the majority of delegates and by the press, although the COS, which was still clinging obstinately to its outmoded tenets, accused Long of capitulating to socialist agitation and complained that the creation of public work by a public authority was 'a most impolitic step'.[7] But in spite of these allegations, the socialists themselves showed little enthusiasm. Hardie was almost alone in welcoming the scheme, referring to it in January 1905 as 'a helpful and hopeful development'.[8] *Justice*, on the other hand, said that the conference had been nothing more than a hollow farce designed to draw attention away from the SDF demand for an autumn session by providing a semblance of action from the central authorities. Everyone was exhorted to keep up the pressure by deputation, resolution, memorial and leaflet. All other work, it pronounced, must be laid aside.[9]

Labour's criticism of Long's plans fell roughly into three main groups. Firstly, there were those who felt that the whole concept of tackling unemployment by means of a committee system was wrong. Blatchford, for example, claimed that its operation would be much too slow.[10] Quelch objected to a committee structure because in his view its composition would be mainly bourgeois.[11] Secondly, many were undoubtedly disappointed that the burden of supporting London's farm colonies was not to be shared between all the capital's boroughs, irrespective of whether they had an unemployment problem or not. This point was made very strongly by Crooks in a letter written to Balfour in December. 'All poor parts,' he complained, 'where work-people are aggregated, have to bear abnormal burdens which should be shared, if not by the nation, then at least by the metropolis.'[12] Closely allied with this particular criticism was the fact that West Ham, one of the worst-affected areas, was excluded from the new structure because it was not a London borough. SDF speakers made much of this at a London Trades Council demonstration held in Trafalgar Square shortly before Christmas. Finally, and probably most deeply felt, came the criticisms of the financial arrangements. It was claimed by some Social Democrats that the whole scheme would fail because the local authorities would refuse to levy any rate.[13] But when working-class representatives tried to oppose a resolution put up at the first meeting of the Central (Unemployed) Body that the necessary monies be raised from voluntary subscriptions rather than from the rates, they were easily outvoted. This voluntary principle annoyed the socialists so much that Hyndman had the effrontery to claim at a public meeting chaired by the Lord Mayor of London, who was the fund's treasurer, that Long's plan was like that of General Trochu at the siege of Paris—it was not designed to work.[14]

If Long had hoped to allay the unrest and relieve the pressure of the unemployed by his plans for London, his hopes were ill-founded. Indeed, as the situation continued to deteriorate the labour organisations began to increase their agitation. At a meeting of the ILP executive, held at the end of October, it was decided to undertake a series of educational public meetings on unemployment, holding them in several important industrial cities. One party member informed the *Labour Leader* that Hardie was thinking of introducing an unemployment Bill in the forthcoming parliamentary session, and possibly this was a further step in the ILP's campaign.[15] But there is no other evidence to support the claim—for example, in the *Minutes* of the party's National Administrative Council —and while it is possible that Hardie may have been intending to introduce such a Bill on behalf of the National Unemployed Committee, it seems unlikely, as this organisation seems to have disappeared by the middle of 1904. At least, no more is heard about it. The SDF, too, was maintaining its pressure for an autumn sitting, and immediately after Long's conference sent a telegram to Balfour congratulating the government on at last ending its long months of inaction. It went on to ask about the possibility of a special session, arguing that some of the ideas which Long had mentioned required legislative orders.[16] This was supplemented by yet another appeal to the branches, this time asking them to contact their local MPs and also the government seeking their views on the matter. But only three branches are recorded as having written to the Prime Minister, and only nine MPs replied to SDF representations.[17]

The government apparently remained passive in the face of this pressure, even when the rest of the labour movement joined with the Social Democrats in demanding immediate parliamentary action. The ILP executive added its voice to the growing chorus by sending a memorandum to Balfour early in November, while Hardie raised a petition signed by fourteen MPs in favour of such a step. This had the support of the TUC, which also contacted Balfour informing him that:

> This meeting of the Parliamentary Committee of the Trades Union Congress, representing 1,500,000 workers, learns with pleasure that an appeal has been made by a number of Labour and other members of Parliament and Local Authorities urging the Prime Minister to call a special short Session of Parliament for the purpose of dealing with the unemployed question, and joins with them in pressing the matter on the Prime Minister's favourable attention.[18]

Balfour replied to all these requests in a similar vein, telling Hardie that 'if I thought that an Autumn Session of Parliament would contribute . . . I should be prepared to accept the suggestion'.[19] In a letter to Crooks he gave his reasons for refusing, stating that he felt it necessary to await the outcome of the new machinery which Long had set up, and adding that it would be unwise to place too much hope on the results of a parliamentary debate.[20]

The TUC responded to Balfour's rejection of its appeal by asking him to make arrangements for a parliamentary discussion at the beginning of the next session. It also asked the Prime Minister to receive a deputation, and in order that it should be able to present him with some concrete proposals a joint labour conference on unemployment was planned for the early new year under LRC auspices. Balfour prevaricated about this request for a deputation, but eventually admitted to his personal secretary, J. S. Sandars, that he could 'see a certain difficulty in refusing' and decided that to see it in the first weeks of February would give him an opportunity to say things which he intended anyway to say in the King's Speech.[21] Early in January 1905 Sam Woods, the TUC secretary, was summoned to Downing Street. In the event he was ill and W. C. Steadman went instead, returning with a promise from the Prime Minister that he would receive a deputation on 7 February.

Once the TUC, the ILP, and the LRC began to interest themselves seriously in the unemployment problem it was almost inevitable that the voice of the much smaller SDF would be drowned. But this should not be allowed to obscure the fact that the campaign for a special parliamentary session at the end of 1904 was started by the Social Democrats. Not without reason the executive complained at the 1905 conference that the federation had 'received little recognition for its initiative in this direction'.[22] It must have been equally galling for Social Democrats when MacDonald issued a press statement about the forthcoming LRC unemployment conference saying that it would lay down the party's official policy and that for the first time 'proposals would be pushed to the front by a permanent and active political organisation'.[23]

The Social Democrats were similarly elbowed out of the spotlight once the government decided to bring in legislation, thereby transferring the focus of attention to Parliament where both the TUC and ILP were represented. The SDF, of course, had no MPs. Long's decision to tackle the problem by Act of Parliament was hardly surprising in view of the continued rise in the unemployment rate—it reached 7 per cent at the end of November 1904—and the widespread fears that violence would soon erupt. The portents were certainly ominous. In appealing for the continuation of agitation *Justice* had claimed that 'there is better prospect than ever before of waking up the authorities to a sense of their responsibility in regard to the unemployed . . . it is our duty to see to it that we bring the requisite pressure to bear upon them'.[24] Thus in many cities Social Democrat agitators successfully channelled spontaneous unrest into effective protest. In Liverpool the complacency of the city council, which had declared that work was plentiful, was rudely shattered by a noisy mass parade of unemployed workers through the city centre, while the main Bradford workhouse was besieged early in November by 2,000 unemployed demanding work. In Manchester SDF members took over a series of meetings originally arranged by a local unemployed confectioner and turned them into mass demonstrations which so alarmed the guardians that they agreed to provide immediate relief. In the south, Brighton's most fashionable church was invaded by a large number of unemployed, again led by local Social Democrats. Fears of violence were clearly increased by London's first major demonstration of the winter, held in Trafalgar Square under the auspices of the London Trades Council, but dominated by speakers from the SDF. The *Graphic* observed that many of them had been 'very violent in tone', while the *Mail* thought that the speeches had been an open incitement to crime.[25]

On 24 January 1905, after more than a year of prevarication, the cabinet at last discussed positive legislative proposals for dealing with unemployment, basing the discussion on a paper prepared by Long. Later, when giving evidence to the royal commission on the poor laws, Long acknowledged the influence of the pressures for action which the SDF had helped to generate.

> It is all forgotten now, but during the eighteen months that the pressure of the unemployed was growing, the methods adopted by the unemployed towards all the authorities were violent in the extreme. There were crowds besieging the offices of the relieving officers . . . the boards of guardians could hardly sit in some places without safeguarding their doors. . .[26]

He went on to admit that his plan had been 'somewhat hurriedly conceived' and said that one of the considerations governing his decision to bring in a Bill had been the fact that many local authorities were constantly calling his attention to the plight of the unemployed and their agitation.[27] In this context it is worth noting that, according to *Justice*, 45 poor law unions, 12 county councils, 40 urban councils, and 3 rural district councils had passed and forwarded to the Local Government Board the SDF resolution demanding a special session of Parliament.[28] 'One of the most active agents in bringing both direct and indirect pressure to bear upon the government,' said Sir Arthur Clay, a leading figure in the COS, 'is the Social Democratic Federation.'[29]

The government was not alone in being compelled to take unemployment seriously. The Liberals, too, frequently twitted in the labour press for supporting a free trade policy that could produce such heavy unemployment and suffering, were also beginning to take an interest. The inspiration behind this was the Liberal whip, Herbert Gladstone, who had written to Campbell-Bannerman in November 1904, suggesting the establishment of one or two unofficial Liberal committees to investigate various aspects of policy, including unemployment.[30] By December these committees had come into being and a memorandum on unemployment, written by Gladstone, was circulating among the Liberal leaders. No copy survives, but its importance may be gauged from the fact that it was seen by most of the prominent men in the party—Campbell-Bannerman, Asquith, Bryce, Spencer, Tweedmouth, Fowler, Morley, and Sinclair. Gladstone took the opportunity of explaining some of his ideas in a speech at Leeds in December, advocating that the government should take a survey of all necessary national works and then use the unemployed to carry them out. This was far too radical for Sinclair and also for Bryce, who thought that the whole matter should be treated with great caution 'lest we should seem to admit that it is the duty of the State to provide work—a doctrine which would cause general alarm'.[31]

Two weeks after the cabinet's first discussion on unemployment policy, the labour deputation waited on Balfour at Downing Street. The ideas which it put to him were substantially those agreed to at the joint labour conference which had been held at the end of January, but the Prime Minister remained unimpressed. He argued against the nationalisation of industry on grounds of principle, opposed schemes of afforestation because of their cost, and rejected proposals to set the unemployed to work on coast and marshland reclamation, claiming that these were merely palliatives and did nothing to solve the basic problem. Nor did he see how the government could effectively control the flow of work in its own establishments. In a sense he could afford to be so negative because his government had at last got some positive ideas of its own, ideas which were mentioned in the King's Speech to the newly assembled parliament on 14 February 1905.

But the announcement that machinery would be set up to deal with the unemployed generally evoked little more than passing comment. Most of the daily papers selected the proposed Aliens Bill or the Redistribution Bill as the most important items of domestic legislation. The Liberal *Daily News* only referred to the Unemployment Bill in order to dismiss it as a piece of bluff that would fool no one.[32] Most labour representatives, however, were cautious, but pleased. Hardie welcomed the announcement as 'the first break in the policy of do nothingness'.[33] Arthur Henderson, who had won Barnard Castle for the LRC in 1903, thought it 'most gratifying that at last the question of unemployment finds a place in the King's Speech'.[34] The ILP decided that for the time being it would issue no more of Hardie's unemployment pamphlets, while the immediate reaction of the LRC was to call a meeting in order to prepare a statement on the Bill's proposals. Only the SDF decided to continue its agitation, arguing that the announcement was a tribute to its efforts and that they must be maintained to prevent the government from weakening. Thus a second public demonstration was fixed for 25 February, a major one already having been held to coincide with the state opening of Parliament. The editor of the *Railway Review*, the paper produced by the Amalgamated Society of Railway Servants, shared the Social Democrats' suspicions, suggesting that the proposed Bill was nothing more than an election gambit, but such accusations were unfounded.[35] It is true that Sandars had written to Balfour about the contents of the King's Speech, saying that it 'ought to be made as attractive as possible for Party reasons' as 'it may be our goodbye', but this does not indicate that the government had no intention of honouring its commitments.[36] Indeed, the Bill was discussed again by the cabinet only three days after the King's Speech was delivered to the Commons.

The memorandum which Long presented for his colleagues' consideration on this occasion dealt at length with a controversial proposal to raise money for the new scheme from the rates. He pointed out that it was generally accepted as necessary to establish some means of meeting unemployment distress before it actually occurred. As he proposed to set up bodies for this purpose, he argued, he could hardly leave them dependent on voluntary finance. One of his main purposes in introducing the Bill, he continued, was to offset the growing demand for state action to solve the problem, a demand that was popular with certain sections of the opposition and with socialists. It was quite probable that his own scheme would fail if it was denied rate aid. In this case, he concluded, the demand for direct state intervention would probably become overwhelming.[37] But this proposal to utilise the rates caused a lot of heart-searching among Conservatives, and the opposition was led by Lord Salisbury who prepared a counter-memorandum, discussed on 2 March.

This paper argued strongly against rate aid because 'it involves principles so novel that they ought only to be adopted upon the most conclusive evidence'.[38] His main fear was that once the principle had been conceded for emergencies there would be nothing to prevent future governments greatly increasing the rate contribution and turning it into a routine practice, thus encouraging the working classes to depend on the community for help rather than on their own efforts. Nor, he felt, was there any adequate safeguard against malingerers, and if rate aid was supplied voluntary aid would dry up. Anyway, he concluded, the present crisis was nearly over and the need for emergency legislation rapidly disappearing.[39] The outcome of this cabinet meeting was apparently a modified Bill, for Salisbury told Balfour a few days later that 'though the new Unemployed Bill is an improvement upon the first, I do not approve of it. I think there should be no direct access to the rates . . . for the purpose of providing work for the unemployed.' [40] He did not object, he added, to rate money being used simply to provide the machinery or to finance emigration, but he re-affirmed his hostility to Long's idea of paying the unemployed with rate monies.

Although Salisbury ended his letter to Balfour by saying that he would not press his views if there was a majority against him in the cabinet, he was not alone in his opposition to the rate aid clauses in Long's Bill, for there were powerful vested interests outside the cabinet that were equally alarmed. One of these was the COS which saw the plan as a further concession to socialist pressure. The society's secretary, C. S. Loch, argued that in practice, if not in so many words, it was admitting the existence of a right to work. He was concerned, too, that voluntary effort would die out if the rates were used, and he also thought it undesirable that by sidestepping the poor law in this way applicants for relief should avoid the penalty of disfranchisement.[41] The idea of rate aid was also opposed by the wealthy London boroughs, which resented the prospect of being rated in order to subsidise operations on behalf of the unemployed concentrated in the poorer areas. Sidney Buxton aptly summed up Long's problem when he told Campbell-Bannerman that 'his chief difficulty is with his own friends, and the richer Metropolitan Boroughs, who do not want to be rated'.[42]

For some weeks after the King's Speech the Labour representatives in the House of Commons waited patiently for the introduction of the promised legislation, ignoring the taunts of the SDF that in not raising the matter they were forgetting the interests of the class to which they belonged and which they were supposed to represent. Early in March, Long was transferred to the Irish Office and replaced at the Local Government Board by the Prime Minister's brother Gerald, but there was still no sign of the Bill, and the SDF responded to the change by circulating yet another letter, asking all local authorities to put pressure on the new minister. On 30 March the patience of the Labour MPs finally ran out and questions were thrown at Arthur Balfour with such vigour that the Speaker twice had to call for order. Three days later Balfour was wriggling even more furiously. Hardie asked if it was the government's intention to introduce the Bill before Easter under the ten minute rule as Balfour had previously hinted, and the Prime Minister replied that if this course was 'one that meets with general approval, I shall be happy to accept it'. But when Hardie pressed him to name a day, Balfour was forced to contradict himself, answering that he could not, 'nor can I venture to say that so important a Bill ought to be introduced under the ten minute rule'.[43] Discretion, however, evidently got the better of the Prime Minister's valour, and on 12 April he informed Hardie that the Bill would be brought in under the ten minute rule after all, along with the Aliens Bill.

It is tempting to interpret Long's removal to the Irish Office as a Balfourian ploy to remove him from a post in which his very genuine desire to help the unemployed had caused dissension within the party and the cabinet. But the main consideration behind Balfour's choice was simply the need to find

D

an experienced Tory squire—a class that Long typified—to satisfy the demands of the Ulster Unionists for a suitable replacement for George Wyndham. In any case, the Bill which Gerald Balfour introduced on 18 April still contained the controversial clause permitting the payment from the rates of men employed on farm colonies established under the scheme. 'It would be impossible,' he said, 'to set up statutory bodies, permanent bodies for statutory duties, and leave them entirely dependent upon voluntary subscriptions for their maintenance.'[44] The plan which he went on to outline involved the creation of local London borough distress committees, the equivalents of the existing joint committees, supervised by a central body which was to be responsible for the creation of labour registries and bureaux. The local committees were not, he emphasised, empowered to provide work—this was the task of the central body. Each borough was to make a financial contribution to the scheme equivalent to a rate of one halfpenny in the pound, to be increased to one penny at the discretion of the Local Government Board. By the time Balfour had finished describing the proposals for London his ten minutes was nearly up and he was unable to say much about the scheme outside London, except that it was to have a more optional basis.

This final statement was one that attracted a considerable amount of adverse criticism from the labour ranks. In an interview with the *Labour Leader* Hardie said that it was a major drawback and made the scheme outside the capital 'very weak and ineffective'.[45] The *Railway Review's* commentator on parliamentary affairs thought that it would lead to a flood of provincial unemployed descending on London in the mistaken belief that work would automatically be found for them there.[46] Immediately after the Bill's first reading, the parliamentary committee of the TUC met and passed resolutions to the effect that no plan would be deemed satisfactory that was not nationally applicable and compulsory. A second general criticism was levelled against the clause which dealt with the wages to be paid to men employed under the scheme's provisions. It was laid down that they had to be less than the amount earned in a week by a general labourer of the lowest class. The general labour unions naturally objected strongly to this, Tillett claiming at the dockers' congress that the Bill was tantamount to a state system of blacklegging.[47] The TUC, mindful of the interests of its unskilled members, also passed a resolution saying that the Bill would be unacceptable if it resulted in the unemployed being used to lower the wages of general and unskilled men. Others attacked the clause which stated that no one could apply to the distress committees for more than two years in succession, while Social Democrats claimed that even a penny rate was insufficient. Fred Knee, a prominent London member of the SDF, challenged the necessity of creating new authorities to deal with the unemployed, arguing that the existing ones could just as easily be used.[48] Quelch thought the distress committees should provide work as well as passing on applicants to the central committee.[49]

But it would be wrong to think that the organised labour movement had nothing but criticism for the Bill. Harry Quelch admitted that it did have a two-fold significance. It recognised state responsibility for the unemployed, and proposed to unify London for rating purposes.[50] His party colleague, James Macdonald, thought that the compulsory nature of the London scheme and the use of public funds were both highly acceptable features.[51] Nearly all sections, whatever else they may have thought of the Bill, interpreted it as the recognition of the state's responsibility for the unemployed. This was the view taken by speakers at both socialist party conferences in 1905, and the *Labour Leader*, while suggesting that the Bill was too timid, welcomed it because 'it establishes the principle that the State is responsible for these crises which drive so many men out of work'.[52] Such claims must have worried the government, for both the Balfours had emphasised that this was not the Bill's intention. When he later gave evidence to the commission on the poor law Gerald again stressed, as he had done in his cabinet paper, that the rate aid provision had been included precisely to avoid giving any such impression.[53] This widespread and contrary interpretation must help to explain the government's subsequent reluctance to persevere with the Bill, although at Canterbury in October Akers-Douglas went to great lengths to show that the slowness of government business during the spring had been due to the time-consuming activities of the opposition before Easter.[54]

By mid-May, however, doubts as to the government's good faith were beginning to manifest themselves, stimulated by the Prime Minister's refusal—or inability—on 19 April and again on 8 May to name a day for the measure's second reading. Unemployment still stood at over 5 per cent and in Leicester 500 unemployed men signed up to join a march on London in emulation of a group of striking boot-makers from Raunds in Northamptonshire, who had won considerable public sympathy by just such an action. Soon similar marches were being organised in other towns, much to the alarm of some of the Labour MPs, such as Crooks.[55] Ramsay MacDonald was also dismayed, feeling that 'these disorganised bodies of unemployed . . . would seriously damage the chances of securing a rational and sympathetic consideration of the Unemployed Problem'.[56] Carefully organised marches, however, were a different proposition, and, after consultation with MacDonald, Hardie set about arranging these under ILP auspices. A circular was sent to all local branches emphasising the need to keep out all rogues when recruiting men for the marches, and it stressed, too, the importance of enrolling as many as possible of the artisan class in order to make the maximum public impact. Each man, it added, was to take his own blanket and food.[57] On 18 May Hardie was able to inform the Prime Minister that marches had been arranged to start from Leeds, Manchester, Newcastle, Liverpool, Glasgow and Birmingham.

The press was full of alarmist rumours, the *Telegraph* claiming that if the Leicester idea was taken up on a wide scale, arms would be needed to quell the marchers.[58] 'The metropolis,' warned the *Express*, 'is by no means prepared to wake up and find itself the Mecca of unemployed pilgrims.'[59] On 15 May a stroke of fortune had enabled Hardie to supplement his campaign to put pressure on the government to pass the Unemployed Workmen's Bill. He explained in a circular to the branches marked 'strictly confidential':

> This is to explain what has been appearing in the Press, about Great Demonstrations in connection with the Unemployed. The whole thing has arisen out of some recent consultations with MacDonald as to how best to increase the prestige and standing of our movement ... and to turn to most account the threatened march of Leicester's unemployed.

He went on to say that the previous day Joseph Fels, the millionaire American disciple of the land reformer, Henry George, had turned up at ILP headquarters with the offer of £200 to back some big effort on behalf of the unemployed, and that he and MacDonald had decided to undertake massive public meetings all over the country, with a major demonstration in London as the culmination of the provincial marches. For tactical reasons they had decided to ask the LRC to arrange the London meeting. 'By this means, we hope to make the gathering a huge success, whilst we get the credit.'[60] The same day, Hardie wrote to Henderson, explaining his plans and asserting that 'I am determined not to allow the bill to go under without making a big effort to save it'.[61] He added that the ILP would provide expenses of up to £150. This offer, in fact, presented some difficulties, for there was some suspicion among trade unionists about the ILP's motives, perhaps justifiably in view of Hardie's circular, but MacDonald suggested that if there was any feeling about the ILP finding all the money they should simply organise a general appeal to which the ILP could subscribe its donation.

But five days after writing to Henderson, Hardie informed his colleagues in the ILP that he had abandoned his plan for marches of the provincial unemployed on London, and it was widely claimed in the labour press that this was done because the Leicester unemployed, refusing to wait, had marched independently and spoilt the total effect. This, however, must have been an attempt to cover up more fundamental reasons, for the Leicester march did not begin until 4 June. Possibly when Hardie made his rather naive attempt to frighten the Prime Minister by telling him that several marches were already fixed, Balfour's firm reply had impressed him. 'I am of opinion that the arrangements of this house in regard to its own business ought not to be modified in one way or the other by any external demonstrations.' [62] Perhaps equally significant was the fact that this statement won the grateful support of the press, for Hardie had sometimes shown himself to be sensitive to public opinion. In any case, as the *Labour Leader* pointed out, the scheme was beginning to run into some practical difficulties.[63] Finally, and perhaps most decisive of all, there was the opposition of several of the Labour MPs. Burns noted in his diary for 24 May that his opposition to the Bill and the attempts to push it through had provoked criticism at a joint labour meeting from Henderson and Crooks, but 'we beat them in their attempt to rush us into the L.R.C. fold. Carried our point well. The rest of the men stood like rocks beside me.' [64]

But even though Hardie had given up the idea of mass marches on London he was still set on saving the Bill, especially when Gerald Balfour told a joint labour deputation on 25 May that only the total weekly wage paid to men given work under the Bill had to be less than that earned, on the average, by ordinary unskilled labourers in normal jobs. The actual hourly rate of pay could be the same, thus meeting the fears about the Bill being used to undercut union wage rates. In an article in the *Labour Leader* Hardie claimed that even with all its faults the measure was worth having because it recognised three vital principles—communal responsibility to find work, public acceptance of the expenses, and the removal of disfranchisement. Once the machinery was in existence, he argued, it would only need a trade crisis for all the restrictions to be swept away.[65] Thus despite the continued opposition of Burns and some difficulty in arranging suitable dates to avoid the holiday season, the plans for the London and provincial demonstrations went ahead. The first meeting took place at Sowerby in Yorkshire on 17 June, and three days later Gerald Balfour opened the debate on the second reading of the Unemployed Workmen's Bill. That the government had been disturbed by the labour interpretation of the measure as implying state responsibility was evident from the speeches of both Balfour and his predecessor, Long. The President of the Local Government Board emphasised again that there was absolutely no question of the state being obliged to find work for its unemployed, while Long accused the Bill's supporters of associating with it ideas which went much further than the government itself was prepared to go. Although the Bill was read a second time it came in for heavy criticism from the government's own back-benchers, especially Sir George Bartley, and from the press, the *Graphic* hopefully predicting that 'the government will recognise the dangers that lurk in this hastily drafted measure and will prudently allow it to drop'.[66]

By the end of June similar rumours were widespread in the labour press, though with varying degrees of optimism. The *Railway Review*, for example, expected that it would reach committee before disappearing.[67] The journal of the Electrical Trades Union on the other hand, expected it to be abandoned almost immediately.[68] At the beginning of July, Harry Quelch suggested that Balfour was deliberately leaving the Bill so that there would be no time to amend it, without which it would be useless.[69] There can be little doubt that this flood of rumours, and a continuing high level of unemployment, help to explain the success of the LRC's programme of demonstrations which continued throughout June, July and August, staggered in this way to allow each to be addressed by a national figure. They were organised on a scale far wider than anything which the SDF, for example, had previously achieved, and some impressively high attendances were claimed, though the accuracy of the estimates is open to question. Meetings were held in almost every major city, as the following list illustrates. Attendances, where given, are in brackets.[70]

Altrincham	Hull (3-4,000)	Portsmouth
Barrow	Hyde	(5,000)
Birmingham	Ilkeston	Pudsey (1,000)
(8-12,000)	Islington	Rochdale
Bradford	Jarrow	Rotherham
Brechin	Kilmarnock	St Helens
Bristol	Leeds	Scarborough
Burnley (2,000)	Liverpool	Sheffield
Burton	(13-14,000)	Stockport
Cardiff (1,000)	Long Eaton	Stockton
Crewe	Loughborough	Sunderland
Derby (2-3,000)	Manchester	Swansea
Dewsbury	Merthyr (2,000)	Wakefield
Dundee	Mexborough	Walthamstow
Ealing	Middlesbrough	Warrington
Eccles	Newcastle	Watford
Felling	Newport (2,000)	West Bromwich
Finsbury	Normanton	(15,000)
Gloucester	Norwich	Willesden
Grimsby	Nottingham	Wishaw
Halifax	Oldham	Woolwich
Hanley	Oxford (500)	Yeadon
Huddersfield	Plymouth (1,000)	York (1,000)

Each meeting passed a resolution welcoming the Bill as an acceptance of public responsibility to find jobs for the out-of-work, but demanding that it apply to the whole country equally, that all wage limits be removed, and that the bulk of the cost be borne by the national exchequer. Almost all the leading personalities of the labour world took part, with the notable exception of Burns. The whole campaign really reached its climax with the London meeting held on 9 July, but although some 250 trade unions and 2,000 unemployed took part the total effect was ruined by torrential rain. Nevertheless, it must have been extremely aggravating that such a successful series of demonstrations costing over £150 passed almost unnoticed. 'No conspiracy of silence, no boycott of popular agitation,' complained the *Labour Leader*, 'was ever more complete than that of last Saturday's and Sunday's Unemployed Bill demonstrations by the London Press . . . not a single reference was made to the huge meetings held in scores of towns.' [71] Nor was the London demonstration any more successful in earning public notice, the *Express* almost laconically observing the day afterwards that suicide as a means of escape from unemployment seemed to be on the increase, an observation of peculiar poignancy for the few relatives of the sixty-nine-year-old unemployed woman whose useless and unwanted body had just been removed from the River Medway.[72]

Some did claim, however, that one result of the demonstrations was a softening in the Prime Minister's attitude. There may well have been an element of truth in this, for on 13 July, just after the London meeting, Balfour announced that the Bill could go through. But he made its passage conditional on the removal of the rate aid clause and it is clear that a great deal of pressure was being exerted on the government behind the scenes, not only by its own supporters, but also by outside interests. Only a week previously the West End London boroughs had made a strong protest against the financial arrangements, and it is significant that on 17 July Balfour told a

deputation of the wives of London's unemployed that a revised
Bill would be drawn up once current negotiations were complete: this on the same day that a Conservative paper advised
the government to relegate the measure 'to the limbo from
which it should never have emerged'.[73]

The discussions about the Bill's future were evidently well
advanced, as less than a week passed before Gerald Balfour
presented the revised version to the House of Commons. It
was now envisaged as an experiment to last for ten years, and
there was to be no rate aid to pay wages to unemployed men.
Instead, all money for the payment of wages was to be raised
from voluntary sources. There were some other minor alterations as well, but these were the ones in which the working-
class movements were vitally interested and the reaction was
predictably hostile. The *Labour Leader* condemned the revision as 'the most indecent fraud ever perpetrated upon the
working classes'.[74] Hardie, who said that the scheme was now
an 'airy superstructure without any solid foundation', wasted
no time in raising a petition signed by 7 lord mayors, 11 leading churchmen, 27 MPs, and 21 others including Lansbury
and Alden, and calling for the government to resist outside
pressures and pass the original Bill.[75] The Labour MPs were
more divided than ever, for at a meeting held with the TUC's
parliamentary committee on 24 July Hardie, Henderson and
David Shackleton all joined Burns in opposing the new draft,
even though the rest were still in favour of getting it through.
Henry Broadhurst, the Lib-Lab member for one of the Leicester seats, and Crooks were among those who still supported
the measure, Hardie later stating during the report stage that
it was only respect for the latter's judgement that was preventing him from dividing against it when the vote was taken.[76]
In spite of these divisions, however, the LRC had no intention
of letting the agitation drop, as MacDonald explained in a
letter sent to all the groups which had participated in the
summer demonstrations:

I am instructed to say that the L.R.C. does not propose to allow the cause of the Unemployed to drop. So soon as we know what the purpose of the Government is exactly we shall consider plans for organising on a national scale an agitation to demand that something shall be done immediately on the lines of the resolutions on unemployment passed at our Liverpool Conference last January.[77]

The government's intentions were apparently made clear when on 31 July Balfour omitted the Unemployed Workmen's Bill from a list of those which were to be pushed through before the session ended. When challenged by Hardie he said that he had no intention of passing a Bill which included the rate aid clause, but without it the Bill's supporters did not seem very keen. At least, he added, he had received very little encouragement for the re-drafted measure.[78] But then, just as it seemed that the government had finally decided to let the Bill die, perhaps hoping to use labour's divisions as a further justification, there came the first sign of the uncontrolled violence which Hardie, for one, had already predicted as a result of the government's procrastination. A large group of Manchester unemployed, allegedly obstructing traffic in Albert Square, refused to disperse when ordered to do so and, inspired by Social Democrat agitators, rioted when the police made a baton charge on them. Hardie promptly sent off a telegram of congratulations, saying that the spirit of Peterloo was once more abroad in England and that now they would win their fight.[79] Certainly the incident produced a good deal of uneasiness in the press.

It was no coincidence that on 2 August, the day after the Manchester riot, the government began manoeuvres to withdraw from the difficult position in which it now found itself. A royal commission to investigate the poor law and the whole problem of poverty and distress was announced in reply to what Beatrice Webb later termed 'an evidently pre-arranged

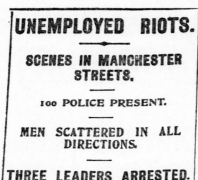

UNEMPLOYED RIOTS.

SCENES IN MANCHESTER STREETS.

100 POLICE PRESENT.

MEN SCATTERED IN ALL DIRECTIONS.

THREE LEADERS ARRESTED.

Scenes occurred in Manchester this afternoon which have no parallel in the history of the city since the dreadful days of Peterloo, nearly a century ago. For some time now the unemployed have been agitating for the passing of the Unemployed Bill, now before Parliament.

Latterly they have been holding weekly and almost daily meetings in the Police Yard in Albert-street, but in order to bring their grievances more prominently before, and obtain the sympathy of, the public the venue was changed in defiance of the civic authorities. from the Police Yard to Albert Square. Several of these meetings have been held with no serious result other than a slight

In the meantime the unemployed made their way to Piccadilly, opposite the Queen Victoria monument. A rally was made, and Mr. Smith was amongst those who spoke.

When it became known that arrests had been made a large crowd of curious people (amongst whom were a few unemployed) assembled in Albert Square, and for a considerable time afterwards stood with their eyes on the front entrance to the Town Hall evidently awaiting further developments.

THE POLICE DENOUNCED.

At the Piccadilly meeting, the unemployed, who by this time were re-inforced by a large number of sympathisers, appeared to resent what one of them called "a gross interference with their rights." Amongst the most indignant were several women, who cried out what they would do to the police.

Several speakers addressed the meeting, and denounced the police for their conduct that day, a sentiment that was received with applause. Mr. Balfour and the Government came in for a share of the general indignation and when "boo's" were called for the right hon. gentleman a chorus of them was given lustily.

Threat To Rescue Prisoners.

One of the speakers, reverting to the occurrence, threatened that if any more arrests were made the unemployed in Manchester would not stop until they had succeeded in effecting their release. They would rescue them, he was heard to say amid the din, and "our comrades," he added, "we will stand by." The orator, who was hoarse with excitement, next appealed to the manhood and womanhood of the unemployed to assemble again in their fullest strength and to assert their right to free public procession and their

The Manchester unemployed riot. *Manchester Evening Chronicle,* 31 Jul 1905

question'.[80] Gerald Balfour's statement that the government was now anxious for the Bill to be tried as a three-year experiment contrasted vividly both with his own previous announcement that it was to last for ten years and with his brother's omission of it from the list of measures to be completed before the session ended. By 7 August the government had successfully steered the Bill through the Commons, resisting in the process two attempts by Hardie to reinstate the rate aid clause.

It was noticeable that during the debates the government speakers, particularly Arthur Balfour, stressed that the royal commission was part of a long-considered strategy. 'I have now to say . . . that, having given full consideration to the question, we are of opinion that the time has now come when full in-quiry . . . ought to be undertaken.'[81] But if the government had been thinking about such a commission for some time, why hadn't it been mentioned previously? The only evidence to suggest that the government had thought about the matter prior to 2 August 1905 consists of a letter written by Long to Balfour—in December 1904. It was in reply to Balfour's query as to how he should answer a letter from Herbert Samuel, the Liberal MP, who had suggested that the government should undertake just such an investigation. Long had replied that there was much to be said for the idea, indicative again of his real wish to tackle poverty and unemployment in a drastic way, but had added that the present time was not suitable.[82] If there had been any serious intention of setting up a commis-sion it would have been a very useful foil against embarrassing questions from labour deputations—but it was never men-tioned. In February the Prime Minister had told Shackleton that any tampering with the poor law would be a dangerous thing.[83] On 9 May Gerald Balfour had said in reply to a question from Hardie that the government had no intention of setting up a small committee to examine the working of the poor law.[84] In either case the announcement of a large-scale inquiry would have done much to offset the unfavourable im-pression given by these essentially negative pronouncements. Again, as late as 26 July the government had said that the Bill was to be a ten-year experiment, though by 2 August it had been reduced to three years, the natural corollary of a royal commission whose report could reasonably be expected within that time. 'Let us confess,' said the *Standard*, 'what ministers will hardly deny, that the Royal Commission was an after-thought suggested by the Parliamentary difficulty in which they found themselves. . .'[85]

It seems clear, then, that the government, alarmed by the ugly incident in Manchester, decided to resurrect a Bill which it had virtually pronounced dead on 31 July, perhaps hoping to offset some of labour's antagonism towards the new version by appointing a royal commission, an act which implied that once more information was available, a more far-reaching solution could be applied. In any case, Balfour must have known that, barring an electoral miracle, it would be a Liberal government which would have the task of putting the commission's proposals into effect. Nor was it unimportant that Balfour himself represented a Manchester constituency, and he may well have had one eye on his future election prospects. There was certainly no doubt in the labour press that he had 'been shaken by events in Manchester' and that the riot was directly responsible for the government's change of heart.[86] One trade union journal claimed that when the riot broke out 'hon. members suddenly developed a great anxiety to pass a Bill which but a short time previously they had in their own minds relegated to the House of Commons waste paper basket'.[87]

Even though Balfour had given in to the anti-Bill lobby and removed the rate aid clause, many labour writers and leaders still interpreted it as an acknowledgement of state responsibility for the unemployed, not now by extending the principle of local financial liability to its logical conclusion that the state was ultimately responsible, but deducing it from the simple fact that the government had legislated on the matter. This was the view of a writer in Robert Blatchford's *Clarion*, although he still termed the Bill a 'poor lopped off measure'.[88] When the dockers' leader, James Sexton, strongly attacked the bill at the TUC conference in September he was censured by the *Labour Leader*, which claimed that it was important because its very existence constituted an admission by the state of its duty towards the unemployed.[89] This same interpretation of the Unemployed Workmen's Act lay behind the decisions of both main socialist parties to insist that it be put into the fullest possible use in order to secure the practical recognition of the right to work. In addition, it was hoped that this would so exploit the measure's weaknesses that it would break down and prepare the way for a more radical scheme. Both the SDF and the ILP, therefore, took steps to organise the unemployed more effectively than ever before.

In August the ILP announced in a branch circular that a series of meetings would be held in leading industrial cities to consider ways and means of utilising the new legislation and also to enrol the unemployed in a permanent organisation pledged to secure the right to work. At the beginning of November, by which time most of these provincial conferences had been held and at least eight local 'right to work' committees already established, Hardie chaired a meeting of delegates from various labour and socialist groups to consider the formation of a National Right to Work Council. Originally it had been hoped that the LRC and the Labour MPs would carry out this task, but only Shackleton had turned up at the October meeting called to consider it. He had been against the launching of such a movement and it was therefore decided that it should be undertaken by the ILP.[90] Now in November a small committee was set up, charged with the job of drawing up a national manifesto and gathering funds. These developments were welcomed by the SDF in contrast with its hostile reception of the National Unemployed Committee in 1903. This favourable reaction may have been due to the fact that —unlike the National Unemployed Committee, which had been the brain-child of a radical, consisted of a Liberal-Labour alliance, and had had a very moderate programme—the new body was committed to a socialist objective and was entirely socialist in composition. George Barnes was the chairman, the treasurer was Lansbury, Frank Smith of the ILP was the secretary, while the committee members included Hardie; Pete Curran, of the gasworkers' union; Frank Rose, an ILP member of the Amalgamated Society of Engineers; Mary Macarthur, the women's labour organiser; MacDonald; Mrs Cobden-Sanderson, socialist daughter of the famous Richard

Cobden; and Harry Quelch. The inclusion of the last two may also explain the federation's support, for both were SDF members. By the beginning of December twenty-one local 'right to work' committees had been set up, and *Justice* was appealing for many more to be formed.[91]

A further explanation of the federation's friendly reception of the Right to Work Council was that it saw in it a means of making its own efforts more effective, even national, in scope. Working through the medium of the London Trades Council, the Social Democrats had secured the summoning at the end of September of a conference of London unions and socialist organisations. No representatives from the LRC were invited, although 96 trade unions, 4 ILP branches, the Fabian Society, and the SDF executive and London District Council all attended. It was agreed to set up the London Central Workers' Committee with the aim of co-ordinating agitation in the capital and establishing local committees in each borough to press the councils to put the new legislation into the fullest possible use. Just how far the SDF dominated this body can be seen from the fact that Quelch was elected chairman and that eight of the fifteen executive members were also Social Democrats—Knee, Harry Kay, John Hunter Watts, G. Patterson, Jack Williams, J. McLeod, T. Wall, and John Stokes. On 3 October the SDF contacted the ILP, suggesting that a national joint unemployment committee be formed to organise agitation on a national scale. The contents of the letter indicated clearly that the SDF had been greatly impressed by the success of the ILP-inspired demonstrations in the summer, which had compared very favourably with the federation's own efforts to organise a national demonstration in January. At this stage the ILP was still hoping that the 'right to work' movement would be organised by the LRC, and it was decided to urge the SDF to co-operate 'with that body'.[92] Just in case the LRC decided not to become involved, however, Hardie, Philip Snowden, and Bruce Glasier were authorised to act on behalf of the ILP in this matter. But there was evidently some disagreement about the attitude to be adopted towards the federation because only one of this trio, Hardie, later supported demonstrations organised by the London Central Workers' Committee in November and December. He was joined by Barnes and Smith, but it seems that Snowden and Glasier shared the view of MacDonald, who was totally against any co-operation with the Social Democrats. When they had first taken steps to set up the London Central Workers' Committee MacDonald had told the secretary of the ILP's metropolitan council that he had 'the best evidence for believing that the matter is only another SDF dodge to hamper the LRC'.[93]

But these efforts at organisation all received a considerable impetus when the Local Government Board eventually issued the orders for the new Act's administration. In addition to re-introducing several rules which had originally been dropped in response to labour pressure—for example, the regulation that a man could not receive work for more than two years in succession—each applicant was now required to fill in a very detailed personal record form. This, claimed Hardie, had the COS stamped across every page and unless an applicant could 'show the rudiments of angels' wings already in the sprouting stage, he or she may go hang for anything the act will do for them'.[94] When Gerald Balfour announced that nothing could be done about any of these unpopular regulations until the distress committees had been set up, both the SDF and the ILP campaigned vigorously for their own nominees. The Social Democrats were quite successful in London, and in West Ham secured no less than five places on the committee for SDF members. The ILP, too, managed to get some representation, scattered up and down the country, but in London the effort was bungled. MacDonald blamed Sanders, the party's London organiser:

So far as I can make out there are several nominations of

E

our kind of people few of whom know that the others are up. Now Sanders is paid to look after the interests of the I.L.P. in London and for his £50 he ought to put himself to the trouble of getting some unity imparted into our action. Instead things have been allowed to drift and once more the I.L.P. looks as if it were going to be out of it . . . it is all very sickening. . .[95]

Nor was the ILP-inspired Right to Work Council achieving very much. By the time Balfour resigned his premiership in early December it had only just managed to produce its manifesto. The London Central Workers' Committee, on the other hand, was extremely active. In one week alone, *Justice* claimed, the organisation had forced the Battersea Distress Committee to endorse the SDF's unemployment programme, led deputations to the authorities in Bethnal Green, Southwark, Hackney, Fulham, and Hammersmith, and had organised propaganda meetings in Kensington, Poplar, Paddington, and Westminster.[96] Large-scale marches through the West End were also arranged, particularly in November, and this campaign was so successful in keeping unemployment in the public eye that the *Daily Graphic* was forced to conclude that 'there is little chance of the London public being allowed to forget the Unemployed problem, even if they had a mind to'.[97] Others were less dispassionate. 'How long,' asked Sir Arthur Clay, 'is this sordid farce to be allowed to continue?'[98]

Balfour seems to have watched this socialist activity on behalf of the unemployed with a mixture of detached amusement and concern. In October he had been sufficiently interested to have his secretary draw up a report on its extent and objectives, but in November, probably encouraged by the downward trend in unemployment, he told the explorer and diplomatist, Sir Frank Younghusband, that 'it is curious that they should suppose . . . they can terrorise us into any such absolutely fatal admission as that it is the duty of the State to find remunerative work for everyone desiring it'.[99] He knew that the SDF was too small to present any real danger, and in any case the London Central Workers' Committee was running into financial difficulties of the sort which had always hampered the federation's work. At the end of November Fred Knee appealed for funds to support Jack Williams as a full-time organiser for the committee. It was again indicative of a new spirit of co-operation between the SDF and some members of the ILP that two of those who responded to this appeal were Hardie and Frank Smith.[100]

CHAPTER 3

The birth of the Right to Work Bill, 1906-1907

EARLY IN DECEMBER 1905 Arthur Balfour finally tendered his resignation to the King. This, said *Justice*, was no excuse for the labour movement to neglect the needs of the unemployed. On the contrary, the matter was all the more important because the past statements of the Liberal leaders, who were to form the next government, had not been very promising.[1] Certainly at various times during the previous three years they had come under heavy fire from labour and socialist writers for their failure to produce an unemployment policy. In November 1904, for example, Campbell-Bannerman had received a deputation of unemployed at Manchester and the *Labour Leader* had commented sadly that 'he could promise to do nothing . . . no opinions . . . no proposals . . . not even a programme'.[2] It is true, of course, that the party had established an unemployment committee late in 1904, but this did not produce any generally accepted policy, nor did it act as a stimulant to the Liberal rank and file. W. H. Beveridge, invited by Herbert Samuel in March 1905 to address a meeting of Liberal MPs on unemployment, gained the impression that his audience had not thought very much about the subject at all, and after the meeting was over C. P. Trevelyan, one of a group of Liberal members who were concerned that the party should have an advanced social policy, apologised to him for the lack of intelligence shown by those who had attended.[3]

Even as unemployment had got worse in 1905, and the government had at last introduced legislation, the Liberal leaders had only reluctantly taken a more active interest, and then mainly for political reasons. Gladstone had pointed out to Campbell-Bannerman that a short speech on the Unemployed Workmen's Bill 'would have a good effect and show that the Opposition takes a keen interest in the Bill'.[4] Similarly, in asking Buxton to move a resolution at a party meeting demanding permanent machinery to tackle the unemployed problem the Liberal MP, Augustine Birrell, stressed that 'it ought to be moved by a front bench man in order to prove our good faith and show that we mean *business*'.[5] But many remained unconvinced by the Liberals. In the *Labour Leader* 'Gavroche' noticed that at the height of the summer's unemployed agitation they were also holding demonstrations, but were not discussing unemployment. Although Liberalism had once meant something, he continued, it had now become a 'kind of lavatory where the parvenus tidy themselves up . . . before they pass in amongst the old nobility'.[6] Hardie, with some foresight, thought that even if the Liberals did intend to do anything for the unemployed once they were in power, there would be all sorts of party disputes, probably involving the House of Lords, and that as a result the unemployed would be forgotten.

Nor were these doubts about Liberal policies in any way modified once it became clear that Balfour's days at Downing Street were numbered. If anything they were increased when Edward Grey, soon to become foreign secretary in the new Liberal Government, said at Dudley on 15 November that the solution lay in education, land reform, housing and temperance legislation. This was followed by a vague statement from Campbell-Bannerman to the effect that 'whatever we do in the matter, I think it will be more deliberate and effectual than this', the reference being to the Unemployed Workmen's Act.[7] Still worse was to follow. At Walthamstow on 20 November another Liberal soon to enter the cabinet, John Morley, declared that he had no remedy at all. Not surprisingly, Campbell-Bannerman told Asquith shortly before Balfour resigned that 'much mischief was being done by the notion that we had little or nothing to say about the unemployed'.[8]

Much obviously depended on who was appointed to the Local Government Board and thus given responsibility for formulating a policy. When John Burns, famous for his role in the unemployed riots of 1886, was given the job it was not entirely unexpected, for in October 1904 one observer had advocated giving him this very post.[9] But Burns' views had mellowed greatly since his appearance at the Old Bailey in January 1888 on riot charges, and the news of his appointment went down badly with his former colleagues in the SDF. His old branch at Battersea issued a press statement claiming that his elevation was 'the crowning act and the reward of a whole series of betrayals of the class to which he belonged'.[10] Harry Quelch also took the view that Burns had received a fair reward for his apostasy.[11] But the less extreme sections of the working-class movement were not so critical. Hardie was cautiously—or, in view of his electoral pact with the Liberals, tactfully—optimistic. Trade unionists generally seem to have been pleased that a working man had at last found his way into the cabinet, and the clash of opinion between moderate and extremist was to some extent symbolised at a London Trades Council meeting on 14 December 1905 when Fred Knee opposed a motion applauding Burns' appointment. He was supported by all the SDF delegates and the resolution was declared lost when the voting went 37-37.

By and large, the first actions of the new government justified the attitude of those who were prepared to give it a chance. A circular, which came into effect in January, was issued from the Local Government Board in December, relaxing the regulation which had denied work under the Unemployed Workmen's Act to any who had previously been in receipt of poor law relief. The government was also thinking of increasing labour representation on the poor law commission. Although the TUC had petitioned Balfour for some representation, he had ignored its requests and when the names of the commissioners were announced at the end of November they were deemed sufficient, in the phraseology of one trade unionist, to send shivers of horror down the backs of all working men.[12] Only three, Lansbury, Beatrice Webb, and Charles Booth, were thought to be sympathetic to labour. The rest included C. S. Loch of the COS, Samuel Provis, permanent head of the Local Government Board, and charity workers Octavia Hill and Helen Bosanquet. The TUC evidently expected a friendlier attitude from the new Liberal administration, for on 20 December it decided to put forward the name of Francis Chandler, secretary of the Amalgamated Society of Carpenters and Joiners, and he was in fact added to the commission. Finally, although it was not public knowledge, a cabinet committee on unemployment was set up, consisting of Burns, Lord Ripon, Asquith as Chancellor, Gladstone as Home Secretary, and Sidney Buxton.[13]

Before this committee could work out any detailed proposals, however, the new government had first to face a general election. But it was no great ordeal, for it resulted in an enormous Liberal majority. Equally noteworthy for contemporaries was the emergence of the LRC which won 29 seats and almost immediately changed its name to the Labour Party. Many gloomy predictions appeared in the press about the policies which the new party would follow. As far as unemployment was concerned, one paper confidently forecast that it would compel the provision of work at public expense, which would, it was claimed, produce widespread pauperisation.[14] But in fact the Labour candidates themselves had suggested a remarkable variety of solutions for unemployment during the election campaign, and even after it was over they were frequently very vague when it came to putting forward concrete proposals.[15] Crooks, for instance, said merely that the Labour Party would take the matter up.[16] This lack of any clearly defined policy simply reflected the fact that the Labour Party had never previously been in a position to introduce detailed pieces of legislation. Notwithstanding the Liverpool unemployment conference of 1905, the Labour Party made its entry on to the parliamentary stage with no detailed programme on unemployment, only a general commitment to two principles: that each man had an inherent right to work, and that the state was financially and morally responsible for the unemployed.

Unemployment as such did not play a very important part in the election campaign and Liberal candidates frequently managed to get away with rather vague and imprecise expressions of sympathy for its victims, but little more. Generally, those who did have any constructive suggestions were advocates of land reforms, although there was some pressure from the party's radical wing for the establishment of national machinery or even the restoration of the original Bill of 1905.[17] After the election this radical group was augmented by newcomers such as Alden and G. P. Gooch. But even by the beginning of 1906 the government had not definitely made up its mind to introduce any unemployment legislation, for the Prime Minister told Asquith in a much-quoted phrase that 'two sops' for labour, a Trades Disputes Bill to offset the effects of the 1901 Taff Vale decision (which had made trade unions' funds liable for damages inflicted by their officials), and a Workmen's Compensation Bill, should be sufficient.[18] Lord Ripon, however, felt that it was imperative for the matter to be dealt with in the government's first session, and early in February the cabinet committee did in fact meet, and, according to Burns' diary, 'settled policy'.[19] When the new parliament assembled on 19 February 1906 it was informed that the Unemployed Workmen's Act of 1905 would be amended, although no details were given.

The labour movement reacted cautiously to this statement, and the Right to Work Council, determined to turn the many vague expressions of Liberal sympathy into something tangible, organised a massive public meeting on 21 February in the Queen's Hall, London, to remind the government that it was expected to honour its commitments. When in the middle of March Burns told Will Thorne, elected for West Ham South, that no day had as yet been fixed for the introduction of the amending Bill, the London Central Workers' Committee also arranged a demonstration in the East End which was addressed by the new Labour member for Sunderland, Tom Summerbell. But Burns steadfastly refused to commit himself and in May the Prime Minister refused to receive a deputation from the Right to Work Council. The response was another militant protest meeting, this time in Hyde Park, which was informed by another new Labour MP, James Seddon, that they would obviously have to 'strike the fear of man into the hearts of the Government'.[20]

Seddon was accompanied at this demonstration by Hardie, Barnes, and Thorne, but none of the other Labour MPs took part, much to the annoyance of Frank Smith. In a circular issued to all socialist bodies he proclaimed that the time for talking was over and that the Labour Party, to justify its existence 'must *act*'.[21] Accordingly, he then contacted MacDonald and asked him to summon a meeting of the Labour members to discuss what could be done to stimulate the government further. It was agreed to put heavy pressure on Burns in the Commons and questions were put by James O'Grady on 23 May, J. R. Clynes on 24 May, Thorne on 28 May, and Hardie two days later. This parliamentary attack was sustained during the Whitsun adjournment debate when Crooks joined Hardie and Thorne in protesting against the government's failure to redeem its promises. In the evening Henderson, Shackleton, and MacDonald presented the Prime Minister with a memorandum asking for a clear statement of the government's intentions. It had been signed by 115 Liberal and Labour members, a total which suggests that there was already considerable discontent with Burns' performance among the Liberal back-benchers. Indeed, only a few days before, one of them,

C. F. G. Masterman, had taken a deputation to see him and urge the necessity of immediate action on the unemployed question, but he had again refused to commit himself.

Burns' apparent lack of concern was all the more remarkable in view of the rising volume of dissatisfaction also expressed by the authorities responsible for the administration of the Unemployed Workmen's Act. The Glasgow Distress Committee condemned it as completely useless after only a few weeks, while in London the St Pancras Committee found the Central (Unemployed) Body far too slow in finding work for the applicants it recommended. Mrs Montefiore, the wealthy socialist who served on another of the London committees, in Hammersmith, later recorded her impressions of it.

> It seemed to me that the men who had formulated all unemployed schemes had veritably tried how not to do things. Long lists of men out of work were put before us week after week, and name after name was struck out as not being eligible.[22]

At its annual meeting the Association of Municipal Corporations overwhelmingly passed a resolution declaring that the present structure of the Act was unworkable.

Behind his mask of indifference, however, Burns was clearly being forced to do some rapid thinking as May drew to a close. His own cabinet colleagues were growing restless, Ripon telling Buxton that:

> It would be most foolish and even dangerous for the Government not to make provision before Parliament is prorogued for a possible want of employment next winter. I care little how it is done, but done it must be or we shall run a very serious risk.[23]

By the time this letter was written Burns had finally produced an idea, stimulated, it seems by Gladstone, Buxton and Ripon. Buxton told Ripon that:

H. Gladstone agrees with us on an exchequer grant to tide the matter over temporarily. . . It is, I think, far the best temporary solution; and as Burns now proposes it himself it is a great thing gained to get him to . . . do something.[24]

But there was clearly some dissension within the cabinet, for when the exchequer grant was discussed on 27 June Burns put 'my view, got my way'.[25] What had happened to the 'settled policy' of February? What, in fact, had then been decided?

Conceivably, the cabinet committee had agreed to do nothing, pending the report of the poor law commission, although this would mean that the statement in the King's Speech had been completely misleading. It is true that the extensive Liberal programme, which envisaged twelve major Bills, was widely interpreted as a profession of faith rather than an indication of the practical possibilities for one session, but many of the proposed measures were of an uncontroversial nature and not expected to take up much time. Further light is thrown on this question by Beatrice Webb, for shortly after the cabinet committee meeting Burns had been to see her and she noted in her diary that there was to be 'an amendment to the Unemployed Act of last session in the direction of great contributions from the rates'.[26] Now Burns had opposed the original legislation of 1905 precisely because it had envisaged using rate aid to pay the unemployed, and it is just possible that Mrs Webb was mistaken. This, however, seems unlikely, if only because the Prime Minister had informed Lord Knollys that the amending Bill would 'have some of the features of the original Bill of last year'.[27] It seems much more likely that Burns had been over-ruled by his colleagues. He had thus prevaricated about producing the amendment, which would explain why *Justice* referred in March to rumours of ministerial splits over unemployment policy, and also why Burns' own diary contains the following, oddly punctuated, entry for

12 May 1906. 'I do not like the Unemployed Bill to amend it is to extend the virtues of pauperised dependency and to inflict I am afraid a serious blow on the morale of the labourers . . . presumably I am for resignation.'[28] His own preference, it seems, was to wait for the report of the poor law commission and he may have hoped all along that if it became necessary to do anything before the report came out he could propose an exchequer grant over which he could keep a tight control. Such a policy would certainly appeal to his departmental officials, the chief of whom was a member of the commission, and it would also appeal to labour, which generally believed that the Unemployed Workmen's Act should be financed from the exchequer. Either way, the differences of opinion within the Liberal cabinet committee had been brought into sharp relief by labour pressure, inside the Commons and in outside demonstrations.

The day after the cabinet finally accepted the proposal for an exchequer grant, Campbell-Bannerman informed the Commons that a full statement would be made on 19 July. But this was too late to prevent popular discontent manifesting itself. Early in July unemployed in Manchester, tired of the labour movement's inability to wrest anything from the government other than statements of future intent, seized a piece of church land and began to cultivate it. They were led by a man named Smith, who had been one of the Social Democrat ringleaders arrested in 1905 after the riot in Albert Square, and who now declared that 'this is the first battleground of a movement that will go down in history'.[29] His aim, he told an interviewer from *Justice*, was to draw public attention to the plight of the unemployed, to dispose of the popular myth that unemployed men were lazy, and to show the immorality of keeping land unused when it was the basic source of the necessities of life.[30] The SDF executive, perhaps impressed by Smith's predictions, but always eager to jump on to any likely bandwagon of discontent, sent Jack Williams to take charge of the Manchester men, and he dispatched a telegram to Burns reminding him of his stormy past. 'Manchester's unemployed have taken your advice of twenty years ago, and have gone back to the land . . . congratulate us.' [31]

Encouraged by his success, Smith next occupied a piece of land near Salford, but he was swiftly evicted by the irate owner. Williams, having established the Manchester men to his satisfaction, moved on to the 'Triangle Camp', which had been set up by a Social Democrat member of the West Ham Corporation, Ben Cunningham, on council property at Plaistow. This camp was short-lived, however, for Cunningham and his unemployed followers were evicted on 4 August after a short struggle with the police. His subsequent attempt to re-occupy the land led to his appearance in court. At Leeds the 'Libertarian Camp' only lasted for three days before hooligans broke in, turned out the unemployed occupants and burnt the tents. Perhaps the most successful of all was the camp organised by Albert Glyde of the ILP on land belonging to the Midland Railway Company near Bradford. By 25 August he estimated, probably very liberally, that 25,000 visitors had been to the camp and that over £50 had been raised by the sale of postcards and vegetables.[32] But these experiments in communalism soon came to an end as the various landowners asserted their rights and turned off their uninvited guests.

The general reaction had been one of tolerant amusement, although the National Right to Work Council had recommended the tactic and Thorne suggested that it might force the government's hand if carried out on a sufficiently wide scale.[33] But the SDF was just not strong enough outside London to organise such a movement, even if it had possessed the necessary financial resources, while most members of the ILP were still expecting the solution to come from parliamentary action, and even those in the National Right to Work Council were not prepared to involve themselves in extra-parliamentary pressure on such a scale.

Thus the government remained totally unmoved by these demonstrations of dissatisfaction, bolstered by the fact that some concrete proposals had finally been brought forward by Burns on 19 July. Burns had begun his speech with a survey of the current problem, asserting that as unemployment had many causes, so it had many solutions. This was why, he continued, the government had agreed to do nothing until the report of the poor law commission came out. In the meantime, a grant of £200,000, to be administered by the Local Government Board, was to be provided for the Unemployed Workmen's Act. Combined with rate money and voluntary subscriptions, this would make available something between £300,000 and £400,000. Legislation on small-holdings, crofters, and the army, all to be introduced shortly, would also make a contribution to improving the situation.

This statement was accepted on behalf of the Labour Party by MacDonald, who promised full support to the government. Although some of his colleagues criticised this action on the grounds that there had been no party meeting authorising him to do this, there can be little doubt that his action was a fair reflection of the views of most sections of the working-class movement. Will Crooks said that he approved of the government's proposals, while Barnes thought that 'an intelligent, if somewhat tardy, appreciation of . . . the problem has been evinced during the month'.[34] The railway workers' MP, G. T. Wardle, claimed that Burns' speech had been listened to with pleasure on the Labour benches.[35] It is true that neither *Justice* nor the *Labour Leader* were so enthusiastic, but it must be stressed that the programme only seems to have been accepted in the belief that the grant was a temporary measure. The railway servants' conference approved of it only 'as an instalment of what we anticipate in the near future'.[36] The editor of the engineers' magazine hoped for legislation in the 1907 session, seeing the £200,000 as a stop-gap.[37] A similar sentiment was evident at the TUC's September conference when the delegates, while agreeing that the sum was not enough, saw hope in the fact that this was the first time a government had ever made a national contribution to help the unemployed.

Thus when the TUC and the General Federation of Trade Unions (GFTU) both rejected a suggestion made jointly by the London Trades Council and the SDF early in 1907 that a demonstration be held to draw attention to those who were still out of work, their refusals were not due solely to the continuing prosperity of the economy—they owed much to the general labour expectation that the government would announce an unemployed programme in the King's Speech at the beginning of the session. This expectation also explains why the Labour Party, meeting in February to finalise the details of its own programme, decided to ballot for only four Bills, none of which had any direct bearing on unemployment. It was hardly surprising that when the Royal Speech concentrated entirely on the matter of constitutional relations between the Lords and Commons and made no reference at all to unemployment, the Labour MPs reacted angrily, and put down a censure motion on the government. Their resentment was well expressed by Clynes in a speech he made to the Commons in March.

> The £200,000 granted last year was surely not given in place of an amendment of the Act. He and his friends at least took it not as a sum which was to replace legislation, but as a sum to aid for some time pending a drastic amendment of the Unemployed Act in keeping with promises previously made by Ministers of the Crown.[38]

Immediately after the disappointment of the King's Speech, Hardie vowed that unemployment and old age pensions, also ignored, would be taken up vigorously by the Labour Party in the Commons, and little time was wasted in implementing his threat. The Joint Board, representing the Labour Party, the TUC, and the GFTU, met on 5 March and decided to appoint two sub-committees to draft reports and recommendations for an unemployed Bill. Hardie, MacDonald, Steadman, and John Ward, all MPs, were charged with the task of compiling the political sections, A. H. Gill (the MP for Bolton), Curran, Walter Hudson (who represented Newcastle in parliament) and Isaac Mitchell of the GFTU the economic parts.

The Labour Party's determination to produce this Bill must have been greatly increased when Burns, in reply to a question from the Labour member for Norwich, George Roberts, stated that he had nothing to say about renewing the exchequer grant and stressed again that he had no intention of amending the 1905 Act. He remained obdurate in the face of a rising tide of criticism about his administration of the Unemployed Workmen's Act and the exchequer grant. Many were annoyed by the petty nature of the regulations which he had added to the original legislation, and Hardie claimed that he had done a similar thing to the exchequer grant, hedging it round with so many restrictions as to make it virtually useless.[39] The same criticism was implicit in MacDonald's assertion, made at the ILP's Easter conference, that with a sympathetic administration the Act might have been 'a most valuable instrument'.[40] Burns was also attacked for breaking his pledges. In announcing the exchequer grant in July 1906 he had stated that the only condition for its use would be the degree of local distress, but it seems that in practice he had insisted on the locality making some contribution before he would sanction any allocation from the grant. This accusation was first made in a *Labour Leader* editorial and was then given more concrete form during an Easter adjournment debate in 1907 when Hardie cited Burns' refusal to give money to the Newport Distress Committee unless it raised funds locally as well.[41] Hardie said the knowledge that the government had set aside a large sum for unemployment relief would inevitably lead to a decline in the size of voluntary local subscriptions.[42]

The unwillingness of the Local Government Board to use any of the grant to finance experiments in relief also came under fire. Lansbury in particular attacked Burns' refusal to allow the Poplar Guardians to buy outright the land which Joseph Fels had leased them in 1904 with an option to purchase after three years.[43] Hardie informed the House of Commons that when the Glasgow Distress Committee arranged to buy land in order to start a farm colony, an arrangement sanctioned by an inspector from Burns' department, Burns himself had stepped in at the last moment to stop the purchase going through, even though the committee was planning to buy the land with money raised locally. He gave as his reason the imminence of the poor law report and the expiration of the 1905 Act, but in fact they were more devious than this.[44] He had always opposed labour colonies, noting after one visit to Hollesley Bay that it was 'a costly and foolish experiment developed by that prize fanatic G. L. . . . a holiday for 250 men from London . . . a process of coddling. . .'[45] He had never shared the view held by Lansbury and his supporters that farm colonies were a useful means of re-training men for future employment on small-holdings. As early as 1893 Burns had written in a Fabian tract that they were 'foredoomed to failure' being 'the revival in another form of the hated casual ward with all its physical and moral iniquities'. They were, he believed, unscientific, presupposing male labour, the absence of family ties, and only unskilled labour.[46]

His general reluctance to finance any experiment of this type was made much worse in labour eyes by the fact that he did not even spend all of the exchequer grant, much to the disgust of the Labour MPs who had generally thought it insufficient anyway. On 13 March 1907 Burns told the Commons that any remaining money would be returned to the exchequer at the end of the month. Two weeks later he revealed that well under half of the £200,000 had actually been spent, and Hardie seized on this during the Easter adjournment debate.

F

It was incomprehensible, he claimed, that with so much money left Burns had consistently refused to give more to schemes such as the workrooms set up in London to provide work for unemployed women.[47] It did little to enhance Burns' reputation that he was still holding so much of the exchequer grant when in February the Central (Unemployed) Body had been compelled to issue a public appeal for more funds.

By the beginning of June both the TUC and the GFTU had endorsed the reports of the Joint Board sub-committees and on 4 June the full board decided that a composite report in the form of a Bill should be forwarded to the Labour members and the trade union group for presentation to the Commons. After surveying the whole question of poverty the reports concluded that unemployment should be tackled in two ways. One was to try and secure the maximum number of workmen to perform such work as was required, the other was to increase the volume of available work, where it was advantageous to do so, in order to absorb surplus labour. The first of these objectives, it was argued, could be achieved by minimising fluctuations in the demand for labour by making time rather than manpower the elastic element in the labour-employment syndrome. The report thus urged all trade unions to make it official policy to abolish overtime working, or at least to restrict it as much as possible. In times of depression short-time working was advocated instead of the wholesale laying off of workers. The TUC had already been working along these lines, arranging conferences on overtime in accordance with resolutions passed at the Liverpool congress in 1906. The first of these had been held in March 1907 for workers engaged in engineering and shipbuilding, some 350,000 workers in these trades being represented by 40 delegates. They showed themselves keen to tackle unemployment by restricting overtime, but there were, as an observer from the National Amalgamated Union of Labour pointed out, many practical difficulties.[48] In June a second conference was held, this time for building-trade workers, and it passed similar resolutions dealing with the standard of wages, the legal restriction of overtime, and the need to establish a committee to coordinate efforts on these lines within the industry.

The second recommendation of the Joint Board report—that the volume of work should be increased where possible—was to be the function of the Bill which the parliamentary group was to prepare, but drawing it up was not without its difficulties. Will Thorne was opposed to the inclusion of any clause penalising those who refused work under the scheme, fearing that it would be harshly interpreted by middle-class administrators, but he was overruled and on 9 July 1907 Ramsay MacDonald took advantage of the ten minute rule to introduce the Labour Party's Unemployment Bill. It proposed the creation of a central unemployment committee to undertake the planning of national works and the appointment of local commissioners to develop and coordinate local works. Each local authority was to set up an unemployment committee charged with the job of finding work for all registered unemployed in its area, and which could use rate money to pay men for any such work. The heart of the measure came in the third clause, embodying the principle of the right to work.

> Where a workman has registered himself as unemployed, it shall be the duty of the local unemployment authority to provide work for him in connection with one or other of the schemes herein-after provided, or otherwise, or failing the provision of work, to provide maintenance should necessity exist for that person and for those depending on that person for the necessaries of life.[49]

It was unfortunate from the Labour Party's point of view that the introduction of this Bill was completely overshadowed by the dramatic collapse in the Commons of the Liberal member for North Staffs, Sir Alfred Billson, who died shortly after MacDonald had resumed his seat. Although it was put down for a second reading on 16 July there was never any real chance of getting it further discussed. Government business had proceeded very slowly in the first half of 1907, owing to the obstructionist tactics of the House of Lords, internal problems within the cabinet, and the outpacing of administrative machinery by the sheer size and complexity of the government programme.[50] This had been appreciated by the Labour Party's strategists, and the Right to Work Bill, as it was soon popularly termed, had been introduced partly so that any weaknesses could be exposed and remedied, partly so that its principles could be well publicised by means of an intensive winter campaign in order to ensure that it would be familiar when it was re-introduced in 1908, the year the Unemployed Workmen's Act of 1905 expired. It would thus be a ready-made and well-understood measure which, it was hoped, the Liberal Government would be compelled to bear in mind when considering how to replace the 1905 legislation. When Parliament met in 1908, said Roberts, the Labour whip, it was anticipated that every party member would ballot for a day on which to bring in the Bill.[51] The *Labour Leader* warned that unless everyone combined to press the Bill upon the country's attention it would be 'obstructed, resisted and lost'.[52]

CHAPTER 4

The battle for the Right to Work Bill, 1907-1908

THE INTRODUCTION OF the Labour Party's Unemployment Bill did little to dent Burns' self-confidence. He condemned it as a prescription for 'universal pauperism' and did no more than renew the exchequer grant for one year, even then refusing to guarantee that it would all be spent.[1] In public speeches the Labour members kept up a constant sniping against his policies, and his obstinacy and growing unpopularity continued to alarm some of his cabinet colleagues, particularly when two socialists won by-elections at Colne Valley and Jarrow, in the last case, it was claimed, because of the candidate's advocacy of the Right to Work Bill.[2] In August Sidney Buxton, fresh from an interview with Burns, told Ripon that he had been able to

> extract nothing except that 'it is all going very well', which it is not (he will lose us all our seats in London if he's not careful). . . It is important for us in our autumn speeches and before cabinets begin again to be able to say the Government intends to deal with the matter by *Bill* in view of the expiring of the act next year. . . I also want Burns to get pinned to something.[3]

The fears increased still more when the Labour Party's propaganda campaign got under way in July against a background of rising unemployment. Although the SDF had kept up local propaganda work in several cities, setting up a farm colony for Manchester's unemployed and raising over £170 for those in Hastings, the unemployed index had remained fairly steady at around 3.3 per cent in the first half of the year, but now its rise, coupled with an increase in commodity prices, indicated that the boom was coming to an end.

The campaign started with the publication in July of a pamphlet by MacDonald, who outlined the defects of the Unemployed Workmen's Act and its poor administration under the Liberals, and then gave details of the proposed new Bill.[4] In addition to this, 20,000 copies of the Bill were printed for general distribution and it was also printed as an official appendix to the party's July *Quarterly Circular*. The main thrust of the campaign, however, was embodied in a series of public meetings which took place in the autumn. By mid-September MacDonald already had 45 speaking engagements arranged for this purpose, Snowden 40, James Parker 12, and Tom Summerbell 8.

In undertaking this effort the Labour Party clearly had one eye on its position in the public interest, for Hardie told Bruce Glasier at some time during the summer that 'somehow we don't seem to bulk so large as we did in the eye of the public'.[5] It was hoped, too, to offset the growth of left-wing criticism which had grown up as a result of the party's failure to achieve anything in Parliament in 1907. Although old age pensions also featured in the speeches, unemployment held price of place and there was a militant tone in the voices of several of the Labour MPs. Summerbell told his Sunderland constituents that the party intended to fight to the death for the unemployed in the coming session.[6] Three weeks later at Nelson, Snowden said they would create such a wave of public feeling that the government would be compelled to legislate.[7] He spoke in similar vein at Maidstone and Chiswick in November and Rochdale the following month. At Newton, Seddon told his audience that if satisfaction was not forthcoming from the government in 1908 then 'wigs will be on the green at St Stephens'.[8]

Early in the new year Barnes brought out a pamphlet very

similar to MacDonald's, while Fred Jowett, MP for West Bradford, and the victor of Jarrow, Curran, took opportunities to stress yet again that unemployment would be the Labour Party's rallying call in the new session.[9] The ILP, too, was playing its part, the Metropolitan District Council organising a conference in January to keep all the London branches in touch with the latest developments and to discuss possible lines of action if the government again ignored the unemployed.

In a way the Labour Party's task was made easier by the continued deterioration of the labour market which produced an unemployment index of 5.8 per cent in the first month of 1908. Depression had set in, consequent upon a financial crisis in the United States and poor harvests in several countries. Unrest in Britain's industrial centres rose accordingly. Three major demonstrations organised by the London SDF in November and December 1907 had already produced some scuffles with the police and several arrests. Violent clashes occurred in Birmingham when in January Jack Williams arrived with a group of Manchester unemployed en route for London, and more arrests were made. Another Social Democrat agitator, A. P. Hardy, was arrested for obstruction when he tried to lead local unemployed into the King's seaside house at Brighton. Edward VII also figured in the plans of a third Social Democrat, Stewart Grey, who tried to present a petition to him. Informed by Gladstone that the King could not comply with its terms, Grey sent his followers to Brighton and took himself off to Windsor in order to fast in the chapel. Failing to achieve much by this gesture he moved on to London, announcing his intention of returning to Windsor at the head of an army of 10,000 unemployed.

The publicity campaign was successful in provoking critical observations about the Bill and several were forthcoming at a special conference assembled in January for the purpose of providing the renewed parliamentary struggle with a good send-off. W. C. Anderson of the ILP, for example, objected to the inclusion of a clause providing for the punishment of men who just refused work. Others were against the use of emigration as one of the remedies which the local unemployment committees could apply. Some wanted it made explicit that the scheme was only temporary, pending the transfer to collective ownership, but a resolution from the floor to insert such a clause in the Bill secured only thirteen votes. For the rest, MacDonald successfully defended the existing structure of the Bill, arguing that all members of distress committees agreed that it was greatly strengthened by the inclusion of the penal clause, and pointing out that emigration was not meant to be a general remedy, but simply one which could be applied in carefully considered individual cases. These points having thus been cleared up, the delegates unanimously passed a resolution approving the Bill.

With this backing the offensive was opened in Parliament by Arthur Henderson during the debate on the King's Speech, which had again ignored unemployment. He accused the government of raising false hopes and demanded to know why the Labour Party's Bill was not adopted if the government could not draft one of its own. The next day MacDonald, supported by Crooks, Snowden, William Brace the miner's MP, and Ward, moved an amendment regretting the omission of any unemployment proposals. But Burns still remained unmoved, claiming that their pessimism was unfounded, and stating that the government was preparing existing machinery for the implementation of the poor law report when it came out. According to the parliamentary correspondent of the *Labour Leader*, many Liberals pulled long faces when Burns went on to say that he would do no more than renew the exchequer grant for a further year, and back-bench discontent was certainly apparent when MacDonald was followed into the opposition lobby by 146 MPs, 70 of whom were Liberals.[10]

George Roberts declared that the support given to this amendment, which was followed four days later by the first reading of the Right to Work Bill, unchanged from its 1907 form, showed that the government could not ignore the matter much longer.[11] Certainly the press covered the debate very fully, all of the papers coming out strongly against the Labour amendment. This did not deter the party, however, from continuing its efforts to publicise the Bill, and early in February a circular was distributed suggesting that all labour organisations draw the attention of local MPs to its second reading, as it was 'desirable that Members of Parliament should be made aware of the interest which organised labour takes in the subject'.[12] This was followed by a second circular directly particularly at trade unionists, who in many cases seem to have been content to shelter from unemployment behind their own relief systems.

> What have you to say to the Bill? You know that the Unemployed man always threatens your wages. He increases the power of the non-Unionists. He is constantly liable to become a blackleg. He drains your funds. You have now to keep him whilst the man whom he enriches pays nothing. . . Wage Earners! Stand by the Unemployed and the Labour Party's Bill![13]

In provincial cities a series of successful demonstrations in favour of the Bill was organised, and the campaign culminated in London with a large public meeting on 12 March. It was addressed by MacDonald and Lansbury, and resolved to ask all the London MPs to be in their places the following day when the second reading debate was due.

The continuance of the labour pressure, the level of public interest, and the violence of unemployed agitation, obviously alarmed many Liberals, hence the large anti-government vote on 30 January. It is also significant that the first reading of the Right to Work Bill had been introduced by a Liberal radical, P. W. Wilson, as none of the Labour members had been lucky in the ballot. The Bill was deemed of sufficient importance to warrant a cabinet discussion on 11 March and it was apparent that the press rumours of ministerial divisions over the measure were well founded. Lloyd George was in favour of it.[14] Asquith told the King that the 'right to work' principle was 'obviously inadmissible', but felt that something should be done for the sake of appearances.[15] Buxton, too, thought that if the government was to oppose the Bill then 'we ought at least . . . to have an alternative'.[16] Lord Ripon, on the other hand, was not prepared to support it, believing that public opinion was not in its favour, but he did tell Buxton that he would not treat it too harshly.[17] Burns was completely opposed to it and left his colleagues in no doubt as to his views which he embodied in a cabinet memorandum. If the Bill was put into operation, he argued, no one would have any incentive to look for work, nor would any casual labourer take a temporary job unless it was well paid. Exaggerating in order to make his point, he went on to express doubts about the ability of an unemployment committee to find work simultaneously for 1,000 housemaids, 2,000 clerks, and 5,000 casual labourers. There was no reason at all, he concluded, to change the current policy of waiting for the report of the poor law commission.[18]

Birrell told a deputation from the Bristol Right to Work Committee that the principle underlying the Labour Party's Unemployment Bill might well 'mean the disruption of the Liberal Party' and it seems that he was not far from the truth, for the rank and file of the party was no less divided than the cabinet.[19] On the one side stood the radicals who had supported the 'right to work' amendment on the King's Speech; men such as Masterman, who was in favour of the government going 'forward boldly in some large and far reaching scheme of social reform'.[20] On the other wing were those like Harold Cox, the member for Preston, who thought that although the 'right to work' slogan was superficially attractive 'it is easier to advertise a quack medicine than to find a real remedy for a long-standing disease'.[21] The possibility of an embarrassing split over the Bill worried the Liberal whips a good deal and they prepared to take careful note of all those who voted against the government on the second reading. The Liberal whip, John Whitley, certainly did not mince his words. Each Liberal member was informed that 'an important division is expected. Your attendance and support of the Government is very earnestly requested.' [22]

So great was the interest generated by the Labour Party's campaign that many papers discussed the Bill's prospects in their morning editions, the *Mail* dismissing it as 'sheer insanity'.[23] The *Standard* published a series of short interviews with selected MPs, giving their opinions and voting intentions.[24] In spite of this interest, the House was little more than half full when P. W. Wilson rose to move the second reading on 13 March, and it seems that a good number of Liberals, including Lloyd George, had decided to escape their dilemma by absenting themselves from the debate, for they were not all paired. Wilson rather spoilt his opening speech by offering to drop the crucial third clause, and it is possible that this was the outcome of a visit he had recently made to Asquith, who was acting head of the government as Campbell-Bannerman was ill, and who wanted to do something, but opposed the 'right to work' principle. Certainly several Liberal members might have voted for the measure had it been made less controversial in this way, but it hardly mattered, for MacDonald, who was seconding, immediately contradicted Wilson by affirming that the Labour Party was not prepared to omit the clause.[25] The government put up two members with trade union interests, Fred Maddison and Henry Vivian, to oppose the Bill, and both claimed that it would create more unemployment than it relieved, arguing strongly that it was the fruit of socialist agitation and not wanted by the trade union movement. This allegation hardly accorded with the way in which the Bill had been drawn up, and it provoked the anger of the miner, Brace, certainly no socialist, who promptly rose

PARLIAMENT AND THE PEOPLE.

EXCITING DEBATE ON THE UNEMPLOYED.

MR. JOHN BURNS BURNS HIS BOATS.
CABINET TROUBLES.

BY OUR OWN CORRESPONDENT.

Friday was a regular field-day. Never before has the House been so thoroughly roused on the occasion of a Labour debate. Never have the chiefs of verbal warfare thrust and parried with a keener edge. At a culminating crisis of the fight Will Crooks arose, flushed and excited, and said of one of Mr. John Burns' characteristic misrepresentations: "It's speech effective enough. It had very little reference to the Bill, and every second or third sentence was diversified by some reference to the fiends called "Socialists"; but the House roared with laughter at many of his references. "I have never had such a lapse in my reason as to become a Socialist," he confessed; and the House evidently believed him.

The Right to Work Bill debate. *Labour Leader*, 20 Mar 1908

to announce that he had not intended to participate in the debate but he wished to state categorically that trade unionists did support the measure.[26] And so, after a lengthy debate, did a good number of Liberals, for when the vote was taken 116 votes were recorded in favour of giving the Bill a second reading. The magnitude of this rebellion again produced considerable alarm. One anti-socialist stated that the introduction of 'this astounding measure . . . from the Liberal benches is pregnant with warning'.[27] The hysteria which afflicted the Conservative press was well illustrated in the *Telegraph's* comment that 'whoever supports the bill is a socialist and ought to wear a red flag as an outward sign of his being a dangerous firebrand'.[28]

With public interest running at such a high level the Labour Party was in no mood to abandon the struggle, and shortly after the debate on the second reading was concluded the order for the second reading of an Eight Hour Bill was read and withdrawn. This Bill had originally been introduced on 11 February by Will Thorne at the request of the TUC

and was down for a second reading on 1 May. It was withdrawn, however, because Pete Curran, successful in the draw
for a day on which to discuss a parliamentary motion, decided
to bring one forward on the eight-hour day. According to the
procedural rules of the Commons, he could not do this when
a Bill on the same topic was still before the House. As his
motion was to be discussed on 18 March it seems that Thorne's
Bill was dropped so that Curran could use the opportunity to
press home the unemployment attack. From the point of view
of publicity he was fairly successful, for there were several
press comments on the discussion, a typical one labelling the
idea as a 'fresh challenge to the country's common sense'.[29] But
the Labour spokesmen did not really make the most of this
opportunity, failing to stress that an eight-hour day would
effectively increase the amount of available work and thus
answering those critics of the Right to Work Bill who had
claimed that the measure gave no indication of how the guaranteed work was to be provided.

It was claimed that the Labour Party's campaign for the
unemployed had been so successful that the government dared
not ignore the problem much longer, and MacDonald told an
audience at Halifax that they would not allow the problem to
sink over the horizon again. But what was to be done before
the next session when the Bill could be brought in again? At
a meeting of the Joint Board held on 17 and 18 March it was
decided to persist with the efforts to keep the measure before
the public.

> The appeal must now be made to the country. At tens of
> hundreds of Socialist meetings during the year the de-
> mand that the Bill be passed must be made, and at every
> meeting in the constituencies addressed by members who
> voted against the Bill their action must be challenged.[30]

In a word of general encouragement to all those who had
joined in the campaign, MacDonald, enclosing copies of the

division list, asserted that there was no intention of letting the principle drop, and he urged everyone to persist with the education of the electorate. The second thread of Labour's future policy was to defend the Bill against those who were misrepresenting it, both in the press and at public meetings. A special pamphlet was issued explaining certain clauses which had been subject to uninformed criticism, particularly clause three, and another circular was prepared stating that the Joint Board repudiated 'most strongly the suggestion that in its working it will be inimical to Trade Unionism'.[31] A policy of this sort was certainly necessary because Liberal politicians especially seem either to have misunderstood the scheme or, more likely, deliberately misrepresented it. There were some, such as the old-school radical H. J. Wilson, who genuinely disliked the Bill, but others seem to have purposely distorted its probable effects. Churchill, for example, said at Dundee that it would entitle a man to claim work 'no matter how bad his character'.[32] Walter Runciman, recently made President of the Board of Education, claimed during the by-election at Dewsbury that

> Any workman out of work for any cause, good, bad, or indifferent—for incompetency, for insobriety, for laziness —could come to the Dewsbury local authority and . . . if they said 'We have no work to give you', he could reply, 'Then you must maintain me and my family.' I venture to say that such a bill would put a premium, not on the best, but on the worst, of our working classes.[33]

Even Lloyd George, speaking in support of Churchill at his Manchester by-election, now proclaimed that the measure was a bad one, his change of heart almost certainly being connected with his recent promotion to the exchequer, which would have had to find the money had the Bill become law.

This spate of by-elections was produced by the ministerial changes made by Asquith when he took over the post of prime minister from the ailing Campbell-Bannerman in April. It is a further indication of the government's embarrassment over the Right to Work Bill that Asquith apparently decided to use this cabinet shuffle as an opportunity to remove Burns from the Local Government Board. At least, this was one of the offices which he offered to Churchill, and even when it was refused in favour of the Board of Trade it was on the understanding that unemployment should now be tackled in the long term from this department.[34] One of Churchill's first actions in his new post was to take on Beveridge and begin the planning of a national system of labour exchanges. Asquith, having in this way bypassed Burns' responsibility for a long-term unemployment policy, then contented himself by sending Masterman, by now very much the radical confidant of Lloyd George and Churchill, to the Local Government Board as Under Secretary in the hope of offsetting the President's conservatism. Burns was apparently none too keen on this arrangement and wrote hastily to Asquith.

> I am not sure . . . whether you have finally decided upon the proposed colleague you mention. . . . If not then I should like a word with you first. If you have decided I will of course receive in a friendly spirit any man you may consider desirable to send here.[35]

He was too late, however, for Masterman got the job, having made it clear that he expected Provis to be replaced by someone with a drastic mandate for reform.[36] It was perhaps indicative of Burns' weakened position that when Sir Berkely Sheffield asked on 23 June whether the government intended to renew the exchequer grant for a further year, the question was answered by Masterman, who said that the matter was being discussed by Churchill and Lloyd George.

The development of some new, long-term unemployment policy, implied by these ministerial changes, was every day becoming more urgent as the depression deepened. By June the unemployed index had risen to 7.9 per cent and violence broke out in several cities. Windows were smashed in Manchester in protest against the government's inactivity, while in Glasgow workers from over forty trades took part in a massive anti-government demonstration at the end of June. But working-class discontent was not directed solely against the government, for many voices were raised against the apparent quiescence of the Labour Party which, apart from one attempt, voluntarily abandoned, to prevent the Unemployed Workmen's Act being included in the Expiring Laws Continuance Bill, had remained strangely quiet since March. In Parliament its attentions were concentrated on the Old Age Pensions Bill, and leaders such as Henderson and Shackleton were also very interested in the fate of the Licensing Bill.

This lack of vigour in Parliament and the necessary but unspectacular policy of educating the electorate about the Right to Work Bill combined to create the impression that the party had forgotten the unemployed. At the ILP conference in April one delegate advocated that obstructionist tactics should be used in the House of Commons in order to force the government's hand.[37] In July the Yorkshire Federation of Trades Councils added its voice to the growing volume of criticism, perhaps taking its cue from J. M. McLachlan, a member of the ILP, who had condemned the Labour Party for following a policy of political opportunism and modest palliatives.[38] The Social Democrats, too, who had welcomed the appearance of the Right to Work Bill and encouraged the party's campaign in the winter of 1907-8, were now highly critical of the party's failure to force it through Parliament by militant means. Two members of the Fleetwood Branch suggested that each local organisation should send postcards to all the Labour MPs asking them to drop all other matters. 'Practically nothing,' complained *Justice*, 'is being done. . . The Labour Party in the House of Commons seems to think that it has done its duty.' [39] Even the *Labour Leader* was moved to admit in August that the party had not managed any 'striking performance from a popular point of view'.[40]

This dissatisfaction was not confined to the party's left-wing critics or even its own non-parliamentary members, for the seemingly apathetic policy followed after the defeat of the eight hours resolution and its failure to make any significant impact also disturbed some of the MPs who had constantly pressed the cause of the unemployed since the election of 1906. The parliamentary pressure of that year, the militant speeches of the 1907-8 campaign, and the bombardment of the government benches in 1908 had been very largely the work of a certain number of Labour MPs—MacDonald, Snowden, W. T. Wilson, Henderson, Crooks, Thorne, Jowett, Seddon, Charles Duncan, Curran, James Parker, T. F. Richards, Hardie, Barnes, O'Grady, Clynes, Roberts, and Summerbell. Now the discontent of some of this group was implicit in the re-convening of the National Right to Work Council in London on 31 July 1908, the day that the parliamentary session ended. The council had been silent since the middle of 1906, mainly because its members had put their faith in a parliamentary policy focused on the Right to Work Bill. The failure to achieve anything in this way and the ensuing disappointment among some of these 'activists' clearly lay behind this meeting, and the executive now decided to collect reliable statistics from the main industrial cities and also to invite trades councils and other working-class organisations to form local committees in order to carry out a winter agitation. By the middle of November Frank Smith had circularised 1,500 trade unions, 250 trades councils, and 1,400 socialist societies, urging them to exert pressure to secure the early re-opening of the distress committees, asking how many men had been on short time during the year, and asking trade unions to state how many of their members were out of work in the third week of September. At least eight, and possibly as many as twenty-five new committees came into existence in response to this appeal from Smith (see Table 2, pages 191-2). In order to strengthen

G

the campaign in London the Right to Work Council also contacted the ILP's Metropolitan Council, asking it to form a
special sub-committee to organise the work, but the council
decided instead to refer the matter to the executive with the
suggestion that all the London branches simply be asked to
release their organisers for two weeks from 11 September,
when the campaign was due to get under way, for special work
with the unemployed. It seems from this that the Right to
Work Council envisaged the London ILP filling the role
played in 1905-6 by the now defunct Central Workers' Committee.

These preparations were assisted to a considerable extent by
the failure of the labour market to recover during the summer
months. By August 8.5 per cent were out of work, and as the
winter approached the unemployed grew still more militant.
In September 200 Glasgow unemployed broke into the council chamber and forced the commencement of several relief
schemes. Two days later they interrupted Prince Arthur of
Connaught as he was inspecting a Glasgow company of the
Boys' Brigade, and then interfered with a civic lunch at which
he was guest of honour by singing the 'Red Flag' outside the
town hall and shouting imprecations against the royal family.
The situation looked so bad at one point that troops in the
nearby barracks were alerted. In Manchester the police, as in
1905, resorted to baton charges to break up a gathering of
unemployed in Stevenson Square, and one of the ringleaders,
a man named Skivington, subsequently led a large number
of the crowd into the cathedral where they punctuated the
sermon with comments. Skivington was only prevented from
seizing the pulpit by a quick-thinking organist who drowned
his attempts to address the congregation. A silent gathering of
some 10,000 unemployed outside the Sheffield town hall so
unnerved the councillors that £10,000 was promptly voted for
relief works. From Nottingham 150 men set out to march to
London, and elsewhere in the Midlands there were clashes

between unemployed and the police. On 4 October, Stewart Grey, who had been leading hunger marchers from city to city, was arrested in Trafalgar Square for obstruction. He was twice rescued by the mob and twice re-captured by the police.

These signs of violence alarmed many who saw behind them the influence of the socialist agitators. 'It is gratifying to learn,' ran one account, 'that the worst excesses are due, not to the distress of starving people, but to the deliberate policy of the Socialist Party.' [41] The editor of the *Express*, Ralph D. Blumenfeld, had already taken steps to formalise the structure of the Anti-Socialist Union, and by the autumn he was issuing constant warnings about the increasing influence of socialism. But there were also those who encouraged the violence. Victor Grayson told the unemployed not to stay in their hovels but to

come out . . . and to thrust their pinched starved faces into the faces of the well conditioned multitudes . . . they would be less than men if they did not use what energy this cursed civilisation had left them to get food immediately.[42]

A writer in A. P. Orage's *New Age* claimed that the Glasgow riot had been the best protest achieved by the unemployed.[43] Even at the TUC the advocates of violence were heard, one Social Democrat delegate claiming that they had to strike the fear of man into the hearts of the ruling classes and that little would be secured while the Labour MPs were content to remain so respectable.[44] Will Thorne told one of his audiences to help itself from the bakers' shops if it was short of bread, advice which resulted in his prosecution for incitement. The Social Democratic Party (the Social Democratic Federation had adopted this new title late in 1907) was also encouraged by this spread of unemployed militancy and decided to try and channel it more effectively by setting up small committees on lines similar to those of 1886 and 1903. Since 1905 the Social Democrats had been comparatively quiet about unemployment, partly because it had not been sufficiently serious to work on very effectively, as the fiasco of land-grabbing in 1906 had shown, and partly because the focus of attention had passed to the Labour Party and Parliament. Even if they had wished to encourage agitation on a wide scale, financial stringency would almost certainly have stopped them. The London Central Workers' Committee had collapsed in 1906 for want of funds, and although Jack Williams had organised daily meetings at Tower Hill and the occasional demonstration he had been working for nothing by March 1907, as the executive could no longer afford to pay him. During the same year it had been necessary to consider raising members' subscriptions, and in the spring Knee had had to report that the London Organisation Fund was 'absolutely bankrupt'.[45]

On 19 September 1908 the London branches of the Social Democratic Party (SDP) set up a central committee to run the agitation, but things did not improve financially, and the party's hopes of fomenting unrest in the provinces were dashed by the poor response to an appeal made for money to finance it. The London effort would probably have failed as well had it not been for the generosity of Lady Warwick, who contributed £40 of the £42 4s 6d (£42.23) raised by the middle of October.[46] The first stage in the London campaign was a demonstration in Trafalgar Square on 10 October, and the threatening slogans on the marchers' banners certainly lived up to Quelch's warnings that their aim was to 'make the unemployed a menace . . . institute a reign of terror . . . make the governing classes howl with affright at the danger to their skins and their stolen wealth'.[47] Will Thorne, who addressed the meeting, again appealed to his Labour Party colleagues to obstruct all legislation until unemployment had been dealt with. Two demonstrators were arrested. It was in this sort of atmosphere that Parliament re-opened on 12 October, the suffragettes adding their contribution to the scenes of violence in Parliament Square. The Right to Work Council had already been organising street demonstrations as well, and some idea of the strain which this agitation helped to impose on the capital's forces of law and order can be seen in a letter received by Gladstone on 11 October.

> Henry [Commissioner of the Metropolitan Police] said that the strain on the police caused by demonstrations of women, unemployed, etc., was heavy and was increasing. Yesterday or Thursday (I forget which day) he had 'hunger marches' taking place in *twenty* divisions. Every march had to be accompanied by a body of police: otherwise they would have begun to break into shops.[48]

Church parades were organised on the morning of 11 October, followed by public meetings in the afternoon and evening. Each meeting, held under Right to Work Council and ILP auspices, appointed deputations to wait on the London MPs on the first day of the autumn session, and when these deputations began to arrive at about six o'clock in the evening considerable pressure was put on the police, some 2,500 of whom were packed around the Houses of Parliament. Several of the Labour Party 'activists' supported the requests of the deputations to meet their respective MPs, who were eventually informed by the police that if they did not receive them, there would be a full-scale riot.

This autumn sitting of Parliament had been called by the government in order to complete the passage of outstanding items of legislation, particularly the Licensing Bill. But the rise in the numbers out of work and the spread of violence meant that the cabinet, further stimulated by Labour demands in Parliament for some statement of its intentions, was almost immediately plunged into discussion about the unemployment situation. On 14 October Burns was informed, somewhat abruptly, that something had to be done straight away, and a small committee consisting of L. Harcourt, the First Commissioner of Works, Churchill, Lloyd George, Reginald McKenna,

Gladstone, Buxton, and Burns himself, was established to draw up a list of proposals for immediate implementation.[49] The same day Asquith announced that he would make a full policy statement the following week. It was either a tribute to the Labour Party's pressure or an indication of Liberal poverty that the Labour Party chairman was called in to give advice. Henderson was well aware of the feelings of some of his colleagues, for on 16 October he warned the cabinet that unless prompt action were taken he would be unable to restrain his extremists.

In fact, one parliamentary extremist, Grayson, had already shown his displeasure on the previous day, leaving the House in disgust when the Speaker ruled that the Licensing Bill must take precedence over his motion for an adjournment in order to discuss the plight of the unemployed. On 16 October he was suspended when he tried to interrupt the committee stage of the same Bill, and as he was being escorted from the Commons he turned and loudly condemned the Labour Party as a traitor to its own class. Grayson, however, was not a member of the Labour Party, having won Colne Valley without its official backing. In warning the cabinet about his extremists, therefore, Henderson must have had in mind somebody else, and it seems that his concern was about a small group of the 'activists' which, as well as working vigorously in Parliament for the unemployed, had also co-operated actively with the Social Democrats on several occasions. Hardie, Seddon, and Thorne, for example, had all supported the 1906 demonstrations held jointly by the Right to Work Council and the London Central Workers' Committee, while Curran and Thorne had both given their support to the tactics of the land-grabbers in the same year. Thorne and O'Grady had both attended the SDF's major protests of 1907 in London, and Roberts, Summerbell, and Thorne again had all appeared at some of Jack Williams' Tower Hill meetings.[50] At least two of this group sympathised with Grayson's action, disagreeing only with its timing. Thorne told his union executive that he would have acted with Grayson had the Labour Party not already agreed to wait for the government's policy statement.[51] Fred Jowett said that although neglecting one's duty and then expecting to make up for it by 'theatrical display' was not war, he would 'make one of a number to court suspension or anything else which would be likely to cause confusion in the ranks of the enemy' if the government's proposals weren't satisfactory.[52]

Now on 19 October this small group, led by Hardie, attended a joint meeting with the SDP's London unemployment committee, and agreed to set up a Joint London Right to Work Committee with the Social Democrat, E. C. Fairchild, as secretary, in order to bring greater cohesion into the London agitation. Hardie had clearly decided that, to be effective, any parliamentary effort really needed the backing of some militant outside pressure. Such pressure was bound to be more effective, both morally and physically, if led from the capital where the SDP was stronger than the ILP and had already organised a successful network of unemployment committees, whereas the ILP's London council had been reluctant to do more than place the various branch organisers at the disposal of the Right to Work Council. That the Social Democrats were prepared to work with members of a party which they had been criticising since 1907 is explained in part by the fact that some of them were still hoping to form a united socialist party, and the 'right to work' slogan was one which they could heartily endorse. Significantly *Justice* said in announcing the formation of the Joint Committee that 'we have entered into active co-operation with the National Right to Work Council and we hope in that, as in other directions, to render effective service to the unemployed *and socialism*' (my italics).[53] Then there was the undoubted attraction of being involved in a national movement, their own efforts at organising on this scale earlier in the autumn having failed miserably. Finally, of course, there was the perennial problem of finance which the National Right to Work Council with its wide trade union support could reasonably be expected to avoid.

Clearly, however, the use to which Hardie and his friends put this new London organisation depended largely on the contents of the government statement. But the cabinet was not finding it easy to make up its mind, and while Hardie negotiated with the Social Democrats, Henderson continued to negotiate with the government. His suggestions that the exchequer grant should be increased and that rate money should be used by local authorities to pay wages to men employed under the terms of the Unemployed Workmen's Act were favourably received by Churchill, Masterman, and Buxton, but were fiercely denounced by Burns in a cabinet memorandum. All he would concede was an increase in the size of the exchequer grant—if it was really necessary—relaxation of some of the regulations issued for the administration of the 1905 Act, and a few other administrative changes. The poor law report was imminent, he claimed, and he could see no reason to change the policy of waiting for its suggestions, especially as it would require legislation to enable the local authorities to pay wages out of the rates.[54] Three days passed before the cabinet eventually resolved its differences and it was Burns who triumphed having, in his own words, 'made a dogged fight. W.C. and L.G. fought equally hard but wore them down by weight of mettle. At end L.G. capitulated and urged economy for Treasury's sake.'[55] The same night Asquith informed the King of the government's plans and it was clear, as Mrs Masterman recorded, that 'J.B. has scored all along the line, partly because he came armed with figures . . . partly because the distrust of the Ll.G.-Churchill combination is so profound in the Cabinet'.[56]

Asquith introduced the government's proposals on 21 October, prefacing his remarks with the comment that he could not anticipate any of the measures to be introduced next session, a thinly veiled reference to Churchill's labour exchange scheme.

For the present it was proposed to increase the exchequer grant to £300,000, to relax some of the regulations pertaining to the Unemployed Workmen's Act, and to provide an extra 24,000 places in the army's special reserve. In addition, Admiralty orders for warships were to be brought forward and repair work in Admiralty shipyards was to be speeded up. Finally, over 8,000 men would be given temporary employment over Christmas in the Post Office. All this, noted Burns with some satisfaction, was a 'real triumph' as the Labour Party had been completely out-generalled over the question of the penny rate.[57]

It was reported in the press that the Labour Party's trade union section was generally satisfied with this programme, although the whole party did back a motion disapproving of it. But when a vigorous offensive of questions, lasting through the rest of the session, was mounted it was noticeable that it was conducted almost entirely by the 'activists'. This campaign concentrated on two themes: the problems of areas where distress committees did not exist, and aspects of the programme which, it was felt, could be extended. According to one report, the aim of this attack was ultimately to swamp Burns' department and cause him to spend all the exchequer grant by Christmas.[58] This was probably an exaggeration, but certainly at the beginning of November MacDonald contacted all local authorities drawing their attention to the effect of Asquith's statement and urging them to secure for their own unemployed a share of the promised relief. He wrote to ILP branch secretaries, too, asking if their local council had applied for permission to form a distress committee and also asking for specific information about local needs.

The parliamentary questions began as early as 27 October when Snowden asked Burns if the authorities at Keighley had requested permission to create a distress committee and with what result.[59] This was the first of a series of such queries, always couched in exactly the same terms, which were put regularly during the autumn session until 3 December when the climax—eight questions in one sitting—was reached. At intervals the Labour members asked for statements about the number of successful applications, and eventually Burns admitted that 52 had been made altogether of which he had sanctioned 14 only. Questions were also raised about areas too small demographically under the regulations of the 1905 Act to have committees. On 11 November Summerbell asked if grants would be made to these areas if they set up their own special committees, but was told that they did not qualify.[60] The same day Hardie asked, unsuccessfully, if the extra £100,000 promised by the government could be provided on conditions which would permit its use by these deprived districts.[61] Curran then suggested on 13 November, again without success, that such areas should be combined and one committee formed for the whole.[62] Ten days later, Hardie repeated his plea for the extra money to be made available to places which did not qualify for the original grant, but was again informed that this was not possible.[63] A second theme of this questioning concerned particular aspects of the government's plans. Thus Richards asked Burns if he would circularise the distress committees with advice about the best sort of work to provide for the unemployed.[64] George Roberts wanted to know how many people had been induced to emigrate by the distress committees.[65]

The most sensational incident springing from this constant pressure on Burns came on 12 November when, in reply to a question from Thorne, he stated that his recently issued circular concerning the removal of restrictions on applicants for work allowed full discretion to local distress committees to relax such barriers. Henderson immediately rose and asked if this was what Asquith had meant in his statement of 21 October, and later in the day he moved the adjournment of the Commons in order to draw attention to the discrepancy between the Prime Minister's promise and Burns' circular. The

covering letter which Burns had sent with the new order,
alleged Henderson, completely contradicted Asquith's own
declaration. Asquith replied that Henderson was quite correct
in supposing that he had not meant to imply simply that the
local committees should have a discretionary power, but that
the restrictions should be lifted entirely. He had talked the
matter over with Burns and the error had now been rectified.[66]
This public rebuke clearly upset Burns and he noted with
almost poetic sadness, that 'I sat serene and endured the spleen
but wondered for its source. . . An unexpected blow from the
P.M. Why?'[67]

The 'activists', faced with this repeated resistance from
Burns, made one final effort in Parliament before the session
ended. Hardie brought in a two-clause Bill on 8 December
which would have amended the 1905 Act to allow local authorities to pay wages from the rates, and which would also have
given the status and power of distress committees to the
smaller bodies created by the Unemployed Workmen's Act to
collect statistics and run labour bureaux in districts too small
to qualify for full committees. Hardie hoped that the government would take up his measure and it was put down for a
second reading the following day. But the session was nearly
over and it never came up for further discussion. It was evident at a Joint Board meeting held on 9 December that in
introducing this Bill, Hardie had been acting on his own
initiative, almost certainly on behalf of the 'activists'. He had
to explain that his action had in no way been meant to reflect
on the status of the Board.[68]

Meanwhile, the SDP had begun to implement the street
campaign in the form of marches into the West End. Williams
was put in charge of this, and he led the first procession of
some 2,500 men through London's richer quarters on 25 November. Shopkeepers promptly began to complain, as they had
done in 1903, and their anger was doubtless exacerbated when
so many men turned out on 16 December that Oxford Street

was completely blocked. Two days previously a question had been asked in the Commons about the possibility of increasing the strength of the London police force in view of 'the great increase of duties recently thrown upon it'.[69] Similar disquiet was apparent when, shortly after Christmas, another Social Democrat organiser, R. Greenwood, began to hold a series of unemployed meetings in the fashionable West End squares. Grosvenor Square was the scene of one such demonstration on 13 January, and a second, held the following week in Belgrave Square, was the occasion of much violence. Typical enough was the case of Joseph Lloyd, arrested for inciting people to attend these gatherings armed 'not with your fists but with something else'.[70] One protester claimed that the only object of these meetings was to insult West End residents.[71] Others feared that only the police stood between London and total riot.[72] Thus it was not surprising that the police resolved to take a much firmer stand in the future, and permission was refused for a second meeting in Belgrave Square which Greenwood had planned for 25 January.

At first sight, then, the alliance between the National Right to Work Council and the SDP was working well, an intensive parliamentary campaign being supported and then sustained over the Christmas recess by street agitation. But when, early in February 1909, the Joint London Right to Work Committee asked the Labour MPs to support a demonstration being arranged to coincide with the opening of Parliament all but O'Grady refused. When this demonstration ended in a rowdy fiasco Barnes firmly denounced it in the House of Commons, saying that while he was glad that 'the sea of suffering surging round our very doors . . . last night even, overflowed into our lobby', he wished to dissociate himself from people who organised great demonstrations and then failed to make adequate provision for those taking part. 'We had nothing to do with that, and will not have anything to do with it.'[73]

There were other indications, too, that the co-operation had not lasted long. The National Right to Work Council was certainly not supporting its London Committee financially. It had no difficulty at all in raising the £250 necessary to finance a national conference which it held early in December 1908, and yet in January the Joint London Committee was appealing for money, Quelch claiming that Greenwood was apparently expected to 'live on air, and grow fat by expanding his lungs by open air speaking'.[74] In the middle of January 1909 Jack Williams appeared in the backruptcy court, while in November, after a summer of complete lassitude, the London Committee reported that it had in hand the paltry sum of 4s 5d (22p). Again, the annual meeting which heard this sad tale was not attended by any of the MPs who had participated in the formation of the London Committee, and the new executive elected by the delegates was dominated by Social Democrats—Fairchild, Greenwood, Williams, W. Lock, Macdonald, John Scurr, Dora Montefiore, and Mrs Hicks all being returned. But the breakdown had clearly taken place long before this.

Finally, it can be noted that in March Frank Rose, a member of the National Committee's executive, claimed in the *Labour Leader* that the Labour Party had recently received a deputation from the Central (Unemployed) Body.[75] In fact, however, as was pointed out in the following week's edition, the deputation had been arranged and manned by the London and District Right to Work Council.[76] Evidently, Rose had no idea of what the London Committee was doing. It was significant that in this disclaimer the words 'joint' and 'committee' had both been dropped from the organisation's title, indicative again of the new independence of the London body.

The co-operation between the inner group of Labour Party 'activists' and the SDP thus lasted at most from late October 1908 to early February 1909, possibly not even as long. Why was it so short-lived? From Barnes' statement in the Commons on 17 February it seems that there may have been some disagreement over tactics. Certainly Hardie had shown himself very sensible of demonstrators' human needs when organising his provincial marches in 1905 and he may have been upset by the SDP's failure to provide sufficient food for the hundreds of women and children who were marched into central London in February 1909. Secondly, some tension was apparently generated by the National Council's December conference. The 'right to work' resolution ran into some difficulty, as many of the distress committee delegates claimed that this was a controversial matter which ought to have been avoided. Thus many Social Democrats, particularly Hyndman, were quite disgusted by the tame nature of the proposals put to Asquith by the conference deputation, and the party decided to hold its own conference under the auspices of the London Committee.

Neither of these reasons was of major significance, however, especially as the National Council could presumably, had it so desired, have given the London Committee the money it needed to provide adequate food for the demonstrators in February. Much more important was the reaction of trade unionists against co-operation with the SDP. Trade union suspicion was implicit in the refusal of the TUC to send delegates to the December conference, and this was certainly not because it felt that the government's proposals had rendered such a meeting irrelevant. Indeed, it had decided to contact the Joint Board with a view to organising a separate conference itself. There were also signs of reaction among provincial trade unionists. Early in the new year the Nottingham Right to Work Committee was suddenly dissolved. Similarly, the Newcastle Trades Council withdrew its representative from its local committee, while in Manchester the trades council left the existing committee and set up a new one, entirely under its own control.

Labour Party members, even 'activists', also disapproved. Clynes disliked the violent tactics which the Social Democrat agitators frequently employed and generally encouraged, telling a group of Manchester unemployed on one occasion that he did not look for a solution in men marching or congregating in town centres but rather in the 'men who were marching intelligently to the ballot box'.[77] MacDonald and Snowden, too, had always been suspicious of the SDP, and they both asserted vehemently that they would have nothing to do with anything organised by that party when they were invited to attend the Joint London Committee's conference in February.[78] As secretary MacDonald in particular had borne the brunt of most of the attacks made on the Labour Party and had frequently been stung into vindictiveness. He told the Oldham Branch of the SDP that he had not been in the least bit surprised to receive its letter applauding Grayson's exit from the House of Commons, 'knowing as I do the general stupidity of the S.D.P. and its incapacity to understand the meaning of any political demonstration'.[79]

Hardie must have known that to work with the Social Democrats would rouse the antagonism of substantial sections of the labour alliance, and yet in October 1908 he had been prepared to take this risk for the sake of the unemployed. What had caused him to change his mind was the fact that Grayson had become the focus of the Labour Party's critics. Resolutions applauding his stand in the Commons and comparing it favourably with the Labour Party's own supine attitude flooded into the *Labour Leader* offices. 'Activists' such as Curran and Snowden were shouted down, respectively at Bradford and Liverpool, when they tried to defend the Labour Party's unemployment policy, and others of the group resorted to attacking Grayson in the press. MacDonald claimed that his supporters showed a lack of understanding of how parliamentary business was conducted.[80] George Roberts said it was sad to see 'purposeless shouting appraised as of greater value than solid insistent work'.[81] By the Christmas of 1908 it was widely rumoured that Grayson, backed by his SDP supporters and

Blatchford's *Clarion* movement, intended to launch a strong attack on the Labour Party executive at the annual conference in January. As it happened, the expected attack never materialised, for Grayson was absent from the vital session of the Portsmouth conference, claiming that he had been kidnapped by two army officers who had driven him into the country and dumped him. But the threat of dissension was real enough, and even though Hardie and some of the other 'activists' had been so frustrated by the Labour Party's failure to press home the unemployed question in 1908 that they were willing to work openly with the more militant Social Democrats, they were certainly not prepared to see their life's work, the creation of an independent working-class political party, destroyed.

Faced with this danger of schism, they decided to close the ranks of the labour alliance and to abandon both the co-operation with the SDP and the formal 'right to work' movement. This explains why the National Right to Work Council disappeared in 1909, and also why in March 1909 O'Grady, certainly one of the most vigorous of the 'activists', was to be found defending the Labour Party against its critics, arguing that it was following the energetic unemployment policy which they were demanding.[82] Any lingering desire to maintain the alliance must finally have been dispelled at the ILP's Easter conference, when the party's 'big four', Hardie, MacDonald, Glasier, and Snowden, resigned from the National Administrative Council in protest against the continuing divisive tactics of Grayson and his supporters.

CHAPTER 5

The decline of the 'right to work', 1909

EVEN THOUGH HARDIE and his colleagues had thus decided to abandon the formal 'right to work' movement sometime between December 1908 and February 1909, the 'activists' did not drop the principle of the 'right to work' or the cause of the unemployed. Despite a small drop in the number out of work in January, unemployment was still rife, particularly in the North East, the Midlands, and parts of Yorkshire, and hunger marchers from these regions were much in evidence. A party from Leeds arrived in Stroud on 3 January and several of the marchers were promptly arrested for provoking a brawl in a public house. Stewart Grey reached South Wales on 7 January and one of his lieutenants, named Williams, attempted to emulate the exploits of the 1906 land grabbers by settling on a piece of land near Cardiff. He was arrested for obstruction. Thus the 'activists' made every effort to keep the matter alive in public speeches, although their efforts were hampered partly by their parliamentary duties, partly by the need to concern themselves with those topics which were claiming public interest. Unemployment had been widely discussed since the autumn of 1908, but even though the Social Democrats organised their demonstrations to coincide with the state opening of Parliament in February, the subject was beginning to lose its news appeal as the numbers out of work decreased, and press and public alike found new topics of interest. A party with serious political pretensions could hardly ignore the great German naval scare which reached almost panic proportions in England in March, or the controversial Lloyd

H

George Budget of April and the constitutional issues to which it gave rise.

Inside Parliament, too, the 'activists' pursued the unemployment question as vigorously as possible. It was they who led the attack on the King's Speech which, failing to mention any measure except labour exchanges, also annoyed many of the trade union members who had expected something more as a result of the government's October promises. During this debate Hardie warned in a spirited speech that 'we shall not accept the present position without such a campaign as . . . will make the Government sorry for its great betrayal', and certainly during the next few months the 'activists' continued to harry the government.[1] At the beginning of March, for example, Clynes and MacDonald attacked Burns' administration of the Unemployed Workmen's Act. A week later Clynes, Barnes, Summerbell, and Hardie all supported Wardle's resolution calling for a reduction of £100,000 in the sum granted to the Local Government Board for expenses incurred in operating the Act. Although no vote was taken, the Labour speakers made it clear that the reduction had only been moved in order to facilitate a further attack on government policy. During the Easter adjournment debate Barnes headed yet another onslaught, twitting the government with its failure to produce the promised amendment of the 1905 legislation. As late as November, by which time the unemployed index had fallen to 6.5 per cent, Barnes, Hardie, and Seddon took advantage of Asquith's motion for the temporary adjournment of the Commons until the 23rd of that month to raise the unemployment question again.

All these gestures, however, were futile because, although the party usually followed the 'activist' lead, the various resolutions and amendments were rarely pressed to a vote. On one occasion Burns withstood one of these parliamentary outbursts so easily, he told Masterman, that at the end of the debate the Labour MPs had 'cooed like doves feeding out of my 'and'.[2]

This, combined with the inability of the 'activists' to stress the subject very much outside Parliament, confirmed many in their belief that the Labour Party had really lost interest in the unemployed and become totally apathetic. Thus outside pressure on the Labour MPs continued to grow. 'The whole party,' claimed an editorial in the SDP monthly, *Social Democrat*, 'has gone to sleep again.' [3]

At the end of March the London Right to Work Council distributed a circular to all labour organisations asking them to put pressure on the Labour members to move the adjournment of the House of Commons in order to discuss unemployment. It was later claimed that over 500 such resolutions were sent into Labour Party headquarters, and certainly both O'Grady and Parker were moved to write articles defending the party's existing policy. [4] Parker pointed out that an adjournment would provide at the most a little over three hours' discussion time, and that the Speaker now would not consider the matter of sufficient urgency to warrant an adjournment. [5] But the critics' hands were undoubtedly strengthened by the debate on the second reading of the Right to Work Bill which took place on 30 April.

The leading Labour speakers were John Hodge and John Ward, the latter not even a Labour Party member although it seems likely that he was put up simply to offset the criticism, freely made in 1908, that trade unionists did not want the measure. Despite the fact that Ward was a GFTU representative on the Joint Board, he had so misunderstood the nature of some changes made in the Bill over Christmas that he had to be openly corrected by Shackleton. This probably helped to produce the verdict of one paper which said that the entire proceedings had been 'lethargic and disappointing'. [6] Several other papers claimed that the Labour speakers had made no attempt to justify the principles underlying the Bill, but had merely used the opportunity to plead with the government for some action. [7] One Labour MP said later in a significant phrase that the Bill would pass 'once labour wakes up'.[8]

The lack of enthusiasm which characterised this debate may well be explained by the fact that it had been completely over-shadowed by the extremely radical and controversial Lloyd George budget introduced the previous day. George Roberts even claimed that the budget speech had been so timed pre-cisely to influence all those who had intended to vote for the Unemployed Bill.[9] There was possibly some truth in this, as the government could not have been unmindful of the embar-rassment it had suffered in 1908 through its failure to produce any realistic counter-proposals. But by this time the govern-ment had in fact got some positive measures of its own and it seems more likely that the lethargy was due to the fact that by 1909 the energies of the labour alliance, channelled for the past two years into the struggle for the Right to Work Bill, had begun to diversify.

For two years the Bill had been the only concrete legislative proposal before the country and its popularity and publicity had depended entirely on the propaganda activities of the labour movement's rank and file. At the ILP's 1909 Easter conference the executive appealed again to branch members to remember 'the great necessity of keeping the Unemployed agitation vigorously active . . . the success of Parliamentary effort will depend upon the strength of the demand outside'.[10] But now in many cases these energies were being taken up with the new schemes and proposals which were appearing in 1909. Many had seen the original introduction of the Right to Work Bill simply as a sort of goad to provoke the government into producing a positive unemployment policy. The *Clarion* had claimed, for example, that the Bill's purpose had been merely to expose the reality and magnitude of the problem.[11] Shackleton had also implied this by stating that the Bill would achieve much if it secured a thorough airing of the subject in the House of Commons.[12] Now at last other suggestions were appearing: proposals designed to show how work could be provided, thus posing an obvious challenge to the Labour Party Bill, which had really done little more than state a principle and outline machinery by which it might be achieved. It had done little, as Herbert Samuel had pointed out, to suggest where the guaranteed work was actually to come from. 'The Right to Work Bill,' he claimed, 'was nothing more than a peroration put into the language of a statute' and they might just as well introduce a 'right to be happy bill' whereby all had the right to be happy and the local authorities had to provide the wherewithal.[13] Once proposals for providing work appeared, little was left of the Right to Work Bill except its principle, and it became very much of an ideal or shibboleth, rather than a statement of practical policy. In this context it is worth noting that shortly after the second reading debate an article in the *Socialist Review* (the monthly produced by the ILP) admitted that it would perhaps 'never pass. It is a manifesto.'[14]

Similarly, the time and energy which the labour movement had devoted to propagating its own ideas were increasingly absorbed by these new programmes. This process began in a tentative way when the royal commission appointed to investigate coast erosion reported in January. Established in 1906, its terms of reference had been expanded in March 1908, largely as a result of Labour Party pressure, to investigate whether it was desirable to make experiments in afforestation as a means of increasing employment at times when the labour market was depressed. The report stated that if the 9,000,000 acres of suitable land were wooded, temporary employment would be provided for 18,000 men in winter and permanent work could ultimately be available for 90,000. Furthermore, there were 'sufficient unemployed persons willing . . . and able . . . who could advantageously be employed without a period of special training'.[15] Labour men received these suggestions very favourably because afforestation schemes had frequently been advocated as a way of absorbing the unemployed, and

Hardie, appearing before the commission on behalf of the Labour Party, had argued strongly in favour of such a remedy, as had Lansbury who also testified.

Not surprisingly, there was a great deal of anger when no place was found for the commission's proposals in the government programme. Henderson grimly reminded Burns that on at least one occasion he had virtually promised to implement the report once it was available.[16] Hardie claimed that he had expected at least £1,000,000 to be set aside for afforestation in 1909, while Snowden told an East London audience that the matter was really 'rotten ripe'.[17] Tom Summerbell, who, along with John Ward, had served on the commission, spent much of his time in 1909 trying to popularise the report's recommendations, and the ILP published a pamphlet which he prepared for this purpose. By the end of February 6,500 copies had been sold.[18] So favourable was the labour reaction to the report that sections of the Conservative press predicted its incorporation into the Right to Work Bill. But there was no time to do this before the second reading debate came on, and after Lloyd George had presented his budget it was widely believed that the Development Bill, to which he then referred, would include some of the afforestation recommendations.

This Development Bill was designed to confer on the government the powers necessary to embark upon schemes of road improvement, marshland reclamation, afforestation, and agricultural experiment, partly to improve facilities in these spheres but also to provide useful work for the unemployed. It was this aspect of the measure which commended it to Hardie, who saw it as the means of giving work to those in need and not covered by another proposed government measure—unemployment insurance. He further argued that, in creating a central authority to frame schemes of work in advance, the Bill had lifted the main idea behind the Right to Work Bill. The Development Bill and the insurance proposals together went, he said, 'a long way towards meeting our demand for

work or maintenance, as set forth in our own Bill'.[19] Barnes
and Roberts supported the measure because they saw it as an
attempt to substitute collective enterprise for private profit-
mongering, and when it passed through the Commons in the
autumn Barnes welcomed it as 'a contribution to the solution
of unemployment . . . the first real attempt to deal with unemployment on the lines of what might be called organic
change'.[20] Thus the Development Bill provided some challenge
to the Right to Work Bill, partly by adopting some of its ideas,
partly by pre-empting the need for any other measure. In
moving an unemployment amendment on the King's Speech
in 1911 O'Grady confessed that the Act contained all labour's
proposals of the past twenty years, and although it failed to
realise many of labour's hopes the *Labour Leader* could still
deem it 'the most Socialistic measure on the statute book'.[21]

The insurance schemes to which Hardie had referred also
began to absorb labour's attention in the course of the year,
and again the claim was made, for example by the Labour
Party executive report to conference, that the proposed state
contributions would be the equivalent of the party's own demand for state maintenance.[22] In February 1909 the GFTU set
up a small committee to gather information about all existing
unemployment insurance schemes in order to submit a report
to the Joint Board. There was apparently some lack of liaison
here, however, for when the matter was raised the Joint Board
secretary informed the federation that the TUC had already
made plans to discuss the question at a special conference to
be held in March. Other trade union leaders spent some time
compiling a detailed list of their criticisms of a draft system
which Beveridge had prepared and submitted to the TUC for
comment.[23]

Perhaps the most potent source of alternative unemployment remedies came, however, in the long-awaited report of
the poor law commission issued on 17 February. Although the
majority report received what Beatrice Webb called a 'magnif-

icent reception', it was not popular with working-class organisations.[24] It was the minority report, signed by Mrs Webb, Lansbury, Chandler, and Russell Wakefield, that captured their imaginations. To tackle unemployment these four recommended that a national system of labour exchanges should be set up and a ministry of labour created to replace the poor law authorities and the distress committees and be responsible for organising the national labour market. In addition, they suggested that trade unions should receive subsidies from the government for their unemployment funds, that the hours of work for all transport workers and those aged under eighteen should be reduced, and that the government should plan its own public works, which were to include afforestation and foreshore reclamation, over a ten-year period, in order to offset fluctuations in the market demand for labour. This set of very practical recommendations was welcomed by almost every working-class group. Mrs Webb had informed leading Labour MPs of the schemes as early as January 1908 and had been pleasantly surprised by their response—'almost a promise of active support'.[25] MacDonald claimed at the ILP conference that the minority report was nothing more than 'our old proposals paraphrased, brought up to date as to facts and experience, and issued at public expense'—in a sense he was right.[26] Proposals for the creation of a labour ministry and for the reduction of hours had long figured in labour programmes. But now these ideas had been blessed as part of a very full attack on unemployment by a government-appointed inquiry, and they were to be popularised by a vigorous campaign under the talented direction of the Webbs. Only the Social Democrats were hostile, and it is significant that one reason for their opposition was the omission of any reference to the 'right to work'.[27]

Trade unionists welcomed in particular the idea that union unemployment funds should receive a government subsidy, and this was put very strongly to Asquith and Lloyd George by a TUC deputation at the end of February. It was pointed out that between 1897 and 1906 the hundred principal unions had spent some £4,000,000 on unemployment relief. By aiding the distress committees, it was argued, the government was indirectly helping the non-unionists and in fairness ought to provide some similar assistance to the unions. In his reply, however, Asquith immediately put his finger on a difficulty, saying that as the unions made no practical distinction between their benefit and industrial funds there would be no safeguard against their using public funds, given as an unemployment subsidy, in order to finance industrial actions. Unless the two funds were separated, he went on, there was no possibility of such a grant being made, and he further suggested that union reluctance to make such a distinction probably explained why the matter had not been raised before.[28] It is a good illustration of the way in which the government succeeded in taking the initiative away from the labour movement during 1909 that a grants-in-aid resolution was defeated at the TUC's September assembly, despite a plea from Charles Bowerman, Labour member for Deptford, that this would reflect unfavourably on the parliamentary committee in view of its earlier deputation to the government. Much of the opposition was based on the same objections, which had been raised unsuccessfully against a similar resolution moved in 1908, but several delegates in 1909 followed the lead of J. Hill of the boilermakers and argued against such grants because they were essentially a sectional solution, unwarranted when the government itself was at last considering working along national lines.

Undoubtedly, however, the greatest appeal of the minority report was to a substantial section of the ILP. Their loss of enthusiasm for the Right to Work Bill was evident when a party demonstration in London to back its second reading had to be abandoned for want of support. Between March and mid-July 1909 the ILP sold 77,850 pamphlets, of which only

800 dealt with the Right to Work Bill and a further 500 with the more general aspects of the unemployment problem.[29] Together, this represents a total of just over 1.6 per cent of the total sold in this period, compared with 20,500 unemployment pamphlets sold out of a total of 141,000 between March 1908 and 20 February 1909, or 15 per cent of the total.[30] Clearly unemployment bulked less large in the party's propaganda activities in 1909.

Much of the impetus behind the ILP's support for the minority report came from the party's national executive, which informed one inquirer in September 1909 that the party was backing the Webbs' National Committee to Promote the Break-Up of the Poor Law established in May. The object of this organisation was explicit in its title and the support given by the ILP's national executive reflected the views of some of the new members elected at the annual conference. One of them, J. M. McLachlan, had advocated as early as 1908 that the Labour Party should abandon the policy of modest palliatives and concentrate on a national campaign ranging over the whole spectrum of poverty.[31] This was just what the minority report offered, and in this way it was a challenge to the almost exclusive support which the Right to Work Bill, essentially a single solution to a single problem, had enjoyed from ILP members.

Sidney Webb was very keen to bring the unemployment proposals into prominence, for even before the reports were issued he was making arrangements with the ILP to hold a major demonstration to publicise them. When this meeting eventually took place, Webb, perhaps unwittingly, criticised the Right to Work Bill. Unemployment, he claimed, would not be solved in one session of Parliament. 'The solution is not to be found in one word, such as Socialism with a big "S" or in two words, such as Tariff Reform. There is no one panacea.'[32] At the ILP's annual conference a delegate from Norwich advocated that they should now strive for unemployment legislation on the lines of the minority report, which he described as 'the last word'. More significantly, he went on to criticise the Right to Work Bill on the grounds that it was not a national solution because local committees were to be created and some of the necessary monies were to be raised from local sources.[33] It was perhaps symbolic of the challenge presented to the Right to Work Bill by the minority report that George Lansbury, formerly an executive member of the National Right to Work Council, became a vice-president of the Webbs' committee in 1909.

The ILP was not alone in withdrawing much of its energy and time from the campaign for the Labour Party's own Unemployment Bill in 1909. As we have seen, there were several who felt that the government had conceded the 'right to work' demand in the Development Bill and the proposed unemployment insurance. A similar view was apparent when, in May, Churchill introduced his labour exchange system. Thus Clynes claimed that it was really a part of the Right to Work Bill.[34] The same implication was behind Henderson's remark that the government had begun to take the measure out in penny numbers.[35] Equally significant in diverting attention from the Bill itself was the amount of time devoted, particularly by the trade union movement, to the actual details of the new scheme.

Exchanges, of course, were nothing new, dating back in London to the 1880s. In 1906 Beveridge, the architect of the present scheme, had pursuaded the Central (Unemployed) Body to set up a system in the capital under the provisions of the Unemployed Workmen's Act. He had even then been aware of the need for trade union support and had done his best to meet the very stringent conditions the London unionists had demanded in return for their blessing. The TUC had been concerning itself with exchanges for some time before the new national programme was brought forward, sending a four-man team to Germany in 1908 to examine at first hand the working of the German system. Once the introduction of a national scheme in Britain was announced, the TUC spent a good deal of time and energy mobilising and organising union opinion. A meeting of 220 delegates, representing 1,550,000 workers, was held in March 1909 in order to discuss both exchanges and insurance, and a constant stream of trade union deputations carried opinions, fears and reservations to the Board of Trade.

So thoroughly did the TUC concentrate on the exchanges that it frequently failed to let the Labour Party know what was being done and in July this produced a heated exchange at a Joint Board meeting. In opening the meeting Shackleton said that Churchill by now was well aware of trade unionists' views, which brought an immediate protest from Henderson and the other Labour Party representatives on the board because, it was claimed, the trade union deputations had acted before any common policy had been agreed upon. Henderson added that he had been forced to deal with many questions concerning the exchanges, often unaware of the attitudes adopted by the various deputies, and constantly 'hampered by the fear that contradictory suggestions might have been advanced'.[36] He further complained that many amendments had been put down of which he had known nothing, although he had been expected to discuss them. (In the light of this complaint it is worth noting that during the committee stage of the Labour Exchanges Bill, Beveridge told his mother of one Labour MP who had put down a whole series of amendments, but because he had acted without first consulting his colleagues he was 'made to stay away when he ought to have moved his amendments and they fell to the ground'.[37]) But the members of the parliamentary committee were not slow to defend their actions. W. J. Davis pointed out that the Labour Party could easily have requested a Joint Board meeting had it really wanted to discuss a common policy, while both Shackleton and Bowerman said that in the past circumstances had sometimes made it necessary for the Labour Party to act without first consulting the other members of the board and the plea of exigency had always been accepted. After some discussion Henderson moved that the board should investigate how far separate action by any one body with regard to prospective labour legislation could be avoided. This was agreed to, despite Shackleton's assertion that he would not do this if it meant that the TUC had to consult the Labour Party every time before it acted.[38]

Although the Labour Exchanges Bill had its first formal reading on 20 May 1909, Churchill had already taken advantage of a discussion on the poor law to indicate the main lines of the scheme. The exchanges were designed, he said, to cope with two deficiencies—the immobility of labour, and the lack of information about the labour market. They would be of use in estimating the seasonal and geographical requirements of certain trades and in encouraging school-leavers to enter prosperous trades rather than dying ones. It was hoped to divide the country into about ten areas, each with a divisional clearing house and with 30-40 first class exchanges (in cities with populations of over 100,000), 45 second class (population 50-100,000), and about 150 minor offices and sub-offices. Although the whole system would be controlled by the Board of Trade there were to be in each area joint advisory committees to ensure impartiality between capital and labour. They were to consist of equal numbers of representatives of workers and management with a neutral chairman.

Labour leaders were not slow to appreciate that there were good reasons for supporting such a system, provided the questions of control and administration were satisfactorily dealt with. It was argued, for example, that the government was set on establishing the system and that to ignore it would mean that it would fall into the hands of the free labourers, a point of no little significance as the National Free Labour Association had already made representations to Churchill seeking some role in the administration.[39] Others pointed out that the exchanges were to be used for registering workers, a necessary step towards dovetailing the supply and demand for labour. Probably the most potent argument for their acceptance, however, was the fact, stressed by Churchill, that they were a necessary preliminary to any insurance plan.

Naturally there were fears and objections which had to be thrashed out. Firstly there were what can be termed the miscellaneous arguments, springing usually from particular trades or interests. Thus the seamen's leader, Havelock Wilson, was totally opposed to any form of exchange system on the grounds that the special bureaux which had been run for sailors over the past sixty years had been a complete failure, and during the second reading debate Wilson moved that the Labour Exchanges Bill be deferred for six months. James Sexton, leader of the Liverpool dockers, was afraid that registration and classification would put some men permanently out of work. In Liverpool, he argued, there were 22,000 dockers of whom 15,000 were in work at any one time. If dock labour was decasualised and registered the unlucky 7,000 would always be the same men.[40] The general labour unions were also disturbed by the prospect of classification, fearing that unskilled men would suffer, and they demanded that their position *vis à vis* the skilled men should be guaranteed.[41]

There were also fears that union wage rates and conditions would not be observed by the exchanges, Curran arguing strongly during the second reading debate that no job should be offered at less than union rates and conditions. Against this, however, other union leaders said that to insist on such a concession would cause the whole scheme to break down, and at the end of July the Joint Board decided to press Churchill for a regulation simply compelling employers to state clearly what they were prepared to pay for a particular job. This he agreed to do, pointing out that it would be extremely difficult to enforce any suggestion for union rates.

Most fundamental of all, however, was the feeling that exchanges were potentially dangerous because they could be used as recruiting agencies during times of industrial dispute, and Curran claimed at the special March conference that all existing bureaux had been used for this purpose. But here the value of the earlier TUC investigation into German exchanges became apparent, for Bowerman was able to point out that this had been one of the main fears held by German unionists, but experience had shown it to be groundless.[42] In any case, as Wilkie later pointed out, if an employer was intent on recruiting blacklegs it was obvious that he would be more successful —and more anonymous—on the back streets of a town than in the exchange, where the moral pressure exerted by the presence of trade unionists would probably be sufficient to deter most potential blacklegs.[43] Despite this, Henderson argued at a later Joint Board meeting in favour of throwing the exchanges out of gear when a dispute was taking place and he was supported by Tillett. O'Grady said that really there was little to fear if information were carefully presented, perhaps by posting notices on the exchange walls about any dispute, and Richards added that if the exchanges did supply blacklegs then a trade union boycott would soon cause them to collapse. Bowerman clinched the argument as far as the Joint Board was concerned by saying that originally German exchanges had been closed during disputes and it had proved a complete waste of time.[44] Although Henderson was thus outvoted at this meeting of the Joint Board, his suggestion was raised again at the TUC conference in September, but it was defeated.

These reservations about the exchanges explain why labour took so much interest in the question of their control and management. Much depended on the quality of the administrators and their impartiality. Clynes claimed that the workers would only accept the exchanges if they were given equal representation on the advisory committees, while Joseph Pointer, a Labour by-election victor making his maiden speech, affirmed that the men would be extremely suspicious if they had no representation.[45] Particularly sensitive on this point were the general labour unions, who were naturally the most subject to exploitation, and also the men in the engineering and ship-building industries who had suffered in the past from the blackleg activities of the free exchange run by the Shipbuild-ing and Engineering Employers' Federation. In fact, there was little to fear, for Churchill had told Asquith as early as Janu-ary that equal representation for workers and management was to be the root principle of trade boards, labour exchanges, and insurance committees. But the slowness of the Board of Trade in appointing the administrative bodies certainly in-creased the workers' suspicions. They had still not been set up by the time the first exchanges opened in January 1910.

Springing directly from this concern with control came labour's interest in the quality of the men appointed to the managerial posts. Some were afraid that civil servants were being offered special incentives to apply, and after consider-able pressure had been put on him in the Commons Churchill announced in September 1909 that all local officers would be selected by three-man committees, representing labour and capital, chaired by a neutral civil servant. The chief appoint-ments, however, he intended to make himself, and he tried to offset any hostility which this might have created by appoint-ing Shackleton to advise him on such positions. It was prob-ably no surprise to trade union leaders when Beveridge was given the post of Director of Exchanges, but the large number of other public school men who got appointments caused alarm in trade union circles and early in 1910 the GFTU set about preparing a report on the social backgrounds of the labour exchanges' administrators.

Undoubtedly, a good deal of the labour movement's caution about the system evaporated when it was seen to be geared into a larger scheme of relief dependent on the financial pro-visions of the budget. Thus long before the budget was presented Hardie dismissed exchanges on their own as 'an insolent attempt to fool the nation'.[46] Barnes adopted a culinary metaphor and damned them as 'mustard without the beef'.[47] He changed his mind, however, when the details of Lloyd George's budget were announced because it was partly designed to pro-

MISS BUDGET: "Is that man a friend of yours?"
LABOUR PARTY: "Oh, he's a poor out-of-work who wants me to help him, but I'll see you home first."
THE UNEMPLOYED: "He seems to have forgotten me since he's taken up with that hussy."

Justice, 6 Nov 1909

J

vide money to link up the exchanges to schemes of development, afforestation and insurance. This must help to explain
the strong support which the labour movement gave to this
Finance Bill. 'Socialists,' wrote Snowden, 'may regard the des-
tination of the new taxation with every satisfaction.' [48] There
were other reasons behind labour's support, of course. Even
more of the revenue was intended for the old age pension
scheme introduced the previous year. The principles behind
the new taxes were highly acceptable as they represented an
attack on landed monopoly, and many of the new or increased
charges had been advocated by a Labour Party conference on
taxation at the beginning of the year. Finally, there was again
the simple political consideration that to have ignored such an
advanced budget would have forfeited the Labour Party's
claim to be a serious radical contender for political power.

But whatever its causes, the interest of the labour alliance
in the budget again served to intensify the processes by which
the amount of time and activity devoted to the Right to Work
Bill was sapped. In November *Justice* printed the cartoon
reproduced on the previous page. Strictly speaking, this charge
was unfair, as support for the budget was not entirely irrelevant to the unemployment question, and most sections of the
labour movement were still anxious to see the problem tackled.
The difference was simply that now the movement's energies
were going into other people's ideas rather than into its own
Right to Work Bill. By the second half of 1909, neither the
Bill nor the ideal occupied the elevated status that they had
enjoyed in the movement's unemployment policy for the previous three years.

CHAPTER 6

A wasted year, 1910

THE PREVIOUS CHAPTER traced the beginnings of the process by which the enthusiasm and time that the labour movement gave to the principles embodied in the Right to Work Bill were side-tracked in 1909 by the appearance of several more practical proposals for relieving unemployment. Naturally such a shift of emphasis did not take place overnight and the fluid state of opinion is well illustrated in the Labour manifestos issued during the general election of January 1910. This contest was brought about by the refusal of the House of Lords to pass the Lloyd George budget and unemployment consequently played a very minor role beside the budget question and the constitutional issues to which the peers' action had given rise. But twenty-two Labour candidates stated that the government's own legislation had made, or would make, a significant contribution towards solving the problem, while others, including MacDonald and Roberts, added that this programme had realised a substantial part of the Right to Work Bill.

The proposals of the minority report were also much in evidence, the eleven candidates who referred to them including Barnes, soon to be made party chairman, Henderson, whom he replaced, and W. C. Anderson of the ILP executive. Six of the eleven also mentioned the 'right to work'.[1] The manifesto put out by the ILP gave almost equal prominence to the two approaches. Both J. H. Belcher, another member of the executive, and George Barnes wrote in the *Socialist Review* that the way to tackle unemployment was through the Right to Work Bill *and* the suggestions contained in the Minority Report.[2] Shortly after the election a certain J. Edwards expressed the hope that the Bill would be amended to include the poor law proposals.[3] A similar view was manifest in the nine unemployment resolutions submitted to the Labour Party's January conference. Five mentioned the Right to Work Bill, two in conjunction with the minority report. Three of six resolutions dealing with the poor law were framed with reference to the unemployment problem.

There were still those, of course, to whom the 'right to work' principle was of more importance than any of the alternative schemes, and they were highly critical of the party's failure to stress it during the election campaign. One delegate to the annual conference, for example, argued that the budget should have been condemned and an all-out stand made on the Right to Work Bill. Another party member wrote to the *Labour Leader* regretting that 'unemployment and the right to work . . . were not the central issue of the Labour campaign during the election'.[4] In the *Clarion* Blatchford used the same line of argument to keep up his almost continuous indictment of the Labour Party. 'The deserters,' he thundered, had been 'so busy defending free trade against the assaults of the Tariff Reformers that (to them) such insignificant problems as unemployment and poverty appear to have been forgotten.'[5] When the election left a forty-strong Labour Party and just over eighty Irish Nationalists holding the balance between a severely weakened government and an opposition almost equal in size, many labour stalwarts anticipated that this favourable position would be used to force through the Right to Work Bill. The expectation was clearly widespread, for H. R. Maynard, who had been the first clerk of the Central (Unemployed) Body, told Beveridge that he was afraid MacDonald might use his party's advantageous position for 'forcing relief schemes or rights to work upon the Board of Trade'.[6]

But the Right to Work Bill did not appear in 1910, nor was

any unemployment amendment moved on the King's Speech, a decision which brought relief to Asquith who seems to have shared Maynard's forebodings. Barnes, Asquith told the King, 'spoke in a more friendly tone than had been anticipated'.[7] It was later explained that O'Grady and Thorne had decided not to move an amendment for fear of bringing down the government, and the priorities implied by this decision—that O'Grady and Thorne preferred to allow the government to get on in peace with the task of curbing the powers of the House of Lords—were shared by many other Labour members, including some of the 'activist' group: Summerbell, Snowden, MacDonald, and Seddon, for example. At Cardiff Snowden said that there was no alternative to the fight with the peers if they wanted the budget, even though such a struggle would take time.[8] Even Barnes, one of the most ardent supporters of the unemployed, said in February that nothing should be allowed to obscure the question of the Lords' veto, which incurred him some criticism at the ILP conference. MacDonald felt that the Labour Party should concentrate on 'stiffening the back of the Government so as to get the supremacy of the Commons settled once for all'.[9] He was so keen on this that in April he was urging the Liberal Chief Whip, the Master of Elibank, to stand firm against the threats of the Irish not to support the budget, saying that to give in would be to strengthen the House of Lords.[10]

Only two of the 'activists' apparently disagreed with this policy. Hardie admitted at the ILP conference that the immediate result of moving a successful amendment on the King's Speech would have been another general election, but it would, he said, have been fought on an exclusively labour issue—unemployment. He had already stated at Swansea in March that questions concerning unemployment and the 'right to work' were the special concern of the Labour Party which could not, therefore, allow itself to be sidetracked into propping up a tottering government.[11] His view was shared by

Jowett who feared that if the party concentrated on the constitutional question social issues like unemployment would be
lost sight of entirely.[12] Perhaps more significant from the point
of view of the party's subsequent history was the disgust of
Leonard Hall, a member of the ILP's National Administrative
Council. 'If there was a firm bargain . . . something tangible,
for instance, for the scores of thousands of poor devils swarm-
ing round the doors of the Labour Exchanges, one could
understand. But there is nothing.'[13] It was no coincidence that
later in the year Hall helped to compose the famous 'green
manifesto', *Let us reform the Labour Party*, which accused the
party, among other things, of neglecting the unemployed for
the sake of political expediency.

But even if the majority of the Labour Party had agreed
with Hardie and Jowett in keeping the unemployed as the
main priority there were other very persuasive arguments
against doing anything very positive. For one thing, if the
party had managed to bring the government down it almost
certainly could not have afforded to fight another election so
soon on any large scale. The January campaign had been a big
strain and now the party's finances were threatened by the
effects of the Osborne judgement. In this action, brought by
W. V. Osborne against his union, the Amalgamated Society
of Railway Servants, the Law Lords had decided that trade
union contributions to maintain MPs were not among the
legitimate objects of unions as defined in the Trade Union
Acts of 1871 and 1875, and that they were thus *ultra vires*.
This struck at the very basis of the Labour Party's independence and made the prospect of a second election distinctly unwelcome. It had also a second effect, and this was to cause the
Labour Party and the union movement to devote most of their
independent activities during 1910 towards securing a reversal
or annulment of the judgement.

As early as 7 January the Labour Party had begun to draft a
Bill to provide for the payment of MPs, and at some time be-

tween January and April, when the 1909 budget was again
passed in the Commons, MacDonald wrote to Lloyd George
saying that unless the government introduced a Bill or resolution providing for the payment of members, or allowed time
for the Labour Party's own Bill, he would withhold party support from the budget.[14] The Liberals, in fact, talked out a
resolution on this subject, but Asquith kept Labour's hopes
high by his sympathetic reception of a deputation in the summer. As the year went on, the campaign to cancel the decision
assumed growing importance, and by August the *Labour
Leader* was terming it the 'question of questions'.[15] The party's
annual autumn campaign was devoted to a drive against war
and to the reversal of the Osborne ruling—'the one thing of
supreme and overwhelming importance'.[16] Not surprisingly,
Osborne was also the burning topic of interest at the TUC's
September conference.

Again, just what proposals were the Labour Party to bring
forward? As indicated in the previous chapter, many were
questioning the usefulness of the Right to Work Bill and seem
to have felt that it was no longer very relevant in the light of
legislation introduced or pledged since it had first been
drafted. MacDonald claimed in February that 'much of the
Bill had already been adopted by the Government . . . much
more of it, owing to the passing of the Development Act, has
been withdrawn from the sphere of legislation and placed in
that of administration'.[17] Snowden shared this view, and one
critic claimed that his acceptance of unemployment insurance
was tantamount to selling the Labour Party's birthright for a
mess of pottage. 'It is absurd for Mr Philip Snowden to assert,
as he does, that the Labour Party's Right to Work Bill is conceded in the above reform unless he holds the view that 7sh
or 8sh is a living wage.'[18] Some ardent supporters of the Bill
were so incensed by these statements that they put down a
censure motion on Snowden and MacDonald at the ILP's
annual conference and were only persuaded to withdraw it at

the last moment. In July Henderson repeated his claim that the government was taking the Bill out in penny numbers, this time to the General Council of the GFTU.[19] Even those who did still feel that the principle of the measure was valuable were compelled to confess that the Bill needed re-drafting. Hardie, for instance, admitted in June that it had been overtaken by events and said that it was necessary to make provision in it for co-ordinating the work of the labour exchanges and development commissioners, and for providing maintenance in the form of insurance administered by a trade union.[20]

Thus, given the differing views about the desirability of passing the Right to Work Bill, the need to revise it, and the general sense of priorities held by most members of the parliamentary Labour Party, it was hardly surprising that the Bill was not even on the party's programme for 1910. First place went to the Trade Union Bill, designed to offset the Osborne decision. In any case, unemployment was not very pressing, being down to 5.7 per cent by February, and four months later Hardie granted that the question had 'ceased to attract that amount of attention it claimed during the depression'.[21] The lack of urgency is clearly seen in the fact that it was not until April that the Joint Board set up a sub-committee to begin the work of re-casting the Bill, and although this task was completed by July the details were still being discussed in October. When the second general election of 1910 took place in December only a third of the Labour candidates mentioned the Bill at all. This compared with the 81 per cent who stressed the Osborne case, perhaps a reflection of the party's general interests throughout the year as well as of declining enthusiasm for the Bill.[22] Significantly, eleven of the thirteen who had mentioned the measure in January and who now omitted it were MPs.[23]

It is doubtful in any case whether the Bill would have received the undivided attention of the labour movement even if it had been re-introduced in 1910. The members of the ILP were still torn between the 'right to work' and the minority report, and when the national council decided to devote the annual summer campaign to propagating the report's proposals for dealing with poverty, destitution, and unemployment, the ardent supporters of the 'right to work' ideal protested so much that in July it was found necessary to issue a public statement to the effect that the council had chosen what it regarded as the best topic for the campaign, even though it was appreciated that some would disagree with the choice. One typical protester expressed the hope that the poor law campaign would not detract from the demand for the 'right to work'.[24] The effort was backed by the Webbs' committee, which had also been responsible for the earlier introduction of the Prevention of Destitution Bill of which George Roberts had said 'it is really the first endeavour to thoroughly analyse the cause and effects of unemployment and to provide a solution'.[25] Little wonder that the devotees of the Right to Work Bill were alarmed by the stress put on the minority report's unemployment programme during the summer campaign. When it culminated in a two-day conference in October, a proposal that the report be implemented was only passed when it was amended to include a clause demanding the recognition of the 'right to work'. This conflict within the ILP between the two programmes caused the *Clarion* to say, early in 1911, that it was about time trade unionists and socialists made up their minds to 'sit on one of two stools'.[26]

It seems unlikely, too, that the trade union movement would have been inclined to spend much time on the Bill in 1910, and Thorne in fact warned delegates at the September congress that there was little chance of its ever passing unless they bestirred themselves. But Osborne hung like a cloud of doom over the movement, and a further distraction was provided by the outbreak of industrial unrest, particularly in the South Wales coalfield where young militants showed every sign of rebelling against the official leadership and its traditional

methods. Both the TUC and the GFTU were also keeping a
very close watch on the teething troubles of the infant labour
exchange system which had come into operation at the beginning of the year. These troubles were apparently quite severe.
Beveridge told his mother that 'every few minutes we get tele-
grams . . . one simply daren't leave the machine alone any more
than one would a locomotive'.[27] Stephen Tallents, who joined
the Board of Trade in 1909, wrote later that 'the new service,
I gathered, was having much difficulty . . . the office was falling
into disorder and public disrepute'.[28]

With this situation at head office it was hardly surprising
that there were mistakes at lower levels, and the Social Democrats, who had been against the exchanges right from their
inception, played up every unfavourable incident in a bitter
press offensive sustained throughout the year. In September,
for example, *Justice* printed the following letter, which had
been distributed to local employers by the manager of the
Bradford exchange.

> Dear Sirs,
> Since the Labour Exchanges opened on February 1,
> 1910 there have been two disputes in the woolcombing
> industry and during the progress of both these unfortun-
> ate occurrences, some Employers applied to the Labour
> Exchange for men, and in both instances we were pre-
> pared to help them all we could. . .
> May I appeal . . . that I may be favoured with your
> orders for men, women, boys and girls, seeing that we
> were prepared to help your trade during troublesome
> times, I believe some reciprocation of our efforts may be
> shown. . .
>   A. Heaton
>   Manager.[29]

Here, it was claimed, was ample evidence that the whole
system was simply one for supplying blacklegs, but the local

trades council, which took the matter up with G. R. A. Askwith, the Board of Trade's industrial adviser, was informed that this circular had been issued without the knowledge or consent of headquarters, and Heaton was suspended pending a full inquiry. The national labour organisations also adopted a more constructive approach and the GFTU asked its member unions to report direct to federation officials any such cases of irregular conduct so that these could be sifted, investigated, and then taken to the Board of Trade. Similarly, when it was announced in July that the working of the system was to be debated in the Commons, the Labour Party executive circularised all local bodies asking if there were particular points or criticisms which might be raised.

There is little indication that the majority of trade unionists shared the dogmatic hostility of the SDP, although there was much dissatisfaction with the everyday running of the exchanges. This accounts for the apparent paradox between the massive TUC vote in favour of a resolution that they were working inimically to trade union interests and the fact that Beveridge was able to tell an international labour conference that English trade unionists had generally accepted the system's advantages.[30] Possibly, too, there was some difference of opinion between the union leaders and the rank and file members who were, after all, most affected. Most of the union secretaries encouraged their members to use the exchanges, but while many local trades councils invited exchange officials to explain the new machinery to them and seem to have been anxious to make use of it, Shackleton had to defend the parliamentary committee at the TUC conference against delegates critical of the failure to insist that the exchanges should only offer work at union conditions and rates. Again, he had to point out that it was the parliamentary committee itself which had decided that they should remain open during trade disputes, a decision which had created several practical difficulties which the committee had done its best to iron out in consultation with Buxton, the new President of the Board of Trade. The degree of rank and file discontent apparently varied from area to area. At a special conference held in the autumn to mark the fiftieth anniversary of the foundation of the London Trades Council all the London delegates attacked the exchanges, although it is not clear how far the criticism sprang from actual experience and how far from the considerable Social Democrat influence in the council. Representatives from Birmingham and Nottingham, in contrast, had few complaints.

Many of the administrative complaints could clearly have been avoided had the advisory committees been appointed earlier, and this was one of the numerous points which TUC deputations raised with Buxton in a series of meetings throughout 1910. But by January 1911 nine were in operation and another four in the process of being set up. Although criticisms of the exchanges continued to be made right up until the outbreak of war in 1914, they had become much less heated by 1911 and in February of that year one trade unionist told Buxton that suspicions now were directed solely against the administration rather than the actual system. Buxton replied that there were only two classes of complaint—those based on bad administration, which would inevitably decrease as time went on, and those founded on unsubstantiated rumour.[31] When labour exchanges were discussed at the TUC conference later in the year some delegates protested that the resolution, which dealt only with the grievances of those actually employed in the exchanges, did not go far enough. The grouping committee explained that it had only been allowed to construct a resolution from those which had been sent in. The result suggests that those which were submitted had been extremely mild.[32]

CHAPTER 7

National Insurance and beyond, 1911-1914

WHEN THE LABOUR PARTY met to draw up its programme at the beginning of the 1911 parliamentary session the Trade Union Bill still had first place. Second was the re-drafted Right to Work Bill. It had been satisfactorily revised, but none of the Labour MPs were lucky in the ballot for a day on which to bring it in and it was decided instead to move a 'right to work' amendment on the King's Speech. There was no fear this time that the Conservatives might vote with the Labour Party in order to bring down the government. All but the most partisan had accepted the electorate's verdict and they were shaken by two successive election defeats in the space of twelve months and unwilling to risk a third. The amendment was moved by two of the 'activists', Clynes and O'Grady, but it was noticeable that several of the others took no part in the debate and this was interpreted in some circles as proof that they felt the amendment to be unrealistic. MacDonald implied that it had been moved purely for tactical reasons when he stated that the debate had been useful in showing that the Labour Party was not necessarily going to be satisfied with the government's insurance plans, outlined in the King's Speech.[1] This use of the 'right to work' simply to put timely pressure on the government explains why Lansbury, who had managed to win a seat in the December election, could say in March that the party had no pledge to the idea at all.[2]

Certainly in the early part of 1911 there was a revival of interest in the eight-hour day as an unemployment solution, attributable in part to the Webbs' campaign on behalf of the minority report. This remedy, of course, had never been very far beneath the surface of labour thought, but had lost much of its early impetus since the struggles of the 1890s. By February 1911, however, Ben Turner, the textile workers' leader, could claim that the matter was once again ranking high in importance. 'We want,' he wrote, 'to regain some of the spirit of the early nineties.' [3] At the same time the ILP was making plans to devote its summer campaign to the eight-hour question.

The move away from the Right to Work Bill was further accentuated in 1911 when for the first time its economic viability was severely challenged in a long debate in the correspondence columns of the *Labour Leader*. This began in February with a letter from a writer signing himself 'Lux', who argued that the maintenance clause had only been included in the Bill because socialists realised that work could not be found under the existing system. But, he went on, if the rates were increased to provide this maintenance, spending power would be reduced and unemployment would therefore rise. Afforestation and similar projects envisaged by the Development Bill and welcomed by the labour movement would also create unemployment because they would merely divert capital from one enterprise to another. [4] This provoked seven replies in the following week's paper, some of which suggested, significantly, that the maintenance should be provided through insurance. A week later G. D. Benson of the ILP wrote to say that no one had grasped the basic point which 'Lux' was making—that the provision of maintenance would divert money from other projects and thus create fresh unemployment in other sectors. 'I am afraid,' he concluded, 'that the I.L.P. will have to overhaul some of its cherished notions and subject them to a very close scrutiny.' [5] In a later letter Benson argued that if the problem was really one about the direction of capital —as most writers seemed to agree—then the answer to unemployment did not lie in a Right to Work Bill. [6] This discussion lasted until 19 May when the editor declared it closed, forty-eight letters having been published.

None of the writers had directly mentioned the minority report and it seems that there was by now a growing feeling in the ILP that the Right to Work Bill was useless, irrespective of the minority report alternative. Others, who had never favoured the minority report, were inclining more and more to the view that the government had adopted most of the Bill's demands, particularly with the announcement of insurance. One writer, lamenting the fact that a 'whole fruitful group of ideas centring round and emanating from the Right to Work' had been 'supplanted by a barren group relating to poor law administration', went on to claim that the Bill had been merely for

> educational purposes and introduced as a kind of quarry
> ... from which Governments could dig solid blocks of
> unemployed legislation... The demand for maintenance
> is translated into a scheme of insurance against unem-
> ployment: the demand for work leads to development
> schemes... It forces the state to assume responsibilities
> which compel it to readjust the economic system which
> results in poverty. That is the value of the Right to Work
> claim. It belongs to those great creative agencies which
> result not in better administration or in any other pallia-
> tive, but in fundamental economic changes which are
> organic and therefore permanent in their value.[7]

Thus when Hardie took advantage of the ten minute rule to bring in the Right to Work Bill on 10 May it passed barely noticed and made no progress, perhaps also overshadowed by the magnitude of the Insurance Bill introduced a few days previously by Lloyd George. The influence of the minority report was very evident in the re-drafted measure, for Hardie affirmed that the 'underlying feature of the Bill is that great undertakings of public utility and Government contracts shall be arranged in advance', and certainly it now envisaged, as the minority report had suggested, that the government should plan its works over a ten-year period.[8] It was significant that Hardie stressed this aspect, for the two main principles of the older version, 'right to work' and rate aid finance, both remained. The new draft also showed the impact of the government's own legislation, as the local unemployment committees were now to be geared to the labour exchanges and to the Board of Trade instead of the Local Government Board. The Social Democrats, who had welcomed the original Bill, were very contemptuous of the new one, Quelch claiming that it was so tame that the government could almost accept it if the 'right to work' clause were replaced by one dealing with insurance.[9]

The insurance scheme had been maturing for some time before Lloyd George introduced it on 4 May. The TUC in particular had kept in close touch with the Chancellor ever since the end of 1909 and the rank and file of the labour movement had exhibited keen interest in it. In 1910 the September congress of the TUC had passed a resolution demanding certain safeguards in any insurance system in order to protect the integrity of the unions. Although Snowden had begun to argue in the same year that the government should put up all the money for any insurance scheme, outright opposition had been limited to a few such as Lansbury and Tillett. Consultations between the government and TUC leaders continued into the new year, and after one such meeting on 9 January Asquith informed the King that it had been decided to merge the two plans for insurance against unemployment and ill-health into one Bill. It was later alleged that this decision was taken as a result of labour pressure, the union leaders feeling that unemployment insurance, on which they were especially keen, would have a better chance of passing if it were part of a larger measure. This seems quite possible in view of the fact that as long ago as July 1909 Churchill had told Runciman that it did not 'seem practicable or desirable to merge the two things'.[10] Certainly the change created many difficulties for the civil servants responsible for drafting the joint Bill, for the two schemes were at different stages of development.[11]

When Lloyd George introduced the new Bill into the House of Commons he spoke for so long on Part I, which dealt with health, that he had little time for Part II, which covered unemployment, but shortly after his parliamentary statement its details were published in a supplementary press announcement. The plan was to cover workers in engineering, shipbuilding, building and construction, with contributions of $2\frac{1}{2}$d (1p) each from the worker and his employer, the state adding 25 per cent of the total thus contributed. Employers were to be able to compound their subscriptions. Benefits were payable for 15 weeks—6s (30p) a week for building workers, 7s (35p) for engineers. There was to be no benefit for men who were sacked for misconduct or who were put out of work by a trade dispute. Nor was any benefit payable for the first week of unemployment. No one was to be able to claim more than one week's benefit for every five weeks' contributions. Men were to be paid through their union which would then claim the requisite amount from a central fund. Non-unionists were to be paid through the medium of the labour exchange.

Once a scheme of such magnitude was actually before the country it was almost inevitable that it would absorb labour's attention and divert attention away from ideas such as the 'right to work' even more. Initial labour reactions were certainly favourable, although there were those such as Snowden, Hardie, and several of the miners' MPs who wished that more workers were included. This also concerned the general labour unions, whose joint council was instructed to press very strongly for their inclusion. Similarly, many speakers at the dockers' triennial delegate meeting were concerned that dock workers had been more or less excluded. Unknown to them, however, Buxton had argued in cabinet for their inclusion on the

K

grounds that this would promote decasualisation and make the measure more defensible.[12] But he was overruled because of the extra cost involved, something which was apparently causing some worry to Lloyd George, for at one time he was thinking of reducing the state's contribution under Part II to 1d per insured man, plus the administrative expenses.[13] Thus when the question of the Bill's scope was raised by Labour members in Parliament it was pointed out by government speakers that it already embraced a third of the adult male working population, the rest either being in unions which paid unemployment donations, or employed in trades not prone to fluctuations in the labour market. Provision was also made for certain other trades to opt into the plan if they wished. In addition, it was argued that the scheme was experimental and before it could be safely extended more actuarial information had to be acquired, an argument with which George Roberts, for one, fully concurred.[14]

Criticism was also made of the clauses concerning the qualifications for, and restrictions on, benefits, particularly the one which stipulated that no benefit would be paid to those who turned down work at a 'fair wage'. As this was not defined it was argued, for example in a Fabian manifesto issued in June, that trade unionists would be penalised for refusing jobs at less than union rates. The clause which denied relief to a man off work because of a dispute was also much attacked because it did not specify that the man had to be directly involved. When an SDP deputation raised this with Buxton it was informed that the clause was included to prevent the insurance fund being depleted by industrial action so that nothing was left for the unemployed. When the matter was discussed at a special conference arranged by the Joint Board in June, Henderson told the delegates that the Labour Party intended to put down a suitable amendment. This was duly moved during the report stage by Alexander Wilkie, the member for Dundee, who claimed that the non-payment of benefit should be confined to those directly concerned in a dispute by virtue of its being between their own employer and their own trade or section. But in his reply Buxton repeated that the unemployment fund was for depressions, not strikes, and added that such an amendment would encourage industrial militancy. In any case he doubted whether it would be possible to demarcate the various trades successfully. Lansbury, Duncan, O'Grady and Clynes all spoke in favour of the amendment, the latter affirming that if it was not allowed then 'the bill will commit an act of the gravest injustice to a poor and suffering class'.[15] But it was rejected 146-69.

Yet a further source of discontent was that the proposed level of benefits was different, and this was most resented, not unnaturally, by building trade workers who were scheduled to get the lower rate. The initiative in challenging this came from the secretary of the amalgamated carpenters and joiners, William Matkin, who wrote to the various building unions urging them to press for equality, and he enclosed with his letter figures to show that over a three-year period they had paid out more in unemployment benefit than the engineering unions. The Joint Board conference also decided that it was inconsistent to have unequal benefits when the contributions were the same in both cases. In July, Buxton told representatives of the building trades federation that he would assist any amendments to this clause that were permissible within the limit of the scheme's financial provisions. When the Bill reached committee W. T. Wilson, himself a building worker, moved that payment be made at a flat rate, and Buxton accepted on behalf of the government, although he strenuously opposed an attempt to include with this amendment another to reduce from one week to three days the waiting period during which no benefit was payable. The cost involved, he said, would be so great that the benefits would have to be cut down in order to finance it.[16]

The provision made for employers to compound their contributions was also unpopular. A. H. Gill said in the Commons that it was not fair that employers could make one reduced annual payment for some men because it would render the rest permanently liable to dismissal.[17] The labour conference also opposed this clause, agreeing that if it were passed pressure would be exerted to gain a similar concession for employees. But this was not very realistic, as Buxton pointed out to a deputation from the engineering unions. Compounding was designed, he said, to make employers regularise employment because they were hardly likely to sack a man for whom a whole year's contributions had already been paid. Only employers had it in their power to regularise work in this way and it would thus be impossible to extend the idea to the men's contributions.[18]

Many felt that the size of the premiums should be graded according to the level of personal income. This was particularly apposite to general labourers who were poorly paid, and it was thus one of the suggestions which the general labourers' council was urged to press on Buxton. Socialists, too, held this view and the ILP executive resolved to support the principle that no one earning less than £1 a week should make any contribution at all.[19] When the Joint Board conference discussed its committee's proposal that employers who paid low wages should bear a larger share of the worker's contribution, Will Thorne moved a resolution which would have exempted lower-paid workers from making contributions at all. This, however, was ruled out of order by Henderson.

It was also feared that the scheme would have an adverse effect on the whole structure of unionism, although most labour leaders were generally prepared to accept this risk so long as amendments were made in the Bill to safeguard the unions. The Joint Board even suggested that the scheme might be beneficial to the union movement on the grounds that as there was nothing to prevent an employer making wage adjustments so that the whole burden fell on the workers, non-unionists would soon realise this and be compelled to join a union in order to protect their wages. But despite this optimism Beatrice Webb voiced a genuine and widespread fear when she said of unemployment insurance that 'if it is carried through, it will lead to increased control of the employer and the wage earner by the state'.[20] W. T. Wilson thought that if employers were allowed to make deductions from wages then it would be almost impossible to persuade men to join a union, and he argued that the Bill should be dropped for a year so that this point could be fully considered.[21] Victor Grayson went much further, purporting to see behind the Bill 'a sinister capitalist purpose . . . it will annihilate your power to fight your employers by strike, or any other form of open aggression'.[22] His view was shared by Hall, who warned that its main object was 'to put an end to trades unionism as a fighting or even defensive force in the nation'.[23]

Because of their dislike of the scheme's contributory nature and their fears about its effects on trade unionism, Grayson, Hall and other malcontents on the left of the labour alliance were prepared to oppose the Insurance Bill outright. Their opposition was augmented by that of the SDP and the Fabian Society. The Social Democrats argued that insurance was not the right way of approaching the problem at all, as it did nothing to reduce the numbers out of work, merely keeping the unemployed worker at subsistence level until such time as he was required again by the capitalist. They were also against the contributory principle, the parliamentary correspondent of *Justice* condemning this proposal as 'mean, petty, and ridiculous'.[24] This was also the Fabians' main objection, and they decided to undertake a vigorous campaign against the scheme, beginning by issuing a critical manifesto. Within two weeks of the Bill being introduced Sidney Webb was urging Sanders to hasten the preparation of this leaflet, expressing the hope that 'the Fabian Society is not going to be as disgracefully incompetent over the Bill as the Labour Party has been'.[25] He was referring, of course, to the general approval given to the plan by the Labour MPs, many of whom were willing to accept it provided the defects were ironed out during its passage through Parliament.

But there was at this stage no unanimity within the parliamentary Labour Party. Lansbury had been arguing since 1910 that insurance would not protect the lower-paid workers, while Snowden had similarly been contending that the government should bear the whole cost. On 24 May Lansbury wrote triumphantly to Webb, telling him that at a party meeting a resolution to abolish contributions from lower-paid workers had been moved with the result that 'we have cut the party exactly in two halves. Snowden came down absolutely on the side of a *non*-contributory scheme. There is more talk among our labour men against the bill . . . now Snowden has come down on my side it is much better.'[26] Although Lansbury did not indicate in his letter who were his other supporters at this party meeting, it can be surmised from their subsequent attitude that Hardie, O'Grady, Jowett, and Thorne were among them. The first three were all members of the ILP, which had voted at its annual conference for a non-contributory system, while Thorne had argued in an article in *Justice* that the whole cost would in practice be borne by the workers, as the state's contribution would come from taxes and the employers' from increased prices. He believed that the expenses should be met from a supertax on incomes of over £300 a year.[27] Lansbury's supporters may have included W. T. Wilson, who had already argued that the workers' burdens were too great, and also Stephen Walsh, the miner, and Joseph Pointer, both of whom voted with Snowden against the money resolution sanctioning the Bill's financial provisions on 6 July.

The official party attitude was laid down by MacDonald in a long *Labour Leader* article. He argued that they were committed to abolishing low wages, but to be continually asking the government for doles, low or non-contributory insurance schemes would simply perpetuate them. Lower-paid workers would come to regard themselves as the objects of state charity and fail to join with their fellows in order to improve their conditions.[28] This argument was promptly assailed by Snowden who condemned it as 'unadulterated, sixty year old, individualism'. If state aid to raise the standard of life was wrong and degrading, as MacDonald suggested, then logically, said Snowden, he ought also to have opposed free meals for needy school children and old age pensions. It might prove impossible to get a non-contributory Bill, Snowden added, but their principles demanded that they should at least fight for one.[29]

These differences all came out at the special conference organised by the Joint Board on 20 and 21 June. Members of the ILP tried to push through a resolution making deductions from wages illegal. MacDonald opposed this, largely on the grounds that the German trade unions, which had been the subject of several Labour Party inquiries, had found a contributory system advantageous. It was also pointed out by those who agreed with MacDonald that labour could hardly demand some say in the control of a machine which it was not prepared to help maintain. Although MacDonald carried the conference with him by 223 votes to 44, this did not deter Margaret Bondfield, Mary Macarthur, and Lansbury moving a resolution to exempt sweated workers from contributing because such people already earned too little to live on. This, too, was defeated on a card vote, 1,164-284. The following day Thorne tried to move a similar resolution, this time applying to all low-paid workers, but he was overruled by Henderson.[30] It was perfectly obvious, as one union journal pointed out, that 'in relation to the trades unions of the country . . . they have not to deal with a non-contributory scheme'.[31] Lansbury was horrified by these decisions and appealed for a nation-wide agitation against the Bill.

But, as the conference had shown, MacDonald was not short of support. According to Lansbury's letter to Webb, at least

half the parliamentary party were even against the abolition
of contributions from lower-paid workers and it seems certain
that the same members would have been opposed to a system
financed entirely by the state. By and large, the trade unionists
in the party backed MacDonald, and it is significant that those
who opposed him most strongly belonged to unions of lower-
paid or unskilled workers—Thorne of the gasworkers and
general labourers, O'Grady of the furniture workers. Although
the Fabian Society had come out strongly against the Bill, one
of its leading members, E. R. Pease, supported the Labour
Party's official policy. There was also some support for Mac-
Donald from members of the ILP executive, for in inviting
Herbert Bryan of the party's London organisation to one of
the Fabian protest meetings, Harry Duberry, one member of
the National Administrative Council who opposed the Bill,
said that the demonstration would 'upset the official element
on N.A.C. but we need not consider that'.[32]

The split within the Labour Party became even more
apparent when the committee stage of the Bill began and the
financial resolution covering both parts was debated. It made
provision for the payment by the state of two-ninths of the
health benefits and one-third (more than originally announced)
of the total contributions made under Part II. Snowden rose
and said he understood that this would be the only opportunity they had of proposing an increase in the state contribution,
and he then argued powerfully for a non-contributory system
of health and unemployment insurance. He only took eight
other members into the lobby with him, however, and it may
be that some of these voted for a free health scheme and had
no strong feelings about the unemployment proposals.[33] When
the financial resolution reached report stage the following day
Jowett moved to abolish all contributions, withdrawing when
he had explained that this was merely his way of registering a
protest.

MacDonald's acceptance of the resolution was severely at-

tacked by those who claimed that it would now be impossible
to move that the state share of the contributions be increased.
He replied by submitting a memorandum (later published) to
the Labour Party executive justifying his action. He argued
that by constitutional practice only a minister could move a
resolution imposing a charge upon the state. Lloyd George
had stated that whatever benefits were paid under Part I the
state would provide two-ninths, and would pay one-third of
the total contributions made under Part II. Thus it was still
possible to move for larger benefits and the party was 'as free
to raise our points and move our amendmnets as we were
before the Money Resolution was carried'.[34] Snowden replied
in the *Labour Leader*, claiming that this statement was a tissue
of mis-statements from beginning to end and adding that there
was no chance of raising the proportion of the state's contribution. Certainly there was no possibility now of abolishing
contributions altogether, which is probably what really infur-
iated Snowden, but he went on to point out that nobody had
known on 6 July that amendments to increase the benefits
would be accepted, for the Speaker had not announced this
until the following day. MacDonald, he concluded, was dis-
honestly sheltering himself behind an interpretation of the
money resolution which no one could have held when the
Labour Party voted.[35]

But Snowden's small support in the division lobby confirms
that very few of the Labour MPs were prepared to support a
non-contributory Bill, and were certainly not willing to jeo-
pardise the whole scheme by voting against the money resolution. Not all of the ILP were prepared to risk splitting the
Labour Party either, and it was George Barnes who conducted
much of the negotiation with the government which took place
during the summer.

MacDonald's own keenness for the measure may have several
explanations. For one thing, he was the leader of an uneasy
alliance of trade unionists and socialists, and there is little

doubt that the trade union majority wanted the Bill. Beveridge stressed to his mother in August, for instance, that the union leaders were particularly anxious to secure the unemployment scheme.[36] Secondly, MacDonald seems genuinely to have believed in a contributory system, for he had written an article some fifteen years previously arguing in favour of workers' contributions to an unemployment insurance plan. Perhaps, too, he was still hankering after office and eager to ingratiate himself with the Liberal leaders. According to one source, he had already accepted one offer of a position in a coalition government projected in 1910 which had never materialised.[37] He was still in very close touch with the Liberal ministers, however. Sir George Riddell noted in his diary that one day in July 1911 when he called at Downing Street he 'found L.G. holding a conference on the Insurance Bill in his garden. Ramsay MacDonald . . . and some Government officials were seated with him under a tree.'[38] W. A. Colegate, secretary of the Prevention of Destitution Committee which had replaced the Webbs' earlier organisation, told Mrs Webb in August that there was a strong rumour circulating that MacDonald was shortly going to get office.[39] But the most likely explanation for MacDonald's attitude was his concern about the effect of the Osborne case on the unions and the Labour Party. Before the end of the session he agreed with Elibank that his party would back the Insurance Bill if provision were made for the payment of MPs.[40] In fact, Lloyd George introduced a government resolution calling for this on 10 August.

Negotiations between the government and the Labour Party continued all through the summer months, Beveridge observing on one occasion when he had spent the day discussing unemployment insurance with the Labour Party leaders that 'they were really very reasonable and pleasant and will be helpful'.[41] But MacDonald's opponents were active as well and spent the summer attacking the Bill. At the end of July the ILP and the Fabians held a joint protest meeting, despite

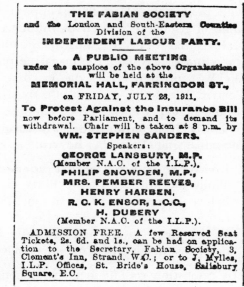

THE FABIAN SOCIETY
and the London and South-Eastern Counties
Division of the
INDEPENDENT LABOUR PARTY.

A PUBLIC MEETING
under the auspices of the above Organisations
will be held at the
MEMORIAL HALL, FARRINGDON ST.,
on FRIDAY, JULY 28, 1911,
To Protest Against the Insurance Bill
now before Parliament, and to demand its
withdrawal. Chair will be taken at 8 p.m. by
WM. STEPHEN SANDERS.
Speakers:
GEORGE LANSBURY, M.P.
(Member N.A.C. of the I.L.P.),
PHILIP SNOWDEN, M.P.,
MRS. PEMBER REEVES,
HENRY HARBEN,
R. C. K. ENSOR, L.C.C.,
H. DUBERY
(Member N.A.C. of the I.L.P.).
ADMISSION FREE. A few Reserved Seat
Tickets, 2s. 6d. and 1s., can be had on applica-
tion to the Secretary, Fabian Society, 3,
Clement's Inn, Strand, W.C.; or to J. Mylles,
I.L.P. Offices, St. Bride's House, Salisbury
Square, E.C.

Protest against the
Insurance Bill.
Clarion, 21 Jul 1911

Labour Party attempts to question whether the Fabian executive had a mandate to participate in such a meeting. One of
Mrs Webb's friends described the scene at the rally.

> Philip Snowden was led on by the enthusiasm of his audi-
> ence to say more against the Bill than he ever imagined
> he could. In fact he was horrified himself and tried to
> hedge but the applause ceased at once and he went back
> to denunciation and wound up with a dramatic appeal.
> Lansbury was great and bellowed in fine style.[42]

The Social Democrats also kept up their opposition, but did
not join formally with the Fabians or the ILP dissenters. In
July, for example, Fairchild published a pamphlet under the
auspices of the London Right to Work Council, claiming that
the scheme should be free. At the TUC conference in September SDP members, backed by some of the ILP rebels, moved
against a contributory system, but were defeated by 940,000

votes to 325,000.[43] Despite this opposition campaign, however, some of its backers, perhaps influenced by this TUC vote, realised that they were going to fail, and C. D. Sharp, who was the editor of *Crusade*, the magazine produced to support the Webbs' campaign against the poor law, wrote despondently to Beatrice Webb that the only effective thing they could now do 'would be to get at the Trade Unions'.[44]

The TUC vote must also have encouraged MacDonald. At the beginning of October he wrote to Elibank again.

> I need not reassure you that the statement I made to you about the attitude of the Party on the Insurance Bill before we separated in the summer holds good. The party came to its decision, and its decision will be carried out by the officers loyally and faithfully, in spite of what two, or at the outside three, members may do to the contrary.[45]

His resolution was further strengthened when, after a long discussion, a censure motion on him in the National Administrative Council was withdrawn. It is not clear how close the debate was or who opposed MacDonald, but there were at least four men present who probably argued against his attitude—Lansbury, Jowett, Duberry, and McLachlan. MacDonald won this particular vote probably because some of the council members—those referred to by Duberry as the official element—had always felt that a contributory scheme was acceptable. Others, such as Ben Riley, thought that as the ILP members were a minority in the parliamentary Labour Party they should abide loyally by its majority decisions.[46] Certainly the split over the Insurance Bill highlighted the problems presented by the complex structure of the Labour Party. What was to be the attitude of those in the Fabian Society and the ILP, which both opposed the measure, who also belonged—by virtue of their ILP or Fabian membership—to a Labour Party which supported it? For the forty or so ILP branches which eventually broke away in the summer to form the British

Socialist Party (BSP) in conjunction with the SDP this problem had been growing for some time, and Hall, one of the dissenters, admitted that the Insurance Bill issue had been 'the last straw that breaks the camel's back'.[47] Others preferred to do what they had always done: remain in the Labour Party and press their own views against the majority view dictated by the trade union element. Thus it was not without significance that those MPs who opposed the Insurance Bill were the remnant of the inner core of 'activists'. Curran and Summerbell were both dead, Seddon and Richards had lost their seats, Barnes and Roberts, along with the trade union section and the rest of the 'activist' group, had accepted that the government programme was satisfactory. Only Hardie, Jowett, Thorne, O'Grady, and Snowden were left, joined now by Lansbury. With the exception of the last two, these were men who had co-operated closely with the SDP, especially in 1908, and it might have been in an effort to resurrect the dead alliance that H. W. Lee, secretary of the provisional BSP committee, contacted the rebels to suggest that they form themselves into a parliamentary group to act in conjunction with the new socialist party.[48] E. C. Fairchild, who had been secretary of the Joint London Right to Work Committee, wrote to Lansbury encouraging him to keep up the fight as long as possible, arguing that if MacDonald prevailed it would be 'the driving under of English Socialism'.[49]

But by the time this correspondence took place resistance to MacDonald's line had to all intents and purposes been broken. Three days after the National Administrative Council threw out the censure motion MacDonald contacted Elibank to inform him of the Labour Party's intentions and to offer advice on the conduct of the rest of the session. The whole tone of the letter bespoke of very close co-operation, almost 'rigging'.

I strongly advise you to adopt the same methods as you did before the summer. It will be a very hard job, but I

believe you can do it. I am sorry to say that there will be
one or two men whom I cannot control, but disagreements between you and the Party as a whole on the Bill
will be on very few points, and upon these we can have
businesslike discussions, and then divisions. I shall also
be willing always to support you on any reasonable application of the closure...[50]

He followed this by issuing a public statement saying that the
Labour Party intended to support the Bill when the autumn
session began. This, said the *Daily News,* dispelled the impression created by the activities of the rebels during the summer
that the party was divided.[51] Ten days later the *Labour Leader*
acknowledged MacDonald's victory, concluding that the dissenters would simply have to make the best of things.[52] The opposition was further undermined when the actuary appointed
by the Labour Party to examine the Bill presented his report.
It would, he concluded, be advantageous for trade unions to
join the scheme because the administrative costs would be
borne by the state, and they would save because the contributions were small compared to the benefits, which the unions
would no longer have to pay. What popular discontent remained was largely among lower-paid workers, and although
there was some resentment at the way in which MacDonald
had acted, the general feeling according to one observer was
'steadfastly in favour of the Labour Party alliance'.[53]

The Social Democrats and the Fabians kept up their opposition, but it had by now lost much of its impetus. The Labour
Party rebels still refused to toe the party line and when a re-
assembled Parliament agreed in October that the unemployment section should be discussed in grand committee Lansbury, supported by Jowett, Thorne, and O'Grady, objected,
but unsuccessfully. During the third reading debate they made
a further protest, claiming that people could not afford the
contributions and that both schemes should be free. But the

third reading was passed by 324 votes to 21.[54]

After a year of internal dissension and negotiation, what had the Labour Party achieved in the way of amendment? Benefits had been made uniform, contributions from young apprenticed workers had been reduced, and the scheme now covered those in the scheduled trades who were aged more than sixteen, not eighteen as originally intended. Some concessions had been granted in the clauses relating to disqualification from benefit because of involvement in trade disputes, and improvements had also been made in the clauses concerning the standard of work offered to unemployed workers. The net result of these changes was an increase in the state contribution of £100,000, twice as much, said the *Labour Leader*, as the transport workers had gained from their recent strike, and readers were invited to draw the appropriate conclusions.[55] Snowden promptly pointed out that this was misleading, as the extra money had come from a surplus on the contributions, not from any increase in the state's share of the cost.[56] The rebels then made a last defiant gesture by issuing a manifesto, signed also by Hardie who had abstained on the third reading, which explained that they had been in general sympathy with the Bill's purpose, but felt that its principles were unsound. Among the objections which they listed to Part II were the contributory basis which compelled men to pay for protection against something for which they were not responsible. They also believed that the price of the benefits was too high in terms of the contributions.[57] This, however, was the last sign of their revolt, and it was perhaps indicative of the labour movement's general acceptance of the Insurance Bill that the *Labour Leader* could state that it had given them something from which to start.[58]

There were, of course, still elements which continued to demand a free scheme, or alterations in the financial arrangements in order to exempt lower-paid workers. Thus the 1912 report of the ILP urged party members to work towards a non-contributory system. In the same year the TUC unanimously passed resolutions calling for the abolition of contributions under Part II from casual workers earning less than 10s a week, and for graduated contributions from those receiving less than £1. At the end of 1912 Ben Tillett was still encouraging the members of his union to agitate for the abolition of contributions, while Thorne successfully secured the passage at Labour Party conferences in 1913 and 1914 of resolutions demanding a universal non-contributory plan. On neither occasion, however, was there any discussion, and while the labour movement may have thus defined its ultimate objective as a free system, in practice it had to accept and work with the existing legislation. In reviewing the outlook for the parliamentary session of 1912 Ben Turner stated that 'he had not much to say about the new Insurance Act. It is now law, and our business should be to make it an Act of usefulness'.[59] The majority of Labour MPs concentrated simply on the principles and administration of the existing measure, W. T. Wilson stressing in 1913 when he moved a reduction in the civil service estimates in order to initiate a discussion on unemployment insurance that 'he was not opposed to Part II of the Act' and that his criticisms would be 'concerned only with its administration'.[60]

Certainly there were plenty of administrative points which required settling. What, for example, was to happen to men who were laid off work because of bad weather? Did they receive their benefit or not? Snowden wanted to know.[61] J. V. Wills, a delegate from the bricklayers, told the 1912 TUC conference that the Umpire, appointed to arbitrate on tricky points, had decreed that in the building trade some men were covered by the Act if working in one type of job, but not in others, which meant that in the course of a single year one man could be in and out of the scheme several times.[62] Another administrative difficulty, pointed out by a TUC deputation to the Board of Trade in 1913, arose from the fact that the authorities often failed to send details of the names of union branches and members on whose behalf benefit cheques were being forwarded. Eventually, in 1914, the government did produce an amending Bill to iron out some of these problems.

The problems of dovetailing the unions' own unemployment relief systems with the state plan also took up a great amount of labour time and energy. A substantial amount of hard work was involved and at least one union secretary expressed relief that his members had decided not to opt into the unemployment scheme, because he was already overworked by the health insurance system.[63] This burden was made even greater by the fact that those unions covered by insurance were generally those which benefited most from the great increase in membership which took place after 1911. In the Operative Bricklayers' Society, for instance, membership went up in 1912 for the first time in many years—by 2,165.[64] In the same year the engineers gained over 22,000 new members.[65] It is tempting to posit some direct connection between the growth of union membership and the establishment of health and unemployment insurance, but it seems more likely that the increase was due to the prospering state of the economy and to the low level of unemployment.[66]

In turn this meant that the Labour Party's Right to Work Bill, already overshadowed by the government's programme, was pushed even further into the shade despite the high place it still occupied in the party programme. Its retention was probably due not so much to any widespread conviction of its usefulness as to the fact that adherence to the principle was one of the few remaining marks of distinction between Labourism and Liberalism. The Bill was re-introduced in 1912 and with the new title of the Prevention of Unemployment Bill in 1913 and 1914, but it was never backed by the sort of effort mounted in 1907-8 and never got beyond a first reading. The influence of the minority report was more marked than ever in the 1913-14 versions, for the Bill was now divided into two sections, the first of which made provision for the estab-

L

lishment of a labour ministry as recommended by the minority report. The 'right to work' clause only survived in the second section, no longer occupying the central place it had enjoyed in the early drafts. Resolutions in its favour were still passed at labour conferences, but the Labour Party executive resisted the few attempts made to commit it to a vigorous policy to push the measure through, and it was clear, as a delegate at the ILP's 1912 conference confessed, that it had become 'a hardy annual'.[67]

The labour movement in general was far more concerned in any case with the high level of industrial unrest which characterised the years between 1911 and 1914. 'No small part of the work . . . during the past twelve months,' reported the ILP in 1912, 'has been to aid the organised workers in their splendid industrial battles and to give legislative expression to their demands.'[68] To this end a fully comprehensive programme was drawn up by the ILP and the Fabian Society which together launched an energetic crusade against all forms of poverty in 1912. Meetings were held all over the country to popularise this programme, which was essentially that of the minority report. Unemployment was largely ignored, partly because of its low level, partly because there was really little new to say about it. But the poverty campaign must have served to strengthen the currents which were carrying the Right to Work Bill into a backwater. It was a measure designed to cope only with one aspect of poverty. The minority report and the ILP-Fabian crusade were based on a much wider concept, well expressed by W. C. Anderson at the ILP's 1913 conference.

Social problems are not isolated and unconnected manifestations; they are interdependent; the roots of one social evil are embedded in other social evils and all find congenial soil in the poverty of the people. Problems like those of wages, hours, housing, health, child-life, unemployment, pauperism, hang closely together, and so we put forward the new people's charter—a social charter this time—demanding for all the workers a standard of life compatible with the gains of civilisation.[69]

It is true that two aspects of the poverty campaign, the demand for an eight-hour day and a minimum wage, were traditional labour solutions for unemployment, but by 1912 they were both seen more as remedies for industrial unrest. Thus the speech made by Clynes at the TUC conference in 1913 advocated an eight-hour day simply on the grounds that that was as much as anybody could reasonably be expected to work in the conditions of modern industry. Similarly, a minimum wage amendment on the King's Speech in 1912 was moved not with reference to unemployment but to the 'existing industrial unrest arising from a deplorable insufficiency of wages'.[70] Unemployment, as a living political issue in Edwardian society, was dead.

CHAPTER 8

Conclusions

THE EDWARDIAN ERA saw a significant change in the attitude of the state towards its unemployed. When the twentieth century began, the worker who had no job usually had recourse to municipal relief works set up under the provisions of the re-issued Local Government Board circular of 1886, to private charity, or to the poor law. If he was a trade unionist belonging to a society that paid unemployment benefit he could, for a time, rely on that. But by 1914 the state had openly admitted its responsibility by legislating for those of its citizens who had no work. The breakthrough came in 1905 with the passage of the Unemployed Workmen's Bill, and four years later the Liberal Government began to lay the foundations of a completely new approach by setting up labour exchanges. In 1911 the National Insurance Act brought approximately one-third of all adult male workers into a state scheme of unemployment protection. It was inevitable that the increasingly articulate working classes should be deeply involved in these changes concerning a problem which affected so many of them, and unemployment thus provides a useful framework in which to study the activity and effectiveness of the Edwardian labour movement.

One can notice first the frequent initiatives taken by the Social Democrats before 1906, both in terms of general policy and direct action. It was the SDF which first interested itself in the recurring problem after the Boer War at a time when the rest of the organised labour movement was still reeling under the impact of the Taff Vale judgement. It was the SDF that first called for a special session of Parliament in the autumn of 1904, a demand subsequently taken up by other labour groups. The following year the idea of working the Unemployed Workmen's Act to death was one first advocated by the Social Democrat, Fred Knee, and soon taken up by Hardie and many of his ILP colleagues. Nor were these initiatives altogether wasted, for the SDF was quite successful in drawing attention to the unemployed, particularly in London. The street marches led by Social Democrat agitators produced considerable annoyance at many levels of society and eventually compelled the government to take steps to limit their effectiveness. This did not deter the SDF, however, and it kept the matter so effectively in the news in 1904 that by the autumn Walter Long had summoned a London conference, largely to placate the rising uneasiness which it had done so much to generate. His decision to legislate also owed much to the SDF's activity. The Liberals, too, frequently twitted in the labour press, including the Social Democrat organs, for not possessing any unemployment policy, were also compelled to give the matter some thought.

These successes were all the more surprising in view of the handicaps under which the federation worked. After November 1903 there were the regulations issued under the government's new legislation to consider, but there were other difficulties, more lasting than those posed by this restrictive measure. Numerical weakness and the uneven distribution of membership limited the scope of the agitation. Real strength was enjoyed only in London, Lancashire, and some provincial towns such as Glasgow and Northampton. Furthermore, power was heavily concentrated in London after 1901 when half of the twenty-four places on the national executive were reserved for representatives from the capital. These administrative weaknesses were well illustrated in 1905 and again in 1908 when the executive could only appeal for, rather than organise, nation-wide demonstrations. Lack of money was another perennial problem which prevented the SDF from undertaking any sustained national campaign of the type organised by the Labour Party in 1907-8. The London Central Workers' Committee collapsed in 1906 for want of funds, and had it not been for the selfless devotion of men such as Williams and Greenwood, both of whom worked on occasion for nothing, the Social Democrats would surely have made less of an impact than they did. In 1908 only the generosity of Lady Warwick made possible the fresh agitation in London, the attempt at national organisation already having failed, partly for lack of finance. But even if the federation had been organically and financially strong, its efforts in the years between 1902 and 1904 at least would still have been hampered by the various internal disputes which, rooted mainly in the question of whether or not short-term palliatives should be ignored for the sake of achieving socialism, divided the movement so deeply that in the space of just over two years it produced two off-spring—the Socialist Labour Party and the Socialist Party of Great Britain.

One other major problem which even a strong organisation would have found it hard to surmount was the frequent complacency of the unemployed themselves, although this can be exaggerated, as the exploits of the land-grabbers in 1906 and the streams of hunger marchers in 1908-9 proves. But even in London's East End, where there was a chronic unemployment problem, it was often difficult to urge the sufferers to act, and it seems more than likely that many of the unemployed only joined the demonstrations because they provided an opportunity to collect money or receive food, hence the problem posed by loafers.

Such apathy towards political and social problems was by no means unique to Edwardian Britain, but still it is strange that those who suffered from unemployment were apparently so reluctant to act on their own behalf. Obviously, unless things were really bad, as they were in 1905 and 1908, men in trade unions which paid unemployment donation had little incentive to participate in any such activity. Similarly, those with some quality or skill which in more prosperous times would usually ensure them a job were hardly likely to risk antagonising potential employers by appearing in violent demonstrations. But there remains the problem of those who had no such skill, who had almost nothing to lose, and who were out of work more often than not. They, argued Robert Tressall, were their own worst enemy who 'not only submitted quietly like so many cattle to their miserable slavery for the benefit of others, but defended it, and opposed and ridiculed any suggestion of reform'.[1] Perhaps their indifference was due to a certain mental dullness produced by months or even years of enforced idleness. W. S. Sanders was perhaps hinting at this when he said that the men who joined the socialist movement had been those who 'still retained sufficient spirit to rebel; this lifted them out of the common ruck of their class, and gave them individuality'.[2] The curious and permanent optimism noticed by Masterman might also have been important.

> There was a time when things were less rosy; when we stood in knots at street corners . . . when work was solicited and solicited in vain. . . . But that time seems long ago. . . We have no faith in its recurrence . . . we possess a genial faith in a Deity who is nothing if not amiable, and we are convinced that tomorrow will see the dawn of the golden age.[3]

Perhaps, too, there was an unwillingness to be exploited for political ends by an organisation with whose politics very few workers agreed, and the SDF made things worse for itself in this respect by its hostile and sectarian attitude towards trade unionists. This explains why it often tried to work through what can best be termed 'front organisations'—the London Trades Council, the Central Workers' Committee, and, later, the 'right to work' movement.

Once the unemployment question was taken up by the government at the end of 1904 it was certain that the spotlight would shift from the streets to the House of Commons. In turn this meant that the leading role which the SDF had played in organising agitation on the question passed into the hands of the other, much larger, labour organisations, the TUC, the ILP, and the body to which both were affiliated, the LRC.

The change took place really in 1905 when the LRC's activity in the House of Commons was supplemented by a national campaign of meetings more massive in scale than anything the SDF could have hoped to arrange. But initially, at any rate, the labour alliance was not free of those very problems which hampered the SDF. It did not, it is true, have the same difficulty of small numbers, as the LRC in 1903 had an affiliated membership of 847,000 trade unionists and 13,000 members of the ILP, against a recorded SDF membership in the same year of only 9,000.[4] But the TUC executive had very little real control over its constituent unions, while the ILP was not very strong in the south of England or, more particularly, in London. This may well explain the attempts made by ILP leaders in 1905 and again in 1908 to harness the London strength of the SDF in the hope that such joint action would be more effective. Nor was the labour alliance free from internal differences of the type which hit the SDF in 1902-4. There was considerable suspicion between socialists and trade unionists, well illustrated in MacDonald's efforts to conceal from the latter the ILP initiative in suggesting and financing the Unemployed Workmen's Bill demonstrations in 1905. Again, some of the ILP rank and file were very wary of their leaders' co-operation with radicals in the National Unemployed Committee, wishing the party to adopt a distinctive socialist line on the unemployed question. In the early days, too, it seems that there may have been something of a financial problem, for the demonstrations of 1905 were apparently made possible only by the timely appearance of Joseph Fels. Despite these drawbacks, however, and the total failure of the efforts to save the original Unemployed Workmen's Bill, once the LRC established a firm foothold in Parliament in 1906 the change of roles was complete and the initiative passed finally into the hands of the new Labour Party.

As a pressure group in the Commons for the unemployed the Labour Party was really quite successful, in spite of the contentions of its left-wing critics. For one thing, the emphasis it placed on the unemployment issue almost from the day of the 1906 session contributed greatly to the eclipse of John Burns. It may be true, as tradition has it, that Burns was a proud, stubborn man in the control of his reactionary departmental officials, but he cannot have been entirely devoid of ability or Campbell-Bannerman, whose glittering cabinet testifies both to the abundance of talent available in the Liberal Party and to his own capacity for choosing able ministers, would hardly have offered him a post in 1905. Certainly the bulk of the labour movement, with the exception of his former SDF comrades, was prepared to give the new Local Government Board President every chance to show what he could do. But his refusal in the face of steady Labour Party pressure to produce any substantial unemployment policy, other than that of waiting for the poor law report, brought him into conflict with his cabinet colleagues and to the verge of resignation as early as May 1906. By early 1908 Asquith had agreed that Churchill should work out a long-term policy, and in October Labour demands for immediate action to cope with a severe depression resulted in the responsibility for a short-term policy also being taken out of his hands and placed in those of a small cabinet committee. The next two years saw the implementation of the long-term policies, and Burns faded from the scene. Small wonder that at the beginning of the 1912 session the veteran northern labour leader, Alf Mattison, could note in his diary that Burns was 'a lonely man and . . . feels his loneliness. It has been noticeable during the past session that Burns has rarely been seen and certainly not been heard in the House.'[5]

The pressure exerted by the Labour Party also succeeded in severely embarrassing the government on at least two occasions, and one Liberal minister confessed that the Labour campaign on behalf of the Right to Work Bill could well divide the Liberal left from its right. Although the actual form of the programme which the Liberals introduced in 1909-11 owed little or nothing to the Labour Party's own Bill, despite the face-saving attempts of several Labour MPs to argue otherwise, the actual fact of the programme was a tacit recognition of the success of the Labour propaganda campaign of 1907-8. It was no coincidence that the outlines of the new legislation were first discussed in government circles in the autumn of 1908, for by that time the Labour Party, aided by a somewhat for-tuitous deterioration in the labour market and a good deal of quite rowdy agitation frequently stirred up by Social Demo-crats, had suceeded in making unemployment, and more particularly the Right to Work Bill, a living political issue. As one commentator said,

> Whatever view one takes of the aims of the Labour Party, one cannot deny that they have succeeded in a way never before realised in focussing the attention of Parliament and the nation upon the . . . growing seriousness of the problem of unemployment.[6]

Considering the smallness and newness of the Labour Party these were impressive achievements. In a sense, however, it was unlucky because the great effort on behalf of the Right to Work Bill reached a climax in March 1908, six months before the worst unemployment crisis of the decade came to a head. The party had effectively shot its bolt too soon and came up against the limitations imposed by parliamentary procedure. Its attempts to keep the matter alive by outside speeches and parliamentary questions naturally appeared to be lifeless and

even irrelevant as unemployment and spontaneous agitation
continued to rise. The party seemed to be frittering away a
golden chance to make a real and lasting impression in one of
the few fields where it had a ready-made policy genuinely
distinct from that of the government.

It was considerations like these which so annoyed the party's
critics and which eventually produced Victor Grayson's out-
burst in October. Undoubtedly, as the critics maintained,
there were Labour MPs who were prepared to wait for the
government to produce its own answers, and who were obliv-
ious of the wider implications of the unemployment problem
because they represented only narrow, selfish trade union
interests. But ever since 1906 one section of the party had
put pressure on the government—MacDonald, Snowden,
W. T. Wilson, Henderson, Crooks, Thorne, Jowett, Seddon,
Duncan, Curran, Parker, T. F. Richards, Hardie, Barnes,
O'Grady, Clynes, Roberts, and Summerbell. These were the
men who launched the question campaign in 1906, made the
militant speeches in 1907-8, and pestered the government front
bench in 1908. It is an over-simplification to interpret their
interest in unemployment as symptomatic of the division between socialist and trade unionist, if only because of the difficulty of allocating each MP neatly into one or other of these
categories. In any case, not all of the group were socialists.
Within this group of 'activists' was an even smaller section,
consisting of Hardie, Curran, Barnes, Seddon, O'Grady, Summerbell, Roberts and Jowett, who, as well as being very vocal
in Parliament, were prepared to work more or less openly with
the SDF on behalf of the unemployed. Some had taken part in
Social Democrat demonstrations, some sympathised with Grayson in his frustration, nearly all of whom were involved in the
formation of the Joint London Right to Work Committee in
October 1908.

This co-operation was short-lived, however. Several of the
other 'activists' were opposed to the idea of working with the

Social Democrats, while others were afraid of the violence which generally seemed to follow them. It is possible that, initially at least, Hardie was prepared to risk their antagonism for the sake of securing something more from the government. What really caused him to forsake the alliance, apart from relatively minor disagreements, was, firstly, the reaction of trade unionists, shown in their desertion of the 'right to work' movement, and, secondly, the way in which Grayson was being used by elements hostile to the labour alliance—elements which included the SDP—to foment a rebellion against it. Hardie often expressed irritation at the cramping effects of the trade union alliance, being 'sore at seeing the fruit of our years of toil being garnered by men who were never of us, and who even now would trick us out', but in the final analysis he was not prepared to see his life's work disrupted either for the sake of the unemployed or of socialist unity.[7] He was vindicated later, for although the BSP failed in 1911 to renew co-operation with those of the 'activists' who had resisted the allurements of the government programme, kept their seats in the elections of 1910, and now opposed the Insurance Bill, it decided three years later to apply for affiliation to the Labour Party. In this way socialist unity was restored, although for a very short time, but within the context of the labour alliance.

But it seems unlikely that the co-operation of 1908 between the SDP and the inner group of 'activists' in the 'right to work' movement would have lasted very long anyway, for by the early months of 1909 the whole impetus behind the movement and the Bill was disintegrating. The Labour Party never did get its Bill through and in this sense its unemployment policy was a failure. However there were those who genuinely believed that in principle, at least, the Development Bill and the Insurance scheme conceded its basic features, while others had never really seen the Right to Work Bill as anything more than a stick with which to beat the government. For all these, the appearance of the government programme did represent the triumphant culmination of the Labour campaign.

It is possible, of course, to adopt a cynical attitude and argue that those Labour MPs who claimed that in effect the Bill had been passed only did so to hide the fact that the government had stolen their thunder. Beatrice Webb seems to have taken this view, for she noted in her diary at the end of 1910 that 'the big thing' of the past two years had been the way that 'Lloyd George and Winston Churchill have practically taken the limelight, not merely from their own colleagues, but from the Labour Party'.[8] Certainly the appearance of constructive proposals from the government benches deprived the Labour Party Bill of the support of those Liberals who had voted for it, some because they believed in it, more because they wished to protest against their leaders' failure to honour election promises. But Mrs Webb herself was partly responsible for the disintegration of support for the Right to Work Bill, because the campaign to popularise the minority report, with its comprehensive plans for tackling poverty, undoubtedly won over large sections of the ILP. It was from this same party that the first large-scale attacks on the Bill's potential came in 1911. By 1914 the Labour Party Bill bore more resemblance to the minority report than to its own antecedents, the clause guaranteeing the 'right to work' having been dethroned and given an insignificant place.

The ideal, it is true, remained as an objective—albeit a somewhat utopian one—to which the British labour movement was committed. In a way, the advent of public assistance in the inter-war period realised it, but the nobility with which Hardie and his friends had originally invested it and the passion with which they had fought for its inception could have had little meaning for the men of whom T. S. Eliot wrote, or indeed for the unemployed of Edwardian England, to whom his words can equally be applied:

No man has hired us.
With pocketed hands
And lowered faces
We stand about in open places
And shiver in unlit rooms.
Only the wind moves
Over empty fields, untilled
Where the plough rests, at an angle
To the furrow. In this land
There shall be one cigarette to two men,
To two women one half pint of bitter
Ale. In this land
No man has hired us.
Our life is unwelcome, our death
Unmentioned in *The Times*.[9]

Notes and references

THE FOLLOWING ABBREVIATIONS are used:

Ann Rep	*Annual Report*
BkL	Beaverbrook Library
BL	Bodleian Library
BLPES	British Library of Political and Economic Science
BM	British Museum
BPP	*British Parliamentary Papers*
EC	Executive Committee
LL	*Labour Leader*
LP	Labour Party
NCL	Nuffield College Library
NLC	National Liberal Club
NLS	National Library of Scotland
PC	Parliamentary Committee
PRO	Public Record Office
RR	*Railway Review*
TLG	*Trades and Labour Gazette*

Chapter 1   The days of the Social Democrats, 1900-4
(pages 13-34)

1 Bosanquet, Helen. *The administration of charitable relief* (1898), 3
2 London, Jack. *The people of the abyss* (Panther edition, 1963), 123
3 For example, 26.5 per cent of the recruits applying at York, Leeds and Sheffield depots between 1897 and 1900 were rejected as unfit. On this generally see Gilbert, Bentley. *The evolution of national insurance in Great Britain* (1966), 21ff
4 Beveridge, William. *Unemployment : a problem of industry* (1909), 148
5 Pease, Edward. *History of the Fabian Society* (2nd edition, 1925), 215
6 Howell, George. *Trade unionism old and new* (1891), 170-205
7 Campbell, D. *The unemployed problem : the socialist solution* (1894)
8 Haw, George. *The life story of Will Crooks MP* (1917), 265-6
9 ILP, *Ann Rep*, 1895, 26

10 *LL*, 9 Feb 1895

11 ILP, *Ann Rep*, 1897, 14

12 *The Times*, 30 Apr 1902

13 *Justice*, 28 June 1902

14 *The Times*, 25 Dec 1902

15 Hobson and Pease had already been investigating unemployment for a Fabian committee. See NCL, Fabian Society, *EC Minutes*, 24 June 1902

16 *LL*, 27 Dec 1902

17 *Daily Mail*, 2 Mar 1903

18 *LL*, 7 Mar 1903

19 A hope expressed in *Justice*, 7 Feb 1903

20 Ibid, 1 Mar 1903

21 Ibid, 29 Nov 1902

22 Ibid, 31 Jan 1903

23 Ibid, 21 Feb 1903

24 *LL*, 21 Feb 1903; *The Times*, 16 Feb 1903

25 *The Times*, 9 Feb 1903

26 Ibid, 26 Feb 1903

27 *Westminster Gazette*, 14 Feb 1903

28 General Union of Operative Carpenters and Joiners, London District Committee, *Half yearly report*, 31 Jan 1903, 1

29 *LL*, 21 Feb 1903

30 Kent Archives Office, Chilston Papers, U 564. CLP 7, ff 10-11. A. Akers-Douglas to Lord Knollys, 12 Feb 1903

31 *Hansard*, 4th series, 118, c137. 18 Feb 1903

32 PRO CAB 37/65. *Unemployed processions*. 22 May 1903

33 SDF, *Ann Rep*, 1903, 17

34 *The Times*, 28 Jan 1903. On the 'impossibilists' generally see Tsuzuki, Chushuchi. 'The impossibilist revolt in Britain', *International Review of Social History*, 1 (1956), 377-97

35 *Justice*, 7 Nov 1903

36 Ibid, 12 Dec 1903

37 Reported in the *Daily Graphic*, 23 Dec 1903

38 *LL*, 19 Sept 1903

39 Ibid, 6 June 1903; 27 June 1903; 25 July 1903; 10 Oct 1903

40 Ibid, 12 Dec 1903

41 Ibid, 9 Jan 1904

42 *The Times*, 7 Nov 1903

43 C/o Mrs J. Clay, Buxton Papers, uncatalogued. L. Maxse to S. Buxton, 26 May 1903

44 *The Times*, 8 Sept 1903
45 Ibid, 12 Apr 1904
46 Ibid. For a full account of this organisation see Brown, Kenneth. 'The Trade Union Tariff Reform Association, 1904-1913, *Journal of British Studies*, 9, No 2 (May 1970), 141-53

Chapter 2   The Unemployed Workmen's Bill, 1904-5
(pages 35-67)

1 *LL*, 20 Feb 1904
2 Ibid, 15 July 1904
3 *Social Democrat*, 8 (July 1904), 392
4 *Justice*, 15 Oct 1904
5 *National Union Gleanings*, 23 (1904), 262
6 See the report in the *Daily News*, 15 Oct 1904
7 *COS Review*, 16 (Nov 1904), 268
8 Hardie, James Keir. 'Dealing with the unemployed : a hint from the past', *Nineteenth Century*, 57 (Jan 1905), 50
9 *Justice*, 22 Oct 1904
10 *Clarion*, 2 Dec 1904
11 *Social Democrat*, 9 (Dec 1904), 720
12 Quoted in Haw, *Will Crooks*, 239-40
13 *Social Democrat*, 9 (Nov 1904), 646-9
14 An incident reported in *Morning Post*, 20 Dec 1904
15 *LL*, 30 Dec 1904
16 *Justice*, 29 Oct 1904
17 The three branches were Bradford, Chorley, and Rawtenstall
18 TUC, *PC Minutes*, 24 Oct 1904
19 Quoted in *National Union Gleanings*, 23 (1904), 268
20 Quoted in Haw, *Will Crooks*, 238-9
21 BM, Balfour Papers, Add MSS 49763, f 14. A. J. Balfour to J. Sandars, 4 Jan 1905
22 SDF, *Ann Rep*, 1905, 17
23 *The Times*, 24 Dec 1904
24 *Justice*, 15 Oct 1904
25 *Daily Graphic*, 19 Dec 1904; *Daily Mail*, 19 Dec 1904
26 *Royal commission on the poor law and the relief of distress, Appendix 8* [Cd 5066] *BPP*, 48 (1910), 69
27 Ibid
28 *Justice*, 19 Nov 1904

M

29 Ibid, 25 Mar 1905
30 BM, Gladstone Papers, Add MSS 41217, ff 134-5. H. Gladstone to H. Campbell-Bannerman, 14 Nov 1904
31 Ibid, Add MSS 46019, f 84. J. Bryce to H. Gladstone, 14 Dec 1904
32 *Daily News*, 15 Feb 1905
33 *LL*, 17 Feb 1905
34 Friendly Society of Ironfounders, *Monthly Report*, Apr 1905, 13
35 *RR*, 17 Feb 1905
36 BM, Balfour Papers, Add MSS 49763, f 73. J. Sandars to A. J. Balfour, 21 Jan 1905
37 PRO CAB 37/74. *The unemployed*. 17 Feb 1905
38 Ibid, 37/75. *The unemploye*d. 2 Mar 1905
39 Ibid
40 BM, Balfour Papers, Add MSS 49758, ff 11-12. Lord Salisbury to A. J. Balfour, 5 Mar 1905
41 In two letters to *The Times*, 9 and 17 May 1905
42 BM, Campbell-Bannerman Papers, Add MSS 41238, f 9. S. Buxton to H. Campbell-Bannerman, 16 Jan 1905
43 *Hansard*, 4th series, 144, c 147. 3 Apr 1905
44 Ibid, 145, c 460. 18 Apr 1905
45 *LL*, 28 Apr 1905
46 *RR*, 21 Apr 1905
47 Quoted in *COS Review*, 17 (May 1905), 284
48 *Justice*, 6 May 1905
49 *TLG*, June 1905, 3
50 *Justice*, 22 Apr 1905
51 *TLG*, May 1905, 2
52 *LL*, 28 Apr 1905
53 *Royal commission on the poor law and the relief of distress, Appendix 8* [Cd 5066] *BPP*, 48 (1910), 14
54 *Kentish Gazette*, 14 Oct 1905
55 'W.C. and others very nervous about the Leicester march...' BM, Burns Papers, Add MSS 46323. Diary, 16 May 1905
56 Transport House, LRC Letter Files, 23, f 40, nd
57 BLPES, *ILP Head Office Circular* (unbound), nd
58 *Daily Telegraph*, 16 May 1905
59 *Daily Express*, 18 May 1905
60 BLPES, *ILP Head Office Circular* (unbound), 16 May 1905
61 *LL*, 19 May 1905
62 *Hansard*, 4th series, 166, c 774. 18 May 1905
63 *LL*, 26 May 1905

64 BM, Burns Papers, Add MSS 46323. Diary, 24 May 1905
65 *LL*, 26 May 1905
66 *Daily Graphic*, 21 June 1905
67 *RR*, 23 June 1905
68 *Eltradion*, July 1905, 49
69 *Justice*, 8 July 1905
70 Compiled from reports in *LL* which reported on 21 July 1905 that over 100 meetings had been held
71 *LL*, 7 July 1905
72 *Daily Express*, 10 July 1905
73 *Daily Mail*, 17 July 1905
74 *LL*, 28 July 1905
75 Ibid, 11 Aug 1905
76 *Hansard*, 4th series, 151, c 429. 7 Aug 1905
77 BLPES, collection of early LRC papers bound as *Infancy of the Labour Party*, I, 331. 29 July 1905
78 *Hansard*, 4th series, 150, cc 981-1018. 31 July 1905
79 *LL*, 4 Aug 1905
80 Webb, Beatrice. *Our partnership* (1948), 317. On the question of the commission's appointment see Brown, John. 'The appointment of the 1905 poor law commission', *Bulletin of the Institute of Historical Research*, 42 (Nov 1969), 239-42, and my reply (which, at the time this book went to press, was expected to appear in the *Bulletin* in Nov 1971)
81 *Hansard*, 4th series, 150, c 1348. 2 Aug 1905
82 BM, Balfour Papers, Add MSS 49776, f 37. W. Long to A. J. Balfour, 6 Dec 1904
83 TUC, *Ann Rep*, 1905. *Report of a deputation on unemployment*, 14
84 *Hansard*, 4th series, 145, c 1346. 9 May 1905
85 *Standard*, 5 Aug 1905
86 *LL*, 4 Aug 1905
87 *Typographical Circular*, Sept 1905, 5
88 *Clarion*, 11 Aug 1905
89 *LL*, 8 Sept 1905
90 Transport House, LRC Letter Files, 26, f 95. Memorandum dated 21 Oct 1905
91 *Justice*, 2 Dec 1905
92 BLPES, *ILP NAC Minutes*, 3 Oct 1905
93 Transport House, LRC Letter Files, 26, f 287. J. R. MacDonald to W. S. Sanders, 25 Sept 1905
94 Hardie, James Keir. *John Bull and his unemployed* (1905), 11

M*

95 Quoted in Thompson, Paul. *Socialists, Liberals, and Labour* (1967), 222
96 *Justice*, 18 Nov 1905
97 *Daily Graphic*, 21 Nov 1905
98 *The Times*, 15 Dec 1905
99 BM, Balfour Papers, Add MSS 49858, f 42. A. J. Balfour to Sir F. Younghusband, 21 Nov 1905
100 List of contributors in *Justice*, 2 Dec 1905

Chapter 3   The birth of the Right to Work Bill, 1906-7
(pages 68-84)

1 *Justice*, 9 Dec 1905
2 *LL*, 9 Dec 1904
3 BLPES, Beveridge Papers, L, I, 203. W. H. Beveridge to his mother, 4 Mar 1905
4 BM, Campbell-Bannerman Papers, Add MSS 41217, f 210. H. Gladstone to H. Campbell-Bannerman, 17 Apr 1905
5 C/o Mrs J. Clay, Buxton Papers, uncatalogued. A. Birrell to S. Buxton, 7 May 1905
6 *LL*, 23 June 1905
7 *The Times*, 17 Nov 1905
8 BL, Asquith Papers, 10, f 173. H. Campbell-Bannerman to H. H. Asquith, 1 Dec 1905
9 *TLG*, Oct 1904, 2; similar suggestions were made in *RR*, 3 Apr 1904, and *Justice*, 4 Apr 1904
10 Quoted in Kent, William. *John Burns : labour's lost leader* (1950), 158
11 *Justice*, 16 Dec 1905
12 *Eltradion*, Dec 1905, 129
13 BM, Burns Papers, Add MSS 46323. Diary, 14 Dec 1905
14 *Standard*, 19 Jan 1906
15 See the candidates' manifestos in NLC, *Election addresses*, 1906
16 Crooks, Will. 'The prospects and programme of the Labour Party', *National Review*, 45 (1906), 627
17 These are the conclusions of Russell, Anthony. *The general election of 1906* (Oxford D Phil thesis, 1962)
18 BL, Asquith Papers, 10, f 200. H. Campbell-Bannerman to H. H. Asquith, 21 Jan 1906
19 BM, Burns Papers, Add MSS 46324. Diary, 1 Feb 1906

20 *The Times*, 15 May 1906
21 A copy survives in BLPES, ILP Watford Branch, Correspondence File 1, f 37. 16 May 1906
22 Montefiore, Dora. *From a Victorian to a modern* (1927), 59
23 C/o Mrs J. Clay, Buxton Papers, uncatalogued. Lord Ripon to S. Buxton, 28 May 1906
24 BM, Ripon Papers, Add MSS 43555, f 255. S. Buxton to Lord Ripon, 27 May 1906
25 BM, Burns Papers, Add MSS 46324. Diary, 27 June 1906
26 BLPES, Passfield Papers, I, 1, Vol 25. B. Webb Diary, 9 Feb 1906
27 BM, Campbell-Bannerman Papers, Add MSS 41207, ff 50-1. H. Campbell-Bannerman to Lord Knollys, 13 Feb 1906
28 BM, Burns Papers, Add MSS 46324. Diary, 12 May 1906
29 *Reynold's Newspaper*, 8 July 1906
30 *Justice*, 21 July 1906
31 *Reynold's Newspaper*, 15 July 1906
32 *TLG*, Sept 1906, 18
33 *Reynold's Newspaper*, 2 July 1906
34 Amalgamated Society of Engineers, *Monthly Journal*, Aug 1906, 6
35 *RR*, 27 July 1906
36 *The Times*, 6 Oct 1906
37 Amalgamated Society of Engineers, *Monthly Journal*, Aug 1906, 5-6
38 *Hansard*, 4th series, 171, c 1861. 27 Mar 1907
39 Ibid, 169, c 107. 12 Feb 1907
40 ILP, *Ann Rep*, 1907, 53
41 *LL*, 1 Mar 1907
42 *Hansard*, 4th series, 171, c 1859. 27 Mar 1907
43 *Justice*, 26 Jan 1907
44 *Hansard*, 4th series, 171, cc 1859-60. 27 Mar 1907
45 BM, Burns Papers, Add MSS 46325. Diary, 13 Apr 1907
46 Burns, John. *The unemployed* (1893), 17
47 *Hansard*, 4th series, 171, c 1853. 27 Mar 1907
48 National Amalgamated Union of Labour, *Quarterly Report*, 30 Mar 1907
49 A Bill to promote work through public authorities for unemployed persons. 7 Edw VII, c 3
50 These are the conclusions of Brown, John. *Ideas concerning social policy and their influence on legislation in Britain, 1902-1911* (London PhD thesis, 1964)
51 *LL*, 16 Aug 1907
52 Ibid, 19 July 1907

Chapter 4   The battle for the Right to Work Bill, 1907-8
             (pages 85-112)

1 BM, Burns Papers, Add MSS 46325. Diary, 9 July 1907
2 See MacDonald's speech introducing the Bill in *Hansard*, 4th series, 177, c 1446. 9 July 1907
3 BM, Ripon Papers, Add MSS 43555, ff 266-7. S. Buxton to Lord Ripon, 19 Aug 1907
4 MacDonald, James Ramsay. *The new Unemployed Bill of the Labour Party* (1907)
5 Quoted in Thompson, Laurence. *Robert Blatchford, portrait of an Englishman* (1951), 185
6 *LL*, 11 Oct 1907
7 Ibid, 1 Nov 1907
8 Ibid, 13 Dec 1907
9 *Clarion*, 17 Jan 1908
10 *LL*, 7 Feb 1908
11 *Typographical Circular*, Feb 1908, 10
12 BLPES, *Infancy of the Labour Party*, II, 73. 10 Feb 1908
13 LP. *The Labour Party and unemployment* (1908)
14 BM, Burns Papers, Add MSS 46326. Diary, 11 Mar 1908
15 BL, Asquith Papers, 5, f 14. H. H. Asquith to the King, 11 Mar 1908
16 BM, Ripon Papers, Add MSS 43555, f 273. S. Buxton to Lord Ripon, 4 Mar 1908
17 Ibid, f 276. Lord Ripon to S. Buxton, 6 Mar 1908
18 PRO CAB 37/91. *The Unemployed Workmen Bill.* 9 Mar 1908
19 Bristol Right to Work Committee, *Ann Rep*, 1908, 2
20 Masterman, Charles. 'Politics in transition', *Nineteenth Century*, 62 (Jan 1908), 16-17
21 Cox, Harold. 'The right to work', *Quarterly Review*, 202 (Jan 1908), 203
22 *The Times*, 14 Mar 1908
23 *Daily Mail*, 13 Mar 1908
24 *Standard*, 12 Mar 1908
25 The Liberal member for Watford, for example, told the local branch of the ILP that MacDonald's stand had decided his own hostile vote. BLPES, ILP Watford Branch, Correspondence File 2, f 33. 13 Mar 1908
26 A censure motion moved on Maddison and Vivian at the 1908 TUC congress was passed, however, by a surprisingly small margin, 826,000 to 821,000. TUC, *Ann Rep*, 1908, 135

27 Raine, George. *Present-day socialism* (1908), 130

28 *Daily Telegraph*, 14 Mar 1908

29 *Daily Graphic*, 19 Mar 1908

30 *LL*, 20 Mar 1908

31 TUC, *Ann Rep*, 1908, 123

32 *LL*, 8 May 1908

33 *The Times*, 20 Apr 1908

34 Churchill, Randolph. *Winston S. Churchill. II. Young statesman, 1901-1914* (1967), 240-4

35 BL, Asquith Papers, 11, f 89. J. Burns to H. H. Asquith, 13 Apr 1908

36 Ibid, ff 95-6. C. F. G. Masterman to H. H. Asquith, 13 Apr 1908

37 ILP, *Ann Rep*, 1908, 60

38 *LL*, 29 May 1908

39 *Justice*, 25 July 1908

40 *LL*, 7 Aug 1908

41 *Daily Graphic*, 19 Sept 1908

42 *LL*, 25 Sept 1908

43 *New Age*, 3 Oct 1908

44 TUC, *Ann Rep*, 1908, 165

45 *Justice*, 15 June 1907

46 Ibid, 24 Oct 1908

47 Ibid, 10 Oct 1908

48 BM, Gladstone Papers, Add MSS 45994, ff 164-5. M. L. Walter to H. Gladstone, 10 Oct 1908

49 Masterman, Lucy. *C. F. G. Masterman* (1939), 110-11

50 *Justice*, 30 Mar 1907; SDF, *Ann Rep*, 1907, 17

51 National Union of Gas Workers and General Labourers, *Minutes of Delegate Meeting*, 17 Oct 1908

52 *Clarion*, 23 Oct 1908

53 *Justice*, 24 Oct 1908

54 PRO CAB 37/95. *The unemployed*, 17 Oct 1908

55 BM, Burns Papers, Add MSS 46326. Diary, 20 Oct 1908

56 Masterman, *Masterman*, 112

57 BM, Burns Papers, Add MSS 46326. Diary, 21 Oct 1908

58 *Standard*, 5 Dec 1908

59 *Hansard*, 4th series, 195, c 46. 27 Oct 1908

60 Ibid, 196, c 296. 11 Nov 1908

61 Ibid, c 270. 11 Nov 1908

62 Ibid, c 713. 13 Nov 1908

63 Ibid, c 1776. 23 Nov 1908

64 Ibid, 195, c 47. 27 Oct 1908

65 Ibid, 196, c 46. 10 Nov 1908
66 Ibid, cc 640-4. 12 Nov 1908
67 BM, Burns Papers, Add MSS 46326. Diary, 12 Nov 1908
68 TUC, *PC Minutes*, 9 Dec. 1908
69 *Hansard*, 4th series, 198, c 1252. 14 Dec 1908
70 *Standard*, 6 Feb 1909
71 *The Times*, 22 Jan 1909
72 *Daily Mail*, 22 Jan 1909
73 *Hansard*, 5th series, 1, cc 98-9. 17 Feb 1909
74 *Justice*, 23 Jan 1909
75 *LL*, 5 Mar 1909
76 Ibid, 12 Mar 1909
77 *Clarion*, 3 Apr 1909
78 *Justice*, 7 Feb 1909
79 Ibid, 31 Oct 1908
80 *LL*, 20 Nov 1908
81 *Typographical Circular*, Nov 1908, 11
82 *Clarion*, 12 Mar 1909

Chapter 5   The decline of the 'right to work', 1909
(pages 113-130)

1 *Hansard*, 5th series, 1, c 184, 17 Feb 1909
2 Masterman, *Masterman*, 128
3 *Social Democrat*, 13 (Apr 1909), 171
4 *Justice*, 27 Nov 1909
5 *LL*, 9 Apr 1909
6 *Morning Post*, 1 May 1909
7 For Example, *The Times*, 1 May 1909; *Westminster Gazette*, 1 May 1909; *Daily Graphic*, 1 May 1909
8 National Union of Boot and Shoe Operatives, *Monthly Report*, May 1909, 223
9 *Typographical Circular*, May 1909, 2
10 ILP, *Ann Rep*, 1909, 21
11 *Clarion*, 20 Mar 1908
12 *LL*, 10 Jan 1908
13 *The Times*, 25 Jan 1909
14 *Socialist Review*, 3 (June 1909), 246
15 *The Times*, 16 Jan 1909
16 *Hansard*, 5th series, 1 cc 54-5. 16 Feb 1909

17 *LL*, 26 Feb 1909
18 BLPES, ILP, *Minutes and Reports from Head Office*, July 1909
19 *Socialist Review*, 4 (Nov 1909), 175
20 *Hansard*, 5th series, 10, cc 983-4. 6 Sept 1909
21 *LL*, 12 Sept 1912
22 LP, *Ann Rep*, 1909, 93
23 BLPES, Beveridge Papers, D 026. Unemployment Insurance: criticisms. Dec 1909
24 Quoted in Muggeridge, Kitty, and Adam, Ruth. *Beatrice Webb. A life* (1967), 189
25 BLPES, Passfield Papers, I, 1, Vol 26. B. Webb Diary, 30 Jan 1908
26 ILP, *Ann Rep*, 1909, 45
27 A point stressed by Quelch when he debated the report with Lansbury in 1910. See *Justice,* 1 Oct 1910
28 Reported in Associated Shipwrights Society, *Quarterly Report*, Mar 1909, 23-6
29 BLPES, ILP, *Minutes and Reports from Head Office*, July 1909
30 *Ibid*, Apr 1909
31 *LL*, 29 May 1908
32 *Fabian News*, 20 (Apr 1909), 40
33 ILP, *Ann Rep*, 1909, 71
34 *LL*, 4 June 1909
35 *Hansard*, 5th series, 5, c 519. 19 May 1909
36 TUC, *PC Minutes*, 11 July 1909
37 BLPES, Beveridge Papers, L, I, 204. W. H. Beveridge to his mother, 7 July 1909
38 TUC, *PC Minutes*, 11 July 1909
39 National Free Labour Association, *Ann Rep*, 1909, 40
40 *LL*, 25 June 1909
41 National Amalgamated Union of Labour, *Quarterly Report*, June 1909, 4-5
42 National Union of Boot and Shoe Operatives, *Monthly Report,* Mar 1909, 158-9
43 TUC, *Ann Rep*, 1909, 150-2
44 TUC, *PC Minutes*, 11 July 1909
45 *Hansard*, 5th series, 6, cc 100-102. 16 June 1909
46 *LL*, 19 Feb 1909
47 Ibid, 26 Mar 1909
48 *Socialist Review*, 3 (June 1909), 256

Chapter 6   A wasted year, 1910
(pages 131-140)

1 NLC, *Election addresses,* Jan 1910
2 Belcher in the *Socialist Review,* 4 (Jan 1910), 336; Barnes in ibid, 4 (Dec 1909), 262
3 *LL,* 11 Feb 1910
4 Ibid, 4 Mar 1910
5 Clarion, 21 Jan 1910
6 BLPES, Beveridge Papers, L, 3, 225. H. R. Maynard to W. H. Beveridge, 2 Feb 1910
7 BL, Asquith Papers, 5, f 190. H. H. Asquith to the King, 22 Feb 1910
8 *LL,* 11 Mar 1910
9 Ibid, 4 Mar 1910
10 NLS, Elibank Papers, MSS 8802, ff 51-2. J. R. MacDonald to Master of Elibank, 13 Apr 1910
11 *LL,* 18 Mar 1910
12 Ibid
13 Ibid
14 BkL, Lloyd George Papers, C/5/11/1A. J. R. MacDonald to D. Lloyd George, nd
15 *LL,* 26 Aug 1910
16 Ibid, 17 Oct 1910
17 Ibid, 4 Feb 1910
18 *TLG,* Feb 1910, 3
19 GFTU, *Annual General Council Meeting,* 2 July 1910, 29
20 Joint Board, *Minutes,* 28 June 1910
21 *LL,* 3 June 1910
22 Blewett, Neal. *The British general elections of 1910* (Oxford D Phil thesis 1966), 575 ff
23 NLC, *Election addresses,* Dec 1910
24 *LL,* 24 June 1910
25 *Hansard,* 5th series, 16, c 819. 8 Apr 1910
26 *Clarion,* 17 Feb 1911
27 BLPES, Beveridge Papers, L, I, 205. W. H. Beveridge to his mother, 24 Jan 1910
28 Tallents, Stephen. *Man and boy* (1943), 178
29 *Justice,* 24 Sept 1910
30 Beveridge, William. ' Labour exchanges in the United Kingdom ', *Conference Internationale du chomâge, Rapport No 26,* Sept 1910

31 TUC, *8th Quarterly Report of the PC*, 48-50
32 TUC, *Ann Rep*, 1911, 190-2

Chapter 7   National Insurance and beyond, 1911-14
(pages 141-163)

1 *LL*, 17 Feb 1911
2 Ibid, 24 Mar 1911
3 Ibid, 17 Feb 1911
4 Ibid, 24 Feb 1911
5 Ibid, 10 Mar 1911
6 Ibid, 5 May 1911
7 *Socialist Review*, 6 (Apr 1911) 87-8
8 *Hansard*, 5th series, 25, c 1219. 10 May 1911
9 *Justice*, 20 May 1911
10 Newcastle University Library, Runciman Papers, Box 12. W. S. Churchill to W. Runciman, July 1909
11 C/o Mrs J. Clay, Buxton Papers, uncatalogued. H. Llewellyn Smith to S. Buxton, 24 Jan 1911, complained about these difficulties
12 Ibid. Unemployment Insurance Memorandum, 16 Mar 1911
13 Ibid. S. Buxton to D. Lloyd George, nd. Buxton said that this was 'endangering the scheme' and added that ' there would be great disappointment, therefore, if the proportion of the State's contribution ... were reduced ... it would make the scheme unworkable'.
14 *Typographical Circular*, June 1911, 10
15 *Hansard*, 5th series, 32, c 827. 30 Nov 1911
16 Ibid, 31, cc 2108-20. 16 Nov 1911
17 Ibid, 26, c 477. 25 May 1911
18 Reported in Amalgamated Toolmakers' Society, *Amalgamated Toolmakers' Monthly*, July 1911, 10-13
19 BLPES, ILP, *Minutes and Reports from Head Office*, 31 May 1911
20 BLPES, Passfield Papers, I, 1, Vol 25. B. Webb Diary, 13 May 1911
21 Amalgamated Society of Carpenters and Joiners, *Monthly Report*, July 1911, 304
22 *The Times*, 31 July 1911
23 BLPES, BSP Papers, f 4. Newscutting, Sept 1911
24 *Justice*, 13 May 1911
25 NCL, Fabian Society Collection, Part A, Box 4, Correspondence from S. Webb. S. Webb to W. S. Sanders, 17 May 1911
26 BLPES, Passfield Papers, II, 4e, ff 33-4. G. Lansbury to S. Webb, 24 May 1911

27 *Justice*, 27 May 1911

28 *LL*, 9 June 1911

29 Ibid, 16 June 1911

30 Ibid, 23 and 30 June 1911

31 Amalgamated Society of Engineers, *Monthly Journal*, July 1911, 5-6

32 BLPES, Herbert Bryan Papers, General Correspondence Va, f 17.
    H. Duberry to H. Bryan, 13 July 1911

33 *Hansard*, 5th series, 27, c 1462. 6 July 1911

34 BLPES, *Infancy of the Labour Party*, II, 204. 14 July 1911

35 *LL*, 21 July 1911

36 BLPES, Beveridge Papers, L, I, 205. W. H. Beveridge to his mother,
    6 Aug 1911

37 Hamilton, Mary. *Arthur Henderson. A biography* (1938), 73-4

38 Riddell, Lord. *More pages from my diary, 1908-1914* (1934), 21

39 BLPES, Passfield Papers, II, 4e, f 72e. W. A. Colegate to B. Webb,
    18 Aug 1911

40 BkL, Lloyd George Papers, C/6/5/5. Master of Elibank to D. Lloyd
    George, 5 Oct 1911

41 BLPES, Beveridge Papers, L, I, 205. W. H. Beveridge to his mother,
    15 Aug 1911

42 BLPES, Passfield Papers, II, 4e, f 64a. M. Reeves to B. Webb, 3 Aug
    1911

43 TUC, *Ann Rep*, 1911, 204-8

44 BLPES, Passfield Papers, II, 4e, f 103c. C. D. Sharp to B. Webb, 20
    Sept 1911

45 NLS, Elibank Papers, MSS 8802, f 334. J. R. MacDonald to the
    Master of Elibank, 4 Oct 1911

46 *LL*, 8 Dec 1911

47 BLPES, BSP Papers, f 4. Newscutting, Sept 1911

48 *The Times*, 27 Oct 1911

49 BLPES, Lansbury Papers, IV, f 231. E. C. Fairchild to G. Lansbury,
    25 Oct 1911

50 NLS, Elibank Papers, MSS 8802, f 337. J. R. MacDonald to the
    Master of Elibank, 9 Oct 1911

51 *Daily News*, 10 Oct 1911

52 *LL*, 20 Oct 1911

53 BLPES, Passfield Papers, II, 4e, f 150. C. M. Lloyd to B. Webb,
    6 Nov 1911

54 *Hansard*, 5th series, 32, cc 1419-1530. 6 Dec 1911

55 *LL*, 24 Nov 1911

56 Ibid, 1 Dec 1911

57 Ibid, 15 Dec 1911

58 Ibid, 8 Dec 1911

59 Ibid, 26 Jan 1912

60 *Hansard*, 5th series, 50, c 1324. 24 Mar 1913

61 Ibid, 42, c 1599. 18 Oct 1912

62 TUC, *Ann Rep*, 1912, 219

63 National Amalgamated Union of Labour, *Quarterly Report*, June
    1913, 4; see also Fyrth, Hubert, and Collins, Henry. *The foundry
    workers* (1968), 134

64 Operative Bricklayers Society, *Ann Rep*, 1912, 111

65 Pelling, Henry. *Politics and society in late Victorian Britain* (1968),
    153

66 On this generally see Pelling, op cit, 152 ff

67 ILP, *Ann Rep*, 1912, 66

68 Ibid, 9

69 Ibid, 1913, 42-3

70 *LL*, 25 Feb 1912

Chapter 8   Conclusions
(pages 164-174)

1 Tressall, Robert. *The ragged trousered philanthropists* (Penguin
   edition, 1940), 33

2 Sanders, William. *Early socialist days* (1927), 18

3 Masterman, Charles. *From the abyss* (1901), 14

4 LRC, *Ann Rep*, 1903, 12. There were also 835 Fabians affiliated.
   For SDF membership see Kendall, Walter. *The revolutionary movement in Britain, 1900-1921* (1969), 311

5 Brotherton Library University of Leeds, A. Mattison Papers, Note-
   book B, 11. 14 Jan 1912

6 Bailey, George. 'The right to work', *Westminster Review*, 170
   Dec 1908), 618

7 Quoted in Pelling, Henry. *A short history of the Labour Party* (2nd
   ed 1965), 21

8 BLPES, Passfield Papers, I, 1, Vol 27. B. Webb Diary, 30 Nov 1910

9 Eliot, T. S. Choruses from 'The Rock'. Reprinted by permission of
   Faber & Faber Ltd and Harcourt Brace and Jovanovich from
   Collected Poems 1909-62

TABLE 1

Unemployment 1900-14 : percentages of all trade unions making returns

	Jan	Feb	Mar	Apr	May	June	July	Aug	Sept	Oct	Nov	Dec
1900	2.3	2.4	2.0	2.0	1.9	2.1	2.2	2.5	3.0	2.8	2.7	3.5
1901	3.5	3.4	3.1	3.4	3.0	3.0	2.9	3.4	3.2	3.2	3.3	4.2
1902	4.0	3.9	3.2	3.4	3.5	3.7	3.5	4.0	4.5	4.5	4.4	5.0
1903	4.9	4.3	3.9	4.6	3.5	3.9	4.4	5.0	5.2	5.6	5.5	6.3
1904	6.1	5.6	5.5	5.5	5.8	5.5	5.6	5.9	6.3	6.3	6.5	7.1
1905	6.3	5.7	5.2	5.2	4.7	4.8	4.7	4.9	4.8	4.6	4.3	4.5
1906	4.3	4.1	3.4	3.2	3.1	3.2	3.1	3.3	3.3	3.9	4.0	4.4
1907	3.9	3.5	3.2	2.8	3.0	3.1	3.2	3.6	4.1	4.2	4.5	5.6
1908	5.8	6.0	6.4	7.1	7.4	7.9	7.9	8.5	9.3	9.5	8.7	9.1
1909	8.7	8.4	8.2	8.2	7.9	7.9	7.9	7.7	7.4	7.1	6.5	6.6
1910	6.8	5.7	5.2	4.4	4.2	3.7	3.8	4.0	4.3	4.4	4.6	5.0
1911	3.9	3.3	3.0	2.8	2.5	3.0	2.9	3.3	2.9	2.8	2.6	3.1
1912	2.7	2.8	11.3*	3.6	2.7	2.5	2.6	2.2	2.1	2.0	1.8	2.3
1913	2.2	2.0	1.9	1.7	1.9	1.9	1.9	2.0	2.3	2.2	2.0	2.6
1914	2.5	2.3	2.1	2.1	2.3	2.4	2.8	7.1	5.9	4.4	2.9	2.5

(* distorted by the coal strike)

Board of Trade, *Seventeenth abstract of labour statistics* [Cd 7733]
BPP, 61 (1914-16), 322

TABLE 2   191

TABLE 2

Right to Work Committees and their source of reference

LONDON BOROUGHS

Battersea	*The Times*, 6 Nov 1908
Bermondsey	Ibid, 5 Nov 1908
*Canning Town	*TLG*, Sept 1908, 9
Finsbury	*Justice*, 7 Nov 1908
Hackney	Ibid, 28 Nov 1908
*Hammersmith	Ibid
Islington	*LL*, 30 Oct 1908
Lambeth	*Justice*, 27 Feb 1909
St Pancras	*The Times*, 23 Dec 1908
*Southwark	*Justice*, 19 Dec 1908
Willesden	Ibid, 9 Nov 1907
Woolwich	*Woolwich Labour Representation Association Minutes*, 24 Nov 1908

PROVINCIAL

*Aberdeen	*TLG*, Sept 1908, 9
Accrington	*Justice*, 2 Dec 1905
Arbroath	Ibid
Barking	Ibid
Birmingham	Ibid
Blackpool	Ibid, 17 Mar 1906
*Bradford	*TLG*, Oct 1908, 10
Bristol	Bristol Right to Work Committee, *Annual Report*
Bury	*Justice*, 2 Dec 1905
Coventry	Ibid, 24 Oct 1908
Croydon	*The Times*, 26 Oct 1908
Doncaster	*TLG*, Nov 1908, 12
East Ham	*Justice*, 2 Dec 1905
Edinburgh	*TLG*, Oct 1907, 11
Erith	*Justice*, 28 Nov 1908
Gorton	Ibid, 17 Feb 1906
Govan	Ibid, 2 Dec 1905
*Halifax	*TLG*, Nov 1908, 12

TABLE 2

Leeds	*Justice*, 2 Dec 1905
Leicester	*LL*, 8 Dec 1905
Lincoln	*Justice*, 27 Feb 1909
Liverpool	Ibid, 24 Jan 1906
Longton	Ibid, 2 Dec 1905
Manchester	Ibid
Middleton	Ibid, 17 Mar 1906
Newark	Ibid, 2 Dec 1905
Newcastle	Ibid
Newport	*LL*, 6 Nov 1908
Nottingham	*Justice*, 2 Dec 1908
Orpington	Ibid, 19 Dec 1908
Oxford	Ibid, 2 Dec 1908
Partick	Ibid
*Reading	Ibid, 24 Oct 1908
St Mary Cray	Ibid, 19 Dec 1908
Southampton	Ibid, 17 Oct 1908
Stoke	Ibid, 2 Dec 1905
Swansea	Ibid
Watford	Ibid
West Ham	Ibid
Wigan	Ibid
*Wolverhampton	*TLG*, Oct 1908, 10
York	*Justice*, 2 Dec 1905

(* committees formed in response to Smith appeal in 1908)

Biographical notes

THESE NOTES COVER most of the important people mentioned in the text. They are not meant to be exhaustive and most of the entries refer only to the years spanned by the book. Further information can be found in almost every case by consulting the *Dictionary of National Biography* or *Who Was Who.*

Akers-Douglas, Henry
(1851-1926)
Conservative MP 1880-1911. Chief Commissioner of Works 1895-1902. Home Secretary 1902-5

Alden, Percy
(1865-1944)
Warden of Mansfield House University Settlement 1891-1901. Liberal MP for Tottenham 1906-18

Asquith, Herbert
(1852-1928)
Liberal MP for East Fife 1886-1918. Chancellor of the Exchequer 1905-8. Prime Minister 1908-16

Balfour, Arthur
(1848-1930)
Entered Parliament 1874. Cabinet rank 1886. Conservative Prime Minister 1902-5. Leader of Conservative opposition in the Commons 1905-11

Balfour, Gerald
(1853-1943)
Conservative MP for Central Leeds 1885-1906. President of the Local Government Board 1905

Barnes, George
(1859-1940)
Secretary Amalgamated Society of Engineers 1896-1908. Labour MP for Blackfriars division of Glasgow 1906-22. Chairman of the Labour Party 1910-11

Beveridge, William
(1879-1963)
Economist and civil servant. Made director of the labour exchange system, which he designed, in 1910

Birrell, Augustine (1850-1933) — Entered Parliament 1889. Liberal MP for North Bristol 1906-18. President of the Board of Education 1905-7. Chief Secretary for Ireland 1907-16

Blatchford, Robert (1851-1943) — Journalist and socialist. Founder and editor of the *Clarion*

Blumenfeld, Ralph (1864-1948) — American journalist. Editor of the *Daily Express* 1902-32. Helped found the Anti-Socialist Union in 1908

Bondfield, Margaret (1873-1953) — Official in the shop assistants' union. Member of the ILP executive 1913-19

Booth, Charles (1840-1916) — Shipowner and writer on social problems. Served on the poor law commission of 1905-9

Bosanquet, Helen (1848-1923) — Noted social worker connected with the COS. Served on the poor law commission of 1905-9

Bowerman, Charles (1851-1947) — General Secretary of the London Society of Compositors 1892-1906. Labour MP for Deptford 1906-31. Secretary of the TUC 1911-23

Brace, William (1865-1947) — Miners' agent. President of the South Wales Miners' Federation 1911-19. Labour MP for Glamorgan South 1906-18

Broadhurst, Henry (1840-1911) — Secretary of the Labour Representation League 1873. Secretary of TUC 1875. Liberal MP 1880-92, 1894-1906

Bryce, John (1838-1922) — Liberal MP 1880-1906. British ambassador in Washington 1907-13

Burns, John (1858-1943) — Member of the SDF 1884-9. Independent Labour MP for Battersea 1892-1918. President of the Local Government Board 1905-14. President of the Board of Trade 1914. Resigned on the outbreak of war

Buxton, Sidney (1853-1934)	Entered Parliament as a Liberal 1883. MP for Poplar 1886-1914. Postmaster General 1905-10. President of Board of Trade 1910-14
Campbell-Bannerman, Henry (1836-1908)	Entered Parliament 1868. Liberal Prime Minister 1905-8
Chamberlain, Joseph (1836-1914)	Liberal President of the Local Government Board 1886. Joined Conservative cabinet 1895. Resigned as Colonial Secretary in 1903 to launch tariff reform campaign. Crippled by a stroke in 1906
Chandler, Francis (1849-1937)	General Secretary of the Amalgamated Society of Carpenters and Joiners 1888-1919. Parliamentary Committee of the TUC 1901-4, 1905-11. Member of the poor law commission 1905-9
Churchill, Winston (1874-1965)	Entered Parliament as a Conservative in 1900. Crossed the floor over tariff reform issue and served as Under-Secretary for the colonies 1905-8. President of the Board of Trade 1908-10. Home Secretary 1910-11. First Lord of the Admiralty 1911-15
Clynes, John (1869-1949)	Member of the National Union of Gas Workers and General Labourers. Labour MP for North East Manchester 1906-31
Crooks, Will (1852-1921)	Mayor of Poplar 1901. Labour MP for Woolwich 1903-18
Curran, Pete (1860-1910)	General organiser of the gas workers and general labourers union. Chairman of the GFTU. Labour MP for Jarrow 1907-10

Davis, William
(1848-1923)

General Secretary of the brassworkers' union 1872-83, and 1889-1920. Parliamentary Committee of the TUC 1881-3, 1896-1902, 1903-20

Duncan, Charles
(1865-1933)

Members of the engineers' union. Secretary of the Workers' Union 1900-28. Labour MP for Barrow 1906-18, and 1922-33

Elibank, Master of
(1870-1920)

Entered Parliament as a Liberal 1900. Scottish whip 1906-10. Parliamentary Secretary to the Treasury 1910-12

Fels, Joseph
(1854-1914)

American soap manufacturer. Promoter of vacant lot farming in Britain and America. Became an ardent advocate of the 'single tax' after 1905

George, David Lloyd
(1863-1945)

Liberal MP 1890-1945. President of the Board of Trade 1905-8. Chancellor of the Exchequer 1908-15

Gill, Alfred
(1856-1914)

Secretary of Bolton spinners and Labour MP for Bolton 1906-14

Gladstone, Herbert
(1854-1930)

Liberal MP for West Leeds 1885-1910. Chief whip 1899-1905. Home Secretary 1905-10

Glasier, John Bruce
(1859-1920)

Socialist propagandist. Chairman of the ILP 1900-1903. Editor of the *Labour Leader* 1904-9

Gooch, George
(1873-1968)

Historian. Liberal MP for Bath 1906-10

Graham, R. B. Cunninghame
(1852-1936)

Liberal MP 1886-92. Became an ardent follower of the socialist William Morris

Grayson, Victor
(1882-?)

Theology student and journalist. Won Colne Valley by-election as a socialist in 1907. Lost the seat in 1910. Helped to form the BSP in 1911. Left Britain in 1914. Place and date of death have not been established

Grey, Edward
(1862-1935)

Liberal MP 1885-1916. Foreign Secretary 1905-16

Harcourt, Lewis
(1863-1922)

Liberal MP for Rossendale 1904-17. First Commissioner of Works 1905-10, 1915-17

Hardie, James Keir
(1856-1915)

Founder of the *Labour Leader* 1889. Founder and Chairman of the ILP 1893-1900, 1913-15. Labour MP 1892-5, 1900-1915. Leader of the Parliamentary Labour Party 1906-8

Henderson, Arthur
(1863-1935)

Labour MP for Barnard Castle 1903-18. Chairman of Labour Party 1908-10, and Party Secretary 1911-34

Hill, Octavia
(1838-1912)

COS worker with special interest in housing. Member of the poor law commission of 1905-9

Hobson, Samuel
(1864-1940)

Irish journalist who helped found the ILP. On the executive of the Fabian Society 1900-1909. Became a guild socialist

Hodge, John
(1855-1937)

General Secretary of the British Steel Smelters' Amalgamated Association 1886-1918. Parliamentary Committee of the TUC 1892-4, 1895-6. Member of the Labour Party executive 1906-23. Labour MP for Gorton 1906-23

Hudson, Walter
(1852-1935)

Secretary of the Irish branch of the Amalgamated Society of Railway Servants. Labour MP for Newcastle 1906-18

Hyndman, Henry
(1842-1921)

Educated at Cambridge. Moving spirit behind the Democratic Federation, which became the SDF in 1884, and he remained as its chairman for many

Jowett, Fred
(1864-1944)

Lansbury, George
(1859-1940)

Lee, Henry
(1865-1932)

Loch, Charles
(1849-1923)

Long, Walter
(1854-1924)

Macarthur, Mary
(1880-1927)

Macdonald, James
(1857-1938)

MacDonald, James
Ramsay
(1866-1937)

Mann, Tom
(1855-1941)

Masterman, Charles
(1873-1927)

years. First chairman of the BSP 1911
Twice chairman of the ILP. Labour
MP for West Bradford 1906-18

Served on the Poplar Board of Guardians 1892. Member of the poor law
commission 1905-9. Labour MP for
Bow and Bromley 1910-12, 1922-40

Secretary of the SDF 1885-1911. Secretary of the BSP 1911-13. Editor of
Justice 1913-24

Secretary of COS 1875-1914. Largely
responsible for the majority report of
the poor law commission

Conservative MP 1880-1921. Parliamentary Secretary to the Local Government Board 1886-92. President of the
Local Government Board 1900-1905,
1915-16

Women's labour organiser and member of the ILP

Member of the SDF executive. Editor
of the *London Trades and Labour
Gazette*. Sometime secretary of the
London Trades Council

Early member of the Fabian Society,
the SDF and ILP. First Secretary of the
Labour Party 1900-1912. Labour MP
for Leicester 1906-18

Member of the SDF and the Amalgamated Society of Engineers. First President of the Dockers' Union 1889-93.
Later became a leader of the English
syndicalist movement

Liberal MP for North West Ham 1906-
11, South West Bethnal Green 1911-

14. Under-Secretary to the Local Government Board 1908-9. Under-Secretary to the Home Office 1909-12. Financial Secretary to the Treasury 1912

Mitchell, Isaac (1867-1952)
Trade Unionist. Member of the TUC Parliamentary Committee 1897-8. Secretary of the GFTU 1899-1907. Joined the Labour Department of the Board of Trade 1907

O'Grady, James (1866-1934)
Furniture worker and Labour MP for East Leeds 1906-18. Member of the ILP

Parker, James (1865-1942)
Member of the ILP and Labour MP for Halifax 1906-18

Pease, Edward (1857-1955)
Founder member of the LRC. Founder member and Secretary of Fabian Society

Provis, Samuel (1845-1926)
Permanent Secretary to the Local Government Board 1898-1910

Quelch, Harry (1858-1913)
Early member of the SDF. Editor of *Justice*, 1887-1912. Chairman of the London Trades Council 1904-6, 1910-13

Richards, Thomas F. (1863-1942)
A national organiser of the boot and shoe operatives' union. Labour MP for Wolverhampton 1906-10

Ripon, Lord (1827-1909)
Entered Parliament 1853. Lord Privy Seal and Liberal leader in the House of Lords 1905-8

Roberts, George (1869-1928)
A member of the typographers' union. Labour MP for Norwich 1906-18

Runciman, Walter (1870-1949)
Shipowner. Liberal MP. Parliamentary Secretary to the Local Government Board 1905-7. President of the Board of Education 1908-11

Samuel, Herbert
(1870-1963)
Liberal MP for Cleveland 1902-18. Postmaster General 1910-14

Seddon, James
(1868-1939)
One-time President of shop assistants' union. Labour MP for Newton 1906-10

Sexton, James
(1856-1938)
Secretary of the National Union of Dock Labourers 1893-1922. President of the TUC 1905

Shackleton, David
(1863-1938)
Labour MP for Clitheroe 1902-10. Member of the TUC Parliamentary Committee 1904-10 and its President 1908-9. Labour Party Chairman 1905. Appointed Labour adviser to Home Office in 1910

Shaw, George Bernard
(1856-1950)
Playwright. Member of the Fabian Society

Sinclair, Archibald
(1860-1925)
Liberal MP 1892. Assistant private secretary to Campbell-Bannerman 1897-1908. Secretary for Scotland 1905-12

Smith, Frank
(1854-1940)
Journalist and one-time Salvation Army Commissioner. ILP member of the London County Council 1892-5, 1898-1901, 1907-13

Snowden, Philip
(1864-1937)
ILP propagandist. Chairman of the ILP 1903-6. Labour MP for Blackburn 1906-18

Spencer, Lord
(1835-1910)
Liberal MP 1857. Cabinet rank 1880. Liberal leader in the House of Lords 1902. Incapacitated by illness in 1905

Summerbell, Tom
(1861-1910)
Member of the ILP. Labour MP for Sunderland 1906-10

Thorne, Will
(1857-1946)
Member of the SDF. A founder of the gas workers and general labourers' union, and its General Secretary 1889-

1934. Parliamentary Committee of the TUC 1894-1933. Labour MP for West Ham 1906-45

Tillett, Ben
(1860-1943)
A founder of the dockers' union and its Secretary until 1922

Trevelyan, Charles
(1870-1958)
Liberal MP 1899-1918. Parliamentary Charity Commissioner 1906-8. Parliamentary Secretary to the Board of Education 1908-14

Turner, Ben
(1863-1942)
President of the General Union of Weavers and Textile Workers 1902-22

Tweedmouth, Lord
(1849-1909)
Entered Parliament as a Liberal in 1880. Became a peer in 1894. First Lord of the Admiralty 1905-8

Walsh, Stephen
(1859-1929)
Miner. Labour MP for Ince 1906-29

Ward, John
(1866-1934)
Early member of the SDF. Founded the Navvies' Union in 1889. A member of the GFTU executive. Lib-Lab MP for Stoke 1906-29

Wardle, George
(1865-1947)
Member of the Amalgamated Society of Railway Servants. Editor of the *Railway Review* 1898-1919. Labour MP for Stockport 1906-20

Warwick, Lady
Frances
(1861-1938)
Member of SDF. Organiser of many social projects and provider of considerable funds for the SDF

Webb, Beatrice
(1858-1943)
Socialist writer and historian. Member of the Fabian Society executive. Served on the poor law commission 1905-9 and was largely responsible for the minority report

Webb, Sidney
(1859-1947)
Socialist, historian, and writer. Member of the Fabian Society executive. Member of the London County Coun-

cil (Progressive) 1892-1910

Wilkie, Alexander (1850-1928)
General Secretary of the Ship Constructive and Shipwrights' Association 1882-1928. Member of the TUC Parliamentary Committee 1890-91, 1895-1903, 1904-9. Member of the Labour Party executive 1900-1904. Labour MP for Dundee 1906-22

Wilson, Joseph Havelock (1859-1929)
Founder of the seamen's union. Lib-Lab MP for Middlesbrough 1892-1900, 1906-10

Wilson, William Tyson (1855-1921)
Member of the Amalgamated Society of Carpenters and Joiners. Labour MP for Westhoughton 1906-21

Woods, Sam (1846-1915)
Vice-President of the Miners' Federation of Great Britain 1889-1909. Secretary of the TUC 1894-1904. MP for Ince 1892-5, for Walthamstow 1897-1900

Bibliography

PART 1   PRIMARY SOURCES

PRIVATE PAPERS

H. Arnold-Forster	BM
H. H. Asquith	BL
A. J. Balfour	BM
G. Balfour	PRO
W. H. Beveridge	BLPES
A. Birrell	Liverpool University Library
R. Blatchford	Manchester Central Public Library
A. Bonar Law	BkL
A. J. Braithwaite	BLPES
H. Broadhurst	BLPES
H. Bryan	BLPES
J. Bryce	BL
J. Burns	BM
S. Buxton	C/o Mrs J. Clay, Newtimber Lodge, Hassocks, Sussex
H. Campbell-Bannerman	BM
A. Chamberlain	Birmingham University Library
J. Chamberlain	Birmingham University Library
Viscount Chilston	Kent County Archives Office
C. Dilke	BM
Master of Elibank	NLS
D. Lloyd George	BkL
E. Grey	PRO
R. B. Haldane	NLS
E. Hamilton	BM
G. Lansbury	BLPES

Lord Lansdowne   PRO
Viscount W. Long Wiltshire County Record Office
J. R. MacDonald   BLPES
A. Mattison   Brotherton Library, University of Leeds
Lord Passfield   BLPES
Lord Ripon   BM
W. Runciman   Newcastle University Library
H. Samuel   House of Lords Record Office
H. J. Wilson   Sheffield Central Library

MANUSCRIPT AND PRINTED MINUTES ETC
Fabian Society, minutes and correspondence   NCL
ILP, Bristol branch minutes   BLPES
    City of London branch minutes   BLPES
    Metropolitan District Council minutes   BLPES
    National Administrative Council minutes   BLPES
    Reports and circulars from head office   BLPES
    Sheffield branch minutes   Sheffield Central Library
    Southwark branch minutes   BLPES
    Watford branch minutes and correspondence   BLPES
    West Ham branch minutes   BLPES
Joint Board, Minutes   Usually bound with the
                                           GFTU reports
LRC, Letter Files   Transport House Library
    The infancy of the Labour Party   BLPES
SDF, Hackney branch minutes   Marx Memorial Library
TUC, PC minutes   Congress House
Woolwich Labour Representation
    Association, Minutes   Woolwich Labour Party
Woolwich Trades and Labour
    Council, Minutes   Woolwich Labour Party

COLLECTIONS OF DOCUMENTS, NEWSCUTTINGS, ETC
British Socialist Party collection   BLPES
Cooke collection   BLPES

Election addresses NLC
Unemployment collection BLPES
POLITICAL REPORTS
BSP, *Annual Report*
Fabian Society, *Annual Report*
ILP, *Annual Report*
  Report of a conference on destitution and unemployment, 1910
Labour Party, *Annual Report*
    Quarterly Report
    Report of a special conference on unemployment and the incidence of taxation, 1909
    The Labour Party and unemployment, 1908
National Liberal Federation, *Annual Report*
National Union of Conservative Associations, *Annual Report*
SDF, *Annual Report*
UNION REPORTS AND JOURNALS

Amalgamated Society of Carpenters and Joiners	*Annual Report*
	Monthly Report
Amalgamated Society of Engineers	*Annual Report*
	Monthly Report
Amalgamated Society of Operative Cotton Spinners	*Annual Report*
	Quarterly Report
Amalgamated Society of Railway Servants	*Annual Report*
Amalgamated Toolmakers Society	*Annual Report*
	Monthly Report
Associated Ironmoulders of Scotland	*Monthly Report*
Associated Shipwrights Society	*Annual Report*
	Quarterly Report
Dock, Wharf, Riverside and General Workers Union	*Annual Report*
	Dockers Record
Electrical Trade Union	*Eltradion*
Friendly Society of Ironfounders	*Annual Report*
	Monthly Report

General Federation of Trade Unions — *Proceedings and Reports*

General Union of Operative Carpenters and Joiners — *Half Yearly Report*

London Society of Compositors — *Annual Report*

London Trades Council — *Annual Report*

Miners Federation of Great Britain — *Annual Report*

National Amalgamated Furniture Trade Union — *Annual Report*

National Amalgamated Union of Labour — *Annual Report* / *Quarterly Report*

National Society of Brassworkers — *Annual Report*

National Union of Boot and Shoe Operatives — *Annual Report* / *Monthly Report*

National Union of Carpenters and Joiners — *Annual Report*

National Union of Dock Labourers — *Annual Report*

National Union of Gas Workers and General Labourers — *Annual Report* / *Quarterly balance sheet*

Operative Bricklayers Society — *Annual Report* / *Trades Circular and General Reporter*

Postmen's Federation — *Annual Report* / *Postmen's Gazette*

Railway Clerks' Association — *Railway Clerk*

Society of Lithographic Printers — *Annual Report*

Trades Union Congress — *Annual Report* / *Quarterly Circular*

Typographical Association — *Half Yearly Report* / *Typographical Circular*

United Society of Boilermakers — *Annual Report* / *Monthly Report*

OFFICIAL PAPERS AND REPORTS
Board of Trade, *Annual Report*
　　　　　　　　Labour Gazette
　　　　　　　　*Reports on unemployment and the state of
　　　　　　　　　trade*
British Parliamentary Papers
Cabinet papers
Hansard
Local Government Board, *Annual Report*

NEWSPAPERS
1　Labour and socialist
British Socialist
Clarion
Clarion Scout
Fabian News
ILP News
ILP Platform
Justice
Labour Leader
Railway Review
Reynold's Newspaper
SDP News
Socialist Record
Trades and Labour Gazette

2　National
Daily Express
Daily Graphic
Daily Mail
Daily News
Daily Telegraph
Morning Post
Observer
Standard
The Times
Westminster Gazette

CONTEMPORARY PERIODICALS
Charity Organisation Review
Christian Commonwealth
Contemporary Review
Cornhill Magazine
Economic Journal
Economic Review
English Review
Independent Review

Labour Record and Review
Liberal Magazine
National Review
National Union Gleanings
New Age
Nineteenth Century
North American Review
Political Science Quarterly

Quarterly Review   *Spectator*
Review of Reviews   *Toynbee Record*
Social Democrat   *Westminster Review*
Socialist Review

MISCELLANEOUS
Bristol Right to Work Committee, *Annual Report*
Charity Organisation Society, *Annual Report*
Conférence Internationale du chomâge, *Rapports*, 1910
National Free Labour Association, *Annual Report* (1909 only)
National Right to Work Council, *Report of a conference on
                                destitution and unemploy-
                                ment*, 1908

PART 2   SECONDARY   SOURCES

THIS LIST IS selective, comprising only those works which the
author found most useful in preparing this book.

CONTEMPORARY BOOKS AND PAMPHLETS
Alden, Percy. *The unemployed : a national question* (1905)
Barnes, George. *The unemployed problem* (1908)
Beveridge, William. *Unemployment : a problem of industry*
    (1909)
Burns, John. *Labour and drink* (1904)
            The unemployed (1893)
Churchill, Winston. *Liberalism and the social problem* (2nd
    ed, 1909)
Dearle, Norman. *Problems of unemployment in the London
    building trades* (1908)
Duffy, T. Gavan. *Mr Lloyd George's insurance scheme* (1911)
Fabian Society. *The National Insurance Bill* (1911)
Hardie, James Keir. *John Bull and his unemployed* (1905)
                   The unemployed problem (1904)

Henderson, Arthur, and Barnes, George. *Unemployment in Germany* (1907)

Hobson, John. *The crisis of Liberalism* (1909)

Howell, George. *Trade unionism old and new* (1891)

Jackson, Cyril. *Unemployment and the trade unions* (1910)

Lansbury, George. *Unemployment—the next step* (1907)

London, Jack. *The people of the abyss* (1903)

LRC. *How the workers of the world began winter* (1905)
Protection perhaps, but what kind (1905)

MacDonald, James Ramsay. *The new Unemployed Bill of the Labour Party* (1907)

Mann, Tom. *The eight hours movement* (1891)
The programme of the ILP and the unemployed (1895)
and Tillett, Ben. *The new trades unionism* (1890)

Masterman, Charles. *From the abyss* (1902)
The condition of England (1909)

Money, Leo. *Insurance against unemployment* (1912)
Work for all (1909)

National Committee for the prevention of Destitution. *How to provide for the unemployed* (1911)
The prevention of unemployment (1911)

Rowntree, Benjamin, and Lasker, Bruno. *Unemployment : a social study* (1911)

Schloss, David. *Insurance against unemployment* (1909)

Smart, Harold. *The right to work* (1906)

Snowden, Philip. *The national insurance schemes explained* (1911)

Summerbell, Tom. *The unemployed and the land* (1908)

Taylor, Fanny. *A bibliography of unemployment and the unemployed* (1909)

Warwick, Countess of. *Unemployment* (1906)

BIOGRAPHY, AUTOBIOGRAPHY AND REMINISCENCE

Aldred, Guy. *No traitor's gait* (Glasgow, 1955)

Asquith, Herbert. *Fifty years of parliament* (two vols, 1926)
                    Memories and reflections (two vols, 1928)

Barnes, George. *From workshop to war cabinet* (1924)

Bell, Tom. *Pioneering days* (1941)

Beveridge, William. *Power and influence : an autobiography* (1953)

Brockway, Fenner. *Socialism over sixty years* (1946)

Churchill, Randolph. *Winston S. Churchill. Vol II. Young statesman, 1901-1914* (1966)

Clynes, John. *Memoirs* (two vols, 1937)

George, Richard Lloyd. *Lloyd George* (1960)

George, William. *My brother and I* (1958)

Gould, Frederick. *Hyndman, prophet of socialism, 1842-1921* (1928)

Hamilton, Mary. *Arthur Henderson. A biography* (1938)

Haw, George. *The life story of Will Crooks MP* (1917)

Hyndman, Henry. *Further reminiscences* (1912)
                 The record of an adventurous life (1911)

Jackson, Thomas. *Solo trumpet* (1953)

Kent, William. *John Burns : labour's lost leader* (1950)

Lansbury, George. *My life* (1928)

McKenna, Stephen. *Reginald McKenna, 1863-1943* (1948)

Mann, Tom. *Memoirs* (1923)

Masterman, Lucy. *C. F. G. Masterman* (1939)

Montefiore, Dora. *From a Victorian to a modern* (1927)

Owen, Frank. *Tempestuous journey* (1954)

Redfern, Percy. *Journey to understanding* (1946)

Riddell, Lord. *More pages from my diary, 1908-1914* (1934)

Samuel, Herbert. *Memoirs* (1945)

Sanders, William. *Early socialist days* (1927)

Snowden, Philip. *An autobiography* (two vols, 1934)

Spender, John. *The life of the Rt Hon Sir Henry Campbell-Bannerman* (two vols, 1923) and Asquith, Cyril. *The life of Herbert Henry Asquith* (two vols, 1932)

Stewart, William. *J. Keir Hardie. A biography* (1921)

Tallents, Stephen. *Man and boy* (1943)

Thomson, Malcolm. *Lloyd George. The official biography* (1945)

Thorne, Will. *My life's battles* (1925)

Tillett, Ben. *Memories and reflections* (1931)

Tsuzuki, Chushichi. *H. M. Hyndman and British socialism* (Oxford, 1961)

Webb, Beatrice. *My apprenticeship* (1950)
Our partnership (1948)

WORKS ON LABOUR HISTORY

Bealey, Frank, and Pelling, Henry. *Labour and politics, 1900-1906* (1958)

Beer, Max. *History of British socialism* (two vols, 1929)

Brand, Carl. *The British Labour Party* (Stamford, 1964)

Clayton, Joseph. *Rise and decline of socialism, 1884-1924* (1926)

Clegg, Hugh, Fox, Alan, and Thompson, Arthur. *History of British trade unionism since 1889* (Oxford, 1964)

Cole, George D. H. *British working class politics, 1832-1914* (1941)

Cole, Margaret. *The story of Fabian socialism* (1961)

Dowse, Robert. *Left in the centre. The ILP 1883-1940* (1966)

Gregory, Roy. *The miners and British politics, 1906-1914* (1968)

Kendall, Walter. *The revolutionary movement in Britain, 1900-1921* (1969)

Lovell, John. *Stevedores and dockers : a study of trade unionism in the Port of London* (1969)

McBriar, Alan. *Fabian socialism and English politics, 1884-1914* (1962)

Miliband, Ralph. *Parliamentary socialism* (1961)

Pease, Edward. *The history of the Fabian Society* (2nd ed,
    1925)
Pelling, Henry. *A history of British trade unionism* (1963)
                    *Popular politics and society in late Victorian
                        Britain* (1968)
                    Short history of the Labour Party (1961)
                    The origins of the Labour Party (1953)
Poirier, Philip. *The advent of the Labour Party* (1958)
Roberts, Benjamin. *The Trades Union Congress, 1868-1921*
    (1958)
Tate, George. *The London Trades Council, 1860-1950* (1950)
Thompson, Paul. *Socialists, Liberals, and Labour* (1967)
Webb, Sidney and Beatrice. *History of trade unionism* (1920)

GENERAL BACKGROUND WORKS
Adams, William. *Edwardian heritage, 1901-1906* (1949)
Bruce, Maurice. *The coming of the welfare state* (1961)
Bunbury, Henry (ed). *Lloyd George's ambulance wagon*
    (1957)
Gilbert, Bentley. *The evolution of national insurance in Great
    Britain* (1966)
Halévy, Elie. *The rule of democracy* (1934)
Mowatt, Charles. *The Charity Organisation Society* (1961)
Nowell-Smith, Simon (ed). *Edwardian England, 1900-1914*
    (1964)
Pelling, Henry. *Social geography of British elections, 1885-
    1910* (1967)
Phelps Brown, Ernest. *The growth of British industrial
    relations* (1959)
Sayers, Richard. *A history of economic change in England,
    1880-1939* (1967)
Williams, Gertrude. *The state and the standard of living*
    (1936)

ARTICLES AND THESES

Blewett, Neal. *The British general elections of 1910* (Oxford D Phil thesis, 1967)

Brown, John. *Ideas concerning social policy and their inflence on legislation in Britain, 1902-1911* (London PhD thesis, 1964)

Brown, Kenneth. *Labour and unemployment, 1900-1914* (Kent PhD thesis, 1969)

Marwick, Arthur. 'The Labour Party and the welfare state in Britain, 1900-1948', *American Historical Review*, 73 (Dec 1967), 380-403

Russell, Anthony. *The general election of 1906* (Oxford D Phil thesis, 1962)

Tsuzuki, Chushichi. 'The impossibilist revolt in Britain', *International Review of Social History*, 1 (1956), 377-97

Acknowledgements

I WISH TO thank the following individuals and institutions for permission to quote from papers in their keeping: the Trustees of the British Museum for the papers of Balfour, Burns, Campbell-Bannerman, Herbert Gladstone and Lord Ripon; the Bodleian Library, Oxford, and Mr Mark Bonham Carter for the Asquith papers; the British Library of Political and Economic Science for the Lansbury, Beveridge and Herbert Bryan archives; the Passfield Trustees for the Passfield Collection; the Right Hon the Viscount Chilston and Kent County Council for the Akers-Douglas papers; Newcastle University for the papers of Walter Runciman; the Trustees of the National Library of Scotland for the Elibank papers; Beaverbrook Newspapers Ltd for the Lloyd George papers; the Fabian Society for their records held at Nuffield College; and Mrs J. Clay for permission to consult the papers of her grandfather, Sidney Buxton.

Librarians, archivists and trade union officers too numerous to list individually all gave generously of their time and knowledge, for which I am very grateful. My colleague in the Department of Economic and Social History at Queen's, Max Goldstrom, kindly read the draft manuscript and offered several helpful criticisms. Above all, my thanks are due to Professor F. S. L. Lyons of the University of Kent who will recognise in this book a much amended version of the doctoral thesis which he supervised between 1966 and 1969.

Kenneth D. Brown

Queen's University, Belfast

Index

Akers-Douglas, Henry, 26-30, 52
Alden, Percy, 31, 58, 72; and NUC, 21-3
Anderson, William, 87, 131, 162
Asquith, Herbert, 45, 69, 72, 110, 114, 120-1, 128, 133, 135, 144; cabinet changes, 94-5; cabinet unemployment committee, 71; on 'right to work', 90, 91; unemployment policy, 102, 104-7, 169

Balfour, Arthur, 20, 35, 40, 47, 68, 69; poor law commission, 60-2, 70; and unemployed agitation, 41-2, 46, 54, 66-7; Unemployed Workmen's Bill (1905), 48, 49, 57-60
Balfour, Gerald, 49; Unemployed Workmen's Bill (1905), 50-8, 60-1, 65
Barnes, George, 65, 73, 78, 108, 109, 119, 131, 133, 153; as 'activist', 97, 114, 157, 171; on labour exchanges, 129; and NUC, 23; in 'right to work' agitation, 63, 86
Beveridge, William, 15, 68, 132, 154; and labour exchanges, 95, 123, 124, 128, 138, 139
Birrell, Augustine, 69, 90
Blatchford, Robert, 18, 40, 62; critical of Labour Party, 112, 132
Bondfield, Margaret, 151
Booth, Charles, 14, 71
Bosanquet, Helen, 13, 71
Bowerman, Charles, 121, 124, 127
Brace, William, 88, 91

British Socialist Party, see BSP
Broadhurst, Henry, 16, 58
BSP (British Socialist Party), 156-7, 172
Burns, John, 21, 26, 70, 71, 169; labour criticism of, 80-2, 114, 169; Liberal dissatisfaction with, 73, 74-5, 85, 88, 95, 169; on 'right to work', 85, 90; in unemployment crisis (1908), 101, 102, 104, 105, 106, 107; unemployment policy, 72-3, 75-6, 78, 88, 104-5, 118; Unemployed Workmen's Act (1905), 54, 55, 57, 58, 75
Buxton, Sidney, 33, 48, 69, 90, 104, 140; critical of Burns, 74-5, 85; serves on Liberal unemployment committees, 71, 102; on unemployment insurance, 145-8

Campbell-Bannerman, Henry, 21, 45, 49, 76, 91, 94, 169; unemployment policy, 68, 69
Central (Unemployed) Body, 40, 74, 82, 109, 123, 132
Chandler, Francis, 71, 120
Charity Organisation Society, see COS
Churchill, Winston, 101, 124, 144, 169, 173; and labour exchanges, 95, 123, 125-6; on Labour unemployment policies, 94, 104
Clynes, John, 147, 163; as 'activist', 97, 110, 114, 141, 171; on labour exchanges, 123, 127; on Liberal unemployment policies, 73, 79

The Idea of Happiness

CONCEPTS IN WESTERN THOUGHT SERIES

GENERAL EDITOR: MORTIMER J. ADLER

INSTITUTE FOR PHILOSOPHICAL RESEARCH

The Idea of Happiness

by
V. J. McGill

FREDERICK A. PRAEGER, *Publishers*
New York · Washington · London

FREDERICK A. PRAEGER, PUBLISHERS
111 Fourth Avenue, New York, N.Y. 10003, U.S.A.
77–79 Charlotte Street, London W.1, England

Published in the United States of America in 1967
by Frederick A. Praeger, Inc., Publishers

Second printing, 1968

© 1967 by Institute for Philosophical Research

Library of Congress Catalog Card Number: 67–22292

Printed in the United States of America

For

Helen

Persons Engaged in the Work of
the Institute for Philosophical Research
1961–1967

RESEARCH STAFF
SENIOR FELLOWS

Mortimer J. Adler
——————

Otto A. Bird
William J. Gorman

Robert G. Hazo
V. J. McGill
A. L. H. Rubin
Charles Van Doren

RESEARCH ASSOCIATES

Betty Beck Bennett
Ann Quinn Burns
Paul Cornelius
Katherine Farnsworth
Ross Firestone

Edgar V. Meyer
Harvey Meyers
Charles T. Sullivan
Gerald Temaner
Jeffrey Weiss

ADMINISTRATIVE AND CLERICAL STAFF

Marlys A. Buswell
Helen M. Kresich
Theresa A. Panek
Denise Ryan

Carter Nelson Sullivan
Frances S. Ward
Celia Wittenber

BOARD OF DIRECTORS
INSTITUTE FOR PHILOSOPHICAL RESEARCH

Mortimer J. Adler
Mortimer Fleishhacker, Jr., Chairman
Robert P. Gwinn
Prentis C. Hale
Daggett Harvey

Louis Kelso
Harold F. Linder
Arthur L. H. Rubin
Hermon D. Smith
Leonard Spacek

Acknowledgments

Many books have been written on happiness and how to be happy by philosophers and citizens concerned about the problem, but the present volume is probably the first to be written on the *idea* of happiness, depicting the conflicts and convergence of all the leading theories of happiness. The proposal that such a study be carried out I owe to Dr. Mortimer J. Adler. The book has been written for the Institute for Philosophical Research, of which Dr. Adler is the director, and follows in large part the method expounded and illustrated in the Institute's first two volumes, *The Idea of Freedom* (1958, 1961), and the reader is referred to Book 1 of Volume I of that work for a full account of the method and problems of this type of "dialectical" research. I should like to thank the Institute for Philosophical Research publicly for the generous stipend which afforded me the time to write this book. I am also indebted to Dr. Adler for a number of suggestions and continual encouragement, to Professors Richard McKeon and Otto Bird for constructive criticism, to Arthur Rubin for helpful cross-questioning, and to Dr. William Gorman for pointing up some features of supernatural happiness. Any errors or misconceptions which may be found in the book, however, should not be laid at their doorstep.

Foreword

The Idea of Happiness is one of a series of studies of basic ideas undertaken by the Institute for Philosophical Research. The Institute was established in 1952 with the avowed purpose of taking stock of Western thought on subjects that have been of continuing philosophical interest from the advent of philosophy in ancient Greece to the present day. In pursuing this task, it hopes to clarify the recorded discussion of such basic ideas as freedom, justice, happiness, love, progress, equality, and law. It aims to transform what, in every case, at first appears to be a chaos of differing opinions into an orderly set of clearly defined points of agreement and disagreement that give rise to real issues and make possible the kind of rational debate that constitutes genuine controversy.

What we are given to start with in each case is a diversity of opinions, the pattern of which is seldom clear. To put order into that diversity and to render it intelligible require a creative effort to construct the controversies that are implicit in it. Only by an explicit formulation of the pattern of agreements and disagreements, together with the reasons for the latter, can we delineate the issues and indicate how they have been or might be disputed. Too often reasons have not been given for positions that have been persistently advanced. In consequence, important issues have not been disputed in a way that carries the controversy forward and brings it nearer to a resolution.

The Institute has proceeded on the assumption that the issues in the field of any basic philosophical idea concern matters about which objective truth is ascertainable. The future resolution of these issues depends upon more sustained and more rational efforts to deal with them than the history of Western thought has so far exhibited, and the initiation of such efforts depends in turn upon a clear and precise understanding of the issues. Providing this has been the sole aim of the Institute's work from the beginning.

To accomplish its aim, the Institute has developed certain procedures and a distinctive method of work. Its approach to the study of the recorded discussion of basic philosophical ideas is essentially dialectical. The materials being studied—the major documents in the literature of any philosophical subject—are historical in the sense that each has a date and place in the history of thought about that subject; but the Institute's study of these materials is *nonhistorical* in aim. It deliberately abstracts from their historical context and pattern. It views them as if they were all contemporary—as if the documents represented the voices of participants confronting one another in actual discussion. The Institute's approach is also *nonphilosophical* in the sense that it does not undertake to develop or defend a theory of the idea under consideration. The only truth with which the Institute is directly concerned is truth concerning the body of thought about a particular subject, not truth about the subject thought about. The Institute therefore refrains from taking part in the discussion that it attempts to clarify. It makes a sustained effort to be impartial in its treatment of all points of view and to deal with them in an objective and neutral manner. It strives to function as a detached bystander or impartial observer, not as a critic or judge assessing the merits of conflicting claims and awarding a verdict.

It should be clear why an intellectual enterprise thus designed and directed is facilitated by a collaborative effort under institutional auspices; it would be almost impossible for a single person working alone to accomplish effectively. On any basic idea, the volume of literature to be examined and interpreted is tremendous, even if only the most significant and representative documents are selected for study. In the process of interpretation and in the attempt to treat all points of view with impartiality, the desired neutrality is more likely to be achieved by many individuals working together than by the most determined effort of a single individual. Collaboration and consultation tend to offset the idiosyncrasies of individual temperaments and intellectual biases. The advantage of teamwork is not only the pooling of diverse abilities, but also the correction of blind spots and the checking of prejudices.

The first product of the collaborative effort of the Institute's staff was a two-volume study, *The Idea of Freedom,* Volume I of which was published in 1958, Volume II in 1961. That study exemplified the Institute's dialectical method in the treatment of a basic idea, and its results provided a good measure of what can be achieved by the application of that method. *The Idea of Happiness,* like *The Idea of Freedom,* is a product of the collaborative effort of the Institute's staff. The names of the members of the Institute's staff and of its Board of Directors, will be found facing the Acknowledgments page.

The treatment of the idea of happiness in the present book differs from the dialectical method of treating basic ideas employed in *The Idea of Progress*, *The Idea of Justice*, and *The Idea of Love*, all of which are adaptations of the method employed in *The Idea of Freedom*. The present book attempts to combine what I would call a historical with a dialectical approach to the study of a great idea. It starts with an exposition of Aristotle's conception of happiness and compares it with other ancient theories of the good life as advanced by Plato and by the Stoics; it then examines the transcendent and otherworldly theories of happiness developed by the great Neoplatonic philosopher Plotinus and by such Christian theologians as Augustine and Aquinas; and turning from them to the era of modern philosophical thought, it concentrates on the contributions to the subject of two German philosophers, Kant and Hegel, and of the English utilitarians, especially Bentham and J. S. Mill.

The exposition of the principal theories, which occupies the first six chapters of the book, aims at setting forth many of the issues that establish the dialectical structure of the controversy. Then follow four chapters concerned with the basic issues in moral philosophy that revolve around the idea of happiness: the issue of self-realization, in which Spinoza is treated as a precursor of modern theories of self-realization and such authors as Bradley and Dewey are treated as modern proponents of Aristotelianism, thus characterizing theories of self-realization as a modern attempt at eudaemonism; the issue of the pursuit of happiness vs. the performance of duty, on which Kant and Aristotle stand opposed; the question of the relation of happiness to virtue, to which the Stoics and Aristotle give conflicting answers; and the issue of the relation of happiness to pleasure, which sets both ancient and modern hedonists and some but not all utilitarians against Aristotle. The final chapter is concerned with the ideal of happiness in the present.

Aristotle is the chief protagonist in all the major issues concerning happiness, and his eudaemonism makes happiness the pivotal term in moral philosophy. For this reason, Dr. McGill treats Aristotle's theory as a framework for the discussion and reviews the literature, beginning with Aristotle, as a background against which a dialectical clarification of the issues and of the arguments pro and con can be given heightened interest and intelligibility. This procedure deviates from that employed in other Institute studies. In *The Idea of Love*, *The Idea of Justice*, and *The Idea of Progress*, as in *The Idea of Freedom*, the dialectical clarification of issues occupies the forefront and center of the stage; the literature concerning the idea in each case is presented only as documentation of the positions taken on the issues or of the arguments pro and con. This book does contain the two components essential to the Institute's handling of a great idea—a dialectical scheme for clarifying the issues that constitute the controversy about it and the employment of this dialectical pattern to order and clarify the discussion of the idea in the literature on the subject.

The Institute for Philosophical Research was established on grants from the Ford Foundation and the Old Dominion Foundation. When the Ford Foundation grant expired in 1956, the Old Dominion Foundation continued to support the Institute's work and was subsequently joined by other benefactors. I wish to express the Institute's gratitude to the sources of financial support that made it possible for it to complete its work on the idea of freedom after the expiration of the Ford grant and, beyond that, to produce not only the present work on the idea of happiness, but also studies of the idea of progress, the idea of justice, and the idea of love. These four studies are now being published simultaneously. Other studies, one on the idea of equality and one on language and thought, are currently being undertaken and should be ready for publication in the near future.

In the period since 1962, the following foundations have made substantial contributions to the Institute: the Old Dominion Foundation, the Houghton Foundation, the General Service Foundation, the Liberal Arts Foundation, the Olive Bridge Foundation, and the Paul Jones Foundation. These acknowledgments would not be complete without an expression of special gratitude for the friendship and support of three men in particular—Paul Mellon and Ernest Brooks, Jr., of the Old Dominion Foundation, and Arthur Houghton, Jr., of the Houghton Foundation.

MORTIMER J. ADLER

Chicago
May, 1967

Contents

*the Causal Role of Pleasure in Happiness/ 1. Does
Pleasure Attend Efficient Operation?/2. Does Pleasure
Cause or Facilitate Activities?/3. Is Pleasure the Main
Goad to Learning?/4. The Plausibility of Psychological
Hedonism/5. How Good a Deterrent Is Pain?/Are
There Qualitative Differences Among Pleasures?/The
Fate of the Hedonistic Calculus and the Pathos of Any
Alternative/1. Is "the Greatest Pleasure of the Greatest
Number" Meaningless?/2. Questions About Pleasure
as the Goal/3. Questions About the Hedonistic Calcu-
lus/4. A Calculus of Pleasures and Pains vs. a Calculus
of Preferences/5. Does the Shift in the Scale of Hedonis-
tic Values Prevent the Calculation of the Greatest Pleas-
ure?/6. Is the Eudaemonian Calculus Any Easier?/The
Relevance of the Altruism-vs.-Egoism Issue/Is There a
Paradox of Hedonism and Does It Extend to Eudaemonism?/The Problem for Utilitarians of Ends and Means*

The Idea of Happiness

Introduction

THIS book investigates the controversy over happiness, which begins with Plato and Aristotle and continues at the present time. How far have the leading philosophers agreed and disagreed about the supreme good, the final end of life, and what reasons do they give in support of their conflicting portraits of the happy man? The arguments often employ the subtle resources of the great philosophical systems, but their pith and content come from everyday experience, so that training in philosophy is not needed to know what the controversy is all about. The book does not attempt to show that one of the rival theories of happiness is right as against the others, nor does it put forward a theory of its own. The intention is rather to make a case for each of the principal theories, as impartially as possible, showing each in its strength and weakness. Perhaps the reader will be tempted to follow through and decide for himself which conception of happiness is closest to the truth, for in the end the decision must be personal. It is possible, too, that renewed soundings of the contours of happiness—which ideally measure the human value of everything else—will help to keep national policy on a humane course. At a time when technological progress and prowess have grown so

3

menacing, there is perhaps a point in examining again the nature of the good life to which, in our tradition, such developments owe their only justification.

The six chapters of Part I describe, in sequence, the main theories of happiness put forward in the Western world, exhibiting in each case their supporting arguments and rationale, whereas the chapters of Part II deal more specifically with the *issues* of happiness, *i.e.*, the controversial questions that either divide one theory from another, or else embroil advocates of the same theory among themselves. Diverse philosophers thus appear on the stage together, and the scene is one of conflict, though analysis suggests that some differences can be avoided or resolved. But though the focus of Part I is on the individual theories rather than on the issues, it does touch on many of the issues, and thus prepares for the more thorough treatment of Part II. Part I prepares for Part II in other ways. It is easier to understand the issues between our theories, and those internal to them, if one has first read an account of each of these theories as a whole, in its unity and individual persuasiveness. For the general reader, also, Part I should serve as a painless introduction to philosophical terms and forms of argument that are presupposed in what follows.

As a framework within which to compare diverse theories of happiness, we take Aristotle's eudaemonism. This does not mean that we take this theory to be the true one and measure the shortcomings of other theories by their failure to conform to it. We adopt Aristotelianism as our framework because it is the most complete and elaborate theory, because it asks the most questions, considers the most alternatives, and combines this amplitude with serious attention to consistency and proof. This theory also appears to have the longest history and to be the most influential. Our Chapter 4 describes Aquinas' "imperfect" happiness, which is derived from Aristotle; Chapter 7 deals with self-realization theory, which is a modern variant of Aristotle's eudaemonism enjoying much influence today; while the last chapter is concerned with contemporary "self-actualization," the dominant conception of positive mental health today, which is greatly indebted to eudaemonism and self-realization theory.

Aristotle's treatment of happiness also anticipates contrary theories. He raises many questions to which later philosophers give answers contrary to his, and presents arguments for alternatives which he rejects but they accept. Aristotle's brief definition of happiness as activity of the soul according to virtue, accompanied by pleasure, and provided with sufficient external goods and fair fortune, will serve to illustrate the point. Aristotle argues that happiness must be an activity rather than a state of the soul, and thereby anticipates the theories of the Stoics, Plotinus, Augustine, Aquinas, and many others, which make happiness (or perfect happiness) a state of the soul. He considers and rejects the view that the possession of virtue *alone* constitutes felicity, and thereby puts himself in explicit opposition to the Platonic Socrates and the Stoics. Again, he gives careful attention to Eudoxus' hedonism, to the view that pleasure is *the* good, the only good that is good in itself, accepting some of the pro-arguments and dismissing others. While repudiating hedonism as such, he embodies a great deal of its *raison d'être* in his own eudaemonism, for pleasure *is* something good in itself, he says, and always accompanies the activity that constitutes happiness. He recognizes that the hedonist's doctrine of the qualitative sameness of pleasures has a certain rationale, and therefore makes a sustained effort to prove the opposite. Even the supernatural view of happiness, which Aristotle dismisses as unattainable by man, he thoughtfully leaves open as a possibility for the gods. In short, Aristotle is remarkably aware in advance of arguable positions partly or wholly opposed to his own views, which were exploited by later thinkers. That is why his treatment of happiness provides the best framework or templet, or whatever one calls it, for the discussion and comparison of theories that are not so complete. Throughout the book we attempt to show how and for what reasons later theories of happiness diverge, not only from one another but also from the baseline of Aristotelianism. But the yardstick, as we said, is not taken to be a measure of truth or adequacy.

There is a kind of eudaemonism in Plato, but there are also diverging tendencies, nor is his eudaemonism complete enough to serve as a regular base of comparison. Even the Aristotelian base is not wide enough to include everything. Aristotle does not have any intimation of the later, utilitarian formula of "the greatest pleasure of the greatest number," with its radical egalitarian implications. Nor does he foresee the possibility of a position like that of Kant, which rejects happiness as the supreme good and puts doing one's duty, or "being worthy of happiness," in its place. Aristotle's base of discussion is broad but he has no suspicion of the later downgrading of happiness by the deontologists.

The problem arises how philosophers who give very different definitions of "happiness" can be talking about the same thing, and if they are not talking about the same thing, how they can disagree—how there can be a controversy? We will say that each of the definitions is a particular refinement of a root meaning which is shared by those who give diverse definitions of it. The root meaning of "happiness" appears to be something like this: A lasting state of affairs in which the most favorable ratio of satisfied desires to desires is realized, with the proviso that the satisfied desires can include satisfactions that are not *preceded* by specific desires for them, but come by surprise. Thus we are suddenly delighted by someone's conversation we had not expected to enjoy, yet, if we had not desired conversation of this *kind* in the past, we should probably not enjoy it now by surprise. Another proviso is necessary: "the most favorable ratio" should read "the most favorable ratio, or some approximation to it," for though some philosophers, *e.g.*, Plotinus, hold that happiness is an absolute optimum, others, *e.g.*, Aristotle, think of it as an approximation and go along with the common judgment that one man can be happier than another.

The most favorable ratio $\dfrac{\text{satisfied desires}}{\text{desires}}$ is elaborated in different ways in different theories of happiness. The most favorable ratio, according to Aristotle, is to be obtained *mainly* by increasing the numerator, whereas the Stoics insist that it can be obtained only by decreasing the denominator. We thus have the contrast between contractive and expansive conceptions of happiness. There are also differences among philosophers as to whether certain *kinds* of satisfactions (or satisfactions in certain *kinds* of objects) make for the optimum ratio, and should be given precedence or preference, or whether the only thing that counts is the intensity and duration of satisfaction (the greatest sum of pleasure). And of course there are differences as to what goods of the mind, body, and external world are necessary, instrumental, or ingredient in the optimum ratio. These examples are sufficient to illustrate our contention that the philosophers whose diverse theories of happiness are discussed in this book are, roughly, talking about the same thing, and that what we are describing is, therefore, a controversy. The crucial disagreement that logically precedes all the rest is whether or not this optimum ratio constitutes the supreme good for man. A limiting case of the ratio is the conception of happiness reached in the eternal felicity of the blessed in heaven, for, here, unsatisfied desires disappear altogether, and the problem of attainability is thus raised to a new dimension.

The subject of happiness ramifies in many directions, and judgments as to what is *directly* pertinent perhaps will differ. Because of the popular interest in the topic, an effort has been made to keep the book within the compass and comfort of general readers. A number of difficult philosophical questions, which would have discouraged such readers, while also enlarging the book disproportionately and blurring its focus, have been omitted.

I

Concepts of
Happiness

Aristotle's Concept of Happiness

The *Nicomachean Ethics* opens with the warning that ethics cannot be an exact science. Whereas Plato pointed to a body of absolute and certain knowledge about the good and the right, attainable at least by philosophers, Aristotle remarks that his discussion will be adequate "if it has as much clearness as the subject-matter admits of." Political science (which includes ethics), he says, investigates actions and goods with regard to which judgments vary and fluctuate so much "that they may be thought to exist only by convention, and not by nature." And what is good in one situation may be harmful in others, for "men have been undone by reason of their wealth, and others by reason of their courage."

> We must be content, then, in speaking of such subjects and with such premises to indicate the truth roughly and in outline, and in speaking about things which are only for the most part true and with premises of the same kind to reach conclusions that are no better.[1]

[1] W. D. Ross (ed.), *Works of Aristotle, Nicomachean Ethics*, 1094b15–22.

The stage is set for an analysis of the moral dimension, which, in its circumstantiality and empiricism, is utterly different from Plato's.[2]

THE TERM "GOOD" AND THE DENIAL OF A UNIVERSAL GOOD

Aristotle agrees with Plato that all arts and inquiries, actions and pursuits are "thought to aim at some good"[3] and that "political science aims at . . . the highest of all goods achievable by action."[4] He disagrees vigorously as to the meaning of "good." Good "cannot be something universally present in all cases and single," as Plato claims, "for then it could not have been predicated in all the categories but in one only."[5] "Good" when applied to man, a relation, a quality, a quantity of any sort, etc., or even to a string of diverse substances, such as a man, a horse, a piece of music, a building, a scientific book cannot in every case have the same meaning.

Aristotle's arguments against a single universal good present in all so-called good things are plausible but have been contested. One most recent challenge is found in G. H. von Wright's *The Varieties of Goodness*. "Varieties of Goods," such as wines, carpenters, and lungs, can all be good, Von Wright says, because they exemplify different "Varieties of Goodness." Thus, "good" applied to wines means pleasant to taste, to carpenters —skillful, and to lungs—healthful. Von Wright contends that Aristotle was led to reject the Form of the Good, because he failed to distinguish between these two sorts of variety.[6] But this is certainly difficult to see. If Aristotle had explicitly recognized these Varieties of Goodness—technical, instrumental, hedonistic, etc.—he still would have had the same reasons for denying a single universal good. As we have seen, Von Wright himself does not claim that there is a single identical good present in all things called "good," but only that there is a "unity" among the Varieties of Goodness. The unity, however, is not one of genus and its species, Von Wright observes; the Varieties of Goodness are not *kinds* of but "forms of goodness," but the meaning of "forms" is not explained. It may be, therefore, that Von Wright, who often agrees with Aristotle, is actually close to him here too.

---

[2] A contemporary English philosopher goes as far as to say that "the impossibility of a 'scientific morality' and the reasons why it is impossible were more clearly understood by Aristotle than by any other philosopher." (Qu. from P. H. Nowell-Smith in *Ethics*, p. 19.)

[3] *Op. cit.*, 1094a1.

[4] *Ibid.*, 1095a16.

[5] *Ibid.*, 1096a28.

[6] See *The Varieties of Goodness*, p. 13.

It is up to Aristotle to explain why, if diverse things called "good" often have no common property, they are all called "good." He does not want to say that the term "good" when applied to plants, horses, virtues, works of art, and men is simply equivocal, like the words "ring," "nut," "seal," and "lock," which can mean something completely different in different applications. We are left with the conundrum that "good" does not mean the same in different applications, yet is not simply equivocal either. Aristotle suggests two alternative solutions. When attributed to diverse things, "good" may mean (1) that they all derive from one good, or all contribute to it; or (2) that the good that belongs to one kind of thing, *e.g.*, a talent, a virtue, or a man, is analogous to the good that is attributed to other kinds of things.[7] According to the first alternative, the goodness in diverse talents, virtues, and men would be *many*, but they would all derive from or contribute to *one* goodness. What "derive" means is not clear. Men owe their diverse merits and goodness to the Form of the Good in which they participate, according to Plato's theory, but this is precisely the theory that Aristotle is rejecting. *Contributing to the one good*—the chief good—is quite a different idea. Could it be said that different kinds of virtue, such as courage and justice, are good simply because they contribute in different ways to the good life? This possibility seems to be excluded by Aristotle when he says that unless some of the virtues or good things are good in themselves the Idea of the good would be empty.[8] It would appear, therefore, that neither alternative under (1) is to be taken seriously.

Alternative (2) is more promising. Diverse human merits and virtues, and assorted goods in general, could be good analogously. "The goodness of temperance is analogous to the goodness of courage," for example, could mean: The goodness of temperance is to human appetite as the goodness of courage is to spiritedness, *i.e.*, our capacity for courage. Von Wright, however, objects that, whenever there are analogous meanings, there is also a primary sense of the word. Thus, "deep" applied to thought is an analogous usage that presupposes a primary use, as when we speak of the deep ocean. But in the case of "good," he argues, there is no primary use—no primary meaning of the word "good," and where there is no primary meaning of a word there can be no analogous meanings either.[9] The argument is ingenious but not conclusive. It could be argued that "good" *does* have a primary meaning, as when we refer to immediate consummations. Analogous meanings of the term would include cases where we refer to acts as good because they are thought to provide future consummations. Moreover, it is not certain that to understand an analogous

[7] See *op. cit.*, 1096b27–30.
[8] See *ibid.*, 1096b20.
[9] *Op. cit.*, p. 15.

meaning of a word one *must* have previously learned a straightforward primary sense of the same word.[10]

That good is radically different from natural properties of an object is contended by G. E. Moore in *Principia Ethica*. To identify good with any set of natural properties is to commit what he calls the naturalistic fallacy. It is to say that good is identical with what it is *not*. For the same reason, it is impossible to give any definition or analysis of good. Much controversy followed. The outcome is that though few, perhaps, would now agree with Moore that good is indefinable and unanalyzable, most would concede that he discovered something distinctive and important about the predicate "good." The linguistic theorist Jerrold J. Katz proposes that Moore's discovery about the nonnaturalness of good is really that the meaning of "good" is syncategorematic.[11] After a lengthy analysis, Katz concludes that, in fact, "the meaning of 'good' does not have the kind of structure that most other English words have. Whereas the meaning of a word such as 'bachelor,' 'honest,' 'hard,' 'cuts,' 'liquid,' etc., is made up of component elements that are attributes in their own right, the meaning of 'good' is a function that operates on other meanings, not an independent attribute. Apart from combination with the conceptual content of other words and expressions, the meaning of 'good' does not make sense. Since the meaning of 'good' cannot stand alone as a complete concept, we shall say that the meaning of 'good' is syncategorematic."[12]

Katz's solution is in line with Aristotle's theory of the meaning of "good," for here also "good" has meaning only when applied along with categorical and other specifications. It is not that "good," as Aristotle understands it, is *ambiguous* when applied to diverse things; it is that the meaning it has in any case depends on the meaning of a group of expressions of which it forms an integral part. Good does not properly have meaning; it is *mitbedeutend*, as Anton Marty says: *It means "with."*

It follows from the rejection of a single universal good that, if we step too far across categories and other distinctions, we come upon x's and y's with regard to which we cannot say, in a quantitative sense, that x is better than y or worse than y, or of equal value either. That is, many goods will be incomparable if "better than" and "worse than" mean containing a greater or less amount of a single good. But, of course, there are other ways of construing these expressions. Better and worse and higher and lower

[10] That we use the same word for things that are neither similar nor, of course, partially identical, in at least seven different types of cases, is convincingly argued by L. J. Austin in the "The Meaning of a Word" in *Philosophical Papers*. See also C. E. Caton (ed.), *Philosophy and Ordinary Language*.

[11] "Semantic Theory and the Meaning of 'Good,'" in *The Journal of Philosophy*, December 10, 1964, p. 766.

[12] *Ibid.*, p. 761.

values can be understood in an ordinal sense as well as quantitatively. Intellectual fulfillment can be better than gustatory satisfactions without being *more* of something.

If a single universal good is the measure of all goods, then any two diverse goods in the universe must be such that either one is better than the other or they are of equal value. If this appears doubtful, as it does to some philosophers, the Aristotelian theory of value will have a certain advantage over the Platonic.

HAPPINESS AS THE HIGHEST GOOD

A highest good, or "final good," if there is only one, will be (1) desired for its own sake, and (2) not desired for the sake of anything else, and (3) will be the only good of which (1) and (2) are both true. All other goods are desired for the sake of something else, even "honour, pleasure, reason, and every virtue," Aristotle says, "for though we would choose the latter for their own sake, even if they did not serve any other end," yet "we also choose them also for the sake of happiness [the highest good for man], judging that by means of them we shall be happy."[13] Aristotle here goes part way with Plato and the Stoics, who say that virtue is the highest good; and also part way with the hedonists, who say that pleasure is the highest good. Virtue and pleasure are both good in themselves. They lack, however, the further qualification—that of *not* being chosen for the sake of anything else. There is a good higher than virtue and higher than pleasure, because these are chosen for it while it is never chosen for them. Men are agreed, Aristotle says, that this highest good is happiness.

But what reason is there to suppose that this highest good exists? Aristotle's argument, introduced in a parenthesis, is that, if everything is desired for the sake of something else, "the process would go on to infinity, so that our desire would be empty and vain."[14] This is impossible. There must, therefore, be a highest good—a good that is not desired for anything else, but only for itself. Let us take an example. If you want sandals on condition that you also want to protect your feet, and you want to protect your feet only on condition that you want to walk long distances, and so on *ad infinitum*, and all of your desires are similarly conditioned, then you do not really want anything at all. Perhaps the argument could also be put as follows: If your every desire for *A* means a desire for *A* on condition that you also have a desire for *B*, and so on *ad infinitum*, then you could never explain what you really desire. You could never finish your statement, since

13 *Op. cit.*, 1097b1–6.
14 *Ibid.*, 1094a20–22.

you would have to substitute a longer expression for "desire for *X*," but in the longer expression "desire for *X*" would always occur.

Aristotle does not, of course, claim that such an argument would prove that there is only *one* superlative good. Maybe there are several goods that are desired for themselves but not for the sake of anything else. Aristotle is cautious in approaching this question. He states that "if there is only one final end, this will be what we are seeking, and if there is more than one, the most final will be the one we are seeking."[15] But he obviously believes that there is only one final end, and he does give a reason for holding this view, viz.: The other candidates for the distinction of highest goods— honor, pleasure, reason, and the virtues—are chosen, not only for their own sake but also for the sake of a fuller lifetime realization, happiness, and perhaps for other reasons, whereas happiness is not chosen, even in part, as something instrumental to another end. All the candidates for the status of highest good except happiness apparently fail to meet one of the requirements.

Whether the existence of a single highest good can be proved or not, it has usually been asserted or taken for granted in the history of Western philosophy; and however differently this highest good may be described, it is almost always called "happiness," or the near equivalent in other languages, though sometimes "welfare," "well-being," or "felicity," or their equivalents, are preferred.

We shall see, however, that there are dissenters, especially in modern times, who argue that there can be no one happiness for all men, that the idea of a single happiness can have no content.

THE UNIVERSAL DESIRE FOR HAPPINESS

Aristotle holds that "all knowledge and every pursuit aims at some good," and that political science aims at "what is the highest of all goods achievable by action."[16] But the marksmanship, where individuals or states are concerned, may be very poor, and is to be trusted only where wisdom rules. That all men aim at good, as they see it, might be called "the postulate of rationality." To aim at evil, knowing it is evil, or knowing it is less good than something else they could obtain, would be to desire that their desires, or their stronger desires, be frustrated. Aristotle agrees with Plato that, when the object of choice is complex, it is some partial good in this object, and not its inherent evil, that is chosen. The robber may spread havoc and misery, but what he aims at is spoils, which are good, at least for

15 *Ibid.*, 1097a28–30.
16 *Ibid.*, 1095a14–16.

himself. He disagrees with Plato in holding that men do sometimes choose one object over another knowing that it contains less good, or more evil, than the other.

"The saying that 'no one is voluntarily wicked nor involuntarily happy,'" Aristotle says, "seems to be partly false and partly true; for no one is involuntarily happy, but wickedness is voluntary."[17] Vice, like virtue, is in our power, since

> where it is in our power to act it is also in our power not to act, and *vice versa;* so that, if to act, where this is noble, is in our power, not to act, which will be base, will also be in our power.[18]

Aristotle thus holds that, although all men aim at what is good, they *can* nevertheless choose something—not through ignorance of any kind—which is less good, or less good in their opinion, than something else they might have chosen. And, of course, what they can do, they do do. But it seems fair to say Aristotle remains in large agreement with Plato even here. Ignorance is at least the main obstacle to right action, hence the importance he attaches to education.

In one place, Aristotle says that all men aim at happiness:

> It may be said that every man and all men in common aim at a certain end which determines what they choose and what they avoid. This end, to sum up briefly, is happiness and its constituents. . . . All advice to do things or not to do them is concerned with happiness, and with the things that make for or against it; whatever creates or increases happiness or some part of happiness, we ought to do; whatever destroys or hampers happiness, or gives rise to its opposite, we ought not to do.[19]

Thus every man and group of men want to be happy, seek happiness continuously, and believe they ought to. This sounds plausible, and remains so when Aristotle goes on to enumerate alternative *conceptions* of happiness:

> We may define happiness as prosperity combined with virtue; or as independence of life; or as secure enjoyment of the maximum of pleasure; or as a good condition of property and body, together with the power of guarding one's property and body and making use of them. That happiness is one or more of these things, pretty well everybody agrees.[20]

From these definitions it follows, he says, that the constituents of happiness are "good birth, plenty of friends, good friends, wealth, good children,

---

[17] *Ibid.*, 1113b14–17.
[18] *Ibid.*, 1113b8–12.
[19] *Op. cit., Rhetoric,* 1360b4–14.
[20] *Ibid.*, 1360b14–18.

plenty of children, a happy old age, and also such bodily excellences as health, beauty, strength, large stature, athletic powers, together with fame, honour, good luck and virtue."[21]

In the *Nicomachean Ethics*, Aristotle sees less agreement among men as to the nature of happiness. *"Verbally,"* he says, "there is very general agreement . . . as to the highest of all goods achievable by action . . .

> for both the general run of men and people of superior refinement say that it is happiness, and identify living well and doing well with being happy; but with regard to what happiness is they differ, and the many do not give the same account as the wise. For the former think it is some plain and obvious thing, like pleasure, wealth, or honour; they differ, however, from one another, and often even the same man identifies it with different things, with health when he is ill, with wealth when he is poor.[22]

From this important passage it follows that men do not aim at happiness—not at the *same* happiness. But perhaps Aristotle is here emphasizing human differences with regard to happiness, whereas in the passage from the *Rhetoric* he is calling attention to basic agreements among human beings; there need be no inconsistency. Aristotle certainly holds that happiness corresponds in part to a common human nature and common human desires, and that some exercise of faculties, lower and higher, and some fruition of desires at all levels, is necessary to happiness. In his view, the wise see happiness as a whole and in proper proportion, whereas the common run of men see it incompletely, or out of proportion, emphasizing instrumentalities like wealth, or lower-order pleasures, in place of the life of reason, which is the quintessence of happiness. All men can thus be said to desire happiness, and to aim at it in an attentuated sense at least: they tend to strive for that which seems to serve their happiness, which they see in some degree of completeness and proportion.

The conversion of a one-sided conception of happiness into an adequate understanding of it must always be possible, for Aristotle tells us that "all who are not maimed as regards their potentiality for virtue may win it by a certain kind of study and care"[23]—barring signal misfortunes, we should add. Education is important, and so is dialectic. The "ordinary man" can be convinced that wealth and sensuous pleasure would not satisfy all his desires, that his one-sided emphasis is a distortion, and that he himself does not really believe it. The voluptuary can be asked whether he would prefer to be an oyster if there were more pleasure in it, and the grasping Croesus can be told the story of Midas, etc. Most men have glimpsed more

---

[21] *Ibid.*, 1360b20–23.
[22] *Op. cit., Nicomachean Ethics*, 1095a17–25. (Italics added.)
[23] *Ibid.*, 1099b19.

of happiness than they have clearly understood, and can often be persuaded that there is more to it than their way of life suggests or exemplifies.

ARISTOTLE'S DEFINITION OF HAPPINESS

We have seen that the highest or final good must be desired for its own sake, and never for the sake of anything else, and that it is unique in this respect. Now it is happiness, Aristotle says, and happiness alone, that meets these requirements. Honor, pleasure, and reason are desired for their own sake, but they are also desired for the sake of other things, whereas we desire happiness for its own sake only. The question "Why do you want to possess knowledge?" makes sense, but the question "Why do you want to be happy?" admits of no answer.

Happiness, briefly defined, is "activity of the soul in accordance with virtue, and if there are more than one virtue, in accordance with the best and most complete," and "in a complete life. For one swallow does not make a summer, nor does one day; and so too, one day, or a short time, does not make a man blessed and happy."[24] Aristotle also adds that the activity is accompanied by pleasure, and that there must be enough external goods and good fortune to enable a man to live out his life in some leisure and dignity.

Let us note first that the above definition of happiness as "activity of the soul in accordance with virtue" is stated as the conclusion of an analogical argument that might be condensed as follows: Just as good lyre-playing consists in an excellence of the function exhibited by lyre-playing, and the same is true in all other cases of the kind, so happiness consists in activity according to virtue, which is the appropriate excellence of the rational function of the soul. A man is happy, then, if he continues to function well in terms of natural teleology up to the end of his life, provided he is furnished with sufficient external goods and does not suffer great misfortunes.

The definition of happiness as "activity of the soul in accordance with virtue" is repeated several times in Book I of the *Nicomachean Ethics,* and occurs also in *Magna Moralia* and the *Eudemian Ethics.* In Book X of the *Nicomachean Ethics,* the formula undergoes a change, viz.:

> If happiness is activity in accordance with virtue, it is reasonable that it should be in accordance with the highest virtue; and this will be that of the best thing in us. Whether it be reason or something else that is this element which is thought to be our natural ruler and guide and to take thought of things noble and divine, whether it be itself also divine or only the most

[24] *Ibid.,* 1098a17–19.

divine element in us, the activity of this in accordance with its proper virtue will be perfect happiness. That this activity is contemplative we have already said.[25]

This *perfect* happiness will correspond to the best element in us, which is theoretic reason, and will consist in the activity of this highest part of the soul. The division of the functions of the soul is as follows:

Parts of the Soul	Divisions of the Soul	Activities of the Soul
Rational	Theoretic, contemplative ...	Philosophy and science
	Practical, calculative	Moral virtue and art
Irrational	Animal, sensitive	Movement, sensation
	Plant, nutritive	Vegetative economy

Man, standing at the apex of the hierarchy of biological forms, exercises rational as well as irrational functions, whereas other animals are capable of only sensitive and nutritive operations, and plants of only nutritive. The higher function depends on the lower ones, with the exception of the highest; the activity of theoretic reason is said to be independent of bodily conditions. This would permit this part of the soul to be immortal,[26] yet, in fact, Aristotle refers to immortality as something "impossible."[27] And this verdict seems to be in accord with the Aristotelian view that the soul is the inner meaning of the body's movement.

In Book I of the *Nicomachean Ethics*, all these functions are said to contribute to happiness, except the nutritive. The reason given is that the nutritive process is passive, does not act on impulse, but depends on the supply of food, and therefore is not capable of virtue. Happiness, however, is activity in accordance with virtue. Moreover, the nutritive part of the soul is not human: it does not obey reason.[28] On the other hand, Aristotle does list health as a constituent of happiness, or as one of the contributing goods. An Aristotelian, therefore, might reasonably hold that the nutritive function does make its contribution, but since it is not directly voluntary, as virtue is, it cannot be a part of happiness, regarded as a creative achievement.

In Book X, Aristotle might seem to be saying that it is contemplation alone that yields happiness; this is how he is often interpreted. We find him arguing that, since theoretic reason is the most distinctive part of the human soul, it is also the highest and best, and its proper virtue will be the

---

25 *Ibid.,* 1177a11–17.
26 See *op. cit., On the Soul,* 430a20–25; and *Metaphysics,* 1070a26.
27 *Ibid., Nicomachean Ethics,* 1111b23.
28 See *ibid., Eudemian Ethics,* 1219b38–43.

crown of human life. The objects of theoretic reason—the objects of philosophy and the sciences—are also better, *i.e.*, eternal and more intelligible. Moreover, "we think happiness has pleasure mingled with it, but the activity of philosophic wisdom is admittedly the pleasantest of virtuous activities."[29] Philosophic activity, or contemplation, is also more self-sufficient than the exercise of the moral virtues, for to be just or temperate or courageous you require occasions and other men, whereas to contemplate these are not needed. It is true that the philosopher, like other men, must have food, shelter, and the like, but, once these requirements are assured, he is independent of other men, according to Aristotle. The disinterested quest of knowledge also seems to be the only activity that is "loved for its own sake," whereas statecraft, war, and all other activities are for the sake of some ulterior end. And happiness, Aristotle says, "is thought to depend on leisure; for we are busy that we may have leisure, and make war that we may live in peace." Summing up the argument, he states:

> So if among virtuous actions political and military actions are distinguished by nobility and greatness, and these are unleisurely and aim at an end and are not desirable for their own sake, but the activity of reason, which is contemplative, seems both to be superior in serious worth and to aim at no end beyond itself, and to have its pleasure proper to itself (and this augments the activity), and the self-sufficiency, leisureliness, unweariedness . . . and all other attributes ascribed to the supremely happy man are evidently those connected with this activity, it follows that this will be the complete happiness of man, if it be allowed a complete term of life.[30]

But the account of happiness in Book X is not inconsistent with the account in Book I. It is not another theory but the development of the same theory. It does contend that happiness is contemplation simply, but that "complete" "perfect" "supreme" happiness is achieved by contemplation, and that this life is *more* self-sufficient and leisurely, and devoted to the "best" objects, and is "pleasantest" and "happiest." The terms are comparative or superlative throughout, and do not exclude a lesser happiness, which Aristotle explicitly recognizes. "In a secondary degree," he says, "the life in accordance with the other kind of virtue [moral or practical virtue] is happy; for the activities in accordance with this befit our human estate."[31] Book I does not discuss the contemplative life or the happiness that arises from it, but promises[32] to do so later. Book X fulfills the promise.

Book I, however, does point to the limitations of a life devoted to honor

[29] *Ibid.*, *Nicomachean Ethics*, 1177a24–25.
[30] *Ibid.*, 1177b16–25.
[31] *Ibid.*, 1178a9–10.
[32] *Ibid.*, 1096a4.

and the practical virtues alone. We read that "people of superior refinement and of active disposition identify happiness with honour; for this is, roughly speaking, the end of the political life." But this political life, Aristotle remarks,

> seems too superficial to be what we are looking for, since it is thought to depend on those who bestow honour rather than on him who receives it, but the good we divine to be something proper to a man and not easily taken from him.[33]

And, in Book IV, a very unattractive picture is drawn of "the proud man," *i.e.*, the man who, possessing all the practical virtues in full measure, gives a correspondingly high estimate of his worth, and seems continually conscious of his superiority.

> Now the proud man, since he deserves the most, must be good in the highest degree. . . . And greatness in every virtue would seem to be the characteristic of a proud man. . . . Pride, then, seems to be a sort of crown of the virtues . . . the proud man is concerned with honours; yet he will bear himself with moderation towards wealth and power, whatever may befall him. . . . For not even towards honour does he bear himself as if it were a very great thing. . . . He does not run into trifling dangers, nor is he fond of danger, because he honours few things; but he will face great dangers. . . . And he is the sort of man to confer benefits, but he is ashamed of receiving them; for one is the mark of a superior, the other of an inferior.[34]

This account of the proud man seems consistent with Aristotle's emphasis on proportion and mean. A man of honor and virtue on a grand scale should be mindful of his true worth as he is mindful of the lesser worth of other men. If he respects virtue, he must respect himself superlatively; if the difference between excellence and baseness is of supreme importance, the sense of it should govern his life. Yet we may suspect that Aristotle's portrait is partly satirical. Perhaps he meant to suggest that the proud man, after all, is absurdly incomplete, that no degree of practical virtue can make up for the lack of theoretic interest and philosophic activity, that leisure cannot be profitably spent in self-esteem, but needs the discipline of impersonal knowledge which is more important than any man. The practical virtue of humor is also lacking to the proud man, but this may spring from the same philosophical deficiency; for humor for Aristotle is intellectual—the ability to perceive incongruities that do not involve pain or moral turpitude.

The brief definition of happiness we have so far considered makes no

[33] *Ibid.*, 1095b23–26.
[34] *Ibid.*, 1123b28–1124b10.

mention of the social dimension. But if happiness in Aristotle's account is self-sufficient in the sense that it "lacks nothing," he does not mean by self-sufficient

> that which is sufficient for a man by himself, for one who lives a solitary life, but also for parents, children, wife, and in general for his friends and fellow citizens, since man is born for citizenship.[35]

And, indeed, the *Nicomachean Ethics* is addressed mainly to the legislator, whose task will be to frame laws necessary for the promotion of virtue and happiness. Nor is the contemplative man as detached and self-sufficient as some of Aristotle's comments might suggest. He also, presumably, needs family and friends as other men do, and his contemplations are not self-contained and useless. In the *Politics*, Aristotle remarks:

> If we are right in our views, and happiness is assumed to be virtuous activity, the active life will be the best, both for every city collectively, and for individuals. Not that a life of action must necessarily have relation to others, as some persons think, nor are those ideas only to be regarded as practical which are pursued for the sake of practical results, but much more the thoughts and contemplations which are independent and complete in themselves; since virtuous activity, and therefore a certain kind of action, is an end, and even in the case of external actions the directing mind is most truly said to act.[36]

For, if theoretical ideas are not creative but sterile, God himself would not be perfect. The same active life, he concludes, "is best for each individual, and for states and for mankind collectively."[37] Thus, Werner Jaeger can say that Aristotle

> is incomparably Greek when he declares that there must be truth in the view that "he who does nothing cannot do well." . . . Clearly Aristotle can combine the philosopher's ideal life with this view of the purpose of state and society only by representing philosophic contemplation as itself a sort of creative "action." Here again he is opening up new roads, and making a new tie to replace Plato's shattered synthesis of knowledge and life. The activity of the creative mind is—building. . . . He now places himself in the midst of active life, and comes forward as an architect of thoughts . . . to build a state in which this intellectual form of action may obtain recognition and become effective as the crown of all human activities that further the common good.[38]

[35] *Ibid.*, 1097b8–11.
[36] *Op. cit.*, Politics, 1325b14–25.
[37] *Ibid.*, 1325b31–32.
[38] *Aristotle, Fundamentals of the History of His Development*, p. 282.

HAPPINESS AS ACTIVITY

It is easy to see why Aristotle makes happiness an activity rather than a state or disposition. The good or end of a thing, in his teleological world view, is its functioning well according to its nature, and functioning is activity. Second, happiness cannot be a disposition, as virtue is, for a man can have a virtue without exercising it. "For the state of mind may exist without producing any good result, as in a man who is asleep or in some other way inactive, but the activity cannot; for one who has the activity will of necessity be acting, and acting well."[39] Aristotle thus agrees with the Stoics that happiness involves virtue, but insists that it is an activity, not a state of mind.

The activity that makes for happiness is that of the soul, but the soul in Aristotle's view is not something separable from the body,[40] nor does it long, like the Platonic soul, to escape from the prison house of the body and fly away into the empyrean. This would be impossible, for the soul is "the essential whatness" of the body[41] as well as the source, by way of its desires, of the body's motion. It is also said to be the inner meaning of the body's motion, and the principle of its functioning. Thus "if the eye had a soul it would be vision." It is also like the axeness of the axe; "if this disappeared from it, it would have ceased to be an axe, except in name"[42] and vice versa, of course. All the affections of the soul, even thinking—as far as it involves imagination—depend on the body, *i.e.*, cease when the body is destroyed.

The activity of the soul that means happiness thus is inseparable from the body and the body's needs. The alienation of the soul from the body is healed, with the result that happiness now belongs to this world alone. The goods of the soul—external goods and those that relate to the body, as well as those belonging peculiarly to the soul itself—are all either constitutive of or instrumental to happiness. The well-functioning of the soul, at all levels except the nutritive, is constitutive.

Since happiness is "activity of the soul in accordance with virtue," it consists of voluntary actions, *i.e.*, actions that are desired and also in a man's power to do or not to do.[43] It is thus impossible to be involuntarily happy, for a man compelled to be virtuous against his will would not be virtuous, though he might appear to be so. Mixed acts—partly voluntary and partly

---

[39] *Op. cit., Nicomachean Ethics,* 1099a1–3.
[40] See *ibid., On the Soul,* 403a–b.
[41] See *ibid.,* 412b12.
[42] *Ibid.,* 412b14.
[43] See *ibid., Nicomachean Ethics,* 1109b30–1110a19.

involuntary—however, belong to happy and unhappy lives. A captain who jettisons his cargo in a storm at sea, as in Aristotle's example, is the knowing cause of his action, though it is not what he desires. That is, he *chooses* something that is undesirable in itself, but is desirable in view of the likely consequences of abstaining from the sacrifice, namely, the loss of the vessel and all on board.

Choice is always voluntary, according to Aristotle, but the voluntary need not involve choice. Animals and children act voluntarily, but not by choice.[44] Whereas volition is desire for things in our power, choice is *"deliberate* desire of things in our own power."[45] Whereas in volition we either do or do not do an act that is available to us, in choice we deliberate between alternative acts that are available, and the act we choose is the outcome of that deliberation. Deliberation, however, is more than the clash of desires; it always involves thoughts or reasons. But reason is not all on one side of an issue and pure desire on the other. The objects we deliberate about can *all* have their reason or rationale, and the role of reason is not simply, as in Plato's allegory of the charioteer, to curb and bridle unruly desires, though it does this too. Reason reproves some desires, but it also sanctions or encourages others, and since it is desire alone that moves the body, it must cooperate with desire to get results.

It is the will, to be sure, that enacts the verdict of deliberation, but is will something different from desire? "Will . . . impulse, and appetite," *On the Motion of Animals* states, "are all three forms of desire, while purpose belongs both to intellect and to desire."[46] The will that commands after choice has been made is thus a kind of desire, and not a separate faculty. Although Aristotle anticipates the later theory of free will, he is in this respect out of line with it. The indeterminacy of nature, as seen by him, leaves open real alternatives for choice, but it is natural desire (the efficient cause of action) instructed by reason (the final cause), that does the choosing. The partnership of desire and reason in choice can be expressed by saying that choice is the work of desiderative reason or, alternatively, of deliberative desire.[47]

[44] See *ibid.,* 1111b4–9.
[45] *Ibid.,* 1113a11–12. (Italics added.)
[46] *Ibid., On the Motion of Animals,* 701a23–24.
[47] Plato, though he relies on the ability of men to make responsible choices as much as Aristotle does, is a thorough determinist. Choice in moral issues is strictly determined by the agent's state of knowledge at the time of choice. If he knows enough, he will infallibly choose to do what is right, but if he is not really *certain* what he ought to do, he may very likely follow some wayward desire and do what is wrong. In the next chapter we point out that whether Plato's or Aristotle's theory of choice should turn out to be the more adequate, the issue probably has few practical consequences, and a decision between the two theories of happiness will not turn upon this point.

The dualism of reason and desire is further eroded in an interesting passage in *Magna Moralia* dealing with happiness, which may represent, according to Ross, a further development of Aristotle's thought:

> Speaking generally, it is not the case, as the rest of the world would have us think, that reason is the principle and guide of virtue, but rather the *feelings*. For there must first be produced in us (as indeed is the case) an irrational impulse to the right, and then later on reason must put the question to vote and decide. One may see this from the case of children and in those who live without reason. For in these, apart from reason, there spring up first, impulses of the feelings toward right, and reason supervening later and giving its vote the same way is the cause of right action. But if they have received from reason the principle that leads to right, the feelings do not necessarily follow and consent thereto, but often oppose it. Wherefore a right disposition of the feelings seems to be the principle that leads to virtue rather than the reason.[48]

Virtue comes about

> when reason being in a good condition is commensurate with the passions, these possessing their proper virtue, and the passions with reason. . . . If, then, the reason be in a bad condition, and the passions not, there will not be virtue owing to the failure of reason (for virtue consists in both).[49]

This Aristotelian account of the interplay of desires and reasons in choice is consistent with a great deal that Aristotle says about particular moral virtues, and the importance of early training and the formation of good habits and a moral character. It can throw new light on the question of how far the virtues are a deliberate choice. Aristotle states flatly that virtue "is a state of character concerned with choice,"[50] but he also leaves no doubt that the virtuous man is a man of virtuous habits. Insofar as virtue is a habit, however, choice is no longer needed; the habits of justice, temperance, etc., suffice. Aristotle's resolution that in the acquiring of virtuous habits deliberation is necessary, but that habits once formed can keep a man to the right course unless, perhaps, exceptional situations arise.[51] Even in the process of creating good habits, where choice plays an essential part, training of desires in youth, so crucial in Aristotle's view, is said to prepare favorable soil for right reason and choice. Virtuous behavior does not always require choice, it would seem, though it is, of course, always voluntary.

The role assigned to choice, volition, desire, and reason—natural func-

---

[48] *Ibid., Magna Moralia,* 1206b18–29.
[49] *Ibid.,* 1206b10–16.
[50] *Ibid., Nicomachean Ethics,* 1106b36.
[51] But habits themselves, as in William James's *Principles of Psychology,* are understood as flexible, selective, and adaptive.

tions of the soul—gives color and contour to Aristotle's theory of happiness, and also, as we shall see, to those of some later philosophers.

HAPPINESS AND VIRTUE

Aristotle's theory displays a bold range of concrete specification unequaled by any other theory except, perhaps, that of Thomas Aquinas. Its strength, that of telling us a great deal about happiness, is also its weakness, for unless the specifications imply one another, the chance of their all being true or acceptable diminishes with their number. But this disadvantage is overcome insofar as Aristotle's treatment is systematic. To keep in mind how far Aristotle distinguishes the kind of activities that make up happiness, it will be well to take a look at the table of moral virtues. With a few important exceptions they are "means" between "extremes"—both vicious.

THE MORAL OR PRACTICAL VIRTUES

Excess	Mean	Defect	Activity[52]
Rashness	Courage	Cowardice	Meeting danger
Profligacy	Temperance	Insensibility	Sensuous enjoyment
Prodigality	Liberality	Stinginess	Giving
Vulgarity	Magnificence	Meanness	Giving, on a grand scale
Vainglory	Self-respect	Humility	Self-love
Excess ambition	(Moderation)	Lack of ambition	Seeking honors, etc.
Irascibility	Gentleness	Poor spiritedness	Aggressiveness
Boastfulness	Truthfulness	Self-deprecation	Truth-telling about oneself
Buffoonery	Wittiness	Dullness	Being humorous
Obsequiousness	Friendliness	Coldness	Being friendly
Bashfulness	Modesty	Shamelessness	Being ashamed
Envy	Righteous indignation	Malice	Reacting affectively to the good and bad fortune of others

The word "virtue" in common English usage often means no more than acceptable sexual conduct and is rarely applied to men. What Aristotle had in mind is more akin to Chaucer's *vertu* when Chaucer spoke of the April showers,

Of which *vertu* engendred is the flour [flower].

The virtue required for happiness is the strength, potency, the excellence of a thing, and the excellence lies in the mean. This explains why insensibility, humility, poor spiritedness, and dullness are classed as vices—

---

[52] Though some of the items in this column are primarily emotions, Aristotle recognizes that we must judge men by their actions and it is clear that virtues, as observed, are activities.

minor vices. They are shortcomings in excellence, and represent failure to exercise powers proper to man in different areas of activity. With regard to insensibility, Aristotle states that people who fall short in the pleasures of the senses (involving contact) "are hardly found"; but many recent writers would certainly deny this, agreeing with Aristotle's classification rather than his commentary on it. But Aristotle regards humility as "commoner and worse" than pride or vainglory, for people who think less of themselves than they deserve "stand back even from noble actions and undertakings, deeming themselves unworthy, and from external goods no less."[53] This judgment would be endorsed by many contemporary psychologists. Dullness, or the chronic difficulty of appreciating humor, also would be regarded as a serious psychological deficiency, though not as a moral fault. Aristotle himself sometimes insists on this distinction (see, for example 1234a24–26), but the table of virtues before us illustrates the extent to which moral and psychological excellence are merged together, or are regarded as the same.

If the mean were a point lying equidistant from the extremes, "happiness" might be much easier to find. The quantitative aspect is of great importance, but is encumbered by complications. The mean is relative to a man's nature, position, wealth, and circumstances. A naturally timid man and a naturally rash one should both aim at the mean of courage, but need not reach the same point of excellence; one man's virtue, since it must be within his power, cannot and need not be the same as another's. Men oppositely inclined—to prodigality or stinginess, to ambition or to the lack of it, etc.—can reach virtue, but it will be a virtue that allows for and reflects their individual differences. This allowance for individual differences contrasts sharply with the uniformity taken for granted by traditional theories of virtue and happiness, and relates Aristotle to modern thinkers such as J. S. Mill and John Dewey.

The mean is also relative to the character of the extremes, and is usually more opposed to one than to the other. We have already seen that humility is more opposed to self-respect than is vainglory or pride. Similarly, cowardice, profligacy, and irascibility are more opposed to their means than are the corresponding extremes. And the mean is likewise relative to the right principle, object, and occasion. What the mean of courage is in a given instance will depend on the principle involved, the dangers, the alternatives, and what one expects to gain. It is a mistake to risk a great deal in small issues. As to emotions toward others, such as fear, anger, and pity, Aristotle says we are "to feel them at the right times, with reference to the right objects, towards the right people, with the right motive, and in the right way."[54] We find out what is right, in the end, by "perception."

[53] *Op. cit.*, 1125a33, 27–28.
[54] *Ibid.*, 1106b20–23.

Some of the means have special complications. Righteous indignation is not really the mean between envy and malice, as Aristotle shows. Malice is not deficient indignation but delight in the misfortune of others. Moreover, Aristotle is quick to point out that some things, such as murder and spite, are bad in themselves, and not only when they occur in excessive or deficient amounts. Bertrand Russell, ridiculing Aristotle's theory of the mean, tells the story of a mayor who boasted that, during his term of office, he had always tried to maintain a proper mean between partiality and impartiality.[55] As a criticism of Aristotle this misses the point, since Aristotle does not consider justice a mean, in any strict sense, but rather an extreme opposed to injustice. Just as murder and spite are bad in themselves, so justice is good in itself. Another virtue that is said to be an extreme that has no excess is the special friendship—or romantic love, as it might be called—that we confer upon a few select persons. The more of this kind of love the better.

The many qualifications that Aristotle is obliged to make clutter his *system* but bring his theory of virtue and happiness closer to the complexities of moral life and judgments. Justice and friendship are especially important in relation to happiness, and Aristotle gives a long account of both. We shall have occasion to discuss them later in connection with the views of other authors. Our purpose here is merely to display at a glance the remarkable amplitude and detail of his account of "the end of human nature."

Happiness and Pleasure

If happiness consists in all this multiplicity of virtuous activities, how can Aristotle say, as he does in Book VII of the *Nicomachean Ethics,* that pleasure is also a good in itself and perhaps even the chief good? After a critical review of the arguments against the goodness of pleasure, Aristotle states

> that it does not follow from these grounds that pleasure is not a good, or even the chief good.[56]

When he has answered these arguments, he concludes:

> And indeed the fact that all things, both brutes and men, pursue pleasure is an indication of its being somehow the chief good.[57]

Is pleasure, then, as well as happiness, the chief good? It is certainly inseparable from happiness:

[55] See *A History of Western Philosophy,* p. 174.
[56] *Op. cit.,* 1152b26–27.
[57] *Ibid.,* 1153b25–28.

It is evident also that if pleasure, *i.e.*, the activity of our faculties, is not a good, it will not be the case that the happy man lives a pleasant life; for to what end should he need pleasure, if it is not a good but the happy man may even live a painful life? For pain is neither an evil nor a good, if pleasure is not; why then should he avoid it? Therefore, too, the life of the good men will not be pleasanter than that of any one else, if his activities are not more pleasant.[58]

Activities will be pleasant whenever they are "unimpeded." Pleasures are a kind of glow which completes and perfects an activity whenever it represents the unimpeded and best use of our faculties. So intimate is the bond between pleasure and the optimum use of our faculties that men, in desiring life and its activities, must also desire the pleasure that completes them:

> . . . whether we choose life for the sake of pleasure or pleasure for the sake of life is a question we may dismiss for the present. For they seem to be bound up together and not to admit of separation, since without activity pleasure does not arise, and every activity is completed by the attendant pleasure.[59]

It makes very little difference whether we say (a) men desire their activities for the sake of pleasure, or (b) men desire pleasure for the sake of the activities they accompany.

The second statement has an air of paradox. It disappears when we take note of Aristotle's further thesis that pleasures are of different kinds, corresponding to the different kinds of activities they accompany. The "intellectual" pleasure of the musician, the "bodily" pleasure of the voluptuary, and the "contemplative" pleasure of the philosopher are all very different. The voluptuary does not desire the pleasure of the philosopher or of the musician, for this would mean engaging in activities for which he has no aptitude or liking. The philosopher would be eventually bored by the pleasures of the voluptuary, and perhaps repelled, for the activities from which they arise are unsuitable to him. Whatever else the philosopher is, William James claims, he cannot be a "lady-killer."

Thus to desire pleasures that match the activities we love is much the same as to desire those activities that match the pleasures we love. When one is chosen for its own sake, it is also chosen for the sake of the other, for, though distinct, they are inseparable. The plausibility of Aristotle's doctrine gains if we try to describe the pleasure of the voluptuary, the musician, the statesman, or the philosopher. We cannot do so without

---

58 *Ibid.*, 1154a1–7.
59 *Ibid.*, 1175a17–22.

describing the corresponding activities, and, if we do not understand these vocations, we cannot understand the pleasure they afford.

Pleasure, Aristotle says, is a glow or radiance that accompanies well-functioning of the senses and rational faculties. It is like "the bloom of youth." It is the flower of a virtuous life, but it is more than this.

> For an activity is intensified by its proper pleasure, since each class of things is better judged of and brought to precision by those who engage in the activity with pleasure; *e.g.*, it is those who enjoy geometrical thinking that become geometers and grasp the various propositions better, and, similarly, those who are fond of music or of building, and so on, make progress in their proper function by enjoying it; so the pleasures intensify the activities, and what intensifies a thing is proper to it, but things different in kind have properties different in kind.[60]

That pleasures are peculiarly united to the activities they accompany, Aristotle says, is indicated by the fact that pleasures alien to a given activity do not facilitate but hinder it. A philosopher who loves the flute will lose the thread of his argument when he hears flute music. And so also in other cases. Alien pleasures, in fact, disturb an activity quite as much as pains do. Their specific nature conflicts with the specific nature of the activity.

Although Aristotle carefully answers the arguments of the disparagers of pleasure, and affirms on his own that pleasure is good and a good in itself—almost the chief good—he nevertheless breaks with hedonism decisively. He holds that pleasures are of different *kinds*, that they differ as do the activities they accompany. Second, he maintains that men desire and treasure, not just any old pleasure but those that accompany the activities they love.

Hedonism, on the other hand, asserts that pleasures do not differ in quality, but only in quantity, *i.e.*, in duration and intensity. Thus, the consistent hedonist will insist that the voluptuary's pleasure is the same as the philosopher's, every bit as good, or even better if it is more intense or lasts longer. For Aristotle, on the contrary, pleasures vary qualitatively as well as quantitatively, and are not additive. "The greatest pleasure of the greatest number" would be an impossible idea. Second, men aim at and cherish, not indiscriminate pleasure but only the kinds that tint the activities of their desire and vocation.

Pleasures differ for Aristotle qualitatively; they differ in worthiness. How are we to judge which are best? They bear the mark of different activities they attend. Those that accompany the highest and most distinctive human activities will be most estimable. The pleasures of the senses are good; those of practical reason are higher; those of philosophic contemplation and

---

[60] *Ibid.*, 1175a31–38.

scientific investigation are best, and verge on divinity. The hedonist also recommends some pleasurable activities over others, but only because they yield a greater balance of pleasure over pain. Aristotle can make some use of this criterion, but it becomes very difficult owing to the qualitative differentiation of the pleasures.

Desires, like pleasures, are specific to the activities to which they relate. The desire to listen to music and the desire to solve a scientific problem differ with their objects.

> But the pleasures involved in activities are more proper to them than the desires, for the latter are separated both in time and in nature, while the former are close to the activities, and so hard to distinguish from them.[61]

It might seem that, since the desire envisages the activity it desires, it would resemble the activity more than the pleasure does. But Aristotle is thinking here of another characteristic of desire—its striving, lack, incompleteness, its character of being *for* something else. Pleasure, on the other hand, is complete in itself, and nothing is wanting to it unless it be more of the same. At the same time it shares the nature of the activity it accompanies by suffusing and, as it were, merging with it. The completeness of pleasure is, however, only for the moment, and it is essentially intermittent, as the hedonist must concede. The completeness of happiness embodies certain guarantees for the future and belongs essentially to a whole lifetime. It is the final goal of men's desire, at least in the sense that nothing less would satisfy.

THE PLACE OF FORTUNE AND WORLDLY GOODS

Solon's saying that a man cannot be called happy until he is dead cannot be true, Aristotle says, because happiness is an activity. Yet there is some truth in it, for how could we say that a man had had a happy life if after his death his children are destroyed or disgraced? Aristotle's answer could be put as follows: If we imagine the dead man alive and capable of responding to the calamities of his descendants, we see his happiness ruined; if not, we say that he died happy, not knowing what would befall.

Reverses of fortune within a man's lifetime, however, can crush his happiness if they are great enough,

> for they both bring pain with them and hinder many activities. Yet even in these nobility shines through, when a man bears with resignation many great misfortunes, not through insensibility to pain but through nobility and greatness of soul.[62]

61 *Ibid.*, 1175b30–34.
62 *Ibid.*, 1100b29–33.

Virtue thus is not sufficient to happiness, though it enables us to bear major reverses with dignity. On the first point Aristotle disagrees with the Stoics; on the second he agrees with them.

The man who is happy, accordingly, lives "in accordance with complete virtue and is sufficiently equipped with external goods, not for some chance period but throughout a complete life."[63] What these external goods are is already clear from the table of the moral virtues. If the happy man is to have *"complete"* virtue, he must be generous, which requires a surplus of goods beyond his own needs, as does also temperance, for this virtue, like the others, is voluntary. The happy man must have courage, too, and this requires arms to defend himself or to serve his country in the army. Nor can he enjoy the urbane friendship of equals, which is the highest type of friendship, without an assured income. And since "plenty of children" and "good children" are important to happiness, he must be able to maintain them. For all the moral virtues he will need an independence and equipoise impossible in the slave and even in the artisan. The work of the artisan is "degrading," and "no man can practise virtue who is living the life of a mechanic or laborer."[64] The slave, in addition to this disability, has no will of his own (as long, as Aristotle says, as he remains and is treated as a slave). Virtue, then, is impossible without independence and leisure,[65] and this is especially true of the intellectual virtue of the philosopher.[66]

"The first principle of all action is leisure," Aristotle says in the *Politics*. "Both [occupation and leisure] are required, but leisure is better than occupation and is its end."[67]

> But leisure of itself gives pleasure and happiness and enjoyment of life, which are experienced, not by the busy man, but by those who have leisure. For he who is occupied has in view some end which he has not attained; but happiness is an end, since all men deem it to be accompanied with pleasure and not pain.[68]

This sharp division of means and ends has been the target of much modern criticism.

THE ATTAINABILITY OF HAPPINESS

It is clear that slaves and artisans, at least the lower artisans, cannot pretend to happiness, though these classes are, of course, necessary to the

---

[63] *Ibid.,* 1101a15–17.
[64] *Ibid., Politics,* 1278a18–19.
[65] See *ibid.,* 1329a1–3.
[66] See *ibid., Nicomachean Ethics,* 1134a–24.
[67] *Ibid., Politics,* 1337b33.
[68] *Ibid.,* 1338a2–7.

state. Children are also incapable of happiness,[69] not only because their lives are so incomplete, but because reason in them is not far enough developed to permit of deliberation and rational choice,[70] and they are lacking in self-control.

Aristotle's views about slaves and artisans reflect conditions in Greece and in the ancient world, and so also his opinion of women, for women at the time were trained to their household duties, but received no liberal education. He does not explicitly say that women are incapable of happiness, but his opinion of them casts some doubt on their eligibility. For "the male is by nature superior, and the female inferior; and the one rules, and the other is ruled."[71] Children are also inferior to the male, but the inferiority of women is permanent. Whereas the child's deliberative faculty, needed for the exercise of virtue, is immature, that of women is said to be "without authority,"[72] *i.e.*, if she hears the voice of reason she does not heed it. Thus Aristotle emphasizes the importance of training women to perform their duties, as children and servants are trained, and their happiness, it would appear, is of a lower kind.

Other citizens, heads of households, men of property and leisure to whom fortune is relatively kind have happiness within their power, and it is thought to be very generally shared,

> for all who are not maimed as regards their potentiality for virtue may win it by a certain kind of study and care.[73]

This, indeed, follows, as Aristotle remarks, from his definition of happiness, at least when his provisos about external goods and fortune have been added.

THE HAPPY MAN AND THE HAPPY STATE

Plato's "perfect state" was excogitated because only in such a state would one be apt to find a just man. Virtue and happiness, as Aristotle conceives them, also presuppose a well-ordered, stable state in the government of which citizens take a part. He goes as far as to say that ". . . the happiness of the individual is the same as that of the state . . . no one denies that they are the same.[74] For those who think wealth is the happiness of the individual think it also the happiness of the state,

[69] See *ibid., Magna Moralia,* 1185a4–5.
[70] See *ibid., Politics,* 1260a10–15.
[71] *Ibid.,* 1254b13–15.
[72] *Ibid.,* 1260a13.
[73] *Ibid., Nicomachean Ethics,* 1099b18–20.
[74] *Ibid., Politics,* 1324a5–8.

while they who approve an individual for his virtue say that the more virtuous a city is, the happier it is.[75]

But how, in terms of Aristotle's definition of happiness, could anything but an individual be happy? Aristotle replies that the best form of government is one "in which every man, whoever he is, can act best and live happily,"[76] and he later characterizes the best governed city as that which has "the greatest opportunity of obtaining happiness,"[77] *i.e.*, the citizens have the greatest opportunity. Aristotle does not hold, as do some modern thinkers, that the state is a super-person who can be happy in himself. It is not really the state that is happy and virtuous, though Aristotle sometimes uses this language, but rather the statesman who directs its course, and the citizens who obey.

It is noteworthy also that the best state provides the *opportunity* of obtaining happiness, and does not undertake to *make* men happy. Aristotle's thought at this point thus appears to anticipate the famous right to "the pursuit of happiness" which makes its appearance in the American Declaration of Independence. For Aristotle, however, it was not a "natural right" but the political ideal, nor did the term "happiness" in the Declaration bear the full Aristotelian meaning. The difference between the Aristotelian idea and that of Jefferson is very significant but so also, we shall see, is the agreement.

Although Aristotle holds that the best government will provide citizens with "the opportunity of obtaining happiness," he often speaks, in a different vein, of the need for making men virtuous by force—by laws and punishments. It is difficult to endue youth with virtue, he says, if they are not

. . . brought up under right laws; for to live temperately and hardily is not pleasant to most people, especially when they are young. For this reason their nurture and occupations should be fixed by law; for they will not be painful when they have become customary.[78]

"Nurture and attention," or teaching and admonition, will not suffice. They must become habituated to virtue, and, for this, laws and punishments are necessary, for "most people obey necessity rather than argument, and punishments rather than the sense of what is noble."[79]

Aristotle naturally praises the Spartan state, which alone has taken an interest in the training and occupations of its citizens.[80] The Spartan

[75] *Ibid.*, 1324a12–13.
[76] *Ibid.*, 1324a24.
[77] *Ibid.*, 1332a6.
[78] *Ibid., Nicomachean Ethics*, 1179b33–36.
[79] *Ibid.*, 1180a3–4.
[80] See *ibid.*, 1180a25–28.

women, however, are badly in need of discipline. The constitution of Sparta succeeded in making the men hardy and temperate, but it neglected to control the women, who, in consequence, grew lax and luxurious, and a danger to the state. Aristotle holds that, because of native differences, women need the discipline of the state even more than men.

Aristotle's doctrine of virtue and happiness thus shows a tension between two opposing tendencies. (a) Virtue, to be virtue, must be deliberately chosen for its own sake and proceed from a good character,[81] nor can happiness be against one's will. (b) On the other hand, virtuous behavior is said to be induced by habituation, compelled by laws and punishments, without proceeding from choice or character; and force, with most people, is the only thing that works. Hence there is need of legislation to produce virtue. But how can such virtue be the real thing? The issue is complex. Part of the answer is: If (a) is *choice* of virtue and (b) is habituation to it induced by laws and punishments, then (b) is usually a preliminary stage and facilitation of (a) and is especially important in youth. Insofar as (b) prevails and (a) fails, there is neither virtue nor happiness, strictly speaking, though there may be order and discipline within the state. We shall see that the tension between (a) and (b) reappears in other theories of happiness.

Although, in Book X of the *Nicomachean Ethics*, Aristotle says that happiness extends "just so far as contemplation does," in the *Politics*, as we have seen, he can insist that if theoretical ideas are not creative but sterile, God himself would not be perfect. Even philosophic contemplation is an activity, and one of its issues is thoughts that could build the state and counsels that should reach the ear of the statesman. In this way, according to Jaeger, Aristotle combines his early ideal of the contemplative life as the highest with his later conviction that the philosopher has a role in statecraft.

Well-being or happiness, we have noted, is the chief end of the state.[82] The best form of government, in practice, is a mixed polity combining elements of aristocracy and democracy, and this is presumably the order Aristotle thought most likely to produce happiness. The superiority of aristocracy is that the few who rule are wiser and more virtuous; the superiority of democracy is that it gives stability to the state, since, when members of the state have a part in the government, they are more contented and loyal. A mixed polity would combine, in a measure, the advantages of both forms of government. It is interesting to observe, however, that the superiority of aristocracy would be canceled if the citizens of a democracy became more wise and virtuous, or the aristocrats turned out

[81] See *ibid.*, 1105a33.
[82] See *ibid.*, *Politics*, 1278b20–29.

to be less so than was thought; whereas the superiority of democracy is permanent, and could not be matched by any aristocracy. It is not surprising, then, that Aristotle's general definition of the citizen as one "who shares in the government" is, as he says, "best adapted to the citizen of a democracy."[83]

In adverting later to the role of government in producing happiness, or facilitating the pursuit of happiness, we shall have to remember Aristotle's adverse criticism of democracy, but also his recognition, in effect, of the permanent advantage of self-rule.

[83] *Ibid.*, 1275b6.

2

Plato's Concept of Happiness

I N the order of chronology and historical influence, this chapter should have preceded the chapter on Aristotle. The exposition of the Aristotelian theory of happiness has been put first because this theory provides the broadest, most detailed, and clearest framework over against which the distinctive traits of rival theories can be seen and compared.

Plato's theory of happiness anticipates the eudaemonism of Aristotle in important respects, but it is not nearly so definite, elaborate, or complete, and it contains crosscurrents of thought that point in other directions. Although it is basically eudaemonist, it also prefigures the austere Stoical conception of happiness and the mystical views of Plotinus and Augustine.

Since Aristotelian eudaemonism has been described in Chapter 1, but nothing has yet been said about later theories of happiness, it seems best in this chapter to look at Platonic eudaemonism as a variant of the more complete and firmer Aristotelian eudaemonism. Indeed, the two theories are so intimately connected that one can scarcely be understood except in comparison with the other. The present chapter, therefore, consists of an enumeration of points of agreement and disagreement. Plato appears to agree with Aristotle in the following respects:

1. All men desire possession of the good, which is happiness. Thus, Socrates readily agrees with the wise Diotima, in the *Symposium*, that all men love the good and want to possess it, and that what they gain by possessing it is happiness.[1] "All of us desire happiness," and we shall be happy "if we have many good things."[2]

2. Happiness is desired for its own sake—not for the sake of anything else. Socrates agrees that there is not "any need to ask why a man desires happiness; the answer is already final."[3]

3. Though all men desire happiness through possession of the good, one sees the good as moneymaking, another as gymnastics, still another as philosophy.[4] For different men, accordingly, the desired happiness takes different forms. Those who identify happiness with a life devoted to pleasure seeking, to gain, or to ambition are, of course, mistaken, in Plato's view, but he sets great store in education, at least when aided by a native superiority of mind, to correct such erroneous interpretations of happiness.

4. Happiness is the life of virtue, and without virtue there is no happiness. Plato never tires of insisting upon this proposition. The virtue necessary for happiness appears in many passages to be practical, but sometimes it is practical and theoretic as well. The main practical virtues are wisdom—wisdom in the conduct of life—courage, and temperance, while theoretic virtue consists in a passionate supererogatory devotion to (mathematical) science and philosophy.

Again and again Plato argues and assures us that the happy man is the just man,[5] and justice here implies or includes temperance and courage, for it is not possible for the just man to be licentious or cowardly. He argues that justice is something good *in itself*, for it is analogous to the health of the body. It is identified in common judgment with the efficient and successful functioning of the soul, just as injustice is associated with malfunctioning and failure. Thus the happy man chooses justice, no matter what the consequences appear to be. But the consequences are, as a matter of fact, generally of a sort that the vulgar as well as the wise think desirable, while the consequences of acting unjustly are generally the opposite.[6] For just men can live together in amity and trustful cooperation, and each can live with himself, whereas the unjust man can have no friend, not even himself.

It turns out, however, that the happiest man of all is the philosopher-

---

[1] See Benjamin Jowett, *The Dialogues of Plato, Symposium,* 204.
[2] *Ibid., Euthydemus,* 279.
[3] *Ibid., Symposium,* 205.
[4] *Ibid.*
[5] See, for example, *ibid., Laws,* 662; and H. D. P. Lee (trans.), *Plato, The Republic,* 353.
[6] See *The Dialogues of Plato, Euthydemus,* 279–282.

king, who is not only just but possessed of scientific and dialectical knowledge implying complete mastery of his lower nature.

> The supremely happy man is the justest and the best, that is, the philosopher king who can govern himself, and . . . the supremely wretched man is the wickedest and worst.[7]

5. The highest happiness results from the exercise of the highest part of the soul, not in the service of the lower parts but in order to gain knowledge and truth. After the philosophical lover has been accepted by his beloved, Plato says,

> their happiness depends upon their self-control; if the better elements of the mind which lead to order and philosophy prevail, they pass their life here in happiness and harmony . . . nor can human discipline or divine inspiration confer any greater blessing on man than this.[8]

That the highest happiness is achieved by the pursuit of scientific and philosophical knowledge is also clearly implied in the *Republic*, where the philosophers, after lifelong study culminating in the Vision of the Good, must be compelled to forsake the studious life they prefer, and devote themselves to the management of the state that bred them. But will this not be unfair, Glaucon protests. "We shall be compelling them to live a poorer life than they might live." That more or less happiness is what is involved is plainly shown by Socrates' answer: "The object of our legislation . . . is not the welfare of any particular class, but of the whole community."[9] The highest happiness thus is enjoyed by the philosophers—at least until such time as they are compelled to make themselves useful. It is fair to conclude also that the daemonic lover described by Diotima[10] would not be represented as inexorably driven by desire to ever higher forms of beauty if the philosophical happiness were not understood to be the best.

6. There are different types of happiness appropriate to the various orders of society. The aim of the founders of the just state is to provide for the happiness of the whole, including all the necessary classes according to their capacities. How happy the philosopher-rulers, the auxiliaries, and artisans would be under the regimented and restricted conditions laid down in the *Republic*, or in the order set up in the *Laws*, is another question. We shall see later that a number of Platonic provisions and laws, designed to produce justice and happiness in the state, are attacked by Aristotle.

7. Pleasure normally accompanies the practice of virtue, and with pleasure, as with happiness, there is a ranking and gradation. The most

---

7 *Plato, The Republic*, 580.
8 *The Dialogues of Plato, Phaedrus*, 256.
9 *Plato, The Republic*, 519.
10 See *The Dialogues of Plato, Symposium*, 202 ff.

unpleasant life is that of the tyrant—the tyrannical man *after* he has seized power in the state, and the most pleasant life is that of the philosopher. Comparing the rival pleasures of the three types of life—the life of reason, the life of ambition, and the life of gain—Plato concludes that only those who live the life of reason will have the experience to decide which pleasures are best, and this decision is in favor of the rational pleasures.[11]

8. There are thus different *kinds* of pleasure. The pleasures of the licentious man are short-lived, mixed with pain, and fraught with painful consequences, whereas the cognitive pleasures are pure, enduring, and redound to happiness since they encourage a continuance of cognitive activity. Pleasure accompanies the well-functioning of the soul in general, but those pleasures are best that attend its highest functions.

9. Hedonism is decisively rejected. Happiness does not consist in pleasure, or the greatest amount of pleasure obtainable, but in the practice of virtue. Men ought to aim at virtue or the good, not at pleasure. Plato continually condemns "the life of pleasure," meaning a career devoted to an increase of pleasure, and it is sensuous or bodily pleasures that he has in mind. It can be argued that two different points are involved here: One is that our main purpose in life should not be to maximize our bodily pleasures; the other is that our conscious aim or purpose should not be to gain pleasures of any kind, even the best. Our geometrical endeavors should aim at understanding or proving theorems, not at securing the pleasure that may result from the activity. Nevertheless, pleasure and pain are for Plato (as for Aristotle) great instructors of mankind, for whether they are aimed at or not they further or hinder, respectively, the activities with which they are associated.

10. Goods such as health, wealth, and beauty are really good, and thus contribute to happiness, but only if they are wisely employed. They are certainly not "goods in themselves, but the degree of good and evil in them depends on whether they are or are not under the guidance of knowledge; under the guidance of ignorance, they are greater evils than their opposites, inasmuch as they are more able to minister to the evil principle which rules them."[12]

11. Friendship and love contribute to happiness, according to Plato's theory (insofar as it compares with Aristotle's eudaemonism), in three ways: (a) Sexual intercourse is a means to the propagation of the species, to the gaining of immortality through offspring (*Phaedrus*), and is regarded as perhaps a necessary stage in the pilgrimage of the soul to higher loves. (b) Although the pilgrimage ends in the contemplation of beauty itself, or of truth, knowledge and the Good—all divinely impersonal, the

[11] See Plato, *The Republic*, 581–583.
[12] *The Dialogues of Plato, Euthydemus*, 281.

lovers of the *Phaedrus* remain ecstatically united in their vision of beauty, and the life of reason, however pictured, is a deferentially shared and cooperative enterprise. (c) On the level of everyday relations among men, Plato sees friendship essential to happiness—to that of the individual and to that of the state—though he says more about the misery resulting from the disturbance of amity than about its positive contribution. Speaking of the happy people of the island of Atlantis, Plato says that they united "gentleness with wisdom . . . in their intercourse with one another," and thought lightly of the possession of gold and other property . . . and saw clearly that all these goods are increased by virtue and friendship with one another, whereas by too great regard and respect for them, they are lost and friendship with them."[13]

12. The happiness of the whole state is something larger and more important than that in the individual, and individual happiness must therefore be subordinated to the happiness of the state.[14]

13. Moderation of the passions in general is the road to happiness, but the passions for justice and the other practical virtues, *and* for truth and knowledge, have no excess, and are good only insofar as they are *not* moderate.[15]

14. Lastly, the arguments by which Plato supports these contentions are often parallel to those of Aristotle. Thus Plato uses the arts-crafts analogy, as does Aristotle, to show what proper functioning in the human soul is, and concludes that, if it functions according to its nature, it functions well, *i.e.*, excellently or virtuously: the soul is healthy and the man who has it is at least subjectively set for happiness. There is also some agreement in the arguments the two philosophers employ against hedonism, but it will be convenient to defer these comparisons to a later stage of exposition and confrontation.

But Plato's theory of happiness also diverges from that of Aristotle in the following respects: Virtue results in happiness *necessarily*, in Plato's view, and nothing else is required. Neither personal gifts, such as health, strength, beauty; nor external goods, *e.g.*, property and income; nor good fortune of any kind or degree, is needed for happiness. In the *Republic*, Book 2, the Platonic Socrates argues that it is better to be just, though one appears unjust, than to be unjust in fact, though one appears just to all the world. The just man, even under the most unfavorable circumstances imaginable, is bound to be happy, whereas the unjust man, though blessed with every advantage, is bound to be miserable. The most miserable of all

13 *Ibid.*, *Critias*, 120–121.
14 See *Plato, The Republic*, 520.
15 See, for example, *The Dialogues of Plato, Philebus*, 66A.

is the tyrant who can do what he pleases, and be as wicked as he wants. For such a man is sick and at war with himself, and the vulgar freedom he first enjoys soon turns into slavery, so that through fear he is driven to currying favor with his own slaves.[16] Only one thing could be worse—that the tyrant, having the finest personal gifts, and limitless wealth and power, should also be immortal, since then, lacking justice and virtue, his misery will have no end.[17] On the other hand, the just man is happy even though he is engulfed in shipwreck and disaster or is tortured on the rack. Suffering, then, is no bar to happiness; it is a boon if it expiates guilt. "You deemed Archelaus happy, because he was a very great criminal and unpunished," Socrates reminds Polus, while he, Socrates, "maintains that he or any other who like him has done wrong and has not been punished, is, and ought to be, the most miserable of all men; and that the doer of injustice is more miserable than he who suffers."[18]

If the doctrine that virtue and happiness, and wrongdoing and misery, are always inseparable, seems fantastically contrary to human experience, we are reminded that men do sometimes freely announce their offenses and demand punishment, and that martyrs under torture or facing a painful death profess the greatest joy or felicity. Evidently conscience, guilt feelings, or a sense of righteousness can, at times, lift men above the worst sufferings and disasters. It is Plato's claim that this must *always* be so which has been found puzzling or incredible. Of the main theories of happiness in the West, only that of the Stoics has agreed with Plato, that only virtue counts.

That virtue and happiness are inseparable should be taught and indoctrinated, even if it is a lie.

> The view which identifies the pleasant and the just and the good and the noble has an excellent moral and religious tendency. And the opposite view is most at variance with the designs of the legislator, and is, in his opinion, infamous; for no one, if he can help, will be persuaded to do that which gives him more pain than pleasure.[19]

Although Plato speaks of pleasure and pain rather than of happiness and misery, it is likely that he does so because the people who need his guidance most are, in his opinion, those who identify happiness with pleasure, and misery with pain. In the following passage another view of happiness is brought in, viz., "the profitable and gainful." The heaviest penalties, Socrates demands, should be inflicted on anyone who dares to say that the profitable and gainful are not also the just, or that "there are

[16] See Plato, *The Republic*, Book 9.
[17] See *The Dialogues of Plato, Laws*, 661–662.
[18] *Ibid., Gorgias*, 479.
[19] *Ibid., Laws*, 663.

bad men who live pleasant lives."[20] And the legislator will seek to persuade the citizens that the just life is more pleasant, even though it should turn out to be untrue.

> ". . . the lawgiver, who is worth anything, if he ever ventures to tell a lie to the young for their good, could not invent a more useful lie than this, or one which will have a better effect in making them do what is right, not on compulsion but voluntarily.[21]

Plato goes on to justify this stratagem, which in the *Republic* he calls "the noble lie," a lie which the rulers tell the citizens for their own good. The extent of Plato's reforming zeal is a point of considerable interest. The extraordinary doctrine that the virtuous man is *always* happy and the bad one *always* miserable may represent Plato's reforming zeal rather than a conviction to which he believes his argument compels him.

The happiness of the philosopher will be prolonged and perfected in an afterlife. Plato believes that his arguments prove the immortality of the soul, or at least give the philosopher "good hope" that this is so. But the immortality of the ordinary soul will be a wandering from one body to another, because this soul is drawn to bodily pleasures; whereas the soul of the philosopher, which is devoted to the highest forms of knowledge and cares nothing for carnal delights, will escape from the round of births and rebirths, and from the trammels of the body, and will live happily forever in the vision of the true, the good, and the beautiful to which its aspiration bends.[22] The real philosophers will understand how much is to be gained by leaving the body behind. "While we are in the body," they will ask, "and while the soul is infected with the evils of the body," how can our desire for the truth be satisfied?

> For the body is the source of endless trouble to us by reason of the mere requirement of food; and is liable also to diseases which overtake and impede us in the search after true being: it fills us full of loves, and lusts, and fears, and fancies of all kinds, and endless foolery, and . . . takes away the power of thinking at all. Whence come wars, and fightings, and factions? whence but from the body and the lusts of the body? Wars are occasioned by the love of money, and money has to be acquired for the sake and in the service of the body; and by reason of all these impediments we have no time to give to philosophy; and, last and worst of all, even if we are at leisure and betake ourselves to some speculation, the body is always breaking in upon us, causing turmoil and confusion in our inquiries, and so amazing us that we are prevented from seeing the truth.[23]

20 *Ibid.*, 662.
21 *Ibid.*
22 See *ibid.*, *Phaedrus*, 245–249.
23 *Ibid.*, *Phaedo*, 66.

Immortality thus offers the philosopher not only an endless prolongation of his truth-seeking but also a perfecting of his endeavors and the happiness they afford by freeing him from the care and tribulations of the body. Ordinary men also desire immortality, according to Plato, but they satisfy the yearning by producing offspring, while the philosopher is content only as he brings forth brainchildren. Aristotle agrees with Plato that men want their happiness extended indefinitely, but also says that there may be a wish even for impossibilities, that is, for immortality. In limiting human happiness to this life, as in requiring a sufficiency of personal gifts, external goods, and fortune, Aristotle's theory is naturalistic, earthbound, and empirical—a sheer contrast to the other-worldliness of Plato's doctrine, with its heaven-storming daemonism and defiance of natural necessities. But there was also a worldly Plato who could go to great lengths, as is shown by his bland praise of the noble lie, in accepting cynical devices for the good that might come of them.

The polar opposition of human desire and reason, which is usually decisive in Plato, has no serious parallel in Aristotle. In the myth of the charioteer in the *Phaedrus,* desire is the black, ungainly, headstrong horse, both comic and evil, who is thrown into a wild turmoil at the very sight of beauty, and would surely wreck the chariot of the soul were he not bridled by the charioteer (reason), and the good white horse (spirit). Desire, if not entirely evil, is always in need of suppression or restraint, whereas reason would seem to be ever in the right, and never wrong in curbing or silencing his unruly colleague. Although Aristotle himself sometimes talks in this vein, too, his conception of human nature, as we have seen in the last chapter, really effects a unity of reason and desire. Reason does not oppose desire in general, for without desire it is powerless; it is rather one desiderative reason that opposes another desiderative reason. The upshot, as far as happiness is concerned, is that a man becomes happy, not so much by successfully curbing desire as by achieving a sane measure of desire (*i.e.,* desiderative reason) between two more or less vicious extremes—one too much and the other too little. Happiness does not mean conquering one part of our nature; in practical life it means achieving a productive balance of all our natural desires. Here again Aristotle's psychology shows the characteristic stamp of naturalism, whereas Plato's picture of a human nature torn between heaven and earth prefigures the views of Plotinus and Augustine, and even Kant.

Only Plato's real philosopher can escape the conflict and torments of a divided soul. As long as he turns steadfastly away from the objects of sense and desire, and remains under the spell of the eternal world of forms, his nature is one and whole. The True, the Good, and the Beautiful are there to lure him, and Eros, which has become his single passion, draws him upward inexorably. Yet we are warned in the *Phaedrus* that desire can be revived; the philosopher may lose his wings and fall again to the earth. And, in the *Republic*, drastic precautions are taken and safeguards instituted to prevent the philosopher-ruler from succumbing to the passions and pleasures of other men. Evidently the happiness of the philosopher is a fragile flower which the hidden beast of desire can too often and too easily destroy. This accounts for the tone of pessimism at the end of the *Republic*, a mood that deepens in later writings.

The Spartan austerity of Platonic happiness: Each member of the *Republic* is to restrict his activity and concern to his own *métier*, for which his proficiency and special training have prepared him; and mind his own business, which is justice. This makes for the unity and efficiency of the state and for the happiness that all classes are to share according to their capacity. The philosopher-ruler experiences rapture in his flight to the empyrean of dazzling archetypes, and the more sober satisfaction of doing his duty when he reluctantly returns to political life. But he is denied the joys of family life and the enjoyments of music and the arts, except for a few items carefully selected for their edifying effect. The happiness of the auxiliaries or soldiery is even more monolithic. There are the satisfactions afforded by combat, bodily exercises, and skill, and by obedience, with occasional freedom during the eugenically controlled festivals, and little else. The artisans are at least permitted some private property and wives and children of their own, but the refinements of life are kept meager after all, and the retention of private families appears to conflict with the eugenics program, which Socrates believes crucial to the continuance of his perfect state. The shepherd, the pilot, and the blacksmith may each reap the joys of workmanship and comradeship, and gladly perform their narrow duty to the state, but all diversification of interests and enjoyments is forbidden.

That democracy fosters "the greatest variety of individual character," and allows everyone to arrange his life as he pleases, is enough to condemn it in Socrates' eyes:

> The diversity of its characters, like the different colours in a patterned dress, make it look very attractive [and many would] judge it to be the best form of society, like women and children who judge by appearances.[24]

> The versatility of the individual, and the attractiveness of his combination of diverse characteristics, match the variety of the democratic society. It's a life that many men and women would envy, it has so many possibilities. . . . One day it's wine, women, and song, the next bread and water; one day it's hard physical training, the next indolence and ease, and then a period of philosophic study.[25]

[24] Plato, *The Republic*, 557.
[25] *Ibid.*, 561.

But all this, according to Socrates, is very bad. Democracy is not only a degenerate order but leads directly to tyranny, which is the worst government of all. Aristotle also condemns the riot of "doing as you please" in "extreme" forms of democracy, but he also sees that blending some elements of democracy with aristocratic rule does not undermine, but actually increases, the stability of the state. He contends that Plato, seeking to give his state maximum unity, fails to see that you can eliminate diversity of characters and functions to a degree to which the state ceases to be a state. To remove all loves and loyalties except those to the state would not increase affection for the state, but more likely replace it by general indifference; for the narrower loyalties to family, friends, and to the profitable reciprocation of men of different kinds are the soil on which the broader loyalty is nourished. Even among equals, Aristotle claims, this productive diversity and reciprocation must be maintained, for it is "the salvation of states." The equals cannot all rule simultaneously, but some will rule while others obey, and then others will take the helm for a period agreed on, according to some order of succession. "The result is that upon this plan they all govern; just as if shoemakers and carpenters were to exchange their occupations, and the same persons did not always continue shoemakers and carpenters . . . it is better that this should be so in politics as well."[26]

We have seen in Chapter 1 that Aristotle insists on plurality and diversity at many points where Plato, desiring as much unity in the state as possible, seeks to reduce them to a minimum. For example, Aristotle states that the moral virtues appropriate to and attainable by a man will depend on his individual abilities and disposition, his occupation, status, wealth, opportunities, etc. Moreover, he emphasizes the multiplicity of the moral virtues, giving much attention to some virtues that Plato hardly ever mentions, if at all; and, indeed, the virtue of humor would seem to have no place in Plato's ideal state, whether that of the *Republic* or that of the *Laws*. And where there is more multiplicity and variety in the virtuous life, there will also be more multiplicity and variety in the corresponding happiness.

In some respects Plato and Aristotle are farther apart in theory than in practice. Aristotle decisively rejects Plato's key doctrine that knowledge alone produces virtue and happiness. A great deal more is required, he contends. For one thing, the virtuous activities of the happy man must be freely chosen, which implies that choice is not determined by knowledge alone but by the agent himself. Here the doctrinal difference seems to be very sharp, but how much difference does this difference make? Though Plato excludes choice in Aristotle's sense, he nevertheless insists on the

[26] Aristotle, *Politics*, 1261a34–37.

practical level that men do have a choice and are strictly responsible for wrong choices, and punishable in proportion to their gravity. In practice, too, Plato and Aristotle agree that all men can choose, at least when they have had a proper education, to acquire the virtues necessary to happiness.

Plato contends, in the *Republic*, though not elsewhere, that the goodness of all things flows from and is caused by the Form of the Good, and suggests that the Vision of this highest form is the highest happiness; whereas Aristotle argues that there is no such thing as the Form of the Good.

The Form of the Good, in Plato's account, seems to have the distinctive attributes of the chief good, or happiness: "It is desired by all though it is difficult to know its nature." It "is the end of all endeavor, the object on which every heart is set, whose existence it divines, though it finds it difficult to say just what it is."[27] It is, of course, desired for itself and not for the sake of something else; and all things that are desired are desired on account of the goodness in them.

On the other hand, the Form of the Good can scarcely be *identified* with happiness. It is an eternal, unchanging being, not an activity of the soul. It is not something that can be worked for and won with effort. The Form of the Good does not depend on human gumption and steadfastness but vice versa. Yet Plato continually insists that virtue and, hence, happiness can be achieved by strenuous exertion.[28] And, indeed, the most that Plato suggests is that the Form of the Good is the one and only *source* of happiness, as it is the only source of every other good, and that the highest happiness, at the pinnacle of the ascending path of mathematical and philosophical studies, is to be found in the Vision of the Good, where the philosopher and his vision are obviously other than the object. In short, the identification of the Form of the Good with happiness is not implied by Plato. We shall see below that it is rather his critic Aristotle who makes this interpretation.

The Form of the Good is a combination, which Aristotle considers very precarious, of the principle of intelligibility, which renders everything that is intelligible, *i.e.*, of a definite kind, and the realization of perfect goodness. As the principle of intelligibility, the Form of the Good is said to be the source and creator of being and goodness:

> Once seen, it is inferred to be responsible for everything right and good, producing in the visible realm light and the source of light and being, and in

[27] Plato, *The Republic*, 505.
[28] Although Augustine and his successors sometimes say that God is happiness, this is evidently an elliptical phrase. What is meant is something like: God is the only source of happiness. Similarly, when it is remarked that a man's happiness is his children, it is presumably meant that he finds his happiness in relation to them, or to them only.

the intelligible realm itself, controlling source of reality and intelligence. And anyone who is going to act rationally either in public or private must perceive it.[29]

But the Form of the Good is not only the source of intelligibility and truth; it is also the perfect realization of truth and goodness, for we must think of it "as being something other than, and even higher than, knowledge and truth [and reality]."[30] The Form of the Good is more than a form; it is "reality," and "the brightest of all realities,"[31] the realization of what it makes possible. This is what puzzled Aristotle. How can a form, whatever its eminence, be something fully actualized—a substance?

The Vision of the Form of the Good, which is the crowning glory of the philosophic career, has all the marks of a mystical experience. It is an immediate, instantaneous awareness in which the totality of reality and value is known, and is of inestimable importance to the knower. Unfortunately, though the highest wisdom is gained, it is ineffable, and the mystic is as little able to convey what he has seen as to explain the visible world to a blind man. And, yet, just as the blind man can be guided by a man with vision, so the philosopher-king is able to guide his fellows among the shadows of the Cave, directing them toward the things that truly partake of rightness and goodness. Although Plato does not explicitly say that the Vision yields the highest summit of happiness, this seems to be implied. Those who have seen the Form of the Good, he says, are loath to return to earth and must be forced to do so for the good of the State. In the analogous case of the philosophical lover's vision of beauty, in the *Symposium* and *Phaedrus,* the ecstasy is made plain.

The rapture of the philosophical lover in the *Symposium* and *Phaedrus* has its parallel in the supreme happiness of disinterested contemplation portrayed in Aristotle's *Nicomachean Ethics,* though the poetic mood and simile are lacking. There is nothing in Aristotle's account of happiness faintly resembling the mystical Vision of the Form of the Good described in the *Republic.*

We have argued above that Plato could scarcely have meant that the highest good for man, or happiness, *is* the Form of the Good. But, now, since the authority of Aristotle is directly contrary, this conclusion should be reconsidered. The Platonists, Aristotle says, introduced one Form of the Good, and claim that other things are good only as they partake of this form, which is made to exist apart and independently. After offering vigorous criticism of this view, Aristotle remarks: ". . . even if there is some one good which is universally predictable of goods or is capable of separate and independent existence, clearly it could not be achieved or

[29] *Op. cit.,* 517.
[30] *Ibid.,* 508.
[31] *Ibid.,* 518.

attained by man." But the good, *i.e.*, happiness, he is concerned with *is* attainable.[32]

It will suffice to say, then, that *if* Plato, or the Platonists, ever held that happiness, or the highest happiness, is the Form of the Good itself, it is a view decisively rejected by Aristotle.

We have confined this chapter to an enumeration of the main points in which Plato's theory of happiness coincides with Aristotle's eudaemonism, and a brief account of the respects in which it diverges. In the chapters that follow, we shall see how greatly the theories of the Stoics, Plotinus, Augustine, and even Aquinas stand in debt to Plato.

[32] *Op. cit., Nicomachean Ethics*, 1096b32–33.

3

The Stoic Concept of Happiness

THE Stoic idea of happiness is an elaboration of one side of the
Socratic-Platonic and Aristotelian conceptions, a contraction, a
retrenchment, suitable to evil times. Whatever is abundant and daring
and creative in the latter gives way in the former to tranquil acquiescence—
submission to nature and usually to the status quo. In an age of uncertainty and trouble, the Stoics retreat to the last line of defense, and seek
to make the mind itself an impregnable citadel, proof against all pain and
adversity. The great exemplar of fearless superiority to fate and to the
opinions of men is Socrates, but Socrates is a martyr to truth and free
inquiry of a sort to which the Stoics profess indifference. It is true that the
Stoic school of philosophy develops its own physics, logic, and psychology,
but these subjects are pursued, not for their own sake but for the sake of
ethics. They provide defenses against attacks by other schools, safeguarding
the calm imperturbability of the Sage.

Unlike the Epicurean school, the Stoics had many leaders who evolved
different versions of their philosophy, and the history of Stoicism displays a
variety of adaptations and expedients designed to defend the doctrine

against continuing attacks from the other schools. The glaring inconsistencies that resulted were not taken too seriously; the consuming aim, which united the school, was to make the mind proof against misfortunes and indignities, and differences as to the *means* were of less account. Throughout all variations and adaptations of the Stoic doctrine, the central thesis remained the same: Virtue, which is desirable in itself, is also sufficient for happiness, and is the only means to it.

In the first part of this chapter, we give a bird's-eye view of typical Stoic views relating to happiness, showing how they diverged from Aristotle's eudaemonism. In the second part, we describe happiness as it was understood by Epictetus (A.D. 60–110), a leading Stoic and a man of austere clarity and nobility.

THE SUPPRESSION OF DESIRE

Plato, we have seen, holds that virtue is sufficient for happiness, but he includes contemplation as the highest virtue, and thinks that the disinterested pursuit of knowledge affords the highest and the only complete happiness. The Cynic Antisthenes (444–368 B.C.) insists that virtue alone yields happiness, but takes a narrow practical view of virtue, and sees no value in the pursuit of knowledge for its own sake. The Stoics agree with Antisthenes, adopting only the practical side of the Platonic theory. Of the relation between virtue and happiness in Stoic theory, Diogenes Laertius says that, according to Cleanthes, who headed the Stoic school after Zeno,

> virtue . . . is a harmonious disposition, choice-worthy for its own sake and not from hope or fear or any external motive. Moreover, it is in virtue that happiness consists; for virtue is the state of mind which tends to make the whole of life harmonious. . . . Virtue, in the first place, is in one sense the perfection of anything in general, say of a statue; again, it may be non-intellectual, like health, or intellectual, like prudence.[1]

Although Zeno calls prudence an "intellectual" virtue, almost everyone takes it to be practical. The Stoics, in general, had no use for Aristotle's intellectual virtues, and this is one way in which they simplified his idea of happiness.

The Stoics also eliminate all degrees between virtue and vice. A man is either perfectly just or unjust, perfectly courageous or cowardly, completely temperate or intemperate, etc. He is either wise or a fool. For though he who acquires some degree of these virtues is moving toward them, he does not have them until he wins them completely. "It is a tenet of theirs," Diogenes Laertius says,

[1] *Lives of Eminent Philosophers*, Vol. II, VII, 89–90, p. 197.

that between virtue and vice there is nothing intermediate, whereas according to the Peripatetics [Aristotelians] there is, namely, the state of moral improvement.[2]

It follows that, since only the completely virtuous are happy, most men are disqualified. By eliminating the Aristotelian degrees of virtue, the degrees of happiness are also eliminated, and a man is either completely virtuous and happy or nothing of either. The scandal of pessimism thus haunts the world of the Stoics, ruled as it is by divine law, and rational and good in all its dispensations, for could it be maintained that anyone is happy in their sense? Later Stoics compromised this position, so odd in an optimistic system, by toning down their denial of the degrees of virtue.

The Stoics, trimming the Aristotelian conception of happiness, sometimes with results they would not have chosen, claim

that the virtues involve one another, and that the possessor of one is the possessor of all, inasmuch as they have common principles.[3]

But this conclusion, together with the denial of degrees of virtue, at once implies that one man's virtue is exactly the same as another's. The Stoic Sage, unless he can claim to be perfect, is no better than anyone else.

The Stoics also diverge from Aristotle in their classification of things into good, bad, and indifferent; for they limit the good to virtues, the bad to vices, while all else is indifferent. Diogenes Laertius says that the virtues are regarded as good both of ends and of means. ". . . in so far as they cause happiness they are means, and on the other hand, in so far as they make it complete, and so are themselves part of it, they are ends."[4] The same is true analogously of vices. They "are evils both as ends and as means, since in so far as they cause misery they are means, but in so far as they make it complete, so that they become part of it, they are ends."[5] But external things are neutral—neither good nor evil. "Life, health, pleasure, beauty, strength, wealth, fair name and noble birth, and their opposites, death, disease, pain, ugliness, weakness, poverty, ignominy, low birth, and the like," are neutral since they "neither benefit nor harm a man."[6] One reason given for this drastic conclusion is that good things are *necessarily* beneficial and evil things *necessarily* harmful; whereas the supposedly good things listed above are sometimes harmful, and the supposed evils are sometimes beneficial.[7] Aristotle answers this argument: A thing may be

---

[2] *Ibid.*, 127, p. 231.
[3] *Ibid.*, 125, pp. 229–231.
[4] *Ibid.*, 97, p. 203.
[5] *Ibid.*, 97, p. 205.
[6] *Ibid.*, 102, p. 209.
[7] See *ibid.*, 103, p. 209.

good even though it is sometimes bad in certain contexts. The fact that some pleasures are mixed with pain or have bad consequences does not prevent pleasure from being good, or even good in itself. Similarly, Aristotle rejects the Stoic contention that "wealth, fame, health, strength, and the like"[8] do not contribute to happiness, and that a man can be happy without any external advantages. He recognizes that external goods are necessary to happiness, and that great misfortunes can destroy it. He sees that the man of excellence or virtue is resilient in the ordinary reverses of life, but that his happiness would succumb to the evils that befell old Priam. Those who claim that a man can be happy while tortured on a rack do not know what they are saying.

Socrates also argues that justice alone ensures happiness, and that no harm can come to a good man. It is left to the Stoics to free the thesis from the dialectical adventure of living dialogue, and to make it a fixed plank in their program of bracing the mind against uncertainty and disaster. The Stoics defend it vigorously, but cannot do so without supplementary theories and concessions. To ensure the happiness of the virtuous man, they advance the theory that "nothing is good or ill but thinking makes it so" (as Hamlet put it), nothing, that is, except virtue and vice. Poverty, disease, ignominy, and death are not evil in themselves, then, for it all depends on the attitude we have toward them.

> Stone walls do not a prison make
> Nor iron bars a cage,

since they can be regarded as a refuge, and a Sir Walter Raleigh or a Cervantes can profit by completing his work in quiet. The idea plays a considerable role in the literature about happiness, especially when Stoic influence is felt. Aristotle often emphasizes its partial truth in the *Nicomachean Ethics* and the *Rhetoric*, but he also sees that there are natural limits to mental powers. The man does not exist who could regard poverty, disease, ignominy, and death, all with indifference.

The Stoics have an ingenious argument to preserve men from the fear of death. Whereas Aristotle says that "death is the most terrible of all things,"[9] the Stoics argue that it is nothing to be concerned about; for where death is we are not; and where we are death is not. What is never experienced can never hurt us, and to fear it is accordingly foolish and irrational. Aristotle, on the other hand, holds that

> the more [a man] is possessed of virtue in its entirety and the happier he is, the more he will be pained at the thought of death; for life is best worth

8 *Ibid.*, 104, pp. 209–210.
9 *Op. cit., Nicomachean Ethics*, 1115a27.

living for such a man, and he is knowingly losing the greatest goods, and this is painful. But he is none the less brave, and perhaps all the more so, because he chooses noble deeds of war at that cost.[10]

Another device of the Stoics for preserving the equanimity of the Sage is famous. As determinists they hold that whatever happens must happen, and from this the following argument issues:

> Whatever happens is necessary, whatever is necessary is rational, whatever is rational is good, and whatever is good is acceptable. Therefore, whatever happens is acceptable.

The conclusion of this argument—called a "sorites"—does not follow, since, for one thing, the word "rational" does not have the same meaning in the two premises in which it occurs. Some Stoics, however, adopt an alternative gambit. They contend that in perception we have the power of giving and withholding assent, so that the Sage could guarantee that nothing evil or unacceptable should come within his purview simply by refusing his assent. This "theory of assent" is like the theory that nothing (except virtue and vice) is good or bad but thinking makes it so, except that it involves sense perception. But perception supplies the materials of all knowledge. This Stoic contention thus implies that knowledge is infected at the source with wishful thinking. The theory of assent was a favorite whipping boy in the schools of philosophy. That we can stop the course of nature by withholding assent seems especially at variance with Stoic necessitarianism.

It is not easy for the Stoic Sage to preserve his "indifference," but without this attitude how could he preserve his tranquil happiness? External things, such as disease, ignominy, and death are said to be neither good nor evil. But would not even the Stoic Sage prefer health to disease, pleasure to pain, life to death? In this quandary, Stoics sometimes make a distinction between good things and "preferred things,"[11] which permits the Sage to *prefer* a good meal to hunger, though the good meal is not *better* than hunger. But this is not an altogether satisfactory solution, for if it is not better, why is it preferred or preferable? These preferred things are also said to be helpful in attaining virtue and happiness, and are thus called "valuable." They are valuable insofar as they contribute to

> harmonious living [or] . . . to the life according to nature; which is as much as to say "any assistance brought by wealth or health towards living a natural life."[12]

[10] *Ibid.*, 1117b9–15.
[11] See *Lives of Eminent Philosophers*, Vol. II, 102–103, pp. 207–209.
[12] *Ibid.*, 105, p. 211.

And the measure of their utility is the expert. The distinction between instrumental value and intrinsic value is, of course, traditional and understandable, but it does not serve the Stoic's purpose. If there are things that are instrumental to virtue, the Stoic cannot remain indifferent to their occurrence or nonoccurrence.

Other bleak and majestic doctrines are toned down. It turns out that "moral improvement" is at least something preferred and valuable[13] and is a step toward virtue. The original doctrine that a man has either perfect virtue or none at all is weakened in the direction of the Aristotelian view that admits of degrees of virtue or excellence. The austere doctrine that virtue is a life of reason without passions or pleasures also tends to be softened. The admission of "preferences" and "rejections" itself entails that some desires and aversions are unavoidable and that some external goods probably are needed. Thus the more concessions made to common sense, the more the Stoic doctrine tends to revert to the more elaborate and qualified theory of happiness that Aristotle had laid down.

THE THEORY OF EPICTETUS

The history of Stoic philosophy shows so many diverse lines of development and revision that it is sometimes hard to see the wood for the trees. It will be useful to confine our attention for a moment to one Stoic philosopher, one who has a great deal to say about happiness and says it with clarity and concrete examples. Epictetus, the slave of a courtier of Nero, takes the usual Stoic view that all men desire happiness, and that happiness really consists in a life in accordance with virtue, with nature or the will of God, or with reason, the highest part of the soul. His development of the theme, however, is original. Happiness, he maintains, results from one thing alone, namely, a steady disposition to restrict our will to what is within our power. What this means, in effect, is that happiness is attainable only if we abandon all desires that we do not have the power to satisfy at all times.

There is a general consensus that happiness or well-being depends on the ratio of satisfied and unsatisfied desires, that is:

$$\text{Happiness} = \frac{\text{satisfied desires}}{\text{desires}}$$

Thus happiness can be achieved, or augmented, in two ways: either (1) by increasing the number of satisfied desires, or (2) by decreasing the

[13] See *ibid.*, 106, p. 211.

number of desires. The first method is expansionist, the second, contractionist. Aristotle makes use of both, but his emphasis is certainly on the first. Epictetus, on the other hand, relies exclusively on the second, and is more contractionist than anyone in history, except, perhaps, the Greek Cynics and the primitive Buddhists, the Vedantists and other cults of India. Epictetus states his position as follows:

> . . . happiness and tranquillity are not attainable by man otherwise than by not failing to obtain what he desires, and not falling into that which he would avoid; such a man takes from himself desire altogether and defers it, but he employs his aversion only on things which are dependent on his will. For if he attempts to avoid anything independent of his will, he knows that sometimes he will fall in with something which he wishes to avoid, and he will be unhappy. Now if virtue promises good fortune and tranquillity and happiness, certainly also the progress toward virtue is progress toward each of these things.[14]

Thus happiness is attainable by any man who restricts his desires to those he can always satisfy. In fact, men are born to be happy and to be happy with one another.

> Let not that which in another is contrary to nature be an evil to you: for you are not formed by nature to be depressed with others nor to be unhappy with others, but to be happy with them. If a man is unhappy, remember that his happiness is his own fault: for God has made all men to be happy, to be free from perturbations.[15]

But how can all men be intended for happiness when there are so many daily obstacles to their desires, and they cannot be happy unless all desires are requited? "For that which is happy," Epictetus says, "must have all that it desires, must resemble a person who is filled with food, and must have neither thirst nor hunger."[16] Plato and Aristotle also subscribe to the view that happiness is "lacking in nothing," but they do not take it too literally, for they know that unfulfilled desire is the mainspring of action. Epictetus, on the other hand, holds that the happy man must go to great lengths to see that none of his desires is unsatisfied; he must abandon all desires that are not completely in his power.

But how is this possible? The wise man, Epictetus counsels, must concern himself with three things: (1) He must so discipline his desires and aversions as to get what he desires, and not get what he is averse to. (2) In moving toward or away from objects, he must do as he "ought," and act according to reason, "and not carelessly." (3) He must avoid painful

[14] *The Discourses of Epictetus*, Book I, Ch. 4.
[15] *Ibid.*, Book III, Ch. 24.
[16] *Ibid.*

affects, for such affects are "produced in no other way than by failing to obtain that which a man desires or a falling into that which a man would wish to avoid. This is that which brings in perturbations, disorders, bad fortune, misfortunes, sorrows, lamentations and envy." Such affects are to be avoided, and this matter is more "urgent," Epictetus says, than anything else. On the other hand, since he is to do his duty, he cannot "be free from affects like a statue, but . . . ought to maintain the relations natural and acquired, as a pious man, as a son, as a father, as a citizen."[17]

The desires whose fulfillment we can control are then as follows: (1) We can eliminate desires and aversions that lead to frustration, and instate those that lead to fulfillment. (2) We can control the will to do our duty and the desire not to do it; acting in accordance with nature or reason is always in our power. (3) We can also eliminate painful affects, and thereby negate the frustration that would otherwise be experienced.

This program of wholesale control of desires and emotions raises serious problems, first, as to its feasibility, and second, as to its desirability in view of wider effects upon the individual and society. Epictetus makes some attempt to answer objections to the feasibility of such drastic controls, but they are in the nature of remonstrance. He asks one objector whether he has been able to resist a pretty girl and to overcome the envy of a neighbor who has inherited an estate. If not, he has not even made a beginning. There is really nothing wanting to him but "unchangeable firmness of mind." "Wretch," he continues his rebuke, "you hear these very things with fear and anxiety that some person may despise you, and with inquiries about what any person may say about you."[18] Is it not easy enough to overcome such vanity? Are you not ashamed of yourself?

Epictetus' formula for eliminating painful affects is as follows: If a man grieves at the absence of his friend, he is told that there is no reason for expecting him to stay perpetually in one place, like a plant. If another complains of his own illness, he is reminded that men are not proof against disease; if he fears his own death or that of his child, he should realize that men are not immortal. The eradication of unwise desires proceeds by a similar formula, viz.: Do you crave wealth, honors, luxuries, pleasures of various sorts? What makes you think they would make you happy? Such things can make you a slave, and arouse the envy and hostility of others. You take great pains to own them, but it ends with their owning you.

From an Aristotelian point of view, and in the eyes of many later philosophers, these are mere half-truths. Although men may be neither stationary nor immortal, it is still regrettable that the friend is absent, and tragic that the child is no longer alive, and to be indifferent would not be

[17] *Ibid.*, Ch. 2.
[18] *Ibid.*

more logical but less human. The Stoic, after all, plays his part as a father, a citizen, a soldier, a senator, or a slave—whatever his sphere of duty may be—and would be naturally affected by the outcome of what he has at heart. Similarly, although the quest of wealth and honors often turns out badly, it need not do so, and, as those who agree with Aristotle insist, some prosperity is necessary to happiness.

Living in accordance with "nature" has also been found perplexing, for how can it be claimed that nature should be our model, that "nature never deceives us"? Critics have pointed out that nature is wildly destructive and cruel, and if it is also purposive throughout, as Epictetus and other Stoics maintain, this hardly makes it a better model. Moreover, the impulses to injustice, cowardice, and intemperance are quite as "natural" as their opposites, in the sense implied by taking nature as our guide. This is so obvious that, in practice, following nature indiscriminately is supplanted by following "nature's plan," which is only a part of nature selected by reason, *i.e.*, in the judgment of Epictetus or of some other Stoic.

The Stoics employ many devices to banish evil from the world. They identify the government of the world with divine reason, which is also the reason of man—his highest nature—so that to complain of disease and death or other natural necessities is completely irrational. In preserving the equanimity of the Stoic Sage, they are abundant in resources, not always consistent with one another. The same problem confronts all the great optimistic systems. The existence of evil, or what men consider evil, in a world that is a reflection or creation of a perfect Being, is also a problem for Plato, Plotinus, and for Christian theologians. This "problem of evil," as it relates to happiness, will be discussed in later chapters.

In one respect the Stoics were far ahead of their times, and unfurled a very modern ideal. Although they advised the individual to give attention to his own virtue and happiness, they also taught that the community of men is equalitarian: everyone is capable of blessedness. Whereas Plato and Aristotle thought in terms of a stratified society, excluding slaves and even artisans from the good life, and all but a few independent gentlemen from the highest happiness, the Stoics recognized "the brotherhood of all men," and welcomed men of all ranks to their school—slaves and emperors on equal terms. They did not recommend *action* to cure social evils, but, relying on education, sometimes looked forward to a universal state in which mankind would no longer be divided by artificial distinctions.

4

The Concept of Transcendent
Happiness

Happiness can be said to be "transcendent" if it is beyond the present life on earth, or if it is something attained in the present life but is beyond the natural powers of man. Such happiness is thus supernatural, and is said to exceed and outshine any ordinary happiness, as the divine does the human. It is "true" or "perfect happiness," whereas any shadowy copy of it realizable on earth and in ordinary life is "imperfect," *i.e.*, deceptive, uncertain, not self-sufficing or self-satisfying. Perfect happiness may be realized temporarily in a mystic experience. In this case it is usually described as "ecstasy," and whomsoever it befalls considers it a rare and priceless boon, the summit of existence before which the rest of his life pales to insignificance. Plotinus holds that the Sage achieves it largely by his own efforts, by his cutting away from the body and turning toward the One, *i.e.*, God. For Christian writers the experience must come, if at all, through the special grace of God conferred upon the individual. The other form of supernatural happiness, which is promised in a future life, is also differently conceived. Plotinus sees it as a *timeless merging* of the soul with God; Augustine and Aquinas as an *everlasting vision* of God. In spite of basic disagreements, there are important agreements too. Plotinus' understanding of the individual soul's relation to God prepared the way for the Christian mystics and for the mystical element in Christian doctrine.

I. The Timeless Merging of the Soul with the One: Plotinus

Happiness Is Independent of Worldly Goods

In his contempt for possessions and prosperity, Plotinus equals, or surpasses, Plato and the Stoics. No goods and no measure of good fortune are necessary for happiness, for this is consistent with pain, torture, the death of dear ones, and ruin.

> Adverse fortune does not shake [the Sage's] felicity: the life so founded is stable ever. Suppose death strikes at his household or at his friends; he knows what death is, as the victims, if they are among the wise, know too. And if death taking from him his familiars and intimates does bring grief, it is not to him, not to the true man, but to that in him which stands apart from the Supreme, to that lower man in whose distress he takes no part.[1]

Not even suspension of consciousness brought on by disease or drugs can destroy happiness, nor can the "miseries of Priam," which Aristotle employs as a signal example of calamities inconsistent with the good life. The reason is that happiness is not concerned with the ordeals of the body but with the soul which has cut loose from the body.

> Now if happiness did indeed require freedom from pain, sickness, misfortune, disaster, it would be utterly denied to anyone confronted by such trials; but if it lies in the fruition of the Authentic Good, why turn away from this Term and look to means, imagining that to be happy a man must need a variety of things none of which enter into happiness?[2]

The Sage is not even disturbed by "the ruin of his fatherland," and it would be very strange if he thought this a disaster at all, even though the state were his own handiwork.[3] The soundest counsel is "Let us flee to the beloved Fatherland," but "the Fatherland to us is There whence we have come, and There is the Father."[4] Such aloofness from one's own state is

---

[1] *Enneads, First Ennead*, IV, 4.
[2] *Ibid.*, 6.
[3] See *ibid.*, 7.
[4] *Ibid.*, VI, 8.

directly contrary to Plato and Aristotle, and even the wholesale indifference of the Stoic does not go to such lengths.

Happiness as the Soul's Journey Toward the One

But if the Sage cuts away the body, an Aristotelian might ask, then, "having no sensation and not expressing his virtue in act, how can he be happy?" Plotinus answers this question as follows: "Wisdom is, in its essential nature . . . The Authentic-Existent [the One, or God]—and this Existent does not perish in one asleep or . . . in the man out of his mind: the Act of this Existent is continuous within him; and is a sleepless activity: the Sage, therefore, even unconscious, is still the Sage in Act."[5]

Nor is death an evil. "Evil to What?" Plotinus asks. He answers, as did the Stoics, that there must be a subject to whom the evil occurs, but there is none. And should there be an afterlife, "then death will be no evil but a good; Soul, disembodied, is the freer to ply its own Act. If it be taken into the All-Soul—what evil can reach it There?"[6]

Neither activity nor consciousness is required for happiness and, indeed, as we shall see, the summit of happiness is a mystic state that transcends all diversity and division, such as are implied by activity and consciousness. Nor can death bring an end to happiness, if happiness is a union with the One, which is absolute and timeless. Nothing external seems to be relevant to the Sage's happiness—only the inner man. There alone we will learn whether a man is happy. Once it is admitted that "the Sage lives within," we must stop looking for his felicity in outer activities or "the object of his desires."[7]

But perhaps we are justified in suspecting a certain amount of rhetorical exaggeration when Plotinus speaks of the independence and invulnerability of the Sage's happiness. Reason, he himself assures us, has "no fundamental quarrel" with so-called objects of men's desires—possessions, good fortune, friends, heightened consciousness, rewarding activities—except as they interfere with the soul's movement toward the One. "Sometimes even it must seek them; essentially all the aspiration is not so much away from evil as towards the Soul's highest and noblest."[8] External and bodily goods and activities of the soul are good insofar as they aid the assent of the soul toward the One, and bad insofar as they conduce to the lower love of the world. They are not good in themselves, nor are they *parts* of happiness, but they are or may be *necessary* to it.

[5] *Ibid.*, IV, 9.
[6] *Ibid.*, VII, 3.
[7] *Ibid.*, IV, 11.
[8] *Ibid.*, 6.

For instance, health and freedom from pain; which of these has any great charm? As long as we possess them we set no store upon them. Anything which, present, has not charm and adds nothing to happiness, which when lacking is desired because of the presence of an annoying opposite, may reasonably be called a necessity but not a Good.[9]

THE NATURE OF THE ONE

Plotinus' Authentic-Existent, the One, the Supreme is modeled after Plato's Form of the Good. It is above knowledge and virtue, and even being and reality, and is the source of everything insofar as it truly *is*. Outside the One is nothing, *i.e.*, nonbeing, matter, "whose very nature is to be one long want," ugliness, which is "matter not mastered by Ideal-Form":[10] Outside of the One is Evil. More clearly than in Plato, the Author of all that is real emerges also as that alone that truly is, other things owing their reality, such as it may be, to their closeness to the One, to the degree to which they resemble it (where "resemblance" is understood as an asymmetrical relation). The One is also absolutely simple, though it is the source of all multiplicity and diversity. It is as if the multiplicity resulted from the dispersal of the rays of the sun which, as they are projected farther and farther from the source, leave more and more interstices of darkness or indetermination between them. But the sun and its light, Plotinus assures us, are inseparable:[11] The multiplicity cannot be multiplicity unless it has a unity, and unity—even the absolute Unity, the One itself—Plotinus sometimes seems to say, cannot be unity without being the unity of something—of something multiple. Yet, on the other hand, the One is said to be absolutely pure, independent, and self-sufficient. The status of the One is further complicated by the fact that it cannot be known, for knowledge implies a duality of subject and object, and that no predicates whatever can be applied to it—not even "one" and "good"—for all predication is limitation, whereas the One is not limited.

The first and noblest emanation of the One is the Intelligible World, the realm of Platonic forms, which is divided between the intelligible forms and the intelligence that knows them. The next emanation of the One, on the blueprint of the Intelligible World, is the World Soul, in which the individual souls merge and yet remain distinct. Farthest from the One is the Material World, which is only partly real; it is real to the extent that its multiplicity partakes of or reflects the "Ideal-Forms" of the Intelligible World.

[9] *Ibid.*
[10] *Ibid.*, VIII, 5.
[11] *Ibid.*, VII, 1.

The Two Loves of the Soul and the
Path to the Higher

The soul thus is suspended between the Intelligible World and the Material World, and is torn between two loves—the love of sensuous delights and the gratification of the body, and the love of philosophical knowledge and ideal beauty. Now it turns toward the lower love, now toward the higher; the turning toward the higher is the path leading to the perfect life or happiness.

There are three stages in the pilgrimage to the supreme goal. First, the stock virtues must be acquired—fortitude, prudence, temperance, practical wisdom, and the rest. Plotinus takes the practical virtues for granted. He is more interested in their relation to the Divine Being. "Does not Likeness by way of Virtue imply Likeness to some being that has Virtue?" he asks. But this cannot be, for, though the Supreme, the One, is the source of the order, distribution, and harmony in which these virtues consist, it has itself nothing of order, distribution, and harmony, and is not itself virtuous. It is true, nonetheless, that by possessing the virtues we become more like the Supreme. In the first place, our becoming like the Supreme does not imply that the Supreme is like us.[12] Second, acquiring of the virtues brings us closer to the Supreme because it is a process whereby we free ourselves from the impurities, passions, and addictions of the body. For Plotinus holds that all the practical virtues can be regarded as purifications—different means of cutting away from the trammels of the body and of avoiding sin. But the first stage is not enough. "Our concern," Plotinus says, "is not merely to be sinless but to be God."[13]

The second stage is one of devotion to beauty, in ever higher forms, to the mathematical sciences, and to philosophy and dialectic, and here Plotinus follows Plato's lead closely. Three types are considered: the musician, "the born lover," and the metaphysician. They represent in every case an advance upward through the Intelligible World toward the topmost peak, though the last is understood to be the highest. Dialectic, as with Plato, is concerned to define the essence of all things and is the most precious part of philosophy.

And while the other virtues bring reason to bear upon particular experiences and acts, the Virtue of Wisdom [*i.e.*, the virtue peculiarly induced by Dialectic] is a certain super-reasoning much closer to the Universal, for it deals with . . . the choice of time for action and inaction, the adoption of

12 *Ibid.*, II, 1–2.
13 *Ibid.*, 6.

this course, the rejection of that other: Wisdom and Dialectic have the task of presenting all things as Universals and stripped of matter for treatment by the Understanding.[14]

The third and last stage in the ascent to the perfect life or happiness is the final transcending of all multiplicity and difference, and of knowledge itself. The soul comes to rest in the ultimate unity—the One. To this we shall return.

THE NATURE OF PERFECT HAPPINESS

Plotinus agrees with Plato, Aristotle, and the Stoics that the perfect life or happiness will be one in which "nothing is lacking." "The sign that this state has been achieved," he says, "is that the man seeks nothing else."[15] But where can this life of greatest plenitude be found? Can it be realized, as Aristotle says, in the realization of theoretic as well as practical virtue? It would not be possible for Plotinus to agree, for he insists that there is something that is beyond and above virtue—the Supreme, the One—and that the man who is happy is lacking in nothing. If a man lacks a good on this criterion he is not happy; if he does not possess *the* Good, or the source of all goodness, how could he possibly be happy? The deprivation, it could be argued, would be infinitely greater. And yet the criterion cannot be wrong, for if happiness does not imply "wanting nothing," then there could be a better state than happiness.

PERFECT HAPPINESS AS THE UNION
OF THE SOUL WITH THE SUPREME

In his account of the mystic encounter with the Supreme, Plotinus agrees with Plato, and yet disagrees too. He speaks of it as a "Vision" which, however, does not belong to the visible world and is also beyond knowledge and predicates and thus ineffable.[16] More clearly than Plato he ascribes to the experience itself an inestimable value, and even identifies it with happiness, which Plato never does. But Plato, like Plotinus, states that the Supreme (Plato calls it the Good) is the author

---

[14] *Ibid.,* III, 6.
[15] *Ibid.,* IV, 4.
[16] We pointed out, however, that though Plato says that the experience is ineffable, he also states that if the philosopher (after his Vision) cannot define and defend the Good—the Supreme Principle—he will not be able to distinguish what is good from what is not, nor to lead the State to justice and happiness. Plotinus may well escape this inconsistency. His Sage, at any rate, is not compelled to put his Vision to work for the good of the State.

and *sine qua non* of happiness, and in fact of everything that is. For Plotinus, however, the vision is something more than a vision; it is a union that is finally identity, without a difference. We are told that the soul, to approach the Supreme, must put good and evil and everything else out of mind, "that alone it may receive the Alone." If that has been done and she has "made herself apt, beautiful to the utmost

> brought into likeness with the divine—by those preparings and adornings which come unbidden to those growing ready for the vision—she has seen that presence suddenly manifesting within her, for there is nothing between: here is no longer duality but a two in one; for, so long as the presence holds, all distinction fades. . . . In this happiness she knows beyond delusion that she is happy . . . linked to This she can fear no disaster nor even know it; let all about her fall to pieces, so she would have it that she may be wholly with This, so huge the happiness she has won to.[17]

The union of the soul with the Supreme lifts the soul, so to speak, out of itself.

> The soul now knows no movement since the Supreme knows none; it is not even a soul since the Supreme is not in life but above life; it is no longer Intellectual-Principle, for the Supreme has not Intellection and the likeness must be perfect; this grasping is not even by Intellection, for the Supreme is not known Intellectively.[18]

In another passage, the union with the Supreme is pictured as the self finding its true self, and the difficulty of speaking of things that transcend knowledge distinctions is recognized.

> In our self-seeing There, the self is seen as belonging to that order, or rather we are merged into that self in us which has the quality of that order. It is a knowing of the self restored to its purity. No doubt we should not speak of seeing; but we cannot help speaking in dualities, seen and seer, instead of, bodily, the achievement of unity. In this seeing, we neither hold an object or trace distinction; there is no two. The man is changed, no longer himself nor self-belonging; he is merged with the Supreme, sunken into it, one with it: centre coincides with centre, for on this higher plane things that touch at all are one; only in separation is there duality; by our holding away, the Supreme is set outside. This is why the vision baffles telling; we cannot detach the Supreme to state it; if we have seen something thus detached we have failed of the Supreme which is to be known only as one with ourselves.[19]

[17] *Op. cit., Sixth Ennead*, VII, 34.
[18] *Ibid.*, 35.
[19] *Ibid.*, IX, 10.

Plotinus himself was said to have had several mystic visions, and there seems no doubt, as William James said, that the mystic experiences reported in many parts of the world, ages, and traditions represent genuine psychological phenomena. But they are, from all accounts, of short duration. Does Plotinus mean that happiness is restricted to these few, fleeting supernatural adventures, of which most men have no inkling? Is it perhaps possible that those who approach the Supreme through steadfast devotion to ideal beauty and philosophy, though without experiencing the mystic union, also approach the happiness that would be their ultimate consummation?

HAPPINESS AS SOMETHING PRESENT, IMMEASURABLE, AND COMPLETE

But perhaps it does not matter that the union with the Supreme is short-lived. Happiness, according to Plotinus, is something that is always *present;* it is not additive, does not increase with time. Thus, a long stretch or even a lifetime of happiness would contain no more happiness than a brief moment of ecstasy. Happiness is something present, and is not augmented by the dead happiness of the past. Nor do memories of past happiness add to present happiness, making it something greater than it was. That bits of time add up does not imply that the happiness accompanying them adds up, for happiness is "indivisible, measurable only by the content of a given instant."[20]

Plotinus' argument is a direct challenge to the Aristotelian theory of happiness, and to all subsequent theories that hold that happiness, to be happiness, must last a full lifetime, or at least a considerable period of time. Felicity is, for him, a changeless moment in the present, and there are no scales to measure a purely internal state that has no parts. That Plotinus is criticizing Aristotle directly is shown by his concluding sentence:

> To put Happiness in actions is to put it in things that are outside virtue and outside the Soul; for the Soul's expression is not in action but in wisdom, in a contemplative operation within itself; and this, alone, is Happiness.[21]

This line of argument will have its reverberations, variations, and rejoinders in later developments of the theory of happiness. For the present it will be enough to point out that Plotinus' conclusion (in the last paragraph) does not appear to follow from his premises. If we grant that happiness exists only in the present, and that it is indivisible and not measurable, it could still be true that a lifetime of happiness is *better than*

[20] *Op. cit., First Ennead,* V, 7.
[21] *Ibid.,* 10.

(or preferable to) a few brief moments of happiness. And it could also be true that there was *more* happiness in the lifetime than in the few moments. Artistic ability may not be measurable, but we can still say that one man has *more* of it than another. As for Plotinus' contention that happiness cannot lie in actions since virtue does not, the Aristotelian answer can be made that if virtue is merely an internal state it can accomplish nothing good, and that if happiness has nothing to do with actions a man could be happy without doing anything, or even existing.

THE REJECTION OF HEDONISM

Plotinus naturally rejects hedonism. If the good life is pleasure, he argues, the good life cannot be denied to any living thing. And if the hedonist contends that the Good requires both feeling and something felt, how can he suppose that "two neutrals can produce the Good?" Moreover, if we recognize that pleasure is the Good, it cannot be by means of sensation or "the faculty receptive of pleasure." Reason or the faculty of judgment will be required. But, in this case, "the cause of the well-being is no longer pleasure but the faculty competent to pronounce as to pleasure's value."[22] The argument, in other words, seems to be that, if we need reason to know that pleasure is the Good, then pleasure cannot be the Good, and reason has a better title. (Hedonists have their answer to arguments of this kind, but, yet, Socrates' case of the oyster richly endowed with pleasure it does not know the value of has often proved disturbing.) Plotinus sees Epicurus' doctrine culminating in selfish self-seeking and "the pursuit of advantage," and his school "convicted by its neglect of all mention of virtue."[23]

Pleasure is no part or requirement of happiness, either. It "cannot be fairly reckoned in with Happiness—unless indeed by pleasure is meant the unhindered Act [of the true man], in which case this pleasure is simply our 'Happiness.' "[24] And in considering why the world should be such that villains prosper and good men suffer, Plotinus remarks that

> since pleasant conditions add nothing to true happiness and the unpleasant do not lessen the evil in the wicked, the conditions matter little: as well complain that a good man happens to be ugly and a bad man handsome.[25]

Yet there is some reason to think that Plotinus, after all, does not exclude all pleasure from happiness, and that he is mostly concerned to divert men

[22] *Ibid.*, IV, 1–2.
[23] *Op. cit., Second Ennead,* IX, 15.
[24] *Ibid., First Ennead,* V, 4.
[25] *Ibid., Third Ennead,* II, 5.

from *bodily* pleasures. No one could condemn pleasure and the life of pleasure more enthusiastically than Plato and the Stoics, and yet they insist that the virtuous life is most pleasant, most cheerful or joyful. In describing the union with the Supreme, Plotinus also speaks of "the joy we have in winning what we most desire,"[26] and even if such terms as "joy" are not used, we would expect that winning what we most desire, and carrying out the unhindered act of fruition, would be pleasant rather than unpleasant or neutral. But this is with the proviso that happiness has qualities. If happiness is literally the identification of the soul with the pure simplicity of the One, which transcends all distinctions, then happiness has no qualities, and we cannot say it is pleasant or anything else.

Happiness as Immanent in All Men

In view of the awful grandeur of happiness, as Plotinus conceives it, one might expect that few men, if any, would be capable of it. But, on the contrary, we are told that "there exists no single human being that does not either potentially or effectively possess this thing we hold to constitute happiness." In those who possess it potentially "it is present as a mere portion of their total being." But there is also the man who is

> already in possession of this felicity, who is this perfection realized, who has passed over into actual identification with it. All else is now mere clothing about the man, not to be called part of him since it lies about him unsought, not his because not appropriated to himself by any act of will.[27]

Such a man has realized the Good. It is himself; it is the Supreme.[28]

We possess happiness potentially since "the Supreme as containing no otherness is ever present with us; we with it when we put otherness away." But what does this mean? Plotinus gives several reasons for the failure to win happiness. Some have drifted away from God and are bound by material interests, or they are lacking in "trust." "The main part of the difficulty" is that the Supreme cannot be known ("seen") without transcending knowledge.[29] Plotinus, like Plato, insists that the road to the Vision is a long and arduous one, and, if it is won briefly, it can also slip away. But the deep longing of the soul to return to its original nature— "the Soul of all"—and to be "alone with the Alone," continues; and one day the soul will escape from the round of birth and death to be eternally what it had been, essentially, all the time, or rather, out of time. For

26 *Ibid., Sixth Ennead,* IX, 9.
27 *Ibid., First Ennead,* IV, 4.
28 See *ibid.*
29 *Ibid., Sixth Ennead,* IX, 4.

while the whole has life eternally and so too all the nobler and lordlier components, the Souls pass from body to body entering into varied forms— and, when it may, a Soul will rise outside the realm of birth and dwell with the one Soul of all.[30]

II. Christian Felicity: The Revelation of a Personal God

In the universe of Plato, Aristotle, and Plotinus, the beings of the highest order are abstract and impersonal; above and beyond the Christian universe is the highest Good—the personal God who created it. This makes a profound difference to the theory of happiness. Historical revelation of a personal God now becomes the predominant fact, and happiness can be conceived only as a relation to Him, to His infinite will, love, and goodness. In their debate with the Greek schools, Christian thinkers used the insights and arguments of Greek philosophy, but they used them to clarify and support what they already knew, or were learning, from Scripture, and to refute rival conceptions of man's highest good.

Plato chides Homer for permitting the great Achilles to say: "I would rather be the meanest hind on earth than ruler of all the dead in Hades." But the truth is that the afterworld of the Greeks was a dim and gloomy place which afforded only a shadowy life. The victory of Christianity over all its rivals in the Roman world is ascribed in part to the radiant afterworld it promised. Here and here alone the highest fulfillment and the ultimate happiness is to be enjoyed, compared to which life on earth is nothing. The Christian dream of an incomparable and scarcely conceivable bliss in the next life naturally led to a relatively pessimistic outlook on the present one. There were, of course, differences in this respect. Aquinas was much more optimistic about the chances of happiness in this life than was Augustine, yet they agree, as most Christian authorities agree, that this life is chiefly a stepping-stone to the next.

The remainder of this chapter will review the two most important theories of Christian happiness, and indicate the main issues to which they give rise.

The Rejection of Pagan Philosophy: Augustine

The Implication of the Desire for Happiness

Augustine, like all his predecessors, begins with the plain fact that all men desire to be happy. Anyone with brains knows this, he says:

[30] *Ibid., Third Ennead,* II, 4.

But who are happy, or how they become so, these are questions about which the weakness of human understanding stirs endless and angry controversies, in which philosophers have wasted their strength and expended their leisure.[31]

A second truth generally accepted is that to be happy is to possess what one desires, but this does not mean that favorites of fortune who amass the wealth and power they want will be happy. In one of his earliest works written shortly before his conversion, *The Happy Life,* Augustine points out that men who set their hearts on riches must fear the loss of them, and that he who is fearful does not have what he wants. Whatever it is the possession of which is needed for happiness must be secure, proof against all change and loss. Moreover, goods such as wealth and power can bring misery as well as joy to those who possess them, depending on other factors that are often beyond control. And suppose the very rich and powerful man were a fool? Would anyone call him happy? Indeed, of all the goods that men seek, knowledge and wisdom alone seem to be good in themselves and steadfast, rockproof against change and disaster.

In point of fact, men desire all sorts of ephemeral goods, but what they *really* desire, as we might say, is that which, once secured, would leave them without desire, free from want, for to be in want is to be miserable. If what men desire in desiring happiness, however, is a state in which nothing is lacking and all desire has come to rest, which is affirmed by Plato, Plotinus, and the Stoics, it would seem that not even wisdom would fill the bill; for wise men are known to have wants and desires and disappointments. It is clear also that, if wisdom is to be the chief good, which to possess is to be happy, it must be an infinite wisdom. For, if it were anything else, we should have to say that that which would satisfy human desire fully would not satisfy it *as fully* as something else could. This would seem to be Augustine's line of thought. The same conclusion is reached by way of Scripture:

> But which should be called wisdom, if not the wisdom of God? We have heard through divine authority that the Son of God is nothing but the wisdom of God, and the Son of God is truly God. Thus everyone having God is happy. . . . But do you believe that wisdom is different from truth? For it has also been said: "I am the Truth" (John 14:6). . . . Whoever attains the supreme measure, through the truth, is happy. This means to have God within the soul, that is, to enjoy God. Other things do not have God, although they are possessed by God.[32]

But do all men, then, desire happiness understood as the wisdom of God? It might be said that they do in the sense that they want not a

[31] *The City of God,* X, 1.
[32] *The Happy Life,* 34.

fragment but all the wisdom there is. Augustine goes on to claim it is God, the Source of truth, Who admonishes and urges us to seek the truth, to seek "and thirst after Him tirelessly." Using Plato's simile, he says that the truth we speak of derives from "this hidden sun [which] pours into our innermost eyes that beaming light," which is God. "Even though, in our anxiety, we hesitate to turn with courage toward this light and to behold it in its entirety, because our eyes suddenly opened are not yet strong enough."[33] This thought recurs in Augustine's writings. Our desire for happiness, *i.e.*, for truth, is a kind of instinct with which we have been endowed by God, that we may be drawn toward Him.[34]

Starting out with two generally accepted propositions—that all men desire happiness, and that happiness is perfect, complete, *i.e.*, leaving nothing to be desired—Augustine concludes that happiness implies the possession of the infinite, and argues this infinite must be infinite wisdom. It also appears to follow that happiness cannot be attained in this lifetime. But should not these also be the conclusions of Augustine's Greek predecessors, since they accept his premises? Plato argues characteristically that the possession of the traditional virtues suffices for happiness, but perhaps he has a higher happiness in mind when he says that happiness is wanting in nothing. Aristotle's reply is seen in his comment on Plato's Form of the Good: ". . . even if there is some one good which is universally predicable of goods or is capable of separate and independent existence, clearly it could not be achieved or attained by man; but we are now seeking something [*i.e.*, happiness] attainable."[35] The Stoics, for their part, might avoid Augustine's conclusions, since they tend to hold that the Sage restricts his desires to what is attainable in this lifetime. And Plotinus' answer could be that the infinity can be apprehended in a brief mystic trance.

Elsewhere, Augustine states the argument somewhat differently: The two conditions of the chief good, or happiness, are said to be, "*first, nothing is better than it: second, it cannot be lost against the will.*"[36] The second condition is really implied in what is said above. Happiness cannot be lost against one's will, since, if this were possible, it would not be a secure possession, and our desire for security would not be satisfied. But the following breakdown of possibilities does show a difference. Though we all desire to live happily, Augustine says, happiness cannot belong "to him who has not what he loves, whatever it may be, or to him who has what he loves if it is hurtful, or to him who does not love what he has, although it is good in perfection."[37] The last two possibilities might seem to be excluded

---

[33] *Ibid.*, 35.
[34] See *The Trinity*, XI, 6, 10; XIII, 8, 11.
[35] *Op. cit., Nicomachean Ethics*, 1096b35.
[36] *The Morals of the Catholic Church*, Ch. 3.
[37] *Ibid.*

if all men desire happiness, and happiness consists in the possession of truth—of God—but there need be no inconsistency. It can be said that men desire the truth in the sense that without it they will never be satisfied, and with it they would; and also that, in point of fact, men do continually pursue hurtful things, thinking that they will be happy thereby, and fail to pursue what would completely satisfy them. Thus, Augustine says that, although "one man joys in this, and another in that . . . all men agree in their wish for happiness, as they would agree, were they asked, in wishing to have joy—and this joy they call the happy life."[38]

THE BEATIFIC VISION AND THE LOVE OF GOD

Happiness consists in the possession of the truth, but the truth is the Second Person of the Trinity. The possession of the truth thus cannot be reduced to mere contemplation of a body of propositions. Besides the knowing there is also the love of God, and love, according to Plato, seeks to possess the beloved, to enjoy eternal possession. But it is not easy to understand what "possession" can mean where the possessed is God. "How, then, do I seek Thee, O Lord? For when I seek Thee, my God, I seek a happy life. I seek Thee, that my soul may live. For my body liveth by my soul, and my soul liveth by Thee. How, then, do I seek a happy life, seeing that it is not mine till I can say, 'It is enough!' in that place where I ought to say it?"[39] How can he know what happiness is before he has attained it? Can it be a nostalgic "remembrance" of something he knew long ago and has half-forgotten? he asks. Can a kind of Platonic "recollection" explain his intimation of a joy that lies in a future life? The soul, which came from God, after all, was once close to Him. Somehow we must know what we are looking for when we seek happiness. But *how* is not clear.

Scriptural promises seem to be Augustine's real guide. At the beginning of his account of the beatific vision in *The City of God*, he asks himself how the saints may be employed in heaven. He confesses that he can know very little, for, the "peace of God," as the apostle says, "passeth all understanding"—all except the understanding of God Himself, Augustine adds.

> Doubtless this passeth all understanding but His own. But as we shall one day be made to participate, according to our slender capacity, in His peace, both in ourselves, and with our neighbour, and with God our chief good, in this respect the angels understand the peace of God in their own measure, and men too, though now far behind them, whatever spiritual advance they may have made. For we must remember how great a man he was who said,

[38] *The Confessions*, X, 19.
[39] *Ibid.*, X, 29.

"We know in part, and we prophesy in part, until that which is perfect is come"; and "Now we see through a glass, darkly; but then face to face." Such also is now the vision of the holy angels, who are also called our angels, because we, being rescued out of the power of darkness, and receiving the earnest of the Spirit, are translated into the kingdom of Christ, and already begin to belong to those angels with whom we shall enjoy that holy and most delightful city of God.[40]

The beatific vision is a vision of the face of God, whereby "face" is meant "His manifestation." Jesus Christ Himself said of the angels of "the little ones," that they "always see the face of my Father which is in heaven" (Matt. 18:10), and "Blessed are the pure in heart: for they shall see God" (Matt. 5:8). Augustine also quotes the Apostle John, "When He shall appear, we shall be like Him, for we shall see Him as He is." Pureness of heart could be expected to make us more "*like* God," though, as Plotinus points out, the likeness is a one-way relation: If we can become like God, God is certainly never like us. And if Augustine sometimes says that we participate in or partake of divine goodness, or in some sense become one with Him, the relation involved, whatever it may be, must be understood as asymmetric. The words "participation," "sharing," "loving," "being like," "one with," etc., help to explain what is meant when it is said that the beatific vision is not purely noetic, but rather a movement of the whole soul toward God; we still "see through a glass, darkly."

Although Augustine takes a dim view of worldly pleasures, he ascribes an incomparable joy to the vision of God. In a sympathetic description of Plato's philosophy, which comes "nearest to the Christian faith," he says that

> no one is blessed who does not enjoy that which he loves. For even they who love things that ought not to be loved, do not count themselves blessed by loving merely, but by enjoying them. Who, then . . . will deny that he is blessed, who enjoys that which he loves and loves the true and highest good? But the true and highest good, according to Plato, is God,[41] and therefore he would call him a philosopher who loves God; for philosophy is directed to the obtaining of the blessed life, and he who loves God is blessed in the enjoyment of God.[42]

But the beatific good requires no extrinsic pleasures, nor is it augmented by "extrinsic" goods, such as "honour, glory, wealth, and the like." Let them be sought as ends, for they can be bad as well as good. Sweeping away conflicting theories that apportion goods between the mind and the body, Augustine welcomes the Platonists who do not claim either that man is

[40] *The City of God*, XXII, 29.
[41] Most Plato scholars deny that Plato identified the Form of the Good with God.
[42] *Ibid.*, VIII, 8.

blessed by the enjoyment of the body or of the mind, but that he is blessed only by the enjoyment of God.[43]

Augustine can agree with Plato and Aristotle that happiness is a life of virtue, but virtue is a perfection of the soul gained only by following God. "As to virtue leading us to a happy life," Augustine says:

> I hold virtue to be nothing else than perfect love of God. For the fourfold division of virtue I regard as taken from the four forms of love . . . temperance is love giving itself entirely to that which is loved; fortitude is love readily bearing all things for the sake of the loved object; justice is love serving only the loved object, and therefore ruling rightly; prudence is love distinguishing with sagacity between what hinders it and what helps it. The object of this love is not anything, but only God, the chief good, the highest wisdom, the perfect harmony.[44]

So theocentric is the universe of Augustine that even the particular virtues having to do, primarily, with the individual's relation to his fellows are absorbed into an all-important relation to God.

Yet, in spite of its radical divergence from Aristotle, Augustine's theory of happiness has something in common with eudaemonism. The individual in seeking God is held to be seeking at the same time his own self—to be realizing his own true nature and destiny, to be fulfilling his deepest yearnings. "For when I seek Thee, my God, I seek a happy life. I seek Thee that my soul may live."[45] But Augustine adds a supernatural dimension to the human nature, which so overshadows the fulfillments composing eudaemonistic happiness as to render them insignificant in his eyes.

THE AFTERLIFE AND THE ATTAINMENT OF PERFECT HAPPINESS

Even if life on earth is blessed with the external goods of body and soul, it is a poor thing and "most wretched" compared to "the peace of freedom from all evil, in which immortals ever abide. . . . And yet if any man

> uses this life with reference to that other which he ardently loves and confidently hopes for, he may well be called even now blessed, though not in reality so much as in hope. But the actual possession of the happiness of this life, without hope of what is beyond, is but a false happiness and profound misery.[46]

---

[43] See *ibid.*
[44] *The Morals of the Catholic Church*, Ch. 15.
[45] *Confessions*, X, 29.
[46] *The City of God*, XIX, 20.

The hope and dim intimation of the joys of heaven are the only approach to happiness in this life, but they are not at all the real thing. They involve uncertainty of attainment, whereas happiness implies secure and serene possession.

Greek philosophers err, Augustine says, when they imagine that this life, which is surrounded by accidents and evil, can be a happy one. Even the virtues of this life, which are our "best and most useful possessions," testify to its ever present miseries. For they would defend and protect us against them, yet they cannot do so. They give witness rather that "by the hope of the future world this life, which is miserably involved in the many and great evils of this world, is happy as it is also safe." And thus the Apostle Paul, speaking of men of true piety, said: "For we are saved by hope; now hope which is seen is not hope; for what a man seeth, why doth he yet hope for? But if we hope for that we see not, then do we with patience wait for it" (Rom. 8:24). Augustine concludes, therefore, that as "we are saved, so we are made happy by hope.

> And as we do not as yet possess a present, but look to a future salvation, so it is with our happiness, and this "with patience;" for we are encompassed with evils, which we ought patiently to endure, until we come to the ineffable enjoyment of unmixed good; for there shall no longer be anything to endure. Salvation, such as it shall be in the world to come, shall itself be our final happiness. And this happiness these philosophers refuse to believe in, because they do not see it, and attempt to fabricate for themselves a happiness in this life, based upon a virtue which is as deceitful as it is proud.[47]

The philosophers accused of conjuring up an impossible happiness on earth are principally the Stoics. Their doctrine, in Augustine's eyes, is not only fabulously false but also impious—a kind of Prometheanism—for how could the Stoic Sage pretend to secure happiness within his own mind, independent of surrounding hazards and evil, and without the aid of God? He asks why, if the world is free from ills, as the Stoics claim, they allow the Sage to commit suicide under some circumstances? What kind of happiness is this which the Sage is said to possess?

But Augustine also attacks a form of eudaemonism, as represented by Varro, viz.:

> The life of man, then, is called happy when it enjoys virtue and . . . other spiritual and bodily good things without which virtue is impossible . . . happier if it enjoys some or many other good things which are not essential

47 *Ibid.*, 4.

to virtue; and happiest of all, if it lacks not one of the good things which pertain to the body and the soul.[48]

To this Augustine replies that those who seek happiness either in the body or the soul, *i.e.*, either in pleasure or virtue, show "a marvelous shallowness," imagining that they can "find their blessedness in this life and in themselves." The Christian, by contrast, knows that there is no happiness except in God. He believes that "the just live by faith," for, Augustine adds, "we do not as yet see our good, and must therefore live by faith; neither have we in ourselves power to live rightly, but can do so only if He Who has given us faith to believe in His help do help us when we believe and pray."[49]

The Consolidation of Christian Thought: Aquinas

Augustine's great energies were spent in combating pagan philosophies and cults, popular in the Roman world in the fourth and fifth centuries, and in crystallizing and consolidating the still wavering Christian doctrine. He argues tirelessly that salvation is the only worthwhile aim of this life, and that felicity belongs to the next. He ridicules the Stoics' pretension to a perfect self-wrought happiness achievable in this lifetime, and shows that their pessimistic utterances were in contradiction to it. Since he knew little of Aristotle, he was not in a position to evaluate, at first hand, his more moderate and realistic view of human prospects and capability on earth. He invokes Plato and his followers frequently, but Plato gives little support for his particular view that happiness is possible only in heaven, and Plotinus, none at all. Augustine perhaps is most effective in arguing the different but related thesis that happiness here is a poor thing compared to that which we can hope to enjoy beyond.

Aquinas lived in a different world. Writing in the thirteenth century, at the peak of the power and influence of the Christian Church, at a time when Christian doctrine and authority had been widely established, he could afford to recognize an imperfect happiness attainable on earth, as well as the perfect happiness reserved for the saints in heaven. The authors to whom Aquinas defers most often are Aristotle and Augustine. He follows Aristotle, though with Christian additions and emendations, in his account of mundane happiness; and he follows Augustine, while making many new distinctions and elaborations, in his exposition of transcendent happiness.

[48] *Ibid.*, 3.
[49] *Ibid.*, 3–4.

The Universal Desire for Happiness

A cornerstone of Aquinas' theory of happiness is laid when he asserts, with Aristotle, that "the good is what all men desire,"[50] and, with Augustine, that "so far as we truly exist we are good."[51] More specifically, Aquinas states that "the essence of good is this, that it is in some way desirable," and "everything is perfect in so far as it is in act. Therefore . . . a thing is good so far as it is being."[52] That which is intended in desiring anything whatever is good and we desire it to the degree that we conceive it to be good. The final desideratum is something illimitably and essentially good, and there can be only one being who answers to this description.[53] This being alone is one with its essence, and therefore necessarily existent and eternal; and it is not only perfect itself but contains the perfection of all things.[54] Thus, since a thing is desired in proportion to its goodness, we must desire God more than anything else; and since He contains the perfections of all species, in desiring anything we desire Him. But it does not seem to be true in fact that all men desire God, though it might be true that they ought to, that He is desirable.

Aquinas recognizes the problem. Some men are not even certain that God exists, he says. "God exists" is self-evident, for the predicate is contained in the subject, but since "we do not know the essence of God, the proposition is not self-evident to us, but needs to be demonstrated by things that are more known to us, though less known in their nature, namely, by effects." But how, then, can we desire God?

"To know that God exists in a general and confused way is implanted

> in us by nature, since God is man's Happiness. For man naturally desires happiness, and what is naturally desired by man must be naturally known to him. This, however, is not to know absolutely that God exists, just as to know that someone is approaching is not the same as to know that Peter is approaching, even though it is Peter that is approaching. For there are many men who imagine that man's perfect good which is Happiness, consists in riches, others in pleasures, and others in something else.[55]

To be happy is "to have all one's desires perfectly satisfied," is a good definition, Aquinas says, if it means that happiness is what *would* satisfy desires completely, for only the vision of God would do this. But it is not

50 *Op. cit., Nicomachean Ethics,* 1094a3.
51 On Christian Doctrine, 1, 32.
52 *Summa Theologica,* 1, Q5, A1.
53 See *ibid.,* Q6, A3.
54 See *ibid.,* Q4, A1–2.
55 *Ibid.,* Q2, A1.

good if it means that happiness consists in the satisfaction of every natural desire, including extravagant sensual desires, which may possess a man, for such desires may hinder true happiness, and lead to unhappiness.[56]

Besides desiring the highest good in the sense that they desire what *would* satisfy all their desires completely (though they may not know what thing would do this), they also desire it in another sense: They are "ordered to one end Who is God." For

> nothing tends toward a thing as an end, unless this thing is a good [and] it is therefore necessary that the good, as good, be the end. Therefore, that which is the highest good is, from the highest point of view, the end of all things.[57]

God is the end to which all things are ordered, for "He is the cause of every end that is an end, since whatever is an end is such because it is a good," and the first cause is always more of a cause than the secondary ones, and further, if there is a series of ends, the ultimate end takes precedence over all the preceding ones. Moreover, "a particular good is ordered to the common good as to an end; indeed, the being of a part depends on the being of the whole [and] the good of a nation [as Aristotle says] is more godlike than the good of one man. Now the highest good which is God is the common good, since the good of all things depends on Him."[58] The love of God is really a desire to "participate somewhat in His likeness," and to be united with Him in some way. For intellectual creatures this is achieved by "understanding God." Thus, "an intellectual substance tends to divine knowledge as an ultimate end."[59]

THE SEARCH FOR THE HIGHEST GOOD: THE KNOWLEDGE AND LOVE OF GOD AS THE ONE LAST END

Aquinas quotes Aristotle to the effect that, if the series of ends is infinite—having no beginning, no final cause—so that a man does *A* for the sake of *B*, and *B* for the sake of *C*, and so on ad infinitum, then "there would be no reason [left] in the world," and "those who maintain the infinite series eliminate the Good without knowing it."[60] Or, as Aquinas puts it, "if there were no last end nothing would be desired." But the argument, he says, holds only if the ends in the series are related to one

[56] See *ibid.*, Part 1 of Part 2, Q5, A8.
[57] *On the Truth of the Catholic Faith, Summa Contra Gentiles*, III, Part 1, Ch. 17.
[58] *Ibid.*
[59] *Ibid.*, Ch. 25.
[60] *Op. cit., Metaphysics*, 994b12–14.

another "essentially," not accidentally; "for accidental causes are not determinate."[61]

We have seen that Aristotle, in the *Nicomachean Ethics,* argues in a similar fashion that there must be a highest good for man. He does not, however, attempt to prove that there is only one highest good, or that men choose all things that they choose for the sake of this highest good or end; Aquinas attempts to prove both.

There are three reasons, he says, why there cannot be more than one last end. First, "it is necessary for the last end so to fill man's appetite that nothing is left beside it for men to desire." Second, the last end can only be one since it is naturally desired, and "nature tends to one thing only." Finally, since "all that can be desired by the will, belong, as such, to one genus, the last end must be one. And all the more because in every genus there is one first principle."[62] If these arguments appear inconclusive there may be other ways in which Aquinas could establish the conclusion. If he is successful in proving the existence of a God having the attributes assigned to the Christian God, and being man's last end, it would easily follow that there are not two last ends.

Whatever is desired is necessarily desired for the sake of the last end, Aquinas argues. A desideratum is necessarily valued either as one's perfect good, or as "tending" to it; for "every beginning of perfection is ordained to complete perfection," which is the last end. It would be impossible, in other words, to desire something *qua* good without desiring more of the same. Moreover, "secondary objects of the appetite do not move the appetite, except as ordered to the first object of the appetite." Thus if a man takes medicine to get well in order to accomplish his work, and this in order to be happy, then, if it were the case that he did not desire to be happy, he would not desire any of the other things either. The conclusion follows from the premises, but some of these seem doubtful. Is it true that we always desire health for the sake of something else?

Aquinas adds an important elucidation:

> One need not always be thinking of the last end whenever one desires or does something; but the force of the first intention, which is in respect of the last end, persists in every desire directed to any object whatever, even though one's thoughts be not actually directed to the last end. Thus while walking along the road one does not need to be thinking of the end at every step.[63]

The view that in desiring anything we desire it—even partly—for the sake of the last end, or happiness, remains controversial. The view that all

[61] *Summa Theologica,* Part 1 of Part 2, Q1, A4.
[62] *Ibid.,* A5.
[63] *Ibid.,* A6.

men have the *same* last end has also met a strong challenge, especially in recent times. It was traditionally asserted by Greek and medieval thinkers, but its meaning varied. Aquinas maintains that all men desire the same last end, for this is simply "the fulfillment of their perfection"—the full realization of their potentials and aspirations, as we might say. As to that in which perfection is to be realized, however, men disagree. Some seek it by way of riches, others by pleasure, etc., yet the disagreement is not hopeless; it can be resolved.

> Thus to every taste the sweet is pleasant; but to some the sweetness of wine is most pleasant, to others, the sweetness of honey, or of something similar. Yet that sweet is absolutely the best of all pleasant things in which he who has the best taste takes pleasure. In like manner that good is most complete which the man with well-disposed affections desires for his last end.[64]

Aquinas is now in a position to answer a number of objections: It is true, he says, that men have different vocations and pursuits in life, that some men live a life of sin, and that they all differ from one another as individuals: They intend the same last end in the sense that all want to perfect themselves, and also by virtue of the fact that, in spite of their individual differences, they agree in their generic nature, which has always the same "tendency." It is implied, moreover, that those who mistake the thing in which the last end lies can be brought, in the light cast by the good man, to see that they are wrong, that what they desired they did not really desire.[65]

Even nonrational creatures concur in this last end, *i.e.*, God, but they do so in different ways. Man, as well as other rational creatures, attains his last end "by knowing and loving God," whereas nonrational creatures can attain it only to the extent that "they share the Divine likeness, according as they are, or live, or even know."[66]

The Denial That Some Good of the Soul Is What Makes Man Happy

If happiness is "the activity of the soul in accordance with virtue," as Aristotle says, then happiness belongs to the soul, and is constituted by its activity. Without alluding to the Philosopher, Aquinas denies that happiness is constituted by "some good of the soul." But does he really disagree with Aristotle? He clearly distinguishes between two ways in which we can speak the "last end," viz., as something desired as an end, and as something attained, and concludes that

[64] *Ibid.*, A7.
[65] *Ibid.*
[66] *Ibid.*, A8.

the thing which is desired as an end is that which constitutes happiness, and *makes* man happy; but the attainment of this thing is called happiness. Consequently we must say that happiness is something belonging to the soul, but that which constitutes happiness is something outside the soul . . . what makes man happy is something outside his soul.[67]

It is clear from this passage that, in denying that happiness is "constituted" by some good of the soul, Aquinas means only to deny that some good of the soul is "what makes man happy." What makes man happy, Aquinas is insisting, is something outside the soul. But does Aristotle disagree? For him, also, what makes man happy is outside the soul; it is the lure of the moral and intellectual virtues. Man does not make *himself* happy except in a secondary sense; he is made happy by meeting the needs of his friends and children, and his country, or by the challenge of science and philosophy.

The disagreement between Aquinas and Aristotle here relates to the *nature* of that which is said to make man happy. God plays only a dim role in Aristotle's theory, but is the be-all and end-all in Aquinas' view.

Closely related to this is another important point of difference. Aquinas insists that "it is impossible for man's last end to be the soul itself or something belonging to it,"[68] for the soul exists in potency, not in act. The soul is always learn*ing* or acquir*ing* knowledge and virtue, but the last end is perfection of knowledge and virtue—the complete fulfillment of desire. Aristotle admits that the difficulty arises in his theory. For it would seem, he says, that happiness cannot be complete until a man is dead, and, if it is incomplete, it is hardly happiness. "Is this not quite absurd," he asks, "especially for us who say that happiness is an activity?"[69] The problem, of course, does not arise in Aquinas' theory of *perfect* happiness, for this is not an activity composed of parts which must be added together until the very end of a man's life before he can be called happy; it is an instant and miraculous attainment of the perfect good, which is complete at every moment. In this respect, and disregarding other considerations, everyone would concede that Aquinas' perfect happiness is greatly superior to Aristotle's happiness, which is admittedly incomplete and imperfect.

VIRTUE AND PERFECT HAPPINESS

Perfect happiness, or ultimate felicity, cannot consist in moral actions, Aquinas argues, since the virtue of fortitude can be ordered to victory in war, and the virtue of justice, to the preservation of peace. Happiness, on

---

[67] *Ibid.*, Q2, A7. (Italics added.)
[68] *Ibid.*
[69] *Op. cit., Nicomachean Ethics*, 1100a12.

the contrary, "is incapable of being ordered to a further end." Similarly, the moral virtues are concerned with establishing a mean of the passions with respect to external conditions, but "such a measuring of passions, or of external things" cannot be "the ultimate end of human life, since these passions and exterior things are capable of being ordered to something else." Aquinas also argues that to become like God is our ultimate end or happiness, but that the likeness cannot consist in moral actions since such actions cannot be properly attributed to God, whereas happiness can. And, finally, Aquinas adds that, since felicity is "the proper good of man," it cannot consist in moral actions; "for some animals share in liberality or in fortitude," though they have no part in man's distinctive trait of intellection.[70]

"Happiness consists in the operation of the speculative rather than of the practical intellect," since the object of the former is the highest of all, and its operation "most delightful" to man. It is carried out mostly for its own sake, rather than being in the interest of action, and, finally, contemplation has most in common with the life of God and the angels.[71]

But perfect happiness does not lie in the pursuit of the speculative sciences, of course, for the speculative sciences are based on the senses, as Aristotle says, and thus "cannot extend further than knowledge of sensibles can lead." But the human intellect is not perfected by something lower than it except "in so far as it partakes of a certain likeness to that which is above the intellect, namely, the intelligible light, or something of the kind." But knowledge of that which is above the human intellect can perfect it directly, not through participation in something higher, and here then must lie man's ultimate felicity.[72] And man's final perfection and happiness does not even consist in a knowledge of the angels, though they are higher than man, for they are what they are by participation in what is higher than they.[73]

The break with Aristotle is not quite so decisive here as one might have expected. Aquinas points out that Aristotle, in his *Nicomachean Ethics*, is concerned with the imperfect happiness such as is enjoyed in this life, and not with perfect happiness, which cannot be attained on earth. "Hence the Philosopher," Aquinas says,

in placing man's happiness in this life, says that it is imperfect, and after a long discussion, concludes: "We call men happy, but only as men." But God has promised us perfect happiness, when we shall be *as the angels* . . . in *heaven* (Matt. 22:30).[74]

[70] See *Summa Contra Gentiles*, Ch. 34.
[71] See *Summa Theologica*, Part 1 of Part 2, Q3, A5.
[72] See *ibid.*, Q3, A6.
[73] See *ibid.*, A7.
[74] *Ibid.*, Q3, A2.

Aquinas concedes that the pursuit of the speculative sciences yields "a likeness or participation" of perfect happiness, and that the intellect is perfected thereby—by being "reduced from potency to act . . . but not in its final and complete act."[75]

Although perfect happiness does not *consist in* moral and intellectual virtues, or their exercise, Aquinas holds that man is perfected by virtues of both kinds, and that neither happiness, perfect or imperfect, is attainable where they are lacking. The Aristotelian moral virtues of justice, fortitude, temperance, and prudence are adopted by Aquinas,[76] and so are the intellectual virtues. They are all "good habits" that we are born with in the sense that we have an aptitude for them, but are acquired in the sense that the natural tendencies must be perfected. But whereas Aristotle says that the virtues are acquired by education, external opportunities, and the efforts of the individual—all natural causes—Aquinas maintains that divine grace is also necessary if the individual is to make all the right choices leading to good habits. And the theological virtues of faith, hope, and charity, which are Aquinas' crowning additions to the Aristotelian table of virtues, are not acquired by habituation at all, but must be infused in us by God.[77]

Because these theological virtues are distinctive and crucial to Christianity, and to Christian conceptions of happiness, we shall have to consider them briefly. Aquinas states that

> man is perfected by virtue for those actions by which he is directed to happiness. . . . Now man's happiness is twofold. . . . One is proportionate to human nature, a happiness, namely, which man can attain by means of the principles of his nature. The other is a happiness surpassing man's nature, and which man can attain by the power of God alone, by a kind of participation of the Godhead.

The principles by which man may be directed to supernatural happiness are called "theological virtues: first, because their object is God, because they direct us rightly to God; secondly, because they are infused in us by God alone; thirdly, because these virtues are not known to us except by Divine revelation, contained in the Holy Writ."[78] Thus, for example, the

[75] *Ibid.,* A6.

[76] On the other hand, Aristotle's virtue of humor is omitted, and friendship seems to be depreciated. Aristotle devotes two long books of his *Nicomachean Ethics* to friendship and says that "no one would choose the whole world on condition of being alone" (1069b18). But Aquinas, though he refers to the same passage, states that "the happy man needs friends," but for one reason alone, namely, "that he may be helped by them in his good work" (*op. cit.,* Q4, A8). And this relates only to the imperfect happiness on earth. Perfect happiness has no need whatever for the companionship of friends.

[77] See *op. cit.,* Q63, A3.

[78] *Ibid.,* Q62, A1.

Apostle says, "Now these remain, faith, hope and charity, these three" (I Cor. 13:13), and "Ye that fear the Lord believe Him," and again, "hope in Him," and again, "love Him" (Ecclus. 2:8). Against the objection that faith, since it is a kind of imperfect knowledge, cannot be more perfect than the moral and intellectual virtues, and is in fact hardly a virtue at all, Aquinas replies that faith and hope relating to mundane things may be less than virtues, but when they relate to the Divine they are more. They surpass all virtues within the power of man, in proportion as their object is more perfect.[79]

Though faith is imperfect compared to knowledge, it precedes hope and charity in the order of generation, for "it is by faith that the intellect apprehends the object of hope and love," and in the same way hope must precede love, for it is by hoping that we come to love. The order of perfection, however, is the reverse of the order of generation, viz., first charity, then hope, then faith.[80]

THE ATTAINMENT OF HAPPINESS IN THIS LIFE AND IN THE AFTERLIFE

The interconnection of the virtues is important for our purpose. If it should turn out that the natural virtues depend on the theological virtues, then even imperfect happiness would depend on Divine intercession, and could not be achieved by any man's efforts alone. Aquinas' answer is as follows: The moral virtues can be acquired without charity "in so far as they produce good works that are directed to an end not surpassing the natural power of man; and when they are acquired thus, they can be without charity, even as they were with many of the Gentiles." But insofar as the good works relate to a supernatural last end, they "cannot be acquired by human acts, but are infused by God."[81] This seems to imply that moral virtues, and presumably also intellectual virtues—so far as they do not bear upon salvation—can be acquired through human efforts, and hence that imperfect happiness might be attained without charity, and the supernatural mediation it entails.

Yet, on the other hand, God "works inwardly in every nature and in every will," Aquinas assures us, and the gifts of the Holy Ghost that are

---

[79] See *op. cit.*, II, I, Q62, A3.

[80] See *ibid.*, A4.

[81] *Ibid.*, Q65, A2. Yet, in the same passage, Aquinas cites Augustine's gloss on "All that is not faith is sin" (Rom. 14:23), namely, "He that fails to acknowledge the truth has no true virtue, even if his conduct be good," which seems quite contrary to Aquinas' conclusion. But possibly the gloss means only that virtue becomes impossible when a man has knowingly and deliberately rejected the faith. And it may be that it expresses Augustine's thought more accurately than it does Aquinas'.

necessary for salvation[82] can also have the effect of increasing imperfect happiness on earth. And the beatitudes also promote perfection, and thus prepare the individual for happiness both here and hereafter. Thus the merits mentioned in the beatitudes, such as meekness, mercifulness, and peacemaking,

> are a kind of preparation for, or disposition to happiness, either perfect or in its beginning; while those that are assigned as rewards may be either perfect happiness, so as to refer to the future life, or some beginning of happiness, such as is found in those who have attained perfection, in which case they refer to the present life. Because when a man begins to make progress in the acts of the virtues and gifts, it is to be hoped that he will arrive at perfection, both as a wayfarer and as a citizen of the heavenly kingdom.[83]

The beatitudes are also said to turn us *away from* "sensual happiness," which is false and perverse, and *toward* the happiness of the active moral life, which is "a disposition to future Happiness," and *toward* contemplative happiness, which, "if it is perfect, is the very essence of future Happiness, and, if imperfect, is the beginning of it."[84]

That happiness on earth is an imperfect image and a preparation for happiness in heaven is expressed in another way. Augustine repeatedly says that no happiness is possible in this life save for the hope for it in the next. Aquinas also remarks that "one is said to possess [happiness] already, when one hopes to possess it,"[85] but he is far from maintaining that hope for future happiness, though important, is the whole of our earthly happiness.

We should expect from these and other considerations that imperfect happiness on earth would be more easily and often obtained than the perfect happiness of heaven, for, indeed, the former is said to be a beginning or preparation for the latter. Yet no one can know who will be saved, and Aquinas assures us that salvation is always *possible*. Since there is in every intellect a natural desire to "see" God, and natural desire must be capable of fulfillment, "every intellect, whatever its level, can be a participant in the Divine Vision. Moreover, it is promised by Scripture."[86]

The assumption that every natural desire must be capable of fulfillment is basic, not only to Aquinas' thought but also to Aristotle's naturalistic philosophy. Aquinas uses the assumption in proving that the ultimate felicity of man in a future life must be possible, and, indeed, it seems to follow that if all men desire this felicity, which can only be enjoyed in a

---

82 See *ibid.*, Q68, A2.
83 *Ibid.*, Q69, A2.
84 *Ibid.*, A3.
85 *Ibid.*, A1.
86 *Summa Contra Gentiles*, Ch. 57. See also *Summa Theologica*, Part 1 of Part 2, Q3, A8; Q5, A1.

future life, and "nature does nothing in vain," then it is possible for every man to realize it. Aristotle, who is equally teleological, and also holds that all men desire happiness wherein "nothing is wanting," nevertheless does not argue that a future life of blessedness must be possible. On the contrary, he states that "there may be a wish even for impossibles, *e.g.*, for immortality."[87] It would seem that the teleological premise that nature does nothing in vain can be invoked on some occasions, and not on others. Its vagueness and a kind of arbitrary generality have left it vulnerable to attack.

THE ROLE OF PLEASURE IN HAPPINESS

In his account of pleasure, Aquinas follows Aristotle's lead in most matters. This is surprising since Aristotle is a naturalist concerned with natural phenomena in this life, whereas Aquinas is mainly interested in the ultimate felicity in the next.

Endorsing Aristotle's insight that pleasure is "at any moment complete, for it does not lack anything which coming into being later will complete its form,"[88] and rejecting Plato's view that pleasure is a becoming, Aquinas concludes, again citing the Philosopher, that pleasure is not in time, though it accompanies processes that are. The object of every pleasure is "a good obtained";[89] and they are divided according as they are natural—arising from the satisfaction of bodily needs, or rational—induced by the activity of reason. Joy is a pleasure of the latter kind, and is never attributed to irrational animals. This is the same as his division of the bodily or sensible, and the spiritual or intellectual pleasures, and Aquinas, of course, agrees with Aristotle that the latter are *greater* than the former. But of all the supporting arguments he marshals, the only one that carries any weight is this—that the one kind is more loved and honored than the other.[90]

Aquinas also undertakes to specify the causes of pleasure, and here again the Philosopher is his guide. Two things are required for pleasure, he claims, the attainment of some good and the knowledge that one has attained it. Since both are operations, every pleasure can be said to arise from operations. But how about the pleasures arising from leisure and rest, when the day's work has been done? Aquinas gives a typically Aristotelian answer to this objection, viz.:

> Operations are pleasant in so far as they are proportionate and con-natural to the doer. Now, since finite power is finite, operation is proportioned to it according to a certain measure. And so if it exceeds that measure, it will no

[87] *Op. cit., Nicomachean Ethics,* 1111b22.
[88] *Ibid.,* 1174a15–18.
[89] *Op. cit.,* Q31, A1–2.
[90] See *ibid.,* A5.

longer be proportionate or pleasant, but, on the contrary, painful and irksome. And in this sense, leisure and play and other things pertaining to rest, are pleasant, since they banish sadness which results from labour.[91]

Movement, also, insofar as it is free and unimpeded, is a cause of pleasure, and so is doing good to another, and, indeed, "whatever we do or suffer for a friend is pleasant, because love is the principle cause of pleasure."[92] And, finally, wonder, which is a desire for knowledge of effects the cause of which surpasses man's power to know, yields pleasure which will be greater in proportion to the strength of this desire to know.

Pleasures, being of different kinds, can conflict with one another, and can hinder as well as aid operations, for, as Aristotle says, "appropriate pleasures increase activity . . . but pleasures arising from other sources are impediments to activity."[93] The pleasures arising from reasoning do not hinder but rather help it by fixing attention; it is the bodily pleasures, as Aristotle shows, that in different ways cause all the trouble. Pleasures are found to *perfect* activities in two ways: as that which completes an activity, making it better than it would have been without it. "And in this sense the Philosopher says that 'pleasure perfects operation . . . as some end added to it,' " as a further good added to it. The second way in which pleasure perfects operation is indicated by Aristotle saying that "pleasure perfects operation, not as a physician makes a man healthy, but as health does,"[94] *i.e.*, a man does not aim at pleasure, which is rather a mark of successful operation. When pleasure accompanies an activity, it is pursued with more eagerness and zeal.

Aquinas rejects a Stoic view that all pleasure is evil. The Stoics are thinking, perhaps, only of bodily or sensual pleasures, but even here they are wrong, "since none can live without some sensible and bodily pleasure." And pleasure perfects spiritual and intellectual operations, as well as bodily activities. But the Epicureans are also mistaken in holding that pleasure is intrinsically good, and that therefore all pleasures must be good. The truth is that some pleasures are good and some evil, and for two reasons: If "pleasure is a repose of the appetitive power in some loved good, and [results] from some operation," the operation may be in accord with "reason and the law of God," or in disaccord. Second, the pleasures are good or evil according as they attach to, or are appropriate to, particular actions that are good or evil.[95]

It turns out that one pleasure is "the greatest good," or at least a part of

91 *Ibid.*, Q32, A1.
92 *Ibid.*, Q6.
93 *Ibid.*, Q33, A3.
94 *Ibid.*, A4.
95 See *ibid.*, Q34, A1.

it. Aquinas says that "Happiness is the greatest good, since it is the end of man's life. But Happiness is not without pleasure, for it is written (Psalms 15:11) *Thou shalt fill me with joy with Thy countenance; at Thy right hand are delights to the end.*"[96]

Plato, Aquinas says, is right in rejecting the opposite errors of the Stoics and Epicureans (which are mentioned above), but wrong in thinking "that no pleasure [could] be the sovereign or greatest good."[97] Plato thinks that pleasure springs from generation and movement, and that it must, therefore, be something imperfect. But in the case of intellectual pleasures, Aquinas points out, we take pleasure not only in acquiring knowledge but in contemplating and using what is already acquired: generation is not always involved. Plato is also misled, Aquinas maintains, by his simple identification of the greatest good with that which is supremely good in itself, apart and unparticipated in; for in this sense, Aquinas says, the Supreme Good is simply God. However, there is quite a different sense of "greatest good," as when we speak of the greatest good *for man*, and this requires that the greatest good be participated in or "possessed," or enjoyed. In the latter sense, the greatest good is something humanly attainable, and it is with this that Aquinas is here concerned.[98]

Thus we can speak of the greatest good in two ways: "Man's last end may be said to be either God Who is the Supreme Good absolutely; or the enjoyment of God, which denotes a certain pleasure in the last end. And in this sense a certain pleasure of man may be said to be the greatest among human goods."[99] But Aquinas asks, how could the greatest good be made better by the addition of pleasure, or any other good? He answers, in effect, that this objection is valid when it is a question of the greatest good, in an absolute sense, but not when the greatest good as experienced by man is meant. You cannot add any good to God, but you can add pleasure or enjoyment to man's experience of God, and get something better as a result. Moreover, Aquinas adds, "it might be said that pleasure is not something extraneous to the operation of virtue, but that it accompanies it, as stated in [Aristotle's] *Ethics*."[100] In this case we could not speak of "adding a good to the greatest good," as if we were adding something separable from it.

Pleasure is greater the higher the operation it accompanies, and greatest of all in perfect happiness—the intellectual vision of God.

[96] *Ibid.,* A3.
[97] *Ibid.,* A4.
[98] Here Aquinas repeats the words and follows the reasoning of Aristotle, in his criticism of Plato's Form of the Good. The passage from Aristotle's *Nicomachean Ethics* is quoted in full in Chapter 1.
[99] *Loc. cit.*
[100] *Ibid.*

THE SENSUAL WORLD AND THE
PERFECTION OF THE BODY

Whether one must have a body to be happy is, for Aquinas, a double question. The enjoyment of *perfect* happiness does not depend on having a body, and this is clear from both authority and reason. For "the Apostle says (II Cor. 5:6) *While we are in the body, we are absent from the Lord. For we walk by faith and not by sight. But we are confident and have a good will to be absent . . . from the body, and to be present with the Lord.* From this it is evident [Aquinas concludes] that the souls of the saints, separated from their bodies, *walk* by *sight*, seeing the Essence of God, in Whom is true Happiness."[101] Reason also supports the same conclusion. Aquinas, concurring with Aristotle, states that the intellect can operate independently of the body, except as it needs "phantasms" (images) to represent the things it knows. But since "the Divine Essence cannot be seen by means of phantasms," which has already been proved,[102] it follows that the body is not needed for perfect happiness.

On the other hand, the body is necessary for happiness on earth. It is necessary to man's perfection, but not as forming his essence; it is necessary to his *well-being*. For example, "beauty of body and keenness of wit belong to man's perfection," not because they are essential traits, but because they are essential to happiness in this life.[103]

The *perfection* of the body thus is necessary if we are to enjoy earthly happiness. "A well-disposed body is of necessity required for it," Aquinas insists, "for 'this happiness consists,' according to the Philosopher, 'in an operation according to perfect virtue'; and it is clear that man can be hindered, by indisposition of the body, from every operation of virtue."[104] But how is this possible? Does it mean that the malfunctioning of the body could not only prevent us from being just and temperate and courageous, but also hinder the operation of the intellectual virtues, including the highest—the vision of God? This would imply that the indisposition of the body could obstruct *perfect* happiness, but Aquinas has just proved that one need not have a body to enjoy perfect happiness, and he maintains also, of course, that before the Day of Judgment, when they will retrieve their bodies, the saints do actually live disembodied in the highest felicity. Moreover, both Aquinas and Aristotle insist that the intellectual operation does not depend on the body.

101 *Ibid.*, Q4, A5.
102 See *ibid.*, 1, Q12, A3.
103 See *ibid.*, Q4, A5.
104 *Ibid.*, A6.

Aquinas' answer is as follows: "Although the body has no part in that operation of the intellect whereby the Essence of God is seen, yet it might prove a hindrance to it. Consequently, the perfection of the body is necessary, lest it hinder the mind from being lifted up." Happiness in heaven, after all, has its beginnings in the happiness here on earth, where the soul may be drawn toward God or weighed down by the body. Thus Aquinas can say that "the perfect disposition of the body is necessary, both antecedently and consequently, for that Happiness which is in all ways perfect." It is necessary *antecedently*, since, as Augustine says, if the body is too difficult to govern "the mind is turned away from the vision of the highest heaven." It is necessary *consequently*, it would appear, since "it is natural to the soul to be united to the body" and it is thus "not possible for the perfection of the soul to exclude its natural perfection."[105] But when the soul of the blessed is reunited with a body, it will be with a purified spiritual body, which, since it is completely controlled by the soul, cannot distract from its vision.

External goods would hardly be needed for the perfect happiness in heaven, but they are required for happiness on earth, which consists in a life of virtue, as Aristotle says. External goods supply "the necessaries of the body, both for the operation of contemplative virtue, and for the operation of active virtue, for which latter he needs also many other things by means of which to perform its operation."[106] But friends, as we have noted, are not so important for Aquinas as they are for Aristotle. They are necessary for happiness in this life only to the degree that they aid in the production of good works.

Although Aquinas, in describing the happiness we can enjoy on earth, continually defers to Aristotle, his account of it is not so complete, and he leaves more questions unanswered. It also depends, in part, on theological tenets, since, for example, virtue cannot be achieved without divine grace. Happiness here is really an understudy for happiness in heaven. It is the saints, who enjoy the latter, who most certainly enjoy the former.

A METHODOLOGICAL NOTE

The issue of perfect happiness in heaven *vs.* imperfect happiness on earth will not be examined in Part II of this book as are other main issues of happiness.

The justification of the belief in perfect happiness—the Christian blessedness—is enmeshed eventually in so many basic doctrines of the

---

[105] *Ibid.*
[106] *Ibid.*, A7.

Church that it would be impossible to give it a fair hearing within the framework of the present book. A presentation of the case against perfect happiness and of the intricate rejoinders of its defenders would also bulk large and lead far beyond the subject of happiness proper. The arguments for the immortality of the soul are involved, and so also are the arguments for God's existence, and for His infinite power, wisdom, goodness and freedom, as instanced by His effects on earth and disclosed by Revelation.

The issue of perfect *vs.* imperfect happiness also is unique in other respects. *Within* the Christian system of Augustine and Aquinas, the two happinesses are not opposed: one is seen as the continuation of the other. *Beyond* the Christian system, the issue usually loses its common ground; the nonbelievers do not argue against perfect happiness, for they do not even acknowledge an afterlife: they argue, at most, against an afterlife. Similarly, they may deny, doubt, or simply disregard the existence of God, and reject or ignore His supposed retributive justice, mercy, and perfect freedom; and here again there can be little meeting of minds on the issue itself. The question of attainability also presents a stumbling block to controversy about perfect happiness. Theories of *im*perfect happiness—the Platonic, the Aristotelian, the Epicurean, the Stoic, for example—specify what you must be, have, or do to be happy, and often cite public examples of happy men, so that a person can form some notion of his chances for happiness, given a certain effort on his part. But no human effort can play any known or probable part in attaining the Christian perfect happiness, nor is a calculation of one's chances feasible. Both are ruled out by the sovereign freedom of God's will, which can elect the greatest sinner as well as a saint, or no one at all: this happiness is not an achievement or a just reward, but a free gift. For this reason, then, as well as for others on which we have briefly touched, the choice between perfect happiness and an imperfect happiness would prove strange and difficult. If a choice were made, it would probably be determined, not so much by a comparison of the merits ascribed to happiness here and happiness there as by relative attainability and other wide-ranging considerations.

5

Concepts of Happiness and Duty

I. The Substitution of Worthiness
for Happiness: Kant

THE philosophers so far considered have disagreed about the nature
of happiness, but they have all agreed that it is the highest good.
Kant is ready to accept a great deal that has been said about the nature
of happiness, but he takes the heart out of everything by his denial that
happiness is the highest good. For what good is happiness if it is not the
highest good, if there is another good that must be continually preferred
to it? Plato and Aristotle confidently exhibit the superiority of true happiness to the possession of wealth and power, and the life of pleasure. Now,
Kant argues that the performance of duty, the "being worthy of happiness," is superior to happiness. Duty is the measure; happiness cannot be
the goal. For Augustine and Aquinas, the supreme good is the perpetual
vision of God, but Kant declares that "nothing can possibly be conceived in the world, or even out of it, which can be called good without
qualification, except a Good Will."[1] In denying that happiness is the

[1] *Fundamental Principles of the Metaphysics of Morals*, First Section, p. 10.

91

highest good, Kant opposes not only the hedonistic conception of happiness, which is especially repugnant to him, but also every other conception of it. Happiness, however conceived, cannot be the supreme good.

Kant was a great challenge, and all theories subsequent to him show his influence. We shall have to give some attention to his ethical views, which resulted in the dethronement of happiness.

VIRTUE AND HAPPINESS

The Stoics hold that virtue is sufficient for happiness. For them, as Kant says, it "was the whole *summum bonum,* and happiness only the conscious-ness of possessing it." (We have seen too that Plato, while tentative about so many things, insists repeatedly that the just man, the virtuous man, is bound to be happy.) On the other hand, the Epicureans[2] "maintained that happiness was the *whole summum bonum,* and virtue only the form of the maxim of its pursuit; viz., the rational use of the means for attaining it."[3] The Stoic and the Epicurean make the same mistake: that of supposing that one can derive one conception from the other analytically. That is, the Stoic holds that virtue implies happiness; the Epicurean, that happiness implies virtue, that is, that from happiness as the *summum bonum* it can be inferred that virtue is simply the means to it. But virtue and happiness, according to Kant, are distinct concepts—the one cannot be derived from the other.

The lack of connection between them is reflected on the practical level, for history is full of suffering heroes and happy villains. Kant thinks it strange that philosophers should have believed that virtue is sufficient for happiness, and that it can be attained by applying reason to this end. For, if in a rational being,

> the proper object of nature were its *conservation,* its *welfare,* in a word, its *happiness,* then nature would have hit upon a very bad arrangement in selecting the reason of the creature to carry out this purpose. For all the actions which the creature has to perform with a view to this purpose, and the whole rule of its conduct, would be far more surely prescribed to it by instinct . . . than it ever can be by reason.[4]

Even if happiness could be conceived as the consummation of "the true wants of nature" with regard to which all men were in accord, or, if man's skills in seeking what he conceives to be his ends were maximized, "never-

---

[2] The Epicurean view is discussed briefly in Chapter 6 in connection with hedonism in general.

[3] *Critique of Practical Reason,* Part I, Book II, Ch. II.

[4] *Metaphysics of Morals,* First Section, p. 12.

theless what man means by happiness . . . would never be attained by him. For his own nature is not so constituted as to rest or be satisfied in any possession or enjoyment whatever." Happiness, according to Kant, presupposes a harmony of nature with one's wish and will, but man is no favorite of nature and must take his chances along with other animals. But worse, perhaps, than all the droughts and plagues of nature that are visited on the species are the misfortunes invented by man—"the oppression of lordly power, the barbarism of wars, and the like."[5]

Virtue and happiness, thus, are two distinct concepts, neither one of which can be derived from the other analytically. Virtue does not, in fact, result in happiness, which is, in any case, unattainable, *i.e.,* unachievable.

THE UNIVERSAL DESIRE FOR HAPPINESS: THE NATURE OF HAPPINESS

"To be happy," Kant says, "is necessarily the wish of every finite rational being, and this, therefore, is inevitably a determining principle of its faculty of desire."[6]

Every philosopher we have discussed so far has claimed that it is desired, as a matter of fact; Kant alone claims that it is *necessarily* desired. He is alone, also (except perhaps for Augustine), in holding that happiness is unattainable on earth. As creatures of sense, living in a mechanically determined world, we necessarily desire a happiness that our best efforts can never achieve; but as moral agents we choose not happiness but duty, and this freedom, Kant holds, is achievable.

What then does Kant mean by "happiness"? In the passage quoted above, he equates it with conservation and welfare. Shortly before, he says that "power, riches, honor, even health, and the general well-being and contentment with one's condition,"[7] are called happiness. In the *Critique of Pure Reason,* we have the famous definition: "Happiness is the satisfaction of all our desires; *extensive,* in regard to their multiplicity; *intensive,* in regard to their degree; *protensive,* in regard to their duration."[8] Elsewhere, in another passage that sounds like a definition, the emphasis is on pleasure, or pleasantness, viz.: "Now, a rational being's consciousness of the pleasantness of life uninterruptedly accompanying his whole existence is happiness."[9] The fact is that Kant sometimes identifies happiness with the satisfaction of all our desires, and more often with maximum

---

[5] *The Critique of Judgment,* 83.
[6] *Critique of Practical Reason,* Part I, Book I, Ch. III, p. 112.
[7] *Ibid.,* p. 10.
[8] *Critique of Pure Reason,* "Transcendental Doctrine of Method," Ch. II, Section II.
[9] *Critique of Practical Reason,* Part I, Book I, Ch. III, p. 108.

pleasure of uninterrupted pleasantness. In either case his "universal desire for happiness" has its plausibility, and in either case his denial of the possibility of happiness makes sense, for it is unlikely that any man could get through life with *all* his desires satisfied, or with no interruption of pleasantness. *Perfect* happiness would be impossible on earth, Kant could have said, but then all the advocates of happiness, except the Stoics and Plotinus, would have agreed with him.

THE IMPOSSIBILITY OF AN ETHICS OF HAPPINESS

If all men necessarily desire happiness, and do what they can to obtain it, how then can it be their *duty* to do what they can to obtain it? The very meaning of "duty," which implies some control and restraint of desire, excludes this possibility, and therefore excludes an ethics of happiness.

Moreover, if happiness is the supreme good, an ethics of happiness will have to formulate a law defining what every man ought to do in order to obtain happiness—stating what is right or obligatory for each in every relevant situation—but is this at all feasible? Actions that would serve one man's happiness would destroy another's. For example, the best way for *A* to promote his happiness might be to go to medical school and to devote his main energies to the profession of his choice, and so it would be his duty to do this. However, the happiness of his classmates would not be served by going to a medical school, but by other courses of action. How then can it be *A*'s duty to do what others are not obliged to do? Could it be some man's duty to tell the truth or keep his promise, while others were under no such obligation? A moral obligation, Kant insists, must be "binding on the will" of every man. Indeed, it must be binding on the will of "every rational being," for rationality is the basis of morals, and, if there are angels, a law that defines our obligation would also be binding on them.

Only a law could establish an obligation, but a law is necessarily universal, applying equally to every member of a class. A law has no exceptions; it would not be a law if it did. Nor can a duty have exceptions. If it is a duty to be honest—except when it is very difficult, dangerous, or what not—then it is not a duty to be honest. And since moral obligation is binding on the will of men, *qua* rational, and not by virtue of any special qualities or vocations they may have, it must be valid for all men equally. But how could an ethics of happiness formulate such a law? What is one man's meat is another man's poison. Without a law, however, there could be no ethics.

Standing in the way of an ethics of happiness is also the notorious uncertainty and precariousness of the future. How could the course of benefit be calculated years and decades in advance, as surely must be done if we are to say, even in the case of one particular man, that he ought—which means he certainly ought—to perform a given act? It would seem that even if it were possible for one man to have a duty that others do not have, it would be impossible to know that a given act would promote his lifelong happiness. We should have to be omniscient, Kant says.

Ethics, according to Kant, must lay down imperatives—rules binding on the will of every rational being. Imperatives are of two kinds—categorical and hypothetical. Categorical imperatives are unconditional, whereas hypothetical imperatives are binding on the will of every rational being only conditionally—only if they accept the condition. Simple examples are:

Categorical imperative: Thou shalt not lie.
Hypothetical imperative: If thou wouldst be believed, do not lie.

The first simply states an obligation for all rational beings; the second is obligatory only for those who accept the condition, *i.e.*, for those who want to be believed. Both, of course, are understood to be binding only on the will of rational beings. A young child or childish adult would not be expected to see or heed the force of either imperative. Hence Kant says that the imperatives are "binding on the will of every rational being," not that they are binding merely on the will of every man.

The principles of ethics must be as irresistible as the principles of logic, Kant holds—in direct contradiction of almost all other philosophers. They must be like $A = A$, or Things equal to the same thing are equal to each other, which are self-evident; or like the syllogism in Barbara, the conclusion of which follows necessarily once the premises are accepted, viz.:

All M is P
All S is M
Therefore, all S is P

There is a big difference, however, which must be kept in mind. The scientific principles are binding on the *intellect* of every rational being. Imperatives are binding on the *will* of every rational being. They alone have to do with *actions* and prescribe what is right or obligatory.

For Kant, however, the parallel between the exact science and ethics is crucial, and in three respects. Just as a theorem of geometry about equilateral triangles must be (a) rationally irresistible and (b) valid for all equilateral triangles, so a moral law must be a priori certain, *i.e.*, incontrovertible, and without exceptions. In fact these two features almost define the moral law. If it is based on ordinary experience, Kant argues, it would not be certain and could have exceptions, and if it has exceptions it could not determine duty in *every* case, and hence could not determine it at all.

Doing one's duty is acting under a law that is necessarily binding on all rational beings, and (c) the motive too, like the judgment of the mathematician, must not be determined by any personal desire. One must be moved by a free and impersonal respect for the subject matter, for those logical connections that accord with reason.

Our original question can be stated in a different form, viz.: Can there be an imperative of happiness, one specifying conduct conducive to happiness in all possible cases? Kant's reply, as suggested above, is that no one has the requisite knowledge of the contents and conditions of happiness. He admits that anyone who wills happiness *necessarily* wills all the means thereto that are in his power, but he adds that

> unfortunately, the notion of happiness is so indefinite that although every man wishes to attain it, yet he can never say definitely and consistently what it is that he really wishes and wills. The reason of this is that all the elements which belong to the notion of happiness are altogether empirical, *i.e.*, they must be borrowed from experience, and nevertheless the idea of happiness requires an absolute whole, a maximum of welfare in my present and all future circumstances. Now it is impossible that the most clear-sighted and at the same time most powerful being (supposed finite) should frame to himself a definite conception of what he really wills in this. Does he will riches, how much anxiety, envy and snares might be not thereby draw upon his shoulders? Does he will knowledge and discernment, perhaps it might prove to be only an eye so much the sharper to show him so much more fearfully the evils that are now concealed from him.[10]

Kant here throws down a serious challenge to eudaemonism, utilitarianism, and every other form of teleological ethics. Their answers will be considered in Chapter 8. Certainly, if his contention is right, there can be no imperative of happiness, nor an ethics of happiness.

But Kant voices other objections. For example, the ethical imperative cannot really be hypothetical; it must be categorical, he says. All men necessarily desire happiness, and if their motive for doing their duty is only this desire, then they do only what they would naturally do anyway, whether it was their duty or not. Duty, to be duty, must be duty for duty's sake, not for the sake of happiness. Thus happiness is irrelevant to moral action, and an ethics of happiness an impossibility.

The Performance of Duty as the Supreme Good

There is still another requirement: The moral act of doing one's duty has no regard to consequences. Kant observes that though you might save a man's life by misdirecting a murderer who is on his trail, you are not

---

[10] *Metaphysics of Morals*, Second Section, pp. 41–42.

justified in doing so. The most that morality permits you to do to save the poor man is to refuse to answer the murderer's question. The moral man will of course suffer if his refusal to lie costs a man his life, but he will not waver on this account. And there is one advantage in his suffering: It proves beyond question that his act was not occasioned by his feeling or desires, but by the command of duty alone.

Thou shalt not steal and *Thou shalt not murder* are also categorical imperatives, and so is Kant's example, "Thou shalt not promise deceit-fully." He is keenly aware of some of the difficulties. How do we know, he asks, that in obeying these precepts we are not actually yielding to "ob-scure" fears and desires? He almost says "unconscious" fears and desires, thus anticipating a criticism later to be brought against every ethics of duty.

It is always possible that fear of disgrace, perhaps also obscure dread of other dangers, may have a secret influence on the will. Who can prove by experience the nonexistence of a cause when all that experience tells us is that we do not perceive it? But in such a case the so-called moral imperative, which as such appears to be categorical and unconditional, would in reality be only a pragmatic precept, drawing our attention to our own interests and merely teaching us to take these into consideration.[11]

But if our real motive in obeying a moral precept, such as "Thou shalt not promise deceitfully," can be concealed or unconscious, is it not difficult to say that any act is motivated by duty alone? And if we cannot determine whether an act is done from a pure sense of duty, is it not as difficult to know whether pure duty has been enacted, in any particular case, as to calculate accurately our future happiness? Kant, of course, does not think so. He is arguing here that it is impossible to make sure by an empirical canvass what all these particular categorical imperatives are, and to know for certain, on empirical grounds, that anyone who obeys them will be acting from duty alone. He is arguing that only an a priori principle can give us a firm guarantee—can certify beyond any question the validity of moral imperatives.

There is only one such principle,[12] he says, and that is:

Act only on that maxim whereby thou canst at the same time will that it should become universal law.

Now if all imperatives of duty can be deduced from this one imperative as from their principle, then . . . at least we shall be able to show what we understand by it and what [duty] means.[13]

[11] *Ibid.,* p. 44.
[12] Kant actually says that "there is but one categorical imperative"; it is really the *one principle of all categorical imperatives,* i.e., it is not an imperative itself since it does not tell you what you must do, but only gives the form of all statements that do.
[13] *Op. cit.,* p. 46.

Deferring the question why we should accept this principle of all imperatives of duty, let us consider some of Kant's examples of the application of the principle. Suppose a man, weary of life, decides on suicide and, being of a moral turn of mind, asserts the following as his maxim: "From self-love I adopt it as a principle to shorten my life when its longer duration is likely to bring more evil than satisfaction." Can he will that this should become a universal law binding on every rational being? No, Kant says, for this would be "a law to destroy life by means of the very feeling whose special nature it is to impel to the improvement of life which would contradict itself and, therefore, could not exist as a system of nature."[14]

But would suicide out of self-love, when life becomes worthless, involve a self-contradiction when made a universal law? Self-love, it will be remembered, is, for Kant, the principle of the pursuit of happiness. That all men should commit suicide when happiness is no longer possible contradicts most religious codes, but does it involve *self*-contradiction?

Kant also considers the case of a man in financial difficulties who adopts the maxim: "When I think myself in want of money, I will borrow money and promise to repay it, although I know that I can never do so."[15] He says that this maxim also becomes self-contradictory when generalized to all men, but here again his critics, and even his followers, find it hard to follow him. For what he says is that if everyone were to break his promises, promises would become impossible, for no one would any longer take them seriously. The maxim, when generalized, might thus lead to a state of society in which the promise-breaker could no longer operate, but this would be quite consistent with the maxim. What is wrong with the maxim, the Aristotelians could claim, is that it leads, not to self-contradiction but to the very opposite of what its author wants, *i.e.*, unhappiness.

Kant's third example is equally infelicitous, but more to our purpose since it deals with a conflict of enjoyment and the development of the higher faculties. The question is whether a man could consistently generalize his maxim, "Live for amusement, sex, and enjoyment only." Kant says that he could not possibly will this as a universal law, since, "as a rational being, he necessarily wills that his faculties be developed."[16] But does a man, simply because he has rational faculties, necessarily will that these faculties be developed? Most people would admit only that men, owing to their rational nature, have a desire, or at least some sort of dumb craving, to develop their powers, and that this may well conflict with a stronger desire for bodily enjoyments. The maxim, if generalized, might lead to a wide-

[14] *Ibid.*, p. 47.
[15] *Ibid.*
[16] *Ibid.*, p. 48.

spread conflict of desire in a society, but conflict of desire is something quite different from logical contradiction.

The ingenious effort to show that it is impossible to generalize unacceptable maxims of duty, it is usually admitted, is a failure. *Thou shalt lie* can be generalized without self-contradiction. If the result is that everyone begins to lie profusely, which is extremely unlikely, then no one could believe anyone, and lies would become impossible. This would be socially undesirable, but no self-contradiction results. Nor is there any logical bar to generalizing *Thou shalt steal* and *Thou shalt kill*. In the first case, there might, in time, be no property left to steal, and, in the second case, there might eventually be no people left to kill. But this would not *contradict* your will, or willingness, that everyone should do as you are doing, namely, stealing or killing. The generalizing of these maxims, Kant's critics argue, is not logically impossible; it does result in bad, *i.e.*, unhappy consequences. That is, Kant's own examples seem to show that, if maxims are to be ruled wicked, it must be because they lead to unhappiness.

There is another alternative: It is held that we have an intuitive certainty that acts such as lying, stealing, breaking promises, killing, etc., are bad. We shall see that some followers of Kant, discarding his attempt to prove that wicked maxims are self-contradictory when generalized, and rejecting at the same time Aristotle's evaluation of acts according to whether they lead to or away from happiness, take the view that we can distinguish right acts from wrong acts simply by understanding their intrinsic nature. It remains to be seen whether this gambit is successful in explaining rightness without reference to consequences and the goal of happiness.

We are now able to return to our question, Why must everyone accept the moral law—the principle of all imperatives of duty? The principle again is:

> *Act only on the maxim whereby thou canst at the same time will that it should become a universal law.*

We can see at once that it has the form of a categorical imperative. It does not say "Act on certain maxims *if* you want good results or a happy event." It says "Act on them no matter what." But why does Kant say that his principle is binding on the will of every rational being? Kant's answer is puzzling. One of his critics suggests that Kant jumps from the plausible conclusion that a rational being would not assent to a self-contradictory principle to the preposterous conclusion that a rational being must assent to every non-self-contradictory principle—including the moral law.[17] It is hard to believe that a man of Kant's logical acumen could make such a

[17] See C. D. Broad, *Five Types of Ethical Theory*, p. 128.

simple error, but, yet, it is also hard to see any alternative explanation of Kant's conviction *proving* that every rational being must necessarily assent to the moral law.

But Kant says more than "assent"; he says that every rational being is necessarily *bound* by the moral law—necessarily obeys it. This can only add new doubts to the old, for a rational being could not be said to necessarily be bound to act in a certain way unless the other parts of his nature are also bound in the same way.

DUTY VS. DESIRE

Plato's dualism of desire and reason leads to unwelcome consequences. When a sharp division is made, desire tends to fall on the side of the body, which is corruptible and which the philosopher seems to regret having, and this leaves the soul with no motive force to soar, which is its destiny. In the *Symposium*, on the other hand, desire is represented as the dynamo of the soul's assent to the highest heaven of beauty. Thus, desire is sometimes a misshapen, unruly beast, cowed only by fear and blows, and sometimes "a mighty hunter," "a perpetual philosopher," and really the same as Eros, the ruler of the world.

Kant's stark dualism of duty and desire also leads to complications. As creatures of desire, we belong to the world of sense in which all our actions are, and must be, causally determined; whereas, as rational beings, we belong to a super-sensuous, noumenal world, in which we are absolutely free, *i.e.*, not determined by causality but self-determined. In the first world, we are necessarily governed by our natural desire for happiness and by the necessities of the physical world. In the second, we are subject to the moral law which we freely adopt because it is in accord with reason, and are emancipated from the tyranny of both desire and physical law. Consequently, every man *can* conform to the moral law. He can conform to it because he ought, for, if it is true that he ought to conform, it is true also that he can conform. Ought implies can, and in the "noumenal" world, which is beyond the sway of both physical and psychological necessity, there is nothing that could stop him. This explains why, though all men, *qua* rational, freely and of necessity, embrace the moral law, most of them in point of fact follow natural desire and seek happiness. They are living in two worlds, mostly in the wrong one.

For 150 years and more, philosophers have been enticed and appalled by this bold conception. Kant deploys his genius in repeated efforts to explain how, as rational beings, we freely and necessarily obey the moral law, while in the flesh we are subject to all the sensuous allurements and physical necessities that might well prevent our doing so. Plato argues that all men would be perfectly good *if* only they knew precisely what the good is in the situation in which they are called upon to act. But this is not so incredible. The knowledge that could make men good is acquired knowledge, and most of us obviously do not have enough of it. Kant's contention is far more drastic. He holds that every man now possesses all that it takes to be morally perfect and that viewed from his rational side he cannot help but be morally perfect.

The divorce of duty from desire and feelings entails another difficulty. Kant admits that we have a feeling of contentment or satisfaction when we do our duty, and calls it "respect" (*Achtung*). But he says it is quite different from other feelings and has no basis in experience. "Duty," Kant says, "*is . . . acting from respect for the law.*" But

> an action done from duty must wholly exclude the influence of inclination and with it every [other] object of the will so that nothing remains which can determine the will except objectively the *law,* and subjectively *pure respect* for this practical law, and to the thwarting of all my inclinations.[18]

The moral law has an austere grandeur, as everyone will admit, and Kant says that it is "holy," and "sublime," like the starry heavens above. The respect it evokes is a fine sense of a higher worth vindicated, as our self-love is thwarted and humiliated. Such a feeling cannot be learned—derived from experience and practice, for in this case its object could not be the same for all men. Men love and approve different things, but they can respect only one.

> But although respect is a feeling, it is not a feeling received through influence but is self-wrought by a rational concept and, therefore is specifically distinct from all feelings of the former kind, which may be referred either to inclination or fear.[19]

When confronted with the moral law, this new and complicated feeling of respect immediately arises, though it is not derived from anything in our previous experience, and has no resemblance to it. It is little wonder that Kant is charged with inventing an *ad hoc* feeling tied up uniquely with the moral law, simply because he cannot explain morality by reason alone, and cannot consistently maintain that feelings generated in experience are involved.

Kant exhibits his respect for the truth by raising a very honest question: Can reason alone be sufficient to move the will of flesh and blood creatures to conform, against their inclinations and fears, to the moral law? As rational beings we might have a sufficient *reason* for conforming; that is the

[18] *Metaphysics of Morals,* Second Section, pp. 19–20.
[19] *Ibid.,* pp. 20–21, fn.

rationality of the law and the fact that our reason freely "legislates" this law, so that we are obeying a law, in a sense, of our own making. But do we also have a sufficient *motive*? Kant replies that, for creatures of sense and passion, a feeling of pleasure or satisfaction is no doubt necessary to morality:

> In order . . . that a rational being who is also affected through the sense should will what reason alone directs such beings that they ought to will, it is no doubt requisite that reason should have a power to *infuse a feeling of pleasure* or satisfaction in the fulfillment of duty, that is to say, that it should have a causality by which it determines the sensibility according to its own principles. But it is quite impossible to discern, i.e., to make it intelligible *à priori*, how a mere thought, which itself contains nothing sensible, can itself produce a sensation of pleasure.[20]

Thus the respect for this law must be pleasurable, but it is impossible to see how it could be, for the pleasure cannot have its usual source in the senses. If it is derived from anything other than the rationality of the moral law itself, the moral will would not be autonomous. We could not be sure that the moral law would be obeyed for its own sake only, for it might be partly determined by that which produced the pleasure. The pleasure or satisfaction must be produced by reason—but how is this possible? "For us as men," Kant says, "it is quite impossible to explain how and why the *universality of the maxim as a law,* that is morality, interests."[21]

Kant's dilemma is that there must be springs of moral action; they must come from reason; they cannot come from reason.

> But to explain how pure reason can be of itself practical without the aid of any spring of action that could be derived from any other source, i.e., how the mere principle of the *universal validity of all its* maxims as law (which would certainly be the form of a pure practical reason) can of itself supply a spring, without any matter (object) of the will in which one could antecedently take any interest; and how it can produce an interest which would be called purely moral; or in other words, *how pure reason can be practical*—to explain this is beyond the power of human reason, and all the labour and pains of seeking an explanation of it are lost.[22]

This passage, which occurs at the close of the *Fundamental Principles of the Metaphysics of Morals,* testifies to Kant's great integrity. It also suggests that it is not easy to seal off duty from desire and the feelings, nor to maintain as an effective goal a moral goal opposed to happiness.

20 *Ibid.,* p. 97.
21 *Ibid.,* p. 98.
22 *Ibid.,* p. 99.

KANT'S FINAL VINDICATION OF HAPPINESS

In his *Critique of Practical Reason,* Kant makes renewed efforts to understand how happiness is related to virtue. "It can never be an immediate duty to promote our happiness," he says, "still less can it be the principle of all duty,"[23] yet we need not, on this account, renounce all claim to happiness. Indeed, it may be our duty to pursue the happiness produced by health or property if the lack of it prevents us from doing our duty. Second, although a person *as* rational, never seeks happiness for its own sake but only moral goodness, this goodness makes him worthy of happiness, and constitutes a claim recognized not only by the person involved but also by disinterested reason.

In Kant's view, then, moral goodness generates a valid claim to happiness. It will be remembered that he is using happiness to mean a life that is continuously accompanied by pleasure, or, as he also puts it, a condition of a rational being with whom everything goes according to his wish and will. The latter formula says that desires are all satisfied, and the former, that pleasure is always present; for the present purpose they come to the same thing.

Now happiness in this sense, though not good in itself, adds a perfection to the supreme good and thus completes it, so that because of it the world is better. The supreme good, as we have seen, is virtue or moral goodness, but this is not

> the whole and perfect good as the object of the desires of rational finite beings; for this requires happiness also. . . . For to need happiness, to deserve it, and yet at the same time not to participate in it, cannot be consistent with the perfect volition of a rational being possessed at the same time of all power, if, for the sake of experience, we conceive such a being. Now inasmuch as virtue and happiness together constitute the possession of the *summum bonum* in a person, and the distribution of happiness in exact proportion to morality (which is the worth of the person, and his worthiness to be happy) constitutes the *summum bonum* of a possible world; hence this *summum bonum* expresses the whole, the perfect good, in which, however, virtue as the condition is always the supreme good, since it has no condition above it; whereas happiness, while it is pleasant to the possessor of it, is not of itself absolutely and in all respects good, but always presupposes morally right behavior as its condition.[24]

The completeness of the moral life thus requires a world in which those who are worthy of happiness are in fact happy. But our world obviously

[23] *Critique of Practical Reason,* p. 187.
[24] *Ibid.,* pp. 206–207.

does not distribute happiness according to deserts. What recourse remains to human beings? The Stoic attempts to wrest happiness from nature by reconciling his mind in advance to everything that fate might bring, and the Epicurean also limits his desires—to the safe, the gentle, and the friendly. Aristotle's virtues are clearly defined with a view to happiness, but if ill fortune destroys the felicity of good men, this is the way of the world and is to be accepted with courage. Another resource is that of the meliorists of the nineteenth century, namely; the world is to be changed. Kant sometimes hopes for progress, but his solution of the dilemma of virtue and happiness, like that of St. Augustine, is religious.

We cannot suppose, Kant says, that God's ultimate purpose in creating the world was the happiness of its rational residents, but rather the *summum bonum,* which is moral goodness. The attainment of moral goodness, however, implies *worthiness to be happy.* Can we conceive that God would desire men to be worthy of happiness without supplying that which would complete the goodness of the *summum bonum* and fulfill the harmony of the world order?

> For nothing glorifies God more than that which is the most estimable thing in the world, respect for His command, the observance of the holy duty that His law imposes on us, when there is added thereto His glorious plan of crowning such a beautiful order of things with corresponding happiness.[25]

Such consideration might justify Kant's "postulate of immortality," but he does not claim to have *proved* that immortality is a fact. In the *Critique of Pure Reason,* he demonstrates that knowledge that goes beyond the possibility of perception is impossible. In his later writings he sometimes talks as if the three postulates of God, freedom, and immortality constitute a kind of higher knowledge, and sometimes as if they are pragmatic demands of our higher nature.

THE DIALECTICAL OUTCOME OF KANT'S THEORY OF HAPPINESS

We shall conclude by stating briefly a number of Kant's conclusions about happiness which impressed other writers on the subject—either positively or negatively, and so played some part in the controversy about this idea. Most of these have already been discussed, but some will be new, and point ahead to further discussion in Chapter 8.

1. The radical opposition between reason and perceptual experience, duty and natural desire, morality and happiness, implies that a serious life is one of incessant conflict—"storm and stress."

25 *Ibid.,* p. 228.

2. The conflict is so fundamental that no resolution of it is possible in this life.

3. The doctrine that pleasure is not good except as a completion of morality—the supreme good—is combined with a pessimistic verdict as to the good man's chances for happiness in this world.

4. Kant's polemic against the hedonic calculus, against the possibility of acting with a view to our total happiness, is influential. How it is possible to make such calculations with the future as uncertain as it is, is a question that is still reverberating.

5. Kant's contention that it is impossible to frame a moral law that would specify the acts all men must perform to obtain happiness has its repercussions. If a virtuous act is one that promotes happiness, and the conditions of future happiness are so various and difficult to foresee, how can we ever know what our duty is, the duty of *everyone*? Moreover, it is commonly recognized that we can know certain acts to be wrong, such as lying and stealing, though we have only the haziest idea of the remote consequences. Kant thus gives heart to those who would replace the ethics of happiness by a morality of duty.

6. Closely related to this is Kant's earnest insistence on the universality of a moral law. No one before had made so much of consistency in morality: every man, including, by implication, all classes of society and backward peoples around the world, must be accommodated within the framework of the one law, in terms of full equality; the moral law is binding on all or none. The more this law appeals, the more the ethics of happiness is discredited, for the latter, as Kant said, could never frame such a law.

7. The general import of Kant's moral law has been anticipated by the Golden Rule, "Do unto others as you would have done unto you," and by other golden rules in ancient cultures. The rigorous monumental structure he builds around it, however, makes a deep impression. Not the least of its attractions is the certainty that it seems to give to moral decisions. Instead of precarious calculations of future happiness, one could determine one's duty by a simple test, *i.e.*, by ascertaining whether one could will consistently that all other men perform the same act, *i.e.*, act on the same maxim as you are acting on.

8. The second form of Kant's moral law, although Kant believes that it follows from the first, seems to have a different import. It is: "*So act as to treat humanity, whether in thine own person or in that of any other, in every case as an end withal, never as means only.*"[26] The inclusion of "thine own person" is puzzling, since Kant does object to a man sacrificing

[26] *Ibid.*, p. 56.

his own life or happiness for his friend or his country, and thus treating himself "as means only." The point of the maxim is to treat every *other* human being as an end in himself, "in a kingdom of ends," and never purely as a means.

At the time Kant was writing, serfs were still owned in Prussia, and there were slaves across the Atlantic and around the world. New forms of exploitation and inhumanity, coming in with the Industrial Revolution, were to raise a storm of protest. The struggles for the right of religious dissent, of sects and individuals, were continuing. All could draw support from Kant's moral law. It favored the English conception of democracy, which emphasized the rights of minorities and individuals, far more than did utilitarianism, which was native to England.

9. Kant holds that it can never be one's duty to pursue one's own happiness. One reason is that happiness is a *natural* end, and men already seek it. "What a man of himself inevitably wills does not come under the notion of *duty*," he says in one of his later writings, "for this is a *constraint* to an end reluctantly adopted. It is, therefore, a contradiction to say that a man is *in duty bound* to advance his own happiness with all his power.

> It is likewise a contradiction to make the *perfection* of another my end. . . . For [only] he is able of *himself* to set before him his own end according to his own notions of duty; and it is a contradiction to require . . . that I should do something which no other but himself can do.[27]

It is likewise irrational *not* to seek the happiness of others, for I naturally desire my own happiness, and therefore want them to help me get mine.

II. Happiness as a Dialectical Achievement: Hegel

In Spinoza's *Ethics*, where the genius of system reaches a new height, happiness fuses not only with virtue but also with the fulfillment of love and freedom. The end result in Hegel is much the same. The impetus to unification is easy to understand. If there is to be a single ideal of human perfection and fruition, all the major goods of life should be reconciled within it. Kant does his best to harmonize the universally recognized goods, but only after playing up their opposition to a point that makes it almost impossible. By defining virtue as obedience to the moral law—a law that we ourselves make, he reconciles it with freedom, conceived as submission to reason. The virtue and the freedom belong, however, to man as a rational being; it leaves the real flesh-and-blood man unfree, unholy,

[27] *Metaphysical Elements of Ethics*, Introduction, IV.

hunting after happiness. Happiness is reconciled with virtue only by a "postulate" which, as is sometimes said, is only "something we *hope* is true." In spite of prodigious efforts, Kant thus bequeaths a set of dualisms which becomes the chief task of the post-Kantians to surmount.

HEGEL'S CRITIQUE OF THE KANTIAN ETHICS

The main tension in Kantian ethics is between desire and duty, or desire and reason. Since duty entails constraint and thwarting of desire, according to Kant, there is a permanent conflict between desire and reason that prevents the natural realization of duty combined with happiness. For Hegel, and for Aristotle, on the other hand, each desire incorporates its own reason or rationale. The desire to eat is a desire to eat *because* one is hungry, or *because* it is healthful. Hence the conflicts of the moral life are really between two desiderative reasons, or, as we can also say, between two deliberative desires. They are conflicts between two desires, each tied up with its own reason or partial justification, or between two reasons, each with its own motive force. Such conflicts are not regarded as permanent; they can be overcome by education, as one desiderative reason corrects or modifies another. In this way, *both* virtue and happiness can be eventually attained. Thus, we have:

Kant: Reason and Desire are in permanent conflict. Hence, the natural outcome cannot be both virtue and happiness; it can be either one or neither.

Hegel and Aristotle: One desiderative reason conflicts with another, but, through learning and education, the conflict is gradually weakened, tending to the final elimination of conflict, and a balance or harmony between the two. In such series the conflict of the desiderative reasons is eventually reduced and the final realization of both virtue and happiness becomes their ideal limit. It would be a mistake, however, to suppose that the reduction of conflict is a purely quantitative process, or that pairs of conflicting desiderative reasons are isolated from one another. The attainment of the mean in Aristotle's theory is not purely a matter of not-too-much and not-too-little, and qualitative factors and interweaving of issues are also very prominent in Hegel's conception of dialectic progress.

It is easy to see why Hegel, in his various studies of the development of moral consciousness in the historical process, is led to associate every moral position with its motivating desire. If a moral idea does not have its dynamic impulse, it cannot lead men to act and suffer. If a desire does not have its reason or rationale, it would have no defense or justification. In criticizing the moral idea of the Terror under Robespierre, or the idea of the "beautiful soul" as conceived by Novalis and Goethe, for example,

Hegel must deal with both motivation and thought. In his *Philosophy of History,* he states:

> We assert then that nothing has been accomplished without interest on the part of the actors; and—if interest be called *passion,* inasmuch as the whole individuality, to the neglect of all other actual or possible interests and claims, is devoted to an object with every fibre of volition, concentrating all its desires and powers upon it—we may affirm absolutely that *nothing great in the world* has ever been accomplished without passion. Two elements, therefore, enter into the object of our investigation; the first the idea, the second the complex of human passions; the one the warp, the other the woof of the vast arras-web of universal history.[28]

The concrete union of the two, Hegel says, is liberty, realized in a state. It is no use regarding passion as sinister and immoral. For when passion is recognized as human activity, as inspired by "private interests," by "self-seeking designs," passion is the key to character and action.[29]

Starting out as an adherent of Kant's ethics—of the moral law and pure duty—Hegel soon becomes critical of their abstract, inhuman character. In his *Early Theological Writings,* he argues that

> between the Shaman of the Tungus, the European prelate who rules church and state, the Voguls, and the Puritans, on the one hand, and the man who listens to his own command of duty, on the other, the difference is not that the former make themselves slaves, while the latter is free, but that the former have their lord outside themselves, while the latter carries his lord in himself, yet at the same time is his own slave.[30]

The man who obeys the moral law simply because he would otherwise be contradicting himself is a slave because he has imposed this law upon himself against his inclinations. The abstract form of the law is alien if not hostile to one side of his nature—his passions, loves, desires, and sensuous experience.

"Woe to the human relations which are not unquestionably found in [Kant's] concept of duty."[31] Hegel says Kant is mistaken in thinking that his moral law has anything in common with Jesus' commandments. The Sermon on the Mount fulfills the law but also annuls it as something now superfluous. Higher than the law is "reconcilability," *i.e.,* a loving disposition. "In reconcilability the law loses its form, the concept is displaced by life; but what reconcilability thereby loses in . . . universality . . . is

---

[28] *Philosophy of History,* Introduction, p. 24. See also *Philosophy of Mind,* Sec. 474.
[29] See *ibid.*
[30] *Early Theological Writings,* p. 211.
[31] *Ibid.,* p. 212.

only a seeming loss and a genuine infinite gain on account of the wealth of living relations with the individuals . . . with whom it comes into connection![32]

He who has the spirit of reconcilability has no contrary desires to conquer and no enmity within him; he seeks rather to overcome the enmity in the other. Young Hegel thus sacrifices the universality of the abstract law for the richness and concrete reality of love. The ideal is a reconciliation of desire and duty, a restoring of the unity of man who has been turned against himself.

In his later writing abstract duty is no longer supplanted by Christian love, but its abstractness, its divorce from desire and feelings, is always criticized. In the *Phenomenology of Mind*, Hegel argues that when sensibility is regarded as irrelevant to duty, or as something that is simply *not in conformity with* duty, the harmonious unity between sensibility and morality, which consciousness ever seeks to achieve, becomes impossible. Sensibility cannot be surrendered for the sake of "pure duty," because duty presupposes sensibility, *i.e.*, some aim or inclination, arising from personal experience and the social formation, to do one's duty. When the aim of the moral consciousness is reduced to mere duty, this consciousness rightly complains of the injustice of a conception obliging it to realize an abstract law, while denying it its own realization.

> The moral consciousness cannot renounce happiness and drop this element of its absolute purpose. The purpose, which is expressed as pure duty, essentially implies retention of individual conviction and knowledge thereof constitutes a fundamental element in morality. This moment in the objectified purpose, in duty fulfilled, is the individual consciousness seeing itself as actually realized. In other words, this moment is that of enjoyment, which thus lies in the very principle of morality, not indeed of morality immediately in the sense of a frame of mind, but in the principle of the *actualization* of morality.[33]

We have seen that Aristotle makes the same distinction. Enjoyment of pleasure is not the proper motive of duty, but it is the normal accompaniment of virtuous activity which is not against our nature but agreeable to it. Hegel goes on to say that since enjoyment attends the actualizing of morality, it

> is also involved in morality, as a mood, for morality seeks . . . to realize itself. Thus the purpose . . . is that duty fulfilled shall be both a purely moral act and a realized individuality, and that nature, the aspect of

[32] *Ibid.*, p. 215.
[33] *Phenomenology of Mind*, pp. 616–617.

individuality, in contrast with abstract purpose, shall be one with this purpose.[34]

Nor does Hegel think much of Kant's final reconciliation of duty with happiness by way of a Postulate of Practical Reason. This amounts to a confession that he has failed to connect morality with reality, which he must do since the moral actors are in this world. He is obliged to resort to *deux ex machina* at the end of the play, and to conjecture that happiness will be distributed according to degrees of worthiness in another world.[35]

In the *Philosophy of Right*, Kant's law stating the correspondence of duty and rationality is approved in principle but condemned for its lack of content. The pronouncement "Act as if the maxim of thine action could be laid down as a universal principle," is too barren to provide a criterion of noncontradiction, or any guide of conduct.[36] Hegel inveighs again against the exclusion of happiness or welfare from morality. When this is done, a view of morality is evolved that "is nothing but a bitter, unending struggle against self-satisfaction as [in] the command: 'Do with abhorrence what duty enjoins.' "[37]

Against all such austerity Hegel upholds the right of the individual to the many forms of happiness embodied in modern life:

> The right of the subject's particularity, his right to be satisfied, or in other words the right of subjective freedom, is the pivot and center of the difference between antiquity and modern times. This right in its infinity is given expression in Christianity and it has become the universal effective principle of a new form of civilization.[38]

The equating of the right of personal satisfaction—an essential phase of happiness—with the right of subjective freedom—an essential phase of freedom—is of great significance, for Hegel says comparatively little about *happiness* as such but a great deal about the growth of *freedom*, which is his principal way of designating the human progress toward goodness and perfection.

THE ATTAINABILITY OF HAPPINESS

For Hegel, as for Kant, happiness is the natural desire of all men, and it is naturally desired for its own sake and not for the sake of anything else. It is taken to mean continual pleasantness or enjoyment, or the satisfaction of

34 *Ibid.*
35 See *ibid.*, pp. 623–624.
36 See *Philosophy of Right*, Addition to 86, Par. 135.
37 *Ibid.*, Par. 124.
38 *Ibid.*

desires—not this or that or every satisfaction, of course, but satisfaction on the whole or at the realistic maximum, when a long period or a lifetime is taken into account. This comes close to Aristotle's eudaemonistic definition of happiness on the subjective side, for the "activity according to virtue" is accompanied by pleasure, and, indeed, our virtues would not be virtues if they were unpleasant to us.

But what do Kant and Hegel say about the relation of happiness to virtue? We have seen that Kant denies there is any natural connection. A Nero might be happy and a saint unhappy, although, if the moral life is to be *complete*, happiness must be apportioned according to the precise degrees of virtue, and unhappiness must match the shades of viciousness. Here too Hegel is much closer to Aristotle than to Kant. Happiness or welfare, he contends, is compounded of natural desire, learning, comparison, choice, a willingness to reject some satisfactions and to accept others, and, hence, implies self-control, prudence, sagacity, and the other virtues as well, for, eventually, the natural desires of the developed consciousness are purified and fused with duty. In seeking its own happiness, natural desire comes to merge with the desire for the happiness of others. At first the happiness of others is willed only abstractly, but eventually it is willed concretely and effectively, through the instrumentalities of the state and other institutions in which the individual has his being, his status, freedom, and worth. Owing to the interdependence of vital and spiritual activities, happiness or welfare becomes a social production. It is inseparable from the state and other institutions and is realized only as a phase of the historical development.

The difficulty of understanding Hegel is notorious, and no one has attempted to separate his theory of happiness from the other themes with which it is mingled and interwoven in his system. We shall, nevertheless, try to see whether the above impressions match what Hegel himself says. He clearly echoes Aristotle and Kant in insisting that happiness must be whole and lasting.

In happiness, thought has already a mastery over the natural force of impulse, since the thinker is not content with the momentary but requires happiness as a whole. This requirement is connected with education in that it is education that vindicates a universal.[39]

The happy man has learned to control impulses and to forgo some enjoyments for others. Education gives us the general knowledge needed.

When reflection is brought to bear on impulses, they are imaged, estimated, compared with one another, with their means of satisfaction and their consequences, &c., and with a sum of satisfaction (*i.e.*, with happiness). In

[39] See *op. cit.*, Addition to 15, Par. 20.

this way reflection invests material with abstract universality and in this external manner purifies it from its crudity and barbarity.[40]

"The sum of satisfaction," which is the same as happiness, is already seen to require some virtues, *viz.*: self-control, prudence, sagacity, refinement, and general knowledge of a kind, though this knowledge ("abstract universality") is said to purify impulse only "externally." What is needed in addition to external knowledge is an *internal* principle of rationality, which, while not excluding the satisfaction of impulse, guides conduct by a different rule, by the rule of duty. Hegel rejects the abstract self-sufficiency of Kantian duty, but he does not reject the duty itself. The duty that was supposed to be irresistible to the rational man is so only when integrated with impulse and its satisfactions. Without personal interest, a man would not act; without a self-imposed rule of reason (duty), he would not be what he is, namely, human.

Hegel ridicules Rousseau's idea of a happy, indolent state of nature, where a man's wants are satisfied without striving, without his "doing anything to produce a conformity between immediate existence and his own inner requirements. . . . But impulse and passion are the very life-blood of all action."[41] Morality is universal, the inactive; passion, interest, desire are the agent. Since

> happiness has its affirmative contents in the springs of action, it is on them that the decision turns, and it is the subjective feeling and good pleasure which must have the casting vote as to where happiness is to be placed.[42]

The particularity of the satisfactions a man chooses (and rejects) to make up his own individual happiness is really the same as the freedom or autonomy of his will.[43] But this freedom of the will is universal—the freedom of man and the happiness the individual seeks are sought by all men. In choosing freely this or that satisfaction, the individual wills first of all the freedom to choose, which is shared with other men. In seeking his happiness in this object or that, he seeks first of all happiness in general, *i.e.*, happiness whose particular content is still unspecified, and this is also the primary object of other men. To be happy is the main thing, not to be happy by means of this or that object.

Hegel's conclusion is that since we have implicitly willed freedom and happiness in general, we cannot consistently will also a particular freedom or happiness for ourselves which is discordant with the freedom and happiness of others. Using "welfare" as tantamount to "happiness," Hegel says that, in the idea of good,

[40] *Ibid.*
[41] *Philosophy of Mind*, 475, p. 236.
[42] *Ibid.*, 479, p. 237.
[43] *Ibid.*

welfare has no independent validity as the embodiment of a single particular will but only as a universal welfare and essentially as universal in principle, *i.e.* as according with freedom. Welfare without right is not a good.[44]

But this does not mean that either the good or happiness could exist, or maintain itself indefinitely, without the other. In his philosophical portrayals of the history of mankind, Hegel shows us long eras that were short of freedom and goodness, but they were also short of happiness. Nor does he disclose any happy epochs that were enslaved or wicked. Kant is so disturbed by the existence of unhappy heroes and gay villains that he postulates an afterlife in which accounts are settled properly. Hegel is also a strong believer in retributive justice, but, though his account is not without its ambiguities, he looks to this world and to world history to balance justice. In considering the complaint that villains often prosper while good men get the worst of it, he counters by asking: But *how* good were the good men? Were they completely good? The goodness of the great man of the past was not separable, in his view, from the goodness of freedom of the state and human institutions in which they were immersed, and these always had decided limitations. Only with the coming of Christianity and the modern state (especially the Germanic) does the era of true freedom even begin. The sufferings of heroes may have their basis also in personal defects—in one-sidedness, incomplete integration, faults unnoticed in the general adulation of striking merits.

We can see that Hegel's moral perspective is very different from Kant's, more realistic in the sense of *Realpolitik*. Instead of drawing a fixed line between fact and moral worth, he fuses the elements of human striving and morality in one historical process. Thus

> . . . abstract right, welfare, the subjectivity of knowing and the contingency of external fact, have their independent self-subsistence superseded, though [they remain distinct]. The good is thus freedom realized, the absolute end and aim of the world.[45]

Hegel chooses, as always, to give special prominence to freedom in this nest of ultimate goods. But he might just as well say that the end and aim of the world is morality, or happiness; insofar as freedom is achieved, so also are these. Indeed, these three objectives, though distinct, are merged in the final goal. In their attainment they are also fused. Thus, according to Hugh Reyburn, Hegel holds that:

> Ethically the individual has the same right to the conditions of happiness as to those of freedom; for in the last resort these coincide.[46]

[44] *Philosophy of Right*, 130.
[45] *Ibid.*, 129.
[46] *The Ethical Theory of Hegel, A Study of the Philosophy of Right*, p. 224.

It should not be thought that, when Hegel contends that you cannot consistently will your particular happiness if it conflicts with general happiness, he has any idea of relying on this abstract argument. Kant maintains that you cannot rationally disobey the moral law, and regards his argument as definitive. Hegel recognizes that his own comparable argument has to do with only the *abstract* idea of happiness or welfare. To will the happiness or the good of other men in the abstract is quite different from willing it concretely and realistically. He never tires of describing the unhappy state of the soul which means well, but is estranged from its reality and instrumentalities, or has lost its integrity.

In the *Phenomenology of Mind,* he ridicules the sentimentalism encouraged by Rousseau, under the heading "The Law of the Heart, and the Frenzy of Self-Conceit."[47] The self-conceit is the conviction that anything that comes from the heart must be good, and is to be approved or at least forgiven. In the *Philosophy of Right,* he declares:

> It is one of the most prominent of the corrupt maxims of our time to enter a plea for the so-called "moral" intention behind wrong actions and to imagine bad men with well-meaning hearts, *i.e.* hearts willing their own welfare [happiness] and perhaps that of others also.

Accordingly, trite thoughts and even crimes are "to be regarded as right, rational, and excellent, simply because they issue from men's hearts and enthusiasms."[48] The sentimental heart is only one of the many abortive forms of consciousness Hegel describes. They are all one-sided and unhappy, failing to fuse the subjective aim with the moral purpose, the moral purpose with the implementing conditions, immediacy with reflection, the concrete with the abstract, the universal with the particular, or the individual with the state and other social institutions in which he has his being, his rationality, welfare, and worth.

Of utmost importance to the attainment of freedom and happiness in Hegel's view are the family, the courts, corporations, police, the economic establishment, the state, and other institutions. In the course of attaining selfish ends, Hegel says,

> there is formed a system of complete interdependence, wherein the livelihood, happiness, and legal status of one man is interwoven with the livelihood, happiness, and rights of all. On this system, individual happiness, &c., depend, and only in this connected system are they actualized and secured.[49]

[47] *Phenomenology of Mind,* pp. 391 ff.
[48] *Philosophy of Right,* 126.
[49] *Ibid.,* 183.

By "system" is meant the organization of society to satisfy human needs, *i.e.*, bodily needs, mental and social needs, including the need for freedom and justice. In the imaginary state of nature, bodily needs could be satisfied, but not the others, and we can therefore know, without personal experiment, that people living in primitive simplicity could not be happy. Man transcends the animal stage by the multiplication of his needs and the means of satisfying them. The increasingly complex interdependence and division of labor turn self-seeking activity into social production, and "each man in earning, producing, and enjoying on his own account is *eo ipso* producing and earning for the enjoyment of everyone else." Happiness or welfare is thus in great measure a social production and accrues to the individual from the efficiency and enlightenment of his society.[50]

What each man contributes to the general welfare depends on his capital, his skill, and on accidental circumstances in which men are dissimilar. Although every individual has a right to his own particularity—his own desires and feelings—this does not negate but rather accentuates the natural inequality of men. The three main classes typical of civil society are (a) the agricultural (the *substantial*); (b) the business (*formal*); and (c) the class of civil servants (the *universal* class). The business class has the task of transforming raw materials furnished by agriculture into commodities, while the civil servants take care of the universal interests of the community. Hegel has a great deal to say about the various functions of this class, of the offices of the legislature, "the prince," the courts, the corporations, the police, etc., and all such activities may be regarded as essentials of welfare, at least under modern conditions.

The Role of the State and of World History

Hegel describes the state as "the actuality of concrete freedom"[51] and its constitution must be regarded as something existing in and for itself, "as divine, therefore, and constant, and so as exalted above the sphere of things that are made."[52] It cannot be imposed from outside, as something a priori good; this was the mistake of the French Revolution. It is indigenous and appropriate to a particular nation.[53] The constitution speaks for all its members and for all classes, but they do not speak for themselves. The people (*Volk*) are denied any voice in government, for it is precisely that

[50] See *ibid.*, 199.
[51] *Ibid.*, 260.
[52] *Ibid.*, 273, note.
[53] See *ibid.*, 274.

section of citizens "which does *not* know what it wills."[54] Thus, for Hegel, as for Plato, democracy means the rule of ignorance. Although Hegel adopts a division of powers between the monarchic, the administrative, and the legislative, the decisive power is concentrated in the monarch, and we have a unity of the state as rigid and organic, in some ways, as that of Plato's *Republic.*

Hegel goes to great extremes to safeguard the prestige and natural authority of the state. In the state, he holds, man finds his rationality, his higher worth and purpose. He is awed by its august power and rectitude, yet he must recognize that this principle of rationality that restrains and punishes him is really within himself. Reflection tells him that its worth and wisdom are far greater and more permanent than his own unchastened desires and interests, and that these must be willingly relinquished for the good of a higher "person."

> Sacrifice on behalf of the individuality of the state is the substantial tie between the state and all its members and so is a universal duty.[55]

The greater truth and morality, as well as power, is on the side of the state, and the authority of the state is vested, to an enormous extent, in the monarch.

What assurance does Hegel have that the monarch will promote the welfare of his subjects? Very little is visible in the way of checks and balances, and, in fact, Hegel seems to reject this principle. He will not hear of democratic or aristocratic elements in a monarchy, such as Aristotle advises in his mixed polity, and, indeed, any checks to the monarch seem inappropriate to Hegel. Nor can the constitution, which defines the broad powers of the monarch, be easily changed, for it is "divine" and "constant."

It might be, though, that the Estates could be convened to correct monarchical policy. Calling together the Estates—delegates from all the classes—might do some good. The delegates are close to local facts and may spur officials to do their duty, and to anticipate the criticism of the "Many." The Estates may also be regarded as a mediating organ between the Crown and the nation,

> preventing both the extreme isolation of the power of the crown, which otherwise might seem a mere arbitrary tyranny, and also the isolation of the particular interests of persons, societies, and Corporations. Further, and more important, they prevent individuals from having the appearance of a mass or an aggregate and so from acquiring an unorganized opinion and volition

[54] *Ibid.,* 301.
[55] *Ibid.,* 325.

and from crystallizing into a powerful *bloc* in opposition to the organized state.[56]

The Estates are convened, generally, when public welfare or happiness is threatened, and may be useful in the above ways, but it is a great mistake to suppose that they have the public welfare more at heart than does the monarch.

As for the conspicuously good will for the general welfare which the Estates are supposed to possess, it has been pointed out . . . that to regard the will of the executive as less good [than that of the ruled] is a presupposition characteristic of the rabble or of the negative outlook generally.[57]

An easy answer to the supposed superiority of the Estates, Hegel suggests, is that the Estates are based on private individual interests, whereas the government aims at the common interest, "the universal end" of the nation as a whole.

The highest freedom of the individual, according to Hegel, is not the freedom of choice, as between rival governmental policies, for example, but a freedom that consists in the willing and—to the developed consciousness—*necessary* acceptance of what is true and good, and this is also our real freedom and happiness. Hegel's contention that "the truth of the particular satisfactions is the universal, which under the name of *happiness* the thinking will makes its aim,"[58] appears to hold for the highly developed consciousness as well as for lower stages. When particular aims become purified, they merge with those of the state, and the subject freely adopts as his happiness such satisfactions as his particular state affords.

Democratic critics charge that, in spite of certain humanitarian features, Hegel's state is completely incompatible with private happiness, as also with freedom, conceived in any common sense. Some claim that, with a view of glorifying the Prussian state, Hegel betrays his own deeper principle of dialectic. Whereas the dialectical movement is seen at work elsewhere inexorably destroying the old and bringing in the new, no opposition is accredited within the state, *i.e.*, acknowledged as having its partial truth as against the monarch. There is, thus, no counterforce to win its rights in opposition. All progress comes to a standstill. There is only one force that transcends the vested rights of the state, according to Hegel, and that is the Spirit of World History. But this has too much the appearance of a general endorsement of the superior rights of stronger nations over against the weak to beguile the liberal mind.

But Hegel's account of happiness in its relation to morality and freedom

[56] *Ibid.*, 302.
[57] *Ibid.*, 301.
[58] *Philosophy of Mind*, 478, p. 237.

is a rich texture, remarkable in its realism and bold combinations, and much of it can fit a different theory of the state. His theory of happiness has been reviewed in this chapter because of its close relation to the opposing theory of Kant. In Chapter 7, however, we shall see that Hegel, along with Spinoza, can be regarded as a spiritual father of a modern philosophy of happiness called "self-realization."

6

The Utilitarian Concept of Happiness

UTILITARIANISM is a continuation of ancient hedonism, with several important innovations. The good or happiness is still a favorable balance of pleasure over pain, and pleasures and pains are still qualitatively alike, differing only in degrees. Pleasures can be added together and balanced against a sum of pains. On the other hand, the ultimate goal of utilitarianism is not the greatest amount of pleasure for the individual but maximum pleasure for the greatest number. This universalistic hedonism, as utilitarianism has been called, is a daring advance over the old egoistic systems of hedonism, and in its equalitarianism and meliorism belongs essentially to the modern world. It means that the pleasure of the lowest servant or workingman is just as valuable as the pleasure of a nobleman or factory owner, and should be preferred if it is greater in intensity or duration. Equal pleasures are equally precious, and are to be valued equally, regardless of who enjoys them. "Each is to count for one, and no one for more than one," Bentham says. The duty of every man is simply to act in a manner calculated to promote the greatest possible balance of pleasure over pain. There is always the implication that the sum of human pleasure could be greatly increased by concerted efforts.

119

This conception did not appear till the seventeenth and eighteenth centuries, and was radical even then. It is true that Aristotle defines commutative justice in terms of equality, insisting that in the just exchange of goods, for example, one man will receive exactly the same as another, power, wealth or eminence being given no advantage. But it is never suggested that the pleasure of the wicked is as good as that of the wise and virtuous, nor that the pleasure of an artisan or slave, other things being equal, should be pursued as much as that of a wise and virtuous man. Aristotle's ethics take for granted a stratified society, in which the pleasurable activities of some men are intrinsically more valuable than the pleasurable activities of others, whether they are *more* in quantity or not.

Nor does Epicureanism recognize the equality of the pleasures of different men. It might be said that *A*'s pleasure is as good for *A* as *B*'s pleasure is for *B*. But *B*'s pleasure is not good for *A* unless it gives *A* pleasure. Friendship is considered the royal road to pleasure, but you value your friend's pleasure only as a means to your own. Hedonism, however, is the doctrine that the good or happiness is pleasure and pleasure alone, or the greatest balance of pleasure over pain. The Epicurean is not a pure hedonist, for he insists that the pleasure must be *mine;* or yours, if you happen to be the person talking. My pleasure is good *for me,* and yours is good *for you,* and the pleasures of different individuals do not add up to a grand total of pleasure. Each individual is to seek his own maximum of pleasure, *i.e.,* happiness; there is no collective happiness.

In recognizing that one man's pleasure is as good as another's, utilitarianism seems closer to pure hedonism. Yet it can be argued that "the greatest pleasure of the greatest number" need not be "the greatest pleasure *possible.*" In some ancient societies, the cultural life of a few depended on the enslavement of a large part of the population, and it is conceivable that the maximum pleasure in such a society could be achieved only by a diminution of the pleasures of the greatest number of its members. Few, however, would challenge the classical utilitarian principle that, *in general,* increasing equality of wealth and opportunity tends to increase the sum total of pleasure, *i.e.,* happiness, in a society (unless, Bentham amends, the rich who are deprived suffer too grievously thereby).[1] Thus, progressive income taxes and other government measures, which have the effect of redistributing national income more equitably, could be justified on utilitarian principles.

Utilitarians agree with the Epicureans in recommending the mild, more lasting pleasures of social life, and in warning against an excess of the more intense sensuous pleasures. There is nothing intrinsically wrong about such pleasures, of course. It is only that they are frequently mixed with pain in

[1] See below, Ch. 10.

the present, and productive of pain in the future, and that they prevent the attainment of the more lasting and dependable satisfactions.

For the eudaemonist, on the other hand, pleasures are of different kinds and values, and are graded according to the worth of the activities they accompany. Sensuous pleasures are of a lower order than intellectual pleasures; they are intrinsically less valuable. The eudaemonist thus remonstrates with the drunkard or libertine as follows:

(1) You are living on the level of an animal and are not realizing your higher potentialities. Your pleasures, like the activities they accompany, are of inferior worth. You are forgoing true happiness, which is the end of human life.

The Epicurean admonishes the voluptuary in a different style, viz.:

(2) Your pleasures are mixed and productive of pain, and destroy opportunity and capacity for the more lasting pleasures. You are inviting pain and passing up the full sum of pleasure of which you are capable.

The utilitarian would say the same, but would add:

(3) You are causing your relations and friends suffering and inconvenience, thus reducing the general happiness.

The eudaemonist—and here we are thinking chiefly of Aristotle—makes (1) his principal contention, but he can also supplement (1) by (2) and (3), or by something like them.

Although anticipated in some measure by ancient hedonism and by eudaemonism, utilitarianism makes a distinctive and important contribution. The end of life is now understood to be a social product admitting of quantitative increase, and the ground is prepared for extensive efforts to augment the sum total of human happiness, conceived simply as pleasure. Plato and Aristotle give attention to the happiness of the state, and the Stoics, though their emphasis is individualistic, sometimes speak of the brotherhood of man. The utilitarians are clearly committed by their doctrine to the happiness of the community and of mankind, one man's pleasure counting exactly the same as another's.

Since Bentham's account of happiness is more elaborate than that of other utilitarians, we shall give it special attention.

THE HEDONISTIC CALCULUS

Bentham begins his exposition of the principle of utility with the famous lines:

Nature has placed mankind under the governance of two sovereign masters, pain and pleasure. It is for them alone to point out what we ought to do, as well as to determine what we shall do. On the one hand the standard of right and wrong, on the other the chain of causes and effects, are fastened to their throne. They govern us in all we do, in all we say, in all we think: every effort we make to throw off our subjection, will serve but to demonstrate and confirm it. . . . The *principle of utility* recognizes this subjection, and assumes it for the foundation of that system, the object of which is to rear the fabric of felicity by the hands of reason and of law. Systems which attempt to question it, deal in sounds instead of senses, in caprice instead of reason, in darkness instead of light.[2]

All men, Bentham declares, seek their own pleasure and avoid pain; when they strive for other things, they are mere means to these sovereign ends. This psychological hedonism is quite different from ethical hedonism, which states that men ought to act so as to achieve maximum pleasure. Bentham adopts both forms of hedonism. They are perfectly compatible, it will be noted, for it may well be true that men are always striving for pleasure, but also true that they usually do so inefficiently, and therefore do not achieve the maximum pleasure possible under the circumstances. What they do is to seek pleasure; what they *ought to do* is to so act as to realize the greatest possible amount.

The ethical hedonism of Bentham, however, is not egoistic: It does not say that men should merely maximize their own pleasure. It is "universalistic": It says that each should so act as to maximize the pleasure of the community. The principle of utility "approves or disapproves of every action whatsoever, according to the tendency which it appears to have to augment or diminish the happiness of the party whose interest is in question . . ., if that party be the community in general, then the happiness of the community: if a particular individual, then the happiness of that individual."[3] Many of our actions concern only ourselves and do not affect the happiness of other individuals. In this case, we are free to choose that act likely to produce the most pleasure or the least pain for ourselves. In other situations, however, we cannot act without affecting the feelings of others, and here we must closely estimate the consequences of our action for all concerned, choosing that alternative likely to produce the best balance of pleasure over pain for the whole group.

A man's first concern is, and should be, his own pleasure, not because it is more valuable than the pleasure of others but because he is in a strategic position to promote it. When a conflict arises between his interest and that

---

[2] *Fragment on Government and* . . . *Principles of Morals and Legislation*, Ch. I, p. 125.
[3] *Ibid.*, p. 126.

of the community, however, he should not stop at balancing the pleasures and pains likely to result to him, but must go on to calculate the balance for others who will be affected. The act he chooses should be the one that tends to maintain the greatest pleasure of the community—or of the part affected. His calculation may not always convince him that the interests of the community come before his own. If a young man were to sell all he has and give to the poor, the pleasure afforded the poor might be counterbalanced by his own sufferings. His calculations might show, however, that if he sacrificed only a half of his goods, there would be a balance of pleasure over pain. This altruistic act would then be in accord with the utility principle.

In calculating the balance of pleasure over pain which would justify a given act, we must consider seven factors of the pain or pleasure, viz.: "Its *intensity*, its *duration*, its *certainty or uncertainty*, its *propinquity or remoteness*, its *fecundity*, its *purity*, . . . and its *extent*, that is the number of persons to whom it extends; or (in other words) who are affected by it."[4]

Intensity and duration are the only dimensions of pleasure usually conceded by hedonists, and Bentham does not really mean to extend the list. Certainty, propinquity, fecundity, and purity are only "circumstances" useful or necessary in computing future pleasures. In calculating future pleasures and pains, we naturally give more weight to the certain than to the uncertain, and, therefore, to the near-at-hand rather than the remote. Of two pleasures of equal quantity, similarly, we naturally prefer the one that gives rise to new pleasures and does not entail pains; and we prefer a pure pleasure to those mixed with pain. The seventh factor, *"extent," may* mean only that, in general, the more pleasure is extended, the more pleasure there is. But it might be taken to mean that the number of persons enjoying the pleasure is important in itself, that it would be intrinsically better to have 100 persons enjoying a certain quantity of pleasure than only 10. This would involve a violation of hedonism, however, and it is hard to believe that Bentham means to imply that anything besides pleasure can add to positive value.

There are no *qualitative* differences among pleasures, Bentham insists. Provided the quantity of pleasure is the same, pushpin is as good as poetry, and the satisfaction of the enlightened statesman has no *intrinsic* advantage over that of the criminal. *It has extrinsic* advantages, however, for it may lead to an improvement in the hedonistic level of the individual or community, whereas the other results in a deterioration.

Bentham's so-called hedonistic calculus has been held up to ridicule by many critics of utilitarianism. In the first place, how is it possible to know

[4] *Ibid.,* Ch. IV, p. 151.

the remote, or even the immediate, consequences of moral acts? The future is precarious. Second, how can the quantities of different pleasures and pains be assessed with the precision necessary for moral decisions? For example, how could a judge calculate that the aggregate sufferings of the community in the future would more than counterbalance the pleasure the defendant would experience as the result of a lenient sentence? How could Bentham know (to use one of his examples) that the pain of disappointed expectation of the hereditary landowner, if his land is divided among landless peasants, would exceed the combined pleasure of the peasants, in the present and future?

Such questions are a challenge to utilitarianism, since, to the extent that the hedonistic consequences of our acts are unpredictable, happiness is unachievable, *unless its increase can be contrived and produced.* What, after all, would utilitarianism be without its melioristic program? No one would give it a second thought.

UTILITARIAN SANCTIONS

Bentham believes that the seven circumstances (mentioned above) relating to the desirability of given pleasures and pains are taken into account by judges, lawgivers, and in the decisions of a private character, though not nearly so much as they should be. But he is far from claiming that such a calculation should be carried out prior to every moral act, and to every judicial and legislative decision. There are also four "sanctions," Bentham claims, that *"bind a man,"* by the imposition of pain and pleasure, "to such or such a mode of conduct."[5] These are the *physical,* the *political,* the *moral,* and the *religious* sanctions. Every individual left to himself learns from nature or the physical world that some actions are generally harmful and painful, and others beneficial and pleasant. Second, he also learns to obey the laws of the state, thereby avoiding the punishment entailed. Third, moral rules or customs instruct the individual as to what pleasures and pains will result from his actions; and, finally, he is guided by the approval or disapproval of his neighbors. There are also religious rewards and punishments promised in this life, or in a future one. The religious sanctions differ from the others in the important respect, Bentham says, that the pains and pleasures involved "lie not open to our observation."[6] It is obvious that religious sanctions cannot play the important part in Bentham's empirical utilitarianism that they do in the theological utilitarianism of Abraham Tucker, Gay, and William Paley. For these thinkers,

[5] *Ibid.,* Ch. III, p. 147, fn.
[6] *Ibid.,* p. 149.

an afterlife in which pleasures and pains are at last distributed according to deserts is absolutely essential to the utilitarian system.

J. S. Mill argues, as does Bentham, that the various sanctions favoring altruistic conduct in other systems of ethics are also available to utilitarianism. Duty, conscience, the goodwill of relatives, friends, and the community, the natural desire to avoid penalties and punishments, and the fear of God's displeasure all operate to promote socially approved conduct in the utilitarian. The only difference is that the utilitarian is guided solely by the pleasant and unpleasant consequences of his actions, whereas others invoke "transcendent" sanctions, such as the will of God. They are mistaken in thinking the transcendence is the important thing, Mill argues, for no one would choose to follow the will of God unless he believed that it was more pleasant (or less unpleasant) to do so than not.[7]

Since these sanctions are in operation, utilitarianism does not require us to compute the distant effects of every moral act on the happiness of the greatest number. Mill points out that

> this is exactly as if anyone were to say that it is impossible to guide our conduct by Christianity, because there is not time, on every occasion on which anything has to be done, to read through the Old and New Testaments. The answer to the objection is, that there has been ample time, namely, the whole past duration of the human species.[8]

By noting the tendency of certain kinds of actions to produce pain, and of other kinds to yield pleasure, men have acquired many subsidiary ethical rules and counsels of prudence; it is by them that most moral actions are governed, and they are often enough reduced to habits. Do not steal, do not bear false witness, and do not take human life, are examples. These maxims serve us on most occasions, but, when doubtful cases arise, we must resort to laborious calculations to determine what is best, whatever ethical creed we may profess. The elaborate hedonistic calculus Bentham proposes, "may," he says, "always be kept in view: and as near as the process actually pursued on these occasions approaches to it, so near will such process approach to the character of an exact one."[9]

In fairness to utilitarianism, we should keep in mind the distinction between the motive for an act and the principle that determines whether the act is right or wrong. The greatest pleasure of the greatest number is seldom the motive of our acts—the end in view.[10] The motive for helping a friend financially may be sympathy, and the motive for punishing a thief

---

[7] *Utilitarianism*, Ch. III.
[8] *Ibid.*, pp. 21–22.
[9] *Op. cit.*, Ch. IV, p. 153.
[10] *Ibid.*, Ch. II, pp. 145–146.

may be antipathy, but the moral standard of these acts is the tendency to augment or diminish the general happiness. Thus Bentham does not hold that the good man is always consciously aiming at the general happiness. It is enough if he promotes it. In this case his act is "naturally right"; if it also has this in view, in addition to his more specific motive, it is "formally right."

The Utilitarian Road to Happiness

Happiness is tied up with morality, as long as happiness is regarded as the highest end of man. In Aristotle's eudaemonism, indeed, activity in accordance with virtue is the very substance of happiness, and for the Stoics it is a special state of virtue. In ancient hedonism and modern utilitarianism, on the other hand, morality is not *constitutive* of happiness, but only *instrumental* to it; it is not good in itself, but good for something else; the means, not the end. The principle of utility, Bentham says, approves of every action whatever that tends to "produce benefit, advantage, pleasure, good, or happiness (all this in the present case comes to the same thing), or (what comes again to the same thing) to prevent the happening of mischief, pain, evil or unhappiness to the party whose interest is considered: if that party be the community in general, then the happiness of the community; if a particular individual, then the happiness of that individual."[11]

Let us consider the two alternatives to the utility principle:

(1) The opposition to the utility principle, Bentham says, assumes two forms: the "principle of asceticism," which *always* opposes it; and "the principle of *sympathy* and *antipathy*," which *sometimes* does. The principle of asceticism, as Bentham defines it, is ludicrous enough. It approves any action that diminishes happiness (pleasure) or increases misery. Philosophers have never gone further in endorsing the principle, he says, than in maintaining that pain is a matter of indifference,[12] although asceticism in religion has made pain a kind of blessedness. But, in its origin, Bentham says, even the self-torture of the pillar saints was inspired by the utility principle, since it was supposed to lead to rewards in the next life. No one, Bentham points out, has ever applied the principle of asceticism consistently. It is seldom suggested, for example, that there is any virtue in inflicting misery on *others*. Applied to legislation and government, he says, the principle would be madness.

Bentham's polemic is directed against ascetic *tendencies* in ethics. He is

11 *Ibid.*, Ch. I, p. 126.
12 *Ibid.*, Ch. II.

insisting that pain or unpleasantness is never good in itself, but evil. He easily shows that this is often forgotten. Mill puts the same point persuasively when he says:

> Unquestionably it is possible to do without happiness; it is done involuntarily by nineteen-twentieths of mankind . . . and it often has to be done voluntarily by the hero or the martyr, for the sake of something which he prizes more than his individual happiness. But this something, what is it, unless the happiness of others, or some of the requisites of happiness? It is noble to be capable of resigning entirely one's own portion of happiness, or chances of it: but, after all, this self-sacrifice must be for some end; it is not its own end; and if we are told that its end is not happiness, but virtue, which is better than happiness, I ask, would the sacrifice be made if the hero or martyr did not believe that it would earn for others immunity from similar sacrifices?[13]

"Happiness" in this passage means a favorable balance of pleasure over pain, and the question raised is whether the hero's sacrifice of his own happiness for others would still be admirable if he knew that the others would remain as miserable as before, though perhaps more virtuous—more disposed to make similar "sacrifices."

Mill's defense of hedonism against ascetic criticism is especially significant in view of a common confusion, previously cited, between "pleasure," meaning sensuous or bodily pleasures, and "pleasure," meaning pleasant feelings. The latter can accompany not only bodily enjoyments but also the highest activities of which man is capable. Owing to this ambiguity, authors who condemn, deprecate, or renounce pleasure in general also regularly insist that the joys of rectitude or faith, or the bliss of heaven, are of incomparable value. This confusion is usually avoided by eudaemonism, for in this view pleasure is strictly speaking only a feeling that accompanies healthy and virtuous activity.

(2) The second alternative to the utility principle, which opposes it only some of the time, is the principle of sympathy and antipathy. This principle, according to Bentham, approves or disapproves of any action if only the agent is disposed to approve it (sympathy), or to disapprove it (antipathy). Thus we automatically approve of a mother's love and care of her infant and disapprove of cruelty. The principle is said to embody the experience of the race and to reflect common sense, but sometimes a man claims higher sympathies than the vulgar are capable of, and, indeed, the principle, Bentham says, takes many forms. A favorite form is "the moral sense" doctrine, that we have a special faculty for discerning right from wrong. Others rely on "the understanding," "the rule of right," "the law of

[13] *Op. cit.,* pp. 14–15.

nature," "the fitness of things," or the law of reason to discriminate right from wrong.

Bentham admits that the dictates of the principle of sympathy and antipathy "frequently coincide" with those of the utility principle. Our feelings of right and wrong often will coincide with our judgments when we make a hedonistic calculation, but not always. What if the feelings of two men disagree? If there is no external standard of judgment, but only feelings, there is no means of resolving disagreements. One man can only say: My feelings tell me I am right; you must be wrong. The other replies in reverse. The result is a stalemate, of a sort often dangerous to the peace. Utilitarianism, on the other hand, provides an external standard, a means to peaceful settlement and understanding.

THE GREATEST-HAPPINESS PRINCIPLE

We must consider whether the utilitarian principle admits of proof. Bentham replies that a proof would be "as impossible as it is needless."[14] What he means is that first principles cannot be proved; another principle more primary than the utility principle would have to be evoked to justify our following the utility principle. There is no such principle, none that could provide a higher reason for maximizing your pleasure. It would be nonsensical to ask, "Why should you maximize your pleasure?" The word "right," Bentham contends, cannot "have a meaning without reference to utility."[15] This implies that the opponents of the utility principle are using language improperly. When they say that it is always right to tell the truth, no matter what the consequences are—regardless of the pain or pleasure that may result—they are using the word "right" in an arbitrary sense, which agrees neither with common usage nor common sense. This linguistic ruling has been vigorously contested. Bentham does not rely on it.

Bentham supports the utility principle mainly by warning against common prejudices and misunderstandings. He asks the reader whether he would discard the principle altogether. If not, why should it be applicable in some cases, and not in others? But, if another principle is to be put in the place of utility, will it have authority for other men, or will it not reduce to a personal sentiment, which other men will regard as caprice? Is it not tyrannical to expect mankind to be governed by one's own persuasions and intuitions? The utility principle has the unique advantage of supplying an objective standard, for all men do actually seek pleasure as their good, and the more the better.[16]

14 *Op. cit.*, Ch. I, p. 128.
15 *Ibid.*, p. 127.
16 *Ibid.*, *passim*.

Mill agrees with Bentham that no direct proof of the utility principle can be given. He has often been accused of arguing from the premise that happiness is universally desired to the conclusion that happiness is therefore desir*able*, *i.e.*, that it ought to be desired, which would be fallacious. But he does not appear to be guilty. The utilitarian doctrine, he says, "is that happiness is desirable, and the only thing desirable, as an end; all other things being only desirable as means to that end." But why should we believe this? Mill answers:

> The only proof capable of being given that an object is visible, is that people actually see it. The only proof that a sound is audible, is that people hear it: and so of the other sources of our experience. In like manner, I apprehend, the sole evidence it is possible to produce that anything is desirable, is that people do actually desire it. If the end which the utilitarian doctrine proposed to itself were not, in theory and practice, acknowledged to be an end, nothing could ever convince any person that it was so. No reason can be given why the general happiness is desirable, except that each person, so far as he believes it to be attainable, desires his own happiness. This, however, being a fact, we have not only all the proof that the case admits of, but all which it is possible to require, that happiness is a good: that each person's happiness is a good to that person, and the general happiness, therefore, a good to the aggregate of all persons.[17]

First, it must be admitted that the analogy between "visible" and "desirable" (in the moral sense) is imperfect. That something is seen is enough to prove that it is visible, whereas that something is desired is not enough to prove that it is desirable. This is obvious, and it is obvious to Mill. He does not claim that the fact that happiness is desired *proves* that it is desirable, but only that this is the only proof that "the case admits of," and that without it there would be no reason to believe that happiness is desirable. First principles admittedly cannot be proved. There is no criterion more evident than the criterion of happiness itself.

In the meantime, utilitarians *need* not deny, as is charged, that virtue and other goods besides happiness are desired. They can concede that virtue is sometimes desired, and even desired for its own sake. Originally, it was not desired at all; it became an object of desire by association with pleasure, viz.: (a) the pleasure entailed by acting virtuously, and (b) the pleasure felt in the possession of virtue. In this way, Mill says, virtue became "a part of happiness." Valued first only as a means to the end, *i.e.*, happiness, it came to be valued as an end in itself.

---

[17] *Op. cit.*, pp. 32–33. The last sentence of Mill's seems to involve the fallacy of composition. The fact that each man's happiness is a good to him does not imply that there is a general happiness that is a good to all persons. But Mill, it is clear, does not depend on this argument. His contention, like Bentham's, is that efficient pursuit of your own happiness tends to the general happiness.

Mill even goes so far as to suggest that virtue cannot be virtue unless it is esteemed for itself. Thus, if the motive of your benevolence is not the relief of another's distress but only your own self-satisfaction, your benevolence is a sham. This conclusion is quite consistent with utilitarianism: The motive is to relieve another's distress, and the act would not afford self-satisfaction unless this *was* its motive; yet the agent would not have acquired motives of the kind had they not afforded him pleasure in the past.

Not only virtue but music and art and all the other luxuries of civilized man are acquired tastes. We esteem them in themselves as parts of happiness, but we should not do so unless they have been associated with pleasure in our experience, and are not associated with pleasure in our present thought. For Mill says that nothing can be desired "except in proportion as the idea of it is pleasant."[18]

Thus, neither Bentham nor Mill believed that the utility principle was the sort of thing that could be proved. It could be rendered most plausible, however, by removing misconceptions and prejudices and by a demonstration that there was no other criterion of action on which men can agree. All other criteria, Bentham thought, reduced to an anarchy of individual judgment, a tyranny of personal preference elevated to a universal rule.

But perhaps the so-called theological utilitarianism can provide a proof of the utility principle. If God's existence could be established independently, and also His benevolence—His desire that His creatures be happy—then the duty to work for the general happiness would be demonstrated. From Scripture and from observations of God's dispensations in the world, Paley concludes that "God wills and wishes the happiness of his creatures,"[19] and by happiness he means "pleasures [which] differ in nothing, but in intensity and continuity."[20] Virtue, therefore, consists in *"the doing good to mankind in obedience to the will of God, and for the sake of everlasting happiness."*[21] A man is obligated *"when he is urged by a violent motive resulting from the command of another."*[22] Accordingly, I am obliged to do something, such as keep my word, "because I am 'urged to do so by a violent motive' (namely, the expectation of being after this life rewarded, if I do, or punished for it, if I do not) resulting from the command of another, namely of God." Although "private happiness is our motive . . . the will of God is our rule."[23]

---

18 *Ibid.*, p. 36. The various ways in which pleasure (and pain) can be thought to motivate choice and action have been mentioned and will be discussed again in Chapter 10.

19 *The Principles of Moral and Political Philosophy*, p. 46.

20 *Ibid.*, p. 15.

21 *Ibid.*, p. 27.

22 *Ibid.*, p. 38.

23 *Ibid.*, p. 39.

Some seventy years earlier, in 1712, George Berkeley argued in a similar vein. Since self-love is the ruling passion of human nature, we naturally pursue pleasure as the good and avoid pain as the evil. At first "we are entirely guided by the impressions of sense; sensible pleasures being the infallible characteristic of present good, as pain is of evil." But the consequences of our actions soon teach us to forgo the pleasures of sense for remote, most lasting enjoyments. But since these latter goods are

> less than nothing in respect of eternity, who sees not that every rational man ought so to frame his actions as that they may most effectually contribute to promote his eternal interest? And since it is a truth evident to the light of nature, that there is a sovereign omniscient Spirit, who alone can make us forever happy, or forever miserable, it plainly follows that a conformity to His will, and not any prospect of *temporal* advantage, is the sole reason why every man who acts up to the principles of reason must govern and square his actions.[24]

Moreover, God, as the maker and preserver of all things, is therefore the undisputed legislator of the world, "and mankind are, by all ties of duty, no less than interest, bound to obey His laws."[25]

Whether one regards this theological proof of the utility principle as strong or weak will depend on whether one accepts the premises, which assert God's existence and His dispensations in a future life. Henry Sidgwick, one of the most subtle and cautious utilitarians, believes the theological argument to be of the greatest importance, since it provides the only final justification for demanding that a man pursue the general happiness rather than his own. In the view of Bentham and Mill, however, the idea of doing God's will influences conduct only in proportion to the pleasure that attends it. It is pleasure rather than a transcendent principle that goads men to action, and when this is lacking, so is the motivation.[26]

If Bentham expects the private citizen and especially the legislator to calculate and promote the general happiness, we should expect him to give some account of the classes of pleasures and pains, of our susceptibility to them, and of the grand strategy of achieving the best hedonistic balance. He does not fail us. He begins with a brief description of the "kinds" of pleasures that the legislator should have in view in devising laws. There are the pleasures of the senses, of health, skill, amity, a good name, power, benevolence or goodwill, antipathy, memory, imagination, expectation, association, etc., and corresponding "kinds" of pain. The list is unsystematic, and serves only to introduce a terminology. "Kinds," of course, does

---

24 *The Works of George Berkeley, Bishop of Cloyne,* Vol. VI, pp. 19–20.
25 *Ibid.*
26 See *Utilitarianism,* p. 27.

not refer to qualitative distinctions among pleasures and pains, but to their various sources.

Bentham's account of "circumstances influencing sensibility" to pleasures and pains is more rewarding. How the individual reacts to external stimulation will depend on his health, strength, and hardiness; bodily imperfection; knowledge; intellectual capacity; firmness of mind; inclinations; moral and religious sensibility and bias; the extent and bias of his sympathies and antipathies; his habitual occupations and pecuniary circumstances, together with "connection" formed by them; and sex, age, rank, education, climate, lineage, government and religious profession.[27] Here we find all the factors essential or favorable to happiness enumerated by Aristotle, except virtuous activity, which is always essential to happiness in his view, and to contemplation, which is necessary to the highest happiness. Contemplation appears to be a clear omission, but virtue is not. Virtue, for Bentham, is simply the outcome of a favorable balance of the factors he mentions, and cannot properly be listed among them.

None of the factors is by itself decisively favorable to the successful pursuit of happiness. It might appear that sympathy would invariably promote utilitarian virtue, and it does greatly increase sensitivity to pleasures and pains, since it prompts a concern not only for our own welfare but that of family, friends, the community, or mankind at large. This widening of concern need not depend on affection, Bentham shrewdly observes, for it frequently extends to relatives on whom no love is wasted, but it has the salutary effect of making the sympathetic man more responsive to the laws of the land or other sanctions. But sympathy has a less propitious side.

> It itself multiplies the sources of antipathy. Sympathy for your friend gives birth to antipathy on *your* part against all those who are objects of antipathy, as well as to sympathy for those who are objects of sympathy to *him*.[28]

This defect of sympathy is also apparent in benevolence, to which it commonly leads, for benevolence toward friends may be at the expense of larger interest. In the general case, however, there is no conflict with the public good. Thus, of all motives, Bentham says, the dictates of goodwill are closest to those of the utility principle.

> For the dictates of utility are neither more nor less than the dictates of the most extensive and enlightened (that is, well-advised) benevolence.[29]

Hobbes denies that sympathy and benevolence are natural human motives. Francis Hutcheson, on the other hand, recognizes a "benevolent

---

[27] Contracted from Bentham's list, *op. cit.*, Ch. VI.
[28] *Op. cit.*, Ch. VI, p. 175.
[29] *Ibid.*, Ch. X, p. 236.

universal instinct," alongside of self-interest, and holds, in fact, that benevolence and virtue are the same. The benevolence is, of course, disinterested. Although "this *Benevolence* is our greatest Happiness," and we should cultivate it as much as possible, we cannot

> be *truly* Virtuous, if we intend only to obtain the Pleasure which accompanies *Beneficence* without the Love of *others*: Nay, this very Pleasure is founded on our being conscious of *disinterested* Love to others, as the *Spring* of our Actions. But *Self-Interest* may be our *Motive*, in chusing to continue in this *agreeable* State, tho it cannot be the *sole*, or *principal Motive* of any Action, which to our *moral* Sense appears Virtuous.[30]

The benevolent actions that Hobbes attributes to self-interest are thus assigned by Hutcheson to an original and powerful instinct, and he argues that this disinterested emotion is the sole ground of moral approbation.[31] Although Joseph Butler admits that benevolence is "the most excellent of the virtues," it is, he says, "by no means the whole of virtue. If this were the case, we should never be able to criticize benevolent actions, even though they might, in supposable cases, produce more misery than happiness."[32]

Bentham, though he recognizes sympathy as an original human motive, believes that it is much weaker than self-interest. The motives that are most powerful, constant, and extensive are "the motives of physical desire, the love of wealth, the love of ease, the love of life, and the fear of pain: all of them self-regarding motives."[33]

The factors listed by Bentham are to be found in other descriptions of the road to happiness, though often by implication only; his enumeration is perhaps the longest of any. It is not meant to be a mere inventory or scrap bag of goods useful to happiness. The unifying and redeeming factor, which can utilize or transform the others in the direction of the greatest happiness, is government, operating as the mentor and educator of the members of the state. "The business of government is to promote the happiness of the society, by punishing and rewarding."[34] Bentham, the incorrigible modern, thus returns to Platonism, but with a difference: Men are to be educated solely by the rational imposition of pains and pleasures,

---

[30] *An Inquiry into the Original of Our Ideas of Beauty and Virtue*, II, p. 194.

[31] *Ibid.*, pp. 197–198.

[32] *The Analogy of Religion*, pp. 407–408.

[33] *Op. cit.*, Ch. XII, p. 279. The differences of opinion as to the relative strength of self-interest and benevolence in human nature, which raised heated debates in the seventeenth and eighteenth centuries, have faded into the background in recent times. Psychotherapeutic ideas and other modern developments have changed the framework in which the advance of general welfare is discussed.

[34] *Ibid.*, Ch. VII, p. 189.

for only thus can they be moved to action. Second, the end is the greatest
pleasure of the greatest number, one man's pleasure counting as much as,
but no more than, another's.

The influence of the magistrate, Bentham says, is widespread and
unceasing. He

> operates in the character of a tutor upon all the members of the state, by the
> direction he gives to their hopes and to their fears. Indeed under a solicitous
> and attentive government, the ordinary preceptor, nay even the parent
> himself, is but a deputy, as it were, to the magistrate: whose controlling
> influence, different in this respect from that of the ordinary preceptor,
> dwells with a man to his life's end.[35]

The influence of the magistrate is especially strong over the "moral,
religious, sympathetic, and antipathetic sensibilities" of citizens. When the
government is well administered, their sympathies and antipathies tend to
be more in accord with the utility principle, whatever the constitution of
the state may be. Their biases will be better directed, less religious, and
"more apt (in proportion) to be grounded on enlarged and sympathetic
rather than on narrow and self-regarding affections, and accordingly, upon
the whole, more conformable to the dictates of utility."[36] Promptness and
regularity in the administration of the laws conduces to happiness, even if
the laws are defective.[37] When the laws are also just, *i.e.*, when they
punish an act in proportion to its tendency to disturb the general happiness, the advantage is far greater.

In the interest of a more rational system of laws and of punishments,
Bentham devoted tremendous time and energy, and many of his publications. His reforming zeal left a deep imprint on the jurisprudence of the
time, and often directed the framing of specific laws and changes in the
penal code.

Both the legislator and the judge, Bentham says, must have in mind the
relevant circumstances by which sensibility may be influenced, and must
compute with the greatest care the punishment that will be most effective
for every species of crime. Since it is the purpose of laws and punishments
to increase the general happiness or to diminish unhappiness, they are to be
judged by how far they succeed in this. The same is true of the acts subject
to law.

[35] *Ibid.*, Ch. VI, p. 182.
[36] *Ibid.*, p. 183.
[37] Bentham, however, is far from condoning unjust laws, just because they are
laws, and is loath to practice law, when it means "making money at the trade of
interpreting a vicious law, at the expense of the public." (Qu. in Elie Halévy, *The
Growth of Philosophic Radicalism.*)

MOTIVES, INTENTIONS, AND CONSEQUENCES

Consequences alone determine what is right by law, as by morality. But, since consequences, nearby or distant, direct or indirect, are bound up with motives and intentions, these two are vital to the realization of happiness, as Bentham conceives it, and are a part of our present subject. We can neglect most of the distinctions Bentham makes in his elaborate discussion, but some are interesting in themselves and too pertinent to miss. A "motive," in the sense that concerns him, is something that can influence the will of an animal, causing him to act voluntarily or to forbear, which is also an act. Avarice, indolence, and benevolence are examples. "Motive" can refer to the immediate pleasure or pain that prompts to action, or to the perception of pleasure or pain in prospect, but the term is also applied to external events that are supposed to result in these perceptions, as, for example, the sight of your neighbor's house burning and the fire coming closer to your own.

If the actual consequences of acting on a motive determine whether this motive is good or bad, it follows at once that no motive is always good and none is always bad. An act inspired by charity can have painful results, and the motive of malice can bring desirable consequences. A great deal of confusion, in Bentham's opinion, has resulted from the assumption that charitable actions are right in themselves, or that they always tend to augment the general happiness. He would not deny, of course, that charity is more apt to have good consequences than malice is, yet insists that even the most highly approved motives, such as the desire "to obtain the favor of the Supreme Being," can result in great absurdities and abominable crimes.[38]

Bentham considers the following objection to his doctrine: Consequences vary from one case to another. How, then, can the goodness or badness of a motive depend entirely on consequences? Are not lust and cruelty *always* considered bad motives? If they are, Bentham wittily replies, it is because we do not call motives by this name when they have good results. We never say, for example, that though his motive was lust, the result was a happy wife and beautiful children, or that a father was cruel to his son, subjecting him to a rigorous discipline, though the result was that the boy got a fine education, and became a success. When the results are good, we do not speak of bad motives.

Nevertheless, Bentham does want to lay down certain propositions about motives in general. The legislator and judge, after all, cannot restrict their

[38] See *op. cit.*, Ch. X.

concern to the unique motives in the individual case, but must be guided by certain rules. We have seen that he admits that benevolence is the motive closest to the utility principle. Next comes "the love of reputation," and after this is "the desire of amity," especially when it extends to many people. But Bentham insists that the self-regarding motives are stronger and more dependable, *as a matter of fact*, than those that have regard to others. The judge and the legislator, aiming at maximum hedonistic results, must keep this relative weakness of benevolent motives in view, and, to some extent, they have done so. There would be much less need for them if this were not so.

Whereas motives are the cause of voluntary acts, and influence the character of the act and the consequences in many ways, intentions play a different part. The *intention* (a) to perform an act, or (b) to produce a certain result, which is elicited by the motive, is not the cause of our actions. It follows that an intention is strictly speaking neither good nor bad: It is neither the "perception" of prospective pleasure or pain, nor the cause of pleasure or pain. We can nevertheless say that the intention is good or bad in a "figurative" sense, because it is connected with consequences or with his motives, which are good or bad.[39]

It is possible for us to intend our act without intending the consequences of it. But it is impossible to intend the consequences of our act without intending our act, since in this case it would not be our act. When the consequences of our act are intended, they can be *directly* or only *obliquely* intended. When a motorist hits and kills a certain man in the street, he may have directly intended this result. On the other hand, a driver who hits a pedestrian and does not directly intend to do so would intend it *obliquely* if he drives at high speed through a stoplight, knowing that, if a pedestrian should be crossing the street at the time, he would not be able to slow down in time to avoid him.

Distinctions of the kind would be useful in determining the kinds of penalties most likely to discourage different types of offenses. Cases can arise in which the intention of an action is "good" but the motive is bad. Malice may motivate you in prosecuting your enemy for fraud, but if he is in fact guilty and is punished, this good consequence confers goodness on your intention. You intended something good, for the worst motive. Similarly, the intention may be "innocent" even when the consequences of the act are harmful, as long as the agent is misadvised as to the circumstances producing the harm. But here again the motive can be reprehensible. The legislator and the judge must always be attentive to the likelihood that unknown circumstances will deflect intention, and that the actual consequences will negate the real motive. Controlling actions in the interest of

[39] *Ibid.*, Ch. VIII, p. 205.

the community is especially difficult in view of cumulative uncertainty of distant consequences. With every step into the future, consequences become more and more entangled in unforeseen circumstances. The increasing uncertainty arises, not only from the multiplication of consequences as we proceed into the future but also by the multiplication of external circumstances influencing these consequences.

Yet a fair degree of certainty is also obtainable, as J. S. Mill and other utilitarians insist, about the consequences of typical moral acts of private individuals. Acts of kindness and justice, or of malice and envy, affect the immediate circle of the agent, and he is forewarned of any distant effects by a great deal of social experience. In most cases, the consequences of an act diminish in importance the more distant they are. This holds for private actions of individuals, however, far more than it does for public, self-perpetuating actions, like the making of laws and penal codes, or passing sentence on a criminal. The effects here do not fritter away, but multiply and accumulate.

Punishments as Productive of the Greatest Happiness

Bentham shoulders, courageously, the responsibility of calculating the effects of laws and penalties on the sum of general happiness. He is blamed for his presumption and dogmatism. How could he foresee the precise meaning of pain entailed by a given punishment, or the degree of deterrence? But from where he stands, there is no alternative procedure. The precedents of the lawyers do not justify a sentence imposed on the prisoner, he argues, nor do antiquity and custom, natural rights or reason, vindicate existing laws. The legal profession, Bentham insists, must be reformed, root and branch. "The business of government is to promote the happiness of the society, by punishing and rewarding,"[40] and the only criterion of law or morals is the tendency to promote happiness. No other standard has application or relevance. The hedonistic calculus is not a luxury of speculation, but a practical necessity—at least for those who hold happiness to be good.

Contrary to Kant and Hegel, Bentham holds that all punishment is an evil. The infliction of pain can be justified only *if and when* it has good results. Punishment is out of place, Bentham says, in four cases:

1. Where it is *groundless:* where there is no mischief for it to prevent, the act not being mischievous on the whole.
2. Where it must be *inefficacious:* where it cannot act so as to prevent the mischief.

[40] *Ibid.*, Ch. VII, p. 189.

3. Where it is *unprofitable,* or too expensive: where the mischief it would produce would be greater than what it prevented.
4. Where it is *needless*: where the mischief may be prevented or cease of itself, without it, that is, at a cheaper rate.[41]

There are four objects of punishment that the utilitarian legislator will have in view.

1. The primary object is revolutionary. It is to do away with all crimes —all acts "which appear to have a tendency to produce mischief."
2. To prevent the most serious offenses.
3. To dispose the offender "to do no *more* mischief than is necessary to his purpose."
4. To prevent harm to society "at as *cheap* a rate as possible," with the smallest penalty.[42]

The principal end of punishment is to control action, either by physically confining the offender or by reforming him. Another associated purpose might be to give pleasure or satisfaction to the injured party, but Bentham says that this should never be the sole purpose of punishment, since the pleasure of the injured party never equals the pain inflicted. This may not always be true, but what is interesting to note is how Bentham remains true to his utilitarianism. Your pleasure in seeing your assailant punished must, in any case, be quantitatively equal to or greater than his pain if it is to be the justification of the punishment.

Bentham methodically lays down a number of rules for obtaining proportion between offenses and punishments. Equal crimes call for equal punishments, for all offenders alike, and the greater the crime, the greater the penalty. But the proportion is to be maintained, not in deference to an abstract rule of retributive justice. Proportion is to be maintained because it is, in general, efficient in preventing crime, and thus contributes to the general happiness. But what would Bentham say about the perhaps exceptional cases in which proportionality and utility do not coincide? Suppose *A*'s crime is worse than *B*'s, but *A* is young and docile, whereas *B* is old and probably incorrigible. *A* might be reformed and re-established as a good citizen after a year in jail, whereas *B* is not likely to change. Should *A*, nevertheless, be given a longer term in prison? Bentham could avail himself of the utilitarian retort that we have already mentioned. He could point out that though the violation of a utilitarian rule in a particular case can have good immediate results, the long-range influence of the violation may more than counterbalance this advantage.

41 *Ibid.,* Ch. XIII.
42 *Ibid.,* Ch. XIV.

THE ROLE OF ETHICS

In the last chapter of his *Principles of Morals and Legislation*, Bentham argues that lawmakers usually go too far in restricting the freedom of citizens. He holds, as we have seen, that laws have no place where punishment will be (1) groundless, (2) inefficacious, (3) unprofitable, or (4) needless. In some degree, private ethics can fill the gap where laws are unsuited to direct men to happiness. Ethics, according to Bentham, is concerned with two kinds of behavior: the behavior that affects only the happiness of the agent himself, and behavior that affects the happiness of others. Every man ought to pursue his own happiness consistently and efficiently; this is his "duty to himself" or "prudence." It would be manifestly absurd to attempt to punish him every time he fails to do so. As for behavior that affects the happiness of others, a man's duty is divided into negative and positive. The negative duty not to harm others is called "probity," whereas the positive duty to promote the happiness of others is "benevolence." Of the three ethical duties, it is obviously probity that requires most reinforcement by laws and penalties. Prudence and benevolence, on the other hand, are much less suited to legal regulation.[43]

The motive to prudence is easily understood. The motives to probity and benevolence, according to Bentham, are not only sympathy but mainly self-interest operating indirectly. Yet, if he stands for egoism, it is a highly social egoism. Whenever the individual *can* produce more pleasure for others than for himself, it is his duty to accomplish theirs and forgo his own.

THE ROLE OF GOVERNMENT AND ECONOMICS

Bentham is primarily interested in laws as instruments for the control of human action, with a view to the promotion of the happiness of the community. In his *Fragment on Government*, which appeared in 1776, early in his career, he dismisses the virtues and shortcomings traditionally allotted to monarchy, aristocracy, and democracy. Whether a government is good or bad is determined not by these distinctions but by the degree to which its laws and administration conform to the utility principle. It appeared that, at the time, an enlightened despot would be more apt to institute the legal reforms he had in view than would a liberal or popular regime. What is important is not who or how many exercised power, but how efficiently power is exercised to control behavior for the sake of the

43 *Ibid.*, Ch. VXII.

general happiness. Utilitarianism has no logical affiliation with democracy, nor with the traditional mixed government. It is clearly opposed to natural law and natural rights, Bentham holds. Natural law gives everyone the right to disregard the laws, if only his interpretation of Scripture convinces him they are wrong. None of the pretended safeguards against the misuse of power gives any assurance that the laws will be justified. All restraint is bad, according to Bentham. It can be justified only on the utility principle, by its consequences. On the other hand, the utilitarian is free to accept democracy if he chooses, as J. S. Mill did, though with reservations. Bentham himself warmed to it when his hopes were raised that the democrats might carry out his legal reforms. Although he remained an avowed disciple of Adam Smith, his solution could not be laissez-faire: His remedy was a rational system of coercive laws.

DISAGREEMENTS AMONG UTILITARIANS

We have already called attention to disagreements among utilitarians that have a bearing on happiness, or on how it is to be achieved.

1. There is a difference between what Sidgwick calls "scientific utilitarianism," found in Spencer, and the "empirical utilitarianism" that distinguishes Bentham's approach. It is largely a difference of emphasis. Whereas Bentham attempts to trace the hedonistic consequences of particular acts, Spencer relies far more than Bentham on "scientific" generalizations about the consequences of various *kinds* of acts, such as theft and benevolence. It is hardly possible to determine the consequences of a particular act before performing it, but the experience of the race has accumulated general rules about the advantage and disadvantage of different *kinds* of acts, which it is safe to follow. A particular act of theft is to be avoided because it belongs to a class of acts having bad consequences. Spencer holds that at least "absolute ethics,"[44] representing the future ideal culmination of moral development, will be securely grounded in hedonistic laws. Sidgwick remarks quietly that, though this may be so, it does not help us now.

2. There is also a difference among utilitarians on the question whether men, as a matter of fact, desire *only* their own pleasure. This thesis can be called psychological-egoistic hedonism. Bentham usually states or assumes this position, but sometimes he implies that the prospect of one's own future pleasure (and/or the avoidance of pain) is not the only human motive, that sympathy with others is also an original spring of action.

[44] *The Data of Ethics*, Chap. XV. In current ethical discussions, these positions are called "rule utilitarianism" and "act utilitarianism," respectively. See, for example, J. C. C. Smart, *An Outline of a System of Utilitarian Ethics*.

Hobbes, it will be remembered, rejects altruistic motives altogether, though he does not, of course, deny what would be called "altruistic behavior." The theological utilitarians, Tucker and Paley, are also psychological egoists. Sympathy and benevolence are of utmost importance, but they are not original impulses. In contrast to these utilitarians are those who contend that sympathy or concern for others is an original trait, as much so as egoistic desire for one's own pleasure. Bishop Cumberland, one of the earliest English utilitarians, takes this view, and so does Hume in his *Enquiry Concerning Human Happiness,* and Henry Sidgwick in his *Methods of Ethics* (Ch. IV). The question, in any case, is one of psychology, not of ethics, of original motives, not of what motives men *ought* to have. All utilitarians hold that we *ought* to so act as to increase the *general* happiness.

3. The difference between the theological and the nontheological utilitarians is chiefly that the former supply an additional sanction for moral conduct—at least for the faithful. If God intended the happiness of His creatures, then, in pursuing it successfully, we are observing God's will as well as our own interests. Moreover, the critical question why a man should strive for the general happiness rather than his own is now susceptible of a new answer. Egoistic desire and altruistic duty can be reconciled by divine justice in a future life, where those who have labored for the happiness of others in this life will be rewarded, and those who have not will be punished. Sidgwick, one of the most cautious and circumspect of the utilitarians, concludes that the existence of God, a being generally assumed to be benevolent and omnipotent, provides the only solution of "the fundamental contradiction" of utilitarianism, the contradiction, that is, between virtue and self-interest.[45] Other utilitarians, on the contrary, do not feel any necessity for theological support. They insist that in our present life *efficient* pursuit of one's own pleasure generally redounds to the pleasure of others, or that the refined pleasures of friendship and altruism are the least mixed with pain and the most enduring and dependable. There is no *need* to postulate a future life.

4. The most sensational difference among utilitarians relates directly to the constitution of happiness, conceived as pleasure. The doctrine that pleasures are quantitatively the same (and so also pains or displeasures) is the bedrock of Bentham's utilitarianism, and of utilitarianism in general. If the hedonistic feelings are not qualitatively alike, there can be no hedonistic calculus. One could not conclude, on the basis of the amount of pleasure involved, that benevolence is generally any better than malice. The very idea of the greatest pleasure of the greatest number would seem to be fraudulent.

[45] See *The Methods of Ethics,* last chapter.

J. S. Mill introduces his revision of utilitarianism quite casually, when he says:

> It is quite compatible with the principle of utility to recognize the fact that some *kinds* of pleasure are more desirable and more valuable than others. It would be absurd that while, in estimating all other things, quality is considered as well as quantity, the estimation of pleasures should be supposed to depend on quantity alone.[46]

Mill argues that men who are acquainted with both animal pleasures and specifically human pleasures, and are alone able to judge between them, show a marked preference for the latter. "No intelligent human being would consent to be a fool, no person of feeling and conscience would be selfish and base,"[47] even though they are convinced that they would henceforth enjoy a much greater quantity of pleasure than would otherwise be their lot.

> It is better to be a human being dissatisfied than a pig satisfied; better to be Socrates dissatisfied than a fool satisfied. And if the fool, or the pig, are of a different opinion, it is because they know only their side of the question.[48]

The tendency of Mill's argument is obviously Platonic and Aristotelian, for the qualitative diversity of pleasures is one of the major theses of eudaemonism. Plato says that no man would choose to be an oyster, whatever its pleasures may be, whereas Mill's example is a pig. Aristotle argues that those who know the pleasure that accompanies rational activity greatly prefer it to bodily pleasures. Similarly, Mill contends that those who are in a position to make comparisons, "give a most marked preference to the manner of existence which employs their higher faculties."[49] Moreover, Mill takes an important step toward Aristotle in maintaining that "the ingredients of happiness are very various, and each of them is desirable in itself, and not merely when considered as swelling an aggregate."[50]

A Note on Mill's Apostasy and a Possibly New Dimension of Pleasure

Mill's return to eudaemonism is far from complete, but it seems decisive as far as it goes. Is it true, as often charged, that he has "betrayed" utilitarianism? If pleasures are qualitatively different, how can it be true that

[46] *Op. cit.*, p. 7.
[47] *Ibid.*, p. 8.
[48] *Ibid.*, p. 9.
[49] *Ibid.*, p. 8.
[50] *Ibid.*, pp. 33–34.

the supreme good is the greatest pleasure of the greatest number? Adding pleasures—whether those of the individual or of the community—into larger and larger quantitative wholes presupposes that they are quantitatively alike. Is not Mill involved in a serious inconsistency?

One escape from this denouement is suggested by W. P. Montague in "The Missing Link in the Case for Utilitarianism," in *The Ways of Things*. Besides duration and intensity, there is perhaps another quantitative dimension, which might be called "extensity." An aesthetic pleasure, let us say, can differ from a gustatory pleasure, not only in duration and intensity but also in extensity. The pleasure of an exquisite meal might be more intense, but shorter-lived, than the pleasure of an evening at the opera; and it could also be narrower, less expansive, and occupy a more limited part of our consciousness at the time, a large part being given, perhaps, to conversation and the watching of friends across the table. The greater breadth of the latter pleasure would then represent *more* pleasure, in the dimension of extensity. The so-called higher pleasures, including those of personal love, generous actions, and cultural and intellectual pursuits, are, in fact, usually thought more pervasive than bodily pleasures. Some pleasures are said to "fill the whole soul," etc.

The Millian utilitarian may thus reduce qualitative differences among pleasures to a quantitative dimension of extensity and so salvage his goal of the greatest pleasure of the greatest number. In view of the disputes in the time of Titchener over the dimensions of sensation, it is not too unlikely that a new dimension of pleasure should be discovered. Not long ago, only three dimensions of auditory tone were recognized—pitch, timber, and intensity—but more recently, a stereoscopic dimension was added, which might be called "voluminousness."

II

Issues of Happiness

II

Issues of Happiness

The Introduction to this book serves notice that Part I expounds the principal theories of happiness advanced in the West, whereas Part II examines the controversial issues, expressed and latent. This division is important, even though the pie could not be cut with a fine line. Theories of happiness owe some of their rational appeal and plausibility to the philosophical systems in which they are enmeshed, and this is conveyed in Part I, since it is concerned mainly with individual philosophers. Part I can also serve as an introduction to Part II in the sense that it is easier to grasp, and understanding of the issues between philosophers presupposes some prior understanding of the rounded systems of each of them. Here, too, context counts.

But, in preparing the way for Part II, it was necessary to give a preview in Part I of quite a few of the issues. Part I, in fact, contains a great deal of controversy, as is inevitable, for the history of philosophy is largely controversy. It was convenient, also, to present some individual theories for the first time in Part II. All the main issues of happiness raised in Part I, however, are elaborated and analyzed in Part II, except the issue of natural *vs.* supernatural happiness. At the end of Chapter 4, we describe the form and scope of this particular confrontation, and explain why it could not be presented in this book. The last chapter deals with a culmination of Aristotelian and self-realization theories of happiness in present-day thought, and the beginning of this chapter explains why main consideration is given to working ideas of current psychology and psychotherapy.

The first chapter of Part II can be regarded as a combination of the two methods, as a compromise, or as a transition from one to the other, since it gives equal attention to individual philosophies and issues.

7

The Issue of Self-realization

WHEREAS ancient hedonism and modern utilitarianism develop only one side of the Aristotelian theory of happiness, self-realization is a restatement or revision of the whole theory. The Aristotelian model is often conceded, or the influence is obvious without admission. Happiness, for self-realization theories, is at once a moral attainment and a fulfillment of human capacities, and it is the one through being the other; by becoming fully ourselves we realize goodness as well. Reason and desire are not seen in radical opposition, but as interfused and inseparable. Every desire has its reason or rationale, and every reason, if it is to instigate action, must have its desire or conation. Man is not naturally divided against himself, an unhappy denizen of two worlds—his reason and duty in one and his happiness and the means of his action in the other, as in the Kantian scheme. In his full self-development, the individual is one and whole, and his happiness is not limited to one element such as pleasure, but consists in the entire fulfillment—a unity of many things in one.

We have already seen, in Chapter 5, Hegel elaborating these ideas in opposition to hedonism, on the one hand, and to Kantianism on the other.

149

An industrious and tenacious student of Plato and Aristotle, Hegel is the first to state the modern self-realization theory, which owes so much to eudaemonism, and his version covers a larger canvas than any other. Well-being or happiness (*Glückseligkeit*) involves a fusion of desire and duty, feeling and reason, freedom and necessity, subjective inclination and objective institutional life, especially that of the state as it evolves to higher forms; and it is to be realized by progressive dialectical steps, only as an outcome of a lengthy historical development. All preceding attempts to define the ultimate goal of human life are supposedly included, as partial truths, in Hegel's all-embracing, all-transforming scheme of realization. The approximation to Aristotle's eudaemonism, which also adopts partial insights from previous theories, is unmistakable, in spite of the astounding originality of Hegel's method.

The great precursor of modern self-realization theories, who preceded Hegel by some 150 years, is Spinoza. The heroic image he carves of man in his strength and weakness, and in his progress toward illimitable understanding, combines scientific realism with uncompromising ideals. Especially interesting from our point of view is his account of self-realization. For Spinoza, it is simply the successful endeavor to persist in one's own being, *i.e.*, self-preservation.

All self-realization theories naturally admit that self-preservation is essential to self-realization—that there can be no question of any attainment unless the self is preserved. Spinoza goes much further. He makes the desire to "persevere in his own being" the essence of man, and identifies the greater perfection a man achieves with greater reality. In striving to persist in his own nature, his understanding, power, and virtue are increased simultaneously. In the section below, we shall see that Spinoza is not only a link between the ancient eudaemonism and modern self-realization but that he also heralds the view of evolutionary theorists who, in the wake of Spencer and Darwin, make self-preservation the final goal of the individual and species.

Self-preservation vs. Self-realization: Spinoza

To understand Spinoza's view of the ultimate good, we must first see what he says about good as such. He takes the traditional view that all men, by their very nature, necessarily pursue what they consider good, just as they *necessarily* avoid what they think evil.[1] But his definitions of "good" and "knowledge of good" sound strikingly egoistic. "Good" is simply

1 See *Ethics*, Part IV, Prop. 19.

"that which we certainly know is useful to us," while "evil is that which
. . . hinders us from obtaining anything that is good."[2] Knowledge of
good and evil, Spinoza holds, "is nothing but an affect of joy or sorrow in
so far as we are conscious of it."[3] An object is called good, accordingly, if it
affects us with joy (*i.e.*, pleasure). But pleasure is not the object that
directs men's desire; Spinoza is no hedonist, but far closer to eudaemonism
in this respect. He defines pleasure as a passage from less to greater perfection (and sorrow as a passage from greater to less perfection). We can say
that a thing is good if it is useful to us and increases our perfection or
reality, but this is equivalent to saying that it "contributes to the preservation of our being" and increases and helps "our power of action."[4] And,
insofar as our knowledge of good is *true* knowledge, our ideas are adequate
and we are self-determined. Pleasure is the mark and crown of our
attainment.

It should not be imagined, however, that the *affect* caused by a thing is
something separate and distinct from the *idea* that the thing is good. "This
idea is united to the affect in the same way that the mind is united to the
body,"[5] which is as much as to say that the idea and the affect are not two
things, but only two aspects of one. The two aspects are easily seen in
Spinoza's definitions of the affects. Love, for example, is "joy [pleasure]
with the accompanying idea of an external cause."[6] The pleasure and the
idea, which refers it to an external cause, are inseparable aspects of the
same affect.[7]

We have seen that Hegel also combines idea with affect in a close unity.
Every realization of idea in the long spiral course of dialectical development is bound up with its distinctive affect; without this it could make no
dent on history, and would never be heard from. Later self-realization
authors also tend to fuse affect and idea, and affect and reason. They reject
the dualism of desire (evil) and reason (good) which appears in some
Platonic formulations. They usually adopt an Aristotelian view that fulfillment of natural desires is always good and makes for happiness, unless it

[2] *Ibid.*, Def. 1 and 2.
[3] *Ibid.*, Part IV, Prop. 8.
[4] *Ibid.*, Demonst.
[5] *Ibid.* See also Part II, prop. 21.
[6] *Ibid.*, end of Part III.
[7] Harry Wolfson argues (*The Philosophy of Spinoza*, Vol. 2, p. 204) that, since
whatever affects us with pleasure is good, we can infer that Spinoza also holds that
"we do not desire a thing because it is pleasant, but, on the contrary, a thing is
pleasant to us because we desire it." (*Ibid.*) If this is correct, Spinoza's conception of
pleasure would be quite similar to Aristotle's. Aristotle holds that pleasure is good in
itself, as we have seen, and Spinoza, that pleasure is "directly good," since by it "the
body's power of action is increased or assisted." (*Op. cit.*, Part III, Prop. 11, and Part
IV, Prop. 41.) Both deny that men aim at pleasure as such, and both regard pleasure
as a superadded perfection of attainment which aids the activity to which it belongs.

interferes with better fulfillments. Indeed, these writers have no love for final dualism; they insist that man, and perhaps his universe too, are integral unities in which oppositions and conflicts are also moments in a continuity of development, or else opportunities for melioristic remedies.

Another way in which Spinoza anticipates self-realization is in his doctrine that things are not desired because they are thought to be good, but, on the contrary, we adjudge them good because we desire them.[8] This follows from the definition of the good as that which we know to be useful to us, *i.e.*, helps each to persevere in his own being. In a famous passage of the *Ethics*, Spinoza explains with fascinating swiftness how this natural egoism of man entails the most disinterested, open-handed generosity and justice. In seeking only our own preservation, *i.e.*, our own happiness, we seek also the happiness of *others*. "Since reason," Spinoza says,

> demands nothing which is opposed to nature, it demands, therefore, that every person should love himself, should seek his own profit,—what is truly profitable to him,—should desire everything that really leads man to greater perfection, and absolutely that everyone should endeavour, as far as in him lies, to preserve his own being. This is all true as necessarily as that the whole is greater than its part. . . . Again, since virtue . . . means nothing but acting according to the laws of our own nature, and since no one endeavours to preserve his being . . . except in accordance with the laws of his own nature, it follows: *Firstly,* That the foundation of virtue is that endeavour itself to preserve our own being, and that happiness consists in this—that a man can preserve his own being. *Secondly,* It follows that virtue is to be desired for its own sake, nor is there anything more excellent or more useful to us than virtue, for the sake of which virtue ought to be desired. *Thirdly,* It follows that all persons who kill themselves are impotent in mind, and have been thoroughly overcome by external causes opposed to their nature. . . . It follows that we can never free ourselves from the need of something outside us for the preservation of our being. . . . Nothing . . . is more useful to man than man. [Accordingly] men who, under the guidance of reason, seek their own profit,—desire nothing for themselves which they do not desire for other men, and . . . are just, faithful, and honourable.[9]

The question why one man should care about another's happiness, a question that haunts all exponents of happiness, is answered by Spinoza in a simple, vigorous style. A man cannot preserve his own being unless he cooperates with other men, and the wider the circle, the greater the gain. Nothing is more useful to the preservation of one man "than that all should so agree at every point that the minds and bodies of all should form,

---

[8] *Op. cit.*, Part III, Prop. 9, Schol.
[9] *Ibid.*, Part IV, Prop. 18, Schol.

as it were, one mind and one body; that all should together endeavour as much as possible to preserve their being, and that all should together seek the common good."[10] What is stated here summarily is elaborated in various theorems of the *Ethics*, which argue that hatred, envy, pride, greed, and other passions that divide men and inflame wars are debilitating and unprofitable to those who indulge them. Spinoza's answer is thus a philosophical variant of the economic theory of *the identity of interests*, viz.: What is really good for the individual is also good, in the long run, for other men and for society. He is far from maintaining, of course, that individual action is sufficient by itself to achieve the general good. But the power of the state, which is necessary for peace and other goods, should be based on the will of all the citizens and must not suppress their freedom of action or thought.[11]

It is quite clear that Spinoza understands by "persevering in one's own being" a great deal more than continued existence. The culmination of the persevering process is a cosmic scientific mind, free from narrow passions, whose blessedness consists in "the intellectual love of God," where God is the ordered system of all that is, or could be. Preservation of one's being becomes identical with the development of one's highest potentialities, and self-preservation thus eventually coincides with self-realization.

SELF-PRESERVATION AND UTILITARIANISM VS. SELF-REALIZATION: DARWIN AND SPENCER

A similar tendency is seen in the evolutionary ethics that arose in the second half of the nineteenth century. Although it is well understood that species sometimes survive by fabulous reproductive rates, by perpetuating for millions of years without change instinctive mechanisms that have been highly successful, or by reverting to parasitic simplicity, the kind of survival that is taken as the model for ethics is, of course, quite different. It is the "survival of the fittest," where *fittest* means the strongest, the most intelligent, and sometimes the most harmoniously shaped and beautiful. Evolutionary ethics could point out that *Homo sapiens* has, in fact, survived all other forms of *Hominidae*, and is infinitely more powerful than any other species, that the deadly struggle for existence has culminated in the triumph of a species incomparably superior to all the rest. Who could doubt that there has been progress, or that it will continue in the future? Natural progress is impeded, however, by misguided humanitarians who call for poor laws that aid the unfit to survive and multiply.

10 *Ibid.*
11 See his *Theological-Political Treatise* in *The Chief Works of Benedict de Spinoza*, Vol. I.

While granting the immense superiority of man over other animals, Darwin argues at length that these advantageous traits evolved gradually and were prefigured in man's recent ancestors. He is intent to show that sympathy and other social emotions—including self-sacrifice for offspring— are found in higher animals. These same traits, magnified in man, became the foundation of civilization. Although the gap between ape and man is enormous, so also is the gap between the savage and the civilized man. There are three reasons for the low morality of savages, Darwin holds: (1) Their sympathy is usually restricted to the tribe; (2) their reasoning powers are insufficient to trace the consequences of their wilful acts and self-indulgence, and (3) they have not yet developed self-restraint and self-discipline.[12]

Morality has a great adaptive value, according to Darwin. It knits the group together in solidarity and common purpose, facilitates cooperative work by rewards and praise, as by blame and punishment.

> The appreciation and the bestowal of praise and blame both rest on sympathy; and this emotion . . . is one of the most important elements of the social instincts. Sympathy, though gained as an instinct, is also much strengthened by exercise or habit.[13]

The moral standard becomes the general good or welfare, or "the greatest happiness."

> As all men desire their own happiness, praise or blame is bestowed on actions and motives, according as they lead to this end; and as happiness is an essential part of the general good, the greatest happiness principle serves as a nearly safe standard of right and wrong. As the reasoning powers advance and experience is gained, the remoter effects of certain lines of conduct on the character of the individual, and on the general good, are perceived; and then the self-regarding virtues come within the scope of public opinion, and receive praise, and their opposites blame.[14]

Darwin goes only part way with utilitarianism. He objects, for one thing, to the doctrine he says he finds in some utilitarians, that men always aim at the greatest pleasure. Many actions are spontaneous, and there are emergency actions, as when one risks his life for others, when there is no time to think of pleasure. Utilitarianism should not be considered a principle of motivation, he thinks, but rather a moral standard. Two prominent utilitarians—J. S. Mill and Henry Sidgwick—he is able to point out, agree with him in this respect. Second, "welfare" or "the general

---

[12] See *The Descent of Man*, p. 135.
[13] *Ibid.*, p. 699.
[14] *Ibid.*

good or welfare" is more appropriate than "the general happiness" to express the state of affairs brought about by sympathy and the other social instincts. "The general good" he defines as "the rearing of the greatest number of individuals in full vigor and health, with all their faculties perfect, under the conditions to which they are subjected."[15] In view of the specific results that the social instincts aim at, Darwin is inclined to believe that it would be better to take "the general good or welfare of the community as the moral standard," rather than the general happiness. He concedes that "the welfare and happiness of the individual usually coincide; and a contented, happy tribe will flourish better than one that is discontented and unhappy."[16] Yet, notwithstanding good-natured concessions, it is obvious that Darwin regards utilitarianism as only part of the truth, and that the goal and standard he is setting up is really successful adaptation to a given environment, assuming, of course, that this will involve a full development of faculties (which need not be the case). If he assigns the greatest value to the moral faculties, based on "the social instincts, including sympathy," and on the development of the intellect, which facilitates moral decisions, it is because they tend to enlarge the adaptive capacity of the group and the individual.

Darwin is keenly aware that the rules, arising from the social instincts, by which societies regulate the conduct of their members, are often ridiculous and cruel, and go directly contrary to the social instincts. As the experience of mankind increases, however, and sympathy is extended to larger and larger groups, he expects that there will be continued progress in rational rules and action tending to the self-preservation, *and happiness*, of all.

Herbert Spencer, like Darwin, takes self-preservation to be the ultimate good, and they both combine self-preservation with happiness conceived as the greatest pleasure of the greatest number. For Darwin, the greatest-happiness principle is a fairly accurate standard of the good, *i.e.*, self-preservation, since the two commonly coincide. Spencer holds that they will fully coincide eventually, for as evolution tends always to increasing self-preservation, it also necessarily yields a greater sum of pleasure, and less pain. As adaptation to existing conditions increases, so does the total pleasure, for nonadaptation is the root of all evil—of all pain. But, though Spencer accepts the utilitarian definition of the ultimate good, he is highly critical of other utilitarian doctrines, especially Benthamism.

In his *Data of Ethics*, as in his *Social Statics*, Spencer says that what we mean by "good" is "conduct furthering self-preservation," and that what we mean by "bad" is conduct that hinders or prevents it.

[15] *Ibid.*, p. 136.
[16] *Ibid.*, p. 137.

All . . . approving and disapproving utterances make the tacit assertion that, other things equal, conduct is right or wrong according as its special acts, well or ill-adjusted to special ends, do or do not further the general end of self-preservation.[17]

Thus we call a mother good who cares for the physical needs and health of her children. So also men who assist others "in reacquiring normal vitality," in protecting their property or defending themselves or aid "whatever promises to improve the living of all his fellows."[18] In all cases, the good is what tends to self-preservation, and self-preservation appears to be something more than mere survival. Good conduct is an advanced product of evolution, if fuller and more complex; and it conduces to more and more permanent life. Evolution "reaches its limits when individual life is the greatest, both in length and breadth," assuring that a sufficient number of the young of the species succeed in growing to maturity and reproducing. It will be clear that "self-preservation," as Spencer employs the term, implies more than is needed for successful adaptation of a species. It implies "the greatest totality of life, in self, in offspring, and in fellow men."[19] (Yet it would seem that the life of the parents, extending far beyond the period necessary for rearing the offspring, might easily be a liability to the species.)

The tie between self-preservation and happiness in Spencer's scheme is easily seen. There exists "a primordial connection between pleasure-giving acts and continuance or increase of life, and, by implication, between pain-giving acts and decrease or loss of life."[20] It is by pursuing the agreeable and avoiding the disagreeable that individuals and species maintain their life from day to day. Second, pleasure accompanies vital functions in their normal degree, whereas pain attends their excess or defect. In a complete life in which faculties function harmoniously, the correlative pleasures arise necessarily.[21] Third, "every pleasure increases vitality; every pain decreases vitality. Every pleasure raises the tide of life; every pain lowers the tide of life."[22]

Although the role assigned to pleasure is reminiscent of Aristotle's theory, Spencer's conception of happiness belongs to a different world. Happiness, for Spencer, is as a correlate of the most perfect adaptation, the culmination of biological and social evolution. In the ideal society, in which, alone, the perfect man is to be found, there will be no virtuous

[17] *Data of Ethics*, pp. 25–26.
[18] *Ibid.*, pp. 26–27.
[19] *Ibid.*, Ch. VI.
[20] *Ibid.*, p. 97.
[21] See *ibid.*, p. 231.
[22] *Ibid.*, p. 103.

activity, in the usual sense, because everyone will automatically do what is virtuous. There will be no duties, because there will be no temptations; everyone will be so perfectly adjusted to the conditions of life that no sanctions, or moral deliberations, or statutes or penalties will be required. Education and the transmission of acquired intelligence and moral proclivity, Spencer thinks, must eventually bring about a general disposition to do the right thing on all occasions, that is, to promote maximum life, and this entails maximum happiness and the elimination of pain. It is by deducing the "absolute morality" of this future state of society[23] that we can understand the "relative morality" of the present—a morality cluttered with uncertainties and confusions. Indeed, the former is as necessary to an understanding of the latter as is physiology to a comprehension of pathology.

Plato maintains that the really just man can only be found in a just state, and that this ideal justice can be used as a yardstick to measure the shortcomings of imperfect states and men. Bentham has his rationalist goal and measure. He holds that men could achieve moral perfection if laws were devised assigning penalities in exact proportion to the tendency of their acts to diminish the general happiness. Spencer, an archoptimist himself, violently opposes the grounds of Bentham's optimism. The greatest happiness is not to be calculated in advance with nice precision, and legislation that is directed to that purpose has turned out to be a series of unhappy guesses. Moreover, Spencer argues, statecraft is becoming more and more discredited as civilization advances, and the state, which is justified only as a means of coping with evil, will wither away as evil recedes. Bentham's legislative program is foolish and dangerous. A strong advocate of laissez-faire, laissez-aller, Spencer holds that the function of the state is limited to protecting its subjects. Governmental interference in other spheres violates biological laws, such as "the survival of the fittest" (Spencer's own phrase), and economic laws, such as "supply and demand": Life would be vitiated and progress retarded by it.

Spencer challenges Bentham on another point, which is of great importance for utilitarianism, and for the theory of happiness in general. Bentham claims, in support of his hedonistic calculus, that every man knows what *happiness* is, whereas *justice* is a matter of dispute on every occasion. Justice must, therefore, be understood in terms of happiness (*i.e.*, pleasure), not vice versa. Spencer maintains, on the contrary, that justice is much more easily determined than the quantity of pleasure, especially when large numbers of people are involved. "For justice, or equity, *i.e.*, equalness, is concerned exclusively with *quantity* under *stated conditions*:

23 See *ibid.*, Ch. XV.

whereas happiness is concerned with both *quantity* and *quality* under *conditions* not *stated*."[24] If it is proposed that two countries exchange shipments of grain for a certain number of sewing machines, world prices of commodities could determine whether the exchange is just, or equal, but how determine whether there would be a gain of total happiness, especially, since, according to Spencer, different *kinds* of pleasure might have to be totaled?

Spencer's recognition that justice is not ascertainable practically by balancing the pleasures and pains involved, brings him closer to the eudaemonistic tradition. Here justice is determined by measuring, not pleasures but by equal value of the goods to be exchanged, and rewards and penalties to be scaled to deserts. Bentham foresees such objections: How does one know that particular exchange-values in the market are just, and particular schedules of rewards and punishment are equitable as opposed to other standards that might be introduced, he asks, except, in the end, by the finding that it makes people happier or less miserable? Is there any other measure than happiness that men can agree upon? Spencer's rejoinder, like Aristotle's, would be that, though pleasure is not a yardstick of the justice or goodness of particular acts, it is always "the concomitant of the highest life,"[25] be it ideal self-preservation, as with Spencer, or virtue in a favored milieu, as with Aristotle.

Spencer veers toward Aristotle in another objection he makes to utilitarianism. Both Bentham and Mill insist that one man's pleasure is exactly as good as another's. Mill states that the greatest-happiness principle

> is a mere form of words without rational significance, unless one person's happiness, supposed equal in degree (with the proper allowance being made for kind), is counted for exactly as much as another's. Those conditions being supplied, Bentham's dictum, "everybody to count for one, nobody for more than one," might be written under the principle of utility as an explanatory comment. The equal claim of everybody to happiness in the estimation of the moralist and of the legislator, involves an equal claim to all the means of happiness, except in so far as the unstable conditions of human life, and the general interest, in which that of every individual is included, set limits to the maximum; and those limits ought to be strictly construed.[26]

Spencer objects that this principle is something over and above the utility principle and needs separate justification, but Mill retorts that it is contained in the utility principle, for this principle implies that one man's

[24] *Ibid.*, p. 196.
[25] This phrase describing the role of pleasure, so reminiscent of Aristotle, is used by Spencer.
[26] *Utilitarianism*, pp. 58–59.

pleasure should count no more than another's. Spencer objects further that institutional action to allocate equal amounts of happiness would be impossible, since pleasure (happiness) is not transferable—not distributable. Moreover, if it *were* possible, it would mean an ignoring of all difference between drones and useful citizens, criminals and virtuous men,[27] the worst characters getting as much as the best. This does not follow, however. Mill's dictum that the pleasure of the scoundrel is as good in itself as that of the hero does not oblige him to hold that a policy should be adopted of equalizing their pleasures. The two men may not have equal capacity for pleasure, and the greatest pleasure of the greatest number may not be served by such a policy. Spencer's criticisms, nonetheless, point to a knotty problem in the logic and implementation of utilitarianism, to which Mill devotes a great deal of thought, viz.: How can the greatest pleasure of the greatest number be squared with the cardinal principle that one man's pleasure is as good as another's? Does not the good of the community call for sacrifices on the part of its members, and more from some than from others? But the difficulty, as Mill points out, confronts other systems of ethics, and is not confined to utilitarianism.

Spencer himself returns again and again to the problem, and his conclusions are not a model of consistency. Justice, he says, is the freedom of a man to appropriate to himself as much pleasure and as much of the means to pleasure as he can, as long as he does not interfere with the equal freedom of other men. But how can interference be avoided if justice and the maximum happiness of mankind are to be realized by the ruthless struggle for existence in which the unfit are eliminated and—though it is sad, Spencer admits—must be eliminated? What is the triumph of the strong but continual interference with the pleasure or happiness of other men? Spencer's ad hoc and disingenuous reply, made in connection with his adverse comments on poor-relief, seems to be that the unfit are miserable anyhow, so that their liquidation would really be humane.

The struggle for existence and natural selection, to which Spencer ascribes the survival of the race and its special powers, are seldom regarded today as a model of justice or a guarantee of maximum happiness in the future. (After a brief heyday of popularity, especially in this country, what is called "Social Darwinism" rapidly receded, and had almost completely disappeared from the scene by 1914.)[28] Spencer sees only the bloody gladiatorial, tooth-and-claw aspect of evolution, and overlooks the benign cooperative side, which Darwin himself often clearly recognizes. Prince Kropotkin, in his *Mutual Aid* (1902), argues that cooperation or "mutual aid" is the mainspring of evolution, and that competition is often harmful

[27] *Op. cit.,* p. 261.
[28] See R. Hofstadter, *Social Darwinism in American Thought.*

to all concerned, and he is able to cite a great deal of evidence. (Authoritative judgment nowadays often veers in the direction of Kropotkin.) Professor Warder C. Allen and his collaborators assert that their whole book, *Principles of Animal Ecology*, is summed up in the following sentence:

> The probability of survival of individual living things, or of populations, increases with the degree to which they harmoniously adjust themselves to each other and their environment.[29]

The doctrine that the struggle for existence and natural selection ensures moral progress and increased happiness is criticized, in a different vein, by Darwin's friend and colleague T. H. Huxley. "The theory of evolution encourages no millennial anticipations," he says. In the animal world

> the struggle for existence tends to eliminate those less fitted to adapt themselves to the circumstances of their existence. . . . But the influence of the cosmic process on the evolution of society is the greater the more rudimentary its civilization. Social progress means a checking of the cosmic process at every step and the substitution for it of another, which we may call the ethical process; the end of which is not the survival of those who happen to be fittest, in respect of the whole of the conditions which obtain, but of those who are ethically best.[30]

The grandson of Thomas Henry Huxley, however, thinks we can learn something ethically important from the course of evolution. It is true, Julian Huxley says, that we can discover no purpose in evolution, but "we can discern a direction—a line of evolutionary progress.

> And this past direction can serve as a guide in formulating our purpose for the future. Increase of control, increase of independence, increase of internal co-ordination; increase of knowledge, of means for co-ordinating knowledge, of elaborateness and intensity of feeling—those are trends of the most general order. If we do not continue them in the future, we cannot hope that we are in the main line of evolutionary progress any more than could a sea-urchin or a tapeworm.[31]

Julian Huxley's contention that we can discover human *values*, as distinguished from human *possibilities*, from a study of *evolution*, has been called a circular argument: If one does not know what is good already, one could not distinguish the good evolutionary developments from the bad and indifferent.

George Gaylord Simpson does not claim that the course of evolution can

[29] *Principles of Animal Ecology*, as quoted by Ashley Montagu in *Darwin, Competition and Cooperation*, p. 59.
[30] *Evolution and Ethics and Other Essays*, pp. 81, 85.
[31] *Evolution: The Modern Synthesis*, pp. 576–577.

instruct us as to the nature of good or right. It does open our eyes, he says, to the awesome prospect of human control, of evolution, and hence of the engineering of human perfection and happiness. He points out that, as his knowledge of evolution advances, man is gaining "the power to modify and within certain rather rigid limits to determine the direction of his own evolution"—biological as well as social.[32] Although the perfect painless utopia predicted by Spencer is not anticipated or even desired, man is achieving the power to greatly increase the means of his own well-being or happiness in the future. Vast progress may be confidently expected, Simpson claims, were it not that man has also achieved the power of self-destruction, and is making rapid progress toward annihilation,[33] as well as toward the improvement of the human lot.

In resolving the conflicting claims of self-preservation and self-realization to be the ultimate good, we have to consider such questions as: Do men desire to go on living even when the hope of happiness has been extinguished, or is survival regarded as a mere means to happiness? There are cases in which men are grateful for a reprise of a few hours before their execution, though they can do little with the interval but breathe and wait. It would seem that a life deprived of happiness in the sense of self-realization, or however else it is defined, could not be regarded as ideal or, perhaps, even human. On the other hand, self-preservation is the *sine qua non* of happiness, and in hard times, becomes a substitute. This is well expressed by a contemporary philosopher who says:

> Man as a docile animal capable of happiness through intelligent guidance of his purposive behavior is also, as a living creature, involved in the dynamics of biological evolution and concerned to live and not to perish. These two evaluative forces, sometimes cooperative and sometimes opposed, are embedded in his make-up and in the dynamic make-up of his society. But if there is a genuine conflict between the two, natural selection overrules man's natural prejudice in favor of happiness. Usually it does this rather quietly by the demand for social conformity. The perverse, uncooperative, solitary or rambunctious man is shouldered away or neglected and has not the opportunity to propagate either his attitudes or his genes. And the greater the pressure in a society the greater the demand for social solidarity among its members.[34]

Self-preservation remains an essential element in the self-realization theory, just as it is an essential feature of eudaemonism, and of every other scheme of happiness. In times of adversity, the individual, and perhaps a whole society, loses hope of happiness, and settles for survival. When a

[32] *The Meaning of Evolution*, p. 329.
[33] *Ibid.*, p. 328.
[34] S. C. Pepper, *The Sources of Value*, p. 654.

society demands high conformity for the security of the individual and his family, the latter may be chosen rather than the dangers and uncertainties of happiness.

Self-realization: Seth, Bradley, Hobhouse, and Dewey

Although self-realization authors have their disagreements, they also agree among themselves,[35] and with Aristotle's eudaemonism, on the following points:

1. Happiness is an activity, not a feeling, state, or condition—a dynamic, open-ended process.

2. It does not come and go like pleasure or good fortune, but belongs to a whole lifetime, or pervades a long segment of a biography.

3. The faculties are fully developed and exercised, especially the highest, and there is

4. Fulfillment of the desires of the individual, especially those that form a durable and consistent whole.

5. The latter involves conflict, requires training, restraint, and self-discipline of desires.

6. Pleasure is the normal concomitant of both the exercise of faculties and the fulfillment of desire, but

7. Pleasure is not generally sought for itself. It should not be aimed at, but rather pleasurable things.

8. The acquisition of virtue is not something different and opposed to the development of faculties and the fulfilling of desires, but is the very same process. (Man is not two souls within one breast.) Ordinary virtues are healthy means between the extremes of desires and of natural functions.

9. The development of the individual's faculties and fulfillment of his desires demand similar development and fulfillment in others, in a stable and enlightened social order.

10. Happiness, *i.e.*, self-realization, is desired by all men, though it may be interpreted narrowly or comprehensively—foolishly or wisely, and may be an unconscious desire.

11. Happiness must be recognized as the highest good for man.

The core agreement among such diverse self-realization theories is almost the same as their common agreement with Aristotle's eudaemonism. Self-realization theories, however, diverge from the Greek model in two general directions:

[35] John Dewey is an apparent exception in one or two respects, which are discussed below, pp. 168, 174–75.

(a) The "self" which is to be realized does not exactly coincide with the "soul" whose happiness consists of virtuous activity. After Descartes, the soul becomes more private and personal, and emerges, at the same time, as the only source of certain knowledge. The soul thus turns into the self, or *myself*, and is contrasted with my body, other selves, and with society. It is not to be understood objectively, but by private introspection. Distinctions are drawn, such as that between the true self and the public self, which has no parallel in the language of the soul. Personality, in its individuality and uniqueness, is more sharply profiled. It assumes the highest moral worth. Its full realization is happiness.

(b) The inner self is posed over against an alien society, and the problem of self-realization is to reconcile the two, whereas the soul in Aristotle's world was integrated in the life of the state from the first, and is meaningless outside of it. The opposition between egoism and altruism, which is marginal in Aristotelian thought, assumes focal importance in modern ethical theories. The ultimate good is now to be attained by overcoming narrow selfish desires by realization of the true self, whose interests extend to friends, neighbors, and all mankind, viewed primarily as individuals, but also as groups or majorities.

To illustrate the common doctrines of self-realization theories listed above, we shall consider the views of four important and very diverse representatives of this position—Seth, Bradley, Hobhouse, and Dewey. We shall undertake to show, from a consideration of their writings, that these self-realization authors do agree as to the eleven features of happiness listed above. The extent of their agreement with Aristotle's eudaemonism will be apparent, as also their wide differences with one another. It should be noted that, though the self-realization authors usually call the supreme good "happiness," they often use "welfare" or "the general good" as names for the same thing. There are two reasons for this. "Happiness," and the corresponding words in German and French (*Glückseligkeit* and *bonheur*), sometimes refer only to the subjective state and not to the qualities of character and the external conditions inherent in, or necessary to, that state. Second, "happiness" is often taken to mean "pleasure" or "a whole made up of pleasure." To avoid subjective and hedonistic connotations, self-realization authors frequently use "welfare" or "the general good" along with "happiness," or alternatively.

(1) and (2): We have seen that, for Aristotle, happiness is always being attained, and is never completely attained. This follows from the fact that happiness is a whole that continues to the end of life, and that new contingencies and problems are always arising. Self-realization is also essentially an unfinished process. As James Seth says,

> The self is never fully realized, it remains always an ideal demanding realization. . . . Ever as we attain in any measure to it, the ideal seems to

grow and widen and deepen, so that it is still for us unattained. . . . It is the infinity of the ideal self that makes it, in its totality, unrealizable, and the life of duty inexhaustible, by a finite being.[36]

From a different angle, but to the same purpose, F. H. Bradley states that in the life of every man the various spheres of action are seen to be "subordinated to and qualified by the whole."

> And most men have more or less of an ideal of life—a notion of perfect happiness which is never quite attained in real life.[37]

Happiness, as self-realization, is one and whole because the self is so, and it is never attained because the self is unlimited and there is always a larger whole beyond. Yet the ideal is not alien to the actual self. Almost any man's life presents a certain unity, and the deepest urge is to attain more.

Another self-realizationist, L. T. Hobhouse, defines the good as "Happiness in the fulfilment of vital capacity in a world adapted to Mind."[38] It is "a mode of consciousness dependent on the relatively stable position and character of the personality as a whole, and endowed with pleasurable feeling-tone."[39] It is achieved in the harmonious development of the self. But the harmony is never complete; the self is never completely fulfilled. If we regard development as a means,

> it is partly because it is a process incomplete and pointing beyond itself. We defined it as progressive fulfilment. Now conversely, we can enlarge the conception of fulfilment to cover not only its ideal completeness, but any state on the way. Fulfilment, then, becomes another name for Development in its static aspect—not as something in process, but as something which has attained a certain level.[40]

Fulfillment, in an absolute sense, is always incomplete, but in a relative sense we can say that it is complete, up to a certain point, or with respect to certain objectives. Hobhouse, however, agrees with T. H. Green that

> self-realization must mean (a) not any kind of experience in which some psychical capacity is fulfilled, but an orderly development of an organic whole, and (b), if it is to form a part of a "common" good, must be conditioned by the equally desirable development of other human beings.[41]

For John Dewey, similarly, happiness is not a transitory experience like pleasure, but depends "upon the standing disposition of the self."

---

[36] *A Study of Ethical Principles*, p. 224.
[37] "Why Should I Be Moral?" *Ethical Studies, Selected Essays*, p. 15.
[38] *The Rational Good*, p. 117.
[39] *Ibid.*, p. 138.
[40] *Ibid.*, p. 113.
[41] *Ibid.*, p. 141.

One may find happiness in the midst of annoyances; be contented and cheerful in spite of a succession of disagreeable experiences, if one has braveness and equanimity of soul. . . . Happiness is a matter of the dispositions we actively bring with us to meet situations.

True happiness, as contrasted with transient gratifications, "issues from objects which are enjoyable in themselves but which also re-enforce and enlarge the other desires and tendencies which are sources of happiness. . . . Harmony and readiness to expand into union with other values is a mark of happiness."[42] When men have alert and active interests in circumstances that promote the development of others, "their exercise brings happiness because it fulfills the self."[43]

If happiness can be looked upon as a fulfilling of the self, the process, of course, remains always incomplete. Dewey never tires of denouncing the pernicious view that some ends are final. Idealists and utopians have always insisted on finality, and as a result have regularly sacrificed the present to the future. In opposition to this absolutist temper, Dewey holds that means and ends form a continuum. The end becomes a means to new goals, and the means, in turn, must come to have a value in themselves. Education, for example, is not a mere preparation for later achievements, and, if it is so treated, the achievements do not occur; it is both means and end.

Every condition that has to be brought into existence in order to serve as means is, *in that connection,* an object of desire and an end-in-view, while the end actually reached is a means to future ends as well as a test of valuations already made.[44]

(3), (4) and (5): Seth cites with approval Aristotle's theory that happiness consists in the perfect fulfillment of the potentialities of both the irrational and the rational sides of human nature. He objects only to there being any "finally irrational element in man, any more than in the universe. For, in man as in the universe, all matter is quick with form; the one is potentiality, the other the actuality of form. Everywhere we have the promise and potency of reason: the irrational is but reason in the making."[45] This revision of Aristotle is not surprising. Self-realization authors evolve from Aristotle's eudaemonism, but are usually influenced by Hegel as well. Hegel, himself deeply versed in Aristotle, introduces a dialectic that sets all the categories into motion and evolution.

What distinguishes true self-realization from counterfeits is coherence, harmony, and the ability to handle conflict. Every part of the temperate

[42] *Ethics*, pp. 213–215.
[43] *Ibid.*, p. 336.
[44] *The Theory of Valuation* in *International Encyclopedia of Unified Science*, Vol. II, No. 4, p. 43.
[45] *Op. cit.*, p. 236.

life is a "partial expression and realization of its total purpose."[46] It is true that a man who seeks only wealth or power may display in his life a certain system and coherence, though he is under the sway of a single passion. In such a life, however, "the part has claimed to be the whole; and the result is necessarily partial, abstract, contradictory.

> The true whole is the unity of all the parts . . . every selfish impulse must be submitted to the control of the rational self, which can alone estimate the relative and permanent value of each.[47]

More than most self-realization authors, Seth insists that the disciplining of desires requires a bitter struggle and self-sacrifice. Complete self-fulfillment can be achieved only through self-renunciation.

The full exercise of the faculties and the realization of a system of consistent desires is implied in the very idea of self-realization, according to Bradley, but so also is the self-restraint and renunciation, without which the system could not endure. Against utilitarianism Bradley argues that happiness or self-realization cannot be the attainment of a mere phase of the self—a series of the self's feelings. Against Kant's "duty for duty's sake" he objects that the will must have concrete content. The self that we and others are to realize, he claims, must be identified with "the station we must fill, and with the appointed functions we are called upon to fulfill." This does not mean that "the false self, the habits and desires opposed to the good will are extinguished." They can be negated but not completely suppressed. The solution comes with a distinction between *will,* which is within our power, and *desires,* which are not. "I must identify myself with the good will that I realize in the world, by my refusing to identify myself with the bad will of my private self."[48]

Whether we identify ourselves with the one self or the other, we realize ourselves. In the one case, we do so perfectly, in the other, imperfectly, and "we cannot possibly do anything else." Accident apart, we can do nothing but realize "our ends, or the objects we desire; and . . . all we can desire is, in a word, self."[49] Yet even the narrow self is suffused with the community life and institutions; when it seeks to escape, it rends itself.

For Hobhouse, happiness is found in the harmonious fulfillment of conation and purpose. When the purpose is clear, "this means the attainment of the end with which the purpose sets out,"[50] but there is also, on lower grades, unintentional fulfillment of latent capacities. Even when a mere potentiality is completed, there is realization.

[46] *Ibid.,* p. 252.
[47] *Ibid.,* p. 253.
[48] *Op. cit.,* pp. 17–18.
[49] *Ibid.,* p. 11.
[50] *Op. cit.,* p. 113.

Thus the good consists in the fulfilment of vital capacity, but the rational good cannot consist in the fulfilment of every sort of capacity, since one fulfilment may destroy another. It can consist only in such fulfilments as are in mutual consistency.[51]

The rational good, which on its subjective side is happiness, is on its objective side "the greatest sense of fulfillment."[52] This fulfillment, however, is not merely the fulfillment of the individual's own powers. It is fulfillment "in all living beings in so far as it can attain harmonious expression."[53] And "the service of society may require the entire sacrifice of happiness or life on the part of the individual." It is a misleading half-truth to say, as Bradley does, that in sacrificing himself the individual "realizes his own highest good." His sacrifice of personal happiness represents a real loss, though it may be, when justified by the good rendered to society, "the least bad thing" for the individual, *"under the circumstances."* "For the full development of every personality is conditionally good—conditional, that is, on its capability of harmonization with the development of others."[54]

For Dewey, all psychology is social psychology. Naturally, therefore, he is concerned with the fulfillment and enlargement of interests, which are inevitably social, rather than with the full development and exercise of faculties; for the latter are included in the former, and do not exist apart. He succinctly expresses the role of interests in the realization of happiness: "The final happiness of the individual resides in the supremacy of certain interests in the make-up of character; namely, alert, sincere, enduring interests in the objects in which all can share." Happiness so entrenched in the self is immune to circumstances.

> The *kind* of self which is formed through action which is faithful to relations with others will be a fuller and broader self than one which is cultivated in isolation from or in opposition to the purposes and needs of others. In contrast, the kind of self which results from generous breadth of interest may be said alone to constitute a development and fulfillment of self, while the other way of life stunts and starves selfhood by cutting it off from the connections necessary for its growth.[55]

Dewey would doubtless concede that individual self-sacrifice is sometimes necessary for the self or community, but it is certainly not one of his themes. Through the use of "intelligence," he continually insists, human beings can avoid human sacrifice of realizations and happiness, both on the

[51] *Ibid.,* p. 113.
[52] *Ibid.,* p. 114.
[53] *Ibid.,* p. 117.
[54] *Ibid.,* p. 143.
[55] *Op. cit.,* p. 335.

level of the individual and of the community. Ethical theories have almost always looked for happiness in the future, and this has meant that they have sacrificed happiness in the present. But "happiness is fundamental in morals," Dewey argues, "only because happiness is not something to be sought for, but is something now attained, even in the midst of pain and trouble, wherever recognition of our ties with nature and with fellow-men releases and informs our action."[56] This does not mean, of course, that we ought not seek the *means* to happiness in the future. Dewey expressly praises Bentham for seeing that "conscience" is genuine "only as it contributes to relief of misery and promotion of happiness."[57] The point involved is that men do not *seek* happiness but spontaneously *find* it. Second, if happiness is ever enjoyed it must be in the present, which, therefore, cannot be considered a mere means; and third, the present happiness includes plans for the future and assurances from the past, and these may be consistent with pain and trouble.

(6) and (7): In spite of differences as to the role of pleasure in self-realization or happiness, our four authors agree that pleasure is the normal accompaniment of self-realization, but that it is not generally, and should not be, sought for itself. When it *is* sought for itself, the quest is self-defeating. This is the so-called paradox of hedonism, viz.: The way to get pleasure is to forget it.

Seth, it is true, thinks that when pleasure is properly understood, the paradox disappears. "The life of pleasure," he says,

> is not an abstract universal; it is a concrete whole, and consists of real particulars. Pleasure, further, is derived from pleasant things; to divorce it from these is to destroy it. But the divorce is entirely gratuitous; no matter how it is reached, the pleasure is our real end. We have not "forgotten" the pleasure after all.[58]

In other words, having *pleasure* in view is having *pleasant things* in view. It is not satisfaction in general that we seek, but particular satisfactions inseparable from their objects. Seth points out that this is actually J. S. Mill's position, and he might have added that it was also that of Aristotle, long before. Seth quotes with approval the famous passage in *Utilitarianism* (already cited above), in which Mill contends that higher activities, such as listening to music, are not mere *means* to happiness, but a part of it. Originally indifferent, and valued because of their association with "the satisfaction of our primitive desires," Mill says, they themselves become sources of pleasures more extensive and continuous than the

[56] *Human Nature and Conduct,* p. 265.
[57] *Ibid.,* p. 212.
[58] *Op. cit.,* p. 71.

primitive sort. Mill eliminates the paradox of hedonism, but only by abandoning a part of hedonism in favor of eudaemonism. Seth is glad to have this distinguished backslider as an ally.

Hedonism is still one side of the truth. Self-realization, for Seth, is the realization of our sentient as well as our rational nature. "If pleasure is not itself the good, it is its natural and normal index and expression, just as pain is the natural and normal index and expression of evil."[59]

Bradley's criticism of hedonism in his essay "Pleasure for Pleasure's Sake" is one of the most effective ever written, yet he recognizes that life would not be worthwhile without pleasure. "Generally," he says, "it is a good thing to aim at the increasing of pleasure and diminishing of pain; but it is a good thing because it increases the actualities and possibilities of life." To make function the end, as Bradley does, "justifies and demands the increase of pleasure and gives you all you can fairly ask in that way. But to say more pleasure is all the end, and life a mere accompaniment, is another matter."[60]

Pleasure, in Bradley's view, is not only the normal accompaniment and spur to function, it is also a test of whether function is operating smoothly or is impeded. Yet, on the other hand, pleasure will not tell you which are the higher functions ". . . if you go by it you must prefer a lower state of harmony to a higher state of contradiction."[61]

Hobhouse also insists that pleasure and happiness are distinct, although they agree in "possessing feeling tone." Pleasure can belong to all sorts of activities, but "happiness is a mode of consciousness dependent on the relatively stable character and position of the personality as a whole, and endowed with pleasurable feeling-tone."[62] He concedes that in the learning process there tends to be a coincidence between desire and pleasure, and that we generally desire what is pleasant, but it does not follow that we generally desire pleasure. The latter does *not* seem to be true, and it also implies that all our actions are egoistic, *i.e.*, aimed in every case at one's own pleasure, which is even more doubtful.

These two points about pleasure, so typical of eudaemonism, are always made by other self-realization authors, though in different ways, and some, like T. H. Green, show less sympathy for hedonism than do others. Dewey, as we have seen, emphasizes the stability of happiness in the face of pain and trouble more than he does the concomitance of pleasantness,[63] but both points are included. As for the doctrine that men desire only

[59] *Ibid.*, pp. 149–150.
[60] *Op. cit.*, p. 76.
[61] *Ibid.*, p. 77.
[62] *Op. cit.*, p. 138.
[63] See, for example, *Ethics*, p. 214.

pleasure, he holds that Bentham and other utilitarians confuse "motive" with "standard." The utilitarians, Dewey says,

> were . . . faced by the problem of conflict between the strictly personal and selfish character of the motive of conduct, and the broadly social and philanthropic character of the standard of approval. Desire for private pleasure as the sole motive of action and universal benevolence as the principle of approval are at war with one another. The chief interest of Bentham was in the standard of judgment, and his acceptance of hedonistic psychology was, in a broad sense, a historic accident.[64]

Bentham, according to Dewey, does not realize that the egoism of motives and his standard of benevolence are inconsistent. What he wants to do is improve conditions of life in England and elsewhere, and his egoistic hedonism is directly contrary to this end. Bentham, as we have seen, has an answer, which we shall consider in Chapter 10.

(8) The four authors, whom we have taken as representative of the self-realization theory, also agree that self-realization is moral growth or enhancement. They all hold, though with characteristic differences, that development of capacities and fulfillment of desires that brings happiness is also a process in which virtue and worthiness are attained. There is even some approximation to the Aristotelian doctrine that the moral virtues, especially temperance, are a mean between extremes. Quotations above have already shown substantial agreement that moral development is equivalent to self-realization. The authors have all reacted against the Kantian divorce of duty and natural desire, and have followed, with great individual variations, the precedent of Aristotle, Spinoza, and Hegel.

(9) A tension between the rights and welfare of the individual and those of the community or State runs through all the main theories of happiness. Plato's *Republic* is concerned with the net happiness of the perfect State, and that of the orders within it, but not with individual self-realization. Aristotle's ethical individualism assumes a natural framework of the State and its institutions, without which happiness is not conceivable. A repressive despotism would exclude happiness; it would thrive best under a mixed polity. The Epicureans find happiness outside the State, but are all the more dependent on the small company of friends, while the Stoics do not thank the State for their tranquillity, and their deeper allegiance is to mankind.

For Seth, the individual is always an end in himself, "and has an infinite worth,"[65] yet the individual and the social are in reality two aspects of one

---

64 *Op. cit.,* p. 263.
65 *Op. cit.,* p. 285.

undivided life of virtue."[66] For this reason there is no conflict between individualism and socialism. In fact, "the true socialism is the true individualism."[67] The true individualism is that which accords to the individual full development of his person or personality; whereas the individualism of the mere individual is anarchy and suicidal. The proper function of the State, accordingly, is the protection of the sphere of personality:[68] "The most perfect State will be that in which there is least repression, and most encouragement and development, of the free life of a full individuality in the citizens."[69] Although Seth deplores narrow patriotism which divides wider allegiances, he warns that mankind, after all, is an "abstract universal," and that the nation remains the permanent framework of self-realization or happiness.[70]

Bradley, in "My Station and Its Duties," also says that the individual cannot carry out his functions or realize himself except as a part of the State. But he goes much further—so much further that the individual seems to get lost or to become a mere cog or cell in the system. Since self-realization is realization of the good will—a will superior to ourselves, and independent of "subjective" liking—it might seem that it is the State rather than the individual self that comes into its own. But the State, as a moral organism, is nothing without its integral members. In affirming it, Bradley says,

> I affirm myself, for I am but as a "heart-beat in its system." And I am real in it, for, when I give myself to it, it gives me the fruition of my own personal activity, the accomplished ideal of my life which is happiness. In the realized idea which, superior to me and yet here and now in and by me, affirms itself in a continuous process, we have found the end, we have found self-realization, duty, and happiness in one—yes, we have found ourselves when we have found our station and its duties, our function as an organ in the social organism.[71]

We have seen that happiness for Hobhouse is "the fulfillment of vital capacity in a world adapted to mind," and that "happiness" means "Happiness of all beings capable thereof; fulfillment of vital capacity means fulfillment in all living beings so far as it can attain harmonious expression."[72] The last phrase is very significant. The happiness of the individual, we have seen Hobhouse insisting, is not inviolable. He is often called upon to sacrifice himself for the good of society. He may prefer to

[66] *Ibid.*, p. 284.
[67] *Ibid.*, pp. 285–286.
[68] *Ibid.*, p. 313.
[69] *Ibid.*, p. 325.
[70] *Ibid.*, p. 333.
[71] *Op. cit.*, p. 101.
[72] *Op. cit.*, p. 117.

give up his life rather than to shirk his duty, but if the sacrifice is real, it is not his happiness, nor self-realization, but tragedy.[73] It will be remembered that during World War I, while German bombs were falling on England, Hobhouse undertook to refute the Hegelian theory of the State,[74] which had been expounded and developed by Bosanquet and T. H. Green. This idealistic theory had made the state into a false divinity, which demanded human sacrifice on a scale, it turned out, that the world had not known before.

This theory, which sanctifies the State at the expense of the individual, is hateful and ominous. Hobhouse finds more sense in Bentham's egoistic hedonism when it insists that a man should be rigidly impartial, as between his own pleasure and that of another person. "Every one to count for one and nobody for more than one" expresses—but also overstates—an austere truth."[75]

Hobhouse's theory of harmony and self-development, however, is concerned to avoid not only one-sided collectivism but also one-sided individualism. The latter attributes to the individual alone what "really belongs to him only as a member of society."[76] Man's happiness cannot be separated from the institutional life in which he is immersed. The objects dear to him are not mere *means* to happiness, as Bentham would have it, but integral parts of it.[77] Of all forms of government, a functional, flexible democracy is most favorable to harmony and happiness.

For Dewey, happiness of the individual is social through and through, and has, for that very reason, a large independence of circumstance.

> No amount of outer obstacles can destroy the happiness that comes from lively and ever-renewed interest in others and in the conditions and objects which promote their development. . . . If we identify the interests of such a self [a self devoted to values shared with others] with the virtues, then we shall say, with Spinoza, that happiness is not the reward of virtue, but is virtue itself.[78]

The attainment of the common good or happiness in society requires a full realization of all the capacities of the individual in all their uniqueness. It is necessary that men be judged by their potential, not by what they have been able to achieve under limiting conditions, at a given time. Democracy is the political form that best assures free individual development.

[73] *Ibid.*, p. 143.
[74] See *The Metaphysical Theory of the State. A Criticism.*
[75] *Elements of Social Justice*, pp. 16–18.
[76] *Ibid.*, p. 31.
[77] *Ibid.*, p. 18.
[78] *Ethics*, p. 336.

For democracy signifies, on the one side, that every individual is to share in the duties and rights belonging to control of social affairs, and, on the other side, that social arrangements are to eliminate those external arrangements of status, birth, wealth, sex, etc., which restrict the opportunity of each individual for full development of himself.[79]

The social side of democracy—Dewey characteristically remarks—is wider than the political. It includes a disposition to criticize and improve existing institutions, and to seek ideal conditions for progress, which, though they are in line with improvements already made, have never been realized anywhere.[80]

(10) The question whether men *do* seek happiness is different from the question whether they *should* seek it. And pursuing objects that make one happy is logically distinct from pursuing them because they make one happy, or for the sake of happiness.

Seth begins with the hedonist thesis that *pleasure* is the actual object of desire. He quotes James's criticism—"a pleasant act, and an act pursuing pleasure, are, in themselves, two perfectly distinct conceptions," and concludes that "the pleasure of pursuit" is psychologically different from the "pursuit of pleasure."[81] He points out that the hedonist Hume and the utilitarian J. S. Mill make the same distinction, though it is against the grain. Mill is even led to accept the paradox of hedonism—that "to get pleasure you must forget it." But on this issue Seth will not join the antihedonists, and insists, as we have noted, that "pleasure itself is our real end," for the pleasurable objects which become ours as the self develops, are inseparable from pleasantness, just as pleasantness is inseparable from them. It will be remembered that Aristotle comes to a similar conclusion in Book X of the *Nicomachean Ethics,* where he says that it makes little difference whether we say that men pursue the distinctive pleasures yielded by certain objects or pursue the objects that yield them.

Bradley rejects, with the vigor of personal distaste, the claim that what men seek is pleasure, though he agrees that it is a good and part of what is sought. "We agree that happiness is the end; and therefore we say that pleasure is not the end. We agree that pleasure is *a* good; we say that it is not *the* good." And this end or standard is happiness, but it is also "self-realization."[82] This is the ethical standard; it is also the psychological principle of motivation. Bradley argues that "every man has a notion of happiness, and *his* notion, though he may not quite know what it is . . . and most men have more or less of an ideal of life—a notion of perfect

[79] *Ibid.,* p. 387.
[80] See *ibid.,* pp. 387–388.
[81] *Op. cit.,* p. 68.
[82] *Op. cit.,* p. 65.

happiness which is never quite attained in real life." Although we may not fully understand it, "what we aim at is self, and self as a whole." This becomes clear if we ask ourselves what we wish for *most,* for then we see that none of us seeks disconnected particular ends—not in themselves. They are subordinated to wider purposes. But are all these wider purposes included within one all-embracing end? Although men may not realize that they are seeking a single goal—the fullest development of self—and often behave inconsistently, the ends they have in view are, roughly speaking, "embraced in one main end or whole of ends."[83]

Diverse echoes of Aristotle, Augustine, Hegel, Emerson, and many others are heard as Bradley attempts to explain how happiness or complete self-development, which is the ethical goal or ideal of human activity, is also the target, dimly perceived or unconscious, of even the most ignorant men.

Hobhouse does not give much attention to the present question. With other self-realization authors, and the eudaemonists, he holds that the object of desire is not pleasure but pleasurable things. These things may be in harmony with one another, or they may be discordant, in which case there is pain or frustration. The harmony resulting from full development of personality means a wider fulfillment of desires and lessened frustration. The overall harmony *should be* desired, or willed, but Hobhouse does not claim that it is generally the end in view. Happiness is, perhaps, for him, as for Bradley, a regulative principle, which embraces desirables that consort in a wider whole, and excludes those that do not.

Dewey argues at length that the notion that men aim at self-development, or happiness, rests upon a confusion between "ends-in-view" and "standards." Men aim at higher wages, prestige, luxuries, a better education for their children than they themselves had, seek to get the best of a rival, or to escape responsibility. The ends they generally have in view are concrete, appropriate to the special circumstances in which they find themselves. Ends-in-view are objects of any desire whatever, but not all desires are approved and sustained by the self who has them; some are never realized. They are excluded, first, by the standards of the community, and, later, by the individual himself, when he internalizes and modifies these standards. Standards are thus criteria to separate approved, acceptable desires from disapproved, unacceptable ones. Self-realization, *i.e.,* happiness, is clearly "a standard of judgment,"[84] and not an end-in-view, not the end of desire. "Indeed, it is hard to imagine its being made the end of desire; as a direct object to be aimed at, it would be so indeterminate and vague that it would only arouse a diffused sentimental state,

83 *Ibid.,* pp. 14–15.
84 *Op. cit.,* p. 214, fn.

without indicating just how and where conduct should be directed. Desire on the other hand points to a definite and concrete object at which to aim."[85]

It is simply impossible to know in advance all the specific things that will be required for our happiness in the future, for our needs change as the world changes, and means to further ends may become unexpectedly dear in themselves. And even if we could aim at, or act in view of, our entire future happiness, the result would be of dubious value. If we must forget pleasure in order to obtain it, Dewey points out, we must also forget virtue and self-realization to attain *them*. The man who consciously aims at virtue and self-realization, instead of particular friends and cultural objects, may well end up a self-centered prig.

Dewey's rejection of self-realization or happiness as the end of man's desire thus seems to be complete. There is only one sense in which men might be said to aim at happiness. Dewey would perhaps agree that all men desire above all else the maximum fulfillment of desire. "No two concrete cases of happiness," he insists, "are just like each other in actual stuff and make-up. They are alike in being cases of fulfillment, of meeting the requirements set up by some desire."[86] This, however, is a "formal trait. It is a mistake to suppose that there is a homogeneity of material or content, just because there is a single name 'happiness.' "[87]

Dewey's insistence that happiness be unique and cut to the pattern of each individual's desires and judgment is of the greatest importance. It may lead him to underestimate the extent to which material and social desirables, in any given culture, are in fact the same for all men, and are sought by all alike. Aristotle, it will be remembered, recognizes that the concrete content of happiness will vary widely among individuals, as their capacities, temperaments, professions, wealth, etc., vary, and hence, also, their virtues. He contends, too, that men envisage happiness differently. Yet he holds, at the same time, that there are essentials and necessary conditions of any human happiness—a common denominator that is more than the formal fulfillment of desires. In a polemical setting, Dewey's emphasis is all on the variety, spontaneity, and unforeseeability of concrete happiness, but in other contexts he seems to acknowledge common features that can be known in advance. Otherwise, there could scarcely be a reform of public education. Along with other self-realization authors, he seems to believe that social and cultural projects are necessary to, and often provide the essentials of, the happiness we share.

[85] *Ibid.,* p. 270.
[86] *Ibid.,* p. 271.
[87] *Ibid.,* p. 270. Dewey's conclusion here resembles Hegel's insight (Chapter 5) that, though all men desire happiness, it is happiness in the abstract; the concrete forms it will take cannot generally be foreseen.

(11) All the self-realization authors agree without ado that happiness, interpreted as self-realization, is the highest good for everyone. This is apparent from the above quotations. Hobhouse, however, takes happiness to be the subjective-feeling side of the good, the objective side of which is harmonious self-development, but this is a mere terminological deviation from the self-realization pattern. He probably thinks of happiness as subjective because, in the English tradition, happiness is associated with hedonism and pleasure, and pleasure is subjective. There is no substantial disagreement.

The main adversaries of the self-realization theory of happiness—Stoic self-containment, utilitarianism, the Kantian repudiation of happiness, and the ideal of a supernatural happiness—are also the main adversaries of eudaemonism. So close is self-realization to the eudaemonism from which it derives that it generally gains and loses with the ups and downs of the parent theory, and controversy that affects the one affects the other in the same way. It is Aristotle's eudaemonism, however, that has the longer history and influence, that provides the fullest, most explicit theory of happiness, and that is far more involved in the controversy over happiness. Accordingly, in the next three chapters, which describe the issues that divide the main theories of happiness, we shall say a great deal about Aristotle's theory, and self-realization will be involved only incidentally. In the last chapter, we shall return to self-realization.

8

The Issue of the Supreme
Good: Happiness vs. the
Performance of Duty

I. KANT'S ATTACK ON THE HAPPINESS PRINCIPLE

I F doing one's duty is the supreme good, happiness is only conditionally
good and should be avoided whenever it conflicts with obligation.
Misery that makes us dutiful would be better than happiness that leaves us
lax. For this reason, the present issue is of primary importance.

The leading antagonist to happiness being the supreme good is Immanuel Kant, and we have traced his main line of argument in Chapter 5.
It remains to state his position on a number of issues, and to indicate the
kind of answers the partisans of the happiness principle can make. Since
Kant usually conceives happiness as pleasure, his attack on the happiness
principle hits the hedonists and utilitarians harder than it does the
eudaemonists. The eudaemonists, after all, could agree with Kant that the
supreme good is not simply pleasure, and that it *is* a life of virtue, though
their understanding of virtue is different from his. On the other hand,

when Kant identifies happiness with "welfare" or "conservation" or the fullest satisfaction of desires, his derogation and downgrading of the happiness principle constitutes a more direct attack on eudaemonism.

We shall also be concerned to show how other deontologists—advocates of duty as the supreme good—argue against the happiness principle; and what answers could be made to *their* contentions. All deontologists seem to take hedonism as their main opponent, but they also repudiate every form of "teleological ethics," *i.e.*, ethics that define right acts or morally good acts as fulfillments of purpose, or as productive of desirable consequences.

How Can Happiness Be Both the Natural and the Moral End of Man?

Although Kant denies that happiness is the supreme good, he asserts that it is the one end and one purpose all rational beings have "by a natural necessity."[1] We have already called attention to his dictum in the *Critique of Practical Reason*:

> To be happy is necessarily the wish of every finite rational being, and this, therefore, is inevitably a determining principle of its faculty of desire.[2]

Although the fact that happiness is universally and necessarily *desired* does not prove that it is *desirable*, that it is the moral end of man, it is a necessary part of such a proof; for if happiness were not desired, J. S. Mill argues, no one would say that it is desir*able*. Kant, however, deduces a contrary conclusion. If men naturally and necessarily pursue happiness, he argues, this cannot be what they *ought* to do; for duty presupposes contrary inclinations and an effort on our part to overcome them. There could never be a creature who "thoroughly *likes* to do all the moral laws," who suffers no temptation to deviate from them. This is an ideal of "holiness" which we should continuously strive to achieve, though we never shall, for the progress toward it is infinite.

> The stage of morality on which man (and, so far as we can see, every rational being) stands is respect for the moral law. The disposition that he ought to have in obeying this is to obey it from duty, not from spontaneous inclination.[3]

It is fanatic and self-conceited to suppose that we can ever become so perfect that our desires will coincide with duty.

[1] *Metaphysic of Morals*, p. 38.
[2] *Critique of Practical Reason*, Part I, Book II, Theorem II, Remark II, p. 112.
[3] *Ibid.*, Ch. III.

Kant' argument here is twofold. First, as denizens of the world of sense, men must naturally desire happiness, which often conflicts with obligation. Insofar as it does, pursuing happiness cannot be what a man ought to do: he ought to fulfill his obligations. The same conclusion is supported by another argument: Even if men's desire for happiness should lead them to obey the moral law on all occasions, which is far from being the case, this would not make them morally good. To be morally good they must not only obey but obey out of pure respect for that austere law "which always humbles them while they *obey* it,"[4] and the respect must be "pure," unmixed with inclination. It must not aim at happiness.

All agree that there is a big difference between natural ends and moral standards, between what is and what ought to be; few have opposed reality and the ideal as radically as Kant. Aristotle says that all men aim at happiness,[5] which is the supreme good and the moral end of human nature,[6] but the point is that most men's aim is not very accurate. "All knowledge and every pursuit aims at some good," and "the highest of all goods achievable by action," which political science aims at, is happiness. "Verbally there is very general agreement; for both the general run of men and people of superior refinement say that it is happiness, and identify living well and doing well with being happy; but with regard to what happiness is they differ, and the many do not give the same account as the wise."[7] Thus some identify it with pleasure, or with honor or wealth, and there is a tendency to identify it with goods one lacks at a given time.

It is nevertheless possible by inductive methods, assuming moral education and a foundation of good habits, to determine what happiness really is;[8] and unless they are "maimed" in their potentialities, all men can achieve it. Though the ends men actually pursue are often inconsistent with their happiness, they can be made to coincide with it. In this case, what a man does from natural desire is precisely what he ought to do. And this, according to Aristotle, is the moral ideal. For if a man did not like being virtuous, how could we call him virtuous?

Aristotle insists, as Kant does, that desires commonly interfere with the performance of duty, or with "the attainment of virtue," as he would have put it. The remedy is to re-educate desires, bringing them closer to rational models and the practice of good men. Reason also cannot produce action. The moral virtues are the work of ratiocinative desires or, which comes to the same thing, desiderative reason. Kant, on the other hand, makes mo-

---

[4] *Ibid.*
[5] See *op. cit., Rhetoric,* 1360b5–7.
[6] See *ibid., Nicomachean Ethics,* 1176a32.
[7] *Ibid.,* 1095a15–21.
[8] See *ibid.,* 1095b1–10.

rality the concern of reason alone, and attempts to insulate it from the realm of desire altogether. The attempt, as we have seen, is beset with difficulties. How it can be natural and *necessary* for us, as creatures of sense and desire, to pursue happiness, and also *possible* (and even *necessary*) for us, as rational beings, to countermand desire out of pure respect for the moral law is never explained. We are not told how we can freely obey the moral law when all our acts are necessarily determined by causality, nor how pure reason alone can move us to act. Kant himself exclaims: ". . . *how pure reason can be practical*—to explain this is beyond the power of human reason, and all the labour and pains of seeking an explanation of it are lost."[9]

The egoistic hedonists and utilitarians are also open to this Kantian attack, for they maintain that men naturally *do*, and also morally *ought* to, pursue happiness, *i.e.*, pleasure, and to value other things only as means to pleasure. It is easy for them to reply, however, that actual practice and the moral ideal remain radically opposed. Whereas men do in fact cherish pleasure for its own sake, and nothing else, what they ought to do is to pursue it efficiently, with clear and unswerving purpose, sacrificing many present desires and entrenched habits for larger gains in the future. This is especially true of the utilitarian, who must be ready to forgo his own happiness whenever a greater happiness of others is obtainable. Thus the "ought" of the hedonists may be opposed by desire, though not always or by all desires. The hedonist, like the eudaemonist, can point to the imbroglio in which Kant lands as a warning against the alienation of the "ought" from the real world of sensation and desire.

Is Happiness Indefinite and Incalculable?

If happiness were the supreme good, it would be the duty of every man to choose the best means to its attainment. But this is impossible, Kant argues, for no one can say what the distant consequences of our acts will be. This would require omniscience. In the first place, every man would need to know the complex pattern of his happiness in the future, for if he does not have this knowledge, how can he possibly select those acts that will conduce to it more than others he might perform? "Unfortunately," Kant remarks,

> the notion of happiness is so indefinite that although every man wishes to attain it, yet he can never say definitely and consistently what it is that he really wishes and wills. The reason of this is that all the elements which

[9] *Metaphysic of Morals*, p. 99.

belong to happiness are altogether empirical, *i.e.*, they must be borrowed from experience, and nevertheless the idea of happiness requires an absolute whole, a maximum of welfare in my present and all future circumstances. Now it is impossible that the most clear-sighted and at the same time most powerful being (supposed finite) should frame to himself a definite conception of what he really wills in this.[10]

Thus, if a man wills riches, knowledge, long life, or health, he cannot be sure which acts of his will definitely secure them in the future, and he may well end up with their opposites. "In short, he is unable to determine with certainty what would make him truly happy; because to do so he would have to be omniscient."[11] He would have to know all the consequences of his acts, but these stretch to infinity.

At first glance this argument may appear devastating, yet answers are available. In the first place, neither eudaemonism nor utilitarianism ever maintains that happiness is "an absolute whole" in the sense that Kant has in mind. Happiness develops in time and is realized sequentially. On the other hand, Aristotle does say that the highest good is supposed to be something complete and perfect, leaving nothing to be desired. But this implies, he thinks, simply that such perfection is only for the gods, that men must be content with a happiness that is never quite complete.

Aristotle insists that all the particulars of happiness cannot be known in advance, and that the best means to it cannot be ascertained with certainty, but adds that precision and certainty are not to be expected in ethics. He avers that his "discussion will be adequate if it has as much clearness as the subject admits of," and warns that it would be "foolish to accept probable reasoning from a mathematician and to demand from a rhetorician scientific proofs."[12] Utilitarians take it for granted that ethics is an empirical study and their rules for attainment of happiness are not intended to be a priori necessary, but only to be probable or consistent with common experience thoughtfully considered.

Against the charge that the very idea of happiness is hopelessly indefinite, it can be pointed out that first principles are always of a general character and do not specify particulars. There is always a gap between principles and concrete instances. Casuistry, the reflective process whereby particular instances are subsumed under general principles, is usually admitted to be necessary to the application of any ethical system. Even for Kant there is always the question whether a particular maxim such as "Always do what you have promised" could be generalized without self-contradiction, and whether commitments you have made may conflict with

---

[10] *Ibid.*, p. 41.
[11] *Ibid.*
[12] *Ibid.*, 1049b12, 26.

the general duty of contributing to the happiness of others. The calculation of uncertain particulars and effects seems unavoidable even in Kant's ethics. Moreover, he admits that it is difficult to know whether a man's motive is pure, whether he acted solely out of respect for the moral law. "It is absolutely impossible," he asserts, "to make out by experience with complete certainty a single case in which the maxim of an action, however right in itself, rested simply on moral grounds and on the conception of duty."[13]

The details of happiness cannot be anticipated precisely nor the effects of our actions known with certainty, but progress can be made in probabilities. Aristotle remarks that

> each man judges well the things he knows, and of these he is a good judge. And so a man who has been educated in a subject is a good judge of that subject, and the man who has received an all-round education is a good judge in general.[14]

J. S. Mill also emphasizes the role of wide experience and expertise in assessing competing hedonic values. He also cites the practical precepts that have accumulated in the long experience of human society, and that are continually improved upon. These relieve us of the necessity of calculating afresh the hedonistic consequences of our individual acts.[15] Early education is of the greatest importance in this connection and the state has the responsibility of seeing that everyone is furnished with it. Both Aristotle and Bentham, it will be remembered, insist that legislation is needed to promote happiness. Moral suasion, example, and early training are fine instructors but cannot always curb headlong passion as the fear of punishment can. Aristotle contends that "it is difficult to get from youth up a right training for virtue if one has not been brought up under right laws."[16] Both authors are thinking of lawmakers, of course, as having longer and wider vision and impartiality than ordinary men, and as having access to far more information. They will be able to guide the citizen realistically to his own happiness, which must be integrated with the well-being of the whole community.

The rapid modern growth of the sciences and technologies is increasing our accuracy in predicting favorable and unfavorable effects of actions aiming at happiness, but it is also exposing unsuspected complexities and sham certainties. The followers of Kant, and many nonfollowers, can still make their point against the feasibility of planning the happiness of

13 *Op. cit.*, pp. 27–28.
14 *Op. cit.*, 1094b28–1095a2.
15 *Utilitarianism*, pp. 22–23.
16 *Op. cit.*, 1179b31.

communities and citizens. One of the most persuasive modern warners of the precariousness of the future, and the hazards and folly of blueprinting one overarching felicity, is John Dewey.

WHAT IS THE RELATION OF DUTY TO INCLINATION AND SELF-LOVE?

Kant agrees with the utilitarians, and also with Aristotle, in a sense, in holding that it is everyone's duty to promote the happiness of other men. He states that

> humanity might indeed subsist, although no one should contribute anything to the happiness of others, provided he did not intentionally withdraw anything from it; but after all this would only harmonize negatively not positively with *humanity as an end in itself,* if everyone does not also endeavour, so far as in him lies, to forward the ends of others. For the ends of any subject which is an end in himself, ought so far as possible to be *my* ends also, if that conception is to have its *full* effect on me.[17]

He argues further that any man would contradict himself if he resolves to do nothing to relieve the distress of his fellowmen or to promote their welfare, and then generalizes this rule of conduct, *i.e.,* if he wills that anyone may do the same. He would contradict himself "inasmuch as many cases might occur in which one would have need of the love and sympathy of others, and in which, by a law of nature sprung from his own will, he would deprive himself of all hope of the aid he desires."[18]

A utilitarian can welcome Kant's recognition of the universal duty of benevolence respecting the argument he offers in support of it. Bentham and Mill also agree with Kant that our duty is to actually *promote* the general happiness, not simply to have a *feeling* of benevolence toward others. Sidgwick, for his part, finds Kant's statement of the duty of benevolence very similar to his own, which is:

> that one is morally bound to regard the good of any other individual as much as one's own, except in so far as we judge it to be less, when impartially viewed, or less certainly knowable or attainable.[19]

Sidgwick believes that this "abstract principle of the duty of Benevolence" is "cognizable by direct intuition,"[20] but he rejects Kant's claim that ethical egoism involves self-contradiction. The ethical egoist may be, as we

[17] *Op. cit.,* p. 58.
[18] *Ibid.,* p. 49. See also *Metaphysical Elements of Ethics,* Ch. VIII (2).
[19] *Methods of Ethics,* 4th ed., p. 382.
[20] *Ibid.*

might put it, "a rugged individualist" who, even in distress, would be too proud to accept help from others. Moreover, even if it were true that everyone in actual distress craves the help of others, the same rugged individualist may decide that, everything considered, more is to be gained by sticking to the egoistic rule of life, and letting other people shift for themselves.[21] Thus the man who adopts the rule of disregarding both the happiness and misery of others need not contradict himself.

Kant, however, would be able to reply that since the egoist, like every other man, "*necessarily*" desires happiness, he will also *necessarily* desire the aid of others *if* only this will relieve his distress. For it is an "analytical truth," Kant assures us, that "whoever wills the end, wills also (according to the dictate of reason necessarily) the indispensable means thereto which are in his power."[22] But there is a flaw in this argument. Can we not imagine, for example, someone (even more rugged than Sidgwick's man) for whom the humiliation of desiring help from others would be worse than any distress it would relieve? If this is the case, Kant cannot claim that the principled egoist would necessarily contradict himself.

Although Kant insists as much as any utilitarian or eudaemonist that happiness is the one thing that all men desire, and that it is every man's duty to promote the happiness of others, even though it is at the expense of his own, he is nevertheless the leading and most influential adversary of the ethics of happiness. The chief reason is his abandonment of happiness as the supreme good, and his substitution of "being worthy of happiness" or the performance of duty. A second reason is his denial that we have a duty to advance our own happiness, and a third is his doctrine that duty must be done only out of respect for the moral law, inclinations and the desire for good consequences having no moral value whatever. Contributing to the happiness of other men because you want them to be happy, or because of sympathy or love for them, is doubtless good, but it is not morally good, Kant insists, and does not make you *worthy* of happiness yourself.

The denial that we have a duty to realize our own happiness and the restriction of morality to duty for duty's sake are closely related, and Kant uses both in his proof that no ethics of happiness can furnish a universal binding moral law—the first essential of all morality.

If what we do from inclination can never have a moral worth, it follows that there is no duty to pursue our own happiness, for, according to Kant, we pursue our own happiness naturally and necessarily. It is our duty to promote our own happiness only in one contingency—when it is seen as necessary to the performance of our duty. If privation or misery should prevent us from meeting our obligations or leave us open to temptation,

---

[21] See *ibid.*, pp. 389–390.
[22] *Metaphysic of Morals*, pp. 40–41.

then we should try to be happy, not because we want to be, of course, but only as an aid to duty.

> Although *"one's own happiness"* . . . is the natural end of all men, this end cannot without contradiction be regarded as a duty. What a man inevitably wills does not come under the notion of *duty,* for this is *constraint* to an end reluctantly adopted. It is, therefore, a contradiction to say that a man *is in duty bound* to advance his own happiness with all his power.[23]

Utilitarians have not been impressed by this contention, and it is possible to go along with Kant on other doctrines and yet reject it. It is interesting that Richard Price, who anticipates so much of Kantian ethics, not only finds no contradiction in a duty to oneself, but argues, on the contrary, that the *denial* of it is "absurd" or "contradictory."

> If it is my duty to promote the good (happiness) of *another,* and to abstain from hurting him; the same, most certainly, must be my duty with regard to *myself.* It would be contrary to all reason to deny this; or to assert that I *ought* to consult the good of another, but not my own; or that the advantage that an action will produce to another makes it right to be done, but that an equal advantage to myself leaves me at liberty to do or omit it.[24]

On the other hand, it is commonly conceded that duty, in one sense at least, implies a constraint that opposes inclination; but this does not worry the partisans of the happiness principle. Even the Epicurean, seeking only his own happiness, has to learn to sacrifice immediate pleasures for more distant ones of greater promise, and the decision could be hard and go against the grain. In this sense, egoistic obligation can involve "constraint to an end reluctantly adopted." The literature of eudaemonism, utilitarianism, and self-realization is full of warnings against the natural inclination to overrate immediate satisfactions which preclude more solid gains in the future. Addressing this point directly, Sidgwick contends that

> the conflict of Practical Reason with irrational desire remains an indubitable fact of our experience, even if practical reason is interpreted to mean merely self-regarding Prudence. It is, indeed, maintained by Kant and others that it cannot properly be said to be a man's duty to promote his own happiness; since "what every one inevitably wills cannot be brought under the notion of duty." But even granting . . . that a man's volition is directed to the attainment of his own happiness; it does not follow that a man always does what he believes to be conducive to his own *greatest* happiness, or his "good on the whole."[25]

[23] *Metaphysical Elements of Ethics,* p. 296.
[24] D. Daiches Raphael (ed.), *A Review of the Principal Questions in Morals,* p. 149.
[25] *Op. cit.,* p. 38.

Moreover, "duty," as the word is used, need not imply unpleasantness. It is a duty to provide for and to educate one's children, and yet no reluctance or constraint may be felt, and this seems to be true of many actions called "duties."

J. S. Mill emphasizes that actions first performed reluctantly as an onerous duty can, when associated with pleasure, become pleasurable in themselves. Thus, keeping one's promises and paying one's debts, when duly associated with public approval and self-satisfaction, may become activities regularly pleasing in themselves, which we rate higher than any losses they entail. To the question how virtue can be instilled where it is lacking, Mill replies:

> Only by making the person *desire* virtue—by making him think of it in a pleasurable light, or of its absence in a painful one. It is associating the doing right with pleasure, or the doing wrong with pain, or by eliciting and impressing and bringing home to the person's experience the pleasure naturally involved in the one or the pain in the other, that it is possible to call forth that will to be virtuous, which, when confirmed, acts without any thought of either pleasure or pain.[26]

Mill's "will to be virtuous" serves as a possible explanation of Kant's pure will to do one's duty, which Kant himself tries in vain to account for in nonempirical terms. If men sacrifice their ostensible happiness for the sake of their children, friends, or fellow citizens, it may be that they have learned to enjoy such actions, that they have become a part—or even an essential part of their happiness. Mill's theory thus might appear to explain in naturalistic terms a psychological fact basic to Kant's antinaturalistic system, a fact without which it could not have been conceived. The theory involves two elements: (a) *Association* of the benevolent act not pleasing in itself with the pleasure of public approval or praise, and consequent self-approval. After a number of associations of the sort the benevolent act may be carried out without any thought of pleasure of public approval or private satisfaction; and (b) the reason is that *such acts are in accord with the human constitution and "naturally" entail pleasure.*[27] They are evidently rooted in sympathy and love of our fellows, which, according to Mill, are as natural to human beings as are self-regarding emotions.

"*Constraint* to an end reluctantly adopted," which for Kant is a mark of every genuine act of duty, is not usually regarded as an essential of the *highest* moral development. Not to enjoy doing what you ought, in Aris-

---

[26] *Op. cit.*, pp. 38–39.

[27] This second element of Mill's theory serves to distinguish it from the theory of "functional autonomy," as G. W. Allport calls it, which was first put forward by Woodworth, in his *Dynamic Psychology*. The first element is in accord with modern associational psychology, or conditioning; the second brings Mill closer to Aristotle.

totle's view, displays a moral defect. Speaking for Aristotle and for himself, Sidgwick says that

> we should surely agree with Aristotle that Virtue is imperfect so long as the agent cannot do the virtuous action without a conflict of impulses; since it is from a wrong bent of natural impulse that we find it hard to do what is best, and it seems absurd to say the more we cure ourselves of this wrong bent, the less virtuous we grow.[28]

The highest form of moral excellence, Sidgwick maintains, calls for effortless conformity with the ideal, but there is also an imperfect form of virtue, in which a man energetically struggles to overcome enticements and temptations, and to come closer to the ideal in which conflict has no place. Kant himself recognizes that the *ideal* of goodness is a coincidence of inclination with duty, but thinks it cannot be attained in this world. His argument against the alliance of duty and inclination, and against the duty to promote one's own happiness, therefore, can scarcely claim to be a priori. It depends on the empirical premise that the world is a scene of continuous moral conflict, of storm and stress throughout.

After long study of Kant's philosophy, the poet Schiller is dismayed by the bleak chasm it presents between duty and desire. "The will," he contends,

> has a more immediate connection with perception and feeling than with knowledge, and it would be regrettable in many cases if it were required to orient itself first to pure reason. I am not predisposed to a man who has so little confidence in the bent of his inclinations that he feels obliged to defer to fundamental moral principles on every occasion.[29]

We respect a man, on the other hand, who trusts his impulses and is not afraid of being misled by them.

The "beautiful soul," which Schiller undertakes to defend against Kant's austere narrowing of moral goodness, has so much confidence in moral feelings that he allows himself to be directed by them without fear that they can result in actions that contradict the moral law. In the beautiful soul, accordingly, feeling and reason, duty and inclination, are in harmony. Here alone nature succeeds in combining freedom of action with moral order and observance, and the natural expression of this harmony is "charm," though not "worthiness." This comes to view only in "the noble soul," at a higher stage of development. Indeed, Schiller is in agreement with Kant when he says that "the satisfaction of inclinations can never be

---

[28] *Op. cit.*, p. 225.
[29] "Ueber Anmut und Würde," *Sämmtliche Werke*, Vol. 4, p. 480.

meritorious." But, though "the beautiful soul is not moral in its individual actions, the whole character is."[30] It represents a moral ideal (though not the highest), which Kant arbitrarily excludes.

Kant's reduction of all virtue and moral excellence to acting out of respect for logical consistency renders all men's other abilities and affections—even the highest—morally worthless. Virtues of the Greeks and Christians alike became morally insignificant insofar as they spring from the inclinations of the agent. The highest ideal of Plato and Aristotle, the contemplative philosopher, is also the happiest man, and delights in his activity. The virtue of the stoic stage is complete, without effort or conflict. The Christian *ideal* of virtue also excludes constraint and reluctance. If Kant is to be believed, however, St. Anthony was virtuous only when he still struggled to overcome his temptations, not after he had succeeded.

The replies to Kant's contentions that what we do for inclination can never have moral worth and that we cannot possibly have a duty to promote our own happiness may be summarized as follows:

(1) An arduous and heroic triumph over temptation is meritorious only when the temptation exists, but nonetheless a man is considered *more* virtuous when he is free from temptation.

(2) If the only *moral* motive to the performance of benevolent actions and acts of loving kindness is respect for reason and logical consistency, then benevolence and loving kindness are not virtues. If your motive in relieving another's distress is not to relieve his distress but to avoid logical inconsistency, you are not really benevolent.

(3) Although it is our duty, Kant says, to contribute to the happiness of others as far as it lies in our power, we are never justified in telling a lie or in deceit, no matter how much happiness of others could be increased thereby, or how much misery prevented.

(4) Although, according to Kant, I ought to recognize that "every rational being is *an end in itself*,"[31] and to make *all* these ends *my* end, "in a Kingdom of Ends," there is one rational being, namely myself, whose end, *i.e.*, happiness, I must *not* make my end on pain of self-contradiction, except perhaps when it is necessary to my performing my duty.

(5) A genuine act of duty is never prompted by inclination, Kant insists, and yet he confesses that it is impossible to understand how "respect" or "reason" can move the will of a creature of the world of sense— how "reason should have the power to *infuse a feeling of pleasure* or satisfaction in the fulfillment of duty, that is to say, that it should have a causality by which it determines the sensibility according to its own principles."[32] And "it is quite impossible to explain how and why the

---

[30] *Ibid.*, p. 481.
[31] *Metaphysic of Morals,* p. 58.
[32] *Ibid.*, p. 97.

universality of the maxim as a law interests."[33] How pure reason can be practical, *i.e., "how freedom is possible,"* remains a mystery.[34]

(6) The Kantian isolation of morality from inclinations and feelings not only leaves the moral act without any effective motivation, it also forestalls moral education. According to Plato and Aristotle, at any rate, attaching pleasures and pains to the right things is of utmost importance in inculcating morals. Thus Aristotle states that "we ought to have been brought up in a particular way from our youth, as Plato says, so as to delight in and to be pained by the things that we ought; for this is the right education."[35] We have seen that Bentham and Mill are equally emphatic on this point.

(1) The Kantian answer to the first criticism, which has already been touched on, is that a creature

> can never be quite free from desires and inclinations, and as these rest on physical causes, they can never of themselves coincide with the moral law, the sources of which are quite different; and therefore they make it necessary to found the mental disposition of one's maxims which *demands* obedience to the law, even though one may not like it; not on love, which apprehends no inward reluctance of the will towards the law.[36]

(2) Kant claims that benevolence and loving kindness, if they spring from natural inclination, have no moral value. For morality has to do with laws that apply universally, and they would not be obligatory if they were not binding on the will of every rational being. But it cannot be true that all men ought to love their neighbors, no matter who they are, since it is not in our power to summon up a feeling like love. For this reason, Kant argues, the biblical command *Love God above everything, and thy neighbor as thyself* must refer to "practical love," not to "pathological love."

> Love to God . . . considered as an inclination (pathological love), is impossible, for He is not an object of the senses. The same affection towards men is possible no doubt, but cannot be commanded, for it is not in the power of any man to love anyone at command; therefore it is only *practical love* that is meant. . . . To love God means . . . to like to do His commandments; to love one's neighbor means to like to practice all duties toward him.[37]

Kant goes on at once to correct this sentence. *Liking* to do something cannot be commanded either: this would be a contradiction. If we know our duty and like to do it, a command would be useless, whereas if we do *not* want to do it, but do it "only out of respect for the law, a command that makes this respect the motive for our maxim would directly counteract

---

[33] *Ibid.,* p. 98.
[34] *Ibid.,* p. 95.
[35] *Op. cit.,* 1104b11–13.
[36] *Critique of Practical Reason,* Part I, Book I, Ch. III, p. 177.
[37] *Ibid.,* p. 176.

the disposition commanded." Thus it cannot be commanded that we have feelings or an inclination to obey the law, but only that we "endeavour after it"[38] (though it is impossible that we should succeed).

(3) Lies and deceit are never justified, for exceptions to the moral law would introduce into it an empirical element of uncertainty. The law would thus not be binding a priori on the will of every rational being. We shall return to this point in the next section.

(4) The only answer to the fourth objection is reiteration: It cannot be our duty to promote our own happiness, since this is something that everyone, by nature, wants to do.

(5) Man is free, Kant says. He *can* obey the moral law out of pure respect for it. He can because he ought. "I ought" implies "I can" is one of the most famous and influential insights in the whole of Kant's philosophy. If he has succeeded in proving that men ought to obey the moral law from pure respect, and against the grain of inclination, then most philosophers would grant that he has proved that it *can* be done, for otherwise it would be our duty to do something that we cannot do, which is nonsense. The fact that Kant cannot see how it is possible for pure reason or "respect" (which is a very peculiar spectral emotion, it will be remembered) to move us to action would not by itself disprove such causation, strange as it is. Kant might still be right about this, if he is right about the nature of our duty.

In some passages, Kant seems to offer another explanation of how reason alone can move us to action. He suggests that the world of understanding, representing the "thing-in-itself," is able to prevail over the world of sense, representing mere appearance. Thus he says that *"the universality of the maxim as a law,* that is, morality," interests us because "it is valid for us as men, inasmuch as it had its source in our will as intelligences, in other words, in our proper self, *and what belongs to mere appearance is necessarily subordinate by reason to the nature of the thing-in-itself."*[39]

In other passages, a pragmatic motif prevails. Kant admits that "the world of understanding as a system of all intelligences, to which we all belong, and to which we owe morality," is largely a *terra incognita;* yet

> it remains always *a useful and legitimate idea* for the purposes of rational belief, although all knowledge stops at its threshold, useful, namely, to produce in us a lively interest in the moral law by means of the noble ideal of a universal kingdom of *ends in themselves* (rational beings), to which we can belong as members then only when we carefully conduct ourselves according to the maxims of freedom as if they were the laws of nature.[40]

[38] *Ibid.*
[39] *Metaphysic of Morals,* p. 98.
[40] *Ibid.,* p. 100. See also p. 88. First italics added.

(6) Pleasures and pains, Kant holds, operate necessarily to determine human conduct, according to the causal laws of the material world. But benevolence caused by pleasure or the fear of pain, though it may be good, is not *morally* good. It is not free and self-determined, but determined by pleasure and pain, which lie outside the self. A maxim of benevolence so determined cannot be made a law of nature binding on all men because the occurrence of pleasures and pains varies widely. The same situation that evokes pleasure in one man causes pain in another. It, therefore, could not be the duty for any man to act benevolently if the act is elicited by the pleasure of giving, or the pain of another's distress; it cannot be what any man *ought* to do, for one man cannot be obligated where another is left free to do as he pleases. The issue raised here will be carried further in the next section.

A word more should be said about the fundamental issue raised in (5) and (6), namely, whether it can be maintained, as Kant's ethics demands, that reason by itself can move the will and initiate action. Aristotle takes a very definite stand on this issue:

> Intellect itself . . . moves nothing, but only the intellect which aims at an end and is practical; for this rules the productive intellect as well, since everyone who makes makes for an end, and that which is made is not an end in the unqualified sense . . . only that which is *done* is that; for good action is an end, and desire aims at this. Hence choice is either desiderative reason or ratiocinative desire, and such an origin of action is a man.[41]

A contemporary English philosopher, very much influenced by Aristotle, criticizes Kant in more or less Aristotelian terms. G. C. Field claims that Kant's notion that intellect or reason can move the will single-handed is "the fundamental fallacy of his theory."[42] "We may," he says, "set against Kant's view the dictum of Aristotle. The intellect by itself moves nothing, has no motive force. Or in other words the mere knowing that an action, or anything else, is of such-and-such a kind cannot possibly move us to act."[43] Field goes on to explain why Kant's view at first glance may appear plausible. It is true that we often cite reasons or knowledge to explain why people behave as they do. For example, we say that a policeman entered a strange house at two in the morning because he was in possession of a bit of knowledge, viz., that a burglar was robbing a safe in this house. On second thought, we see that it was not the knowledge alone that made him act; if he had had no desire to catch the burglar, he would not have gone after him. "The reason why the knowledge moves us to action," Field

---

[41] *Op. cit.*, 1139a35–1139b4.
[42] *Moral Theory, An Introduction to Ethics*, p. 46.
[43] *Ibid.*, p. 47.

points out, "is because it is the knowledge that that particular kind of action will have an effect that we want or desire. But the bare knowledge that a particular action is of a certain kind or will have a certain effect has no influence on us unless we have an interest in that effect or that kind of action, unless, that is, we have some feeling towards it."[44]

CAN THE HAPPINESS PRINCIPLE FURNISH A MORAL LAW THAT WILL BE OBLIGATORY?

We have seen that the moral law, according to Kant, cannot take the form of a hypothetical imperative. The law does not say that you ought to perform or refrain from actions of a certain kind, *if you want something else*. The moral law is a categorical imperative. The obligations it asserts must be binding on the will of every rational being, *unconditionally, i.e.*, no matter what else is the case.

The happiness principle appears to provide us with a moral law in the form of a hypothetical imperative, not a categorical imperative. The partisans of happiness as the supreme good do not say: "Do X, no matter what." They say: "Do X if or since it is a means to or a part of happiness." Happiness is that which gives to every action its worth, according to the utilitarians, and their supreme worth, according to Aristotle.

This might seem to settle the question out of hand. The happiness principle can provide a moral law only in the form of a hypothetical imperative. But let us look a little closer at this hypothetical imperative. It might read as follows:

If you want happiness, *then* you ought to cultivate certain virtues, skills, instrumentalities which conduce to this end, or a part of it.

This imperative is hypothetical because of the if-clause "if you want happiness," but Kant agrees with the partisans of the happiness principle that all men *do* want happiness. In fact, he says that all men desire happiness "by a natural necessity." But if the if-clause is true, so is the then-clause; it is true that

you ought to cultivate certain virtues, skills, instrumentalities which conduce to happiness, or are a part of it.

But the moral law is now a categorical imperative. It is a law based on the happiness principle and is yet "unconditionally binding on the will of every rational being." It holds unconditionally for all men because all men continually, and "by a natural necessity," desire happiness. What more could Kant ask?

[44] *Ibid.*

Kant replies, in effect, that when I state a law of the form *"I ought to do something . . . because I wish for something else . . .* another law is assumed in me as its subject, by which I necessarily wish this other thing, and this law again requires an imperative to restrict this maxim."[45] It will be noted, however, that Kant would here neglect the pertinent point: When the "other thing" is happiness, no infinite regress is involved, for he himself insists that all men naturally and necessarily desire happiness. Nor will the above eudaemonic law of duty be "contingent," as Kant claims such a law must be.[46]

(a) Kant is on stronger ground when he argues that

> the principle of happiness may, indeed, furnish maxims, but never such as would be competent to the laws of the will, even if *universal* happiness were made the object. For since the knowledge of this rests on empirical data, since every man's judgment on it depends very much on his particular point of view, which is itself moreover very variable, it can supply only *general* rules, not *universal;* that is, it can give rules which on the average will frequently fit, but not rules which must hold good always and necessarily; hence, no practical *laws* can be founded on it.[47]

Since the requirements of happiness are empirical and variable, a law stating what one ought to do to obtain happiness cannot be necessarily valid for all men at all times.

(b) Kant also argues that in order for a moral law to be universal and binding on the will of all men in all circumstances it must be a priori necessary. If it is a priori necessary, then, like the theorems of geometry, it must hold in all cases; if not, there is no such assurance. Men differ in desires, tastes, competence, and everything else, but not in reason, and it is reason alone that yields a priori necessity. Accordingly, the moral law must contain no empirical elements; it must be independent of the changing objects of the world of sense.

We have already considered Aristotle's answer. Ethics is not an exact, not a mathematical discipline, and it is foolish to pretend that it is. Bentham repeatedly indicates that the hedonistic calculus is concerned with the "tendency" of acts, not with exact forecasts. In this case, however, the critical question is whether moral rules can have the required universality and certainty.

Mill, replying to the objection that we do not have time before performing an act to determine its effects on the general happiness, points to the vast experience of mankind to which we are heir:

[45] *Op. cit.,* p. 76.
[46] See *ibid.*
[47] *Critique of Practical Reason,* Part I, Book I, Ch. I, VIII, Theorem IV, Remark II, p. 125.

This is exactly as if anyone were to say that it is impossible to guide our conduct by Christianity, because there is not time, on every occasion on which anything has to be done, to read through the Old and New Testaments. [But] there has been ample time, namely the whole past duration of the human species. During all that time mankind has been learning by experience the *tendencies* of actions; on which experience all the prudent, as well as all the morality of life, are dependent.[48]

Mill also contends that the difficulty of assessing the effects of moral actions is not peculiar to utilitarianism, but is shared by other ethical systems. But would this be true of Kant's ethics? As if in reply to this question, Mill asserts that "to all those *a priori* moralists who deem it necessary to argue at all, utilitarian arguments are indispensable."[49] Citing Kant's moral law in one of its formulations—"So act, that the rule on which thou actest would admit of being adopted as a law by all rational beings"—he claims that when Kant

> begins to deduce from this precept any of the actual duties of morality, he fails, almost grotesquely, to show that there is any contradiction, any logical (not to say physical) impossibility, in the adoption by all rational beings of the most outrageously immoral rules of conduct. All he shows is that the *consequences* of their universal adoption would be such as no one would choose to incur.[50]

It is true, in point of fact, that Kant does not specify any positive duties, even in the abstract, except the duties of promoting the happiness of others and our own perfection. And the latter, as Sidgwick points out, tends to reduce to the first, for it is not clear from what Kant says what *my* perfection can be except the disposition to make the ends of other rational beings *my* end. But how can I pretend to make others happy if I do not calculate the consequences of my benevolent acts, if I do not employ "empirical data," if I do not make an empirical study of the kinds of things that are likely to make men of different tastes happy, and of the kinds of acts that are likely to achieve this result? If we are serious about making our neighbors happy, must we not also be serious about the empirical ways and means of doing so? Kant himself insists that it is impossible to will an end without also willing the means necessary to it. Is not Kant, then, in the same boat with the utilitarians—*his* moral acts subject to the same caprices and uncertainties as theirs?

(c) If the moral law is to be universal and unconditional, Kant says, it must not be *"based on any interest."* Would the eudaemonist and the

48 *Utilitarianism*, pp. 21–22. (Italics added.)
49 *Ibid.*, p. 3.
50 *Ibid.*, p. 4.

utilitarian grant that this is a requirement of moral laws? If so, can they satisfy it within their systems?

It would seem that since interest varies from one individual to another, there could not be a universal moral law. As far as interest enters in, Kant concludes, there can be no real moral laws, but only maxims or counsels of prudence, suitable for some men but not binding on all.

Eudaemonists and utilitarians grant that a certain disinterestedness is indispensable to morality. Aristotle's elaborate discussion of justice makes clear that the *intention* is to establish equality in exchange or proportion in awards and punishments. The foreseen consequences may be to the advantage of the agent, or they may be against his interest; it does not matter. Justice consists not in serving his own interests but in instituting equality or proportion. Justice, like other virtues, is good in itself, and a part of happiness. But it is not the whole of happiness. Justice does not always contribute to a man's happiness. On the contrary, it may oblige him to condemn his own son. The just act is thus disinterested in intention, but also in the sense that the consequences may be disadvantageous to him. The good man, it is true, enjoys being just, and no one can be happy who is *not* just. It might be said, therefore, that being just, even when the agent loses by it, is at least doing something without which he could not be happy. Even so, this would not be the intention or purpose of the just act; the intention is to establish a just state of affairs.

Friendship and liberality are disinterested too, since, if your intention in giving aid to your friend or to the poor is only to serve your own interest, you would not be considered generous, but shrewd or calculating. Other Aristotelian virtues, such as temperance, seem to be largely the agent's own affairs, though the community is not unaffected. The highest virtue of contemplation is said to be completely "disinterested," but in a special sense that does not concern us here.

When Bentham is described as a psychological egoist, one may not expect disinterestedness or impartiality to play much part in his system. Yet the hedonistic calculus, as Bentham describes it,[51] involves a sustained detachment from self-centered and selfish interests and passions. It is necessary to consider the whole general tendency of the act (or the kind of act) to be performed, to weigh impartially the probable pleasures and pains accruing to all persons who are likely to be affected, now and at later periods, always assigning equal values to equal pleasures no matter whether friends or foes are to enjoy them. The principle underlying the calculus would indeed appear, as J. S. Mill points out, to be a hedonistic version of the Golden Rule, with which Kant's moral law is often compared. As the calculator does, so he would have others do.

[51] See *Principles of Morals and Legislation*, Ch. IV.

But could a utilitarian moral law, viz., that one should so act as to advance the general happiness, be universally binding on all men? After long consideration of Kant's challenge, Sidgwick concludes that he could certainly will it as a universal law

> that men should act in such a way as to promote universal happiness; in fact it was the only law that it was perfectly clear to me that I could thus decisively will, from a universal point of view.[52]

It is evident, however, that neither eudaemonists nor utilitarians provide the total disinterestedness that Kant demands. They are not much disturbed by this, however, for they do not agree that *morality* demands total disinterestedness, and they can point out that Kant himself does not see how his moral law can be binding on anyone unless he has some "interest" in obeying it.

Kant complains that a moral law based on general happiness would have to take into account empirical differences between men. The friends of the happiness principle can reply that it would be inhumane to do otherwise. The trouble with the Golden Rule, G. B. Shaw remarked, is that tastes differ. Kant himself raises the question: Are we to promote the happiness of others as we see it or as they see it? But he does not really answer it.[53]

THE PROBLEM OF FREE WILL

The moral law states that "I ought to do so and so, even though I should not wish for anything else,"[54] whereas the moral rule of happiness says: "I ought to do so and so, since I want happiness." In the former case the will is determined by the a priori structure of the law itself, which is an embodiment of reason, and will (*i.e.*, pure will, *i.e.*, pure practical reason) that obeys the voice of reason obeys itself. The law it obeys is the law it makes or legislates: the will is free. In the latter case, on the contrary, the will is determined by an object external to it, namely, happiness: the will is not free, *i.e.*, not self-determined. It is determined necessarily by the causal laws of the sensible world—laws that we do not ourselves make, but to which we are subject. It follows, Kant thinks, that the ethics of happiness cannot provide for free choice, nor responsibility, nor merit. There is no blame or credit in conforming to the laws of nature if you can do nothing else.

This is not the place for a general discussion of free will. Let us merely indicate the kind of criticism to which Kant's particular conception of free

---

[52] *Methods of Ethics*, Preface, p. xx.

[53] Neither alternative is acceptable to him, and both immerse actual duties in a sea of uncertainties.

[54] *Metaphysic of Morals*, p. 72.

will (as the foundation of morality) has been subjected, and then consider whether the partisans of happiness can accommodate freedom of choice in their system.

Kant himself admits grave difficulties in his conception of free will. First, it seems to involve a contradiction, for the same will that is totally free in obeying the moral law is also necessarily determined by the goal of happiness, which is alien to it. The same will that resists the beguilements of desire to obey the moral law is also determined irresistibly in an opposite direction—to pursue the means to happiness. Otherwise expressed, we are completely free as members of "the world of understanding" (or reason), but at the same time necessarily determined by external objects as members of the sensible world. This freedom must exist, Kant holds, since it is implied by the moral law, which we know to be true. But he has no confident solution of the contradiction that this involves.

There is another paradox in Kant's conception of free will that is never resolved—or even recognized. "Kant's resting of morality on Freedom," Sidgwick says, "involves the fundamental confusion of using 'freedom' in two senses—'freedom' that is realized only when we do right, when reason triumphs over inclination, and 'freedom' that is equally realized when we choose to do wrong, and which is apparently implied in the notion of ill-desert."[55]

The freedom of choice is necessary if we are to choose what is morally good, but after we have chosen—once our reason has seen itself reflected in the moral law—it disappears and is replaced by quite a different freedom, which is at the same time an irresistible necessity. As members of the intelligible world (the world of the understanding), it will be remembered, we necessarily obey the moral law: we have no choice. Morality depends absolutely on the freedom of choice, for without it there would be neither blame nor credit, nor responsibility. But it also depends entirely on the other freedom, the freedom of perfection, for without it we should not, as rational beings, necessarily obey the law that we legislate. But if we do necessarily obey the law we legislate—reason being obliged to assent to reason—we have forfeited the freedom of choice, and with it the "*constraint* to an end reluctantly adopted," which, for Kant, is necessary to a moral act.

Aristotle rejects the possibility of formal, a priori principles in ethics, and if his account of voluntary action amounts to a free will theory, it is very different from Kant's, and not attended with the same difficulties. "*Man* alone among animals," he says, "is . . . the source of certain actions" and he alone is said "to act."[56] For men are the sources of contingent results.

[55] *Op. cit.,* p. xvii. See also pp. 511 ff.
[56] *Op. cit., Eudemian Ethics,* 1222b19.

So it is clear that all the acts of which man is the principle and controller may either happen or not happen, and their happening or not happening—those at least of whose existence he has control—depend on him. . . . And since virtue and vice and the acts that spring from them are respectively praised and blamed . . . it is clear that virtue and vice have to do with matters where the man himself is the cause and source of his acts. . . . It is clear then that virtue and vice have to do with voluntary acts.[57]

There is a great deal in Aristotle's account of voluntary acts that seems to resemble what Kant says about the freedom of choice, but, as Sidgwick says, Kant confuses this freedom with the freedom of perfection, and the result is that any resemblance is superficial. Thus, although Kant agrees that men are the sources of contingent results and can choose between virtue and vice, he also holds that the good man *necessarily* conforms to the moral law out of pure respect for it.

Leading utilitarians, such as Bentham and J. S. Mill, reject or dismiss free will and explain freedom and responsibility in a manner consistent with determinism. How successful they are is still an open question. Many will agree with the temperamentally calm and judicious Sidgwick when he concludes, in opposition to Kant, that

if happiness, whether private or general, be the ultimate end of action on a Libertarian [*i.e.*, free will] view, it must be also on a Determinist view. . . .

And the same would be true of the ultimate end of "perfection," by which term Sidgwick means to include the Aristotelian conception of happiness. "Perfection" would remain admirable whether it is brought about by the confluence of experience and natural endowment or by free will, unless "the notion of perfection includes that of Free Will. . . . The manifestations of courage, temperance and justice do not become less admirable because we can trace their antecedents in a happy balance of inherited dispositions developed by a careful education."[58]

Although Kant is the greatest adversary of the ethics of happiness, it is well to keep in mind some respects in which he agrees with Aristotelian eudaemonism and utilitarianism, for it is only on the basis of certain agreement that sharp disagreements can arise.

1. Kant agrees with both utilitarianism and eudaemonism that men naturally and universally pursue happiness, as they understand it.

2. He also holds that it is our duty to pursue the happiness of others, as far as it lies within our power.

3. Although he denies that it is our duty to pursue our own happiness,

---

[57] *Ibid.*, 1223a4–20.
[58] *Op. cit.*, Book I, Ch. 5, p. 69.

he makes an interesting exception. Cultivating our own happiness becomes a contingent duty when it is necessary to the performance of other duties.

4. Kant agrees with Aristotle's eudaemonism and with utilitarianism (especially Mill's) in insisting that it is our duty to develop our natural faculties. "As a rational being," Kant says, a man "necessarily wills that his faculties be developed, since they serve him, and have been given him, for all sorts of possible purposes."[59]

5. We have noted that although virtue, or worthiness to be happy, is the *supreme* good according to Kant, it is not the whole or *perfect* good, for it requires happiness for its completion.

> For to need happiness, to deserve it, and yet at the same time not to partici-pate in it, cannot be consistent with the perfect volition of a rational being.[60]

II. FURTHER ATTACKS ON THE HAPPINESS PRINCIPLE

In 1758, some thirty years before Kant wrote his main ethical works, the philosopher Richard Price, who was also a mathematician and clergyman, published his *Review of the Principal Questions in Morals,* a remarkable book that anticipated a number of Kant's distinctive conclusions in ethics. His arguments against the happiness principle, though often similar to Kant's, have a distinctive quality and force of their own, and the same is true of the arguments of the deontological followers of Kant in the present century, such as H. A. Prichard, Sir William Richard Ross, A. C. Ewing, and E. F. Carritt. To better understand the strength and resources of the deontological position, we shall briefly review the stand taken by Price, Prichard, and Ross against the happiness principle.

Unlike Kant, all these philosophers—perhaps because they are all true Englishmen—give a great deal of weight to common sense, and to the plain facts they believe will be apparent to all, upon reflection, except perhaps a few philosophers who have become detached from their fellows. They ask us to consider the natural meaning of statements to the effect that certain acts are *right,* that we *ought* or *should,* or are *in duty bound* or *obligated,* to do them.

If we reflect, Price argues, we shall find that we do not attempt to calculate the total happiness that will result to all parties before we do our duty. When confronted with certain situations and certain past actions of ours, we know at once what we ought to do. It is *prima facie* clear without

[59] *Metaphysic of Morals,* p. 48.
[60] *Critique of Practical Reason,* Part I, Book II, Ch. II, p. 206. For a discussion of this point, see Chapter 5, Section 6.

an elaborate tracing of consequences. We simply pay the debts we have incurred and refrain from lying, or at least we know we *should*. And in case we did succeed in computing the balance of happiness over misery that would result from our paying a certain bill, this would not explain why we *ought* to pay it, though it might give us a good motive for doing so, viz.: the prospect of contributing to the happiness of others. For the finding that the general happiness would be increased by an act would not prove that it was our duty to do it. It is sometimes our duty to do things which, in fact, diminish the general happiness, as when we have made a promise to a person that precludes an act of gratuitous generosity we had planned. But if it is not always our duty to promote happiness, and it *is* our duty to sometimes act in ways that diminish happiness, then happiness is not the supreme good.

Price agrees with Kant that it is certain "that every being must desire happiness for himself," and that it is not a possible object of aversion.[61] He partly disagrees with Kant when he says that "happiness is the *end* and the *only* end conceivable to us, of God's Providence and government," but he adds that God "pursues this end in subordination to rectitude, and by those methods only which rectitude requires."[62] Kant would agree to this as relates to the *next* life, and also with Price's inference that it can scarcely be *our* duty to promote happiness indiscriminately, with no regard to merit. Yet Price asserts that we have a duty "to secure and promote the happiness of the species," and our own happiness as well. It will be remembered that Kant finds the latter duty self-contradictory.

We can see, also, certain broad agreements with Aristotle. Thus Price holds—contrary to Kant—that duty must be our chief delight because we esteem it most highly.

> What we love most, and have the greatest esteem and relish for, must be the source of our greatest pleasure. —Well therefore may he suspect his character, who finds that virtuous exercises, the duties of piety, and the various offices of love and goodness to which he may be called, are distasteful and irksome to him. Virtue is the object of the chief complacency of every virtuous man; the exercise of it is his chief delight.[63]

It is not virtue, of course, if it has the accompanying pleasure as its main *motive*. Price also emphasizes the pleasure inherent in cognitive activities and their objects. "Truth is the proper object of the mind, as light is of the eye, or harmony of the ear . . . reasonable beings love *truth, knowledge and honour* [as] they love and desire *happiness*."[64]

---

[61] *Op. cit.*, pp. 45, 70.
[62] *Ibid.*, Ch. IV.
[63] *Ibid.*, p. 222.
[64] *Ibid.*, p. 73.

Price's conception of happiness is far less elaborate than Aristotle's. He usually equates happiness and misery with pleasure and pain, but sometimes with pleasurable and painful *activities,* which brings him closer to eudaemonism. By first noting how he veers toward Aristotle we can better understand the scope of his dissent. His *bêtes noires* are egoistic hedonism and moral sense theory; he is too much the altruist and clergyman to tolerate the first, and too much the mathematical intellectualist to stomach the second. His agreements with the utilitarians are fairly extensive, yet he disagrees with them more sharply than with eudaemonism, which he does not choose as an adversary.

THE RIGHTNESS OF ACTS VS. THEIR CONSEQUENCES

Right and wrong can be apprehended by the understanding immediately without adding up the total consequences of our actions in terms of happiness and misery, Price maintains.

We have an immediate approbation of making the virtuous happy, and discouraging the vicious, abstracted from all consequences.

He asks, how do we know which acts are right?

Not merely on account of the effects; (which in these instances, we are far from taking time always to consider) but *immediately and ultimately right;* and for the same reason that beneficence is right, and that right objects and relations, in general, are what they are.[65]

Closely related to this general thesis is Price's contention that no one really approves of happiness, or the promotion of happiness, if the recipients are unworthy. Even if this were denied, it would have to be admitted that we would all think it better for the worthy to be happy and the wicked miserable than vice versa, and it would follow from this that we believe there is some ultimate criterion of right and goodness other than happiness. If we imagine that there are only two men in the world, Price says, it would still appear wrong to us "that the good being should be less happy, or a greater sufferer, than his evil fellow being." And suppose we have to choose to give a benefit to one of two persons of very different moral stripe. "The virtuous person, everyone would think, is *worthy* of the benefit; the other *unworthy.*" All of us indeed would think it better, where only two individuals are involved, for the unworthy one to suffer and the worthy one to be happy, than that they should both be happy. But this is an admission that happiness is not the supreme good.

[65] *Ibid.,* p. 80.

"Is there no other kind of wrong in so governing a system of beings," Price asks, "than in producing a *smaller* quantity of happiness rather than a *greater?*"[66] You will at least have to admit, he says, that of two worlds containing an equal measure of happiness, the one in which it is distributed according to merit would be preferable to the one in which it is apportioned helter skelter. But if happiness is the end that justifies all others, how can this judgment be justified?

If happiness is the highest good, moreover, why reform a criminal by *punishment?* If the same reform could be effected by re-education under pleasant conditions, would not this be better?[67] Would it matter that virtuous men, meanwhile, enjoyed no such advantages, as long as there is a net increase in happiness?

In discussing justice, Price says:

> If public good be the sole measure and foundation of property and the rights of beings, it would be absurd to say innocent beings have a right to exemption from misery, or that they may not be made in any degree miserable, if but the smallest degree of *prepollent* good can arise from it. Nay, any number of innocent beings might be placed in a state of absolute and eternal misery provided amends is made for their misery by producing at the same time a greater number of beings in a greater degree happy. . . . Might a man innocently ruin any number of his fellow-creatures, provided he causes in a greater degree the good of others? Such consequences are plainly shocking to our natural sentiments; but I know not how to avoid them on the principles I am examining.[68]

H. A. Prichard, in a famous article in *Mind*, in 1912, also denies that the moral rightness of actions can be determined by their consequences. Some of his arguments echo Price's; others are new. It is natural, he says, to explain why we should do a certain act by saying that doing it will get us what we want, viz., happiness. But, if we take this view, disturbing questions arise on the distinctively moral level, such as—"Why should we keep our engagements to our loss?"—questions that imply that doing what we *ought* need not get us what we *want*, and indeed, frequently entail a severe sacrifice of personal happiness. What motive can induce a man to do his duty against interest? We have seen that Kant, after the most heroic efforts, is unable to explain how mere reason can get a flesh-and-blood creature of desire into action. Prichard faces up to the same problem: Reason or a sense of obligation seems to be unable to move the will; desire can, but mostly in the wrong direction.

Suppose a man is told that he ought to keep his promises because it conduces to the general good or happiness. He can reply: "Why should I

66 *Ibid.*, p. 82.
67 See *ibid.*
68 *Ibid.*, pp. 159–160.

contribute to the good or happiness of others? *My* happiness is *my* concern." Or he might say: "I know I should generally keep my promises, but I do not see how in the present instance I can afford to do it." Although he keeps his promises as a matter of fact, he may still feel, as Prichard suggests, that a kind of fraud is being perpetrated. There is a big gap, after all, between *Act A will contribute to the general happiness* (including that of total strangers and Tibetans), and *I ought to do A.* How can any factual state of the world generate an "ought," i.e., put a man under obligation to bring it about? What is the connection between general happiness and ought? G. E. Moore asserts that the good (which includes happiness and something more) is something that *ought to be,* and that this *ought to be* justifies the *ought to do.* Prichard, however, rejects this remedy, since, he says, "ought" refers to actions, never to things or states of affairs.

The gap between general happiness and the individual's duty to contribute to it, Prichard thinks, is a serious flaw in utilitarianism, since it means that it can give the individual no reason for performing his duty when it is against his interest to do so. It is not the only flaw in this ethics. The notion that we should keep our promises, pay our debts, and tell the truth *for the reason that* it will make people more comfortable and prosperous, or happier, Prichard says, is "plainly at variance with our moral consciousness." It is so plainly at variance with our understanding of moral obligation, "that we are driven to adopt [another] view, viz., that the act is good in itself and that its intrinsic goodness is the reason why it ought to be done. It is this form which has always made the most serious appeal; for the goodness of the act itself seems more closely related to the obligation to do it than that of its mere consequences or results."[69] But this view is also false, for it leads to the dilemma of the Kantian theory of the good will. Thus, if we make our parents happy from an intrinsically good desire to do so, we will not feel that we are *obliged* to do it, that it is our *duty.* If, on the other hand, we make them happy from a *sense of obligation,* it is not the intrinsic goodness of the act that makes us do it, but rather its obligatoriness.[70] The challenge here is no longer to utilitarianism but to Kant, and indirectly to Aristotle and eudaemonism.

Aristotle's eudaemonism is challenged by Prichard's contention that it can never be our duty, or a part of our duty, to act from a good motive, for Aristotle holds that virtue requires that the virtuous act not be only performed but performed for the "right" reason or with a "good" motive. Prichard naturally admits that we can have good motives for doing our duty, but yet denies that the good motive is a part of doing our duty, and that a man is under any *obligation* to have a good motive. It is too obvious, he says, that men do their duty for different reasons, some good, some bad,

[69] "Does Moral Philosophy Rest on a Mistake?" in *Moral Philosophy,* p. 5.
[70] *Ibid.,* p. 6.

and some, perhaps, indifferent. The man who pays his debts only to avoid being sued has done his duty as much as his neighbor who has acted from a noble motive, for the duty is simply to honor an obligation.

Ross supports this conclusion, that having a good motive is never part of doing our duty, by an argument that has proved very influential. That action from a good motive, or any motive, is never morally obligatory, he argues, follows from the Kantian principle, which he says is generally admitted, that "I ought" implies "I can."

> It is not the case that I can by choice produce a certain motive . . . in myself at a moment's notice, still less that I can at a moment's notice make it effective in stimulating me to act. I can act from a certain motive only if I have the motive; if not, the most I can do is to cultivate it by suitably directing my attention or by acting in certain appropriate ways so that on some future occasion it *will* be present in me, and I shall be able to act from it.[71]

The main target of this argument is the Kantian doctrine that you do not perform your duty unless you do it out of pure respect for the moral law.

For both Prichard and Ross, then, a good motive is irrelevant to the performance of duty, and Ross goes a long way with Prichard in ruling out the relevance of consequences. What, then, is left to establish duty except the formal structure of commitment? The apprehension of obligation, Prichard says, "is immediate in precisely the sense in which a mathematical apprehension is immediate, e.g., the apprehension that this three-sided figure, in virtue of its being three-sided, must have three angles."[72] We may have to pause to consider the consequences of a proposed action, but this is only, by inspection of its formal character, to assure ourselves that the action is to be classified as right. As soon as we realize that the time has come to pay a debt, we know at once that we ought to pay it, and without considering whether those affected will gain or lose in happiness.

CAN "OUGHT" BE DEFINED IN TERMS OF HAPPINESS?

If "right" is defined as *what God commands,* or *what produces happiness,* Price argues, then "the propositions '*obeying a command is right,*' or '*producing happiness is right,*' would be most trifling, as expressing no more than that obeying a command, is obeying a command, or producing happiness, is producing happiness."[73] But these propositions are so far from being trifling that they are subject to violent and prolonged dispute.

[71] *The Right and the Good,* pp. 4–5.
[72] *Op. cit.,* p. 8.
[73] *Op. cit.,* pp. 16–17.

If "right" did mean *what produces happiness,* however, any inquiry as to whether right actions do, as a matter of fact, produce happiness would amount to an inquiry as to whether right actions are right actions, or what produces happiness is what produces happiness. In this case, also, it might be added, the denial that right actions always produce happiness would be self-contradictory, which does not appear to be true. Therefore, "right" cannot be defined as what produces happiness, nor as obeying God's commands.

Another *reductio ad absurdum* argument against the identification of *right* or *duty* with *what produces happiness* is expressed by the question: "Would one, who should happen to be convinced, that virtue is what tends to his happiness here and hereafter, be released from every *bond* of duty and morality?" Would not a man, in this case, be justified in committing the worst crimes as long as he believed they led to happiness? Actually, most people would say only that "virtue tends to our happiness," not that it must produce happiness in every case. It is thereby admitted, Price argues, that there may be virtue that is against our interest. If such people continue to identify virtue with producing happiness, they will then be maintaining that "that which is *advantageous* to us, may also be *disadvantageous* to us."[74] Price argues further that those who define "duty" in terms of happiness can be shown to use the term, unwittingly, in quite a different sense. Several authors, including Bishop Cumberland, call obligation *"the necessity of doing a thing in order to be happy,"* which leads Price to ask:

> What, if this be the only sense of obligation, is meant when we say, a man is *obliged* to study his own happiness? Is it not obvious that *obliged,* in this proposition, signifies, not the necessity of doing a thing in order to be happy, which would make it ridiculous; but only, that it is *right* to study our own happiness, and wrong to neglect it?[75]

This underlying sense of "right" or "obligation" also appears, Price thinks, when the question is raised: "What ought to be the end of our deliberate pursuit, *private* or *public* happiness," or "which ought to give way (that is, which *right* should give way) in case of opposition, the calm selfish, or the calm benevolent affection?" This very question assumes, Price contends, that "the perception of *right* influences our choice," for otherwise how could an answer be expected? It presupposes

> that the appeal in all cases is to our moral faculty, as the ultimate judge and determiner of our conduct; and, that the *regard to right,* to *duty,* or to *moral excellence,* is a superior affection within us to *benevolence;* for it comes in, in cases of interference between self-love and benevolence, to turn the scales

[74] *Ibid.,* p. 107.
[75] *Ibid.,* pp. 115–116.

in favor of benevolence . . . to make the determination of public happiness the supreme one in the soul.[76]

Ross, too, criticizes the definition of "right" or "what is obligatory" as the production of some result, such as happiness, and distinguishes three forms that the objectionable definition may take, viz.: Obligatory actions are actions which (a) aim at some result; (b) are likely to produce some result; or (c) *will* produce it. All three forms are defective. (a) The first is unsatisfactory, Ross argues,[77] since having a motive to bring about something can never be part of our duty. Moreover, if what is involved is returning a book we have borrowed from a friend, I do not do my duty by merely *aiming* at its return; I keep my promise only by actually returning it. (b) This objection also holds against the second form of the definition, for if it is only *probable* that my act will produce the result; it may not do so; I should then have done my duty though I failed to keep my promise to return the book. (c) The third form of the definition avoids this objection. It can also avoid the first objection if it is understood to mean that *right* consists of certain acts, and does not include the motive for doing them.

This third definition, which Ross describes as the utilitarian alternative, is thus more plausible than the other, he thinks, but still not true. For it makes the *rightness* of packaging and mailing the book consist in the consequences of doing so, and the consequences of this action, as of other actions, may be multifarious and incalculable. Our duty, Ross says, "is to fulfill our promise, *i.e.*, to put the book into our friend's possession. This we consider obligatory in its own nature, just because it is a fulfillment of a promise, and not because of its consequences."[78]

Another very general argument against the definition of "right" and "ought" in terms of happiness is that no definition of any ethical term— "ought," "right," "duty," or "good"—is possible wholly in nonethical terms. Such definitions commit, according to G. E. Moore, the "naturalistic fallacy."[79] If "ought" or "right" is defined as what produces happiness, for example, the paradox is apparent. We can always question whether a particular obligatory action will produce happiness, or that happiness, in a particular case, has been brought about by a right action, without contradicting ourselves. On the other hand, if we were to question whether a particular triangle is a plane, closed, three-sided figure, we should certainly be contradicting ourselves.

The argument, it is often pointed out, depends on a certain conception of "definition," *i.e.*, one that requires that the *definiens* and the *definiedum*

[76] *Ibid.*, p. 217, fn.
[77] See p. 204, above.
[78] *Op. cit.*, pp. 43–44.
[79] *Principia Ethica.*

be synonymous. It will be noted, too, that, though the argument is pertinent to utilitarianism when it claims that the *meaning* of "right" or "ought" in ordinary usage is *productive of happiness,* it has no immediate application to eudaemonism. In Aristotle's ethics, "right" is not defined purely in nonethical terms: "right" is defined in terms of happiness, but this happiness is itself defined as "activity in accordance with virtue."

The deontological position has considerable *prima facie* plausibility. People do appear to recognize obligations and right actions in a great range of common situations without calculating the quantity of happiness likely to result—without even thinking specifically of consequences. (This is more obviously true, however, of keeping our promises and paying our debts, where we are committed by our past actions, than it is of being merciful and caring for our children; and it is not surprising that the deontologists prefer to take the former as examples of obligatory acts.) It is also undeniable that to predict the balance of happiness over misery resulting from a given act is most difficult. The act itself, as Prichard and Ross stress, is complex, frequently being good in one aspect and bad in another; and consequences are particularly hard to trace since they interact with unforeseen events, for which we are not responsible. For this very reason, a well-meaning ruler, calculating future happiness of his people, may embark on a policy that has, in fact, abominably cruel consequences.[80]

III. Rejoinders on Behalf of the Happiness Principle

The questions raised by the deontologists' attack on the happiness principle have deep ramifications in ethics and psychology. We shall attempt to deal with them only as they bear upon the one issue that concerns us, viz.: whether happiness is or is not the supreme good. We shall first see what friends of happiness can say to the contentions that we immediately apprehend what is right and obligatory; that happy consequences need not be, and are not in fact, calculated; and that this would be irrelevant if they were.

Is Duty Independent of Consequences?

When asked why you keep your promises, you may reply, "Because it is my duty to do so." No one is likely to object. But if you then go on to explain that by your duty you mean an act that, in the given circumstances, will produce the greatest happiness or the least misery, you will

---

[80] See the contention of Bishop Butler in the next section.

have taken a position that can easily be attacked. You can be asked whether you would break a solemn promise if you found that slightly more general happiness would result from breaking than from honoring it. A promise is a promise, the man to whom you have pledged yourself will say. If you have intended to keep your promise only conditionally, you should not have committed yourself unconditionally. The promise is a specific commitment and says nothing about the future happiness of anyone.

The utilitarian, as we have seen, has an answer. He points out that the disutility of breaking a promise usually outweighs any immediate gain that can be had. The general practice of keeping promises is so precious that human society itself must be founded on it, and every exception made tends to weaken the rule and to make new violations more likely. Thus the good utilitarian will recommend a general observance of promise-keeping, even in cases where the immediate effect is a loss in happiness; the long-range effect, he believes, will be a gain.

This reply does not satisfy the deontologists. Ross, while admitting that the keeping of promises has tremendous advantages for general well-being or happiness, insists that "to make a promise is not merely to adopt an ingenious device for promoting the general well-being."[81] It is to engage oneself to a specific duty to another person, not respective to the welfare of society. He admits that it is important to estimate, as far as we can, the net good that will be effected by our keeping our promise, and the net good to be gained by our breaking it. But, even if the latter should turn out to be greater than the former, this would not at all prove that we should not fulfill our promise. Ross says:

> It may be suspected, too, that the effect of a single keeping or breaking of a promise in strengthening or weakening the fabric of mutual confidence is greatly exaggerated by the theory we are examining. And if we suppose two men dying together alone, do we think that the duty of one to fulfill before he dies a promise he has made to the other would be extinguished by the fact that neither act would have any effect on the general confidence? Any one who holds this may be suspected of not having reflected on what a promise is.[82]

Ross concludes that "right" and "optimific," *i.e.*, producing the best results, "are not identical, and that we do not know either by intuition, by deduction, or by induction that they coincide in their application." He concedes, however, that when we are not bound by a special duty by reason of a debt, a promise, or by gratitude, "we ought to do what will produce the most good,"[83] and that their optimific tendency is important in deter-

[81] *Op. cit.*, p. 38.
[82] *Ibid.*, p. 39.
[83] *Ibid.*

mining the rightness even of special duties. Thus, though he is a leading opponent of the ethics of happiness, Ross is willing to accept it *practically*, on a large scale.

Now, how can the partisans of happiness answer these deontological objections? The utilitarians in general recognize the semi-independent role of rules of conduct, such as promise-keeping and paying debts. We have seen that J. S. Mill ridicules the idea that the utilitarian must decide on every occasion whether a particular act, let it be telling the truth or keeping a promise, or anything else, will promote the general happiness. Mankind has learned in the course of long experience that certain practices pay and others do not. There is no need to prove it again in the case of every example. Confronted by any ordinary obligation entailed by his promise to another, the utilitarian can consistently fulfill his promise without calculating the consequences.

Though Bentham has a great deal to say about calculating the net profit of individual acts, he also lays weight on the critical employment of general rules that have proved themselves in practice. The new legislative measures on which he counts to augment or maximize the public happiness, obviously must deal with classes of acts, not individual ones. Even Bentham does not recommend the breaking of promises when a gain in immediate happiness is realizable. Certain kinds of acts should be performed promptly, as a rule, simply because of their general tendency to promote happiness.

> Why ought we to fulfill our engagements? Because the faith of promises is the basis of society. It is for the advantage of all that the promises of every individual should be faithfully observed. There would no longer be any security among men, no commerce, no confidence . . . if engagements did not possess an obligatory force. [Yet] it is their utility which makes them binding.[84]

This is part of Bentham's answer. We shall see later that the utilitarians turn this defense into an offense.

But let us now turn to the special borderline cases brought up by Price, Prichard, and Ross in their campaign against the ethics of happiness. We have just seen that Ross argues that a man would be under obligation to keep a promise to another though they were both on the point of death, and the general happiness could not be affected one way or the other. What would the utilitarians say to this hypothetical case, and numerous others of the kind, which have been invented to refute utilitarianism and teleological ethics in general? They can begin by pointing out that because ethics is not an exact science there will always be borderline cases, in any

[84] *The Theory of Legislation*, p. 82.

ethical system, that present difficulties. They can argue that the borderline cases are so exceptional or improbable that they have no practical importance. The example of the dying man keeping his promise to another dying man, both being sealed off from the rest of humankind, seems artificial, nor is it completely foolproof. For, if the promiser has had the usual sort of social training, he will be happier if he keeps his promise than if he breaks it, especially since the promisee is a dying man. And this happiness of the promiser (and of the promisee too?) could easily outweigh any imaginable advantage that might accrue, under the circumstances, from breaking the promise. Hedonistic consequences might thus favor the honoring of the promise. Although this loophole could be remedied with a little care, the result would be to make the example even more artificial and improbable.

A more interesting utilitarian retort is suggested in an article by John Rawls, in which he maintains that the issue we are discussing has been confused by the failure to distinguish between "the justification of a particular practice [or rule] and the justification of a particular action falling under it." It is thus mistakenly assumed that the promiser is free to decide in every particular case, on the basis of utility, whether to keep his promise. In fact, however, the promiser is allowed no such discretion.

> Indeed, the point of the practice is to abdicate one's title to act in accordance with utilitarian and prudential considerations in order that the future may be tied down and plans coordinated in advance. There are obvious utilitarian advantages in having a practice which denies to the promisor, as a defense, any general appeal to the utilitarian principle in accordance with which the practice itself may be justified. There is nothing contradictory or surprising in this.[85]

A chess player may believe that people would get more enjoyment from the game if the rules were changed, but he would be clearly unjustified in breaking the rules as he plays. He has agreed, for better or for worse, to play according to the present rules. In the same way, the man who has given a promise has tied his own hands, and can no longer decide on utilitarian grounds whether to fulfill it or not. The utilitarian may thus consistently maintain that one should keep promises, even though the general happiness is not affected thereby, or is even reduced.

The promiser is deprived of a *general* appeal to consequences as a justification for breaking a promise, even if he has taken into account the usual bad effects of the rule that you must keep promises. He would not be entitled to say: "I will not keep the promise I made to you, since I think that *on the whole* the results would be better if I don't." But he may be

---

[85] "Two Concepts of Happiness," in *Philosophical Review*, Vol. 64, pp. 3–32. See also R. Brandt (ed.), *Value and Obligation*, p. 233.

justified in appealing to *very serious* consequences of keeping faith. Suppose the promise was made under duress, or threats, or that keeping it will conflict with other obligations, or that the promiser or others will lose their lives if the promise is kept!

These eventualities bring us to the positive case for utilitarianism as against deontology. In a continuation of the passage quoted above, Bentham says that with political contracts (including the so-called social contract), it is the same as with private engagements, "it is their utility which makes them binding."

> When they become injurious they lose their force. If a king had taken an oath to render his subjects unhappy, would such an engagement be valid? If people were sworn to obey him at all events, would they be bound to suffer themselves to be exterminated by a Nero or Caligula, rather than violate their promises? . . . It cannot be denied, then, that the validity of a contract is at bottom only a question of utility—a little wrapped up, a little disguised, and, in consequence, more susceptible of false interpretations.[86]

The utilitarian can therefore answer the above objections, and also claim positive advantages over his critics. He can agree that in promise-keeping, paying debts, and in other cases where we have incurred a specific obligation by our conduct in the past, we see the obligation at once without calculating consequences, and that a *general* appeal to consequences never justifies the violation of a special obligation we have incurred; yet still maintain that an appeal to "very serious" consequences certainly does justify the violation of strict obligations in many cases of the greatest importance. It is true that utilitarians do not always make the clear distinction, pointed out by John Rawls, between the justification of the particular case that falls under it, which is *prima facie* not utility; but the point is that it is always open to them to do so.

The distinction made by Rawls has been utilized by other authors. Austin Duncan-Jones calls attention to passages in which Bishop Butler, who generally approves of the utilitarian rule, definitely limits its application, as when he says that it is dangerous for men to imagine that "the whole of virtue" consists

> in singly aiming, according to the best of their judgment, at promoting the happiness of mankind in the present state; and the whole of vice in doing what they foresee . . . is likely to produce an overbalance of unhappiness in it: than which mistakes none can be conceived more terrible. For it is certain that some of the most shocking cases of injustice, adultery, murder, perjury, and even of persecution, may, in many supposable cases, not have

[86] *Theory of Legislation,* p. 82.

the appearance of being likely to produce an overbalance of misery . . . perhaps may have the contrary appearance.[87]

On behalf of utilitarianism, Duncan-Jones points out that, among other things, the utilitarian, in condemning an act of treachery, for example, can take into account not only its effect on happiness but also the relation of the act to the past conduct and present situation of the agent. "The whole of virtue" does not consist "in singly aiming . . . at promoting the happiness of mankind," Duncan-Jones says.

> For we must distinguish between (1) the rule or rules which must be acted on in particular situations; and (2) the justification of any rule. A utilitarian is not obliged to hold that, in every situation, a man should form an estimate of the happiness and misery [implied] so as to maximize happiness and minimize misery. He may hold that actions of certain kinds should always be avoided, and [others] performed whenever possible, without any calculation of the particular sequence of happiness and misery which will follow: but that these choices and avoidances are justified by reference to the consequences they tend to have in general.[88]

Duncan-Jones is not satisfied with Butler's appeal to what he calls the "common moral consciousness" to determine, without appeal to consequences, the odiousness of injustice, infidelity, treachery, etc., in every possible case. Here, he says, we have to do with intuitions that can vary from one society to another.

> If we are not allowed to appeal to consequences, it is hard to see any ground which could be given, for the moral odiousness of treachery, which could convince a doubter . . . surveying mankind at all times and places, we are forced to acknowledge substantial diversity of conscience, and appeals to common moral consciousness may therefore rest on local idiosyncrasies.[89]

A great advantage of utilitarianism over deontology is that it is able to explain, as can be claimed with some plausibility, why rules enjoining promise-keeping, paying debts, and the like come to be generally adopted by societies of all sorts, why such rules are sometimes modified with wide approval, as when a government eases the burden of debtors, and why in special cases we all think a man—and also of course a government—justified in breaking a promise. Deonotologists, on the other hand, tend to veil in mystery the choice of moral rules of the kind, and have no explanation of the authority or tenure of these rules. So, at least, it appears to the partisans of happiness. Kant, Price, and Prichard, it is true, compare the

---

[87] "Of the Nature of Virtue," qu. in Duncan-Jones, *Butler's Moral Philosophy*, p. 118.
[88] *Butler's Moral Philosophy*, pp. 119–120.
[89] *Ibid.*, p. 120.

perception of obligation to insight into mathematical relations. The difficulty here, of course, is that moral rules vary from one society to another, as mathematics does not, and are often modified as the result of historical developments and changes in socioeconomic conditions. The deontologist, accordingly, leaves himself open to the charge of sanctifying, by a specious mathematical analogy, the norms of his own society.

Aristotle and the eudaemonists, as far as this deontological attack is concerned, are not in the direct line of fire. The reason is that, for eudaemonism, virtue, including promise-keeping, paying debts, etc., is an integral part of happiness. The good man, as Aristotle conceives him, will keep his promises and pay his debts for the sake of happiness, and also for virtue's sake. He will also meet his obligations even when the results are against his interest, and he will do so more readily since he has come to enjoy being virtuous. Although "duty" has no Greek equivalent, nor is it a Greek emphasis, Aristotle points out that the good man will naturally pay his debts before he disperses money to friends or for charity. Obligations and commitments generally come first. Yet common sense and a care for consequences are rarely lacking in Aristotle's account. One would not be praised for returning a sword on the agreed date, he says, if at that time the owner is in a suicidal mood. In short, the good man will fulfill his obligations promptly and cheerfully, and will be dissuaded from it only when the consequences involve a serious conflict of goods. Like the utilitarian, Aristotle's good man can refer to a standard to resolve conflicts of good and obligations, whereas the deontologist does not have this resource.

DISTRIBUTIVE JUSTICE VS. THE GREATEST-HAPPINESS PRINCIPLE

Distributive justice requires the distribution of happiness and misery according to deserts, but such distribution conflicts with the happiness principle, which calls for the greatest possible balance of happiness over misery. The far-reaching, unavoidable issue, therefore, is whether the best possible world is one in which happiness is maximized, or one in which heroes and villains receive their exact due of happiness and misery. The implications for political policy, legislation, and the theory of punishment are fundamental and obtrude tenaciously on the levels of both theory and practice. A conflict of opinion also develops in theology. Kant and Price are convinced that it is God's intention that men should be rewarded and punished in exact proportion to their degree of virtue and sin, but there are other strains of Christian thought that emphasize the forgiveness of sins and a divine beneficence, and these have a different tendency.

It is apparent at once that this issue is a far more direct challenge to utilitarianism than it is to eudaemonism. Although a virtuous man might well be unhappy in Aristotle's scheme, a villain could not possibly be happy. On the other hand, it is quite possible (though it would be most unlikely) for a villain to be "happy" in the utilitarian sense, since "happiness" so understood does not contain virtue as an integral part. The Aristotelian can be asked to choose between a world in which distributive justice is strictly applied throughout, and a world in which it is relaxed or modified for the sake of more happiness; but this quantitative approach to happiness on a worldwide scale is somewhat alien to Aristotelian thought, and far more congenial to utilitarianism. We shall consider first the utilitarian response to the issue.

Is there any other measure of right and wrong, the utilitarian may be asked, than the production of happiness and misery? If not, would it not be right, Price asks, to deprive an innocent man of his property or life if the total happiness of the community could be augmented even slightly thereby? The Athenians sometimes drove an innocent man from the city and stoned him to death. Would this be justified if there were a consequent improvement of the morale and well-being of the whole body of citizens? The resort to scapegoats to relieve public tensions, and to arbitrary confiscations to replenish government funds for general use, have been common enough practices. How can the utilitarian condemn them? There is also the possibility of reforming the criminal by agreeable instruction in pleasant surroundings, without punishment. Would this not be in accord with the utility principle?

The utilitarians in general oppose arbitrary and discriminatory penalties and exactions, and they oppose them on grounds of utility. The immediate result of victimizing an innocent man may be an increase of the public happiness; the long-range effects would be mischievous. Bentham, a recognized authority on legal codes, insists that laws be *consistent among themselves*, as well as with the happiness principle; and that they be *known in advance* and not, save for exceptional cases, in conflict with "natural expectations."[90] He upholds the proportionality between punishments and offenses, but not with pedantic precision, and weighs in various complicating hedonistic factors in order to better achieve the one and only purpose of the laws, which is the promotion of happiness. Distributive justice has no *intrinsic* value, and, indeed, all punishment is evil in itself.

> On the principle of utility, if it ought at all to be admitted, it ought to be admitted in so far as it promises to exclude some greater evil.[91]

[90] *Op. cit.*, pp. 148ff.
[91] *Principles of Morals and Legislation,* p. 281.

It is useful insofar as, in deterring from crime or reforming the criminal, it contributes to the happiness of the community. If these ends could be accomplished by instruction of the criminal, punishment would be only a gratuitous increase of evil.[92] Confiscation of property for the general welfare receives little support from Bentham's utilitarianism. Although he argues that the equality of property in a society would *ideally* make for the greatest pleasure of the greatest number, he also warns that once men have come into possession of land and other property their legitimate expectations of continued ownership have to be taken into account. The pain of disappointing such expectations, which increase with the time the owners have been in possession, will, he claims, be prohibitive from the standpoint of utilitarianism.

It may be concluded that, when they are persuaded that there is a *real* conflict between distributive justice and the general happiness, not only Bentham but other utilitarians as well will choose to suspend or modify the former. To do otherwise would be to abandon happiness as the supreme good, and to countenance a gratuitous increase of evil. Yet there are differences of emphasis. Mill's radical individualism and his doctrine that there is a higher, more precious *kind* of pleasure—of which the pleasure of being fair to every person, regardless, might be an instance—could be expected to make him more averse than Bentham was to the sacrifice of the "rights" of individuals and minorities to the greatest happiness of all. Such differences could be profitably explored, however, only by way of an extensive comparison of the politicoeconomic measures that the two utilitarians endorse.

Although Aristotle makes distributive justice a preeminent virtue, he too sees that it is not infallible, but is to be ameliorated sometimes in the interest of happiness. Equity, he says, corrects the harshness of general laws, and, in the practice of the good men, justice must harmonize with all the other virtues. Rules specifying when distributive justice can be properly relaxed in the public interest are naturally not provided (though particular examples are given). Here, "perception," as Aristotle says, and the example of the good man, must be our guide.

DOES THE HAPPINESS PRINCIPLE PROVIDE A SUFFICIENT MOTIVE TO THE PERFORMANCE OF DUTY?

Prichard argues that, if we do our duty *because* it will make us happy, this motive will be sufficient to get us into action, but then we shall not

[92] See *ibid.*, pp. 281ff.

feel that it is our duty, that we are *obliged* to so act. Whereas, if we do our duty *because* it will make others happy, or because it is good to make others happy, we shall not *always* have a sufficient motive to do it. He says:

> Suppose, when wondering whether we really ought to act in the ways usually called moral, we are told . . . that those acts are right which produce happiness. We at once ask: "Whose happiness?" If we are told "Our own happiness," then, though we shall lose our hesitation to act in these ways, we shall not recover our sense that we ought to do so. But how can this result be avoided? Apparently, only by being told one of two things; either that anyone's happiness is a good thing in itself, and that *therefore* we ought to do whatever will produce it, *or* that working for happiness is itself good, and that the intrinsic goodness of such an action is a reason why we ought to do it. The advantage of this appeal to the goodness of something consists in the fact that it avoids reference to desire, and, instead, refers to something impersonal and objective. In this way it seems possible to avoid the resolution of obligation into inclination. But just for this reason . . . to be effective it must neither include nor involve the view that the apprehension of the goodness of anything necessarily arouses the desire for it.[93]

To promote the happiness of others appears to be a real duty, but suppose this duty conflicts with interest, *e.g.*, the desire to pursue our *own* happiness. We can then have no motive for doing our duty. According to the Kantian formula accepted by the deontologists, "I ought" implies "I can," that is, "If I can't do a thing, it is not my duty to do it." It seems to follow that, though it may be *virtuous* to promote the happiness of others, it is not our *duty* or *obligation* to do so. Insofar as our motive is to promote happiness, we might possess all the virtues and yet never do our duty, strictly speaking.

This argument constitutes a clear-cut criticism, not only of utilitarianism but also of Aristotle's eudaemonism. If the criticism is valid, the ethics of happiness, though it may shelter the whole range of human virtue (excellence), excludes "duty" and "ought," in the moral sense. Let us first consider what answer hedonists and utilitarians can make.

Even egoistic hedonism can offer motives to altruistic conduct. Epicureanism teaches that happiness is to be attained only if one has friends, and it goes without saying that you cannot keep friends unless you are good to them. For the sake of your own happiness, therefore, you ought to cultivate the happiness of friends. But the Epicurean can supply no reason for altruism in a case where it is against the individual's interest. He does not want to, for that matter. But this is not to say that egoism is incapable of developing a motive for altruism. In Spinoza's *Ethics,* the "intellectual

[93] *Op. cit.,* pp. 3–4.

love of God" is evolved out of the primary desire of the individual to "persevere in his own being." In fact, self-realization authors often hold that if the interests of the self expand enough they finally include the interests of other selves, so that their happiness is necessary to one's own.

Bentham agrees with Epicureanism that men *do* seek their own happiness, and that they *should* seek it efficiently, but he adds that they *ought* also to promote the general happiness. "Morality," he says, "is the directing of the actions of men in such a way as to produce the greatest possible sum of good. . . . Morality commands each individual to do all that is advantageous to the community, his own personal advantage included."[94] Although all positive laws and all moral constraint are bad in themselves, since they deprive them of the liberty to do as they please, they are nevertheless, he insists, a necessary means to happiness. Insofar as moral suasion and the laws are wisely appropriate, prudence will tend to the public good. If private interest coincides, or ideally coincides, with public interest (the so-called theory of "the identity of interests"), it is because certain forces are in operation:

> It is true that there is a natural connection between prudence and probity; for our interest, well understood, will never leave us without motives to abstain from injuring our fellows. . . . I say that, independently of religion and the laws, we always have some natural motives for consulting the happiness of others. 1st. The motive of pure benevolence, a sweet and calm sentiment which we delight to experience, and which inspires us with a repugnance to be the cause of suffering. 2nd. The motives of private affection, which exercise their empire in domestic life, and within the particular circle of our intimacies. 3rd. The desire of good repute, and the fear of blame. This is a sort of calculation of trade. It is paying, to have credit; speaking truth, to obtain confidence; serving, to be served.[95]

The various motives enabling men to do their duty—to promote the happiness of others as well as their own—are thus the desire to avoid punishment under the laws, religious sanctions, the feeling of benevolence, "which we delight to experience," private affection, and the desire of good repute and avoidance of blame. The nonlegal motives can be very strong, especially as education refines sentiment and improves understanding of the interlocking of individual and public happiness. For most men, however, the penalties of the law are needed to correct an ignorant and unimaginative narrowing of the scope of self-interest. Legal codes, applying pains to undesirable conduct, must therefore be constructed with the greatest care if the aim of the laws, the advancement of happiness, is to be realized.

[94] *The Theory of Legislation*, p. 60.
[95] *Ibid.*, p. 64.

Prichard asks: Can utilitarianism provide a sufficient motive to the performance of duty when it is against the individual's interest? Bentham's answer seems to be that there are at least five kinds of motives that can prompt us to serve the happiness of others and avoid doing harm to them. But suppose the act of altruism were *really* against the individual's interest, that in increasing the happiness of others he would certainly decrease his own. Could any or all of these five motives be counted on to move him to do his duty? If not, he could not do his duty; and, according to Prichard, it could not *be* his duty to attend to the happiness of others. Moreover, what right has Bentham to make use of benevolence and private affection as separate motives if, as he says, pleasure and pain are the only sovereign masters of human action?

With regard to the first question, Bentham might say that prudence, properly understood, results in probity, that in serving ourselves we serve others. But, No. This is at best only *generally* true. What about the exceptions? Bentham holds that if the individual interest does not in fact coincide with the community interest it should be made to do so. Education should be improved and the laws reformed, especially the latter. To this end he devoted his main energies for many years. The "identity of interests" is something to be brought about. If it were here already, there would be no need of the reforms. Utilitarianism is a program. The exceptions Prichard conjures up require corrective measures.

As for the second question, Bentham points out that benevolence becomes a "delight" to us, and so also does private affection. Instead of spending our money on ourselves, we give it to friends, the poor, or our children. This is consistent with acting according to our greatest pleasure, for the pleasure of generosity is commonly greater than the pleasure of self-indulgence. Yet what is intended in the act of generosity is not our own pleasure. If it were it would not be generosity, and would not yield the pleasure that comes from generosity. The utilitarian can concede that often the way to get pleasure is to intend something else. We must distinguish the standard by which an act is judged to be right or good and the intention the act must have if it is to meet the standard. Acting benevolently or from natural affection can thus be consistent with utilitarianism.

But if it should turn out that Bentham has successfully dealt with this problem, he is at once caught on the other horn of Prichard's dilemma, namely: If self-interest provides a sufficient motive for doing your duty, so that you would do it even if it were not your duty, how can you call it your *duty*? Bentham and other utilitarians point out that acting in accordance with the greatest pleasure principle, though it is what you decide to do and want to do, can involve much tension and thwarting of interest—the sort of thing Prichard implies is necessary for the observance of duty. Doing your duty can involve the sacrifice of a present good, which is live and warm, for a greater good, which is cool and distant in the future. It can entail the sacrifice of the welfare or peace of mind of one's friend or child. The performance of duty can cause us pain and anguish even though we know that our failure to perform it would, in the end, be *more* painful. But the utilitarian can also point out that many common cases of observance of duty, *e.g.*, as when a man does his duty by raising his children, need not involve a restraint upon the will or a thwarting of interest, but may be decidedly pleasant.

Prichard's dilemma, which we are discussing, might be restated as follows:

> If duty were acting from interest, it would not be duty. If duty were acting without (or against) interest, it could not be done. But either it is done from or without (the motive of) interest, and, therefore, it is either not duty or it cannot be done.

The first premise can be challenged, as we have seen, on two counts: Self-discipline and restraint of desire can be needed when a man observes his duty, even though he acts with his (larger) interest in view. But, on the other hand, there are typical duties commonly recognized to be in accord with the interest of the man who fulfills them. With regard to the second premise, Bentham could say that there are five kinds of human motives that can prompt the consistent utilitarian to altruism—to actions promoting the happiness of the community—and the altruism becomes so delightful that it is preferred to ordinary self-regarding pleasures. But utilitarianism has other defenses.

W. D. Falk argues that Prichard unwittingly employs "duty," "ought," "obligation," and other such terms in two different senses. In the objective sense, "duty" is an *external* demand or requirement, objectively grounded in the nature of things, while in the subjective sense it is an inner compulsion, a dictate of conscience. "The external and internal uses of 'ought' remain undifferentiated, and are imperceptibly juxtaposed and confused," in Prichard's argument, as in ordinary thinking on the subject.[96] Prichard's question, "Why should I do my duty?" makes sense when "duty" (or "ought") is taken in the objective sense, but not when it is understood subjectively, for in this case it is like asking, "Why ought I do what I am convinced I ought to do?" This is hardly a sensible question.[97]

The problem for Bentham would thus be: Why ought the individual to

---

[96] See " 'Ought' and Motivations," in *Proceedings of the Aristotelian Society,* 1947–8, 48. See also W. Sellars and J. Hospers (eds.), *Readings in Ethical Theory,* p. 509.

[97] *Ibid.,* pp. 509–510.

promote the happiness of others, in the objective sense of "ought," when "ought" in the subjective sense is lacking? Bentham's answer, as already pointed out, is that where knowledge of cause and effect, moral experience, education, and the sentiment of benevolence does not give the individual a sufficient motive for doing his duty, a system of wise laws will succeed.

In the meantime, to say of such a man that he ought to promote the general happiness when he is not yet convinced that he ought may be taken as a prediction that if certain reforms were to be introduced he would eventually be convinced, and would thus have a subjective "ought" to match the objective utilitarian "ought." Bentham is always the reformer.

Another explanation of the motivation of obligatory acts is elaborated by J. S. Mill. The idea is really Aristotle's, and we have seen it appear even in Bentham, but Mill adds his own distinctive emphasis, giving it the quality of a fresh discovery. This is the insight that things first desired only as a *means* to happiness or pleasure frequently become enjoyable in themselves. All the pleasures of culture, morality, refinement, and civilization are of this sort, Mill points out. Virtuous activities thus come to be desired for their own sake, and these desires are sometimes stronger than the primary drives for food, shelter, etc., with which they were originally associated. Does the utilitarian doctrine, Mill asks,

> deny that people desire virtue, or maintain that virtue is not a thing to be desired . . . disinterestedly, for itself? [No.] What was once desired as an instrument for the attainment of happiness, has become desired for its own sake . . . desired as part of happiness. The person is made, or thinks he would be made, happy by its mere possession.[98]

Mill, no doubt, is closer to Aristotle at this point than he is to fellow utilitarians, yet he has not abandoned his hedonism, for if virtue is desired for itself, even when it is against interest, it is because it has *become* a remarkably pleasant activity in itself. Mill's recognition of sympathy as an original source of altruistic actions (though it may not agree *prima facie* with his theory that it is impossible for men to desire anything "except in proportion as the idea of it is pleasant"[99]) also provides a motive to the performance of duties against interest.

The question raised is whether Mill can satisfy Prichard's demand that the ethics of happiness provide a sufficient motive to the performance of duty when the performance is against interest. It might seem that he can, for Mill's contention that men possess a disinterested desire to act morally is precisely Prichard's own solution, put forward in another essay, viz.:

[98] *Op. cit.*, pp. 33–35.
[99] *Ibid.*, p. 36.

For if we admit the existence of a desire to do what is right, there is no longer any reason for maintaining a general thesis that in any case in which a man knows some action to be right, he must, if he is to be led to do it, be convinced that he will gain by doing it. For we shall be able to maintain that his desire to do what is right, if strong enough, will lead him to do the action in spite of any aversion from doing it he may feel on account of its disadvantages.[100]

In this passage, Prichard concedes all his adversary J. S. Mill could desire.

The conflict between egoistic hedonism and utilitarianism dominates Sidgwick's *Method of Ethics.* Greatly influenced by Kant, Sidgwick takes a much more drastic view of this conflict than do other utilitarians.[101] Indeed, he concludes that the reconciliation of duty and self-interest can be achieved only by supposing that there is a deity or moral order of the world that will reward men for obeying rules of duty, and punish them for transgressing them—in an afterlife—which is conjectural. Without accepting such a hypothesis, he says, we should doubtless be led, not only by self-interest but also by sympathy and inculcated sentiments and social reciprocation, to do our duty, especially in ordinary cases in which duty is in harmony with self-interest. "But in the rarer cases of a recognized conflict between self-interest and duty, practical reason, being divided against itself, would cease to be a motive on either side; the conflict would have to be decided by a comparative preponderance of one or the other of two groups of non-rational impulses."[102]

Sidgwick is as certain as he is of any axiom of arithmetic or geometry that he should do unto others as he would be done unto by them, under similar circumstances, and that he should do what he believes "to be ultimately conducive to universal Good or Happiness," but, unfortunately, he has no corresponding certainty that there exists a system of equitable rewards and punishments that would provide a rational justification for doing what one should in difficult cases. If there is no such system connecting virtue and self-interest, we are forced "to admit an ultimate and fundamental contradiction in our apparent intuitions of what is Reasonable in conduct."[103]

[100] *Op. cit.,* "Duty and Interest," pp. 467–468.
[101] It should be noted that, though Sidgwick is one of the very greatest spokesmen for utilitarianism, he is not strictly a utilitarian himself—not in the usual sense of the term. For him, the good or happiness comprises something else besides pleasure. This modification of utilitarianism, however, is not relevant at this point. As we have previously pointed out, the term "utilitarianism" is often used at present in another sense, viz., as the doctrine that "right" and "wrong" depend wholly on consequences. In this sense, Sidgwick *is* a utilitarian.
[102] *Op. cit.,* p. 508.
[103] *Ibid.*

Although deontologists may be gratified to see a very distinguished utilitarian confess that duty presents a nearly insoluble problem for the ethics of happiness, they can take little comfort from his formulation of the problem. If men did their duty, in cases where it clashed cruelly with self-interest, only (or mainly) because of a calculation that a benevolent deity would be bound to make it worth their while in the next life, the deontologists could not claim that they had acted morally, or from a moral motive. Duty, they always insist, is not to be confused with long-range calculation of interest.

The Aristotelian answer to Prichard's dilemma is like that of Bentham and Mill in important respects, but different in others.

In relation to the second promise of the dilemma, that if we do our duty from a motive of interest and advantage it ceases to be duty, Aristotle reminds us that even what is to our best interest may involve sacrifice and suffering.

> Both art and virtue are always concerned with what is harder; for even the good is better when it is harder. Therefore for this reason also the whole concern both of virtue and of political science is with pleasures and pains; for the man who uses these well will be good, he who uses them badly bad.[104]

Although Aristotle does not talk about duty as such, he is nevertheless concerned with something quite similar to what Prichard has in mind, viz.: virtuous actions that are difficult or painful for a man to perform, and that are highly praised for that reason. But Aristotle, like Plato, Bentham, and Mill, is thoroughly convinced that such adverse virtue is only to be realized by education and the laws, by early association of pleasure with noble actions and pain with base. In this way the citizen learns to desire what is noble, however hard. The good man, Aristotle says,

> does many acts for the sake of his friends and his country, and if necessary dies for them; for he will throw away both wealth and honours and in general the goods that are objects of competition, gaining for himself nobility; since he would prefer a short period of intense pleasure to a long one of mild enjoyment. . . . They will throw away wealth on condition that their friends will gain more; for while a man's friend gains wealth he himself achieves nobility; he is therefore assigning the greater good to himself. The same too is true of honour and office; all these things he will sacrifice to his friend [and he will also give his friend opportunity for noble actions]. In all actions, therefore, that men are praised for, the good man is seen to assign to himself the greater share of what is noble. In this

[104] *Op. cit., Nicomachean Ethics,* 1105a9–12.

sense . . . a man should be a lover of self; but in the sense in which most men are so, he ought not.[105]

This is also a part of the Aristotelian answer. The pursuit of virtue may lead a man to sacrifice what is dear to him, including his own life, and yet be worth it to him, since he "takes for himself a larger share of what is noble." When the sacrifice is hard and the decision painful, we praise the act; when it is easy and pleasant, we praise the character that makes this possible, for a good character, as Aristotle says, is hard to acquire. In either case we praise a hard-won victory; but we also praise the good character for itself, for the moral ideal is not only to do right but to love doing it.

Prichard, however, agrees with Aristotle that a virtuous act "must be done willingly or with pleasure,"[106] but holds that duty or obligation is altogether different from virtue. The same radical division of duty from virtue is adopted by Ross. How can the Aristotelian reply to this?

Obligations are inculcated and good habits formed, he could say, which vary somewhat from one society to another, according to the form of government, the customs, etc., and from one man to another, according to differences of constitutions, dispositions, status, occupations, wealth, and circumstances. As denoting a spring of action, "ought" is thus a *biographical* term,[107] being respective to differentials of training, constitutions, past choices, and commitments. But the duties that the deontologists are concerned with are those said to be incumbent on all men in exactly the same way, such as promise-keeping and paying one's debts independent of customs and training. Where then does the motive to duty come from? Aristotle recognizes that actions to which a person has committed himself have a certain priority. A man should in general pay his debts and keep his promises before engaging in noble acts of generosity, which make the former impossible. And, yet, even these duties are not immediately self-evident. Such obligations are acquired through training, which varies from one society to another, as, for example, in Sparta, where stealing was sometimes praised. Nor are they categorical. Should we return a sword to its owner when he is in a homicidal mood? And must not the deontologist recognize, with Aristotle, that duties should be in harmony with virtues, *i.e.*, not conflict with them? If so, must not the former depend on consequences, at least indirectly, as the latter admittedly do, directly?

If actions are to be completely virtuous, according to Aristotle, they must also be inspired by good motives. But we have seen that Prichard and Ross insist that it can never be part of our *duty* to act from a good motive. Ross

[105] *Ibid.*, 1169a18–1169b2.
[106] *Op. cit.*, p. 11.
[107] Wilfred Sellars has recognized the importance of this side of "ought." (Sellars and Hospers, *op. cit.*, pp. 511 ff.)

adds that it cannot be part of our duty to act from a good motive, because it is not in our power to *have* a good motive and to see that it is effective in getting us to act. We have seen that Kant makes a similar point. The commandment "Love thy Neighbor. . ." cannot mean anything like "Have a warm feeling toward your neighbor," he argues, but relates only to actions, viz.: "Relieve his distress and serve his needs."

The Aristotelian agrees that meeting one's obligations is meeting one's obligations, whatever the motive is, and that this much is a necessary part of virtue, though not its ideal. Generally, a man does right to keep his promise, if he can; but he does better if he does so from a good motive. Almost everyone admits this. If Prichard and Ross did, they would insist that the good motive has nothing to do with duty itself. But, in this case, are they not merely insisting on their own special sense of the term "duty," which excludes the bettering of duty by a good motive?

The answer to Ross's particular contention that it cannot be obligatory to act from a good motive because it is not in our power, at a particular time, to *have* a given motive (as it is in our power to perform a certain act, like returning money we have borrowed), might be as follows: If a man has had a moral education enabling him to perform a certain duty, he will have (or can have) acquired a good motive for doing it at the same time. In answer to Ross's claim, G. C. Field argues that "in any sense in which we can choose what action we shall do, we can choose what motive we shall act from."[108] Why should one ability be more difficult to acquire or call forth than the other? And there may be a related difficulty in the deontological position. Mere cognizance of the situation in which a debt we owe falls due, or in which people expect us to keep our promise, is perhaps not sufficient to instigate action. The intellect alone, Aristotle says, moves nothing.

Prichard finds Aristotle's account of the moral life extremely unsatisfactory. The reason is that

> Aristotle does not do what we as moral philosophers want him to do, viz., to convince us that we really ought to do what in our nonreflective consciousness we have hitherto believed we ought to do, or if not, to tell us what, if any, are the other things which we really ought to do, and to prove to us that he is right.[109]

Aristotle's systematic account of the virtues and the virtuous man and his goal of self-improvement, "cannot possibly satisfy this demand."[110] In fact, Prichard goes on, surprisingly, to explain that *nothing could* satisfy it. One

[108] "Kant's First Moral Principle," in *Mind,* Vol. XLI, p. 33.
[109] *Op. cit.,* p. 13.
[110] *Ibid.*

can give no reason for the performance of duty, and none is needed. An analysis of a situation simply discloses with immediate certainty that we are obligated.

In opposition to this closed, self-contained conception of duty, P. H. Nowell-Smith contends that, though "ought" sentences "are used for a variety of jobs . . . such as choosing, advising, exhorting, and command-ing, they are also used under certain fairly rigid conditions." If a man "says I ought to do X he lays himself open to a request for reasons and he must be prepared with an answer."[111] That a man is "logically bound" to give a reason in such a case, as Nowell-Smith contends, may be challenged. But many will insist that the *ability* to give a person a reason why he ought to do what we say he ought gives the ethics of happiness—both eudaemonism and utilitarianism—a decided advantage over deontology.

The ethics of happiness has also the advantage that it can explain, where deontology fails, the variation of duties in different societies:

> The weakness of the deontological view is its claim to intuition of the "ought" as a unique relation that is not part of the psychological or social structure. This leaves the position wide open to the counter-argument . . . that these alleged intuitions are emotional aftereffects of a process of social conditioning which begins in childhood. In support of this criticism [oppo-nents can] point to the tendency of moral judgments to conform to tradi-tion, and also to the disagreements among individuals and among different traditions.[112]

But deontological ethics is far from being at the end of its rope. Ross's position in particular has been restated and qualified. Many philosophers are convinced that it embraces or at least *conceals* a basic truth.

[111] *Ethics*, p. 190.
[112] A. C. Garnett, *Ethics, A Critical Introduction*, p. 278.

9

The Issue of the Satisfaction of Desire: Fulfillment vs. Prudence

RUNNING through all the famous theories of happiness is the tension between two tendencies, one to self-realization, the other to self-control. Now the maximum fulfillment of the individual's desires and powers is recommended, now the suppression of desires that are seen as too hazardous and costly, entailing pain and disappointment. Generally, of course, both abundance and security are recognized as essentials of happiness, for without security there is no abundance, and without abundance —something beyond the bare necessities of life—there is felt to be nothing in the long run worth securing. Stoicism is one exception to the rule; it relies completely on security and self-control, and dismisses all worldly goods and achievements of the self as unnecessary, if not obstructive of happiness. In the primitive Buddhism of India, similarly, a subjective bliss is evolved out of complete eradication of desire, *i.e.*, of craving or clinging.

Aristotle remarks that men tend to identify happiness with the good they lack at a particular time and feel the greatest need for. Impoverished men will see their happiness in wealth, slaves, theirs in freedom. In evil times, when life and honor and fortune are uncertain, the playthings of tyrants, security appears more precious than anything else, but as attainable only by a remarkable *tour de force*—by transforming the evil of life into something neutral, indifferent, or even good. The Cynics and the Stoics go much further than any schools of the West in reducing happiness to self-discipline and self-control. Stoicism overcomes all desire except for virtue, and virtue, they hold, is always within the power of the wise man. It is the only good that *is* in his power to achieve and keep. Happiness, thus, is a state of virtue that cares nothing for possessions or good fortune, and is proof against adversity—largely for the reason that adversity has been exposed as an illusion. The Stoic sage is his own assurance of happiness, and nothing more is needed. He might develop his talents, and even carry out great enterprises if they are in the line of duty; but all this is completely inessential to happiness, for this state can be maintained in solitary confinement, darkness, and torture.

The Epicureans also seek to make themselves independent of possessions and the shifts of fortune, but their prudence has a different method and purpose. Their retreat is a physical withdrawal from all self-cultivation and enterprise that does not have tranquil pleasure as its aim and end. And yet the Epicureans do not go nearly so far as the Stoics in suppressing desire. They repudiate military ambitions and the zest for honor and reputation, so highly esteemed by the rest of the world, but they give all encouragement to desires for gentle, amiable pleasures, which are commonly condemned as effeminate and unworthy. The Epicureans are also sensible in admitting that the needs of the body must be cared for. Yet, their frugal, simple lives present a remarkable contrast to the luxury of well-to-do Stoics, whose happiness, in theory, owes nothing to external circumstance, not even to necessities.

There is an expansiveness about Aristotle's conception of happiness which sets him apart from the Epicureans and into polar opposition to the Stoics. For him, the happy man is one who mobilizes all his resources and operates at the top of his abilities. This is sometimes not appreciated, for the doctrine of the mean is misunderstood. The mean that is virtue for Aristotle is not a kind of average behavior, a fainthearted compromise between too much and too little, a cautious retreat before the hazards involved in a fuller and richer experience. The mean that is observed in one kind of human activity sets the individual free to employ his energies in other directions. Moderation maintained in eating, drinking, liberality, amatory affairs, and with respect to self-esteem and indignation can provide the time and disposition for an all-round development of abilities and talents. The mean is also determined in relation to the situation and what is involved. When the stakes are high enough or nobility is the goal, the sky is the limit. Thus, Aristotle says

> that the good man does many acts for the sake of his friends and his country, and if necessary dies for them; for he will throw away both health and honours and in general the goods that are objects of competition, gaining for himself nobility; since he would prefer a short period of intense pleasure to a long one of mild enjoyment, a twelve-month of noble life to many years of humdrum existence, and one great and noble action to many trivial ones.[1]

Thus the noble mean of giving can be pushed to the uttermost limits when abilities and the cause are proportionately great, and the ultimate in "self-sacrifice" may be at once the most virtuous and rewarding of actions.

When the occasion is important and the actor has the capacity, the mean calls for heroism and superabundance. It will be remembered, too, that the highest Aristotelian virtues admittedly outrun the mean of moderation, and are best precisely in their excess. Thus, Aristotle says that "love is ideally a sort of excess of friendship,"[2] and that for this reason it cannot be extended to more than a very few persons. The intellectual virtues, which are the crowning glory of human life, are also extremes rather than means, for there cannot be too much devotion to truth, and the surplus is what is admired. Nor is moderation to be sought, of course, on the plane of practical reason, in limiting the amount of artistic activity, or the number of art works produced. Believing, as he does, that life is "good and pleasant,"[3] Aristotle could curb human activities and desire only where doing so would free other desires instrumental to a fuller self-realization.

The necessities of life and a measure of good fortune are certainly necessary to happiness, according to Aristotle, but he does not set any upper limits to prosperity. A prince or a man of great wealth has far more freedom than a man of modest means, and can enlarge the scale of his virtues, improving the happiness of his fellow citizens by his largesse or perhaps by helping to frame legislation that will increase the level of virtue or excellence in the state. To achieve this is the central aim of the *Nicomachean Ethics*. For though the end of the state is the same as that of the single man, the happiness of the state seems "something greater and more complete whether to attain or to preserve,"[4] and the prince or man of great fortune is in an exceptional position to further this end.

[1] *Op. cit., Nicomachean Ethics*, 1169a19–25.
[2] *Ibid.*, 1171a12.
[3] *Ibid.*, 1170a25.
[4] *Ibid.*, 1094b8.

Is Happiness an Activity or a State of Mind?

For the Stoics, happiness is a virtuous state of mind, variously described as tranquillity, imperturbability, independence, indifference, fortitude, harmony with the laws of the world, obedience to God, etc.[5] It is regarded as more or less permanent once it has been acquired, but it can last for a lifetime or for only a brief period. The perfection of happiness can be completely present at one time without continuing into future times, for if this were not so the Stoic's happiness would depend on his keeping alive, and would be overcast by uneasiness or anxiety. For the same reason, it does not depend on an active life, the development of talents and sensitivities, the pursuit of science or the arts. If it did, the Stoic would not be independent; he would be a slave to changing fortune. He will generally do his duty in the station to which he has been assigned, living strenuously, but, if thrown into a dark dungeon, he will be no less happy, since he is no less virtuous.

For Aristotle, on the other hand, happiness is *necessarily* an activity. It makes no small difference, Aristotle says, "whether we place the chief good in the possession or in use, in a state of mind or in activity. For the state of mind may exist without producing any good result, as in a man who is asleep or in some other way quite inactive."[6] Moreover, the possession of virtue seems compatible with "the greatest suffering and misfortunes; but a man who was living so no one would call happy, unless he were maintaining a thesis at all costs."[7] Thus, whereas the Stoics go as far as to argue that, since it is never experienced, death is no loss to anyone, Aristotle could say, as if in answer, that "death is the most terrible of all things."[8]

If the supreme good is an ongoing activity that is never completed, as Aristotle holds, then a man cannot view his own death with the indifference the Stoics require. It is like leaving the theater before the show is over, when he himself still has important parts to play, and everyone else remains to play theirs. Of course, there are compensations and extenuations. He may take comfort from the conviction that he has played his parts well, that people dear to him remain to honor him and carry on in his place, and that everyone will eventually have to leave while the lights are

[5] See Chapter 3 above for a general account of Stoicism, and for references to Stoic writings.
[6] *Ibid.*, 1092a2–1098b32.
[7] *Ibid.*, 1096a1–2.
[8] *Ibid.*, 1115a27.

on and the show is still humming. Happiness is never completed; unrequited desires must remain.

The Stoic happiness, on the contrary, is perfect and complete at any point in time. It is not cumulative—it has culminated and nothing can be added to it. There are no desires that do not find immediate satisfaction in the present, or that cannot be quickly transmuted into cheerful resignation, nor are there any anxieties about the future. A variety of metaphysical and psychological stratagems are devised to eliminate cravings and worries, to protect the composure of the sage, making his happiness self-sufficient at all times. His happiness is already complete and cannot be taken from him by death. It is a state of mind, not an activity. In being proof against death and disaster, it is like the perfect happiness enjoyed by the blessed in heaven, according to St. Augustine, St. Thomas, and other Christian writers. But the picture of perfect happiness on earth, arising amidst countless evils and uncertainties, is as fragile as it is appealing. Crumbling under the criticism of the other schools, especially the Middle Academy and the Epicureans, it is recast again with new arguments and patched up with compromises and concessions to psychology and common sense. Even in the same Stoic author, we can often find a portrait of happiness as perfect serenity, independence, and self-sufficiency, side by side with concessions that blur the picture but also give it plausibility.

Aristotelians must agree with the Stoics that, if happiness is an activity spurred on by desire, it is never complete until a man is dead, for it may be destroyed at any previous moment. No one's happiness, however virtuous he may be, Aristotle says, could bear up under the calamities suffered by old Priam at the end of the Trojan War. "Must no one at all, then, be called happy while he lives?" he asks.[9] But to suppose that a man is only happy when he is dead is absurd, especially when happiness is regarded as an activity. Moreover, if we should argue in this way, even the dead man's happiness would not be secure, for suppose great reverses overtook his descendants. The problem might be resolved in this way: Aristotle is inquiring under what circumstances we can say that happiness has been attained. We should hesitate to speak of a man's life as happy if he died without knowing the calamities that would overtake his children, for it would seem that he had been the victim of a grisly joke, and had lived in a fool's paradise. However, if we take the point of view of the man himself, we must say that the unknown disasters could not have spoiled his happiness.

At the same time, Aristotle insists that happiness is considered "something permanent and by no means easily changed." The happy man is not

9 *Ibid.*, 1100a10.

a chameleon, changing with every wind. What is it that can give happiness the required stability? His answer is similar to that of the Stoics, but also instructively different. The Stoics say that the wise man's virtue is indestructible, and, since happiness is simply this state of virtue, it, too, is indestructible. For Aristotle, also, it is virtue that gives stability to happiness:

> For no function of man has so much permanence as virtuous activities (these are thought to be more durable even than knowledge of the sciences), and of these themselves the most valuable are the more durable because those who are happy spend their lives most readily and continuously in these; for this seems to be the reason why we do not forget them.[10]

They readily and continuously prefer virtuous activity and contemplation to everything else because early training has instilled habits, which are further reinforced by the pleasantness of these habits: Because of his virtue, also, the happy man is resilient to adversity and can cheerfully bear misfortunes that would oppress others. Yet he is no cool, invulnerable Stoic. If too many great events turn out against him, "they crush and maim happiness; for they both bring pain and hinder many activities."[11] But even here "nobility shows through," Aristotle says, if he courageously bears his great misfortunes through nobility of soul, and not from "insensibility to pain."[12] This last qualification is important. The Stoic Sage, as often pictured, seems to shoulder misfortunes serenely only because he is impervious to pain, or as if his misfortunes were not really misfortunes after all. As far as these tendencies prevail in Stoic doctrine, there seems to be nothing for the happy man to endure or to be noble about.

In criticism of its Stoics, Augustine could thus write that

> to be quite free from pain while we are in this place of misery is only purchased . . . at the price of blunted sensibilities both of mind and body. . . . And if some, with a vanity monstrous in proportion to its rarity, have become so enamored of themselves because they can be stimulated and excited by no emotion, moved or bent by no affection, such persons rather lose all humanity than obtain true tranquillity. For a thing is not necessarily right because it is inflexible, nor healthy because it is insensible.[13]

This objection to Stoic doctrine, made also by philosophers of other schools, seems to reflect Aristotle's comment:

> People who fall short with regard to pleasures and delight in them less than they should are hardly found; for such insensibility is hardly human. Even

---

[10] *Ibid.*, 1100b11–16.
[11] *Ibid.*, 1100b28–29.
[12] *Ibid.*, 1100b32.
[13] *The City of God*, Book XIV, Ch. 9.

the other animals distinguish different kinds of food and enjoy some and not others; and if there is any one who finds nothing pleasant and nothing more attractive than anything else, he must be something quite different than a man.[14]

Aristotle goes on to describe the temperate man, who is a mean between the self-indulgent and the insensible. Whereas self-indulgence is a common failing, he says, insensibility is hardly to be found. What he is warning against is thus not a dangerous human tendency but an inhuman and absurd doctrine.

The attitude toward desire is of key importance. The Stoics hold that a state of virtue can be won and sustained by suppressing desires for things that lie beyond our power, whereas Aristotle contends that happiness is a continuous activity and that it is caused by desire, which must also be continuous. Few of these desires will be certain of satisfaction, for certainty does not belong to the practical sphere. The issue with the Stoics is even more sharply drawn when we remember that Aristotelian happiness requires that the activity be such as to develop and exercise the human faculties, especially the higher ones, and that this exercise is normally accompanied by pleasure, even though our leading desire remains unsatisfied—our main goal unattained. Unless there is some impediment, it is pleasant to walk, to employ eyes and ears, to think of the best course of conduct, or of what might be the shortest proof of a mathematical problem, whether or not success attends one's quest or remains only a hope for the future. We see now the deeper meaning of Aristotle's conclusion, already cited, that it makes a great deal of difference whether happiness is an activity or a state. "For the state of mind may exist without producing any good result, as in a man who is asleep or in some other way inactive."[15] The uncompromising Stoic position is that we must suppress all desires the outcome of which we cannot be certain. If we should and could succeed in this, Aristotle thinks, we should accomplish nothing. Without risks there is no victory, no achievement.

The tradition of eudaemonism and of the modern self-realization theory both reject the self-sufficiency of the happy man, and affirm happiness as a ceaseless striving. Thus, Rousseau points out that happiness may be self-sufficient, but not the happy man:

> If any imperfect creature were self-sufficing, what would he have to enjoy? To our thinking he would be wretched and alone. I do not see how anyone who has need of nothing could love anything, nor do I understand how he who loves nothing can be happy.[16]

14 *Op. cit.*, 1119a5–11.
15 *Ibid.*, 1099a1–2.
16 *Emile*, p. 182.

That man's chief good or happiness depends on a continual striving for what lies beyond, but not necessarily on the success of this striving, is well illustrated by Spinoza's goal, at infinity, of "the intellectual love of God," by man's long road to freedom and happiness in Hegel's philosophy, which we briefly sketched in Chapter 5, and by the angels' promise at the end of Goethe's *Faust,* Part 2, that

> Who e're aspiring, struggles on,
> For him there is salvation.

FULFILLMENT VS. SECURITY: STOIC VS. ARISTOTELIAN VIRTUE

The Stoics agree with Aristotle that virtue is the stuff of happiness: they disagree with him as to the nature of virtue. The original and distinctive doctrine of the Stoics is that virtue alone is sufficient to happiness, that nothing else is required. Virtue consists of a serene state of mind which nothing external can mar or disturb. Only the subjective intention matters, not the actual accomplishment of virtuous purposes. Either one has this intention or not; hence virtue is without degree and without kinds. Special virtues, such as justice, kindness, and courage, are recognized, but they tend to be subordinated or assimilated to the overall aim of acquiring one's own happiness, defined as a state of mind proof against suffering, fear, and disappointment, a state of mind that does not really care what happens in the external world. The virtues thus basically become only one virtue, a single-minded psychotherapeutic achievement of the individual—for himself.

Although the Stoics are reluctant to modify the clear logic of this prescription for happiness,[17] they are obliged, under vigorous attacks from other schools of philosophy, to make numerous concessions to psychology and common sense, which, it turns out, are not always consistent with it.

The happy man is supposed to be completely self-sufficient—independent of everything outside himself—but how can he be independent of his friends? If only virtues are good, and only vices evil, then the Stoic must class friends among the things that are indifferent to him—but how can we regard the existence and well-being of our friends with indifference? Stoic doctrine has to be developed so as to permit the happy man to be concerned with the fortunes of friends and fellowmen, while retaining, if possible, his complete self-sufficiency. Why retain the self-sufficiency? Without it, happiness would not be secure against changes in the external world, including friends and fellowmen. But why, then, concede that the happy

[17] As developed by Epictetus, for example. See Chapter 3 above.

man has a concern for the well-being of his friends? Because a happy man without friends would be too incredible. The question is, then, whether the two things can be consistently maintained.

We shall see in this section that insofar as they insist on the absolute self-sufficiency and other extreme doctrines contrived to support it, the Stoics and Aristotle are poles apart. When these are de-emphasized or toned down, on the other hand, Stoicism shows less originality, and resembles a thin image of the Platonic or the Aristotelian model. But even in the last of the Stoics, the Emperor Marcus Aurelius, we find the rigid self-sufficiency doctrine and a gospel of brotherly love side by side. Have they been reconciled or is this a *mariage forcée?* And are the special virtues—justice, courage, kindness, etc.—which are so highly praised, good on their own account or good only as they contribute to the self-sufficiency of the happy man? Or, can they be good in both respects? Insofar as self-sufficiency is the one goal, Stoic happiness is narrow, impoverished of content, merely negative and protective; if, on the other hand, the variety of particular virtues are made to carry their own endorsement, happiness is more variegated and ample, answering more specifically to the range of human needs and capacities. In the following passage from Aurelius, these questions come to a head:

> Suppose then that thou hast given up this worthless thing called fame, what remains that is worth valuing? This, in my opinion, to move thyself and to restrain thyself in conformity to thy proper constitution, to which end both all employments and arts lead. For every art aims at this, that the thing which has been made should be adapted to the work for which it has been made; and both the vine-planter who looks after the vine, and the horse-breaker, and he who trains the dog, seek this end. But the education and training of youth aim at something. In this then is the value of the education and the teaching. And if this is well, thou wilt not seek anything else. Wilt thou not cease to value many other things too? Then thou wilt be neither free, nor sufficient for thy own happiness, nor without passion. For of necessity thou must be envious, jealous, and suspicious of those who can take away these things, and plot against those who have that which is valued by thee. Of necessity a man must be altogether in a state of perturbation who wants any of these things; and besides, he must often find fault with the gods. But to reverence and honour thy own mind will make thee content with thyself, and in harmony with society, and in agreement with the gods, that is, praising all that they give and have ordered.[18]

Fame and fortune and all such fragile and ephemeral things, Aurelius says, are simply worthless. *What does have value is living in conformity with one's own proper constitution. Seek nothing else!*

[18] W. J. Baks (ed.), *The Stoic and Epicurean Philosophers, Meditations,* Book VI, 16.

STOIC POSITIONS AND THEIR PERILS

All the Stoics tell us to live in conformity with human nature, or with nature at large, and usually with both; but how are we to select from nature's prodigal varieties those that are truly "natural"—the exemplars that will be our guide to virtue and happiness? We can determine our "proper constitution," Aurelius says, by analogy with the arts. The end of an art, such as vine-growing, declares itself unmistakably; the natural end of man is no less evident. Whatever the logical force of this famous analogical argument in other cases, the Stoic use of it is open to obvious retorts. The hedonists—both Epicurean and utilitarian—could claim that man's natural end is pleasure, and the theological utilitarians of the eighteenth century contend that man is *made for pleasure*. What other end could God have had for creation? The analogical argument could lead to results which, for the Stoics, are simply despicable.

Moreover, Plato and Aristotle, who originally formulated the arts-crafts analogy, infer quite a different end for man, viz.: full development and exercise of all the faculties, especially the highest—disinterested reason.

The Stoic use of the analogy is especially vulnerable. How can it be argued, for example, that just as all the arts have an end that their own nature discloses, so man has a natural end apparent in his proper constitution, which involves his being indifferent to whether he is cold or warm, starves or eats, lives or dies? Yet this is Aurelius' idea of the proper condition of man:

> Let it make no difference to thee whether thou art cold or warm, if thou art doing thy duty . . . and whether dying or doing something else.[19]

And can it be concluded from man's constitution that one should never grieve at the death of one's child or friend, and never be fearful for their safety? Marcus Aurelius is far from recommending a callous disregard of suffering, as we shall see, and yet he plumps for complete autonomy to be gained by indifference to everything external, and friends and children are, of course, external. The same dilemma grips the thought of other Stoics. It is even more conspicuous in Epictetus, as we have seen in Chapter 3.

Living in conformity with one's "proper constitution" is not a clear guide to virtue, since unless you already know what virtue is you cannot know what is "proper." *Living according to nature* is not a clear signpost pointing the way convincingly to justice, courage, self-control, and independence of mind, since nature displays not only these virtues but also their opposites. Obeying God's will is also unsatisfactory, for God's will could be inter-

[19] *Ibid.*, 2.

preted differently by Stoics and critics of Stoicism. Fortunately, the Stoics do not need to depend on these supporting arguments, though they continue to use them.

They could fall back on their central ethical doctrine, which is independent of metaphysical and theological supports. This is what Aurelius seems to do in the long passage quoted above. After arguing from our "proper constitution," he goes on to another argument, which, as we have seen, Epictetus relies on almost exclusively—an argument that every man could test in his own experience, with visible results. If you value anything else than doing your duty in the station of life to which you have been assigned, Aurelius warns, you will be "envious, jealous and suspicious," full of "perturbation," which no one wants to be. You will be "neither free, nor sufficient for your own happiness." Desire only that which lies within your power, Epictetus says, and you will find a happiness proof against all adversity. An attractively simple prescription for the reverses and uncertainties of life! Unlike the complex Aristotelian theory of happiness, it ignores commonly recognized requirements of the good life, is inconsistent with beliefs of Stoic leaders themselves, and thus has to be continually revised.

When criticism is directed against the psychological possibility of preserving a state of joyful equanimity in the face of calamity and shipwreck, with death of dear ones, and disaster, a rather weak compromise is made: One thing is as acceptable as another, but some are *preferable* to others.

There is also the problem of how a man can be "free" and "sufficient for his own happiness," and yet subordinate to the good of society of which he is a part, and to which he owes service. The well-known historian of Stoicism, Eduard Zeller, points out that with the "the introduction of the idea of society, opposite tendencies arise in Stoic ethics—one towards individual independence, the other in the direction of a well-ordered social life. The former tendency is the earlier one, and continues throughout to predominate."[20] And yet the latter idea is not adventitious, Zeller says, but has basic roots in Stoicism. It is only because he is a rational being that the individual can become independent of everything external, including his fellowmen. But the reason that makes him free is also the reason of other men, and binds all together in a harmonious whole of which he is a very insignificant part. The individual, therefore, must not place his interests above the rational whole of which he is a mere part, but live for society. According to Aurelius, men are united by intelligence and sympathy.

> There is one soul, though it is distributed among infinite natures and
> individual circumscriptions (or individuals). There is one intelligent soul,

[20] *The Stoics, Epicureans and Sceptics,* p. 311.

though it seems to be divided . . . intellect in a peculiar manner tends to that which is of the same kin, and combines with it, and the feeling for communion is not interrupted.[21]

As a part of such a whole, Aurelius continues, and "intimately related to the parts which are of the same kind with myself, I shall do nothing unsocial . . . I shall turn all my efforts to the common interest." Life will flow on happily for one who serves his fellow citizens, "and is content with whatever the state may assign to him."[22]

The difficulty of retaining complete independence of external things, while living for others, and voluntarily subordinating oneself to the will of the state, speaks for itself, and other theories of happiness prefer to avoid such embarrassments by recognizing a certain dependence of external things from the first. This difficulty is closely connected with another.

How can the Stoic be just or fair or kind to his fellows, as he is in duty bound, if what happens in the external world is a matter of indifference to him? Acting justly, it would seem, is not merely a subjective intention, but involves a desire that a certain state of things should exist in the external world. Similarly, to act with kindness and humanity is to will that the distress of one's fellowmen actually be relieved. According to the usual Stoic doctrine, however, the Stoic is indifferent to everything external to his tranquil state of mind. Things are divided into good, evil, and indifferent. Only virtue, understood as subjective intention, is good; only vices are evil; everything else, including the *realization* of virtuous intentions, must accordingly be indifferent. The Stoic cannot consistently care whether or not the justice or kindness he intends is actually accomplished in the world. He cannot desire that the world be different through his actions, because to do so would be to expose himself to disappointment, and thus destroy his happiness, which is by definition, free from trouble.

The same result follows when the Stoic boldly asserts that things are not only all good but *equally* good. In this case, it does not matter to him if those he intends to help go on suffering, or if the injustice he intends to correct continues, for whatever happens is good, or at least necessary for the good. The wise man will, therefore, desire, as Epictetus says, only his own virtue. He cannot consistently desire, it would appear, that his desires be satisfied, *i.e.*, that his virtuous intentions be realized in the external world. Plato and Aristotle and most other philosophers, on the contrary, assume as obvious that to desire a thing and to be indifferent to its realization is a self-contradiction, or at least a serious confusion of thought.

If the Stoic is to refrain from all desires except those he can be certain of

21 *Op. cit.*, XII, 30.
22 *Ibid.*, X, 6.

realizing, must he not refrain from most virtuous desires—from all that aim to bring about good in the world or to remove evil? Or is virtue always realizable—even on the rack?

Stoic self-sufficiency and virtue thus are seen to be in conflict. Insofar as self-sufficiency is the aim, the virtues of justice, kindness, courage, temperance, etc., become simply means to the attainment of the peaceful isolation of sedate but joyful indifference, and are virtues only to the extent that they contribute to this result. If what the Stoics regard as injustice were to make a greater contribution, would it not be more virtuous? Insofar as the virtues, on the other hand, are valued for their own sake, the Stoic ideal comes closer to the variegated Aristotelian happiness, and loses its self-sufficiency.

The self-sufficiency ideal has had a great appeal, and even today it is often adjudged the aim of psychotherapy, viz., to render the individual independent of any changes of his physical and social surroundings. "The happy man," Aristotle says, "needs friends . . . and no one would choose the whole world on condition of being alone";[23] and yet no one can have a friend who is indifferent to whether he comes or goes, lives or dies. It is true that the Stoics also praise friendship on occasion. Cicero says that it is "the first and absolute essential . . . that we have the devotion of friends, who value our worth."[24] The big difference is that the Stoics can rule friendship absolutely essential only by forgetting about their primary objective of self-sufficiency.

The central self-sufficiency doctrine results in an impoverishment of the Stoic conception of happiness, for it implies that the variety of virtues have no worth of their own, and are to be pursued only insofar as they contribute to a permanent equanimity or indifference. The question indeed arises whether virtues such as justice and friendship do not lose their character completely. Aristotelian happiness, demanding full development and exercise of all the faculties, especially those that are most human, is a profusely rich pattern by comparison. The varieties of virtue are not only good for happiness but also good in themselves, and are desired for themselves. Thus, Aristotle says that

> honour, pleasure, reason, and every virtue we choose indeed for themselves (for if nothing resulted from them we should still choose each of them), but we choose them also for the sake of happiness, judging that by means of them we shall be happy. Happiness, on the other hand, no one chooses for the sake of these, nor, in general, for anything other than itself.[25]

[23] *Op. cit.*, 1169b22, 17.
[24] *De Officiis*, Book II, viii.
[25] *Op. cit.*, 1097b2–7.

Honor, pleasure, the exercise of reason and every virtue need not lead to happiness, for good fortune is also required; when happiness is realized they give it a structure physiognomic and expressive of the species. This pluralism of Aristotle also gives his ethics a concrete perceptual footing, and marks one of his main differences with Platonism. In criticizing Plato's theory that all good things are good by virtue of their participation in one Idea or Form of goodness, Aristotle says that, if "intelligence, sight, and certain pleasures and honours," are not good in themselves, and "nothing other than the Idea of good [is] good in itself," then the Form of good "will be empty." The account of one good thing will be the same as that of another. "But of honour, wisdom and pleasure, just in respect of their goodness, the accounts are distinct and diverse. The good, therefore, is not some common element answering to one Idea."[26]

It will be remembered, also, that, in contrast to the uniform nobility and stark simplicity of the Stoic posture, Aristotle describes no fewer than twelve diverse moral virtues, including wittiness or a sense of humor. Such virtues as courage, temperance, liberality, self-respect, gentleness, friendliness, and modesty are means between extremes, but they are means not only with respect to the extremes but also in relation to the situation, the seriousness of the issue and the stakes involved, and the natural propensities, training, wealth, office, and profession of the individual in question. Men may be naturally disposed to one extreme or the other, and the mean that is virtue for one may be impossible for another. Differences as to position, wealth, and *métier* also determine where the just mean lies for a given man. In a very wealthy man, ordinary liberality would be meanness; he must be magnificent in his outlay. The soldier who has been schooled in danger will be expected to be more courageous, at least in martial situations, than other citizens. Every virtuous man will, of course, possess all these virtues, but, realized in different men, they mirror their individuality as well as their common nature.

Only the common nature is recognized by the Stoics. Thus, though they assume with Aristotle that all men are capable of virtue, they can be charged with setting up a regimen available only to a few prodigies of will and self-discipline. They attack, to take a drastic example, Aristotle's program of regulating the emotions, insisting that what is evil, *i.e.*, contrary to reason, must not be moderated, but extirpated.[27] Anger, which in moderation becomes Aristotle's virtue of righteous indignation, is simply evil for the Stoics, and not needed in order to act against injustice.

The intellectual virtues add complexity and abundance to the Aristote-

[26] *Ibid.*, 1096b20–26.
[27] Cicero, *Tusculan Disputes*, iii, 10, 22; iv, 17, 39, 18, 42. See also Seneca, *Epistles*, 85, 5.

lian scheme. They represent the summit and culmination of human happiness, without which it remains incomplete and inhuman, since the most distinctive powers of man would remain unfulfilled. In contrast, it will be remembered, the Stoics dismiss all knowledge that is not practically useful, *i.e.*, that is not designed to promote moral virtue. If they elaborate a physics, a metaphysics, a psychology, and make important developments of logic, it is not because they value theoretic knowledge for its own sake, but in order to support and safeguard their practical ethical program. Epictetus tells us to throw away our books if they do not tell us how to make ourselves self-sufficient. Even the works of the great Stoic leader Chrysippus may leave the reader with mere knowledge, he says, and divert him from his one true concern, which is with desire and aversion. "Your work," he insists, lies in "desire and in aversion, that you may not be disappointed in your desire, and that you may not fall into that which you would avoid."[28] Chrysippus would have agreed. He objects that the intellectual life is only a refined pursuit of pleasure, which is almost the worst thing that a Stoic could say about a manner of living.

Another persistent tendency in Stoicism is to eliminate the degrees of both virtue and happiness. Diogenes, as we have seen, attributes to the Stoics the view "that between virtue and vice there is nothing intermediate, whereas according to the Peripatetics there is, namely, the state of moral improvement."[29] And if there is no such thing as a half-virtuous man, according to the Stoics, it follows that there cannot be a half-happy one either. Indeed, what could degrees mean if happiness depends on complete self-sufficiency, which nothing on earth can disturb? One either possesses perfect virtue and happiness, or one has nothing of either. Aristotle, too, as we have noted, talks of a happiness that is perfect and complete, but assigns it to the gods, not to "mere men." That happiness admits of degrees in his view is also quite evident, although he says very little about the subject. The hierarchy of faculties, however, furnishes a guide. The greatest as well as highest happiness is afforded by the activity of theoretic reason. It is not denied that a man who possesses the moral virtues, but not the intellectual, can be happy; it is only denied that he can have the highest happiness, for this belongs only to the man who possesses both moral and intellectual virtue. Children, on the other hand, are said to be incapable of happiness, insofar as reason in them is not sufficiently developed. Yet reason is developing in the child; rapid progress is being made. Similarly, the slave cannot be happy *qua* slave, that is, as long as he obeys his master's will, not his own. But Aristotle points out that slaves act freely on some occasions. Artisans and laborers are also excluded from happiness, but only insofar as they lack leisure and sufficient income.

28 *Op. cit.*, Book I, Ch. 4.
29 *Op. cit.*, 127, p. 231.

Probably it is more in accord with Aristotle's meaning to speak, in all these cases, of some degree of happiness, rather than of none at all. All men, it will be remembered, are capable of happiness insofar as they are not "maimed in their potentialities for virtue."

The harsh denunciation of pleasure by the Stoics marks, from the Peripatetic point of view, a further impoverishment of their idea of happiness. Cicero and Seneca explicitly attack the Aristotelian-like view that happiness is to be defined as virtue combined with pleasure. Cicero condemns this view as worse than the opinion that pleasure alone is good. "I maintain," he says, "that all sensual pleasure is opposed to moral rectitude.

> And therefore Calliphon and Diomachus, in my judgment, deserve the greater condemnation; they imagined that they should settle the controversy by coupling pleasure with moral rectitude; as well yoke a man with a beast! But moral rectitude does not accept such a union; she abhors it, spurns it. Why, the supreme good, which ought to be simple, cannot be a compound and mixture of absolutely contradictory qualities.[30]

In a similar rhetorical manner, Seneca denounces the idea that "the blending of virtue and pleasure into one" constitutes the highest good. "The honourable," he says, "can have no part that is not honourable," and would lose its integrity and power if it could.

> For it begins to need the help of Fortune, and this is the depth of servitude. . . . How is such a man to obey God and to receive in cheerful spirit whatever happens, and . . . never to complain of Fate, if he is agitated by the petty prickings of pleasure and pain? But he is not even a good guardian of his . . . friends if he has a leaning toward pleasures. . . . But Virtue is alone able to mount to this height.[31]

The main target of Cicero and Seneca, as of other Stoic writers, is *sensuous* pleasure. They are ready enough to assert that virtue brings the highest joy, a joy that eclipses all others, but they refuse to see this joy as anything akin to pleasure, which they condemn or dismiss as sensuous and unworthy, at least when it is relished and pursued. In itself it is neither good nor bad, but indifferent. But is not the pleasure attending the satisfaction of natural wants itself natural, and therefore good? Sextus Empiricus concludes that "the Stoics hold pleasure to be a thing indifferent and not preferred in that class; Cleanthes held that it is not according to nature, any more than a wig or rouge, and has no value in life; Archedemus admitted it to be according to nature in precisely the same sense as the hairs which grow in the armpits; Panaetius distinguished between

---

[30] *De Officiis*, Book III, 119.
[31] "On the Happy Life," in *Moral Essays*, XIV–XV, 5.

pleasures according to nature and pleasures contrary to nature."[32] The variety of opinion on the subject signalizes a serious conflict in Stoic thought. They are morally fascinated by the Socratic-Platonic dualism, which they take to imply that reason and pleasure are opposites and incompatible. But can this dualism be reconciled with their monistic doctrine that it is the world soul, rational and good throughout, that is responsible for all the works and orderings of nature—a doctrine that removes at one stroke all external bars to happy self-sufficiency?

THE DEPENDENCE OF HAPPINESS ON FORTUNE AND EXTERNAL GOODS

We have here several interrelated questions: Are external goods and fortune, in some amount, *necessary* to happiness, or are they completely *unnecessary and irrelevant*? The former position is taken by Aristotle and by most other philosophers who discuss the matter; the latter is maintained only by the Cynics and Stoics, by St. Thomas and other Christian philosophers, in speaking of the ideal of the monastic life or of the happiness of the blessed in heaven, and by certain schools of Indian thought. The first position is supported by common-sense considerations; the latter, by quite a variety of philosophical or theological considerations. We shall be concerned in our brief discussion of this issue mainly with the representative contrast between the view of Aristotle, on the one hand, and the Stoics and St. Thomas, on the other.

When it is conceded that some amount of external goods and fortune is necessary for happiness, it is usually held that only a modest amount is *needed,* and the addition of more is of doubtful value. In the centuries preceding the Industrial Revolution, in fact, the tendency was to think wealth and high position a greater hazard to virtue and happiness than privation and poverty. We shall review briefly the typical arguments against luxuries and in favor of the simple life, and suggest why they have lost their popularity in recent times. By the time of Bentham we shall f happiness associated, not with modest means but with abundance.

Another related issue on which there has been a change of conviction will be touched on. This is the issue as to which ways of getting money are "natural," good, economically and ethically justifiable.

ARE EXTERNAL GOODS AND FORTUNE NECESSARY TO HAPPINESS?

Aristotle's words are fairly typical of the affirmative answer. External goods are needed

[32] *Outlines of Pyrrhonism,* XI, 73.

for it is impossible, or not easy, to do noble acts without the proper equipment. In many actions we use friends and riches and political power as instruments; and there are some things the lack of which takes the lustre from happiness, as good birth, goodly children, beauty; for the man who is very ugly in appearance or ill-born or solitary and childless is not very likely to be happy, and perhaps a man would be still less likely to be happy if he had thoroughly bad children or friends or had lost good children or friends by death . . . happiness seems to need this sort of prosperity in addition.[33]

Happiness is not overturned by small misfortunes, but great ones "crush and maim" it. Greatness of soul may enable a man to endure hardships with noble resignation, but there would be no nobility in it if he did not suffer, if his happiness were not affected by disaster.[34]

The opposite is maintained by the Cynics and Stoics. Virtue alone is good, and vice alone is evil, according to Antisthenes, and all else is a matter of indifference.[35] A man requires only virtue to be happy. We have seen that the dominant view of the Stoics is the same. It remains dominant even when it is conceded, with doubtful consistency, that wealth and the gifts of fortune are *preferable* to poverty and misfortune; for the Stoic can still maintain that the former are not *necessary* to happiness. Thus Seneca, himself a very rich man, says that

> the wise man does not think himself undeserving of any of the gifts of Fortune. He does not love riches, but he would rather have them; he does not admit them to his heart, but to his house, and he does not reject the riches he has, but he keeps them and wishes them to supply ampler material for exercising his virtue.[36]

The wise man will prefer riches to poverty, since poverty allows for only one virtue—the virtue of not being "bowed down and crushed by it, whereas riches give a wider scope to liberality, diligence, grandeur and orderliness. Do not, therefore make a mistake—riches are among the more desirable things. . . . As a favorable wind, sweeping him on, gladdens the sailor, as a bright day and a sunny spot in the midst of winter and cold give cheer, just so riches have their influence upon the wise man and bring him joy." If, however, the ordinary rich man fails to see anything out-of-the-way in this attitude, Seneca replies:

> In my case, if riches slip away, they will take from me nothing but themselves, while if they leave you, you will be dumbfounded, and you will feel that you have been robbed of your true self; in my eyes riches have a certain

[33] *Op. cit.*, 1099a32–1099b8.
[34] *Ibid.*, 1100b23–32.
[35] See Diogenes Laertius, *Lives of Eminent Philosophers*, vi, 104.
[36] *Op. cit.*, xxi, 2.

place, in yours they have the highest; in fine, I own my riches, yours own you.[37]

Although Seneca says, as Aristotle before him, that wealth enables the wise man to perform certain virtues on a larger scale, and is desirable on that account, he also claims that virtue and happiness are in no way disturbed if all of it is lost. Would any among the Stoic wise men, he asks, deny "that even those things we call 'indifferent' do have some inherent value, and that some are more desirable than others? To some of them we accord little value, to others much."[38]

The logic of this position has invited obvious criticism. If riches, far from being a matter of indifference, bring the wise man joy and cheer, how can their disappearance take from him only themselves, and nothing else? It is also pointed out that Seneca himself stoops to gross flattery of Nero to retain his place and possessions, but this *ad hominem* argument does not tend to discredit the Stoic doctrine unless it can be shown that other Stoic leaders are also unable to combine a keen appreciation of riches with an indifference to their loss.

Seneca also concedes that health, beauty of person, strength, and even pleasure are desirable and that they contribute to happiness. "The wise man will prefer to be tall than to be a dwarf, strength of body to feebleness, good health to illness. They contribute something to happiness, though they are trifles in comparison with the whole, and can be withdrawn without destroying the essential good." Pleasure is another such trifle.[39]

We see again that, insofar as the Stoics forget for a moment their doctrine of the autarchy or self-sufficiency of the virtuous man, they tend to recognize the same factors of happiness that we find in Aristotle's account. But whether they are insisting on it or momentarily forgetting about it, they continue to hold that external goods and fortune, though they may be *preferable*, are not *necessary* to happiness.

The same thesis is also embodied in the Christian ideal of the ascetic life, though here the goal and wherefore are transcendental. It will be remembered that Jesus counseled the rich young man: "If thou wilt be perfect, go and sell all thou hast, and give it to the poor, and thou shalt have treasure in heaven; and come and follow me." The young man went away sadly, because of his great possessions, and Jesus then said "that a rich man shall hardly enter the kingdom of heaven" (Matt. 19:20–24). Augus-

---

[37] *Ibid.*, xxii.

[38] *Ibid.*

[39] See *ibid.* Pleasures of the wise man must be approved by reason, which delights in temperance, but temperance "reduces our pleasures." To the hedonist, Seneca retorts: "You embrace pleasure, I enchain her; you enjoy pleasure, I use it; you think it the highest good, I do not think it even a good; you do everything for the sake of pleasure, I, nothing" (*ibid.*, x, 2).

tine and Aquinas conclude, in the words of the latter, that "the religious state is an exercise and discipline to the attaining of the perfection of charity." To attain this perfection "it is necessary that a man wholly withdraw his affections from worldly things,"[40] for the love of earthly things stimulates desire for them, and thus diverts from the love and service of God.

In arguing that poverty is necessary for the religious life, Aquinas brings up a number of objections to this conclusion. For example, does not wealth contribute to man's "ultimate perfection"? Liberality and noble offices require property, according to Aristotle, and so does Christian almsgiving. How then can poverty be necessary to perfection? Scripture itself seems to say that in giving a man should hold back that which he himself needs (II Cor. 8:12 and I Tim 6:8); and that poverty exposes a person to the danger of spiritual sin, viz.: theft and the denial of God (Eccles. 27:1 and Prov. 30:9); and Aristotle can be quoted to the effect that to give too much is to ruin one's life. Moreover, the episcopal state is considered "more perfect than the religious state," yet bishops are allowed to have property.

Replying to these objections, Aquinas explains:

> Happiness or felicity is twofold. One is perfect, to which we look forward in the life to come; the other is imperfect, in respect of which some are said to be happy in this life.[41]

The happiness of this life, which is active, does require external goods, but the contemplative happiness does not; and Aquinas supports his position by citing Aristotle. Although the exercise of the *moral* virtues requires external goods, Aristotle says, "the man who is contemplating the truth needs no such thing, at least with a view to the exercise of his activity; indeed, they are, one may say, even hindrances, at all events, to contemplation."[42]

It is Aquinas' contention that possessions hinder the attainment of charity "by enticing and distracting the mind." But man, he says, "is directed to future happiness by charity; and since voluntary poverty is an

---

[40] *Summa Theologica*, II, 2, Q186, A3.

[41] *Ibid.*, Reply to Obj. 4.

[42] *Op. cit.*, 1178b3–7. Aquinas is comparing Aristotle's contemplative man, who contemplates the subject matter of science and philosophy, with the religious, who contemplates God in this life with a view to perfection and happiness in the next, in one respect, viz.: The contemplation in neither case requires external goods, and may be hindered by them insofar as they disturb the quiet of the soul. It should be remembered, however, that Aristotle's contemplative man needs a private income to support both his moral virtues and the leisure required for theoretic activity. The religious, on the other hand, needs no personal income since he has institutional support.

efficacious exercise for the attaining of perfect charity, it follows that it is of great avail in acquiring the happiness of heaven."[43]

The fact that the poverty is voluntary is important. Spiritual danger arises when the poverty is *not* voluntary. It is in this case that *they will become rich, fall into temptation and into the snare of the devil* (I Tim. 9). Nor do those who voluntarily embrace poverty risk loss of health and sustenance. For "bodily danger does not threaten those who, intent on following Christ, renounce all their possessions and entrust themselves to divine providence."[44] The renunciation is to be complete. The Apostle (II Cor. 8:12) must not be taken to imply that every man is to give alms "according to what a man hath," and hold back what he needs for himself. He fears that the weak will not be capable of renouncing all their temporal goods; he does not mean that it is not better to give all. As for the objection that bishops are allowed to have property, Aquinas points out that the episcopal state has as its object, not the acquiring of perfection but the administration of temporal as well as spiritual things, and that to this end wealth is instrumental. When perfection is the end, he adds, the Aristotelian mean in giving is raised to a new dimension, the degree being proportionate to the value of the end in view.

Aquinas, like the Stoic, upholds a perfect happiness, independent of possessions—even of the means of life, and both argue that possessions tend to divert and entice the soul from its highest goal. But the Stoic goal of self-sufficiency and perfect happiness *on earth* appears both foolish and impious to Christian philosophers, while the reliance on a perfection beyond nature and not based on perception would have been rejected by the Stoics, and is, in fact, rejected by Marcus Aurelius as idle speculation.

Is Happiness Favored by Modest Means and Fortune or by Abundance?

It might be expected that in periods in which economic goods are in short supply, at least for most men, and the fortunes of life uncertain, we should be told that *more* goods and greater security are prime requisites for happiness. As a matter of fact, we hear much more about the moral hazards of wealth, the corruption caused by luxuries, and the folly of making one's happiness dependent on position and possessions. We have listened to the warnings and admonitions of the Stoics, and to Aquinas' arguments for the utter poverty of the religious life. But even those philosophers who concede that external goods are essential to happiness tend to limit them to bare

[43] *Loc. cit.*
[44] *Op. cit.* Reply to Obj. 2.

essentials, and to praise a simple life with few needs. Even the Epicureans, having no religious motive, rule that only necessaries and a few comforts are productive of happiness, most comforts and all luxuries being hindrances. The motif of renunciation running through many Christian centuries is expressed in New Testament passages, such as:

> And having food and raiment let us be therewith content. But they that will be rich fall into temptation and a snare, and into many foolish and hurtful lusts, which drown men in destruction and perdition.
>
> For the love of money is the root of all evil, they have erred from the faith, and pierced themselves through with many sorrows (I Tim. 9–10).

In a very different vein, Socrates consigns the Guardians of his Republic to poverty. Those who are alone fit to rule the "perfect" state must have no property except what is "absolutely necessary. . . .

> And they alone of all the citizens may not touch or handle silver or gold, or be under the same roof with them, or wear them, or drink from them. And this will be their salvation, and they will be the saviours of the State. But should they ever acquire homes or lands or moneys of their own, they will become housekeepers and husbandmen instead of guardians, enemies and tyrants instead of allies of the other citizens; hating and being hated, plotting and being plotted against, and they will pass their whole life in much greater terror of internal than of external enemies, and the hour of ruin, both to themselves and to the rest of the State, will be at hand.[45]

Their poverty will not only be necessary for the State; it will be best for the Guardians themselves. The philosophers who devote themselves to contemplation, exercising the highest faculty, will not only guard the happiness of the State but will themselves be the happiest of all the members of the State. The artisans too will not have too much property. If they do they will not care to work. Similarly, the State must not have more than it needs; for if it is rich it will excite the envy and cupidity of its neighbors, and will be involved in unnecessary wars.

Plato's arguments have often been repeated, but there is no occasion to follow the history of their influence. But let us turn, for a moment, to a similar passionate denunciation of luxuries and unproductive wealth in modern times. Jean-Jacques Rousseau regards happiness as a life of virtue attended with pleasure (when it is above the level of primitive simplicity), but this virtue does not include, of course, the theoretic virtue, which for Plato and Aristotle is the summit of human achievement. While they are especially interested in the few who live for contemplation, he is mostly concerned with the many who toil and go hungry. "Luxury," Rousseau says,

[45] *Op. cit., Republic,* 417.

is in itself the greatest of all evils, for every State, great or small; for, in order to maintain all the servants and vagabonds it creates, it brings oppression and ruin on the citizen and labourer . . . and sooner or later depopulates the State.[46]

Owing to the establishment and sanctity of private property, Rousseau says, great crimes first become the order of the day: "assassinations, poisonings, highway robberies, and even the punishments inflicted on the wretches guilty of these crimes."[47] "For, according to the axiom of the wise Locke, *There can be no injury, where there is no property.*"[48] The desire for superfluities and delicacies now becomes insatiable. The great man must have "immense wealth, then subjects, then slaves." And

> the less natural and pressing his wants, the more headstrong his passions, and, still worse, the more he has it in his power to gratify them; so that after a long course of prosperity, after having swallowed up treasures and ruined multitudes, the hero ends by cutting every throat till he finds himself, at last, sole master of the world. Such is in miniature the moral picture, if not of human life, at least of the secret pretensions of the heart of civilized man.[49]

Conveniences produced by the progress of the arts also had the effect of enervating and enslaving both mind and body. They lost

> with use almost all their power to please, and even degenerated into real needs, till the want of them became far more disagreeable than the possession of them had been pleasant. Men would have been unhappy at the loss of them, though the possession did not make them happy.[50]

Yet it was not Rousseau's mature intention to condemn the institution of property and the fruits of civilization. His brilliant essay from which we have just quoted was rather a denunciation of the inequalities of wealth, which left grinding toil and poverty on one side, and parasitic depravity and licentiousness on the other, and had so perverted the image of man that no trace of his original goodness appeared. Rousseau's solution was not a return to the so-called primitive state of man, to a life of instinct, which would have been too absurd as a program, but rather the reinstatement of an idyllic pastoral era, a golden age, which would combine something of the simplicity of primitive life with improvements, moral and material, made possible by civilization. In later works, Rousseau no longer condemned the arts, but he continued to praise the simple life free from cares

[46] *On the Origin of Inequality*, p. 244.
[47] *Ibid.*, p. 242.
[48] *Ibid.*, p. 213.
[49] *Ibid.*, p. 241.
[50] *Ibid.*, p. 211.

and superfluities. The appealing picture he drew of the simple joys of the poor was, at the same time, a pointed criticism of the extravagance of the French Court, which was doing its best to impoverish the richest nation in Europe; it made him the hero of all the forces which were moving toward reform and revolution. As popularly interpreted he also gave strong support to the "back to nature" movement and to the cult of "the noble savage," which idealized life in the wilds and the character of the savage.

The fire and vehemence of Rousseau's polemic against luxury stems largely from the implied inequality of wealth, and the impoverishment of the many. If luxuries debase the few who can afford them, he seems to argue, their effect on the rest of the population is far worse. The extreme inequalities of wealth, which divide the State into two hostile factions, is also the key to Socrates' passionate denunciation of extravagance. The tendency of timocracy to degenerate into plutocracy comes about through "the accumulation of gold in the treasury of private individuals." Those who had prized honor before everything now love money more, and they vie with one another to accumulate the largest fortune. "They invent illegal modes of expenditure" not permitted to the defenders of the State, "for what do they or their wives care about the law?"[51] The rich become richer and the poor, poorer, and the government is directed, not by knowledge but by the desire of the few. There thus comes about "the inevitable division; such a State is not one, but two States, the one of poor, the other of rich men; and they are living on the same spot and always conspiring against one another."[52]

Such a State will not be able to defend itself, either, for the oligarchs are unused to fighting and love money more, nor will they dare to arm the people. And all this degeneracy will overtake the State, Socrates argues, if officers and heroes are given a taste of luxuries and exposed to the lure of money. He therefore specifies in detail that they are not to be permitted luxuries of any kind, neither Syracusan dinners nor Athenian confectionary nor any other refinements of life, and "to have a Corinthian girl as his fair friend"[53] also is definitely forbidden. Socrates was indeed a great admirer of Spartan austerity, and seems not to have noticed that Spartan generals, precisely because of their poverty, succumbed again and again to bribery by the enemy.

Later philosophers often echo Plato's warnings that license and an interest in money are the ruin of valor, yet the lack of sufficient pay, or of prompt payment, or a share of spoils, etc., are as commonly claimed to dampen martial ardor. Property, Aristotle observes, can be a great incentive

[51] *Republic*, VIII, 550.
[52] *Ibid.*, 551.
[53] *Ibid.*, 405.

to courage, and men are braver when they have something to fight for. When the battle becomes desperate, it is the untrained citizens who will continue to defend their homes, he says, while their allies, the professional soldiers, falter and retreat. Among the few who have raised their voice on this side of the argument is the philosopher-economist David Hume. Luxuries and the arts, he contends, have not spoiled the fighting spirit of the French and English, "whose bravery is as incontestable as is their love of the arts, and their assiduity in commerce . . . and industry," which are nourished by luxury.[54]

The reasons offered for rejecting riches and luxuries run through endless variations, but they seem to be summed up under the following headings: They are hostile to happiness because

(1) they destroy a man's independence and peace of mind, fill him with anxiety and leave him cruelly exposed to the turns of fortune;

(2) they distract and entice men from higher activities—intellectual and aesthetic—since they trammel the mind with cares;

(3) the pleasure possessions afford thus conflict with other pleasures which are more durable and dependable and less mixed with pain;

(4) possessions and luxuries spoil the simple joys of a life close to nature;

(5) they encourage idleness and quench the spirit of industry;

(6) they engender passions repugnant to happiness—greed, ambition, envy, servility, hatred—and invite war and plunder;

(7) they divide every city and nation into hostile factions, the rich and the poor, the rich becoming ever richer and the poor poorer, until civil war ensues;

(8) they undermine real friendship, sympathy, cooperation among men;

(9) honor, valor, and martial enterprise on which the happiness of the individual and the state depend, are weakened, and;

(10) the love of wealth lures men from the love of God, and endangers salvation.

These contentions, or most of them, were answered, not so much by counterarguments as by historical developments. For many centuries men had either rejected progress or seen it as possible for men only in the sphere of moral or intellectual improvement. But, beginning with the nineteenth century, when the Industrial Revolution and the Agricultural Revolution had revealed, to the farsighted at least, that economic production could, for the first time in history, be expanded to satisfy the needs of the whole population, a change of attitude became apparent. Reformers were less worried about the evils of luxury and too much wealth than about the evils

[54] See "Of the Refinement in the Arts," *Essays, Moral, Political and Literary*, pp. 281, 284.

of poverty and too little wealth. They could denounce the pauperization of the wage earners and poor who made up a great part of the population of rich industrial nations, since in terms of the productive potential it was avoidable. It was not unnecessary wealth, or luxuries, or the delicacies and refinements of life that menaced happiness, but rather the fact that only a few had them while the rest went without, or lacked even necessities. Formerly, these superfluities were condemned because they were necessarily in short supply, and thus divided society into two hostile factions—the haves and the have-nots. But, now, increasingly, what was denounced was not these civilized trimmings and adornments of life but rather the predatory or myopic policies that prevented the whole population from enjoying them.

It is now pretty obvious that modern productivity and productive potential, aided by the spread of democracy, have largely discredited or deflected the old arguments against possessions and luxuries. Let us hear from one outstanding representative of the new outlook.

Jeremy Bentham, whose utilitarianism we have already discussed, was one of the strongest opponents of asceticism in general, and of property-asceticism in particular. J. S. Mill called him "the great subversive." He not only carried out a broad frontal attack on all forms of "the principle of asceticism," which stands for the restriction of pleasure; he and his followers also spent years in laborious endeavor, eventually quite successful, to effect the repeal of laws embodying that principle, and to see that new laws aiming at the general happiness were enacted.

The business of government, Bentham teaches, is to promote the greatest happiness of the greatest number, and it does so chiefly by guarding against pains, for "the care of his enjoyments ought to be left almost entirely to the individual."[55] In promoting happiness, four subordinate ends—Subsistence, Abundance, Equality, and Security—demand attention. Subsistence and Security are the most basic, for there could be no Abundance or Equality without them, yet it is through the latter that the general happiness is realized and expanded.

No laws are needed to compel men to seek abundance, Bentham says, for the attraction of pleasure and the accumulation of new wants, while the old are being satisfied, drive men naturally to new acquisitions. Far from "dulling the edge of husbandry," acquisitions sharpen zeal.

> Desires extend with means. The horizon elevates itself as we advance. . . . Opulence, which is only a comparative term, does not arrest this movement once begun. On the contrary, the greater our means, the greater the scale on which we labour. . . . Now what is the wealth of society, if not the sum of

[55] *The Theory of Legislation*, p. 95.

all individual wealth? And what is more necessary than the force of these natural motives, to carry wealth, by successive movements, to the highest possible point?

It appears that abundance is formed little by little, by the continued operation of the same causes which produce subsistence. Those who blame abundance under the name of luxury, have never looked at it from this point of view.[56]

Those who condemn luxuries also forget the security they provide, and the vulnerability of countries that produce no superfluities.

But countries in which luxury abounds, and where governments are enlightened, are above the risk of famine. Such is the happy situation of England. With a free commerce, toys useless in themselves have their utility, as a means of obtaining bread. Manufactures of luxury furnish an assurance against famine. A brewery or a starch-factory might be changed into a means of subsistence.[57]

Bentham's insertion of the phrase "where governments are enlightened" warns us that abundance does not by itself ensure the general happiness. Where luxuries are not attended by a measure of equality in rights and income, they may go hand in hand with starvation.

His remark that "opulence . . . is only a comparative term" is very important in the context. The comforts and luxuries of one time become necessities in a later period. Under modern conditions of economic growth and diversification, all these terms are relative, and what is assailed as wasteful or sinful indulgence at one time becomes, at another, an essential item in the minimum inventory of a decent life. The historical shift in the meaning of "necessities" was clearly recognized by Marx, when he wrote:

The number and extent of the labourer's so-called necessary wants, as also the mode of satisfying them, are themselves the product of historical development, and depend therefore to a great extent on the civilization of a country, more particularly on the conditions under which, and consequently on the habits and the degree of comfort in which, the class of free labourers has been formed. In contradistinction therefore to the case of other commodities, there enters into the determination of the value of labour-power a historical and moral element.[58]

The "historical and moral element" evidently consists of expectations and habits engendered by economic and social development, and what is a luxury of the rich in one country may, in another, be the natural expectation of everyone.

[56] *Ibid.*, p. 101.
[57] *Ibid.*, p. 102.
[58] *Capital*, 1, p. 90.

The problem for the consistent utilitarian is to determine which distribution of wealth will maximize the total pleasure or happiness of society. Assuming that the distribution of wealth in a society has long existed, Bentham derives from the utility principle five propositions as to "the effect of a portion of wealth upon happiness":

(1) For each unit of wealth there is a corresponding amount of happiness, or "a certain chance of happiness."

(2) Given men of contrasting fortunes, those who are richer will be the happier. If this were not so, men would not care for wealth beyond a certain amount.

(3) "The excess happiness of the richer will not be so great as the excess of his wealth." Thus a landowner who has an income greater than the combined income of a thousand farm laborers who work for him may enjoy much more happiness than any one of these men, but surely not so much as the sum total of their happiness.

(4) "The greater the disproportion between two masses of wealth, the less it is probable that there exists a disproportion equally great between the corresponding masses of happiness."

(5) "The nearer the actual proportion approaches equality, the greater will be the total mass of happiness."[59]

The more equal the distribution of wealth the greater the sum of happiness, but this is obvious only where the distribution is age-old. It does not mean that happiness could be maximized by *re*distributing wealth on an equal basis in a society long accustomed to inequality. Where property rights are old and long protected by law and custom, confiscation may entail, for men of property, pains of disappointed expectation that outweigh, Bentham holds, the gains of equality for the whole society. Thus the process of equalizing wealth would not necessarily increase the total happiness of a society. Moreover, the very principle of Security on which civilized life depends—the principle that assures men the enjoyment of the fruit of their labor—would be put in jeopardy. The consequences could be far-reaching.

There is another principle of Bentham's that has a bearing on the redistribution of wealth: The loss of happiness suffered by a man due to the confiscation of a part of his property will be in proportion to the amount of property he has left. It follows that, if a man gains a sum of money from another of equal fortune, there is a net loss of happiness; the fraction representing the winner's gain will be smaller than that which represents the loser's loss. This unfavorable factor must be taken into account in any contemplated redistribution of wealth. If it deprives the loser of his

[59] *Op. cit.,* pp. 105–106.

subsistence, the loss of happiness may be regarded as infinite. And, in general, the poorer a man is the more he stands to lose by the alienation of a portion of his property. "If the richer is the loser," on the other hand, "the evil done by an attack on security will be compensated in part by the good which will be great in proportion to the progress toward equality."[60] It follows that, if there is to be a redistribution of wealth, any gain in the sum total of happiness will be greater to the degree that inequalities are reduced.

Bentham's arguments for equality are adopted, revised, and reduced to mathematical form by W. Stanley Jevons[61] and by many other economists. They furnish theoretical justification for the present-day graduated income tax and welfare legislation, designed to bring about a more equitable distribution of the national income. Their special interest for us, in the present inquiry, is that they constitute a vigorous answer to centuries of attacks on luxuries and possessions. There is absolutely nothing wrong with them, Bentham implies, except that most people do not have enough of them or else do not know how to enjoy them, which is a deficiency that education is able to correct. Indeed, abstracting from special circumstances, happiness is increased by wealth.

The feasibility of an economy of abundance could be seen in the nineteenth century by men of vision. In the fourth century B.C., on the other hand, there was no example or prospect of an economy of abundance. Every city, as Plato said, was in fact divided into two cities, a few rich who lived in plenty and the many poor who barely subsisted. The only conceivable alternative was the distribution of the very limited income of the State among the citizens on an equal basis, or with an approach to equality, but this meant reducing everyone to a rather bleak Spartan regimen. There were simply not enough goods produced to divide so that everyone, including artisans and laborers (not to speak of slaves), would get a decent share of the good things of life. The complete lack of education of the laboring section of the population of Greek cities also rendered equalitarianism unattractive. It was easy to believe that these uneducated men were what they seemed—naturally inferior, lacking in nobility. In the light of such circumstances, Aristotle's discussion of the topic concedes more to equality, in the end, than one would expect.

Phaleas of Chalcedon, Aristotle says, was the first to recognize that revolution might be warded off by equalizing the possessions of citizens. This would be difficult to accomplish in a State already established, but might be easily introduced in a new colony. Plato's *Republic*, as we have seen, reduces the Guardians to an equality of poverty, while the *Laws*

60 *Ibid.*, p. 108.
61 See *Theory of Political Economy*.

forbids any citizen to possess more than five times the amount held by the poorest. Aristotle raises a number of objections to the regulation of property. Reformers are apt to forget, he says, that laws limiting property of a man must also limit the number of his children. Moreover, rich men whose fortunes have been confiscated will be inclined to stir up revolution, and the nobles will think themselves worthy of a larger share. It seems clear that men will desire to possess a lot more than they need, and that therefore

> the legislator ought not only to aim at equalization of properties, but at moderation in their amount. . . . [But this] will be no nearer the mark; for it is not the possessions but the desires of mankind which require to be equalized, and this is impossible, unless a sufficient education is provided by the laws. But Phaleas will probably reply that this is precisely what he means, and that, in his opinion, there ought to be in states, not only equal property, but equal education.[62]

Aristotle quickly dismisses this alternative, which is a little surprising, since he elsewhere insists that the State should undertake the education of the youth and that wise laws can inculcate virtue.[63] Moreover, the best laws will be ineffective "unless the young are trained by habit and education in the spirit of the constitution, if the laws are democratical, democratically, or oligarchically, if the laws are oligarchical."[64] The main thing in either case is to train youth to honor the constitution. Democracies of the extreme type, however, become unconstitutional regimes. "Men think that what is just is equal; and that equality is the supremacy of the popular will; and that freedom means the doing what a man likes. . . . But this is all wrong; men should not think it slavery to live according to the rule of the constitution; for it is their salvation."[65]

Manifest in all Aristotle's criticism of democracy is his conviction that men are fundamentally unequal. "The beginning of reform," he says, "is not so much to equalize property as to train the nobler sort of natures not to desire more, and to prevent the lower from getting more; that is to say, they must be kept down, but not ill-treated."[66] On the other hand, he also believes that men should be "molded" in accordance with the government under which they live, even if it is democratic and egalitarian:

> And since the whole city has one end . . . education should be one and the same for all, and . . . should be public . . . not private . . . the

[62] *Op. cit., Politics,* 1266b27–33.
[63] See, for example, *ibid., Nicomachean Ethics,* Book X, 9.
[64] *Ibid., Politics,* 1310a16–18.
[65] *Ibid.,* 1310a30–36.
[66] *Ibid.,* 1267b5–9.

training in things which are of common interest should be the same for all.[67]

Though Aristotle also says that private education is better than public insofar as men are to carry out different functions, this does not conflict with his judgment that all citizens, as citizens, should receive the same training in self-restraint and the moderation of desire. On this central point, therefore, he does not seem to disagree much with Phaleas after all.

The agreement on this central point also reduces or eliminates other disagreements. To Phaleas' contention that it is disparities of possessions that produce highwaymen,[68] Aristotle replies that "the greatest crimes are caused by excess and not by necessity. Men do not become tyrants in order that they may not suffer cold."[69] But if this is so, will not the universal public education recommended by Aristotle as well as Phaleas be able to correct in youth the excesses of potential tyrants? It seems clear that Aristotle's healthy fear of revolution, shared, of course, by Bentham, and indeed most other philosophers, has two roots. First, he is dismayed by the bloody strife that has disrupted constitutional government and order in so many Greek cities. Second, revolutions usually (though not always) brought into power uneducated men, unrestrained in their passions, whom Aristotle regards as ignoble. His own preference is for an enlightened, constitutional, aristocratic government, but he sees that such a regime would be more secure and stable if it contained certain democratic elements.

The wealth of the State should be moderate, Aristotle says. It should not be so great as to excite the envy of its neighbors, but yet great enough to repel invasion. "Abundance of wealth is a great advantage," but only within limits. The wealth of the individual, on the other hand, is not restricted. Riches are not *needed* for happiness, but they are useful and facilitate special virtues, though they belong of necessity to a very few. Aristotle does not object to luxuries in the few, and it is hard to see how he could have objected to luxuries for the many as well, had he conceived it to be possible. Had an economy of abundance, such as obtains in the United States and Europe today, been on hand or in prospect, and had good examples existed of the salutary effects of the universal public education he so warmly recommended, it is easy to believe that his views might not have been too far removed from those of Bentham and Mill, and Dewey—or even Galbraith. There is no egalitarian principle in Aristotle comparable to

[67] *Ibid.,* 1337a22–27.

[68] We have seen that Locke and Rousseau trace crime to the establishment of property.

[69] *Op. cit.,* 1267a13–14.

Bentham's and Mill's doctrine that one man's happiness counts as much as, but no more than, any other's, but, given further data, there might have been.

The attitude toward luxuries and other goods that can add to the amenities of life is bound to change when the economic plant is able to produce enough of them for everyone, and may be stalled if it does *not* produce them. In the light of the vast increase of productive capacity, the ten objections summarized on p. 250 seem to lose vitality. Replying to them in the order in which they are listed, one could perhaps suggest the usual view today by saying:

(1) that peace of mind is more commonly disturbed by poverty than by ample means;

(2) that poverty is more apt to prevent intellectual and aesthetic activity than riches;

(3) and (4) that the pleasures considered durable and also "the joys of a simple life close to nature" usually require an independent income, and are more secure and dependable if it is ample;

(5) that men, given the chance, will work even more effectively for a high standard of living than for bare subsistence;

(6) that though the pursuit of wealth engenders undesirable passions it can also counteract them, and, in any case, there is no viable alternative;

(7) that society may be united by wealth, rather than divided, if there is enough to go around;

(8) that, for the same reason, friendship and sympathy may be increased rather than diminished;

(9) that the security of nations no longer depends on valor and martial enterprise, but, if it should be thought to, they are in general not lacking;

(10) that it is not at all clear that the poor are more pious than the rich.

It is not claimed, of course, that these rejoinders are in the least probative, but only that they reflect a general view of thinkers today, though it is a view more frequently assumed than actually expressed. It holds not only for the "affluent society" of the United States and Europe, but also for the rest of the world which is mostly poor and hungry. No statesman in any country today would dare to say that his nation or people would be better off if they had less wealth or fewer luxuries.

What Ways of Getting Wealth Favor Happiness?

The question of what ways of getting wealth favor happiness, like the one we have just discussed, is answered very differently by authorities in different centuries, depending in large part on the existing structure of economic life. Unlike the other question, however, it is seldom answered by philosophers, or with direct reference to happiness. Whether one kind of activity, agriculture or trade, for example, contributes most to the wealth of a nation, is a topic in economic history and the history of economic theories; it is not a topic in the comparative study of theories of happiness. The productivity of various types of economy is of immense value for the practical implementation of happiness, but the subject extends far beyond *our* subject. We shall confine ourselves to one example of how economic history, rather than philosophical arguments, tends to prevail.

The change in attitudes toward usury provides a good illustration. The Old Testament repeatedly forbids the practice, and Aristotle also condemns it vigorously in the famous passage:

> There are two sorts of wealth-getting . . . one is a part of household management, and the other is retail trade: the former necessary and honourable, while that which consists in exchange is justly censured; for it is unnatural, and a mode by which men gain from one another. The most hated sort, and with the greatest reason, is usury, which makes a gain out of money itself, and not from the natural object of it. For money was intended to be used in exchange, but not to increase at interest.[70]

Aquinas upholds the Old Testament's judicial precept forbidding the exaction of usury for loans that are made,[71] and rejects it also, following Aristotle, on the ground that it is "unnatural" and "unjust." But he weakens the prohibition, as far as "strangers" are concerned, when he says: "It was not the intention of the Law to sanction the acceptance of usury from strangers, but only to tolerate it on account of the proneness of Jews to avarice, and in order to promote a more peaceful feeling towards those out of whom they made a profit."[72] After the thirteenth century the increasing growth of trade and the needs of an expanding, diverse, more stabilized economy made it more and more difficult to uphold the prohibition, and it was eventually dropped. The Biblical interdiction remained, nor did Aristotle's line of argument change. What changed was the world. It was no longer the scene of scattered local markets of a predominantly agricultural economy, and could no longer profit by the regulations of manufacture, trade, pricing, employment, etc., which had served a useful purpose in the past. The Aristotelian conception of fair exchange, based on the equality of labor costs, like the insistence on the "just price," gave way before the new demands of commerce, and eventually usury was no longer a mortal sin.

70 *Ibid.*, 1258b5.
71 See *Summa Theologica*, Part I, II, Q105, A2, Reply to Obj. 4.
72 *Ibid.*, A3, Reply to Obj. 3.

THE MOODS OF HAPPINESS

We have been concerned in this chapter with conflicting views as to the part played by possessions in the realization of happiness. The Stoics represent one extreme, Bentham the other; between the two, but much closer to Bentham, in spirit, is the position of Aristotle. We have discussed philosophical positions. It remains to call attention to the corresponding moods. A "mood" is a state of mind in which we discern one side of life with an intensity of feeling and conviction. It is a personal vista rather than a comprehensive assertion, a way one feels at times, not a reasoned conclusion; and one mood is not in contradiction with another. It may be that the Stoic sometimes confuses his mood with a philosophical position, that the extremity of his tenets does not represent a steady and studied conviction. From his more flexible, common-sense viewpoint, Aristotle is able to recognize that moods, out of line with his general conception of happiness, may have a supreme value, on occasion. Thus, the great-souled man who suddenly loses all he has is able to rise above his misfortune. The great-souled man still has himself; and he is able to turn his gaze back upon himself with serenity because he finds virtue or excellence there. But this is a mood; it is not evolved into a philosophical theory of happiness.

Poetry seems to be the natural language of moods, and one of the moods most commonly portrayed is an aloof independence of honors, high station, treasures, and all the fickle enticements of the world. But the glory of appropriation and achievement is also a favorite theme. Faust's engineering project has brought industry, prosperity, and happiness to the people. As Mephistopheles says:

> Your will, your people's industry,
> Have won the prize of earth and sea.

But Faust is still unsatisfied, for two old folks live on the hill, dominating the scene of his exploits, where he wishes to build his palace. The disappointment stings his heart.

> It is impossible to bear it,
> And yet I'm ashamed to say the thing.
> The old folks there should make concession,
> I'd have the lindens for my throne;
> The few trees there, not my possession,
> Spoil me the world I call my own.
> There I would fain, for world-wide gazing
> From branch to branch a scaffold raising.
> Open to view the course I've run,

That I might see all I have done,
View at one glance, before we brought,
The masterpiece of human thought,
Which made a fact shrewd wisdom's plan
And won broad dwelling-place for man.
Thus suffer we the sorest rack,
Midst riches feeling what we lack.
The chime, the scent of linden-bloom,
Close round me as with church and tomb.
The power of my all-conquered will
Breaks down before that sandy hill.
How shall I ever free my spirit?
The bell rings and I rage to hear it![73]

But poetry more often deals with serene detachment from the rewards of
the world—a Stoic theme with a thousand variations. As an occasional
mood, let us hope that it is universal, for the most successful man who
could not sometimes see all his possessions and conquests as vain and
worthless would be an object of pity. So at least the poets seem to say. As
an expression of a Stoiclike mood, we may take the poem *A Gentle Wind,*
by Fu Hsuan, a Chinese poet of the third century.

A gentle wind fans the calm night:
A bright moon shines on the high tower.
A voice whispers, but no one answers when I call:
A shadow stirs, but no one comes when I beckon,
A kitchen man brings a dish of lentils:
Wine is there, but I do not fill my cup.
Contentment with poverty is Fortune's best gift:
Riches and Honour are the handmaids of Disaster.
Though gold and gems by the world are sought and prized,
To me they seem no more than weeds or chaff.

Some poets have seen that a mood of detachment, while quietly steeling
against possible disaster, is also consistent with great intensity of feeling.
More than anyone else, perhaps, Emerson is the philosopher of expansive
individualism. There are no common men, he says. "Each is uneasy until
he has produced his private ray into the concave sphere, and beheld his
talent also in its last nobility and exaltation."[74] His poem entitled "Give
All to Love" begins with the lines:

Give all to love;
Obey thy heart;
Friends, kindred, days,

[73] Goethe, *Faust,* Second Part, V.
[74] B. Atkinson (ed.), *The Complete Essays and Other Writings of Ralph Waldo
Emerson,* "Uses of Great Men."

Estate, good-fame,
Plans, credit and the Muse,
Nothing refuse.

Yet a certain detachment is necessary. While giving all to love, the lover must be ready to depart the instant the girl's thoughts turn to another. Thus:

Leave all for love;
Yet, hear me, yet,
One word more thy heart behoved,
One pulse more of firm endeavor,
Keep thee today,
Tomorrow, forever,
Free as an Arab
Of thy beloved.[75]

The readiness to steal away like an Arab at a moment's notice, is not, of course, to be understood as a continuing state of mind. It is rather an occasional mood in which, conceiving an irreparable loss, a man feels and knows what he must do in that event. Without occasional moods of calm detachment, in which he sees himself separated from all he cherishes, a man lacks dignity and perspective. Here the Stoics were on strong ground. But to live continuously in such moods, and to equate serene indifference with happiness in all circumstances of life, invites the comment of Aristotle and St. Augustine that such a state would be either impossible or less than human.

[75] B. Atkinson (ed.), *The Selected Writings of Ralph Waldo Emerson*, pp. 773–774.

10

The Issue of Pleasure:
Eudaemonism vs. Hedonism

Can There Be Happiness Without
Pleasure?

It is hard to see how a joyless happiness can be seriously recommended, or even a happiness that is admittedly less pleasant than some other state men might attain to; and so far we have encountered no theory that deliberately takes the pleasure out of happiness. Although "pleasures" or "a life of pleasure" is often condemned, joy or delight or some other variant of pleasure is then made a feature of the highest good.

When Socrates and the Stoics inveigh against "pleasures," what they mean, as we have noted, are bodily or sensuous pleasures. The joy of the mind, on the contrary, is considered the natural flower of virtue, which, however, is never pursued for its own sake, nor regarded as a reward of virtue. Thus, Seneca says that

> the life of the happy man must, whether he wills it or not, necessarily be attended by constant cheerfulness and a joy that is deep and issues from deep within, since he finds delight in his inner resources. . . . Should not such joys as these be rightly matched against the paltry and fleeting sensa-

262

tions of the wretched body? The day a man becomes superior to pleasure he
will also be superior to pain. Therefore we must make our escape to
freedom. . . . Then will be born the one inestimable blessing, the peace
and exaltation of a mind now safely anchored and . . . the great and stable
joy that comes from the discovery of the truth.[1]

This passage will serve to remind us of others we have quoted from Stoic
writers. The Platonic Socrates is the model for this attitude, and we have
seen that for the lover of the highest truth he recommends an audacious
and selfless quest, and promises a joy that is sheer ecstasy.

Even St. Augustine, who says that the things of "this world must be
used, not enjoyed, that so the invisible things of God may be clearly seen,"
nevertheless assures us that "the true objects of enjoyment"—the persons of
the Holy Trinity—are "delights" capable of making us truly happy.[2] The
"delights" and "enjoyment" attainable in heaven can only be conceived as a
higher, more intense form of pleasure.[3]

But is not the ancient Greek school of Cynics an exception to the general
rule that pleasure is always considered a part of happiness?[4] Antisthenes is
reported to have held that pain is a good thing, referring especially to the
pains of Hercules, and that pleasure is the greatest evil. The pains of
Hercules, however, are encountered in the midst of heroic exploits, and we
may suspect that the pleasures Antisthenes has in mind are also of a special
kind. For both Antisthenes and his disciple Diogenes are said to have
lauded the pleasures of poverty, independence of mind, and justice,
claiming that the happiness attained through a just life exceeds all others
in pleasure. Thus, Zeller attributes to Diogenes and the Cynics the view
that

happiness consists in that true joy which can only be obtained by an
unruffled cheerfulness of mind. Moreover, the Cynics when wishing to set
forth the advantages of their philosophy, did not fail to follow in the
footsteps of Socrates, by asserting that life with them was far more pleasant
and independent than with other men, that their abstemiousness gave the
right flavor to enjoyment, and that mental delights afforded a far higher
pleasure than sensual ones.[5]

[1] "On the Happy Life," IV, 3–4.
[2] *On the Christian Doctrine,* Book I, Chs. 4–5.
[3] Joy, Augustine says, is the attainment of our wish. When consent of the will
"takes the form of enjoying the things we wish, this is called joy" (*City of God,* XIV,
Ch. 6). Aquinas explicitly classes joy as a higher form of pleasure—a pleasure that
"follows reason." Joy is a spiritual or intellectual pleasure, and greater than the bodily
pleasures (*Summa Theologica,* Part I, II, Q31, A3–5).
[4] Another possible exception is Plotinus, but we have seen (Chapter 8) that his
denial that the Sage needs pleasure (unless this means mere unimpeded activity)
refers to bodily pleasures. He leaves no doubt that the Vision of the One is a supreme
joy.
[5] *Socrates and the Socratic School,* pp. 308–309.

Zeller agrees with Ritter that the Cynic doctrine, which is poorly developed, means only that pleasure should never be taken as an *end* of action, and is to be avoided when it has this pretension, for the true end is virtue alone.

It might be thought, too, that pleasure would be excluded from happiness by all authors who hold that pleasure is the mere relief from pain, and therefore nothing really existent. This view is put forward by Socrates in the *Philebus*[6] and refuted by Aristotle in the *Nicomachean Ethics*.[7] Aristotle argues that, though we are pleased by the relief ("replenishment") from pain, the relief is not the whole of pleasure.

But this does not happen with all pleasures; for

> the pleasures of learning and, among the sensuous pleasures, those of smell, and also many sounds and sights, and memories and hopes, do not presuppose pain.[8]

In spite of this sensible criticism of the theory that pleasure is the mere absence of pain, it has been adopted by many thinkers, including Kant and Schopenhauer.

In his *Anthropologie*, Kant claims:

> Pleasure is the feeling of the furtherance of life, pain of the hindrance. . . . Pain must thus precede pleasure; pain always comes first. For what could result from a continual furtherance of life, beyond a certain point, than a speedy death from joy? Nor can pleasures immediately follow upon others; between them pain is always to be found. There are small hindrances of the vital force interspersed with furtherances of it, which make up the condition of health. But we mistakenly interpret this as a continual state of well-being. . . . Pain is the goad to activity, and in this we feel our life first and foremost; without it death would supervene.[9]

Underlying Kant's argument is the conviction that human life is haunted by an uneasiness or irritation, a desire to escape from the present, whether we are engaged in thought or action. Pain is the prod to change; pleasure never is.

Did Aristotle answer these contentions in advance? Whether pleasure is always immediately preceded by pain is an empirical question. Aristotle reminds us, in effect, that we can be pleasantly surprised by a landscape, a delicious taste, a new intellectual insight, when the pleasure is not preceded by pain. But even if pain always *did* precede pleasure, he adds, this would not at all prove that pleasure is a mere relief from pain.

Schopenhauer repeats Kant's argument with many variations and color-

---

[6] See *Philebus*, 42, 44.
[7] See *op. cit., Nicomachean Ethics*, 1173b8–18.
[8] *Ibid.*, 1173b15–19.
[9] E. Cassirer (ed.), *Immanuel Kant's Werke, Anthropologie*, Vol. 2.

ful illustrations, but there is no need to discuss them here. Our object now is to determine whether there are any theories of happiness that exclude pleasure. Schopenhauer's theory is not an example in point, since, for him, happiness is unattainable. It is an illusion. Hence, the question whether it excludes pleasure does not arise. And when, on the other hand, Schopenhauer suggests, and he does sometimes, that the holy man *can* overcome the cruel Will to Live and yet go on living, we get the distinct impression that the "blessedness" he will enjoy involves something more than an absence of pain. Nor is Kant's theory of happiness an exception to the general rule. In his basic writings on ethics, where the goal of happiness is contrasted with the ideal of duty, happiness is defined in terms of pleasure (or the satisfaction of desire), and happiness is certainly not the mere absence of pain.

The failure to recognize that pleasure is (typically) a feeling may account in part for the centuries of disparagement of pleasure. When it is taken to be a sensation, and the opposite of pain, a man who nobly endures his pains cannot easily be thought to be at the same time pleased. It is well known, however, that the joy of winning an athletic contest, or of self-approval, or achievement of any kind is consistent with even intense pains of injuries or disease. A man is happy in spite of his pains, and sometimes hardly notices them. This can be explained if pleasure is a feeling, for the feeling is not the opposite of pain, but of the feeling of unpleasantness. Pleasure thus can coexist with pain, though not with unpleasantness. It thus can be cherished, not only by the weakling who cannot endure pain but also by the strong and courageous.

When pleasure, again, is put on the same level as pain, it is regarded as physical, as belonging to the body. Thus, when the body is downgraded or despised, as we have seen with Socrates, the Stoics, and their followers, pleasure is also disparaged and considered beneath the notice of the wise man. But, yet, the joy of the wise man is said to be as incomparably fine as "the life of pleasure" is contemptible. Such confusions are avoided once it is recognized that pleasure is not tied to the senses, as pain is, but is typically a feeling pervading the thought of *anything* desired. Or, as Aristotle puts it, "pleasure is a state of the *soul,* and to each man that which he is said to be a lover of is pleasant."[10]

THE CLAIM THAT SENSUOUS PLEASURES ARE THE BEST

If there is general agreement that pleasure is essential to happiness, the question is—which pleasures contribute *most*—the sensuous pleasures, usually thought to be intense and short-lived, or those associated with friend-

[10] *Op. cit.,* 1099a8.

ship, self-approval, and intellectual and aesthetic activity, usually regarded as milder and more lasting? This question is quite different from the issue that divides the hedonists from the eudaemonists, and that will be discussed later, viz.: Whether pleasures are qualitatively alike or qualitatively different. With regard to the first question, almost all hedonists and all eudaemonists agree: the mental pleasures are best and contribute most to happiness.

We shall thus confine our attention in this section to (1) hedonists who have been supposed to prefer sensuous pleasures, and (2) those who really do.

(a) Since Epicurus is the undisputed leader of the Epicureans, his position is that of the whole school. It is easy to see that he is no voluptuary or epicure. He begins by saying that

> pleasure is the beginning and end of the blessed life. For we recognize pleasure as the first good innate in us, and from pleasure we begin every act of choice and avoidance, and to pleasure we return again, using the feeling as the standard by which we judge every good.[11]

But though every pleasure, "because of its natural kinship to us is good, yet not every pleasure is to be chosen," nor every pain avoided.[12] Some pleasures are mixed with pain and lead to pain, and some pains to greater pleasures. If we are content with a few things, Epicurus says, we shall not be unhappy if deprived of luxuries; and when bread, cheese, and wine are available, they will seem like a feast. Even the Stoic Seneca could praise the spirit of the following passage:

> When . . . we maintain that pleasure is the end, we do not mean the pleasure of profligates and those that consist of sensuality . . . but freedom from pain in the body and from trouble in the mind. For it is not the continuous drinkings and revellings, nor the satisfaction of . . . which produce a pleasant life, but sober reasoning, searching out the motives for all choice and avoidance, and banishing mere opinions, to which are due the greatest disturbance of the spirit.[13]

The "mere opinions" are the superstitions that threaten us with the wrath of the gods. It is the great value of philosophy that it dispels these chimerical notions, and offers proof that we are free to choose what is most useful to a pleasant life.

Maximum happiness is afforded, not by sensuous enjoyments but by the gentle communion of friends. "All friendship," Epicurus says, "is desirable

[11] W. J. Oates (ed.), *The Stoic and Epicurean Philosophers, Epicurus to Menoeceus*, 129.
[12] *Ibid.*, 129–130.
[13] *Ibid.*, 132.

in itself, though it starts from the need of help." Even here prudence is necessary, yet too much is unwise, for friends we must have. "We must not approve either those who are always ready for friendship, or those who hang back, but for friendship's sake we must even run risks."[14] Our friend may be put to torture and then we suffer as much as he does, and, when he betrays us, our whole life is "confounded by distrust."[15] In spite of these risks, Epicurus praises friendship as the royal road to happiness. It is also the means of spreading the doctrine of pleasure to all men in all lands: "Friendship goes dancing round the world proclaiming to us all to awake to the praises of the happy life."[16]

It is the mild, safe, lasting pleasures—consisting, according to Epicurean theory, of gentle movements of atoms in the body—that are recommended. Friendship, rather than passionate love. Yet the *final* test is the maximum pleasure attainable, and the needs of individuals vary. To a pupil who has asked for advice, Epicurus answers in an amusing vein:

> You tell me that the stimulus of the flesh makes you too prone to the pleasures of love. Provided that you do not break the laws or good customs and do not distress any of your neighbors or do harm to your body or squander your pittance, you may indulge your inclination as you please. Yet it is impossible not to come up against one or the other of these barriers: for the pleasures of love never profited a man and he is lucky if they do him no harm.[17]

The counsels against love are clearly prudential, not puritanical.

Another hedonist who is sometimes supposed to hold that sensuous pleasures, if given free rein, make the greatest contribution to happiness, is Sigmund Freud. Let us see if this is so. "What is called *happiness* in the narrowest sense," Freud says, "comes from the satisfaction—most often instantaneous—of pent-up needs which have reached great intensity, and by its nature can only be a transitory experience." When a desired condition continues for any length of time, only "mild comfort" is experienced, for we are so constituted that only contrasts afford intense enjoyment. "Our possibilities of enjoyment are thus limited from the start by our very constitution. It is much less difficult to be unhappy."[18]

> It is little wonder if, under the pressure of [possible suffering from our body, the external world, and our fellowmen], humanity is wont to reduce its demands for happiness . . . if a man thinks himself happy if he has merely

[14] *Ibid.*, 23, 28.
[15] *Ibid.*, 56–57.
[16] *Ibid.*, 52.
[17] *Ibid.*, 51.
[18] *Civilization and Its Discontents*, II.

escaped unhappiness or weathered trouble; if in general the task of avoiding pain forces that of obtaining pleasure into the background.

But, though some pain is avoided by curbing desire, the craving for satisfaction still remains, and enjoyment is greatly reduced. The avoidance of pain, at the expense of pleasure, is one way of dealing with the ever present threat of suffering, and it takes many forms, none of which assures happiness. Sublimation affords an escape for the few really creative artists, but the lot of most men is frustration. There remains, of course, the alternative of heedless surrender to the pleasure principle, but this, according to Freud, is self-determining.

> Unbridled gratification of all desires forces itself into the foreground as the most alluring guiding principle of life, but it entails preferring enjoyment to caution and penalizes itself after short indulgence.

The causes of man's unhappiness are not all in the external world or in his relations to his fellowmen, but mainly in himself. External progress cannot be expected to bring happiness, but the hope for it never dies.

> The goal towards which the pleasure-principle impels us—of becoming happy—is not attainable; yet we may not—nay, cannot—give up the effort to come nearer to realization of it by some means or other.[19]

Freud thus cannot be said to recommend sensuous pleasures as the key to happiness, for happiness is not to be attained in this way, or in any way. He recognizes sexual intercourse as the most intense pleasure that men can enjoy; he also believes that complete satisfaction would require complete sexual freedom, which would conflict outrageously with the reality-principle. Guilt and self-destructiveness—the death instinct—would remain.

(b) There may be many men who hold, or live as though they believe, that sensuous pleasures are the high road to happiness; there are almost no philosophers who have maintained this view publicly. We shall therefore consider only one example: the ancient Greek school of Cyrenaics.

In all cases there is emphasis on the uncertainty of human affairs and the ephemeral character of all the distinctions and achievements on which men set their hearts. The future not only is uncertain, according to the Cyrenaics, but unknowable. In perception we have sensations, but these tell us nothing about the external things that caused them. We are aware of whiteness or hardness, but this does not permit us to infer that something is white or hard. Following Protagoras, the Cyrenaics hold that we can know only our subjective sensations and feelings, and that we can be

[19] *Ibid.*

perfectly certain of these. We can be sure of pleasures of the moment, but cannot successfully calculate future ones. The study of natural causes is fruitless. Thus it is said of Aristippus (435–350 B.C.), the founder of the Cyrenaic school, that "he derived pleasure from what was present, but did not toil to procure the enjoyment of something not present."[20] Neither the past nor the future are objects of concern.

"Particular pleasure," the Cyrenaics hold, "is desirable for its own sake, whereas happiness is desired only for the sake of particular pleasures."[21] By happiness they understand a sum of pleasures over a lifetime or a considerable period, and the sum is valuable only because the particular pleasures are valuable, even if there should be no sum. Moreover, though future pleasures are evidently good in themselves, the process of obtaining them is often painful, "so that to accumulate pleasures that are productive of happiness appears . . . a most irksome business."[22] It is better to enjoy each pleasure as it comes, for the future is uncertain, and no man knows whether the pleasure he works for will arrive.

The Cyrenaics insist, according to Diogenes Laertius, that bodily pleasures are far better than mental pleasures, and bodily pains far worse than mental pains, and this is the reason why offenders are punished with the former.[23] Friends are to be valued, not for their own sake but as a means to our pleasure. We can have no knowledge of the friend's feelings, in any case, and too much concern for him would be unprofitable. When censured for enjoying the favors of Lais, Aristippus is said to have retorted: "I have Lais, not she me; and it is not abstinence from pleasures that is best, but mastery over them without ever being worsted."[24]

(c) An absorption in the immediate pleasures of personal love, gaiety, and the arts, is portrayed by David Hume in his essay, "The Epicurean." When his Caelia is tearful over the prospect of death and the uncertainty of everything else, the Epicurean begs her not to waste precious time. For,

if life be frail, if youth be transitory, we should well employ the present moment, and lose no part of so perishable an existence. Yet a little moment, and *these* shall be no more, We shall be as if we had never been. . . . Our fruitless anxieties, our vain projects, our uncertain speculations, shall all be swallowed up and lost. Our present doubts, concerning the original cause of all things, must never, alas! be resolved. This alone we may be certain of, that if any governing mind preside, he must be pleased to see us fulfil the ends of our being, and enjoy that pleasure for which alone we were created

---

20 Diogenes Laertius, *op. cit.*, 66.
21 *Ibid.*, 88.
22 *Ibid.*, 90.
23 See *ibid.*
24 *Ibid.*, 75.

. . . but while youth and passion, my fair one, prompt our eager desires,
we must find gayer subjects to intermix with these amorous caresses.[25]

The persistent reasons for preferring sensuous pleasures are that they are
immediate and certain, while all else, except death, is uncertain and
precarious. It is best, therefore, to make quick and sure use of the moment
we are allotted, so that, at the end, we can "turn down an empty glass." Or,
as Edna St. Vincent Millay puts it:

> I burn my candle at both ends,
> It will not last the night;
> But ah, my foes, and oh, my friends
> It gives a lovely light.[26]

Sometimes the preference for sensuous pleasure is not tied to immediacy, but is calculating, laying careful plans for future enjoyment. An
example is furnished by the conduct of the cynical hero of Kierkegaard's
Diary of a Seducer, who plans in advance the successive stages of a
seduction in order to maximize his pleasure. The theories of this voluptuary are not, of course, Kierkegaard's, and the *Diary* forms only one
dialectical part of the larger work, *Either/Or,* which points in precisely the
opposite direction. The works of Marquis de Sade, which have recently
been revived, state the case for planned indulgence of the senses, but it
would appear that licentiousness and profligacy are more easily made a rule
of life than seriously defended. Most philosophers writing on happiness
would be inclined to agree with Aristotle, who contends, in his *Eudemian
Ethics,* that if life contained only the pleasures of eating and sex, and were
to continue indefinitely, no one would really, "on account of these experiences choose existence rather than non-existence."[27]

QUESTIONS ABOUT THE CAUSAL ROLE OF PLEASURE IN HAPPINESS

Whether we accept eudaemonism or hedonism, or some other theory of
happiness (or of nonhappiness) will depend in part on what they say
about the causal role of pleasure, and on whether we can accept what they
say. An affirmative answer to the first two questions below, (1) and (2),
will support both hedonism and eudaemonism, though not in exactly the
same way. A negative answer will discredit both. In fact, however,

---

[25] "The Epicurean," in *Essays, Moral, Political and Literary,* p. 146.
[26] *A Few Figs from Thistles,* "First Fig."
[27] *Op. cit., Eudemian Ethics,* 1215b30.

evidence favors both (1) and (2): There is a great deal of agreement that pleasure both accompanies and facilitates efficient and successful activities.

In (3), below, we report a recent physiological discovery that supports the ancient theory that pleasure is one of the two main roads to learning. This result is congenial to hedonism, of course, but also backs up Aristotle's eudaemonism, though perhaps not perfectly. In (4), we distinguish three different views, often confused, as to *how* pleasure determines human activities. One of these views, we see, affords a much more plausible psychological base for hedonism (including most forms of utilitarianism) than do others, and disarms some favorite criticisms of hedonism.

Finally, in (5), we cite findings of psychologists to the effect that pain does not instruct as pleasure does, and is not a good deterrent. Centuries of abject respect for punishment are hereby called in question, and all positive theories of happiness, envisaging better instruction and correction of human beings with less pain, would be strengthened as against pessimistic adversaries.

1. DOES PLEASURE ATTEND EFFICIENT OPERATION?

We have seen that, according to Aristotle, all healthy activities are accompanied and completed by pleasure. The exercise of the senses is pleasant, for we speak of pleasant sounds and sights; and thinking is even more so, since it is an activity of the part of the soul that is highest and distinctive to man. Pleasure is not a state by itself, but pervades the activity to which it belongs, and "supervenes as the bloom of youth does on those in the flower of their age."[28] It is true that even when our faculties are in good order we are not always pleased, but this is only because we are not continuously active. We tire of things: They cease to afford pleasure because we no longer attend to them closely; their novelty, which led us to study and analyze them, has worn off. As the activity subsides, so does the pleasure.

Aristotle's theory that all healthy, "unimpeded"[29] activity is accompanied by pleasure has sometimes been criticized as follows: While it is true that we generally enjoy seeing, unless our eyes are inflamed, and listening, unless we are partly deaf, etc., this is not always the case. It is not pleasant to see or hear or smell something repulsive, even when sense organs are functioning perfectly. Thus, unimpeded perception is not

[28] *Ibid., Nicomachean Ethics*, 1174b32.
[29] *Ibid.*, 1153a15.

always pleasant; it is sometimes quite unpleasant.[30] The criticism seems to have some force, and Aristotle does not directly answer it. The answer might be that people *do* like to examine bloody accidents and other hideous, terrible, and repulsive things. As long as they awaken curiosity, the attentive observation that follows will have the kind of pleasantness that usually goes with successful discriminations. We may be horrified by what, with rapt attention, we are examining. The observing can be pleasant, while that which is being observed is highly unpleasant.

The objection that unimpeded activity is not always pleasant is matched by the objection that impeded activity is sometimes pleasant. Do not the hindrances and difficulties that are encountered in perception and thought actually provide pleasure—whet our interest and add zest and drama? The encountering and overcoming of the hindrances are precisely what gives us pleasure. G. C. Field defends Aristotle's position as follows:

> . . . such an argument misconceives the place taken by the difficulties in such an experience. What they do is not by themselves to produce pleasure, but to rouse us to greater activity. It is because there is, so to speak, more activity, because our powers are more completely brought into play, that there is greater pleasure in overcoming big difficulties than small ones. And of course the pleasure only comes when the difficulty has been overcome and the activity has thus perfected itself.[31]

This reply to the objection seems to be one that Aristotle himself might make, except, perhaps, for the last sentence. Pleasure, for Aristotle, is primarily an accompaniment of *activity,* and the activity of overcoming hindrances to clear perception and thought, or effective action, could be expected to be pleasant itself, even before the hindrances have been overcome—before "the activity has perfected itself." The virtuous activity that, according to Aristotle, is always accompanied by pleasure is full of difficulties, especially when one must make choices, and the virtuous habit is not yet established. What takes the pleasure out of an activity is not the impediment we find we can overcome with effort but rather the one we find we cannot.

The British psychologist and philosopher G. F. Stout, writing at the turn of the present century, gives a balanced statement of the Aristotelian position. "The antithesis between pleasure and pain," he says, "is coincident with the antithesis between free and impeded progress towards an end." This does not mean, however, that pleasure arises only when there are no impediments at all. A lack of all impediments would be consistent only with sleep or death.

[30] Anthony Kenny, in *Action, Emotion and Will,* Chapter 6, makes this criticism, among others.
[31] *Moral Theory,* pp. 95–96.

Unimpeded progress is pleasant in proportion to the intensity and complexity of mental excitement. An activity which is thwarted or retarded either by the presence of positive obstruction, or by the absence of cooperative conditions, or in any other conceivable way, is painful in proportion to its intensity and complexity, and to the degree of the hindrance. . . . The type of the painful state is *Tantalus,* continually reaching after the fruit which continually evaded him. . . . The counterpart on the side of pleasure to the state of Tantalus is not, however, that of immediate and complete attainment. It is the smooth and prosperous progress towards attainment. With ultimate attainment, the mental tendency ceases to operate, and the pleasure ceases also. It is in the intermediate activity that enjoyment arises. Disturbance of equilibrium is not, as such, painful; otherwise all consciousness would be painful. Nor is equilibrium itself pleasant; otherwise all pleasant states would be states of unconsciousness.[32]

That pleasure is the normal accompaniment of varied action and endeavor, when the hindrances are not too great, is also the view of the distinguished physiologist C. Judson Herrick:

The simplest view seems to the author to be that the normal activity of the body within physiological limits is intrinsically pleasurable, so far as it comes into consciousness at all. There is the simple joy of living for its own sake, and the more productive life is, within well-defined physiological limits of fatigue, good health, and diversified types of reaction, the greater the happiness. The expenditure of energy within these physiological limits is pleasurable *per se* except in so far as various physiological factors enter to disturb the simple natural physiological expression of bodily activity. . . . The expenditure of intelligently directed nervous energy along the lines of fruitful endeavor is probably the highest type of pleasure known to man.[33]

This Aristotelian view usually goes unchallenged, and, if it is seldom explicitly stated, this is because it is taken for granted. Schopenhauer and all pessimists deny it, by implication at least. Heidegger and some other existentialist authors, together with Freud and the Freudians, exclude, by their doctrine that men are ridden by inescapable anxiety or guilt, the very possibility of unimpeded action and thought. Self-realization, on the other hand, subscribes to the Aristotelian view. Hedonism tends to do the same. Epicureanism assumes that pleasure attends a life according to nature—a life of moderation free from ambition, frenzy, and superstition. The religious utilitarians hold that man is created and intended for happiness, which implies that pleasure is normal,[34] while J. S. Mill, as we have seen, goes far toward agreeing with Aristotle in this matter.

[32] *Analytic Psychology,* Vol. 2, pp. 270–271.
[33] *An Introduction to Neurology,* p. 355.
[34] Sometimes the point is made explicitly. See, for example, Paley, *Natural Theology,* Ch. XXVI, p. 359.

2. Does Pleasure Cause or Facilitate Activities?

The causal efficiency of pleasure is asserted by both Aristotelianism and hedonism, but with a difference; the Aristotelian account *is more complex because it takes pleasures to be of different qualitative kinds,* and insists that their causal effect varies according to their kind, and the kind of activity to which they belong. Thus the pleasure peculiar to doing geometry sustains this activity and improves proficiency, while the distinctive pleasure of building a house intensifies and improves performance of this sort, and so for other activities. Hedonists, on the other hand, hold that pleasures are qualitatively the same, and that what reinforces (strengthens) an activity is simply the *amount* of pleasure associated with it, or the *amount* of pain (unpleasantness) avoided.

We have seen that, according to Aristotle, it is desire alone that moves the body, but the object of desire is pleasant,[35] and pleasure "accompanies all objects of choice: for even the noble and the advantageous appear pleasant."[36] Far from being an impediment, pleasure is actually an incentive to action, and generally virtue cannot be without the pleasure that comes from it.

Compare this with Bentham's:

> Nature has placed mankind under the governance of two masters, *pain* and *pleasure*. It is for them alone to point out what we ought to do, as well as determine what we shall do. On the one hand, the standard of right and wrong, on the other the chain of causes and effects, are fastened to their throne. They govern us in all we do, in all we say, in all we think: every effort we make to throw off our subjection, will serve but to demonstrate and confirm it.[37]

Bentham is saying that pleasure and pain are the only determinants of human thought and behavior, and that they ought to be. (The difference between the "are" and "ought to be," it will be remembered, is the difference made by intelligence, calculation, and enlightened laws, which render the pursuit of pleasure more successful.)

Aristotle would not at all admit that pleasure and pain are the only determinants of human action (or that they should be), for health, honor, and the virtues, as well as pleasure, are desired for themselves. Yet health, honor, and the virtues are all pleasant, as are other objects of desire. What

[35] See *Nicomachean Ethics,* 661a8.
[36] *Ibid.,* 1104b35.
[37] *Principles of Morals and Legislation,* Ch. 1, p. 125.

moves men to action, therefore, is not always pleasure; but it *is* always the pleasant. Thus, Aristotle concludes that pleasure completes for every man the activities that he loves best, and therefore completes the life that each desires.

> It is with good reason, then, that they aim at pleasure too, since for every one it completes life, which is desirable. But whether we choose life for the sake of pleasure or pleasure for the sake of life is a question we may dismiss for the present. For they seem to be bound up together and not to admit of separation, since without activity pleasure does not arise, and every activity is completed by the attendant pleasure.[38]

Pleasantness, thus, is the necessary but not sufficient cause of human behavior. It must be a pleasantness that attends and completes the activities each of us loves. The pleasure of the music lover heightens his attention and understanding, that of the geometrician improves his acumen and persistence; but the pleasure proper to one activity does not intensify, but may impede, an activity of a different kind. Thus a man who loves flute playing will be distracted by this pleasure from a philosophical conversation to which he is listening. One pleasure conflicts with and excludes the others. Each intensifies only the activity to which it is proper.[39]

A famous passage in Hobbes shows how a hedonist theory can go a long way in agreeing with Aristotle. When an external object, according to Hobbes, acts upon our senses, an appetite or aversion is set up in the organism, which is an "endeavor," *i.e.*, a motion of matter. It is the sense (or "appearance") of this motion which we call "Delight or Trouble of Mind."

> This Motion, which is called Appetite, and for the apparance of it *Delight*, and *Pleasure*, seemeth to be, a corroboration of Vitall motion, and a help thereunto; and therefore such things as caused Delight, were not improperly

---

[38] *Op. cit.*, 1175a16–22.

[39] It is interesting to note that Bentham also refers to the distinctive pleasure afforded by a particular musical instrument. Whoever *plays* a harpsichord, he says, "experiences a pleasure *perfectly distinct* from that of hearing the same piece of music executed by another." (*Principles of Legislation*, p. 22. Italics added.) The question is what he means by saying that the one pleasure is "perfectly distinct" from the other. If he had meant "a greater pleasure," he probably would have used this expression. The most natural interpretation of "perfectly distinct" in the context is "qualitatively quite distinct," and this would be consistent with Aristotle's theory of pleasure, though not with Bentham's. It is possible that Bentham (who was himself an accomplished harpsichord player) was thinking of the actual experience rather than his theory, of the particular concrete quality he knew so well rather than of that abstract nature which all pleasures have in common. What he is illustrating is what we might now call "the joy of workmanship"—one of the assets and motivations of the good life.

called *Jucunda* (à *Juvando*,) from helping or fortifying; on the contrary, *Molesta, Offensive*, from hindering, and troubling the motion vitall.

Pleasure therefore, (or *Delight*,) or the apparance, or sense of Good; and *Molestation* or *Displeasure*, the apparance, or sense of Evill. And consequently all Appetite, Desire, and Love, is accompanied by some Delight more or lesse; and all Hatred, and Aversion, with more or lesse Displeasure and Offence.[40]

This helping and strengthening of vital motion by pleasure is the more important since all appetite, desire, and love are attended with pleasure, and felicity in this life, according to Hobbes, is not a state in which desires have been fulfilled, but a continuing process in which they are being fulfilled.

For there is no such thing as perpetuall Tranquillity of mind, while we live here; because Life itself is but Motion, and can never be without Desire, nor without Feare, no more than without Sense . . . the word of Schoole-men *Beatificall Vision* is unintelligible.[41]

Since desire is present most of the time, presumably, so also is the helping and reinforcement of activities, and the opposite effect of aversion would be exceedingly frequent too.

Thus, though Hobbes agrees with Aristotle that pleasure abets the activity that it attends, he gives the abetting a wider scope, for Aristotle does not concede that desire is *always* accompanied by pleasure. On the other hand, Aristotle insists that pleasures are as specific as the different activities they accompany, each pleasure assisting only that activity to which it is proper, and this is excluded by Hobbes.

Whether or not pleasure accompanies, facilitates, and prolongs healthy and successful activities seems crucial for both eudaemonism and hedonism. If it does, they are partially confirmed; if it does not, they can hardly be true.

For the same reason, the role of pleasure and pain in human learning is important. The evidence for and against the traditional view, in contemporary learning theory, is too voluminous to summarize here. It may be mentioned, however, that the "drive-reduction" theory, which is the main alternative to the pleasure-pain theory, has been subject recently to increasing criticism, and that the discovery of centers for pleasure in the brain constitutes an additional setback, as it gives new support to the pleasure-pain theory.

[40] *Leviathan*, Part 1, Ch. 6, p. 25.
[41] *Ibid.*, p. 30.

3. Is Pleasure the Main Goad to Learning?

In order to induce experimental animals to repeat a certain response and to desist from other alternative responses, it was thought necessary to reward the desired response with food, water, etc., or to punish alternative responses by annoyances such as electric shocks. In 1954, James Olds and Peter Milner discovered that the same result could be obtained without external reward of any kind. They implanted electrodes permanently in the lower centers of the brain, and put the animals into a Skinner box, wired so that, by depressing a bar, the animals could stimulate their own brains. When the placements were made at given points in the area, the rats tirelessly continued to depress the bar, just as if they were being rewarded by pellets of food, though unfed for long periods. The number of responses in a twelve-hour period varied from 3,000 to 7,500, depending on the precise places being stimulated. When the current was turned off, however, the animals gradually ceased to respond. There seemed little doubt that the response was being reinforced or rewarded by electrical stimulation of certain tiny areas of the posterior hypothalamus and midbrain.[42]

In later experiments, the rate of self-stimulation ran to an incredible 8,000 responses an hour, and the insatiable rats often persisted in pressing the bar at this rate for as many as twenty-four or even forty-eight hours continuously. And, when deprived of food for twenty-four hours, and then given a chance to eat, the hungry animals continued to press the bar instead, leaving the food at the other side of the cage untouched. It was found, too, that under self-stimulation they could learn to run a maze as fast as when the usual reward of food was given, and, when it came to running across a painfully charged grille, self-stimulation was twice as effective as twenty-four-hour hunger.[43]

In the "do-it-yourself" situation contrived by Olds, it is up to the rat whether its brain will continue to be stimulated. "Presumably," Dean Wooldridge says, "if it enjoyed the sensation, it would be motivated to learn to press the lever for its electric reward; if there were no actual enjoyment, its rate of lever-pressing should be no greater than the random

[42] See "Positive Reinforcement Produced by Electrical Stimulation of Septal Area and Other Regions of Rat Brain," in *Journal of Comparative and Physiological Psychology*, 47, 1954. See also R. C. Birney and R. C. Teevan, *Reinforcement: An Enduring Problem in Psychology.*

[43] See James Olds, "Self-stimulation of the Brain," in *Science*, 127, 1958, pp. 315–324.

rate characteristic of any ordinary rat running curiously around its cage and occasionally stepping on a lever that happened to be in its path."[44] This would happen only ten to twenty-five times per hour, as against thousands of times per hour when the rat is allowed to stimulate its brain.

Loci for pain or fright also have been discovered; when the electrodes are placed in these loci, adjacent to the pleasure centers, the rats never pressed the bar a second time, and would do anything to avoid stimulation. When, in other experiments, monkeys were used, they gave every indication of severe pain or fright, or both: they shrieked, quivered, tried to escape, etc. It was concluded that it could not be "sham" pain—*mere* external symptoms of pain. The animal "bites and tears any object near the mouth hard enough to break teeth out of its jaw."[45]

One implication of these discoveries, according to Olds, is that pleasure is now reinstated in learning against pain, and that the classic conception, that a response is learned simply because it is repeatedly followed by the reduction of a painful need or drive, has been discredited. As Olds points out:

> In classical theory . . . drive and punishment are synonymous . . . and a reward is held to be fundamentally nothing more than the reduction of a drive. . . . The hedonistic view that behavior is pulled forward by pleasure, as well as pushed forward by pain, is rejected in classical theory for the more parsimonious notion that pain supplies the push and that learning based on pain reduction supplies the direction. The work reported in this article clearly shows one implication of the drive-reduction theory to be incorrect, for massive inputs to certain parts of the central nervous system are shown to have rewarding effects. Further, by showing that there are anatomically separate mechanisms for reward and punishment in the brain, it points directly to a physiological basis for the motivational dualism suggested in the hedonistic theory. In fact, it appears, that the area producing rewarding effects upon electrical stimulation, is far larger than the area producing punishment.[46]

Deep stimulation of the brains of human beings is, of course, not experimental but therapeutic, and the mapping of pleasure and pain centers has not advanced as far as in the case of animals. Hundreds of patients, however, have been treated by implantation of electrodes in analogous areas of the brain, and confirmatory results have been obtained. Thus, Wooldridge reports that:

> electric stimulation in various brain centers has produced sensations described by the patient as ease and relaxation, joy, and great satisfaction. For

[44] *The Machinery of the Brain,* p. 127.
[45] *Ibid.,* p. 130.
[46] *Op. cit.,* p. 315.

other centers, anxiety, restlessness, depression, fright and horror have been reported. When arrangements are provided for self-stimulation in pleasure centers, patients have sometimes stimulated themselves into convulsions somewhat similar to those produced by electroshock treatment. After these self-stimulated convulsions, however, the patients are found to lie relaxed, smiling happily, contrary to the restless fighting frequently observed after shock treatment. As with animal experiments, pleasure and punishment centers are frequently found situated close to one another.[47]

The discovery of pleasure and pain centers favors hedonism, as against the drive-reduction theory, for it means that positive reinforcement is not simply the reduction of a drive. As the findings are further confirmed, pleasure will be accorded its own distinct physiological base, and the persistent theory that pleasure is merely the absence of pain will be, more than ever, discredited. Moreover, hedonists will no longer feel compelled to talk as if the mere mental feeling were itself the causal agent. Experimental testing of the effect of pleasure on behavior will become a real possibility for the first time.

The discovery may eventually give more backing to Aristotle's eudaemonism. For Aristotle, pleasure is a bloom that supervenes upon bodily activities, and pleasures vary qualitatively with the different kinds of activities they accompany and are appropriate to. Some physiological support for this doctrine is now accumulating. Pleasure centers have been differentiated into those that are sensitive to hunger and those that are sensitive to sex. When electrodes are implanted in the former centers, the animal will stimulate itself only when it is hungry; when they are implanted in the latter centers, it is shown, by a more complicated procedure, that it will stimulate itself only when the sexual urge is present.[48]

4. THE PLAUSIBILITY OF PSYCHOLOGICAL HEDONISM

Hedonism maintains the psychological thesis that men naturally pursue pleasure and avoid pain. Aristotle agrees that men naturally pursue what is pleasant and avoid what is painful or unpleasant. Hedonism often goes further, maintaining that pleasure and pain are the only motivations, but this is rejected by Aristotle's eudaemonism. This doctrine is called "psychological hedonism."

Forty years ago, L. T. Troland distinguished three kinds of psychological

[47] *Op. cit.,* p. 133.
[48] See *ibid.,* p. 128.

hedonism—hedonism of the future, hedonism of the present, and hedonism of the past,[49] and held that these quite different theories are often confused with one another. Hedonism of the future says that we always consciously choose to do the actions we think will give us the most pleasure in the future, or the least pain. This theory is too implausible to be maintained consistently for very long, for it is too obvious that *all* of our choices are not dictated by a *conscious* expectation of the most pleasure or the least pain. This theory, therefore, tends to pass over into hedonism of the present or hedonism of the past, without any notice of the change.

Hedonism of the present says that whatever alternative of action is most pleasant to us at the moment (or least unpleasant), is the one chosen. We see Socrates denying this doctrine in the *Protagoras*. Men are not overpowered by pleasure or by pain, he contends. They make mistakes because of ignorance. The real disadvantage of hedonism of the present is that it would be hard to establish introspectively *i.e.,* we frequently seem to choose the more unpleasant act in the present for the sake of some good in the future, and the expectation of the future good does not always make the present act less unpleasant. In any case, the introspective evidence for this theory would be ambiguous and debatable, and no other kind of evidence is available. *Faute de mieux,* then, the hedonism of the past becomes more attractive.

Hedonism of the past is the view that our acts are determined by past pleasures and pains: we are attracted to situations that have afforded pleasure in the past and repelled by those that were painful. Just as the white rat learns to avoid blind alleys and electric shocks, and to find its way to food in minimum time, without much thought or introspection, so we too are conditioned by our hedonistic experience in the past. No conscious calculation as to the course of action that will yield the most pleasure is needed, nor is it necessary to suppose that people always succumb to what is immediately pleasant and always recoil from what is painful. They simply tend to do what has repeatedly had pleasant consequences in the past, and to refrain from doing what has proved painful. It is thus apparent that hedonism of the past might well be true, though the other forms of psychological hedonism are both false. It also admits of objective testing in a sense in which *they* do not. Whether human beings tend to be governed by past hedonistic experiences—with inference, of course, playing a part— is, in principle, confirmable.

In this sense of psychological hedonism—hedonism of the past—almost everyone has said that pleasure and pain are somehow the governors of education and the learning process in general. In either of the other senses

[49] See *The Mystery of Mind,* pp. 137 ff.

of psychological hedonism, no one would make this claim and stick to it consistently. This is why it seems important to distinguish these three distinct senses of the term. Bentham's psychological egoism can be ridiculed, if it is taken to imply that we *always* consciously aim at our own individual pleasure; but not if it is taken to imply hedonism of the past, *i.e.*, that we tend to perform actions that have led to pleasure in our experience, and to desist from those that have led to pain. This would be quite consistent, of course, with Bentham's contentions that we do *sometimes* consciously calculate the balance of pleasure and pain to be expected from certain acts, and also with his view that we *ought* to do so on important occasions, with full information and utmost intelligence. The hedonism of the past seems to be basic to Aristotle's eudaemonism, too, especially in relation to *habits*, virtuous as well as vicious and neutral; and it need not exclude choices in which virtue is *formed*, for virtue is the most important thing of all, he says, and it is natural to choose it. But when habits are formed, choice is not necessary.

5. How Good a Deterrent Is Pain?

Recent psychological studies suggest that pain is not so effective a deterrent and educator as had always been thought. The legislation and criminal codes with which Bentham was primarily concerned were calculated to improve conduct mainly by the imposition of pain. But there was another side to Bentham's thought. He held that as men become enlightened they apprehend the identity of their own interests with the interests of the whole community, and punishment and the threat of punishment are less needed. The only justification for the infliction of pain was the promotion of the general happiness; obviously the less pain needed the better. Aristotle's eudaemonism also would only gain in attraction if it proved true that pleasure is a more efficient educator than pain. And as the pain of punishment declined, so also would the moral obloquy and pain of inflicting pain and death.

Here, then, are a few of the findings and afterthoughts about pain. Experiments of N. R. F. Maier show that punishment often produces a state of frustration in which the animal repeats the same painful mistake time and time again.[50] B. F. Skinner found that punishment deterred the punished responses only temporarily; the learning did not last. "The effect of punishment was a temporary suppression of the behavior, not a reduction of the total number of responses. Even under severe and prolonged

[50] See *Frustration: A Study of Behavior Without a Goal.*

punishment, that rate of responding will rise when punishment has been discontinued. . . . It is found that after a given time the rate of responding is no lower than if no punishment had taken place."[51] The tendency to respond remains after all the punishment designed to eradicate it. This agrees, Skinner points out, "with Freud's discovery of the surviving activity of what he called repressed wishes,"[52] for these wishes continue to be active, in one way or another, though the responses are punished. Doubts about pain as a dependable deterrent are also stirred by experiments on rats in which learning to make a response is facilitated by electric shocks, when followed by food. Pain does not always result in avoidance. Once the pain stimulus has been organized on a cerebral level, D. Hebb says, it *may be* positively motivating.[53] Thus punishment *may* actually reinforce the behavior it is designed to obliterate.

Pain, however, usually functions as a deterrent, and the question raised is how efficient and dependable it is as a deterrent. One disadvantage of pain, as compared with pleasure, is that it does not tell us *what to do* but tells us *what not to do*. The punished response is prevented from occurring (temporarily, at least) by the substitution of another response that is incompatible with it. But this substitute response may involve chronic fear or anxiety, or any of numerous incapacitating psychosomatic or hysterical symptoms. The substitute response may be worse in its effects than the socially disapproved response that was eliminated by the punishment. There seems to be a good consensus among authorities that psychotherapy deals largely with the byproducts of punishment. The ways in which neurosis arises from pain and frustration is illustrated by numerous studies of experimentally induced neurosis in animals, and even in man.[54]

An increasing concern of the social sciences is to investigate the extent to which rewards and painless techniques can be substituted for punishment and still maintain social controls in a complex modern society. To the extent that civilized goals can be achieved without punishment, happiness would seem to be more generally attainable, whether it is defined as the greatest pleasure of the greatest number, or as activity in accordance with virtue, accompanied by pleasure. Only Price, Kant, and others who esteem retribution above happiness would disagree with this objective.

[51] *Science and Human Behavior*, p. 184.
[52] *Ibid.*
[53] *The Organization of Behavior*, pp. 189–190.
[54] See, for example, A. R. Luria, *The Nature of Human Conflicts*; P. E. Huston, et al., "A Study of Hypnotically Induced Complexes by Means of Luria Techniques," *J. of Gen. Psychology*, 11, 1934; and, for a general account of experimentally induced neuroses, J. H. Masserman, *Behavior and Neuroses*; and "Comparative Conditioned Neuroses," in *Annals of the New York Academy of Sciences*, 56, Art. 2, 1953.

ARE THERE QUALITATIVE DIFFERENCES AMONG PLEASURES?

We have seen that, according to Aristotle, there are not only lower and higher pleasures; pleasures differ from one another as much as do the activities they accompany. Here are his arguments and a few others:

1. Things of different kinds are *completed* by things of different kinds. "Now the activities of thought differ from those of the senses, and both differ among themselves, in kind; so, therefore, do the pleasures that complete them."[55] The pleasure of drinking a certain wine could be said to "complete" *that* activity, but not the activity of solving a geometrical problem; to this it would be inappropriate. The argument hangs on the meaning of "complete." In his *Metaphysics*, Aristotle distinguishes three meanings of the word. A thing is called complete (a) if it is impossible to find a single one of its parts outside itself, or (b) if it is unexcelled in excellence by anything of its kind, *e.g.*, "a complete doctor, a complete flute-player," or (c) if it has attained its end, and this is good.[56] An activity might be completed by pleasure in sense (a) if pleasure is conceived as part of the activity. The drinking of wine would at least be *more* complete if it is pleasant than if it is not. And an activity, *e.g.*, solving a geometrical problem, might be completed by pleasure in sense (b) insofar as the pleasure increases proficiency and perseverance, at least Aristotle assures us it does. But sense (c) would be inapplicable since Aristotle holds that pleasure is not generally the end of activities.

The argument, however, raises a fundamental doubt. It does not exclude the possibility that the pleasantness that in some sense *completes* an activity is qualitatively the same in the case of the diverse activities. The activities might well be diverse, while the pleasure that *completes* them is homogeneous.

2. Aristotle also argues that

each of the pleasures is bound up with the activity it completes. For an activity is intensified by its proper pleasure, since each class of things is better judged of and brought to precision by those who engage in the activity with pleasure; *e.g.*, it is those who enjoy geometrical thinking that become geometers and grasp the various propositions better, and, similarly, those who are fond of music or of building, and so on, make progress in their proper function by enjoying it.[57]

[55] *Op. cit., Nicomachean Ethics*, 1175a26–28.
[56] See *ibid., Metaphysics*, 1021b12–1022a3.
[57] *Ibid., Nicomachean Ethics*, 1175a30–35.

The pleasure proper to a given activity intensifies it and increases proficiency, but pleasures proper to other activities hinder it. Thus the pleasure of listening to flute music may prevent music lovers from attending to an argument and, in general, the more pleasant activity obstructs or completely eliminates the less. "Now since activities are made precise and more enduring and better by their proper pleasure, and injured by alien pleasures, evidently the two kinds of pleasure are far apart. For alien pleasures do pretty much what proper pains do."[58]

That the pleasantness of an activity stimulates and improves performance is generally admitted, though some would add that the effect is not due to the pleasantness (alone), but (also) to the underlying physiological processes. Aristotle affirms the role of the physiological processes, except in the case of the purely intellectual or contemplative activities, and this seems to be out of line with his general position. The crux of the argument, however, is the claim that the contrary effects of different pleasures on an activity prove that one pleasure is proper to that activity, and the others are alien—and that pleasures are thus qualitatively very different. The objection made to the argument can be put as a question, viz.: Why cannot the contrary effects be explained by the contrary activities? It is very difficult to attend to an argument while listening to music. The moves required by the one are presumably incompatible with those required by the other. But if the activities themselves exclude or hinder each other, as simultaneous performances, there is no need to invoke qualitatively different pleasures to explain the exclusion or the hindrance.

3. "Each animal is thought to have a proper pleasure, as it has a proper function; viz. that which corresponds to its activity. If we survey them species by species, too, this will be evident; horse, dog, and man have different pleasures."[59] Different men also prefer different pleasures. The best pleasures are those that attend the activities preferred by "the supremely happy man." Here again the retort of critics is: The activities that yield pleasure to various species are universally conceded to be quite different. The variation in their constitution, habits, etc., are perhaps sufficient to account for this. There is no reason to think that no explanation is possible unless we assume qualitatively different pleasures.

4. "Now for most men their pleasures are in conflict with one another because these are not by nature pleasant, but the lovers of what is noble find pleasant the things that are by nature pleasant. . . . Their life, therefore, has no further need of pleasure as a sort of adventitious charm, but has its pleasure in itself."[60] There are thus said to be two kinds of

[58] *Ibid.*, 1175b14–17.
[59] *Ibid.*, 1176a3–6.
[60] *Ibid.*, 1099a12–16.

pleasures: Those which conflict among themselves and are adventitious, and those which steadily accrue to the virtuous man by reason of his virtue, and which are, like the virtues, without conflict.[61] If this is taken as an argument for different *kinds* of pleasure, it would be inconclusive. It might be true that the pleasure of making money is adventitious and conflicts with other pleasures, and also that the pleasure proper to virtue is steady and built-in, but this could be explained by the *causal effects* of the two kinds of pleasant activities. It would have no tendency to prove that the pleasure of making money is qualitatively different from the pleasure belonging to virtue.

5. Another argument, which begins its career with Plato, is to the effect that, since reason is higher than sensation, and distinctive of man, whereas sensation is shared with animals, the pleasure proper to reason is a better and finer pleasure than the pleasure proper to sensation and sensuality. So far, the argument has little force. The hedonist readily replies that rational pleasures are better than sensuous because they are *greater,* in duration or intensity, and less mixed with pain; they *need* not be *qualitatively* superior.

J. S. Mill joins Plato and Aristotle in contending that, as he puts it, "some *kinds* of pleasure are more desirable and more valuable than others."[62] "It is better to be a human being dissatisfied than a pig satisfied; better to be Socrates dissatisfied than a pig satisfied. And if the fool, or the pig, are of a different opinion, it is because they only know their side of the question. The other party to the comparison knows both sides."[63]

Does it follow that pleasures differ from one another qualitatively? Could not Bentham or any other regular-line hedonist reply: "It is better to be a cultivated man than a pig. True enough. But the reason is that the cultivated man, in spite of his anxieties and disappointments, which the pig is free from, enjoys a greater balance of pleasure over pain." Sheer quantity of pleasure would explain the cultivated man's choice as well as qualitative differences among pleasures could.

But has not Mill excluded this answer? Suppose the cultivated man's choice is between being himself, and enjoying a considerably less quantity of pleasure, and being a pig, which enjoys much more, and, at the same time, suffers less pain. If the alternative is put this way, it follows that something other than the quantity of pleasure and pain determines the choice of the cultivated man. But why must that *something* be the higher value of the pleasures of a cultivated life? It might be the higher value of the cultivated activities themselves. Another objection to Mill's alternative has been that it is decidedly artificial. Can Socrates really put himself in

---

[61] *Ibid., Magna Moralia,* 1200a2–10.
[62] *Utilitarianism,* p. 7.
[63] *Ibid.,* p. 9.

the place of the pig? If not, how can he make the required comparison? Another objection, considered by Mill, is that some men capable of higher pleasures actually come to prefer sensual indulgence. Mill admits the fact. Men capable of the higher pleasures sometimes do succumb to the lower. "But this is quite compatible with a full appreciation of the intrinsic superiority of the higher. Men often, from infirmity of character, make their election for the nearer good [pleasure], though they know it to be the less valuable."[64] In other cases, a man, as he ages, may really lose his ability to enjoy the higher pleasures though he knows full well that they are more valuable.

Mill's argument for higher pleasures is not so much that men do usually *prefer* those that come from exercise of the higher faculties, as that all men capable of them *recognize* them as more valuable, even though they should be less in amount than sensuous pleasures. The biological conception of man, on the contrary, regards the exercise of the higher faculties as a mere means to biological satisfactions, and to securing them for the future. It should be clear, however, that it is possible to oppose the biological conception of man without recognizing different *kinds* of pleasure. One can take the view that the higher activities afford *more* pleasure than the lower.

6. In Plato's *Philebus,* Socrates argues that pleasures are of two kinds, true and false, and the contention has been revived in recent years by a number of philosophers. At first, it lacks all plausibility. But, if pleasure is expressed by the common idiom of "pleased with," we see at once that what we are pleased with may turn out to be nonexistent, or to be quite repugnant. A man may be pleased with his inheritance, though he subsequently finds that there was nothing to be pleased *with*—that he has, in fact, inherited nothing. But are not such pleasures mistaken, and perhaps false? Similarly, are not the pleasures that have true objects correct and true?

The discussion of this issue brings out important aspects of pleasure, but they do not concern us here. Even if it should be decided that some pleasures are true and others false, these two classes of pleasures would not constitute *kinds* of pleasure, in the sense we are discussing. The true pleasures would be true because they corresponded with a fact, and the false would be false because they clashed with a fact. Or, in any case, they would be true or false according to their relations to something else. They would not have been shown to be qualitatively different. The same is true when Socrates interprets true and false pleasures as "good" and "false," respectively.

7. The strongest support for different kinds of pleasure may come, after all, from introspection. Are not pleasures so closely bound up with **different**

[64] *Ibid.*

kinds of activity as not to admit of separation, as Aristotle claims; and do we not prefer the pleasure that comes from the things we love most? Does the artist want indiscriminate pleasure, or does he want the specific enjoyment of artistic achievement? If what he wants is pleasure in general, he would be as well content to have it coupled with prowess on the stock market or success on the tennis court. It could scarcely be contended that the *only* reason he actively desires the pleasure to be had by artistic success, and not the pleasure to be had from other activities, is that he thinks he has some chance of getting the former, but has no hope of the others.

But, if what the artist, the mathematician, the merchant, the mechanic, the gambler, etc., each chiefly wants is the pleasantness bound up with the activity he loves, and would not be content with the pleasantness associated with other activities, we do have some reason to think that there are, in fact, kinds of pleasure. It could be said, of course, that, if the artist had been educated as a mathematician, a merchant or a mechanic, his taste would have differed accordingly. This would mean that a lengthy education is necessary for a full appreciation of certain pleasures, and that without it the exuberance and success of certain activities could not be experienced. All men start out life with the same biological satisfactions. It is through the association of these biological satisfactions with activities that are at first neutral, Mill contends, that they acquire such widely different tastes in pleasure. Yet the cultivated man, Mill also holds, knows enough of the pleasures of a number of vocations and stages of life to make comparison among them, and to testify that they are qualitatively quite different.

A hedonistic answer to all these arguments in favor of qualitative differences is summed up succinctly by Sidgwick:

> When . . . we judge of the preferable quality (as "elevation" or "refinement") of a state of consciousness as distinct from its pleasantness, we seem to appeal to some common standard which others can apply as well as the sentient individual. Hence I should conclude that when one kind of consciousness is judged to be qualitatively superior to another, although less pleasant, it is not the feeling itself that is preferred, but something in the circumstances under which it arises, in the active or passive relations of the sentient individual to other persons or things or permanent objects of thought. For certainly if we in thought distinguish any feeling from all its circumstances and conditions (and also from all its effects on the subsequent feelings of the same individual or of others) and contemplate it merely as a transient feeling of a single subject; it seems impossible to find in it any other preferable quality than that which we call its pleasantness, the degree of which is only cognizable directly by the sentient individual.[65]

[65] *Methods of Ethics*, 4th ed., pp. 128–129.

It will be seen that the above passage is a generalization of the particular objections we have noted to seven arguments for qualities of pleasure. The third sentence deals especially with the introspective case for such qualities. In direct contradiction to 7, above, it states that we introspect qualitative differences of feeling only because we fail to separate the feelings themselves from all sorts of surrounding circumstances. If we attended to the feelings by themselves, "it seems impossible to find in it any other preferable quality than that which we call its pleasantness." Aristotle and Mill are just as certain of the contrary, and insist that the pleasure of the seducer is quite distinguishable from that of the philosopher. The feelings are distinguishable in their effects, morally distinguishable, Bentham and Sidgwick would reply, but not in themselves.

Here, perhaps, is the crux of the controversy. Can the explanation of the disagreement be that Aristotle never learned to introspect in the modern sense, while Mill forgot, for the moment? Were not feelings a great deal more subjective for Sidgwick than for Aristotle? One will not find in Aristotle anything comparable to Sidgwick's demand that we discriminate the feeling itself from every sort of surrounding circumstance. On the contrary, pleasure is described as a bloom that supervenes upon an activity and "completes" it. The pleasantness is like a color that suffuses the operation, and it is as if every diverse operation has its own distinctive color. This analogy, however, is misleading in one important respect. Objects change their colors under many conditions, and very different objects can have the same color. We can thus describe colors apart from the objects they characterize. The reverse is true of Aristotle's pleasures, for each of these is bound up with its own distinctive activity, and inseparable from it. How, in this case, can a pleasure, we may ask, be described as anything different from the particular activity it characterizes? And what can virtuous and vicious pleasures have in common to justify us in calling them both pleasures?[66] And, again, if pleasure is simply a name for an assort-

---

[66] Protarchus asks Socrates this question in *Philebus* [12]. When Socrates claims that it would be absurd to hold that "opposite pleasures," such as the pleasure of the wise man and that of the fool "are severally alike," Protarchus objects: "Why, Socrates, they are opposed in that they spring from opposite sources, but they are not in themselves opposite. For must not pleasure be of all things most absolutely like pleasure—that is, like itself?" Socrates replies that pleasures are alike as pleasures, just as colors are alike as colors, but that this does not prevent white and black from being absolute opposites. In the same way, some pleasures are opposites, viz., good and bad pleasures, though they are alike in being pleasures.

A recent author has criticized Socrates' analogy between pleasure and color: "The relation of colour to colours is not the same as the relation between pleasure and pleasures," he contends. "One learns what colour is by learning to distinguish black from white and other colours; one does not learn what pleasure is by learning to discriminate between the pleasures of golf and the pleasures of sonateering." (Anthony Kenny, *Action, Emotion and Will*, p. 133.) No evidence, however, is offered for the latter judgment.

ment of pleasant activities, what can Aristotle mean by saying that any pleasure "intensifies" and "brings to precision" the activity to which it is proper? Would it not come to saying that some activities, called "pleasant," are self-stimulating and self-improving?

In Sidgwick's view, these difficulties could be expected to result when one fails to separate the feeling of pleasure itself from all the surrounding circumstances. How deep the difficulties go is debatable. At present it is only necessary to recall that the stimulating agent, in Aristotle's account, is not a mere *feeling* of pleasure. Implicated also are physiological processes (except perhaps where the intellectual virtues are concerned[67]) and the activity upon which the pleasure supervenes. Pleasant activities, however diverse, have a common nature: Many are desired for their own sake by all men, and all by some; and, this being the case, they are self-sustaining and, where skill and success are involved, performance tends to be improved. And painful activities are observed to have a directly opposite effect. This does not imply that pleasures are identical with the activities they attend, but only that they are very "close" to them in time and nature, and in fact hardly distinguishable:

> But the pleasures involved in activities are more proper to them than the desires; for the latter are separated both in time and in nature, while the former are close to the activities, and so hard to distinguish from them that it admits of dispute whether the activity is not the same as the pleasure. (Still, pleasure does not seem to *be* thought or perception—that would be strange; but because they are not found apart they appear to some people the same.) As activities are different, then, so are the corresponding pleasures.[68]

This Aristotelian theory is not plausible in the abstract. It becomes very plausible the moment we are called upon to describe, to explain or render understandable or credible, the pleasure we find in our activities and their objects; for what we do in describing a pleasure particularly is to describe these activities or objects. When we remark that we greatly enjoyed a concert by the Budapest Quartet, there seems no way of explaining what we mean more particularly except by praising the program and analyzing the fine points of the performance. We need not be justifying ourselves in the face of possible criticism. It is very unlikely that we are consciously detailing the acoustic events that *caused* in us a feeling of a certain intensity and duration. We are rather filling in the superficiality of "How I enjoyed the concert!" or "What pleasure!" with our actual meaning, and specifying what our pleasure or enjoyment was like.

It could not be maintained, of course, that the concrete specification that somehow amplifies the statement that something is pleasing must always be

---

[67] See *op. cit.*, *Eudemian Ethics*, 1220a9–10.
[68] *Ibid.*, *Nicomachean Ethics*, 1175b30–35.

an amplification of the *meaning* of the statement. It might serve other purposes on occasion. Our concern here is to point out that saying that a concert, an art exhibit, or a vacation was enjoyable is normally (unless one's auditor was himself present) taken to be promissory of further statements specifying the *nature* of the enjoyment, which specification is generally a description of the activities or objects in which the pleasure was experienced.

We have seen that pleasure, according to Aristotle, is not a separate state or a process of any kind. Pleasure is no movement or process: It "seems at any moment complete, for it does not lack anything which coming into being later will complete its form."[69] That is, it never becomes *more* complete in form if it lasts longer. Movements and processes, on the contrary, are only complete at the final moment. They also require time, whereas we can be pleased at a single moment, for pleasure is a whole without parts.

Gilbert Ryle is largely in agreement with Aristotle, at this particular point. He remarks that:

> When I enjoy or dislike a conversation, there is not, besides the easily clockable stretches of conversation, something else, stretches of which might be separately clocked, some continuous or intermittent introspectable phenomenon which is the agreeableness or disagreeableness of the conversation to me. I might indeed enjoy the first five minutes and the last three minutes of the conversation, detest one intermediate stage. . . . But if asked to compare in retrospect the durations of my enjoyings and dislikings with the durations of the stretches of the conversation which I had enjoyed or disliked, I should not be able to think of two things whose durations were to be compared. Nor can my pleasure in contributing and listening to the conversation be some collateral activity or experience which might conceivably clamour for a part of my interest or attention, in the way in which a tickle might distract my attention from the butterfly.[70]

Ryle concludes that his liking and disliking are not introspectable objects over and above the conversation and his interest in it. They are rather "special qualities" of his interest in the conversation, which, in turn, is "the special quality" of his "active and receptive conversational activities."[71]

The issue over qualities of pleasure finds its real testing ground in the intricacies of introspection. If Bentham and Sidgwick are right, Aristotle fails to distinguish the feeling of pleasure from an assortment of surrounding circumstances, and hence does not clearly realize that one pleasure can only be better than another by being *more, i.e.,* quantitatively greater. If Aristotle is right, and Ryle's elaboration is accepted, then there is no feeling

---

[69] *Ibid.*, 1174a15–16.
[70] *The Tarner Lectures,* "Pleasure" in *Dilemmas,* Ch. VI, p. 60.
[71] *Ibid.*, p. 60.

of pleasure that can have a longer or shorter duration, or perhaps any degree of intensity, apart from the duration and the properties of the activity to which it belongs, or to which it is "proper." This outcome has an important bearing on the next question to be considered.

The Fate of the Hedonistic Calculus and the Pathos of Any Alternative

Whatever its difficulties may be, the hedonistic calculus is essential to hedonism. Happiness cannot be the greatest possible balance of pleasures over pains unless there *is* such a balance, and it cannot be achieved unless this can be calculated and distinguished from lesser sums. An analogous problem haunts every teleological system of ethics. However happiness is defined, it always involves a summation of goods, a weighing and comparison of values in the future, and, as realized by different individuals, a computing of what will be most and best. The fact that nonhedonistic systems do not have much to say about their own calculating process does not mean that it is less of a problem for them; it may mean just the opposite.

Since we have already described the hedonistic calculus (Chapter 6), especially the account of it in Bentham—which is by far the most elaborate—we can now consider the standard objections to it, and the replies that hedonists can make in each case.

1. Is "the Greatest Pleasure of the Greatest Number" Meaningless?

T. H. Green, whose self-realization view we have mentioned (Chapter 7), is a determined opponent of hedonism, and would correct it in a direction that can be recognized as mainly Aristotelian. We can see, Green begins, why hedonism has proved so attractive to many thinkers. Defining the highest good as "the greatest possible net sum of pleasures has seemed to afford a much more positive and intelligible criterion than the conception of a full realization of human capacities, which we admit to be only definable by reflection on the partial realization of these capacities in recognized excellences of character and conduct." It also promises an escape, he says, from the circle in which "virtue" and "ought" are each defined in terms of the other. But far from being more intelligible, he argues, the notion of "the greatest possible net sum of pleasures" is "intrinsically unmeaning . . . a phrase to which no idea really corresponds."[72]

[72] *Prologomena to Ethics,* p. 400.

Green does not mean that it is meaningless to speak of "a greater pleasure of a greater number," for anyone can see that if there are more people pleased there will be more pleasure.

> The ability, however, to compare a large sum of pleasure . . . is quite a different thing from ability to conceive a greatest possible sum of pleasures, or to attach any meaning to that phrase. The sum of pleasures plainly admits of indefinite increase, with the continued existence of sentient beings capable of pleasure . . . but it will never be complete while sentient beings exist. To say that the ultimate good is a greatest possible sum of pleasures . . . is to say that it is an end which for ever recedes; which is not only unattainable but . . . can never be more nearly approached; and such an end clearly cannot serve the purpose of a criterion, by enabling us to distinguish actions which bring men nearer to it from those that do not.[73]

How can "the greatest possible sum of pleasure" furnish a criterion for right conduct, *i.e.*, tell us which of our acts will contribute most to it, if this sum is always changing and is never the same? It would be like measuring our conduct with a ruler that is always changing and growing longer. Yet hedonism and utilitarianism cannot get along without this criterion, Green says. If we substitute a new utilitarian criterion, which says only that actions are to be approved that yield more pleasure to more people, and omit any reference to "a perfect state of existence," then approval and disapproval lose their meaning. It would seem, therefore, that we can really *approve* of moral action only in terms of an ideal that is changeless!

Green is also arguing that, since pleasures come one by one, with spaces in between, and are never experienced as a sum, they cannot form a sum. Pleasures, he may have meant, are nothing if not experienced, and therefore the greatest sum of pleasures, which itself must be a pleasure on the hedonistic criterion, is nothing.

Sidgwick answers Green's argument as follows:

> Each pleasure, we are told, "is over before the other is enjoyed": a man "cannot accumulate pleasures; if he experiences a pleasure every hour for the next 50 years, he will have no more in possession, and will be in no better state, than if he is pleased the next minute and then comes to an end."
>
> But unless the transiency of pleasure diminishes its pleasantness . . . I cannot see that the possibility of realizing the hedonistic end is at all affected by the necessity of realizing it in successive parts. The argument seems to assume that by an "end" must be meant a goal or consummation, which, after gradually drawing nearer to it, we reach all at once: but this is not, I conceive, the sense in which the word is ordinarily understood by ethical writers.[74]

[73] *Ibid.*, p. 401.
[74] *Op. cit.*, p. 134.

Sidgwick shows his usual cool restraint. He might have pointed out that, if pleasures do not add up, neither do hours or days or good deeds, and one should be as much as many. He concludes that,

> so long as one's prospective balance of pleasure over pain admits of being made greater or less by immediate action in one way or another, there seems no reason why "Maximum Happiness" should not provide as service-able a criterion of good conduct as any "chief good" capable of being possessed all at once, or in some way independently of the condition of time.[75]

2. QUESTIONS ABOUT PLEASURE AS THE GOAL

In an effort to make sense out of the utilitarian goal, Green suggests that what the utilitarian *could* reasonably mean is "a state in which all human beings . . . shall live as pleasantly as is possible for them, without one gaining pleasure at the expense of another . . . a certain sort of social life . . . pleasant to all who share in it," but which is not particularized in any other respect.[76]

Green has no positive objection to this reformulation of the theory, and is, in fact, as much in favor of the pleasant life as he is opposed to "a sum of pleasures." His only complaint is that

> instead of having that definiteness which, because all know what pleasure is, it seemed at first to promise, it turns out on consideration to be so abstract and indefinite. It tells us nothing of that life, to the attainment of which our actions must contribute if they are to be what they should be, but merely that it would be as pleasant as possible for all persons, or for all beings of whose consciousness we can take account.[77]

This serious shortcoming of "universal pleasantness," Green implies, is overcome by his own ideal of "the absolutely desirable life," which consists of the full realization of the individual's capacities. Although "pleasure must be incidental to such realization, it is in no way distinctive of it, being equally incidental to any unimpeded activity, to the exercise of merely animal functions no less than to those that are properly human."[78] It is true that we do not know precisely what a *full* realization of capacities would be like, but we do know a great deal about partial realizations. We can be certain that the ideal of full realization provides "a definiteness of direction, which the injunction to make life as pleasant as possible does not supply."[79] The former points pretty clearly to a standard of knowledge and

[75] *Ibid.*
[76] See *ibid.*, pp. 402–403.
[77] *Ibid.*, p. 403.
[78] *Ibid.*
[79] *Ibid.*, pp. 403–404.

art, an attainment of virtues and excellences, which may be far in advance of what has been realized in a given society; whereas the latter comprises no such inherent aspiration to a fuller, more human life.

We have seen that the eudaemonists, and the four self-realizationists discussed in Chapter 7—Seth, Bradley, Hobhouse, and John Dewey—all make the same point, though in very different ways. They all insist that pleasure is the normal accompaniment of the process of self-realization; they all contend that the goal sought is rather pleasant things than pleasure as such, and that pleasure divorced from the activities to which it belongs is too indefinite to supply the guidelines to a truly human life.

Bradley, for example, holds that, while it is good to maximize pleasure and minimize pain as far as we are able to do so, it is good "because it increases the actualities and possibilities of life" (see above, Chapter 7, p. 169). Yet pleasure will not tell you which are the higher functions; ". . . if you go by it you must prefer a lower state of harmony to a higher state of contradiction." For his part, John Dewey contends that "pleasures are so externally and accidentally connected with the performance of a deed, that an attempt to foresee them is probably the stupidest course which could be taken in order to secure guidance for action."[80] Though pleasures are generally goods to be enjoyed, those of the dissolute, the dishonest, the mean and stingy are morally condemned. "And this fact is fatal to the theory that pleasures constitute the good because of which a given object is entitled to be the end of action."[81] The long-range calculation of our future pleasure is self-defeating since the occurrence of pleasures is too fortuitous, and it gives us no assurance that the pleasures we realize will be such as we can approve and really want.

What answers can hedonists make to this two-pronged objection? Are the pleasures projected into the future too indefinite to be computed and counted on, and are they such a poor guide to the kind of life men think they should have? The objection assumes that hedonists want a kind of life in which distinctive human abilities are duly developed and exercised, but this assumption, as we have seen, is justified by-and-large.

Everyone, of course, knows what pleasure is. The objectors do not deny this. The question is whether everyone knows what the maximum pleasure of the community, or even of any individual, will be like in the distant future, and how it is to be promoted, especially as it relates to the goal of being a complete human being. Hedonists can admit that the future is more or less uncertain, and there are undeniable difficulties in calculating future pleasures, especially those of other people. But has it been shown

80 *Ethics*, p. 207.
81 *Ibid.*, p. 209.

that there is any alternative good which could be calculated with greater certainty? Would it be any easier to know what actions would promote our maximum self-development or make the largest contribution to the culture of the future? Dewey, who insists that pleasures are not to be calculated, often insists that other goods are in the same boat. The future is "precarious." Second, even though some other good could be better calculated than pleasure, pleasure would have a certain immense advantage: Other goods are matters of taste and are enjoyed only by some men, or at certain times, whereas pleasure is always to everyone's taste and no surfeit is possible. Thus it will always make sense to say that men ought to pursue a certain line of conduct because it will result in pleasure or relief from pain, but, if we say they ought to act in certain ways because it will achieve some other good, the sense, or good sense, will be lacking unless they happen to want this good. Only something valued universally can furnish a basis for injunctions binding on all men. Third, whatever the difficulties about the commensurability of pleasures and pains, they are at least commensurable to some degree, which is more than can be said of other goods that compete with pleasure. How, for example, can one compare the relative value of two lines of self-development—one cultural enterprise with another, for example—and say that one is more of a self-development than the other? But if self-developments are not commensurable, where is the guidance? No documentation, at this stage, is needed to see that these are the retorts implicit in the literature of hedonism and utilitarianism.

To the charge that, if maximum pleasure alone is the goal "you must prefer a lower state of harmony to a higher state of contradiction," and wind up with the fleshpots rather than with music and mathematics, hedonists point out that this presupposes that the fleshpots afford more pleasure than the higher pursuits. But this is certainly debatable. The Epicureans and most other hedonists hold that friendly and intellectual engagements provide a much better balance of pleasure over pain. Hobbes holds that the pleasure of curiosity is far more intense than that of any carnal delights, though Freud maintains just the reverse. Can we say in the usual manner that only the connoisseur, who knows *both* the delights of the fleshpots and of philosophy, can know which is greater, and that the connoisseur always decides in favor of philosophy? Commenting on this argument, as it is expressed by Plato, Sidgwick says: "But who can tell that the philosopher's constitution is not such as to render the enjoyment of the senses, in his case, comparatively feeble? while on the other hand the sensualist's mind may not be able to attain more than a thin shadow of the philosopher's delight."[82] Thus it would be hard to *prove* that the doctrine

[82] *Op. cit.,* p. 148.

that pleasures alone are intrinsically valuable would have the practical effect of directing men along the primrose path.

The hedonists have other lines of defense. Bentham insists that those who say that men ought to cultivate activities that yield less pleasure than do others they might pursue are really embracing the "Principle of Asceticism." They are, in effect, maintaining that less pleasure is better than more. It might also well be that some men would fulfill themselves better by cultivating the pleasures of the simple life, or by cooperating, on a modest level, in a larger social enterprise, than they would by straining for the highest fulfillments in science and art. On the political level, the advocacy of policies entailing less general pleasure, or more pain, than others that might be introduced is, from a democratic viewpoint, always suspect, whatever reasons for it may be given.

3. QUESTIONS ABOUT THE HEDONISTIC CALCULUS

"One can make an estimate on the basis of the general tendency of a proposed action upon welfare and suffering," John Dewey says; "no one can figure out in advance all the units of pleasure and pain (even admitting that they can be reduced to unit quantities) which will follow."[83] It is not only that the future is uncertain and of a baffling complexity. There is also the prevailing circumstance that the train of actions you embark upon to secure some future sum of pleasures all have side effects, and that these side effects may be very undesirable. The comparing of a present pleasure with the anticipation of a future one—a warm, living experience with a spectral thought of a proposed one in the future—is difficult enough; weighing your pleasure against the pleasures of other people, especially those remote in space, in culture, or circumstance, is even worse. It is also

> difficult to make a regard for general happiness the standard of right and wrong, even in a purely theoretical estimate. [It] goes contrary to our natural tendency to put first our own happiness and that of persons near to us. This difficulty, however, is slight in comparison with that of making the intellectual estimate effective in action whenever it conflicts with our natural partiality in our own favor.[84]

The alternative to "the alleged precision for which Bentham was praised," but which "introduces an impossibility into actual conduct," is reliance on our own good character.

[83] *Op. cit.*, pp. 264–265.
[84] *Ibid.*, p. 264.

We are sure that the *attitude* of personal kindliness, of sincerity and fairness, will make our judgment of the effects of a proposed action on the good of others infinitely more likely to be correct than will those of hate, hypocrisy and self-seeking.[85]

Dewey wants to agree with J. S. Mill, as against Bentham, that kind hearts are more trustworthy than any calculation of maximum pleasure in the future.

Herbert Spencer, although he is himself a "universalistic hedonist" (utilitarian), also denies the feasibility of long-range calculation of pleasures. He cites Sidgwick's criticism of *egoistic* hedonism, but claims that the difficulties are compounded when the aim is the greatest surplus of pleasures over pains—of the whole community.

> Making general happiness the immediate object of pursuit, implies numerous and complicated instrumentalities officered by thousands of unseen and unlike persons, and working on millions of other persons unseen and unlike. . . . So that even supposing valuation of pleasures and pains for the community at large is more practicable than . . . valuation of his own pleasures and pains by the individual; yet the ruling of conduct with a view to the one is far more difficult than the ruling of it with a view to the other. Hence, if the method of egoistic hedonism is unsatisfactory, far more unsatisfactory for the same and kindred reasons, is the method of universalistic hedonism, or utilitarianism.[86]

The utilitarian answers to these objections have been anticipated above. One can be a good utilitarian without undertaking to prove in the case of every action, or every important action undertaken, that it will yield the best balance of pleasure over pain. Ethical codes and every practical art, Mill points out, provide us with proven rules of conduct. "Honesty is the best policy" is not supplanted and superseded by the utility principle.

> It is a truly whimsical supposition that if mankind were agreed in considering utility to be the test of morality, they would remain without any agreement as to what *is* useful, and would take no measures for having their notions on the subject taught to the young, and enforced by law and opinion.[87]

Bentham himself is far from proposing that we calculate at the drop of the hat. The hedonistic calculation is most useful in testing commonly accepted rules of conduct, in cases where they are in conflict or doubt. Since Bentham is mainly interested in introducing new legislation and in reforming cruel and capricious criminal codes, he naturally gives a great deal of attention to the pleasure-pain arithmetic. He justifies his proposals

[85] *Ibid.*, p. 265.
[86] *The Data of Ethics*, p. 184.
[87] *Op. cit.*, p. 22.

radically by a showing that the hedonistic calculus is necessary and feasible. But in proportion as a rational system of laws was adopted, there would be much less need for individuals to calculate remote consequences of their acts.[88]

But if the dubieties of the hedonistic calculus appear too costly to the utilitarian, could he, perhaps, abandon it, while yet retaining intact the basic utilitarian principle that the final good or happiness is the greatest pleasure of the greatest number? This is, in any case, the alternative chosen by Spencer, who says:

> It is quite consistent to assert that happiness is the ultimate aim of action, and at the same time to deny that it can be reached by making it the immediate aim.[89]

It is feasible to compute the balance of pleasure and pain over short periods, while it is futile over longer ones; but this does not disprove that happiness is the end of action. In the first place, it is feasible to compute the balance of pleasure over pain in ever so many cases, and the fact that we cannot do so in other cases does not prevent us from being utilitarians. A businessman does not cease the practice of choosing the best bargain he can for the reason that in some cases he cannot determine which of two bargains is better. A utilitarian need not give up the ideal maximum pleasure because pleasures and pains do not form a graduated quantitative series, and are not perfectly commensurate with one another.

But this is not Spencer's main contention. In a letter to J. S. Mill, repudiating the name "anti-utilitarian" that Mill had applied to him, Spencer says:

> The view for which I contend is, that Morality, properly so-called—the science of right conduct—has for its object to determine *how* and *why* certain modes of conduct are detrimental, and certain other modes beneficial. These good and bad results cannot be accidental, but must be necessary consequences of the constitution of things; and I conceive it to be the business of Moral Science to deduce, from the laws of life and the conditions of existence, what kinds of action necessarily tend to produce happiness, and what kinds to produce unhappiness. Having done this, its deductions are to be recognized as laws of conduct; and are to be conformed to irrespective of a direct estimation of happiness or misery.[90]

[88] Those who hold that the pleasure of the community is best advanced by following moral rules, *e.g.,* The Golden Rule, are now called "rule utilitarians," whereas those who believe that calculation of the effects of individual acts is best are called "act utilitarians."

[89] *Op. cit.,* p. 184.

[90] *Ibid.,* p. 66.

Just as astronomy has evolved from an accumulation of individual observations to a deductive system, so will Moral Science. This "Absolute Ethics," of course, belongs to the remote future, though it can be a guide to the "Relative Ethics" of the present.

Sidgwick is not willing to admit that individual calculations of pleasures and pains can be avoided in this way. The science affording deductions of hedonistically right conduct does not exist, and may never exist.[91] Moreover, Spencer's Absolute Morality presupposes a "final perfect form of society," in which pleasure will be at its maximum for everyone, and pain will have disappeared. Sidgwick thinks it would be "quite impossible to forecast the nature and relations of the persons composing such a community with sufficient clearness and certainty" to define their moral code, even in outline. We could not even *begin* to imitate the behavioral rules of society so unlike our own that it has no place for punishment.[92]

4. A Calculus of Pleasures and Pains vs. a Calculus of Preferences

The measuring of the moral rules of present society against those governing a perfect society is valuable, nonetheless, and utopias play an important and perhaps a necessary part in the development of ethics. But the hedonist need not go to such extremes to avoid the embarrassing assumption that pleasures form a quantitative series, and are in strict ratio to one another. Moritz Schlick formulates his "law of motivation" as follows: "In the conflict of motives the decision goes to the most pleasant or least unpleasant."[93] It will be seen that this is close to what Troland calls "the hedonism of the present." He admits that the phrases "most pleasant" and "least unpleasant" have given rise to criticism that is all too justified; for pleasantness, as a mental state, "cannot actually be measured, cannot be determined quantitatively . . . [where] a calculus of pleasure and pain with sums and differences of feelings would be meaningless."[94]

The difficulty is easily overcome. Instead of talking about quantities of pleasure and pain, we can simply say, as we all do on innumerable occasions that we *prefer this to that.*

When two ends-in-view, *a* and *b*, appear alternately before one, they are not directly balanced one against the other; but we find that, for example, the transition from *a* to *b* is an unpleasant experience, while the transition from

91 See *op. cit.*, p. 179.
92 See *ibid.*, p. 465.
93 *Problem of Ethics*, p. 41.
94 *Ibid.*, p. 92.

b to *a* is pleasant. Thus we are able to say, by way of definition, that *a* with respect to *b* is the more pleasant or the less pleasant idea. . . . Thus we see how one can speak sensibly of more or less with respect to pleasure and pain, without actually presupposing quantitative differences. We require nothing more than the opposition of pleasure and pain in the transition from one idea to another.[95]

Heroism and self-sacrifice are quite consistent with this analysis, Schlick holds. One may prefer *a* to *b* even when *a* represents almost certain death, while *b* means safe retreat from an unequal contest. This is as much as to say that the alternative *a* may be, in moments of great enthusiasm, more pleasant to a man, or less unpleasant, than *b*. But the quantities of pleasure can be replaced by introduction of the asymmetrical, transitive relation of preference. Has not Schlick, therefore, succeeded in keeping hedonism while shelving the quantification of pleasure, an exploit Sidgwick thinks impossible?

It should be added that Schlick has no desire to defend utilitarianism. In his opinion, "the *real* 'greatest happiness of the greatest number' is not a tangible concept."[96] For one thing, the consequences of our acts extend indefinitely into the future and are "simply incalculable."[97] And the utilitarian is confronted by absurd questions such as: "How should I act when the circumstances are such that my conduct can lead either to a certain definite amount of happiness in each of four persons, or double that amount for each of two?"[98] Can we assign any meaning to "*A* is three and one-half times as happy as *B*"? Such difficulties, which haunt the utilitarian at every step, are to be avoided by dropping the "summation of pleasures" altogether, and substituting the analysis in terms of preference.

But can *utilitarianism* be salvaged if assertions of preference are substituted for assertions that one sum of pleasures is twice or three times as great as another? According to Davidson, McKinsey, and Suppes, such numerical assertions of value acquire definite meaning when "a coherent theory of measurement is given by specifying axiomatically conditions imposed on a structure of empirically realizable operations and relations. The theory is formally complete if it can be proved that any structure satisfying the axioms is isomorphic to a numerical structure of a given kind."[99] It is understood, of course, that what is being directly measured, in one way or another, is not quantities of pleasure or other values but preferences of an individual.

95 *Ibid.*, p. 40.
96 *Ibid.*, p. 196.
97 *Ibid.*, p. 88.
98 *Ibid.*, pp. 88–89.
99 D. Davidson, J. C. C. McKinsey, P. Suppes, "Outlines of a Formal Theory of Value, 1," in *Philosophy of Science*, 22, 2, 1955, p. 151.

These authors, as well as Schlick, are concerned exclusively with the order of preferences of the individual among his own experiences, and do not admit the possibility of extending the theory from a personal calculus to an interpersonal calculus, as would be required by utilitarianism, in its usual form. The individual can give a hedonistic rating of his own experiences, but how can he honestly say that he *prefers* the pleasurable experience of other individuals A, B, and C, to his own? What would be the basis of the comparison? Schlick would say that the preference for serving others rather than oneself would be the pleasure afforded by passing from the thought of serving ourselves to the thought of serving others. This answer would not satisfy the utilitarian, who wants to maintain that the preferences of the altruist are generally more *justifiable* than those of the egoist.

An attempt has been made recently to extend the measurement of pleasures from the personal to the impersonal level. Robert McNaughton argues that this can be done if two assumptions needed for the personal calculus are carried over to the interpersonal calculus, and one new assumption is added. Indifferent (unconscious) experiences are equivalent; secondly, equals added to equals give equal results, and equals added to unequals give unequal results. These assumptions are conceded for the individual calculus. Would they hold also for sets of pleasures belonging to different individuals? "Indifferent moments are equivalent," McNaughton contends, "regardless whose moments they are," since they are all unconscious. "It seems reasonable to say that two unconscious people are equally happy, since neither is happy nor unhappy."[100] But to be able to determine that the combined pleasures of A, B, and C are greater than those of D, E, and F, for example, it is necessary to assume also that "when unequals are added to equals the results are unequal in the same order." The *additional* assumption needed for the interpersonal calculus is:

> For every two individuals, there is a pair of moments, one from each individual, either both happy or both unhappy, which are empirically equivalent.[101]

By "empirically equivalent" is meant that the two moments can be said to be equivalent by an outside observer. The two criteria suggested for such equivalence are: similarity in the backgrounds of the two individuals who are in a given situation, and second, similarity of their overt responses in the same situation. If the equivalence can be established for distinct individuals, then, given the other assumptions, the utilitarian principle that

[100] "A Material Concept of Happiness," in *Philosophy and Phenomenological Research*, 14, 2, 1953, p. 178.
[101] *Ibid.*, p. 179.

the pleasure of the greatest number is preferable to the pleasure of any lesser number of persons clearly follows.

Although McNaughton, in this paper, talks about happy (pleasant) and unhappy (unpleasant) moments, he is really dealing with preferences:

> The concept of happiness as outlined in this paper supposes no sixth sense [as do both Bentham and Mill], but assumes that happiness is based on a sort of preference for certain moments in experience over others. In short, happiness is not perceived in the way that redness is perceived. And the treatment of this paper allows that some reflection may be needed before one can decide how happy an experience is.[102]

McNaughton's assumptions are "unrealistic," in the opinion of Davidson, McKinsey, and Suppes, but they would probably admit that his pioneer attempt to set up an interpersonal calculus is highly suggestive. They themselves point out that even some of the best contemporary philosophers reject too hastily the possibility of measurement of hedonistic preferences, insisting on too strong a sense of measurement, without considering alternative meanings of measurement that are currently useful in science. It is commonly objected, for example, that preferences corresponding to different intensities of pleasure cannot be measured because the different intensities do not add up to a combined intensity, but the same is true of intensities of tone, and other intensities, which are admitted to be measurable. We have seen that philosophers have dismissed hedonism, and *a fortiori* utilitarianism, on the ground that it would be absurd to say that one pleasure is three and one-half times greater than another, yet it is clear that things can be measured that do not form extensive magnitudes. There are stronger and weaker senses of measurement. The weakest sense consistent with hedonism might involve a ranking of pleasurable events according as they would be rationally preferred or found equivalent to one another, the preference relation being strictly transitive and asymmetric, and the equivalence relation transitive and symmetric.

In the last sixty years, analysis in terms of preference has assumed increasing importance in economics. Instead of attempting to measure utility, a scale of preferences of the individual as among varying quantities of two goods can be substituted, with the help of Edgeworth's indifference curves. "Utility is thus eliminated, because we are left merely with a series of more preferred, less preferred, and indifferent combinations of quantities of two goods."[103] In decision theory, also, preference is a central concept, and some believe that it holds great promise for aesthetics. George Henrik von Wright, who wrote the first study of preference from the point of view

102 *Ibid.*, p. 181.
103 Erich Roll, *A History of Economic Thought*, p. 509.

of formal logic, thinks it very plausible "that preferences, at least of some basic kind, can be studied independently of utility and probability," but that "neither utility nor subjective probability can be defined independently of preferences."[104] For methodological and practical reasons, measurement of preferences has also become more and more prominent in psychology as concern with introspected feelings has receded.

In view of such developments, the usual arguments against the hedonistic calculus, to the effect that it is impossible because pleasures cannot in any sense be measured, lose a great deal of their plausibility. It seems likely that the future status of this calculus will depend in part on the results turned up by studies of preference and choice in numerous areas of behavioral science. The appraisal of specific results in these areas lies outside the very general scope of the present book. But there is one point relating to the measurement of pleasures which, because of its prominence in the philosophical literature, must not be neglected.

5. Does the Shift in the Scale of Hedonistic Values Prevent the Calculation of the Greatest Pleasure?

The only effective argument against the hedonistic calculus, according to Ernest Albee, is put forward by Spencer in his early work *Social Statics.* Albee's own statement of the argument, which is succinct and more comprehensive than Spencer's, is as follows:

> . . . the hedonistic calculus is impossible, because there would necessarily be an important shifting of the scale of hedonic values with every stage of intellectual or moral progress (or decadence), whether on the part of the individual, the community, the nation, or the race. . . . It will be seen to have an important theoretical, as well as practical, bearing; for if the assumed ultimate, happiness [pleasure], be found to vary in proportion as something else varies, external conditions remaining the same, there is at least a strong presumption that it may prove not to be the true ultimate after all.[105]

In what shall the greatest happiness be thought to consist? Is it to be found in the immediate satisfaction of bodily needs, or are the mental needs more important? What is the ideal ratio between bodily and mental enjoyments? "Shall we consider the total absorption of time and energy in business [which, Spencer says, distinguishes his own age] as constituting the 'greatest happiness,' and act accordingly?"[106] Or shall it be thought

[104] *The Logic of Preference,* p. 17.
[105] *A History of English Utilitarianism,* pp. 387–388.
[106] *Social Statics,* p. 10.

that the greatest happiness consists in the exercise and gratification of all the faculties? But beyond a certain point, will this not produce pain rather than pleasure? What, then, would be this turning point? Will it not depend on the balance of desires, which varies from one age, community, and individual to another? In this case, "the notion of happiness must vary with the disposition and character; that is, must vary indefinitely."[107]

> Not only, therefore, is an agreement as to the meaning of "greatest happiness" theoretically impossible, but it is also manifest that men are at issue on all topics which, for their determination, require defined notions of it. So that in directing us to this "greatest happiness of the greatest number," as the object towards which we should steer [what our pilot] shows us through his telescope is a *fata morgana,* and not the promised land.[108]

This argument against the hedonistic calculus, advanced by one of the greatest of the hedonists, is certainly interesting, but far from conclusive. The fact that tastes differ widely as to the *means* to pleasure does not cancel the fact that all men have the same taste for pleasure, and the more the better. It does not at all prove that it is "impossible" to choose acts that tend to produce the greatest pleasure of the greatest number, but merely reminds us that in doing so we must be sure to take into account "the disposition and character" of the persons affected by our acts who, in the overwhelming majority of cases, as Bentham points out, are limited to a few of our associates.

The weakness of the argument stands out clearly in Albee's statement. If happiness varies with the state of intellectual and moral development, "external conditions remaining the same," he says, we cannot assume that happiness is the ultimate, and we *can* conclude that the hedonistic calculus is "impossible." It is true that, if intellectual and moral development (and thus also the choice of pleasurable *objects*) could change without any change in the external conditions (!), it might be more difficult to know that the change has taken place, and, therefore, more difficult to know what would please the people who have undergone the change. But surely it would not be impossible. They could make their preferences known, and we could take them into account in our calculations—not perfectly, of course, but perfection is an exorbitant demand to make of any teleological ethics.

Meanwhile, it is well to remember that utilitarians have not been unaware of the wide range of variation among men in their susceptibility to pleasure and pain from different sources. Mill, in particular, insists on respect for individuality, and Bentham, in his methodical way, draws up

107 *Ibid.,* p. 8.
108 *Ibid.,* p. 10.

elaborate instructions for determining the best hedonistic consequences in particular cases. It is true that Bentham is interested primarily in framing laws providing for justice and facilitating prosperity, objects all men can enjoy, but he is also intensely concerned that individual action should not be restricted more than is necessary for these ends, which are conducive to the general happiness.

The argument might take a deeper turn if we consider the possibility that the neutral point in the pleasure-pain scale, "the hedonistic zero," as Sidgwick calls it,[109] can be shifted up and down the scale. For, if this neutral point, or area, between the weakest pleasures and the weakest pains can be shifted up and down the scale, then it would seem that the very same feeling can be pleasant at one time and unpleasant at another time. In this case, an unhappy man can be made happy either (a) by providing him with new and better feelings, or (b) by shifting his neutral area farther down the scale, so that feelings formerly experienced as somewhat unpleasant are now experienced as somewhat pleasant. Thus, a man who has spent several ghastly years in a concentration camp and returns to his former life finds that feelings formerly dull or neutral—such as the feeling of looking out the window into the empty, quiet, rather ugly street—are now decidedly pleasant. Something like this happens, no doubt, in common experience. But are the feelings really the same as they were formerly? Is it merely his appraisal of them that has changed? If so, something besides pleasure must be recognized as good. Hedonism must be abandoned, or remodeled as a system of preferences.

Experiments have shown that in a great many perceptive situations the neutral point, or "adaptation level," as it is called, can be shifted in one direction or the other. When subjects are asked to estimate weights lying between 200 and 400 grams, they fix upon 250 grams as the neutral point; everything above this point is heavy, everything below is light. But if the subjects previously have lifted heavier weights, the neutral point no longer lies within the series 200 to 400; all these weights now feel light. In recent experiments, also, "affective states are . . . seen to behave in much the same manner that sensory dimensions do and to be closely dependent upon them. Like sensory dimensions, affects 'above' the indifference region have one quality and affects 'below' the indifference region have the opposite or complementary quality."[110] Such studies of affect, however, are not geared to decide the question that interests us, namely, whether the indifference region can be shifted while the range of feelings remains unchanged.

[109] See *op. cit.*, pp. 124–125.
[110] H. Helson, "Adaptation Level Theory," in S. Koch (ed.), *Psychology: A Study of a Science*, Vol. 1, pp. 599–600.

Until this can be established affirmatively, the shift of the indifference region furnishes no argument against the hedonistic calculus. It still may be true, of course, that the same feelings are differently appraised, that some men are more tolerant of pain and painful feelings than others, not because they are less sensitive but because they have made a positive adaptation to such experiences, as by learning to divert attention to other things or by eliminating fear and apprehension that attach to unaccustomed pains.

6. IS THE EUDAEMONIAN CALCULUS ANY EASIER?

Whereas utilitarianism is wholly and explicitly an ethics of consequences, eudaemonism is so only in part. Aristotle does not tell us clearly, as Bentham does, how far the attainment of virtue and happiness hangs upon a correct estimation of the consequences of our actions. If we ask how we are to determine which actions will result in happiness, Aristotle seems to have several answers. Virtue has a strong tendency to happiness, but it is recommended, not only because of its good consequences but also because (a) it is an activity in accordance with reason, which is the distinctive nature of man, and therefore appropriate to man, as swimming is appropriate to a fish. And there seems to be still another criterion of actions conducive to happiness. Some virtues—distributive justice, for example—(b) appear to be intuitively self-justifying, quite apart from their consequences.

The utilitarian would deny that these two criteria are independent of consequences in the larger sense. If someone were to question whether living according to reason is necessary to human happiness, it would not suffice to answer that reason is distinctive of man, that animals do not have it. One would have to argue that, in the lives of one's contemporaries and in the history of the human race, rational behavior, *e.g.*, courage, temperance, justice, friendship, etc., have generally paid off with desired results; and that irrational conduct, as commonly understood, has netted undesired consequences. The utilitarian would make similar objections to the intuitive criterion. It also fails to dispense with a study of consequences. For, suppose that, whenever rewards and punishments were distributed according to the merits of the persons receiving them, people tended to be dissatisfied, and rancor and quarrels broke out more frequently than when any other principle of division was employed! Would it still be maintained that distributive justice was right and conducive to happiness, or that it was a necessary part of happiness?

If an Aristotelian, in short, were to claim that we do not have to study consequences because we know by his nature what is good for man, the utilitarian would reply, as Bentham and Mill did: By studying the consequences of actions in history we acquire general rules specifying that some classes of actions yield desirable results in general, whereas others do not. Since these rules have been proved by experience, we can rely on them in typical cases, and are spared the trouble of calculating particular effects. We have seen that Mill considered the Golden Rule a most valuable guide, and that Bentham, in spite of his emphasis on the calculation of the effects of individual actions, also relied on ethical rules and laws which summed up general experience in a compendious manner. Spencer, for his part, looked forward to a stage of science so advanced that psychological, physiological, and sociological laws would be able to direct man, even in the smallest particulars, to his greatest good. But this was a utopian conception.

Since the general rules often conflict in particular cases, and there is frequently a question whether a proposed action falls under one rule or another, or several, or none, casuistry is continually required. Aristotle seems to insist on this as much as do the hedonists and utilitarians. When considering particular cases, he often refers to consequences, but sometimes to what is fitting or appropriate to the situation. But may not what is fitting or proper have become so owing to desirable consequences it had in the past, especially when these include the immediate effects on the feelings of the persons involved? This, at least, is what the utilitarian suggests. The only alternative is an immediate, self-certifying intuition of the rightness of a particular act.

Thus, Albee contends that difficulties attending the hedonistic calculus also appear in any other system of ethics "which seriously attempts to explain how we are to determine the rightness or wrongness of particular classes of actions." This primarily practical problem is sure to arise "the moment we transcend the crudest form of Intuitionism, which refuses to go beyond what is conceived to be the infallible verdict of 'conscience' in each individual case."[111]

In calculating consequences, Aristotelian eudaemonism appears to be at a disadvantage as compared to hedonism. The disadvantage is that the goods it recognizes are activities that have no common denominator, and are, in this sense, incommensurable. Thus, while the hedonist can legitimately say that of two alternative courses of conduct one will produce *more* good than the other, meaning more pleasure, the Aristotelian cannot make such a comparison, because the choice is often between different kinds of goods, which have no goodness in common.[112] Not even the pleasures that

[111] *Op. cit.*, p. 388.
[112] See *op. cit.*, *Nicomachean Ethics*, 1096a12 ff.

accompany excellent or virtuous activities provide a common measure, for they vary in quality *inter se* as much as these activities do. Yet, on the other hand, eudaemonism has one decided advantage over utilitarianism—the goods it must calculate to determine the rightness of an action are largely open to perception and publicly observable.

There is nothing to prevent the ultimately diverse goods from being ordered on an ascending scale, according to the graded preferences of "the good man," who will always prefer the higher to the lower. In determining what line of action will redound most to our happiness, Aristotle advises us to imitate the good man. No one will question that this is feasible, to a degree, though there are great and obvious complications. But here again the utilitarian points out that the good man is no better than he *does,* and is known only by the consequences of his actions. When the arguments have been stated on both sides, in short, it becomes doubtful whether the eudaemonistic calculus is any easier than the hedonistic calculus.

THE RELEVANCE OF THE ALTRUISM-
VS.-EGOISM ISSUE

By egoism, *i.e.,* egoistic hedonism, Sidgwick means "a system that fixes as the reasonable ultimate end of each individual's action his own greatest possible Happiness [*i.e.,* pleasure]; or more strictly . . . the greatest possible surplus of pleasure over pain."[113] The egoist, so understood, need not be forever thinking of or calculating his maximum pleasure. He may believe that the most pleasure is to be attained by following what he understands to be God's commands, and will accordingly be intent on that, Sidgwick says. Or, he may believe, "as Aristotle seems to do," that virtuous activity is the most pleasant of all, and therefore will concentrate on being virtuous.[114]

Nor need the egoist be indifferent to the pleasures of his family and friends, or of people in general. The Epicurean is an egoist *par excellence,* but that does not prevent him from attending to the pleasures of his friends, or from regarding friends as essential to happiness. When he aids his friend in distress, his *aim* and *intention* can be to do just this. His *motive* need not be to augment his own balance of pleasure over pain, but to improve that of his friend. His being an egoist, in the sense explained, simply means that in his opinion the reasonable ultimate *justification* of action is each individual's own greatest pleasure. The egoist may, thus, in effect, be as generous and unselfish as the altruist, who holds that egoism is

113 *Op. cit.,* pp. 120–121.
114 See *ibid.,* p. 122.

immoral. He may firmly believe that giving pleasure to others is the very best way of getting pleasure for himself, and conduct himself accordingly. The real distinction between the generosity of the refined egoist and that of the man who makes altruism his principle may be only that the former enjoys what he is doing. Or is it that the latter will be generous *whether he enjoys it or not?*

This is the nub of the present dispute. The egoist *may be* as altruistic as you please, but suppose he prefers to serve his own interests selfishly, and believes this is the way to his maximum pleasure. What argument or principle can we invoke to dissuade him? Even those who oppose both hedonism and egoism can admit that one's own pleasure naturally comes first, Sidgwick remarks. He quotes the following testimony from Bishop Butler:

> . . . though virtue and moral rectitude does indeed consist in affection to and pursuit of what is right and good as such: yet, when we sit down in a cool hour, we can neither justify to ourselves this or any other pursuit till we are convinced that it will be for our happiness, or at least not contrary to it.[115]

Sidgwick's own statement of the superior claims of egoism is forthright:

> . . . common sense assumes that "interested" actions, tending to promote the agent's happiness, are *prima facie* reasonable; that the *onus probandi* lies with those who maintain that disinterested conduct, as such is reasonable.[116]

It is not too much to say that Sidgwick assumes this burden of proof through a great part of his *Methods,* and that the clash between egoism and utilitarianism becomes, for him, the principal issue of ethics. What reason can be given to a person—binding on every man *qua* rational—for tending to the welfare of others, when it is against his own interest? After drawing on all his resources, he all but confesses, as we have seen, that no sufficient reason can be given unless, perhaps, there should be another world in which the generous are rewarded for their self-sacrifice.

Sidgwick, who was influenced by Kant, seems to be seeking a principle of benevolence that can be considered just as reasonable, and can be acted upon just as readily by everyone, as is the principle of self-interest. Aristotle does not look for a general self-evident principle, but instead relies on education and the laws to correct antisocial behavior in the particular forms in which it appears. He agrees that "the love of self is a feeling implanted by nature and not given in vain, although," he adds, "selfishness is rightly censured."[117] But though love of parents, children, etc., are also "natural,"

[115] *Op. cit.,* p. 119.
[116] *Ibid.,* p. 120.
[117] *Op. cit., Politics,* 1263b1.

benevolence in general is not, but must be cultivated. What reason, then, can be given for unselfishness? In the next line or two, Aristotle suggests an interesting answer. Selfishness, he says,

> is not the mere love of self, but love of self in excess, like the miser's love of money, for all, or almost all men, love money and other such objects in a measure.[118]

Selfishness is like miserliness: both are excesses of fairly universal human emotions which are in themselves respectable. Both damage the individual as well as the state, and the same can be said, with differences of degree, of the extremes of all the moral virtues. In all cases the individual has personal reasons for reform, which education, example, and the laws direct and encourage. It is true that in many instances these agencies, because something or other is lacking, will be ineffective; men will persist in being bad. This does not mean that they have no good reason for reforming their conduct, but only that they do not have the training and enlightenment to see their own advantage. All men are capable of happiness, Aristotle says, unless they are maimed in their potentialities. Persuading a man to eliminate his selfishness should not be more difficult, in principle, than persuading him to take watchful and prudent care of his own personal interests. They are equally essential to his happiness. Thus the antagonism between egoism and altruism, which for Sidgwick is the great theoretical problem of ethics, is, for Aristotle, part and parcel of the practical task of instilling the virtues by education, example, and the laws.

For Bentham, also, the program of eliminating selfish behavior is not unlike the program of discouraging foolishly short-range actions, which tend to be injurious to the agents themselves. Enlightened self-interest is what is required by the public interest, and Bentham relies upon good laws even more than Aristotle to bring about this enlightenment, as he, no doubt, gives less weight to education brought about by other means. He is criticized for holding that men ought to act in their own interest, and also to pursue the greatest pleasure of the greatest number; and he is sometimes gratuitously credited with the view that "the identity of interests" is effected automatically through the unhampered operation of economic forces. But this is to forget all about his primary role as a reformer. The identity of interests is to be brought about by good laws, to the framing and promotion of which he devoted most of his life, as also by clear, pragmatic thinking in moral matters, by avoidance of outmoded and pious-ascetic prescriptions.

In one broad aspect of benevolence, it has been argued, Bentham and

---

[118] *Ibid.*, 1263b2–4.

other utilitarians too, were well ahead of Plato and Aristotle. This is the clear recognition of a basic equality of human dignity and worth. Bentham's insistence that, in the summing up of pleasures of which happiness is composed, one man's pleasure should count as much as another's, and no more, had no counterpart in Plato or Aristotle, and was indeed something new in the history of ethics. It followed that the landlord should share his land with his tenants and laborers, that the manufacturer should share his profits with his factory hands, that the master should wait on his servant, *if* only more pleasure was to be had by this means. We have seen that Bentham blunted this radical egalitarianism with other hedonistic considerations that cut the other way, yet it can hardly be doubted that its influence has continued to grow.

Bentham was also one of the first to see—what the ancients had not dreamed of—that poverty and a rankling sense of injustice, which have always afflicted the majority of the people, could be eliminated *without* an equal distribution of goods, or even an approach to equality. All that was required was that economic production be greatly expanded, enough to supply the basic needs and some luxuries for all. This is the "affluent" stage our own society has reached, according to Galbraith, and the demand for equality has turned into a demand for a fair share of the abundance.

Is There a Paradox of Hedonism and Does It Extend to Eudaemonism?

The paradox is to the effect that the amount of pleasure attained varies inversely with the degree to which it is consciously pursued. Or, as Dewey puts it, "the way to attain pleasure is not to seek it."[119]

Why do so many thinkers agree that the pursuit of pleasure is self-defeating? A number of reasons can be cited: (a) If we are to attain the objects we desire, we need to concentrate on the *means* to their attainment. But pleasure is not such a means, and thus the conscious pursuit of pleasure will distract from and prevent its attainment. If a mathematician actively seeks pleasure rather than the proof, the proof may not be achieved; and the musician, with his mind on the pleasantness of giving a brilliant performance and of hearing the applause, may perform badly. (b) Concrete pleasures are distinctive to and inseparable from the *different kinds* of activities they accompany. Only by pursuing the latter do we realize the former. (c) Conscious pursuit of pleasure robs us of the pleasure of disinterested generosity—the joy of helping friends for *their*

[119] *Op. cit.*, p. 270.

sake. (d) It also is said to deprive us of the pleasure of surprise and the pleasures that come as a surprise. The joys of life, in Dewey's view, are more like a jewel we suddenly find than game we hunt down and snare. Schlick is of the same mind when he says:

> Everyone knows, or experience teaches him as he grows older, that happiness seems to vanish in direct ratio to the eagerness with which it is pursued. One cannot pursue it, one cannot seek it; for it cannot be recognized from afar, and only unveils itself suddenly, when present. Happiness, those rare moments of life in which the world by a coincidence of apparently insignificant circumstances suddenly grows perfect, the contact of a warm hand, the look of crystal clear water, the song of a bird, how could one "strive" for such things? Nor does it depend on these things, but upon the soul's receptivity which they find awaiting them. It depends on the capacity of the soul to respond to the proper vibration.[120]

In place of the pursuit of happiness (pleasure), Schlick would put furtherance by the individual of his "capacity for happiness."

But perhaps the paradox of hedonism has been overstated. F. H. Bradley, who is no friend of hedonism, points out that, though the search of the individual for his own pleasure is doubtless self-defeating, common opinion does not take the same view of the search for the pleasure of the greatest number.[121] A number of the objections to pursuing pleasure seem to be blunted or avoided altogether when the pleasure in view is that of other men. The paradox, in fact, may derive its plausibility largely from the consideration of thoroughly selfish and self-indulgent persons who are continually engrossed in their private sensations and feelings.

For Bradley, however, utilitarianism is still paradoxical. Like Green and many others, he fails to see how we can aim at a feeling state of "all sentient organisms."

The evaluation of the "paradox" cannot get very far without observing a few other distinctions. In the first place, it is one thing to consciously aim at future pleasure, and quite a different thing to aim at external objects, such as food, wealth, information, or understanding, which experience has proved to be attended with pleasure. Eating is undoubtedly "commonly attended with an agreeable feeling," Sidgwick says, "but it cannot, I think, be strictly said that this agreeable feeling is the object of the hunger." It is true also that an anticipation of the pleasure of eating often accompanies hunger, but it is no less clear that the one can appear without the other. And much the same can be said of the desire for wealth, information, or

---

[120] *Op. cit.*, pp. 197–198.
[121] See "Pleasure for Pleasure's Sake," in *Ethical Studies*, p. 31.

understanding, and the anticipation of the pleasure of having them. "Throughout the whole scale of my impulses, sensual, emotional, and intellectual alike," Sidgwick asserts, "I can distinguish desires of which the object is other than my own pleasure."[122]

The utilitarian thus need not be ensnared by the paradox of hedonism. By pursuing pleasure he does not have to mean that we always are or should be consciously motivated by the prospect of future pleasure. Pursuing pleasure can also mean aiming at those external things that have been attended by pleasure in the past,[123] and if these two kinds of pursuing can sometimes coexist "by a sort of alternating rhythm,"[124] though they are often mutually exclusive, too, has not the paradox lost its sting? What the utilitarian can maintain—and the egoistic hedonist, too, for that matter—is that sometimes we act with a view to obtaining future pleasure, while at other times we reach for food, reputation, or understanding, which has been associated with pleasure in our experience, but with no *thought* of future pleasure. What is self-defeating about the search for pleasure, it may be asked, when the end-in-view is only occasionally the obtaining of pleasure?

It is only fair to consider, now, whether eudaemonism may not suffer from a similar paradox. Dewey maintains that

> the so-called hedonistic paradox, that the way to attain pleasure is not to seek for it . . . may be paralleled by another paradox, namely, that the way to achieve virtue is not to aim directly at it. For the standard is not the same as the end of desire. Hence contribution to the general good may be the standard of reflective approval without its being the end-in-view. Indeed, it is hard to imagine its being made the end of desire; as a direct object to be aimed at, it would be so indeterminate and vague that it would only arouse a diffused sentimental state, without indicating just how and where conduct should be directed.[125]

Max Scheler contends, furthermore, that to aim at virtue is a kind of Pharisaism, that virtue should be *worn* rather than directly sought (*Der Formalismus in der Ethik und die materiale Wertethik*). Others insist that to make the pursuit of virtue the main thing is to become a prig, a result quite opposite to what was intended. To be generous you must aim at the welfare of others, not at achieving virtue for yourself.

[122] *Op. cit.*, p. 46.
[123] It will be remembered that this distinction marks the difference between what Troland calls "hedonism of the future" and "hedonism of the past."
[124] *Op. cit.*, p. 136.
[125] *Op. cit.*, p. 270.

The question now is how this bears upon Aristotle, who describes happiness as activity according to virtue. Aristotle might well agree with Dewey: Although the virtues are valuable in themselves, Aristotle does not say that they are to be aimed at directly and primarily. The virtues in the virtuous man tend to become habits, and the habits are ways of dealing with concrete situations, not general aspirations to virtue. In the beginning the virtues were created by acts of choice, where the choice is between specific lines of conduct. Virtue itself is not aimed at, except abstractly, for who knows in advance what form it should take? The objects of desire are all sorts of concrete things. Virtue enters as a standard in terms of which some of them are chosen, others rejected. "For there must first be produced in us (as indeed is the case) an irrational impulse to the right, and then later on reason must put the question to the vote and decide it."[126]

Nor can happiness itself be an object sought after, an end-in-view, according to Dewey. Happiness is not one thing; it is different for every man. The miser finds his happiness in one thing, a kind philanthropic man finds his in another. All that the diverse happinesses have in common is "the fact of being fulfillments. . . . In material content, the two cases differ radically; in form they are alike, since both occupy the same status and play the same role—that of satisfying a desire." Which desires are to be gratified in a given case depends on the standard, which discriminates "between the various material kinds of satisfaction so as to determine which kind of happiness is truly moral; that is, approvable."[127]

As we have seen, Aristotle also says that "verbally there is very general agreement" that happiness is "the highest of all goods achievable by action,"[128] but, yet, men differ exceedingly as to what happiness is, some finding it in wealth or honor, while others identify it with moral virtue or contemplation. It is clear, then, that men do not aim at one thing called "happiness," but rather at particular objects they think will satisfy their desires. Nowhere does Aristotle say that we *aim at happiness;* he says we *choose it* "for itself and never for the sake of something else."[129] This seems to mean that what all men *want* is the greatest possible balance of satisfied over unsatisfied desires, but what they *aim at* are particular actions that will achieve this end. For happiness, however interpreted, is always taken to be "living well," but to live well we must not only choose objects of desire which truly satisfy us; we must choose those that fit in with a full lifetime that is satisfying.

[126] *Op. cit., Magna Moralia,* 1206b19–21.
[127] *Op. cit.,* p. 271.
[128] *Op. cit., Nicomachean Ethics,* 1095a16.
[129] *Ibid.,* 1097b1.

Aristotelian happiness, it seems fair to conclude, is not something *really* aimed at or pursued; and hence the pursuit of it could not be self-defeating.

THE PROBLEM FOR UTILITARIANS OF ENDS AND MEANS

This question has already been discussed in Chapter 8, in relation to deontological ethics, and requires only a brief notice in the present connection. Literally, all ethics that defines "right" and "morally good" in terms of consequences makes the end justify the means. The only alternative is to hold that what is right or obligatory is self-evident, self-justifying, and intuitively certain—on sight or after reflection. The difficulties of this position have been lengthily reviewed.

The challenge to utilitarianism is usually put as follows: Suppose the pleasure of the greatest number could be greatly increased by the murder of a wicked old moneylender, or by depriving innocent individuals of their rights or means of livelihood, or by lying, cheating, stealing, or an act of treachery! Would the end then justify the means? Bentham, Mill, all the leading utilitarians, address themselves to this question. The answer they offer, as we have seen, is that the long-range effects of such violations of sacred human rights would more than counterbalance the immediate gain, and result in a net loss of pleasure. But the critic retorts that it is easy to imagine cases in which the crime committed would be secret and have no possible influence on public morals, or in which the influence would be negligible. Are a few such doubtful borderline cases sufficient, the utilitarian may then ask, to upset an ethical system with so much in its favor? And how can intuitive certainty about moral truths, which in fact varies from one age, community, and individual to another, be thought a viable alternative to utilitarianism? So the argument runs.

The question we wish to raise is whether Aristotle's eudaemonism can also be charged, in a pejorative sense, with making the end justify the means. We have just quoted a passage in which Aristotle says that we choose honor, pleasure, reason, and every virtue for themselves. Here, he adds in parentheses: "for if nothing resulted from them we should still choose each of them." The good man will continue to choose virtue even if it does not contribute to his happiness, or have any other effects. But will he continue, refraining from every injustice and wrongdoing, even in exceptional cases in which it is possible by an act that is bad in itself to save his fellow soldiers from death, or the State from disaster? This is a question to which it is difficult to find an answer. Would not a general's injustice toward a soldier or civilian be justified if it enabled him to carry out a larger act of justice later on?

We know that Plato has Socrates defend the thesis that justice is better than injustice, no matter how much the individual may suffer for it. But this does not mean that injustice is always to be avoided when the good of the State is at stake. The "noble lie," the deception of the citizenry on the highly sensitive point of who their own children are, is recommended because of its salutary consequences for the State. Since the statesman will know what is for the good of the State—what actions will have the best consequences—it will be his task to see that it is carried out by the citizens, whatever means may be necessary. There is no higher standard for action than the good of the State.

The position of Aristotle is more complex. He holds that, though monarchy might be *theoretically* best, a mixed polity is *practically* the best government, and that the constitution should provide for the participation of citizens and guarantee certain rights. On the other hand, he examines the most diverse types of government in Greece with understanding and some sympathy. Believing that even a bad government is better than complete breakdown and anarchy, and knowing that ideal conditions are not to be had for the choosing, he is disposed to make the best of existing regimes, and not to insist on *ideal* morality in rulers. Like Machiavelli, he offers advice to tyrants on how to preserve and stabilize their regimes. The tyrant, he says, should not follow the common practice of robbing his subjects of power, and humbling and dividing them by distrust, for this will probably not serve his purpose. On the other hand, he must be careful, above all else, to "keep power enough to rule over his subjects, whether they like him or not, for if he once gives this up he gives up his tyranny. But though power must be retained as the foundation, in all else the tyrant should act or appear to act in the character of a king . . . he should pretend a care of the public revenues . . . maintain the character of a great soldier, and produce the impression that he is one."[130] This advice would curtail the wickedness of the tyrant, which ordinarily knows no limits,[131] but he is still obliged to do whatever is necessary to maintain his power. If loss of his power means the collapse of government altogether, dire measures might be justified.

In answering the question whether injustice is ever justified by the good it brings, utilitarianism and eudaemonism seem to be in the same boat. In an ideal society, wicked acts would not be expected to lead to desirable

[130] *Op. cit., Politics*, 1314a36; 1314b23.
[131] *Ibid.*, 1314a13.

results, but, in actual societies, we know that they sometimes do and that a decision must be made. It might be thought that Aristotelianism, since it defines virtue in functional terms—as perfect functioning of all capacities —could reject the bad act without bothering with its good consequences. It turns out in practice that this cannot be done.

III

The Contemporary Pursuit of Happiness

II

The Ideal of Happiness
in the Present

CONTEMPORARY philosophers have not been concerned to develop new theories of happiness, though they have contributed valuable criticism and fresh substantiation of parts of the old theories, some examples of which have already been cited. Their energies have been devoted to other subjects. Popular books about happiness, which might be called "philosophical," it is true, appear with predictable frequency. They offer advice as to how to achieve happiness, which may be helpful to some people but do not provide anything like a general grounded theory of human nature and choice in relation to opportunities. They sometimes show insights and perspectives, but they are not systematic and do not seem to contribute much to our subject.

In the meantime, the social sciences, psychology, and psychotherapy have undergone great expansion, and are giving more systematic attention to goals and normative considerations. Anthropologists who study societies in which standards are very different from each other and from our own are eventually tempted to make comparative value judgments of a sort

321

implying that one conception of the good life is truer than another. If they are willing to see the gifts of Western civilization—including medicine—transform the values of technologically backward societies, they can scarcely take the view that diverse ideals of a successful life are incomparable, or that the scientist, as scientist, can make no value judgments. The historian, the sociologist, and the psychologist also are confronted with the same problem. They sometimes announce a program of sticking to facts and eschewing all valuations. Does this mean that, as scientists, they are willing to devote their knowledge and skills to any task the authorities assign and pay for? In effect, this would be anything but value-neutral. In some areas of psychology and the social sciences, at any rate, value-judgments appear to be unavoidable. A view of the good life is implied, or sometimes explicitly elaborated.

In this final chapter we shall confine our attention to the most important current development of the theory of the good life, *i.e.*, the good-enough, the better, and the best or ideal life. The disciplines that are obliged, more than any others, to say what they *mean* by an improvement of the individual's general condition, and hence what they mean by a satisfactory or ideal life, are personality theory and psychotherapy. Both are concerned with undesirable symptoms and their removal, but their interest often goes beyond this negative result to a positive conception of "mental health," which is close to what we have been discussing under the name of "happiness." The fact that this conception is logically connected with medical therapy or with objective tests and controlled studies gives it a significance lacking in earlier theories.

We shall begin with a review of the ideas of leading psychologists and psychotherapists who represent what is called the "self-actualization" theory of personality development and the aim of psychotherapy. We shall see that some of these authors use "happiness" as an equivalent of self-actualization, that others apparently hesitate to do so because there is a tendency, especially in English-speaking countries, to equate happiness with hedonism, and that, in all cases, their description of self-actualization resembles, significantly, the description of happiness given by Aristotle and by self-realization authors (see Chapter 7). Next, we briefly note objections to the self-actualization theory and the defense that can be made. Alternative theories of the aim of psychotherapy also will be mentioned. It is contended that, whatever technical advantages they may have, they are concerned only with partial goods or with therapeutic *means* to full self-actualization. At the end, we shall summarize a number of respects in which the three theories—eudaemonism, self-realization, and self-actualization—appear to agree.

THE CONCEPT OF SELF-ACTUALIZATION

Kurt Goldstein, who was the first to employ the term "self-actualization," carries to a holistic extreme a tendency found in all self-actualization authors. They all reject the mechanistic idea that personality is wholly the product of successive linkages of responses into larger and larger wholes, by conditioning or any other piecemeal process; and insist that it acts more or less as an integrated whole. Goldstein, however, maintains that the *only* drive "is to actualize the individual capacities as fully as possible."[1] The reflexes, local responses, and separated drives that are supposed to interact to form the unity of the organism or of personality are wholly incapable of doing so. These part-processes either are artifacts of the laboratory or else arise in a catastrophic situation where personality breaks down and is disorganized. "The concept of different separate drives," Goldstein says,

> is based on observation of the sick, of young children, and of animals under experimental conditions—that is, on observations made under circumstances in which some activities of the organism are isolated from the whole. This is the case in pathology; it is the case in children because the organism of the child lacks a center; and it is the case in experiments with animals because of the experimental conditions. . . . The impression that there are separate drives arises easily . . . when the organism is living under inadequate conditions. If the human being is forced to live in a state of hunger for a long time, so that he is forced to relieve this feeling, it disturbs the actualization of his whole personality. Then it appears as if he were under a hunger drive. The same may be the case with sex. A normal organism, however, is able to repress the hunger feeling or the sex urge if it has something very important to do, the neglect of which would bring the whole organism into danger.[2]

The unity of personality is not imposed on it by external stimulation, in Goldstein's view. To a great extent, normal integration or "ordered behavior" is self-produced, suggesting at times that an Aristotelian entelechy is at work, and, indeed, Goldstein calls the governing principle "actualization" or "self-actualization." The organism, he says, "is determined by the . . . tendency to come to terms with the requirements of the outer world in the best possible condition of the whole."[3] The influence coming from the outer world "does not occur by direct causation," but "by way of the functional organization of the whole."[4]

[1] *Human Nature*, p. 141.
[2] *Ibid.*, pp. 142–143.
[3] *Ibid.*, p. 186.
[4] *Ibid.*, p. 188.

It is easy to see that, though ordered or integrated behavior of the whole person is, for Goldstein, the mark of normality and success, the integration is for the sake of "self-actualization." All the "instinctive" and voluntary actions by which it comes to terms with its environment successfully "make possible the organism's actualization of its capacities." The only drive "is to actualize individual capacities as fully as possible."[5]

Intermediate between the holism of Goldstein and the atomistic behaviorism of Dollard and Miller is the integrative theory of G. W. Allport. He is far from reducing all drives to one, as Goldstein does, and he also avoids the reduction of drives to the biological, which characterizes Freudian and behaviorist theories. His conception of "functional autonomy," as we have noted in connection with J. S. Mill's similar theory, explains how cultural and social drives may become independent of biological needs. His theory is mainly genetic. "Integration," he says, "means that from disparate units of behavior larger and more exclusive integers are formed."[6] The units of integration vary in scope and complexity, forming a hierarchy, viz.: conditioned reflexes, habits, traits, "selves" (in James's sense of plural selves belonging to a normal individual), and total personality. Simplest of all are the conditioned reflexes, and most complex is the all-embracing total personality, which is never completely integrated; the intervening structures are progressively larger in scope and complexity.

For Allport, however, the integration is only a part of "growth," only one aspect in the development of personality. Other aspects are "self-esteem," "functional autonomy," "extension of self," "self-objectification: insight and humor," and "personal *Weltanschauung*." He points out, too, that it may be achieved at the expense of *richness of personity* and suggests that it would be better to go on growing, though embroiled in conflict, than to be a well-integrated mediocrity. "Growth motives," he points out in another book,

> maintain tension in the interest of distant and often unattainable goals. As such they distinguish human from animal becoming. By growth motives we refer to the hold that ideals gain upon the process of development. Long range purposes, subjective values, comprehensive systems of interest are all of this order.[7]

Like Goldstein,[8] Allport rejects pleasure as the key to motivation. Pleasure,[9] he states, in good Aristotelian fashion, is "the glow which attends the integration of the person while pursuing or contemplating the attain-

[5] *Ibid.*, pp. 139, 141.
[6] *Personality, A Psychological Interpretation*, p. 142.
[7] *Becoming, Basic Considerations for a Psychology of Personality*, p. 68.
[8] See *op. cit.*, p. 229.
[9] He actually says "happiness," but there is no doubt that he means pleasure.

ment of goals. . . . It is not a motivating force but a by-product of other-wise motivated activity."[10] And, again like Goldstein, Allport sees integration—the hallmark of normality—as a phase of the over-all process of growth or actualization of capacities.

Another variant of self-actualization is expressed by Nevitt Sanford, when he says that "the psychological approach to personal problems . . .

> rests upon the psychology of personality development and seeks to conceptualize the goals of such development—differentiation, wholeness, autonomy, utilization of potentialities, and the like. Psychological well being, from this point of view, does not mean absence of disease but rather a state of relatively advanced development. Psychological maladjustment is conceived of as a relative failure with respect to diverse goals of development. Psychological analysis . . . is an attempt to assess the developmental status of the individual with particular attention to the potentialities for and the obstacles to further growth. . . . In his practice of psychotherapy, the psychologist seeks, most essentially, to further the growth of the individual, to help him to become what he can.[11]

Opposing the drive-reduction theory that man acts only to reduce tensions, and the view that he acts only to restore an equilibrium that has been disturbed, Sanford argues that there are dynamic higher needs as well. "Growth and development," involving "expansion and increasing complexity," he says, "are certainly the best candidates for the status of natural tendencies."[12] Sanford also emphasizes the contrast between the state of stable integration, which on a simple level of development may be free from conflict, with the process of continual growth and enterprise, which cannot escape conflict. The latter gives a more reliable measure of health and soundness, since a growing person can bear the strains and assimilate the rapid changes of modern life, while the person of stable integration is comparatively inflexible and without many resources.

Lawrence S. Kubie practically defines mental health as high resistance to stress and "freedom and flexibility to learn through experience, to change and to adapt to changing circumstance,"[13] and we find the same emphasis in many prominent psychologists and psychotherapists. The keynote for some is "ability to learn," for others it is "continuous growth" or development of the "whole man," "productiveness," or "actualization," but their idea of soundness or excellence in human activity seem to widely overlap or merge.

[10] *Loc. cit.*
[11] "The Findings of the Commission in Psychology," in *Annals of the New York Academy of Science*, 63, 1955, pp. 341 ff.
[12] J. Katz *et al.* (eds.), "Normative Conceptions in Psychology" in *Writers on*
[13] "The Fundamental Nature of the Distinction between Normality and Neurons," in *Psychoanalytic Quarterly*, 28, 1954, p. 172.

Robert W. White contends that the popular ideals of *mental health, adjustment,* and *emotional maturity* have not "been derived from the contemplation of successful life-patterns. They all spring from the mental hospital and psychiatric consulting room, from studies of sick aspects of sick people. For the most part they are simply the logical opposites of the things that are troubling people, things like dependence, inferiority, competitiveness, a harsh superego."[14] These ideals consequently get expressed in abstract formulae, which do not relate to the concrete exigencies and decision-points of an adult life. A finding that an individual has complete faith in himself, for example, gives "little hint of the problems involved in being happy and creative in one particular life-pattern with its enduring commitments and inescapable restrictions as well as its rewards and its changes."[15]

"It is now generally recognized," White says, "that emotional disorders can be traced to blocks in the learning process. . . . These blocks are produced by defenses against anxiety so that development can be resumed. It is implicit in this account that normal growth signifies unblocked learning, a process of *continuous change.*"[16] The "growth trends" that characterize "the process of natural growth," in White's view, have some resemblances, as Sanford notes, to the phases of normal personality development in Allport's account. They are: The Stabilizing of Ego Identity—the finding out who you are and what your role is—The Freeing of Personal Relationships—the overcoming of anxiety and defensiveness, which enlarges the ability to form friendships—The Deepening of Interests—the growing capacity to become absorbed in and fascinated with external objects on their own account, or disinterestedly—The Humanizing of Values—increasing awareness and activation by human values.

A. H. Maslow has written widely on motivation and personality, and is known especially for his efforts to give cognitive and other higher needs due place in psychological explanation. He agrees with Goldstein that there are powerful human urges to upset and go beyond a present equilibrium as well as to restore an equilibrium that has been disturbed. His emphasis on the distinction between "coping" behavior, which is "instrumental, adaptive, functional, purposive," and "expressive" behavior, which is nothing of the sort, is especially important for our theme. To overlook or slight the expressive side of our activity in psychology is to leave out the consummatory phase and all forms of enjoyment. Unfortunately, Maslow says, contemporary psychology has been far more concerned with practical results and technology, with means, than with ends.

14 *Lives in Progress,* pp. 357–358.
15 *Ibid.,* p. 358.
16 *Ibid.,* p. 328.

It has notoriously little to say . . . about beauty, art, fun, play, wonder, love, happiness, and other 'useless' reactions. It is therefore of little or no service to the artist, the musician, the poet, the novelist, to the humanist, the connoisseur, the axiologist, the theologian, or to other end- or enjoyment-oriented individuals. [It] offers little to the modern man whose most desperate need is a naturalistic or humanistic value system.[17]

Maslow sets himself to fill the gap and, as a matter of fact, is able to cite many allies—psychologists who are going in the same direction.

"Various recent developments," Maslow says, "have shown the necessity for the postulation of some sort of positive growth or self-actualization tendency within the organism, which is different from its conserving, equilibrating, or homeostatic tendency, as well as from the tendency to respond to impulses from the outside world. This kind of tendency to growth or self-actualization, in one or another vague form, has been postulated by thinkers as diverse as Aristotle and Bergson, and by many other philosophers. Among psychiatrists, psychoanalysts, and psychologists it has been found necessary by Goldstein, Rank, Jung, Horney, Fromm, May, and Rogers."[18] Under Maslow's direction, a study was made of the healthiest 1% of a college population, negatively selected on the basis of standard tests, and positively, by indications of self-actualization. This "syndrome" was, roughly and tentatively: "the full use and exploitation of talents, capacities, potentialities, etc." People of this sort "seem to be fulfilling themselves and to be doing the best that they are capable of doing, reminding us of Nietzsche's exhortation, 'Become what thou art!' They are people who have developed or are developing to the full stature of which they are capable."[19] Many of these potentialities are peculiar to individuals, but others are shared by the group. It would seem, however, that much more clarity is needed in drawing this distinction.

The headings under which the group of self-realization students are described, which often overlap, and need at least a catchword of explanation, are: More Efficient Perception of Reality and More Comfortable Relations with It—perceiving what is given, rather than one's own hopes, anxieties, etc.; and hence—Acceptance (Self, Others, Nature)—relative lack of guilt, shame and defensiveness, etc.; Spontaneity—motivation rooted in the need for "character growth and character expression"; Problem Centering—centered on problems rather than on the ego, with wide frame of reference; The Quality of Detachment; The Need for Privacy; Autonomy; Independence of Culture and Environment—rewards, status, honors are less important than "self-development and inner growth";

[17] *Motivation and Personality*, pp. 179–180.
[18] *Ibid.*, p. 124.
[19] *Ibid.*, pp. 200–201.

Continued Freshness of Appreciation; The Mystic Experience—ability to detach oneself momentarily from the noise and struggle; *Gemeinschafts-gefühl*—the feeling of sympathy and identification with human beings as such; Interpersonal Relations—deeper feelings of the sort; Democratic Character Structure—humility and honest respect for others; Discrimination Between Means and Ends—generally seeks ends, and is not confused about the distinction; Philosophical, Unhostile Sense of Humor; Creativeness; Resistance to Enculturation—ability to keep a little aloof from the culture in which one is enclosed.[20]

Like the other self-actualization authors we have discussed, Erich Fromm rejects hedonism. "Pleasure cannot be a criterion of value," he says, "since some people derive pleasure from submission and not from freedom . . . from hate and not from love, from exploitation and not from productive work."[21] In its place he elaborates a humanistic ethics, in which actualization of man's potentialities—realization of his productive power to create material things, works of art and science and especially, to create and recreate himself—is the same as virtue. Fromm says:

> Productiveness is man's ability to use his powers to realize the potentialities inherent in him. If we say we must use his powers we imply that he must be free and not dependent on someone else who controls his powers. We imply, furthermore, that he is guided by reason . . . that he knows what they are, how to use them, and what to use them for. Productiveness means that he experiences himself as the embodiment of his powers as the "actor"; that he feels himself one with his powers . . . that they are not masked from him.[22]

In self-actualization theories, there is a natural tendency for the normal to become the ideal; since to be normal means to become oneself, to realize one's true worth, and this cannot be much less than the accomplishment of

---

[20] See *ibid.*, pp. 203–228. We have reviewed all these particulars because Maslow's account of the self-actualizing man is the most complete one we know, and because it illustrates best the tendency of the picture of the normal man to become a picture of the ideal man, even if this is not the author's intent. The gratifications of the self-actualizing man, it might be added, tend to the maximum on all levels of actualization, and it is clear that the ideal man is a "happy" man too. But not in the sense of hedonism at all. The ideal belongs in the broad tradition of eudaemonism and the self-realization theory. Without access to Maslow's materials, it is a little difficult to see how all the traits he lists, of which some indication has been given above, fit together with plausible consistency. The self-actualizing person, for example, is said to be centered on objects and problems rather than on the ego, and yet he is more concerned to achieve self-development or personal growth than anything else. Perhaps what is meant is that he cares for objects that will, in fact, enable him to grow, for to take self-development as thematic, as the end-in-view, might well impair efficiency, which requires absorption in the object, as Maslow himself clearly implies.

[21] *Man for Himself*, p. 15.
[22] *Ibid.*, p. 84.

happiness. According to Fromm, "happiness is an achievement brought about by man's inner productiveness and not a gift of the gods. Happiness and joy are not the satisfaction of a need springing from a physiological or psychological lack; they are not the relief from tension but the accompaniment of all productive activity, in thought, feeling, and action." While joy belongs to a single act, happiness may be regarded as "a continuous or integrated experience of joy." In realizing his potentialities the individual spends his energies while increasing them; he "burns without being consumed." Happiness does not exclude pain and grief, but only depression and a sense of worthlessness; it can grow from the former as it is destroyed by the latter. *"Happiness is the criterion of excellence in the art of living, of virtue in the meaning it has in humanistic ethics."*[23]

Symbolically, Fromm suggests, the genital stage of man's sexual development, which for Freud is the ideal of health and excellence, denotes exactly what productiveness does.[24] All we have to do is extend productiveness, which Freud emphasizes only in the biological sphere, to the material, social, political, artistic, scientific, and humanistic sectors of man's activity. This is quite an extension. But we find Erik H. Erikson making the same point. He recalls that, when Freud was once asked "what a normal man should be able to do well," he replied: *"Lieben und arbeiten"* ("love and work"). When he said "love," Erikson explains, "he meant *genital* love, and genital *love;* and when he said love *and* work, he meant a general work-productiveness which would not preoccupy the individual to the extent that he loses his right or capacity to be a genital and a loving being. . . . We cannot improve on the formula which includes the doctor's prescription for human dignity—and for democratic living."[25] The orgasm is not merely sexual:

> The total fact of finding, via the climactic turmoil of the orgasm, a supreme experience of the mutual regulation of two human beings in some way breaks the point off the hostilities and potential rages caused by the oppositeness of male and female, of fact and fancy, of love and hate. Satisfactory sex relations thus make sex less obsessive, overcompensation less necessary, sadistic controls superfluous.[26]

Properly understood, Erikson insists, "the utopia of genitality" includes:

> 1. mutuality of orgasm, 2. with a loved partner, 3. of the opposite sex, 4. with whom one is able and willing to share a mutual trust, 5. and with whom one is able and willing to regulate the cycles of a. work, b. procrea-

[23] *Ibid.*, p. 189.
[24] See *ibid.*, pp. 83–84.
[25] *Childhood and Society*, p. 229.
[26] *Ibid.*, p. 230.

tion, c. recreation, 6. so as to secure to the offspring, too, a satisfactory development.[27]

It might be said, then, that, while the revisionist Fromm goes beyond Freud's genital ideal, Erikson, a staunch upholder of Freudian doctrine, carries Freud beyond himself. Fromm develops his idea of *productiveness* into a complete self-actualization theory; Erikson, taking up the same idea, makes some progress in the same direction.[28]

Putting the patient in a position to find his happiness might be said to be the aim of psychotherapy, according to Fromm, and this is also Karen Horney's view. Horney's special emphasis, however, is on the actualization of the self via the gratification of its need for love and affection and recognition. It is as if she declared: "Take care of that, and the other things will follow." Like Fromm and the other self-actualization authors we have mentioned, and in line with the eudaemonistic and self-realization tradition from Aristotle on, Horney insists that happiness is an achievement that involves effort and entails risks which may frighten many from the pursuit. "Most patients," she says, "have known merely the partial satisfaction attainable within the boundaries set by their anxieties; they have never experienced true happiness nor have they dared to reach out for it. . . . The neurotic has been altogether engrossed in his pursuit of safety and has felt content when merely free from haunting anxiety, depressions, migraine and the like." Or, he has been so absorbed in his own pretended "unselfishness" that he fears to make claims for himself. Or, "he has expected happiness to shine on him like sunrays from the sky without his

---

[27] *Ibid.*, pp. 230–231.

[28] As we have seen, Freud himself takes a dim view of the possibility of human happiness. For him, as Herbert Marcuse points out, "free gratification of man's instinctual needs is incompatible with civilization: renunciation and delay in satisfaction are the prerequisites of progress." "Happiness," says Freud, " 'is no cultural value.' Happiness must be subordinated to the discipline of work as full-time occupation, to the discipline of monogamic reproduction, to the established system of law and order. The methodological sacrifice of libido, its rigidly enforced deflection to socially useful activities and expression, *is* culture." (*Eros and Civilization*, p. 3.) The price we have paid for the sacrifice of happiness, Marcuse says, is not too great; for it has resulted in civilization. He criticizes Fromm's proposal that the therapist enter into a positive relation to his patient, unconditionally affirming his "claim for happiness," as follows: "The 'claim for happiness' if truly affirmed, aggravates the conflict with a society which allows only controlled happiness, and the exposure of the moral taboos extends this conflict to an attack on the vital protective layers of society." In a "repressive" society, the claim will not be tolerated. "The affirmative attitude toward the claim for happiness then becomes practicable only if happiness and 'the productive development of personality' are redefined so that they become compatible with prevailing values. . . . In a repressive society, individual happiness and productive development are in contradiction to society; if they are defined as values to be realized within the society, they become themselves repressive." (*Ibid.*, pp. 244–245.)

own active contribution." Analysis helps the patient to realize that the ground for happiness must be prepared within himself, that if he gives up the self-defeating demand for unconditional love, "he need not despair of obtaining happiness through love." The more he sheds his neurotic trends, "the more he becomes his own spontaneous self and can take care of his quest for happiness himself."[29] In speaking of the difficulties of self-analysis, Horney says, "The ultimate driving force is the person's unrelenting will to come to grips with himself, a wish to grow and to leave nothing untouched that prevents growth. It is a spirit of ruthless honesty toward himself, and he can succeed in finding himself only to the extent that it prevails."[30] It would be too much to say that Horney has developed a full-length self-actualization theory, but the tendency is in this direction, and in no other.

It should not be thought there are no differences among the authors we are discussing as to the nature of self-actualization or the self-actualization process, but in many cases they will be found to be minor. Their failure to criticize one another on the specific matters that concern us is significant. What seem to be outright differences may turn out to be matters of selective interest or emphasis. It will be remembered that Fromm, in his *Escape from Freedom*, maintains, as his central thesis, that many men—in fact the majority of the German electorate at the end of 1932—prefer security to freedom, dependence with protection to independence with its risks. Carl R. Rogers, on the contrary, says that

> the urge for a greater degree of independence . . . the tendency to strive, even through much pain, toward a socialized maturity . . . is stronger than the desire for comfortable dependence, the need to rely upon external authority for assurance. . . . I have yet to find the individual who, when he examines his situation deeply, and feels that he understands it clearly, deliberately chooses to have the integrated direction of himself undertaken by another. When all the elements are clearly perceived, the balance seems invariably in the direction of the painful but ultimately rewarding path of self-actualization or growth.[31]

Men do sometimes, in effect, prefer dependence to self-actualization, Rogers concedes, but when they do so they do not so much *choose* as drift into dependence without knowing exactly what they are doing. But this explanation of the matter is not wholly consistent with what Fromm says in *Escape from Freedom*.

Rogers is in close agreement with Goldstein when he states, as one of his

29 *New Ways in Psychoanalysis*, pp. 289–290.
30 *Self-Analysis*, p. 175.
31 *Client-centered Therapy*, p. 490.

basic principles, that *"the organism has one basic tendency and striving—to actualize, maintain, and enhance the experiencing organism . . .* all organic and psychological needs may be described as partial aspects of this one fundamental need."[32] The same accentuation of the self-actualization theory is to be found in Donald Snygg and A. W. Combs in their book *Individual Behavior* in which learning experiments are used to support the self-actualization thesis, and its advantages are shown in the sphere of counseling. In psychoanalysis, too, Rogers says, the therapist finds a powerful ally, even when he is dealing with patients on the brink of psychosis, in "the organic tendency toward ongoing growth and enhancement."[33]

That the psychotherapist should take advantage of the particular growth potentials present in the patient also is emphasized by Sanford. Endeavoring to state the function of psychotherapy with maximum breadth and acceptability, he says that its purpose "is to help the individual achieve fuller development." There are strict limitations to what the therapist can do, of course. He cannot endow an adult with potentialities he lacks. He can, and must, "create conditions under which the individual's inherent tendencies to growth have a fresh opportunity to express themselves." By discussion and interpretations, he can help the patient to see his stance in the world in a different light, and to gradually restructure "his internal organization and . . . his system of interpersonal relationships [so] that obstacles to growth are removed and unused potentials are released." Unlike education, which utilizes *general* capacity for growth, psychotherapy concentrates on *individual* capacity, employing the affect aroused to bring the patient to a new insight into his situation. Sanford remarks, however, that:

> just as some procedures which have been called group therapy do not differ essentially from education, there is a tendency in education to move in the direction of group therapy, using for teaching purposes the emotional processes operating in the teacher-class situation.[34]

[32] *Ibid.*, pp. 487–488.

[33] *Ibid.*, pp. 489–490. The urge to self-enhancement does not aim at pleasure, but its success is accompanied by pleasurable emotions, Rogers says. The striving to maintain and enhance the organism tends to be painful, but the painful emotions are not typically disintegrating, as some have claimed, but rather marshal and organize the effort. In one respect this formulation seems out of line with the tradition we are tracing, for this tradition maintains that perhaps the greatest pleasure man can have comes from the actualizing process itself—from the striving against opposition for the objects which enhance or are enhancing the self. But in the light of other things that Rogers says it seems likely that he does, after all, recognize that the excitement of the struggle itself is an important source of pleasure.

[34] "The Findings of the Commission in Psychology," in *Annals of the New York Academy of Science,* 63, 1955, pp. 341 ff.

The self-actualization theories define the *ideal* of normality—or human excellence or happiness—in terms of growth, development, or actualization, and insist that the *positive* goal is the main thing.[35] It is essential to eliminate mental inflexibilities and rigidities, constrained dependence, anxiety—unconscious determination of thought and action; the chief reason is that they are the obstacles to continued learning and growth. The accent is not on the avoidance of risks and dissatisfactions on a simplified level of existence but on the more or less hazardous quest of larger satisfactions. Recently, the National Opinion Research Center at the University of Chicago turned up some evidence that positive feelings of satisfaction are a much better indication of happiness than is freedom from dissatisfaction. Persons in four small Illinois towns (two of them economically depressed, one prosperous, and one on the upgrade) were questioned and interviewed about their state of happiness ("very happy," "pretty happy," and "not too happy"), and about the frequency of their positive or "good" feelings and their negative or "bad" feelings, the balance of which seemed to correlate with the assessment of happiness. The study of some 2,000 subjects carried out so far supports the "central theme" of Dr. Norman M. Bradburn, the director of the project, that the relative unhappiness of the people living in the depressed communities derives, *not* from the greater number of negative feeling experiences but from the fact that there are far fewer opportunities to enjoy those life experiences that make a person feel "good." Those experiences that "contribute to happiness by increasing the number of good feelings" were found to be "a high degree of social interaction and participation in the environment: seeing friends and relatives, talking with friends on the telephone, meeting new people, traveling, eating out, and belonging to organized groups." But all forms of social interaction were reduced in the depressed communities. Thus, Dr. Bradburn concludes: "It is the lack of joy in Mudville rather than the presence of sorrow that makes the difference."[36]

There are quite a number of other self-actualization theories we should have to mention if this review were to be complete. But the task now is to sum up briefly the respects in which self-actualization agrees with eudae-

[35] A very full account of human potentialities, and of their fulfillment as the urge and goal of the individual and race, is to be found in Gardner Murphy's *Human Potentialities*.

[36] *In Pursuit of Happiness*. Eugene Heimler, of Middlesex, England—a World Health Organization's mental health consultant to the U.S.—reports the finding that continued positive satisfactions are necessary even to normality, to effective functioning in society. The five areas of sanity-saving satisfaction, he says, are financial, sexual, emotional (parental and marital), friendship, and work. Normal functioning in society does not require satisfaction in every one of these areas, but in a certain proportionality which is now being measured quantitatively by tests devised for the purpose. (Reported in the *San Francisco Chronicle*, Aug. 9, 1964.)

monism and self-realization, and also to indicate some ways in which it differs.

Let us begin by noting that, though it is a rare thing for contemporary psychologists and clinicians to relate themselves to the work of philosophers, some of our self-actualization authors do compare their theories to Aristotle's eudaemonism and Spinoza's self-realization theory. Fromm, for example, compares the "productiveness," which for him is the measure of man's happiness, with the productiveness that plays an important role in Aristotle's ethics. In Aristotle's view, Fromm says, "One can determine virtue . . . by ascertaining the function of man. Just as in the case of a flute player, a sculptor, or any artist, the good is thought to reside in the specific function which distinguishes these men from others and makes them what they are, the good of man also resides in the specific function which distinguishes him from other species and makes him what he is."[37] Fromm then quotes a passage (1098b32, which we have given above) in which Aristotle says how important it is to take the chief good, or happiness, to be an *activity* rather than a state, and concludes, with approval, that, for Aristotle, the happy man is one "who by his activity, under the guidance of reason, brings to life the potentialities specific of man."[38] Fromm also finds his conception of productiveness delineated in Spinoza's system in which, as we have seen, virtue consists in the realization of the natural powers of man.[39] In the same way, Plato, Aristotle, and Spinoza are cited for their views as to the relation of pleasure and happiness: Pleasure as an accompaniment of natural activities that perfects them, and that is the most valuable when it corresponds to our highest nature—theoretic reason; the qualitatively different kinds of pleasure; and the doctrine that the chief good is not pleasure, but happiness—the activity that actualizes human nature. In Spinoza's system, Fromm particularly calls attention to the definition of joy, as "a passage from less to greater perfection" (or power); the famous last Proposition of the *Ethics*, "Blessedness (or happiness) is not the reward of virtue, but virtue itself . . ." and the implied doctrine that productive activity is the end of life, and pleasure merely its accompaniment.

Maslow also finds his key conception—self-actualization—anticipated in part by Aristotle and Spinoza. The difference is that these philosophers did not know as much about human beings as we do today—nothing about recent discoveries in human motivation and psychopathology. Consequently, he says, "we may agree with Aristotle when he assumed that the

---

[37] *Op. cit.*, p. 91.
[38] *Ibid.*, p. 92.
[39] "Virtue," he contends, "is the unfolding of the specific potentialities of every species; for man it is the state in which he is the most human." (*Ibid.*, p. 26.)

good life consisted in living in accordance with the true nature of man, but we must add that he simply did not know enough about the true nature of man."[40]

In her monograph, published by the Joint Commission on Mental Illness and Health, Marie Jahoda describes and evaluates, in a provisional way, six current concepts of mental health, viz.:

1. Growth, Development, Self-actualization
2. Attitudes Toward the Self
3. Integration
4. Autonomy
5. Perception of Reality
6. Environmental Mastery

The first concept is, of course, the self-actualization we have been discussing. The authors representing the second concept emphasize one or more of the following points: "The accessibility of the self" to the consciousness of the subject, the correctness of the subject's judgments about the self, and self-acceptance, *i.e.*, easy acceptance of unavoidable limitations of the self, together with a readiness to consider the gains and cost of removing remediable faults.

Under the third concept, Integration, Jahoda mentions "a balance between psychic forces," an example of which is the ideal interplay of ego, superego, and id. According to Kubie and others who follow Freud in this respect, the conscious forces should be at the helm and the influence of the unconscious forces reduced to a minimum. This favors flexibility, readiness to learn and to change, and excludes automatic or compulsive repetition which characterizes neuroses, in Freud's view, and the misery that attends them. There are two other aspects of Integration that may be given prominence: "A unifying outlook on life," and "resistance to stress."

Concerning the three last concepts, or "criteria," of mental health, Jahoda states that they all "share an explicit emphasis on reality-orientation."[41]

Autonomy, as Jahoda understands it, has to do either with the process of decision-making or the independent behavior that results, and the author, insisting on one, naturally gives some attention to the other. The broadest characterization of this concept, perhaps, would be that the autonomous individual is self-determining rather than "self-surrendering," that is, determined by the person or character rather than by chance exigencies in personal or social life. (A similar division of the goal of the autonomy is made by Fr. Duyckaerts, in his *La Notion de Normal en Psychologie*

[40] *Op. cit.*, p. 341.
[41] *Current Concepts of Positive Mental Health*, p. 43.

Clinique; namely, independence in relation to oneself, and independence in relation to others. The first means that the individual can determine his own actions by choice and determine his own character, to some extent at least. The second means that the adult has been able to overcome his childish dependence on the attitudes of others, his need to bow to their superior wisdom or authority, and relies mostly on himself. Such a man is independent, self-reliant, "inner-directed" as opposed to "other-directed," whereas the neurotic is characterized by submission and dependence.)

The fifth concept, Perception of Reality, is described under two headings, which are self-explanatory, viz.; "perception free from need-distortion," and "empathy or social sensitivity." Here the requirement of cognitive correctness is not to be understood as excluding individual differences in perception and appraisal. Sound people can see and feel things differently, Jahoda says, as long as they do not distort reality to fit their wishes. "The mentally healthy person will *test* reality for its degree of correspondence to his wishes or fears. One lacking mental health will assume such correspondence without testing."[42]

The sixth concept, Environmental Mastery, is discussed under headings that again speak for themselves: The ability to love; Adequacy in love, work, and play; Adequacy in interpersonal relations; Meeting of situational requirements; Adaptation and adjustment; and Problem-solving.

A number of observations now can be made about these concepts as they relate to happiness: (a) Jahoda's classification is based on the literature; any other sophisticated roundup of the prevailing requirements for positive mental health would be quite similar. Thus the French philosopher Duyckaerts lists the following leading conceptions of "the normal" as Integration, Autonomy, Adaptation, the Average or statistical mean, and Creativity, as opposed to frustration. The last seems to resemble very closely Fromm's "productiveness," and other conceptions of the self-actualization authors. (b) There is a great deal of overlap of Jahoda's six concepts, as she herself points out. The authors who stand for self-actualization, she says, include in it the elements of concept 2, *i.e.*, accessibility of the self, self-acceptance, etc. Some of them—Maslow, Allport, and Dr. M. Mayman, she adds, adopt elements of most of her concepts. It will be clear from the first section of this chapter that Fromm certainly adopts such a "multiple-criterion" position, and that other self-actualization authors appear to do so. There is indeed a tremendous amount of overlap. Conceptually it is difficult to see how Environmental Mastery, as described, can be realized without the realization of all the other five concepts. (c) Concepts 2–6 are not opposed to concept 1, unless they are taken as sufficient in

---

[42] *Loc. cit.*

themselves, apart from self-actualization, *or* self-actualization authors reject or ignore them.

Consider the first alternative: If Integration is conceived as independent of Growth, Development, Self-actualization, then a man could achieve a fine integration on a level far below his gifts and capacities, and come out of a successful analysis only half alive. If care were taken to eliminate every vestige of the requirement that full potentialities must be actualized from concepts 2 and 4–6, would not the result be the same? The goal of therapy would be the adjustment of a man to his environment, or self-awareness and self-acceptance, or perception and mastery of the environment as it is, or all of these at once, by the easiest, most convenient route, even though potentials should be sacrificed. Autonomy itself might turn out to be governed by prudence.

Concepts 2–6, if clearly demarcated from self-actualization, often seem to be viewed as *means* to self-actualization, that is, to the fulfillment of human desires when gifts and capacities are fully exploited. We have seen, in fact, that self-realization authors, though they assign focal importance to growth, development, self-realization, also tend to recognize the need for the other requirements in the Jahoda list. The more elaborate the description of self-actualization, the more these subsidiary concepts are acknowledged.

(d) In criticism of the self-actualization concept, Jahoda complains that it is not clear whether the process is supposed to be going on in all organisms, or only in healthy ones.

> It is not always easy to distinguish these two meanings in the mental health literature. This lack of clarity probably has something to do with the controversial philosophical concept of Aristotelian teleology, to which the notion of realizing one's potentialities is related. The need for making the distinction in a discussion of mental health becomes urgent if one realizes that not only the development of civilization but also self destruction and crime . . . are among the unique potentialities of the human species.[43]

The Aristotelian answer, in brief, would be that self-destruction would not be an actualization of human nature, but rather the annihilation of human faculties and potentialities, and that crime, similarly, would be inconsistent with moral virtues, such as friendship, prudence, self-esteem, and justice, which are necessary for self-actualization or happiness. A like answer might be made on behalf of contemporary self-actualization authors. They all understand self-actualization to be an ongoing process, development being a means to further development, not to frustration. Moreover, as Jahoda points out, they all include "self-accessibility" and "self-acceptance" as

[43] *Op. cit.,* p. 31.

requirements. We have seen also that those self-actualization authors who go into detail include also the other main requirements 3–6 as subsidiary concepts. Could a destructive nature meet all these requirements?

Jahoda makes the sound observation, which we find also in Sanford, Allport, Fromm, and other self-actualization authors, that self-actualization cannot mean actualization of *all* the individual's potentialities; the full development of his mathematical potential might prevent the full development of his musical capacity. She points out that no one would say that because a man made a great success of music while neglecting his mathematical talent he must lack mental health. Nor is it likely that anyone would claim that such a man could not be happy. Differentiation and specialization could be as important as breadth, in one case as in the other.

(e) The question remains whether self-actualization can be identified. Jahoda complains that empirical criteria are scarce and imprecise, but goes on to mention the useful classification of students into "under-achievers" and "over-achievers," and the further criterion furnished by time budgets, showing what percentage of his time a man spends in interests that go beyond his job and the requirements of living. There are other criteria, it might be added, such as the percentage increase of cultural expenditures with rising income, and the relation between IQ, and scores on aptitude and ability tests, on the one hand, and achievement levels, on the other. In the analytic situation, Duyckaerts argues, "the notions of creativity and frustration correspond to real properties of behavior, which can be apprehended directly, by minute and patient analysis, in the phenomenal field of the individual."[44] When the examination of the potentialities and progress of the individual toward actualizing them is superficial, the criteria are rough and ready, and leave much to be desired; when it is concrete and exhaustive, the results are generally found pretty reliable. And since self-actualization authors usually recognize the auxiliary role of the other concepts in Jahoda's list, the tests available for these concepts can be expected to give some support to the tests for self-actualization as well.

(f) It naturally makes some difference that Jahoda is concerned with "positive mental health," whereas we are interested in happiness, but not much. Happiness without positive mental health would be a dubious combination, however the two are conceived, and impossible, we hold, if they are conceived according to eudaemonism and self-actualization, respectively; while positive mental health without a share of happiness would not be worth the therapeutic costs. Self-actualization authors often use happiness as synonymous with self-actualization, we have noted, and probably all

[44] *La Notion de Normal en Psychologie Clinique,* p. 194.

of them would do so if they did not associate "happiness" with hedonism, a view they all wish to reject. Secondly, the tests for positive mental health seem to be relevant to happiness as well, and the decision is rated the same in importance.

It perhaps will be useful to point out again why the self-actualization conception of positive mental health is uniquely pertinent to the theory of happiness. With regard to all the other concepts in Jahoda's list, we may ask what purpose they serve; they do not seem to be final ends but rather high-order means. We may ask why the self should be accessible, and why the self is to be accepted, why a certain kind of integration is desirable, why more rather than less autonomy should be sought, why facing reality is better than wishful thinking, and why mastering the environment is better than taking it easy. All such questions make sense. On the contrary, the question why you want to cash in on your assets, *i.e.*, to satisfy as many of your desires as possible, given continuing development of your potentials, sounds somewhat preposterous. It is understood that everyone automatically wants to satisfy as many of his desires as possible, and that, if the cultivation of one's capacities results in more or better satisfactions, the gain is self-evident.

Maximum satisfaction[45] of desires corresponding to a full development of human faculties and individual abilities may be the ideal, some will say, but because its achievement is dangerous and precarious it is better to settle for a poorer but surer level of satisfaction. Whatever the wisdom of this advice may be, it is not the prevailing counsel in this "affluent" society. Politicians and educators no longer tell the people to be content with a modest lot, really below their capacities, but proclaim, as the economy continues to expand, the indefinite enlargement of individual life.

SELF-ACTUALIZATION, EUDAEMONISM, AND SELF-REALIZATION

In Chapter 7 we summarized a number of resemblances between eudaemonism and the self-realization theory. In the present chapter we have seen both of these theories reflected in the contemporary self-actualization theory. The doctrines and emphases shared by the three theories, with great differences of accent, are as follows:

1. Man's chief good or happiness consists in the fulfillment of his human nature and individual potentialities.

---

[45] "Satisfaction" here includes surprise satisfaction, which is experienced prior to the desire for it. Thus one is surprised by the beauty of the landscape, which one had not anticipated, though one would not enjoy it now if one had not desired this kind of thing in the past. Some call it "serendipity."

2. There are higher needs and higher desires that have "functional autonomy," *i.e.*, satisfying them is not simply an indirect way of satisfying biological needs and desires, and they can continue to activate behavior even when the latter are satisfied.

3. The best life or happiness requires that the higher (cultural) needs and desires be satisfied in some degree. The tendency is to hold that the more they are satisfied, the better the life, even if it is at the expense of biological needs. A physically sick genius is better off than a healthy boor. What seems to be assumed in general is that man is a cultural animal, so that without culture he would not be quite human.

4. The *ideal*, however, is all-round development, biological as well as cultural.

5. This requires more or less continuous exercise of all the human capacities, especially the highest, but this cannot be routine or repetitive, for, by their very nature, reasoning and aesthetic activity demand ever fresh materials and problems, and the same would be true of social activity.

6. The good life or happiness is not a state but an activity, and the activity seems to be regarded as an exercise of both mind and body, function and structure, bound up in an inseparable unity. In the tradition we are describing, at any rate, no basic causal dualism or opposition between mind and body is to be found.

7. The self is active in achieving its highest good. It is not only determined from outside but also by its own human endowment and acquired nature, and the power of choice.

8. The chief good or happiness is an achievement rather than an issue of fortune. But this does not mean that one achieves happiness by pursuing it as an end-in-view, for the implication is that the ends-in-view most likely to result in happiness may be concrete and delimited objects obtainable by a given individual, and not by others, such as winning a particular woman or completing a certain program of painting or a set of experiments. Although seldom clearly expressed, the chief good or happiness seems to play its part in determining conduct, not as an end-in-view but as a standard by which to judge the acceptability of competing ends-in-view.

9. The achievement of the good life or happiness is consistent with pain, grief, crisis, and struggle, and is generally not possible without them, but there is high "resistance to stress."

10. The conception of the good life or happiness is expansive rather than prudent and contractive. It is to be attained, not so much by the reduction of one's desires as by the increase of satisfied desires. There are serious engagements—a big "investment in living."

11. Virtuous activity and the natural process of self-fulfillment are the same thing. The criterion of the growth or development that results in self-

fulfillment—and therefore happiness—is said to be conscious choice on the basis of a continuing readiness to learn and relearn the complex and changing conditions favorable to the maximum satisfaction of desires, together with a willingness to try out new desires and conduct experimentally and to judge the outcome by this standard, provided, of course, that the environment is in some degree hospitable to such efforts. The basic opposition between desire and virtue is thus rejected. If a virtuous desire prevails over another, it is because it is or becomes a stronger or preferred desire.

12. The fundamental dualism of desire and reason is also transcended. Desire, not reason, is the moving force of human action. But, in the course of natural development, reasons—as criteria, strategies, and prudential considerations—become embedded in desires. Desires thus become desires-for-such-and-such-a-reason. Desires turn out to be "ratiocinative desires," as Aristotle puts it, while reasons are actually "desiderative reasons." Unless it is simply an elliptical way of speaking, the tradition we are concerned with does not talk of reason subduing desire.

13. The dilemma of egoism *vs.* altruism—of selfish desire *vs.* the duty of unselfishness—is transformed by the claim that unselfishness, properly understood, is the expansion of the self to include a concern for others. Selfishness is the narrowing and freezing of the self by fear and frustration, whereas unselfishness is growth and expansion of the range of interests. The unselfish man has his conflicts of interest, of course, but, when he decides to sacrifice the narrower interest for the larger one, his unselfishness has the sanction of real preference or desire. He is not only unselfish but wants to be.

14. Self-esteem, exempt from self-illusion, self-escape, guilt, and anxiety, is an essential feature of the ideal.

15. Since achievement in the arts and sciences is a crowning phase of self-fulfillment, there is a tendency to regard this kind of achievement, not as something morally indifferent but as a continuation of moral excellence in another sphere, as a growth or enhancement of the self which, since it is possible, ought to be.

16. When moderation is urged in the matter of eating, drinking, etc., or with regard to certain social activities, it is urged, not for the reason that excess is bad in itself but because it involves inflexibility or fixation, excludes opportunities for learning, and narrows the range of self-fulfillment.

17. Pleasure is not generally the end-in-view, nor is it the standard that measures the excellence of different activities. The view, stated or implied, is that pleasure regularly accompanies the exercise of human functions and individual abilities, when they are not too much impeded, as well as the

successful attainment, partial attainment, or anticipated attainment of individual goals. In the latter case, the accompanying pleasure is simply the indisputable pleasantness of satisfying desires. There is some tendency, at least, to recognize that the pleasure may accompany experiences that have not been desired—many come as a surprise or serendipity.

18. The process of self-fulfillment is never completed. Whereas pleasure, as Aristotle claims, is in a sense complete in itself, the good life or happiness is never finished, is always pointing beyond. The growing self can never stop learning and emendation, nor escape the chance of shipwreck and ruin, and can rest on its oars only momentarily. The Faustian man can never avow he has had enough. Venturing a thought he is said to have borrowed from Spinoza, Goethe has the Angel in *Faust* II declare that he who ceaselessly strives is never lost.

19. It is hardly necessary to add that the tradition we have been discussing recognizes that economic goods, a stable social order, and constitutional rule are essentials of the good life or happiness. There is no tendency to asceticism or to a posture of Stoical independence.

As to the differences between the three conceptions of the good life or happiness, it will be granted that there have been tremendous developments in recent times that are bound to affect the outlook on happiness, especially as regards its possible *attainment*, not only by favored individuals and classes but by entire populations. The developments relating to the *nature* of happiness seem to be largely psychological. If happiness is interpreted as a process of self-fulfillment, it will probably be conceded that modern discoveries about the specifics of maturation, learning, educational techniques, the effects of punishment, the role of the unconscious and repression, the regularity of ambivalence in love and friendship, and so on, have thrown a good deal of light on this process. The self-actualization authors we have discussed are immersed in theories and facts relating to the abnormal—to obstructions to a satisfactory life. The reason is that their focus is on therapy, and they have at their disposal knowledge and techniques not available to earlier centuries. It is in their improved knowledge of these obstacles and of the means to their removal that the self-actualization authors go beyond earlier conceptions and make their main contribution to the theory of happiness.

In the specification of the moral content of happiness, on the other hand, the earlier theories—eudaemonism and self-realization—seem to go far beyond the self-actualization theory, which, wishing to remain "objective," tends to reduce ethics to psychology. But how deep does this ethical neutrality go? The self-actualization theory does not analyze and recommend the Aristotelian virtues, or endorse any other list of virtues in general, but the therapist seeking to aid his patient in actualizing his powers naturally predisposes him to a kind of courage at one concrete juncture, and influences him in the direction of prudence, generosity or other virtues at other points of the therapeutic process. It may be argued, in fact, that self-actualization authors really take the standard virtues for granted, and invoke them when needed in the concrete therapeutic situation. In this case there would be less difference between self-actualization and the earlier theories. It will be remembered, too, that, while the self-actualizing is a natural process, it is also an ideal, and that eudaemonism and the self-realization theory are distinguished by the same blend of the natural and ideal. Thus, while there is a big difference between the psychologizing of the therapists and the moral language of the earlier philosophers, the substantive difference between them may not be so great as it seemed at first sight.

In tracing developments of the theory of happiness in present thought, we have concentrated on the efforts of psychologists and psychotherapists to define positive mental health, because they seem to have the most relevance to the *nature* of happiness, whereas pertinent developments in the social sciences relate mostly to its implementation. The literature strongly suggests that what we have called "self-actualization" theory is a continuation of eudaemonism and self-realization theory, and that when psychotherapists prefer other norms of the normal or satisfactory life, this might be explained in one of two ways: Either, like Freud, they do not believe human happiness possible, or they wish, understandably, to delimit the professional commitment to the removal of symptoms and their recurrence, and to restrict themselves to healing the sick.

THE PURSUIT OF HAPPINESS

Psychotherapy can do nothing, of course, except in the framework of a stable political order. Self-actualization, like self-realization and eudemian happiness, actually presupposes a welfare state. In this 2,000-year tradition, the state is assumed to be a *natural* institution indispensable to human survival, and also to the good life. And it is considered a chief means to happiness. The aim of the kingly art or science, Plato holds, is to make men happy, mainly by making them good,[46] for, if they are virtuous, they must surely be happy. For Aristotle, similarly, the aim of politics is to make men happy.

> It ordains which of the sciences should be studied in a state, and which class of citizens should learn and up to which point they should learn them; and we see even the most highly esteemed of capacities to fall under this, *e.g.*

[46] See *Euthyphro*, 288–292.

strategy, economics, rhetoric; now, since politics uses the rest of the sciences, and since, again, it legislates as to what we are to do and what we are to abstain from, the end of this science [the production of happiness] must include those of the others.[47]

Aquinas agrees with Aristotle's verdict that " 'we call those legal matters just which are adopted to produce and preserve happiness and its parts for the body politic,' since the state is a perfect community."[48] For "the last end of human life is happiness," Aquinas says, "and to this principle chiefly and above all law must be referred."[49] The making of the laws, since they are to promote the common good, is the prerogative of the whole people or a representative of it.[50] And Aquinas also agrees with Aristotle when he says that happiness *is* a perfecting of the soul, though the perfecting is not, of course, the end or cause of the happiness.[51]

Utilitarians generally go further. Bentham insists that the *only* justification the restraints of law and administration can have is that they augment the net sum of pleasure for the greatest number. But this is all the justification they need. Pleasure and pain, especially pain, are the great instructors of mankind, as Plato and Aristotle say. A rational system of laws, making sagacious use of these powerful motives, could in time increase the general happiness indefinitely, and also, as a byproduct, improve moral conduct. Indeed, it is only as conduct is improved that the community's sum of pleasure is augmented. It is true that the utilitarian's definition of "right" and "moral" is not accepted by the other schools, but these schools themselves differ in this matter. It is sufficient for the present purpose to keep in view the just, prudent, generous, courageous, temperate conduct that utilitarianism, like other schools, actually enjoins. It is by making men virtuous, by way of a rational system of laws, that Bentham would make them happy. This is also true, with proper qualifications, of the other philosophers mentioned above, and of Rousseau and many others. The state also provides security and certain liberties, but if the people remain unhappy it has failed in its purpose.

In John Locke we find a complete reversal of this traditional view. "The great and chief end . . . of Mens uniting into Commonwealths, and putting themselves under Government, *is the Preservation of their Property.*"[52] The preservation of life and liberty are also ends of the State, according to Locke, but need not always be mentioned, since they depend

---

[47] *Op. cit., Nicomachean Ethics,* 1094b1–7.
[48] *Ibid., Politics,* 1, 1, 1252a5.
[49] *Summa Theologica,* Part I of Part II, Q90, A2.
[50] *Ibid.,* A30.
[51] *Ibid.,* Q2, A7.
[52] The Second Treatise Concerning Civil Government, pp. 368–369.

on the preservation of property, and are understood to be included under it. But the promotion of happiness is certainly not an end of government, in Locke's judgment, except incidentally, insofar as the safeguarding of life and property contribute to it. Nor is virtue an end. Matters of conscience in religion or morals should be of no concern to the magistrate. It is of utmost importance that he confine himself to things that are strictly political.[53]

In his passionate defense of the individual and of his right to any idiosyncrasy that does not result in injury to his fellows, J. S. Mill goes a long way toward endorsing the dictum that "the state which governs least governs best." But, as is well known, Mill is of two minds on this question, and one of his most striking exceptions to the laissez-faire doctrine is his insistence that the State has the duty of seeing that all its citizens receive an education, if need be, entirely at public expense. One important test of the goodness of political institutions, accordingly, is "how far they tend to foster in the members of the community the various desirable qualities, moral and intellectual. . . . The government which does this best has every likelihood of being best in all other respects, since it is on these qualities, as far as they exist in the people, that all possibility of goodness in the practical operations of government depend." A government is good or bad, then, insofar as its tendency is "to improve or deteriorate the people themselves."[54] Yet, in spite of this, Mill is far from agreeing with Bentham that it is the business of government to make men happy; its role is rather to equip them with the intellectual and moral wherewithal to find happiness themselves, each in his own unique way.

The documents that mark the advent of the American republic present a startling variation of doctrine. The Declaration of Independence states that "all men are endowed by their Creator with certain unalienable rights; that among these are life, liberty, and the pursuit of happiness. That to secure these rights, governments are instituted among men, deriving their just powers from the consent of the governed." And the Preamble to the Constitution announces that "We, the people of the United States, in order to form a more perfect union, establish justice, insure domestic tranquility, provide for the common defense, promote general welfare . . . do ordain and establish this Constitution of the United States of America."

Although a great deal happened in the eleven years between the Declaration and the Constitution, we need not suppose that the "promote general welfare" of the second document is out of line with the "pursuit of

[53] *A Letter Concerning Toleration, Great Books of the Western World,* Vol. 35, pp. 16–17.
[54] *Utilitarianism,* p. 193.

happiness" of the first. On the contrary, it would seem that the *program* of promoting general welfare provides implementation of the inalienable *right* to pursue happiness, that is, promises that the external means would be provided for citizens to pursue their happiness, each in his own way.

It is notable that the intention to promote morality, so much a part of the Platonic-Aristotelian tradition, is entirely lacking in both documents, and that the establishment of a religion is expressly prohibited by the Constitution. Only the subsequent ill-fated 18th Amendment undertook to reform morals, and it was not long after rescinded by the 21st Amendment. It is significant, too, that the arguments in favor of the Constitution put forward in the *Federalist Papers* continually urge the consideration of happiness, or the conditions of it, but seldom invoke morality. Again and again it is argued that only through the proposed Union can happiness, along with security and liberty, be preserved and enlarged, and that this is the end and justification of government. But we do not find it urged on behalf of self-government or "the more perfect union" of the states that it will improve morals of citizens or make them better men, though much, indeed, is said about its effect on security and welfare.

A thousand historical circumstances no doubt bid for a share in explaining this deliberate reticence. What concerns us here is the dialectical relation between this reticence and "the pursuit of happiness." Had the aim been to *make* men happy, something would have been said about making them just and moral, for it is unlikely that happiness was envisaged without virtue. But nothing *was* said about making men virtuous, presumably, because the laws have no jurisdiction, as Locke said, in matters of conscience in religion and morals. The conclusion of this hypothetical argument would be that the aim was not to *make* men happy, but to make this possible. Happiness, then, was not something that could be designed and produced by government, even the wisest, but could only be prepared for and perhaps found.[55] What government by the consent of the governed *could* provide were some absolute essentials of a successful pursuit.

There seems no doubt that in the competition of forms of government, democracy is now winning the race, but the victory is perplexed by division and uncertainty. In a recent series of lectures,[56] C. B. Macpherson contrasts three contemporary forms of democracy: Liberal-capitalist democracy, nonliberal communist democracy, and the nonliberal, noncommunist

---

[55] The individual, unique, largely incalculable, and serendipidous character of happiness is emphasized, it will be remembered, by John Dewey and Moritz Schlick, but in most authors it remains obscure, overshadowed if not crowded out by the formal features of the common good.

[56] See *The Real World of Democracy*.

democracy being realized in underdeveloped nations of Africa and Asia. Many would prefer to reserve the title of democracy to one of the three forms alone, yet each can claim usage and models, ancient or modern, and a body of theory in its support. Many speak and act on the conviction that the people's happiness would be best served by the one real democracy in every country the world round, no matter what the native traditions, economic conditions, and realistic prospects may be. Is not the same medicine and the same science of engineering good for all countries alike? The counterthesis is to the effect that people can borrow science and technology with sheer advantage, but that one's happiness, like one's virtues, is more personal, and should be selected with a practiced eye to all the indigenous circumstances and opportunities, studied with loving care inspired by community or self-interest alone, and that the political forms in which the very possibility of happiness is enshrined are also an intimate choice.

This issue of happiness is not, unfortunately, merely academic, but the airing of differences at least discourages the worst results.

Bibliography

Albee, Ernest. *A History of English Utilitarianism*. New York: Macmillan, 1901.

Allport, G. W. *Becoming: Basic Considerations for a Psychology of Personality*. New Haven, Conn.: Yale University Press, 1955.

————. *Personality: A Psychological Interpretation*. New York: Henry Holt, 1937.

Aquinas, Thomas. *On the Truth of the Catholic Faith (Summa Contra Gentiles)*, trans. by Vernon J. Bourke. Garden City, N.Y.: Hanover House, 1956.

————. *Summa Theologica*.

Aristotle. *Eudemian Ethics*, in *The Works of Aristotle*, ed. by W. D. Ross.

————. *Magna Moralia*, in *The Works of Aristotle*, ed. by W. D. Ross.

————. *Metaphysics*, in *The Works of Aristotle*, ed. by W. D. Ross.

————. *Nicomachean Ethics*, in *The Works of Aristotle*, ed. by W. D. Ross.

————. *On the Motion of Animals*, in *The Works of Aristotle*, ed. by W. D. Ross.

————. *On the Soul*, in *The Works of Aristotle*, ed. by W. D. Ross.

————. *Politics*, in *The Works of Aristotle*, ed. by W. D. Ross.

————. *Rhetoric*, in *The Works of Aristotle*, ed. by W. D. Ross.

Ashley Montagu, M. F. *Darwin: Competition and Cooperation*. New York: Henry Schuman, 1952.

Atkinson, B. (ed.). *The Selected Writings of Ralph Waldo Emerson*. New York: Modern Library, 1962.

Augustine. *On Christian Doctrine*, in *The Works of Augustine*, ed. by Marcus Dods.

————. *The City of God,* trans. by Marcus Dods. New York: Modern Library, 1950.

————. *The Confessions,* trans. by E. B. Pussey. New York: Pocket Books, 1951.

————. *The Happy Life,* trans. by L. Schopp. London: B. Herder, 1939.

————. *The Morals of the Catholic Church and the Morals of the Manicheans,* in *The Works of Augustine,* ed. by Marcus Dods.

————. *The Trinity,* in *The Works of Augustine,* ed. by Marcus Dods.

Austin, J. L. *The Meaning of a Word,* in *Philosophy and Ordinary Language,* ed. by Charles E. Caton. Urbana, Ill.: University of Illinois Press, 1963.

————. *Philosophical Papers.* Oxford: Oxford University Press, 1961.

Bentham, Jeremy. *A Fragment on Government and the Principles of Morals and Legislation.* Oxford: Basil Blackwell, 1948.

————. *Theory of Political Economy,* in *Complete Works,* ed. by J. Bowring. New York: Russell, 1962.

Berkeley, George. *The Works of George Berkeley, Bishop of Cloyne,* Vol. VI. London: Thomas Nelson & Sons, 1953.

Birney, R. C., and Teevan, R. C. (eds.). *Reinforcement: An Enduring Problem in Psychology.* New York: Van Nostrand, 1961.

Bradburn, Norman, M. *In Pursuit of Happiness: A Pilot Study of Mental Health Related Behavior.* In press.

Bradley, F. H. "Why Should I be Moral?," in *Ethical Studies: Selected Essays.* New York: Liberal Arts Press, 1951.

————. "Pleasure for Pleasures Sake," in *Ethical Studies: Selected Essays.* New York: Liberal Arts Press, 1951.

Brandt, R. (ed.). *Value and Obligation.* New York: Harcourt, Brace, 1963.

Broad, C. D. *Five Types of Ethical Theory.* London: Routledge & Kegan Paul, 1951.

Butler, Joseph. *The Analogy of Religion.* London: Bell & Daldy, 1857.

Caton, Charles E. (ed.). *Philosophy and Ordinary Language.* Urbana, Ill.: University of Illinois Press, 1963.

Cicero. *De Officiis,* trans. by W. Miller. Loeb Library. Cambridge, Mass.: Harvard University Press, 1913.

————. *Tusculan Disputations,* trans. by J. E. King. Loeb Library. Cambridge, Mass.: Harvard University Press, 1927.

Darwin, Charles. *The Descent of Man.* New York: A. L. Burt, n.d.

Davidson, Donald, McKinsey, J. C. C., and Suppes, Patrick. "Outlines of a Formal Theory of Value," in *Philosophy of Science,* 22, 2, 1955.

Dewey, John. *Human Nature and Conduct: An Introduction to Social Psychology.* New York: Henry Holt, 1922.

————. *The Theory of Valuation,* in *International Encyclopedia,* Vol. II, No. 4. Chicago: University of Chicago Press, n.d.

Dewey, John, and Tufts, James H. *Ethics,* rev. ed., New York: Henry Holt, 1952.

Diogenes, Laertius. *Lives of Eminent Philosophers,* Vols. II and VII, trans. by R. D. Hicks. Cambridge, Mass.: Harvard University Press, 1958.

Dods, Marcus (ed.). *The Works of Augustine.* Edinburgh: T. & T. Clark, 1873.

Duncan-Jones A. (ed.). *Butler's Moral Philosophy.* Hammondsworth, Middlesex, England: Penguin Books, 1952.

Duyckaerts, Father. *La Notion de Normal en Psychologie Clinique.* Paris: Librairie Philosophique J. Vrin, 1954.

Epicurus. *Epicurus to Menoeceus,* in *Fragmenta Epicurea.*

Epictetus. *The Discourses,* in *The Stoic and Epicurean Philosophers,* ed. by W. J. Oaks. New York: Random House, 1940.

Erikson, Erich, H. *Childhood and Society.* New York: W. W. Norton, 1950.

Falk, W. D. "Ought and Motivation," in *Proceedings of the Aristotelian Society,* 48, 1947–48.

Field, G. C. "Kant's First Moral Principle," in *Mind,* Vol. XLI.

————. *Moral Theory: An Introduction to Ethics.* New York: E. P. Dutton, 1921.

Freud, Sigmund. *Civilization and Its Discontents,* trans. by J. Riviere. Reprinted from the Hogarth Press Edition, n.d.

Fromm, Erich. *Man for Himself.* New York: Rinehart, 1947.

Garnett, A. Cambell. *Ethics: A Critical Introduction.* New York: Ronald Press, 1960.

Green, T. H. *Prologomena to Ethics,* 3rd ed. Oxford: Clarendon Press.

Goldstein, Kurt. *Human Nature in the Light of Psychopathology.* Cambridge, Mass.: Harvard University Press, 1951.

Halévy, Elie. *The Growth of Philosophic Radicalism.* Boston: Beacon Press, 1955.

Hebb, D. O. *The Organization of Behavior.* New York: John Wiley, 1949.

Hegel, G. W. F. *Early Theological Writings,* trans. by T. M. Knox and Richard Kroner. Chicago: University of Chicago Press, 1948.

————. *The Phenomenology of Mind,* trans. by J. B. Bailie, 2d ed. London: George Allen & Unwin, 1949.

————. *The Philosophy of History,* Stroud Trs. London, 1914.

————. *The Philosophy of Mind,* trans. by W. Wallace. Oxford: Clarendon Press, 1894.

————. *The Philosophy of Right,* trans. by T. M. Knox. Oxford: Clarendon Press, 1942.

Helson, Harry. "Adaption Level Theory," in *Psychology: A Study of a Science,* Vol. 1, ed. by S. Koch. New York: McGraw-Hill, 1959.

Herrick, Judson, C. *An Introduction to Neurology.* Philadelphia: W. B. Saunders, 1915.

Hobbes, Thomas. *The Leviathan,* Everyman's Edition. New York: E. P. Dutton, n.d.

Hobhouse, L. T. *Elements of Social Justice.* London: George Allen & Unwin, 1922.

————. *The Metaphysical Theory of the State: A Criticism.* London: George Allen & Unwin, 1918.

————. *The Rational Good: A Study in the Logic of Practice.* London: George Allen & Unwin, 1921.

Hofstadter, Richard. *Social Darwinism in American Thought,* rev. ed. Boston: Beacon Press, 1955.

Horney, Karen. *New Ways in Psychoanalysis.* New York, 1939.

————. *Self-Analysis.* New York: W. W. Norton, 1942.

Hume, David. *Enquiry Concerning Human Happiness.*

————. "Of the Refinement in the Arts," in *Essays, Moral, Political, and Literary.* London: Henry Foude, World's Classics, 1904.

Hutcheson, Francis. *An Inquiry into the Origin of Our Ideas of Beauty and Virtue,* Vol. II: *Concerning Moral Good and Evil,* 2d ed. London: Printed for J. Darby *et al.,* 1726.

Huston, P. E., *et al.* "A Study of Hypnotically Induced Complexes by Means of Luria Techniques," in *Journal of General Psychology,* 11, 1934.

Huxley, Julian. *Evolution: The Modern Synthesis.* London: George Allen & Unwin, 1945.

Huxley, T. H. *Evolution and Ethics and Other Essays.* New York: D. Appleton, 1898.

Jaeger, Werner. *Aristotle: Fundamentals of the History of His Development,* trans. by Richard Robinson. Oxford: Clarendon Press, 1934.

Jahoda, Marie. *Current Concepts of Positive Mental Health.* New York: Basic Books, 1958.

James, William. *The Principles of Psychology,* 2 vols. New York: Henry Holt, 1898.

Jevons, W. Stanley. *Theory of Political Economy,* ed. by H. S. Jevons. London: Macmillan, 1931.

Jewett, Benjamin (ed.). *The Dialogues of Plato.* New York: Random House, n.d.

Kant, Immanuel. *Anthropologie,* in *Immanuel Kant's Werke,* ed. by Ernst Cassirer. Berlin: Bruno Cassirer, 1923.

————. *The Critique of Judgment,* trans. by James Creed Meredith. Oxford: Clarendon Press, 1911.

————. *Critique of Practical Reason and Other Works on the Theory of Ethics,* trans. by T. K. Abbott. London: Longmans, Green, 1926.

————. *The Critique of Pure Reason,* trans. by J. M. D. Meiklejohn. New York: John Wiley, 1943.

————. *Fundamental Principles of the Metaphysic of Morals,* in *The Critique of Practical Reason and Other Works on the Theory of Ethics,* 10th ed., trans. by T. K. Abbot. London: Longmans, Green, 1926.

————. *Metaphysical Elements of Ethics,* in *Kant's Critique of Practical Reason and Other Works on the Theory of Ethics,* trans. by T. K. Abbott. London: Longmans, Green, 1926.

Katz, Jerrold J. "Semantic Theory and the Meaning of Good," in *The Journal of Philosophy,* December 10, 1964.

Kenny, Anthony. *Action, Emotion, and Will,* London: Routledge & Kegan Paul, 1963.

Kropotkin, Peter Alexeivich. *Mutual Aid: A Factor of Evolution.* New York: Knopf, 1925.

Kubie, Lawrence S. "The Fundamental Nature of the Distinction Between Normality and Neurons," in *Psychoanalytic Quarterly,* 28, 1954.

Locke, John. *A Letter Concerning Toleration,* in *Encyclopaedia Britannica Great Books of the Western World,* Vol. 35.

————. *The Second Treatise Concerning Civil Government,* in *Two Treatises on Government,* ed. by Peter Laslett. Cambridge: Cambridge University Press, 1960.

Luria, A. R. *The Nature of Human Conflicts.* New York, 1932.

Macpherson, C. B. *The Real World of Democracy.* Oxford: Clarendon Press, 1966.

Maier, N. R. F. *Frustration: A Study of Behavior Without a Goal.* New York: McGraw-Hill, 1949.

Marcus Aurelius. *Meditations,* in *The Stoic and Epicurean Philosophers,* ed. by W. J. Oates. New York: Random House, 1940.

Marcuse, Herbert. *Eros and Civilization.* Boston: Beacon Press, 1955.

Marx, Karl. *Capital.* Chicago: Charles H. Kerr, 1932.

Maslow, A. H. *Motivation and Personality.* New York: Harper & Brothers, 1954.

Masserman, Jules H. *Behavior and Neuroses.* Chicago: University of Chicago Press, 1943.

McNaughton, Robert. "Comparative Conditioned Neuroses," in *Annals of the New York Academy of Sciences,* 56, Art. 2, 1953.

———. "A Metrical Concept of Happiness," in *Philosophy and Phenomenological Research,* 14, 2, 1953.

Mill, John Stuart. "Utilitarianism," in *Utilitarianism, Liberty and Representative Government.* New York: E. P. Dutton, 1944.

St. Vincent Millay, Edna. *A Few Figs from Thistles.* New York: Harper, 1922.

Minor, Ralph W. (ed.). "Comparative Conditioned Neuroses," *Annals of the New York Academy of Sciences,* 56, Art. 2, 1953.

Montague, W. P. "The Missing Link in the Case for Utilitarianism," in *The Ways of Things.* Englewood Cliffs, N.J.: Prentice-Hall, 1940.

Moore, G. E. *Principia Ethica.* London: Cambridge University Press, 1903.

Murphy, Gardner. *Human Potentialities.* New York: Basic Books, 1958.

Nowell-Smith, P. H. *Ethics.* Baltimore: Penguin Books, 1954.

Olds, James. "Self-Stimulation of the Brain," in *Science,* 127, 1958.

Olds, James, and Milner, Peter. "Positive Reinforcement Produced by Electrical Stimulation of Septal Area and Other Regions of Rat Brain," in *Journal of Comparative and Physiological Psychology,* 47, 1954.

Paley, W. *The Principles of Moral and Political Philosophy.* Dublin, Ireland: Brett Smith, 1743.

———. *Natural Theology.* New York: Bobbs-Merrill, 1963.

Pepper, Stephen C. *The Sources of Value.* Berkeley, Calif.: University of California Press, 1958.

Plato. *Critias,* in *The Dialogues of Plato,* ed. by B. Jowett.

———. *Gorgias,* in *The Dialogues of Plato,* ed. by B. Jowett.

———. *Euthydemus,* in *The Dialogues of Plato,* ed. by B. Jowett.

———. *Euthyphro,* in *The Dialogues of Plato,* ed. by B. Jowett.

———. *Laws,* in *The Dialogues of Plato,* ed. by B. Jowett.

———. *Phaedo,* in *The Dialogues of Plato,* ed. by B. Jowett.

———. *Phaedrus,* in *The Dialogues of Plato,* ed. by B. Jowett.

———. *Philebus,* in *The Dialogues of Plato,* ed. by B. Jowett.

———. *Protagoras,* in *The Dialogues of Plato,* ed. by B. Jowett.

———. *The Republic,* trans. by H. D. P. Lee. Baltimore, Md.: Penguin Books, 1955.

———. *Symposium,* in *The Dialogues of Plato,* ed. by B. Jowett.

Plotinus. *The Enneads,* trans. by Stephen MacKenna and B. S. Page. New York: Pantheon Books, 1959.

Price, Richard. *A Review of the Principal Questions in Morals,* ed. by D. Daiches Raphael. Oxford: Clarendon Press, 1948.

Prichard, H. A. *Does Moral Philosophy Rest Upon a Mistake?*, in *Moral Philosophy, Essays and Lectures*. Oxford: Clarendon Press, 1949.

Radhakrishnan, Sarvepalli, and Moore, Charles, A. (eds.). *A Source Book in Indian Philosophy*. Princeton: Princeton University Press, 1957.

Raphael, D. Daiches (ed.). *A Review of the Principle Questions on Morals*. Bloomington: Indiana University Press, 1960.

Rawls, John. "Two Concepts of Rules," in *Philosophical Review*, Vol. 64, 1955, pp. 3–32.

Reyburn, Hugh A. *The Ethical Theory of Hegel: A Study of the Philosophy of Right*. Oxford: Clarendon Press, 1921.

Rogers, Carl R. *Client-Centered Therapy*. New York: Houghton Mifflin Co., 1951.

Roll, Erich. *A History of Economic Thought*. Rev. ed. New York, 1942.

Ross, W. D. *The Right and the Good*. Oxford: Clarendon Press, 1930.

———. (ed.). *The Works of Aristotle*. Oxford: Clarendon Press, 1926.

Rousseau, J. J. *Emile*. New York: Everyman's Editions, 1961.

———. *On the Origin of Inequality*, in *The Social Contract and Discourses*. New York: Everyman's Library, E. P. Dutton & Co., 1932.

Russell, Bertrand. *A History of Western Philosophy*. New York: Simon & Schuster, 1945.

Ryle, Gilbert. "Pleasure," in *Dilemmas, The Tarner Lectures*. Cambridge: Cambridge University Press, 1962.

Sanford, Nevitt. *The Findings of the Commission in Psychology*, in *Annals of the New York Academy of Science*, 63, 1955.

———. "Normative Conceptions in Psychology," in *Writers on Ethics*, ed. by J. Katz, *et al.*, New York: D. Van Nostrand Co., 1962.

Schiller, F. *Ueber Anmut und Wurde*, in *Schiller's Sammtliche Werke*. Band 4, Stuttgart: Cotta'sche Buchhandlung, 1883.

Schlick, Moritz. *Problems of Ethics*, trans. by David Rynin. New York: Prentice-Hall, 1939.

Sellars, W., and Hospers, J. (eds.). *Readings in Ethical Theory*. N.Y.: Appleton-Century-Crofts, 1952.

Seneca. *Moral Letters*, ed. and trans. by R. M. Gummere. 3 Vols. Loeb Library. New York: Putnam Publishing Co., 1920.

———. *On the Happy Life*, in *Moral Essays*, trans. by J. W. Basore. 3 Vols. Loeb Library. New York: Putnam's Publishing Co., 1928–1935.

Seth, James. *A Study of Ethical Principles*. Sec. ed. New York: Charles Scribner's Sons, 1895.

Sextus Empericus. *Outlines of Pyrrhonism*, in *Philosophical Works*. Cambridge: Harvard University Press, 1942.

Sidgwick, Henry. *Methods of Ethics*. 4th ed. London: The Macmillan Co., 1890.

Simpson, George Gaylord. *The Meaning of Evolution*. New Haven: Yale University Press, 1949.

Skinner, B. F. *Science and Human Behavior*. New York: Macmillan Co., 1953.

Smart, J. C. C. *An Outline of a System of Utilitarian Ethics*. Victoria (Australia): Melbourne University Press, 1961.

Snygg, Donald, and Combs, A. W. *Individual Behavior*. New York: Harper & Brothers, 1949.

Spencer, Herbert. *Social Statics*. Abridged and Revised. New York: D. Appleton & Co., 1904.

―――. *The Data of Ethics*. New York: A. L. Burt Co., 1901.

Spinoza, B. *Demonstrations.*

―――. *Ethics.*

―――. *Theological-Political Treatise*, in *The Chief Works of Benedict de Spinoza*, trans. by R. H. M. Elwes. New York: Dover Publications, 1951.

Stout, G. F. *Analytic Psychology*. New York: Macmillan & Co., 1896, Vol. 2.

Troland, L. T. *The Mystery of Mind*. New York: D. Van Nostrand Co., 1926.

Von Wright, G. H. *The Logic of Preference*. Edinburgh: Edinburgh University Press, 1963.

―――. *The Varieties of Goodness*. London: Routledge, Kegan, & Paul, 1963.

White, Robert. *Lives in Progress*. New York: Holt, Rinehart and Winston, 1952.

Wolfson, Harry. *The Philosophy of Spinoza*. Ambridge, Mass.: Harvard University Press, 1948.

Wooldridge, Dean, E. *The Machinery of the Brain*. New York: McGraw-Hill, 1963.

Woodworth, Robert, *Dynamic Psychology*. New York: Henry Holt, 1918.

Zeller, Eduard. *Socrates and the Socratic Schooes*. 2d. ed. London: Longmans, Green, 1877.

―――. *The Stoics, Epicureans and Sceptics*. Rev. ed. London: Longmans, Green, 1880.

Zimmer, Heinrich. *Philosophies of India*. New York: Pantheon Books, 1951.

Index

357